FAVORITE BRAND NAME RECIPES COOKBOOK

PUBLICATIONS INTERNATIONAL, LTD.

Pictured on the front and back covers: Row 1: Cool and Creamy Cucumber Spread
(page 11), Caribbean Fudge Pie *(page 325)*, New Orleans Crumb Cake *(page 350)*, Broccoli
and Pasta *(page 218)*. Row 2: Northwest Cheesecake Supreme *(page 306)*, Marinated Beef
Salad *(page 84)*. Row 3: Marinated Shrimp and Vegetables *(page 90)*, Ginger Pineapple
Mold *(page 73)*. Row 4: Fluffy Grasshopper Pie *(page 326)*, Golden Gate Grill *(page 243)*,
Ham Pasta Primavera *(page 205)*, Fresh Vegetable Salad *(page 64)*. Row 5: Rainbow Fruit
Salad *(page 75)*, Marinated Kabobs *(page 134)*, Garden Chicken Salad *(page 84)*, Shantung
Chicken *(page 148)*.

CONTENTS

Your Guide to Great Cooking

FAVORITE BRAND NAME RECIPES COOK-BOOK is just that—a collection of all-time favorite recipes developed and tested by America's top food companies, using their brand-name products. Expert home economists at leading American food companies have developed, tested, and written these recipes to help you use their products. We have selected the most popular recipes for this book, many of which have been collected from the pages of our best-selling FAVORITE BRAND NAME RECIPES Magazine. Now you have a convenient volume containing all of your favorites.

The variety of these recipes is apparent as you glance through the book. You'll find recipes for any occasion. We've included appetizers, beverages, soups and salads, main dishes of all kinds, breads and rolls, and a variety of desserts. From breakfast to supper and even midnight snacks, there are recipes for any time of day. For busy days, you'll find terrific recipes that get you out of the kitchen in a hurry. When you have time to be creative, choose one of the gourmet specialties. Recipes with the international flair of Italy, the Orient, Mexico, and France are included, along with home-style dishes that represent American cooking from every region. You can try new ideas for family meals, or present something elegant for a special occasion.

When looking through this book, you'll notice that a large number of these recipes can be prepared in your microwave oven. Some have been developed especially for microwave cooking. Although these recipes have been thoroughly tested, the microwave cooking times given must be considered approximate. Higher-wattage microwave ovens cook foods more quickly than those with low wattage. In addition, the starting temperature of the food, the shape and size of the pieces, and the food's depth in the cooking utensil can affect cooking time. Most recipes will give a test for doneness. It's best to use the cooking times in the recipe as a guideline; check to see if the food is done before adding more time.

Some recipes in this book are followed by a nutritional analysis, giving numeric values for the number of calories and amount of protein, fat, carbohydrates, sodium, and cholesterol in each serving of the recipe. This information is based on the ingredients listed in the recipe. For cases in which a choice of ingredients is given, the first option was used in computing the nutritional analysis. If the ingredient list calls for "2 tablespoons butter or margarine," for example, the nutritional information applies to the recipe made with butter, not margarine. Ingredients listed as "optional" or "if desired" were not included in the analysis. If a range of servings is given in the recipe, the analysis was computed for the largest number of servings. Please remember that, just as individual foods of the same type are different, their nutrition content can vary. Consequently, these figures should be viewed as approximations.

As wonderful as these recipes are, you'll also find that this book is appealing to browse through to get hundreds of great ideas for menu and meal planning. And with a collection of recipes this comprehensive, you can be sure you'll always have just the right recipe at your fingertips. So start cooking—and enjoy the delicious results!

APPETIZERS

Good friends and good times call for these tempting appetizers. Look for easy dips and spreads to welcome impromptu guests, elegant first courses to set the tone for an important meal, and wonderful party fare for gatherings large and small. You'll find a variety of sensational starters to let your hospitality shine.

Bacon-Horseradish Dip

1 pouch CAMPBELL'S® Onion Soup and Recipe Mix
2 cups sour cream
5 slices bacon, cooked and crumbled
1 tablespoon prepared horseradish
1 teaspoon Dijon-style mustard
Cooked bacon curl for garnish

1. In medium bowl, combine soup mix, sour cream, crumbled bacon, horseradish and mustard; mix well. Cover; chill until serving time, at least 2 hours.
2. Garnish with bacon curl. Serve with chips or crackers.
Makes 2 cups.

Colorful Carrot Dip

1 8-ounce package *Light* PHILADELPHIA BRAND Neufchâtel Cheese, softened
½ cup finely shredded carrot
1 teaspoon parsley flakes
⅛ teaspoon salt
Dash of pepper

Combine neufchâtel cheese, carrots and seasonings, mixing until well blended. Chill. Serve with vegetable dippers.
1 cup.
Variations: Substitute freeze-dried chopped chives for parsley flakes.
Substitute ½ teaspoon dried basil leaves, crushed, for parsley flakes.
Substitute ¼ teaspoon dill weed or lemon pepper for parsley flakes.

Cracked Black Pepper and Herb Spread

1 package (8 ounces) cream cheese, softened
6 ounces goat cheese (Montrachet, Chèvre or feta)
¼ cup WISH-BONE® Italian Dressing
½ cup chopped red onion
1 teaspoon fresh chopped thyme leaves*
1 teaspoon fresh chopped sage leaves**
1 teaspoon cracked black pepper

In food processor or blender, process all ingredients until blended; cover and chill. Garnish, if desired, with additional cracked black pepper and serve with assorted fresh vegetables, crackers and breads.
Makes about 2 cups spread.
***Substitution:** Use ½ teaspoon dried thyme leaves.
****Substitution:** Use ½ teaspoon dried sage leaves.
Note: Also terrific with Wish-Bone® Robusto Italian, Herbal Italian Blended Italian, Lite Italian or Lite Classic Dijon Vinaigrette Dressing.

Curried Peanut Dip

- 1 pouch CAMPBELL'S® Onion Soup and Recipe Mix
- 1 cup sour cream
- 1 cup plain yogurt
- 1/4 cup creamy peanut butter
- 2 teaspoons curry powder
  Chopped peanuts for garnish
  Fresh pear slices for garnish

1. In medium bowl, blend soup mix, sour cream, yogurt, peanut butter and curry powder. Cover; chill until serving time, at least 2 hours.
2. Garnish with chopped peanuts and pear slices. Serve with vegetable or fruit dippers.
Makes 2 1/4 cups.

Layered Taco Dip

- 1 pound lean ground beef
- 1 (4-ounce) can chopped green chilies, undrained
- 2 teaspoons WYLER'S® or STEERO® Beef-Flavor Instant Bouillon
- 1 (16-ounce) container BORDEN® or MEADOW GOLD® Sour Cream
- 1 (1 1/8-ounce) package taco seasoning mix
- 1 (16-ounce) can refried beans
- 1 (6-ounce) container frozen avocado dip, thawed
  Shredded cheese, chopped tomatoes, sliced green onions, sliced ripe olives
  WISE® BRAVOS® or LA FAMOUS® Tortilla Chips

In large skillet, brown meat; pour off fat. Add chilies and bouillon; cook and stir until bouillon dissolves. Cool. In small bowl, combine sour cream and taco seasoning mix; set aside. In 7- or 8-inch springform pan or on large plate, spread beans. Top with meat mixture, sour cream mixture and avocado dip. Cover and chill several hours. Just before serving, garnish with cheese, tomatoes, onions and olives. Serve with tortilla chips. Refrigerate leftovers.
Makes 12 to 15 servings.

Creamy "Philly" Guacamole Dip

- 2 medium avocados, peeled
- 1 tablespoon lemon juice
- 1 8-ounce package PHILADELPHIA BRAND Cream Cheese, softened
- 1/4 cup finely chopped onion
- 1/2 teaspoon salt
- 1/4 teaspoon garlic salt
- 1/4 teaspoon hot pepper sauce
- 1 10 1/2-ounce can bean dip
  Shredded lettuce
  Chopped tomato
  Ripe olive slices
  100% Natural KRAFT Mild Cheddar Cheese, shredded

Mash avocados with juice. Combine avocado mixture, cream cheese, onions and seasonings, mixing until well blended. Evenly spread bean dip onto serving platter. Top with remaining ingredients. Serve with avocado mixture and corn or tortilla chips. Garnish with additional chopped tomato and ripe olive slices, if desired.
6 to 8 servings.
Variation: Substitute 16-ounce can refried beans for bean dip.

Clam Onion Dip

- 1 (16-ounce) container BORDEN® or MEADOW GOLD® Sour Cream
- 1 or 2 (6 1/2-ounce) cans SNOW'S® or DOXSEE® Minced Clams, drained
- 1 (1.5-ounce) package MRS. GRASS® Onion Recipe, Soup & Dip Mix
- 3 tablespoons REALEMON® Lemon Juice from Concentrate
- 2 to 3 teaspoons prepared horseradish

In medium bowl, combine ingredients; mix well. Chill. Stir before serving. Serve with assorted fresh vegetables. Refrigerate leftovers.
Makes about 2 1/2 cups.

Vegetable Tuna Dip

- 1 cup mayonnaise or salad dressing
- 1 (8-ounce) container BORDEN® or MEADOW GOLD® Sour Cream
- 1 (6 1/2-ounce) can tuna, drained
- 1 (1.7-ounce) package MRS. GRASS® Homestyle Vegetable Recipe, Soup & Dip Mix
- 2 tablespoons REALEMON® Lemon Juice from Concentrate
- 1 teaspoon prepared horseradish, optional

In medium bowl, combine ingredients; mix well. Chill 3 hours to blend flavors. Stir before serving. Serve with fresh vegetables or potato chips. Refrigerate leftovers.
Makes about 4 cups.

Blue Cheese Walnut Spread

1 envelope KNOX® Unflavored
 Gelatine
3/4 cup cold water
1/2 cup sour cream
1/3 cup milk
1 tablespoon lemon juice
1 teaspoon Worcestershire
 sauce
4 ounces blue cheese, crumbled
1 package (8 ounces) cream
 cheese, softened
1/2 cup walnuts

In small saucepan, sprinkle unflavored gelatine over 1/4 cup cold water; let stand 1 minute. Stir over low heat until gelatine is completely dissolved, about 3 minutes.

In blender, process sour cream, remaining 1/2 cup water, milk, lemon juice, Worcestershire sauce and cheeses until blended. While processing, through feed cap gradually add gelatine mixture, then walnuts; process until blended. Pour into 7 1/2×3 3/4×2 1/4-inch loaf pan or 4-cup bowl; chill until firm, about 3 hours. Unmold onto lettuce-lined platter and serve, if desired, with crackers, party-size breads and fruits.
Makes about 3 3/4 cups spread.

Garlic Spread

1 8-ounce package
 PHILADELPHIA BRAND
 Cream Cheese, softened
1/2 cup PARKAY Margarine,
 softened
2 tablespoons chopped parsley
2 tablespoons chopped onion
1 garlic clove, minced

Combine cream cheese and margarine, mixing until well blended. Add remaining ingredients; mix well. Chill.
Approximately 1 2/3 cups.

Baked Cream Cheese Appetizer

1 4-ounce package refrigerated
 crescent dinner rolls
1 8-ounce package
 PHILADELPHIA BRAND
 Cream Cheese
1/2 teaspoon dill weed
1 egg yolk, beaten

Unroll dough on lightly floured surface; press together seams to form 12×4-inch rectangle. Sprinkle top of cream cheese with half of dill; lightly press dill into cream cheese. Place cream cheese, dill-side down, in center of dough. Sprinkle cream cheese with remaining dill. Enclose cream cheese in dough by bringing sides of dough together, pressing edges to seal. Place on lightly greased cookie sheet; brush with egg yolk. Bake at 350°, 15 to 18 minutes or until lightly browned. Serve with assorted crackers and apple slices.
8 servings.

Variations: Substitute combined 1/2 teaspoon dried rosemary leaves, crushed, and 1/2 teaspoon paprika for dill weed.

Substitute *Light* PHILADELPHIA BRAND Neufchâtel Cheese for Cream Cheese.

Eggplant Caviar

1 large eggplant, unpeeled
1/4 cup chopped onion
2 tablespoons lemon juice
1 tablespoon olive or vegetable
 oil
1 small clove garlic
1/2 teaspoon salt
1/4 teaspoon TABASCO® pepper
 sauce
 Sieved egg white (optional)
 Lemon slice (optional)

Preheat oven to 350°F. Place eggplant in shallow baking dish. Bake 1 hour or until soft, turning once. Trim off ends; slice eggplant in half lengthwise. Place cut-side-down in colander and let drain 10 minutes. Scoop out pulp; reserve pulp and peel. In blender or food processor combine eggplant peel, onion, lemon juice, oil, garlic, salt and Tabasco® sauce. Cover; process until peel is finely chopped. Add eggplant pulp. Cover; process just until chopped. Place in serving dish. Garnish with egg white and lemon slice, if desired. Serve with toast points.
Makes about 1 1/2 cups.

Chili con Queso

2 tablespoons CRISCO® Oil
1/4 cup minced onion
1 can (7 1/2 ounces) whole
 tomatoes, drained and finely
 chopped
1 can (4 ounces) chopped green
 chilies, undrained
1/4 teaspoon salt
2 cups shredded Cheddar or
 Monterey Jack cheese
 (about 8 ounces)
1/3 cup whipping cream
 Nacho chips

Heat Crisco® Oil in 1-quart saucepan. Add onion. Cook over medium-high heat, stirring occasionally, until onion is tender. Add tomatoes, chilies and salt. Stir to blend and break apart tomatoes. Heat to boiling. Reduce heat to medium-low. Cook, stirring occasionally, 15 minutes. Remove from heat. Stir in cheese and cream. Cook over low heat, stirring constantly, until cheese melts. Serve with nacho chips.
About 1 3/4 cups.

Variation: Hot Chili con Queso. Follow recipe above, substituting jalapeño peppers (drained) for green chilies.

Vegetable Dip Verde

1 cup cottage cheese
1 cup firmly packed parsley sprigs
½ cup chopped green onions
⅓ cup capers, drained
2 hard-cooked eggs, peeled, quartered
2 cloves garlic
1 tablespoon lemon juice
¼ teaspoon salt
¼ teaspoon TABASCO® pepper sauce

In container of blender or food processor combine all ingredients. Cover; process until smooth. Remove to serving bowl. Cover; refrigerate at least 1 hour. Serve with cut-up fresh vegetables.
Makes about 1½ cups.

Creamy Chili Dip

2 packages (8 ounces each) cream cheese or reduced-calorie cream cheese, softened
¾ cup V8® Vegetable Juice
1 can (4 ounces) chopped chilies
½ cup VLASIC® or EARLY CALIFORNIA® Chopped Pitted Ripe Olives
½ cup chopped sweet red pepper
2 teaspoons grated onion
¼ teaspoon hot pepper sauce
Fresh cilantro for garnish

1. In medium bowl with mixer at medium speed, beat cream cheese until smooth and fluffy.
2. Gradually beat in V8 juice until smooth and thoroughly blended.
3. Stir in chilies, olives, red pepper, onion and hot pepper sauce. Cover; refrigerate until serving time, at least 4 hours.
4. Garnish with fresh cilantro. Serve with fresh vegetables or chips for dipping.
Makes 4 cups.

Per tablespoon: 28 calories, 0 g protein, 3 g fat, 1 g carbohydrate, 50 mg sodium, 8 mg cholesterol.

Toasted Sesame Cheese Spread

2 tablespoons KIKKOMAN Soy Sauce
1 package (3 oz.) cream cheese
4 teaspoons sesame seed, toasted
Assorted crackers

Pour soy sauce over cream cheese block in small dish, turning over several times to coat all sides. Cover; refrigerate 2 hours, turning cheese block over often. Remove cheese block from soy sauce and roll in sesame seed. Refrigerate until ready to serve with crackers.
Makes 4 to 6 appetizer servings.

Manhattan Clam Dip

1 (3-ounce) package cream cheese, softened
¼ cup mayonnaise or salad dressing
1 (8-ounce) container BORDEN® or MEADOW GOLD® Sour Cream
½ cup BENNETT'S® Cocktail Sauce
1 or 2 (6½-ounce) cans SNOW'S® or DOXSEE® Minced Clams, drained
2 tablespoons chopped green onion
1 teaspoon REALEMON® Lemon Juice from Concentrate

In small mixer bowl, beat cheese and mayonnaise until smooth. Stir in remaining ingredients. Chill. Garnish as desired. Serve with assorted fresh vegetables or WISE® COTTAGE FRIES® Potato Chips. Refrigerate leftovers.
Makes about 2 cups.

Tropical Fruit Dip

½ cup mayonnaise
¼ cup sour cream
3 tablespoons lime juice
1 teaspoon honey
½ teaspoon ground cumin
¼ teaspoon TABASCO® pepper sauce
½ cup shredded coconut

In medium bowl combine mayonnaise, sour cream, lime juice, honey, cumin and Tabasco® sauce; mix well. Stir in coconut. Cover, refrigerate at least 1 hour. Serve with cut-up fresh fruit.
Makes about 1 cup.

Quick Paté Mold

½ pound liverwurst, cut into small pieces
1 (8-ounce) package cream cheese, softened
2 tablespoons finely chopped onion
1 teaspoon WYLER'S® or STEERO® Chicken-Flavor Instant Bouillon
Parsley, optional
Melba rounds

In small mixer bowl, combine liverwurst, cheese, onion and bouillon; beat until smooth. Turn into well-oiled 2-cup mold. Chill. Unmold; garnish with parsley if desired. Serve with Melba rounds. Refrigerate leftovers.
Makes 1 appetizer mold.

Chicken with Oriental Dipping Sauce

2 packages (12 ounces each) SWANSON® Frozen Fried Plump & Juicy® Chicken Dipsters® or 1 package (28 ounces) SWANSON® Frozen Fried Chicken Nibbles®
¾ cup V8® Vegetable Juice
¼ cup packed light brown sugar
2 tablespoons rice vinegar or dry sherry
1 tablespoon soy sauce
1 tablespoon cornstarch
¼ teaspoon grated fresh ginger

To Microwave:
1. Prepare chicken dipsters according to package directions.
2. In medium microwave-safe bowl, stir together remaining ingredients. Cover with waxed paper; microwave on HIGH 3 minutes or until hot and bubbling, stirring once during cooking. Serve chicken with sauce for dipping.
Makes 1 cup sauce.
   Note: This sauce is also great to use for dipping MRS. PAUL'S® fish sticks, fried eggplant, zucchini sticks and onion rings.

Eggplant Spread

¼ cup olive oil
1 medium eggplant, peeled and coarsely chopped (about 1 pound)
½ cup chopped onion
1 clove garlic, minced
¾ cup V8® Vegetable Juice
¼ cup toasted chopped pine nuts
2 tablespoons chopped fresh parsley
2 teaspoons soy sauce
1 teaspoon sugar
⅛ teaspoon pepper
Pita bread wedges

1. In 10-inch skillet over medium heat, in hot oil, cook eggplant, onion and garlic about 15 minutes or until eggplant is tender, stirring often.
2. In covered blender or food processor, blend eggplant mixture until smooth.
3. In medium bowl, combine eggplant mixture, V8 juice, pine nuts, parsley, soy sauce, sugar and pepper. Stir until thoroughly mixed. Cover; refrigerate until serving time, at least 2 hours. Serve with pita bread wedges.
Makes 3 cups.

Per tablespoon: 18 calories, 0 g protein, 2 g fat, 1 g carbohydrate, 28 mg sodium, 0 mg cholesterol.

Chicken Liver Pâté

2 packages (8 ounces each) SWANSON® Frozen Chicken Livers
¼ cup water
1 pouch CAMBPELL'S® Onion Soup and Recipe Mix
2 slices bacon, chopped
¼ cup butter or margarine, cut up
2 tablespoons brandy
½ teaspoon dry mustard
¼ teaspoon dried thyme leaves, crushed
¼ teaspoon pepper
Fresh parsley for garnish
Chopped hard-cooked egg for garnish

To Microwave:
1. Remove frozen livers from boxes but do not remove from pouches. Place in 2-quart microwave-safe casserole. Microwave, uncovered, at 50% power 5 minutes, turning pouches over once during cooking. Let stand 5 minutes. Remove livers from pouches and place in same casserole.
2. Add water, soup mix and bacon. Cover with lid; microwave on HIGH 5 minutes, stirring twice during cooking. Reduce power to 50%. Cover; microwave 4 minutes or until livers are no longer pink, stirring once during cooking.
3. In covered blender or food processor, combine liver mixture, butter, brandy, mustard, thyme and pepper. Blend until smooth.
4. Spoon mixture into 3-cup crock. Cover; refrigerate 4 hours or overnight. Garnish with parsley and egg. Serve with crackers.
Makes about 3 cups.

Guacamole

3 ripe medium avocados,
    seeded and peeled
2 tablespoons REALIME® Lime
    Juice from Concentrate *or*
    REALEMON® Lemon Juice
    from Concentrate
½ teaspoon garlic salt
½ teaspoon sugar
¼ teaspoon pepper

In blender container or food processor, mash avocados. Add remaining ingredients; mix well. Chill to blend flavors. Garnish as desired. Serve with WISE® BRAVOS® or LA FAMOUS® Tortilla Chips or fresh vegetables. Refrigerate leftovers.
Makes about 2 cups.

Variations: Add 1 or more of the following: sour cream, cooked crumbled bacon, chopped water chestnuts, chopped fresh tomato, chopped chilies.

Molded Cheese

2 packages (4-serving size) or
    1 package (8-serving size)
    JELL-O® Brand Orange or
    Lemon Flavor Gelatin
1½ cups boiling water
½ pound (2½ cups) finely grated
    sharp Cheddar cheese
1 package (8 ounces) cream
    cheese, softened
1 cup (½ pint) sour cream
½ cup chopped scallions
¼ cup chopped parsley
3 tablespoons prepared
    horseradish
1 tablespoon Worcestershire
    sauce

Dissolve gelatin in boiling water. Combine remaining ingredients in large bowl; with electric mixer at medium speed, beat until well blended. Gradually blend into gelatin. Pour into 6-cup mold. Chill until firm, about 3 hours. Unmold. Garnish with fresh fruit or vegetables, if desired. Serve as an appetizer with assorted crackers.
Makes 5½ cups or 11 servings.

Cool and Creamy Cucumber Spread

3 medium cucumbers
1 (8-ounce) *plus* 1 (3-ounce)
    package cream cheese,
    softened
½ cup sour cream
¼ cup snipped fresh dill*
1½ teaspoons lemon juice
1 envelope LIPTON® Vegetable
    Recipe Soup Mix

Thinly slice 1 cucumber and arrange in bottom of lightly oiled 4-cup ring mold; set aside.

Peel, seed and coarsely chop remaining cucumbers. With food processor or electric mixer, combine cream cheese, 1 cup chopped cucumber, sour cream, dill, lemon juice and vegetable recipe soup mix until smooth. Stir in remaining chopped cucumber. Turn into prepared mold; chill until firm, at least 3 hours. To serve, unmold onto serving platter and fill center, if desired, with cherry tomatoes and leaf lettuce. Serve with assorted crackers.
Makes about 3½ cups spread.

Substitution: Use 2 tablespoons dried dill weed.

Savory Herbed Baked Brie

1 wheel (1 kilo) Brie, about
    8 inches in diameter
¼ cup chopped parsley
1 small clove garlic, minced
1 teaspoon dried rosemary
    leaves
1 teaspoon dried thyme leaves
1 teaspoon dried marjoram
    leaves
8 very thin slices hard salami,
    finely chopped
1 sheet frozen puff pastry,
    thawed according to
    package directions
1 egg, lightly beaten

Place Brie in freezer 30 minutes. Preheat oven to 350°F. In small bowl combine parsley, garlic, rosemary, thyme and marjoram. Remove Brie from freezer; slice in half lengthwise with a long thin-bladed knife. Spread herb mixture over cut side of 1 Brie half. Sprinkle with chopped salami. Press Brie halves back together.

On floured surface roll pastry to 18×12-inch rectangle. Place Brie in center of pastry. Bring edges of pastry over top to seal; cut off excess. Seal corners by brushing with egg and pressing pastry together. Place Brie seam-side-down on lightly greased jelly-roll pan. Brush with egg and make 4 holes in top of pastry.* Bake 30 minutes or until pastry is golden and puffed. (Cheese inside should be runny.) Let stand at least 15 minutes on wire rack before serving. Serve with crackers.
Makes 15 to 20 appetizer servings.

*A design for top may be made from excess pastry dough. Brush design with egg and press on top to seal.

Garden Vegetable Spread

1 8-ounce container Soft
 PHILADELPHIA BRAND
 Cream Cheese
1/2 cup shredded carrot
1/2 cup shredded zucchini
1 tablespoon chopped parsley
1/4 teaspoon garlic salt
 Dash of pepper

Combine ingredients; mix well. Chill. Serve with party rye or pumpernickel bread slices or assorted crackers. *1 1/3 cups.*

Variation: Serve with LENDER'S Pre-Sliced Frozen Plain Bagelettes, toasted.

Hot Crabmeat Appetizer

1 8-ounce package
 PHILADELPHIA BRAND
 Cream Cheese, softened
1 7 1/2-ounce can crabmeat,
 drained, flaked
2 tablespoons finely chopped
 onion
2 tablespoons milk
1/2 teaspoon KRAFT Cream Style
 Horseradish
1/4 teaspoon salt
 Dash of pepper
1/3 cup sliced almonds, toasted

Combine all ingredients except almonds, mixing until well blended. Spoon mixture into 9-inch pie plate; sprinkle with almonds. Bake at 375°, 15 minutes. Serve with crackers. *Approximately 1 1/2 cups.*

Variations: Substitute 8-ounce can minced clams, drained, for crabmeat.

Omit almonds; sprinkle with dill weed.

Warm Herb Cheese Spread

3 (8-ounce) packages cream
 cheese, softened
1/4 cup BORDEN® or MEADOW
 GOLD® Milk
1/4 cup REALEMON® Lemon Juice
 from Concentrate
1/2 teaspoon *each* basil, oregano,
 marjoram and thyme leaves
1/4 teaspoon garlic powder
1/2 pound cooked shrimp,
 chopped (1 1/2 cups), optional

Preheat oven to 350°. In large mixer bowl, beat cheese until smooth. Gradually beat in milk then ReaLemon® brand. Stir in remaining ingredients. Pour into 9-inch quiche dish or pie plate. Cover; bake 15 minutes or until hot. Garnish as desired. Serve warm with crackers or fresh vegetables. Refrigerate leftovers.
Makes about 4 cups.

Microwave: In 9-inch pie plate, prepare cheese spread as above. Cook on 50% power (medium) 5 to 6 minutes or until hot. Stir before serving.

Florentine Dip

1 8-ounce package *Light*
 PHILADELPHIA BRAND
 Neufchâtel Cheese, softened
1/2 cup plain yogurt
2 tablespoons milk
1 10-ounce package frozen
 spinach, thawed, well-
 drained, chopped
2 hard-cooked eggs, finely
 chopped
1/4 teaspoon pepper
1/4 teaspoon salt

Combine neufchâtel cheese, yogurt and milk, mixing until well blended. Stir in remaining ingredients. Serve with vegetable dippers. *2 1/2 cups.*

Hearty Herbed Cheese Spread

1 pouch CAMPBELL'S® Onion
 Soup and Recipe Mix
2 packages (8 ounces each)
 cream cheese, softened
2 cups shredded sharp Cheddar
 cheese (8 ounces), at room
 temperature
1/2 cup chopped fresh parsley
2 tablespoons milk
1 teaspoon dried basil leaves,
 crushed
1 teaspoon dried tarragon
 leaves, crushed
1/2 teaspoon dried dill weed,
 crushed
2 tablespoons cracked pepper
 Paprika for garnish

1. In medium bowl, combine soup mix, cheeses, parsley, milk, basil, tarragon and dill; beat with wooden spoon until well blended.
2. Line 9-inch pie plate with plastic wrap, letting wrap hang over edge. Spoon cheese mixture into pie plate, packing down firmly. Cover; chill until serving time, at least 4 hours.
3. Invert pie plate over serving dish and remove pie plate and plastic from cheese. Smooth surface of cheese with a knife to remove any wrinkles. Press cracked pepper into sides of cheese; sprinkle top with paprika. Serve with crackers.
Makes 3 1/4 cups.

Note: To make a fancy design on cheese spread, first cut a piece of cardboard into desired shape (flower, Christmas tree, etc.), and lay cardboard on cheese spread. Sprinkle paprika around design. Carefully remove cardboard to leave a stenciled design in paprika.

Tijuana Taco Dip

1 can (16 ounces) refried beans
1 can (8 ounces) tomato sauce, divided
1¼ teaspoons TABASCO® pepper sauce, divided
1 large tomato, chopped
¾ cup shredded Monterey Jack cheese
¾ pound ground beef
2 teaspoons chili powder
1 cup sliced ripe olives
1 cup shredded Cheddar cheese
1 cup sour cream
   Chopped green onions, ripe olives and tomatoes for garnish
   Taco or tortilla chips

Preheat oven to 350°F. In medium bowl combine refried beans, 3 tablespoons tomato sauce and ½ teaspoon Tabasco® sauce; mix well. Spread evenly in 1½-quart baking dish. Top with chopped tomato and Monterey Jack cheese.

In large skillet cook beef and chili powder; stir frequently until meat is cooked. Remove from heat; drain off fat. Stir in remaining tomato sauce, sliced olives and remaining ¾ teaspoon Tabasco® sauce. Spread evenly over cheese in dish. Sprinkle with Cheddar cheese.

Bake 15 to 20 minutes or until cheeses melt and beans are hot. Remove from oven. Spread sour cream over top; garnish with green onions, olives and tomatoes. Serve warm with taco or tortilla chips.
Makes 12 appetizer servings.

Hot Beef Dip

¼ cup chopped onion
1 tablespoon PARKAY Margarine
1 cup milk
1 8-ounce package PHILADELPHIA BRAND Cream Cheese, cubed
1 3-ounce package smoked sliced beef, chopped
1 4-ounce can mushrooms, drained
¼ cup (1 ounce) KRAFT Grated Parmesan Cheese
2 tablespoons chopped parsley

Saute onions in margarine. Add milk and cream cheese; stir over low heat until cream cheese is melted. Add remaining ingredients; heat thoroughly, stirring occasionally. Serve hot with French bread slices, if desired.
2½ cups.
Variation: Substitute 2½-ounce package smoked sliced turkey for 3-ounce package smoked sliced beef.
Serving Suggestion: For a colorful variety, serve with French, whole-wheat or rye bread cubes.

Mexican-Style Appetizer

1 can (11½ ounces) CAMPBELL'S® Condensed Bean with Bacon Soup
1 package (1¼ ounces) taco seasoning mix
¼ teaspoon hot pepper sauce
1 cup sour cream
1 can (4 ounces) chopped green chilies, drained
½ cup VLASIC® or EARLY CALIFORNIA® Sliced Pimento-Stuffed Olives
1 cup shredded longhorn cheese (4 ounces)
½ cup alfalfa sprouts
½ cup chopped CAMPBELL'S FRESH® Tomato
Tortilla chips

1. In small bowl, combine soup, taco seasoning mix and hot pepper sauce; stir until blended. On large serving plate, spread mixture into a 6-inch round. Spread sides and top of bean mixture with sour cream to cover.
2. Layer chilies, olives, cheese, alfalfa sprouts and tomato over sour cream. Cover; refrigerate until serving time, at least 4 hours. Surround with tortilla chips.
Makes 10 appetizer servings.

Hot Artichoke Dip

1 package (9 ounces) frozen artichoke hearts, thawed
½ pint (8 ounces) sour cream
¼ cup grated Parmesan cheese
1 envelope LIPTON® Golden Onion Recipe Soup Mix
Buttered bread crumbs
Suggested Dippers*

Preheat oven to 350°.

In food processor or blender, puree artichokes. Add sour cream and cheese; process until smooth. Stir in golden onion recipe soup mix. Turn into 2½-cup casserole, then top with bread crumbs. Bake uncovered 30 minutes or until heated through. Serve with Suggested Dippers.
Makes about 2¼ cups dip.
   Suggested Dippers: Use carrot or celery sticks, whole mushrooms or sliced zucchini.
   Microwave Directions: Omit bread crumbs. Prepare mixture as above. Heat at HIGH (Full Power), turning casserole occasionally, 8 minutes or until heated through. Let stand covered 5 minutes. Serve as above.

Party Cheese Ball

2 8-ounce packages PHILADELPHIA BRAND Cream Cheese, softened
2 cups (8 ounces) shredded CRACKER BARREL Brand Sharp Natural Cheddar Cheese
1 tablespoon chopped pimento
1 tablespoon chopped green pepper
1 tablespoon finely chopped onion
2 teaspoons worcestershire sauce
1 teaspoon lemon juice
Dash of ground red pepper
Dash of salt
Chopped pecans

Combine cream cheese and cheddar cheese, mixing at medium speed on electric mixer until well blended. Add all remaining ingredients except pecans; mix well. Chill several hours. Shape into ball; roll in pecans. Serve with crackers.
Approximately 2 cups.
Variations: Omit pecans. Roll in finely chopped parsley, dried beef or toasted chopped almonds.

Shape into log. Coat top and bottom of log with chopped parsley. Slice; serve with crackers or cucumber slices.

Shape into 1-inch balls. Roll in chopped nuts, dried beef, toasted sesame seed or chopped parsley.

Shape into pyramid. Coat one side with chopped nuts, second side with chopped parsley and third side with chopped dried beef. Serve with party rye bread.

Shape into football; coat with pecans. Top with pimento strips to form lacing.

Quick Mexican Spread

1 8-ounce package *Light* PHILADELPHIA BRAND Neufchâtel Cheese, softened
1 4-ounce can chopped green chilies, drained

Combine neufchâtel cheese and chilies, mixing until well blended. Chill. Serve with tortilla chips or spread over warm tortillas or corn bread.
1 cup.

Pine Nut Cheese Spread

1 8-ounce package PHILADELPHIA BRAND Cream Cheese, softened
2 tablespoons KRAFT Grated Parmesan Cheese
1/4 cup chopped green pepper
1 tablespoon finely chopped onion
2 teaspoons chopped pimento
Dash of ground red pepper
1/3 cup pine nuts or slivered almonds, toasted

Combine all ingredients except pine nuts, mixing until well blended. Chill. Shape into log. Coat with pine nuts just before serving.
1 cup.
Variation: Substitute *Light* PHILADELPHIA BRAND Neufchâtel Cheese for Cream Cheese. Increase Parmesan cheese to 1/4 cup (1 ounce). Spoon into serving container. Top with pine nuts just before serving.
Hint: Homemade cheese spreads in colorful containers make great hostess gifts. Include the recipe for an added personal touch.

Zucchini Chive Dip

1 8-ounce container Soft PHILADELPHIA BRAND Cream Cheese
3 tablespoons milk
1 small zucchini, shredded
3 tablespoons chopped chives
1/8 teaspoon salt

Combine cream cheese and milk, mixing until well blended. Add remaining ingredients; mix well. Chill. Serve with vegetable dippers or chips.
1 cup.

Nutty Blue Cheese Vegetable Dip

1 cup mayonnaise or salad dressing
1 (8-ounce) container BORDEN® or MEADOW GOLD® Sour Cream
1/4 cup (1 ounce) crumbled blue cheese
1 tablespoon finely chopped onion
2 teaspoons WYLER'S® or STEERO® Beef-Flavor Instant Bouillon
1/2 to 3/4 cup coarsely chopped walnuts
Assorted fresh vegetables

In medium bowl, combine mayonnaise, sour cream, blue cheese, onion and bouillon; mix well. Stir in nuts; cover and chill. Stir before serving. Garnish as desired. Serve with vegetables. Refrigerate leftovers.
Makes about 2 cups.

Hawaiian Coconut Spread

1 8-ounce container Soft
    PHILADELPHIA BRAND
    Cream Cheese
2 tablespoons KRAFT Apricot,
    Pineapple or Peach
    Preserves
1/3 cup flaked coconut

Combine cream cheese and preserves, mixing until well blended. Add coconut; mix well. Chill. Serve with nut bread slices.
1 1/3 cups.

Variations: Add 1/8 teaspoon anise seed.

Substitute 1/4 cup whole berry cranberry sauce for KRAFT Preserves.

Savory Cheddar Spread

1 8-ounce package
    PHILADELPHIA BRAND
    Cream Cheese, softened
1/2 cup MIRACLE WHIP Salad
    Dressing
1 cup (4 ounces) 100% Natural
    KRAFT Shredded Mild
    Cheddar Cheese
2 tablespoons green onion
    slices
8 crisply cooked bacon slices,
    crumbled
1/2 cup crushed buttery crackers

Combine cream cheese and salad dressing, mixing until well blended. Add cheddar cheese and onions; mix well. Spoon into 9-inch pie plate; sprinkle with combined bacon and crumbs. Bake at 350°, 15 minutes. Serve with additional crackers.
2 cups.

Variation: Substitute 1/4 cup bacon flavored bits for crumbled bacon.

Microwave: Microwave cream cheese on Medium (50%) 30 seconds. Assemble recipe as directed except for sprinkling with bacon and crumbs. Microwave on High 4 minutes or until thoroughly heated, turning dish every 2 minutes. Sprinkle with combined bacon and crumbs. Serve as directed.

Pineapple-Almond Cheese Spread

2 cans (8 ounces each) DOLE®
    Crushed Pineapple
1 package (8 ounces) cream
    cheese, softened
4 cups shredded sharp Cheddar
    cheese
1/2 cup mayonnaise
1 tablespoon soy sauce
1 cup DOLE™ Chopped Natural
    Almonds, toasted
1/2 cup finely chopped DOLE™
    Green Bell Pepper
1/4 cup minced green onion or
    chives
    DOLE™ Celery stalks or
    assorted breads

Drain pineapple. In large bowl, beat cream cheese until smooth; beat in Cheddar cheese, mayonnaise and soy sauce until smooth. Stir in pineapple, almonds, green pepper and onion. Refrigerate, covered. Use to stuff celery stalks or serve as dip with assorted breads. Serve at room temperature.
Makes 4 cups.

Refreshing Cucumber Dip

1 8-ounce package
    PHILADELPHIA BRAND
    Cream Cheese, softened
1/2 cup sour cream
1 tablespoon milk
1 teaspoon grated onion
1/4 teaspoon worcestershire
    sauce
1/3 cup finely chopped cucumber

Combine all ingredients except cucumbers, mixing until well blended. Stir in cucumbers. Chill several hours or overnight. Serve with chips or vegetable dippers.
1 2/3 cups.

Layered Crab Spread

2 (8-ounce) packages cream
    cheese, softened
2 tablespoons REALEMON®
    Lemon Juice from
    Concentrate
1 teaspoon Worcestershire
    sauce
1/4 teaspoon garlic powder
2 tablespoons finely chopped
    green onion
3/4 cup BENNETT'S® Chili Sauce
1 (6-ounce) can ORLEANS®
    White Crab Meat, drained

In large mixer bowl, beat cheese, ReaLemon® brand, Worcestershire and garlic powder until fluffy; stir in onion. Spread evenly on 10-inch plate. Top with chili sauce then crabmeat. Cover; chill thoroughly. Garnish as desired. Serve with assorted crackers. Refrigerate leftovers.
Makes 10 to 12 servings.

Peppy Bean Dip

1 pouch CAMPBELL'S® Onion Soup and Recipe Mix
½ cup sour cream
1 can (16 ounces) refried beans
½ cup salsa
1 large clove garlic, minced
    VLASIC® or EARLY CALIFORNIA® Sliced Pitted Ripe Olives for garnish

1. In medium bowl, combine soup mix, sour cream, beans, salsa and garlic; mix well. Cover; chill until serving time, at least 2 hours.
2. Garnish with olives. Serve with corn chips or vegetable dippers.
Makes 2½ cups.

Roasted Red Pepper Mousse Spread

1 envelope KNOX® Unflavored Gelatine
½ cup cold water
2 cups (1 pint) whipping or heavy cream
1 jar (8 ounces) roasted red peppers, drained and coarsely chopped
½ cup mayonnaise
1 cup loosely packed basil leaves*
¼ cup grated Parmesan cheese
1 small clove garlic, finely chopped
½ teaspoon salt
⅛ teaspoon pepper

In small saucepan, sprinkle unflavored gelatine over cold water; let stand 1 minute. Stir over low heat until gelatine is completely dissolved, about 3 minutes. Remove from heat and let stand until lukewarm, about 2 minutes.

In large bowl, with electric mixer, beat cream until soft peaks form. Gradually add red peppers, mayonnaise, basil, cheese, garlic, salt and pepper. While beating, gradually add lukewarm gelatine mixture and beat until blended. Pour into 7-cup mold or bowl; chill until firm, about 3 hours. Unmold and serve, if desired, with sliced Italian bread, toasted.
Makes about 6 cups spread.

*Substitution: Use 1 cup chopped fresh parsley plus 1 teaspoon dried basil leaves.

Shrimp Spread

2 (8-ounce) packages cream cheese, softened
½ cup REALEMON® Lemon Juice from Concentrate
2 (4¼-ounce) cans ORLEANS® Shrimp, drained and soaked as label directs
1 to 2 tablespoons finely chopped green onion
1 tablespoon prepared horseradish
1 teaspoon Worcestershire sauce
¼ teaspoon pepper
⅛ teaspoon garlic powder

In small mixer bowl, beat cheese until fluffy; gradually beat in ReaLemon® brand. Stir in remaining ingredients. Chill to blend flavors. Garnish as desired. Serve with crackers or fresh vegetables. Refrigerate leftovers.
Makes about 3 cups.

Mustard Sauce

2 tablespoons CRISCO® Oil
2 tablespoons all-purpose flour
2 tablespoons dry mustard
½ teaspoon salt
1 cup milk

Blend Crisco® Oil, flour, mustard and salt in small saucepan. Cook over medium-high heat 1 minute. Stir in milk. Cook, stirring constantly, until sauce thickens and bubbles.
About 1 cup.

*Favorite Recipe from **Crisco Oil/Procter & Gamble***

Salmon Mousse

2 envelopes KNOX® Unflavored Gelatine
1 can (15½ ounces) salmon, drained (reserve liquid)*
1 stalk celery, cut into 3-inch pieces
1 small onion, quartered
½ medium cucumber, peeled, seeded and quartered
1 cup (½ pint) whipping or heavy cream
¾ cup mayonnaise
¼ cup lemon juice
1 teaspoon dried dill weed
½ teaspoon salt (optional)

In medium saucepan, sprinkle unflavored gelatine over reserved salmon liquid blended with enough water to equal 1 cup; let stand 1 minute. Stir over low heat until gelatine is completely dissolved, about 5 minutes.

In blender or food processor, process gelatine mixture, vegetables, cream, mayonnaise and lemon juice until blended. Add salmon, dill and salt; process until blended. Pour into 6-cup mold or bowl; chill until firm, about 3 hours. Unmold and serve with assorted crackers.
Makes about 5½ cups spread.

*Substitution: Use 2 cans (6½ ounces each) tuna, drained (reserve liquid).

Mini Monte Cristo Sandwiches

2 tablespoons butter or margarine, softened
2 tablespoons prepared mustard
8 slices white bread
4 slices fontina or Swiss cheese (about 4 ounces)
4 slices cooked ham (about 4 ounces)
3 eggs
½ cup milk
1 envelope LIPTON® Golden Onion Recipe Soup Mix
¼ cup butter or margarine

Blend 2 tablespoons butter with mustard; evenly spread on each bread slice. Equally top 4 bread slices with cheese and ham; top with remaining bread, buttered side down. Cut each sandwich into 4 triangles.

Beat eggs, milk and golden onion recipe soup mix until well blended. Dip sandwiches in egg mixture, coating well.

In large skillet, melt ¼ cup butter and cook sandwiches over medium heat, turning once, until golden.
Makes about 16 mini sandwiches.

Country Pâté

4 slices bacon
1 pound ground beef
½ pound cooked ham, cut into ¼-inch pieces
½ pound raw skinless boneless chicken breast, cut into ¼-inch pieces
2 eggs
1 pouch CAMPBELL'S® Onion Soup and Recipe Mix
2 tablespoons brandy
½ teaspoon pepper
¼ teaspoon ground nutmeg
Watercress for garnish
Cherry tomatoes for garnish

To Microwave:
1. Arrange bacon slices ½ inch apart across bottom and up sides of 9- by 5-inch microwave-safe loaf dish; set aside.
2. In medium bowl, thoroughly mix beef, ham, chicken, eggs, soup mix, brandy, pepper and nutmeg. Spoon meat mixture into bacon-lined dish, packing down firmly. Fold ends of bacon over filling.
3. Cover with waxed paper; microwave on HIGH 8 minutes, rotating once during cooking. Carefully pour off fat. Cover; microwave on HIGH 8 minutes or until center is firm, rotating dish twice during cooking. Let stand, covered, 10 minutes. Pour off fat. Invert onto serving plate. Cover; refrigerate until serving time, at least 4 hours.
4. Cut loaf into thin slices. Garnish with watercress and cherry tomatoes. Serve with crackers and mustard.
Makes 18 appetizer servings.

Note: If you are using a temperature probe, cook pâté to an internal temperature of 175° to 185°F.

Spicy Appetizer Dip

1 (8-ounce) can crushed pineapple in its own juice
1 cup COLLEGE INN® Chicken or Beef Broth
3 tablespoons cornstarch
2 tablespoons soy sauce
2 tablespoons white wine vinegar
2 tablespoons firmly packed light brown sugar
¼ teaspoon crushed red pepper
Cocktail franks, ham cubes or fresh vegetables

Drain pineapple, reserving juice. In small saucepan, blend reserved juice, broth, cornstarch, soy sauce, vinegar, brown sugar and red pepper. Cook and stir until mixture thickens and boils. Stir in pineapple. Serve hot or cold with cocktail franks, ham cubes or vegetables.
Makes 2 cups.

Piña Pepper Spread

1 can (8 ounces) DOLE® Crushed Pineapple, drained
½ cup bottled taco sauce
1 package (8 ounces) cream cheese, softened
Taco chips or crackers

Combine pineapple and taco sauce in small bowl. Place cream cheese on serving plate in block or cut into individual servings. Spoon pineapple mixture over top. Serve with taco chips or crackers.
Makes 4 servings.

Mexicali Nacho Platter

1 envelope LIPTON® Nacho Cheese Recipe Soup Mix
1¼ cups milk
1 pound boneless chicken breasts, cooked and cut into thin strips
Corn tortilla or nacho chips
Assorted Nacho Toppings*

In 2-quart saucepan, with wire whip or fork, thoroughly blend nacho cheese recipe soup mix with milk. Bring just to the boiling point, stirring frequently, then reduce heat and simmer covered, stirring occasionally, 5 minutes. Stir in chicken and heat through. To serve, arrange chips on large serving platter. Top with ½ nacho sauce and Assorted Nacho Toppings, then add remaining sauce and toppings.
Makes about 4 main-dish servings.

***Assorted Nacho Toppings:** Use any combination of the following—sliced pitted ripe olives; chopped green onions, tomatoes, green chilies and avocado; and crumbled cooked bacon.

Herbed Cheese Pinwheel Canapes

- 1 8-ounce package PHILADELPHIA BRAND Cream Cheese, softened
- 2 tablespoons chopped parsley
- 2 teaspoons lemon juice
- ½ teaspoon dried basil leaves, crushed
- ⅛ teaspoon pepper
- ⅛ teaspoon garlic powder
- 1 1-pound unsliced whole-wheat bread loaf, crusts trimmed Soft PARKAY Margarine
- ¼ cup finely chopped pecans
- ¼ cup sesame seed
- 1 tablespoon worcestershire sauce

Combine cream cheese, parsley, juice and seasonings, mixing until well blended. Slice bread lengthwise into ½-inch slices. Roll each slice to ¼-inch thickness. Evenly spread each bread slice with cream cheese mixture; roll up, starting at narrow end. Spread bread rolls with margarine, excluding ends. In small skillet, combine remaining ingredients; cook 3 minutes or until worcestershire sauce evaporates. Cool. Coat bread rolls with pecan mixture. Cover; chill at least 30 minutes. Cut each bread roll crosswise into ½-inch slices.
Approximately 2½ dozen.

Mexican Shrimp Cocktail

- ½ cup WISH-BONE® Italian Dressing
- ½ cup chopped tomato
- 1 can (4 ounces) chopped green chilies, undrained
- ¼ cup chopped green onions
- 1½ teaspoons honey
- ¼ teaspoon hot pepper sauce
- 1 pound medium shrimp, cleaned and cooked
- 2 teaspoons finely chopped coriander (cilantro) or parsley

In medium bowl, combine Italian dressing, tomato, chilies, green onions, honey and hot pepper sauce. Stir in shrimp. Cover and marinate in refrigerator, stirring occasionally, at least 2 hours. Just before serving, stir in coriander.
Makes about 6 servings.
Note: Also terrific with Wish-Bone® Robusto Italian, Lite Italian, Blended Italian or Herbal Italian Dressing.

Cheese & Nut Stuffed Bread Slices

- 1 loaf Italian or French bread (about 16 inches long)
- 1 (8-ounce) *plus* 1 (3-ounce) package cream cheese, softened
- 4 tablespoons butter or margarine, softened
- 1 cup shredded Cheddar cheese (about 4 ounces)
- 1 envelope LIPTON® Vegetable Recipe Soup Mix
- ½ cup chopped walnuts

Trim ends of bread, then cut bread crosswise into 4 pieces. Hollow out center of each piece, leaving ½-inch shell; reserve shells (save bread for fresh bread crumbs).

With food processor or electric mixer, combine cream cheese with butter until smooth. Add Cheddar cheese, vegetable recipe soup mix and walnuts; process until blended. Pack into reserved shells. Wrap in plastic wrap or wax paper, then chill at least 4 hours. To serve, cut into ½-inch slices.
Makes about 2 dozen slices.
Note: Store any remaining cheese mixture, covered, in refrigerator and serve as a spread with crackers.

Cheesy Potato Skins

- 4 large baking potatoes, baked Oil
- ¼ lb. VELVEETA Pasteurized Process Cheese Spread, cubed
- 2 tablespoons chopped red or green pepper
- 2 crisply cooked bacon slices, crumbled
- 1 tablespoon green onion slices Sour cream

Cut potatoes in half lengthwise; scoop out centers, leaving ¼-inch shell. Fry shells, a few at a time, in deep hot oil, 375°, 2 to 3 minutes or until golden brown; drain. Place on cookie sheet. Top with process cheese spread; broil until process cheese spread begins to melt. Top with remaining ingredients.
8 appetizers.

Preparation time: 60 minutes
Cooking time: 10 minutes

Herb Appetizer Cheesecake

1 cup dry bread crumbs
1/4 cup PARKAY Margarine, melted
1/4 cup olive oil
2 cups fresh basil leaves
1/2 teaspoon salt
1 garlic clove, cut in half
2 8-ounce packages PHILADELPHIA BRAND Cream Cheese, softened
1 cup ricotta cheese
3 eggs
1/2 cup (2 ounces) KRAFT Grated Parmesan Cheese
1/2 cup pine nuts

Combine crumbs and margarine; press onto bottom of 9-inch springform pan. Bake at 350°, 10 minutes.

Place oil, basil, salt and garlic in blender container. Cover; process on high speed until smooth. Combine basil mixture, cream cheese and ricotta cheese, mixing at medium speed on electric mixer until well blended. Add eggs, one at a time, mixing well after each addition. Blend in parmesan cheese; pour over crust. Top with pine nuts. Bake at 325°, 1 hour and 15 minutes. Loosen cake from rim of pan; cool before removing rim of pan. Serve warm or at room temperature. Garnish with tomato rose and fresh basil, if desired. Chill any remaining cheesecake.
16 servings.

Variation: Substitute 1 cup chopped parsley and 1 tablespoon dried basil leaves for fresh basil leaves.

Cheese Stuffed Tomatoes

1 cup BORDEN® or MEADOW GOLD® Cottage Cheese
1/4 cup (1 ounce) crumbled blue cheese
1 teaspoon celery seed
1 teaspoon prepared mustard
1/4 teaspoon onion powder
30 cherry tomatoes, tops removed and seeded

In medium bowl, combine cheeses and seasonings; mix well. Spoon cheese mixture into tomatoes; cover and chill. Refrigerate leftovers.
Makes 30 appetizers.

Beef Kushisashi

1/2 cup KIKKOMAN Soy Sauce
1/4 cup chopped green onions and tops
2 tablespoons sugar
1 tablespoon vegetable oil
1 1/2 teaspoons cornstarch
1 clove garlic, pressed
1 teaspoon grated fresh ginger root
2 1/2 pounds boneless beef sirloin steak

Blend soy sauce, green onions, sugar, oil, cornstarch, garlic and ginger in small saucepan. Simmer, stirring constantly, until thickened, about 1 minute; cool. Cover and set aside. Slice beef into 1/8-inch-thick strips about 4 inches long and 1 inch wide. Thread onto bamboo or metal skewers keeping meat as flat as possible; brush both sides of beef with sauce. Place skewers on rack of broiler pan; broil to desired degree of doneness.
Makes 10 to 12 appetizer servings.

Beer Batter Fried Veggies 'n Things

Oil
1 envelope LIPTON® Golden Onion Recipe Soup Mix
1 cup all-purpose flour
1 teaspoon baking powder
2 eggs
1/2 cup beer
1 tablespoon prepared mustard
Suggested Veggies 'n Things*

In deep-fat fryer, heat oil to 375°.

Meanwhile, in large bowl, beat golden onion recipe soup mix, flour, baking powder, eggs, beer and mustard until smooth and well blended. Let batter stand 10 minutes. Dip Suggested Veggies 'n Things into batter, then carefully drop into hot oil. Fry, turning once, until golden brown; drain on paper towels. Serve warm.
Makes about 4 cups veggies 'n things.

***Suggested Veggies 'n Things:** Use any of the following to equal 4 to 5 cups—broccoli florets, cauliflowerets, sliced mushrooms or zucchini, or chilled mozzarella sticks.

Baked Artichoke Squares

**3 tablespoons CRISCO® Oil
1 cup chopped fresh
    mushrooms
1/4 cup thinly sliced celery
1 clove garlic, minced
1 can (14 ounces) artichoke
    hearts, drained and chopped
1/3 cup chopped green onion
1/2 teaspoon dried marjoram
    leaves
1/4 teaspoon dried oregano leaves
1/4 teaspoon cayenne
1 cup shredded Cheddar cheese
    (about 4 ounces)
1 cup shredded Monterey Jack
    cheese (about 4 ounces)
2 eggs, slightly beaten
Pastry:
1 1/2 cups all-purpose flour
1/2 teaspoon salt
1/2 cup CRISCO® Oil
1/4 cup milk**

Preheat oven to 350°F. Heat Crisco® Oil in medium skillet. Add mushrooms, celery and garlic. Sauté until celery is tender. Remove from heat. Stir in artichoke hearts, onion, marjoram, oregano and cayenne. Add Cheddar cheese, Monterey Jack cheese and eggs. Mix well. Set aside.

For pastry, combine flour and salt in medium mixing bowl. Blend Crisco® Oil and milk in small mixing bowl. Add to flour mixture. Stir with fork until mixture forms a ball. Press dough in bottom and 1 1/2 inches up sides of 13×9-inch pan. Bake at 350°F, 10 minutes.

Spread cheese mixture on baked crust. Bake at 350°F, about 20 minutes, or until center is set. Cool slightly. Cut into 24 squares. Serve warm.
2 dozen appetizers.

Appetizer Ham Logs

**2 cups ground ham
1 egg, beaten
1/4 teaspoon pepper
1/4 cup seasoned fine dry bread
    crumbs
1/2 cup horseradish sauce
1 tablespoon prepared mustard
1/8 teaspoon celery salt
    Vegetable oil for frying
    Pimiento strips**

Combine ham, egg and pepper in medium bowl; mix well. Shape into 1-inch logs or balls. Roll in bread crumbs. Refrigerate, covered, 1 hour.

To make mustard sauce, combine horseradish sauce, mustard and celery salt in small bowl until well blended. Refrigerate, covered, until serving time.

Heat 3 inches oil in heavy, large saucepan over medium-high heat until oil is 365°F; adjust heat to maintain temperature. Fry ham logs, a few at a time, 2 to 3 minutes or until golden. Drain on paper towels. Garnish with pimiento strips. Serve with mustard sauce.
Makes about 24 appetizers.

*Favorite recipe from **National Pork Producers Council***

Baked Stuffed Clams

**12 clams, well scrubbed*
    Water
1 envelope LIPTON® Vegetable
    Recipe Soup Mix
2 cups fresh bread crumbs
1 teaspoon oregano
1/8 teaspoon pepper
2 tablespoons oil
2 tablespoons grated Parmesan
    cheese**

In large skillet, arrange clams, then add 1/2 inch water. Cook covered over medium-high heat 5 minutes or until clams open. Remove clams, reserving 3/4 cup liquid; strain liquid. (Discard any unopened clams.) Remove clams from shells, then chop clams; reserve 12 shell halves.

Preheat oven to 350°. In small bowl, combine vegetable recipe soup mix, bread crumbs, oregano and pepper. Stir in clams and reserved liquid. Stuff reserved shells with clam mixture. Arrange on baking sheet; drizzle with oil, then sprinkle with cheese. Bake 15 minutes or until golden.
Makes 12 stuffed clams.
Substitution: Use 2 cans (6 1/2 ounces each) minced or chopped clams, drained (reserve 1/4 cup liquid). Mix reserved liquid with 1/2 cup water. Shells can be purchased separately.
Microwave Directions: Omit oil. Cook and stuff clams as above. On plate, arrange clams and heat uncovered at HIGH (Full Power) 5 minutes or until heated through, rearranging clams once.

Ham-Wrapped Oysters

**3 tablespoons prepared
    horseradish
1/2 pound ham, cut into
    3×1×1/4-inch strips
2 dozen fresh oysters, shucked
3 tablespoons butter or
    margarine, melted
1 tablespoon lemon juice
1/4 teaspoon garlic powder**

Spread horseradish on 1 side of each ham strip. Place 1 oyster on each ham strip; roll up and secure with wooden pick. Arrange on broiler pan. Combine butter, lemon juice and garlic powder in small cup. Brush each ham roll with some of the lemon-butter. Broil, 5 inches from heat, 10 to 15 minutes or until edges of oysters curl, brushing occasionally with the remaining lemon-butter.
Makes 24 appetizers.

*Favorite recipe from **National Pork Producers Council***

Saucy Shrimp

½ pound medium-size raw shrimp
¼ cup KIKKOMAN Teriyaki Baste & Glaze
2 tablespoons dry sherry
1 tablespoon lime juice
1 tablespoon sliced green onions and tops
3 to 4 drops Tabasco pepper sauce

Peel, devein and butterfly shrimp. Combine teriyaki baste & glaze, sherry, lime juice, green onions and pepper sauce in medium bowl; stir in shrimp. Cover; refrigerate at least 1 hour, stirring occasionally. Remove shrimp and place on rack of broiler pan. Broil 2 to 3 minutes on each side, or until shrimp are opaque and cooked. Serve immediately with wooden picks.
Makes 6 appetizer servings.

Stuffed Mushrooms with Crabmeat

12 to 15 large mushrooms
1 envelope LIPTON® Vegetable Recipe Soup Mix
package (6 ounces) frozen crabmeat, thawed and squeezed dry
½ cup sour cream
3 tablespoons plain dry bread crumbs
1 tablespoon snipped fresh dill*
3 dashes hot pepper sauce
⅛ teaspoon pepper
2 tablespoons butter or margarine, melted

Preheat oven to 350°.
Remove and finely chop mushroom stems. In medium bowl, combine chopped mushroom stems, vegetable recipe soup mix, crabmeat, sour cream, bread crumbs, dill, hot pepper sauce and pepper; set aside.
On lightly greased baking sheet, arrange mushroom caps; stuff with crabmeat mixture, then brush with melted butter. Bake 15 minutes or until tender.
Makes about 12 appetizers.
*Substitution: Use 1 teaspoon dried dill weed.
Make-Ahead Directions: Mushrooms can be partially prepared up to 1 day ahead. Simply prepare and stuff as above. Cover and refrigerate. To serve, brush with butter, then bake as above.

Teriyaki Scallop Roll-Ups

12 slices bacon, partially cooked and cut in half crosswise
⅓ cup REALIME® Lime Juice from Concentrate
¼ cup soy sauce
¼ cup vegetable oil
1 tablespoon light brown sugar
2 cloves garlic, finely chopped
½ teaspoon pepper
½ pound sea scallops, cut in half
24 fresh pea pods
12 water chestnuts, cut in half

To make teriyaki marinade, combine ReaLime® brand, soy sauce, oil, sugar, garlic and pepper; mix well. Wrap 1 scallop half, 1 pea pod and 1 water chestnut half in each bacon slice; secure with wooden pick. Place in shallow baking dish; pour marinade over. Cover; refrigerate 4 hours or overnight, turning occasionally. Preheat oven to 450°. Place roll-ups on rack in aluminum foil-lined shallow baking pan; bake 6 minutes. Turn; continue baking 6 minutes or until bacon is crisp. Serve hot. Refrigerate leftovers.
Makes about 2 dozen.

Baked Stuffed Shrimp

1 pound jumbo raw shrimp (about 12 to 16), peeled, leaving tails on
1 cup chopped mushrooms
⅓ cup chopped onion
1 clove garlic, finely chopped
1 teaspoon WYLER'S® or STEERO® Chicken-Flavor Instant Bouillon
¼ cup margarine or butter
1½ cups soft bread crumbs (3 slices bread)
1 tablespoon chopped pimiento
Melted margarine or butter
Chopped parsley, optional

Preheat oven to 400°. In large skillet, cook mushrooms, onion, garlic and bouillon in margarine until tender. Remove from heat; stir in crumbs and pimiento. Cut a slit along underside of each shrimp; do not cut through. Remove vein; brush entire shrimp with margarine. Mound stuffing mixture in hollow of each shrimp. Place in greased shallow baking dish. Bake 10 to 12 minutes or until hot. Garnish with parsley if desired. Refrigerate leftovers.
Makes 6 to 8 servings.
Microwave: In 1-quart glass measure, microwave margarine on full power (high) 45 seconds or until melted. Add mushrooms, onion, garlic and bouillon. Microwave on full power (high) 3 minutes or until onion is tender. Stir in crumbs and pimiento. Prepare shrimp as above. Place in 2 greased 12×7-inch shallow baking dishes or 1 (12-inch) round glass platter. Microwave on full power (high) 3 minutes or until hot. Proceed as above.

Marinated Mushrooms

1/2 cup WISH-BONE® Italian & Cheese Dressing
2 pounds fresh mushrooms
2 teaspoons lemon juice

In large saucepan, heat Italian & cheese dressing and cook mushrooms over medium heat, stirring occasionally, 5 minutes. Add lemon juice. Remove mushrooms with dressing to large shallow baking dish. Cover and marinate in refrigerator, stirring occasionally, 4 hours or overnight.
Makes about 4 cups mushrooms.
Note: Also terrific with Wish-Bone® Italian, Robusto Italian, or Lite Italian Dressing.

Marinated Antipasto

1 1/2 pounds medium raw shrimp, peeled, deveined and cooked
6 ounces Provolone cheese, cut into cubes
1 (6-ounce) can pitted ripe olives, drained
1/2 cup sliced green onions
1 cup vegetable oil
2/3 cup REALEMON® Lemon Juice from Concentrate
2 tablespoons Dijon-style mustard
2 teaspoons sugar
1 1/2 teaspoons thyme leaves
1 teaspoon salt
4 ounces Genoa salami, cut into cubes
1 large red pepper, seeded and cut into squares

Place shrimp, cheese, olives and onions in large shallow dish. In small bowl or jar, combine remaining ingredients except salami and pepper; mix well. Pour over shrimp mixture. Cover; refrigerate 6 hours or overnight, stirring occasionally. Add salami and pepper; toss. Drain; serve with toothpicks. Refrigerate leftovers.
Makes about 8 cups.

Thai Chicken Strips

1/2 cup WISH-BONE® Italian Dressing
1/4 cup dry white wine
1 tablespoon sugar
1 tablespoon soy sauce
1 tablespoon finely chopped coriander (cilantro) or parsley
1/2 teaspoon ground ginger
1/2 teaspoon ground cumin
1/4 teaspoon paprika
1/4 cup sesame seeds, well toasted
1 1/2 pounds boneless chicken breasts, cut into lengthwise strips

In food processor or blender, process Italian dressing, wine, sugar, soy sauce, coriander, ginger, cumin and paprika until blended. In large shallow baking dish, combine dressing mixture, sesame seeds and chicken. Cover and marinate in refrigerator, stirring occasionally, at least 3 hours.
Remove chicken and marinade to large shallow baking pan or aluminum foil-lined broiler rack. Broil chicken with marinade, turning occasionally, 10 minutes or until done. Garnish as desired.
Makes about 20 appetizers.
Note: Also terrific with Wish-Bone® Robusto Italian, Classic Dijon Vinaigrette, Herbal Italian, Lite Italian, Blended Italian or Lite Classic Dijon Vinaigrette Dressing.

Buffalo-Style Chicken Wings

Oil
12 chicken wings (about 2 pounds)
1/2 cup all-purpose flour
2 tablespoons butter or margarine
1/4 cup sliced green onions
1 medium clove garlic, finely chopped
1 cup (8 ounces) WISH-BONE® Sweet 'n Spicy® French Dressing
1 teaspoon thyme leaves
1 teaspoon oregano leaves
1 teaspoon ground cumin
1/2 teaspoon hot pepper sauce* WISH-BONE® Chunky Blue Cheese Dressing
Celery sticks

In deep-fat fryer or large heavy skillet, heat oil to 375°.
Cut tips off chicken wings (save tips for soup). Halve chicken wings at joint. Lightly coat chicken with flour, then carefully drop chicken, a few pieces at a time, into hot oil. Fry, turning occasionally, 15 minutes or until golden brown; drain on paper towels.
Meanwhile, in large skillet, melt butter and cook green onions with garlic over medium heat, stirring occasionally, 3 minutes or until onions are tender. Remove from heat and stir in sweet 'n spicy French dressing, thyme, oregano, cumin and hot pepper sauce. Add chicken and toss to coat. Serve with chunky blue cheese dressing and celery sticks.
Makes 24 appetizers.
Variations: First Alarm Chicken Wings: Add 1 teaspoon hot pepper sauce.
Second Alarm Chicken Wings: Add 1 1/2 teaspoons hot pepper sauce.
Third Alarm Chicken Wings: Add 2 teaspoons hot pepper sauce.
Note: Also terrific with Wish-Bone® Lite Sweet 'n Spicy French, Russian or Lite Russian Dressing.

Miniature Teriyaki Pork Kabobs

1 pound boneless pork, cut into 4×1×¹⁄₂-inch strips
1 can (11 ounces) mandarin oranges
1 small green bell pepper, cut into 1×¹⁄₄×¹⁄₄-inch strips
¹⁄₄ cup teriyaki sauce
1 tablespoon honey
1 tablespoon vinegar
¹⁄₈ teaspoon garlic powder

Soak 24 (8-inch) bamboo skewers in water 10 minutes. Thread pork strips accordion-style with mandarin oranges on skewers. Place 1 pepper strip on end of each skewer. Arrange on broiler pan.

For sauce, combine teriyaki sauce, honey, vinegar and garlic powder in small bowl; mix well. Brush sauce over kabobs. Broil, 6 inches from heat, about 15 minutes or until pork is done, turning and basting with sauce occasionally.
Makes about 24 appetizers.

*Favorite recipe from **National Pork Producers Council***

Rumaki

16 slices bacon
1 pound chicken livers, cut into quarters
1 can (8 ounces) sliced water chestnuts, drained
¹⁄₃ cup soy sauce
2 tablespoons packed brown sugar
1 tablespoon Dijon-style mustard

Cut bacon slices in half crosswise. Wrap ¹⁄₂ slice bacon around piece of chicken liver and water chestnut slice. Secure with wooden pick. (Reserve any remaining water chestnut slices for another use.) Arrange on broiler pan. Combine soy sauce, brown sugar and mustard in small bowl. Brush over bacon rolls. Broil, 6 inches from heat, 15 to 20 minutes or until bacon is crisp and chicken livers are done, turning and brushing with soy sauce mixture occasionally.
Makes about 32 appetizers.

*Favorite recipe from **National Pork Producers Council***

Chicken Wings with Honey & Orange Sauce

12 chicken wings (about 2 pounds)
1 envelope LIPTON® Golden Onion Recipe Soup Mix
¹⁄₃ cup honey
¹⁄₄ cup water
¹⁄₄ cup frozen concentrated orange juice, partially thawed and undiluted
¹⁄₄ cup sherry
1 tablespoon prepared mustard
2 teaspoons soy sauce
¹⁄₄ teaspoon ground ginger
3 dashes hot pepper sauce

Preheat oven to 350°

Cut tips off chicken wings (save tips for soup). Halve remaining chicken wings at joint.

In 13×9-inch baking dish, blend remaining ingredients; add chicken and turn to coat. Bake uncovered, basting occasionally, 40 minutes or until chicken is done and sauce is thickened.
Makes 24 appetizers.

Microwave Directions: In 13×9-inch baking dish, prepare chicken wings and sauce as above. Heat uncovered at HIGH (Full Power), basting and rearranging chicken occasionally, 20 minutes or until chicken is done and sauce is thickened. Let stand uncovered 5 minutes.

Filled New Potatoes

2 pounds (18) small new potatoes
1 8-ounce container Soft PHILADELPHIA BRAND Cream Cheese
Caviar
Chopped chives

Cook potatoes in boiling salted water 15 to 20 minutes or until tender; drain. Cut thin slice from bottom to form base; scoop out top with melon ball cutter. Fill with cream cheese; top with caviar or chives. Serve warm.
1¹⁄₂ dozen.

Golden Chicken Nuggets

1 envelope LIPTON® Golden Onion Recipe Soup Mix
³⁄₄ cup plain dry bread crumbs
1¹⁄₂ pounds boneless chicken breasts, cut into 1-inch pieces
¹⁄₄ cup butter or margarine, melted

Preheat oven to 400°. Combine golden onion recipe soup mix with bread crumbs. Dip chicken in bread crumbs mixture, coating well. In lightly greased large shallow baking pan, arrange chicken, then drizzle with butter. Bake, turning once, 10 minutes or until chicken is done.
Makes about 2 dozen nuggets.

Crispy Fried Mushrooms

- ½ cup all-purpose flour
- ½ teaspoon salt
- ¼ teaspoon dry mustard
- ¼ teaspoon paprika
  - Dash pepper
- ½ cup buttermilk
- 8 ounces whole fresh mushrooms
  - CRISCO® Oil for frying

Mix flour, salt, mustard, paprika and pepper in large plastic food storage bag. Set aside. Place buttermilk in small bowl. Dip a few mushrooms at a time in buttermilk. Place in bag with flour mixture. Shake to coat.

Heat 2 to 3 inches Crisco® Oil in deep-fryer or heavy saucepan to 375°F. Fry a few mushrooms at a time, 2 to 3 minutes, or until deep golden brown, turning over several times. Drain on paper towels. Serve hot with *catsup*, if desired.
4 to 6 servings.

Grilled Cheese

- 1 piece raclette cheese*
  - (12 to 16 ounces)
- 1 tablespoon olive or vegetable oil
- ½ teaspoon ground oregano
  - Sliced crusty French bread or large crackers

Place cheese in 10-inch iron skillet; brush with oil. Sprinkle oregano on top. Place bread slices around cheese in skillet.

Grill cheese, on covered grill, over medium-hot **KINGSFORD® Charcoal Briquets** 10 minutes or until cheese is very soft. Remove to table; spread cheese on bread slices.
Makes 6 servings.

*Raclette cheese is available at specialty cheese shops. You can try another soft cheese, such as Swiss, but cooking time may vary.

Deviled Stuffed Eggs

- 12 hard-cooked eggs
- ⅓ cup finely chopped VLASIC® Country Classic Sweet Gherkins
- ⅓ cup MARIE'S® Refrigerated Buttermilk Spice Ranch Style Salad Dressing
- 2 tablespoons finely chopped onion
- ¼ teaspoon salt
  - Finely chopped VLASIC® Country Classic Sweet Gherkins for garnish

1. Remove egg shells. Cut eggs in half lengthwise. Remove and chop egg yolks. Dice 1 egg white.
2. To make filling: In medium bowl, combine yolks, diced egg white, ⅓ cup gherkins, salad dressing, onion and salt.
3. Spoon about 1 tablespoon filling into each remaining egg white half. Cover; refrigerate until serving time, at least 4 hours.
4. To serve: Top each filled half with chopped gherkins.
Makes 22 appetizers.

Golden Mini Quiches

- 1 envelope LIPTON® Golden Onion Recipe Soup Mix
- 1½ cups light cream or half and half
- 3 eggs, beaten
  - Pastry for double-crust pie*
- 1 cup shredded Swiss cheese (about 4 ounces)

Preheat oven to 400°.

In medium bowl, thoroughly blend golden onion recipe soup mix, cream and eggs; set aside.

On lightly floured board, roll pastry ⅛ inch thick; cut into 36 (2½-inch) circles. Press into 7½×9¾-inch muffin pans. Evenly fill prepared pans with cheese, then egg mixture. Bake 25 minutes or until knife inserted in center comes out clean and pastry is golden. Serve warm.
Makes 3 dozen mini quiches.

Variation: For one 9-inch quiche, bake one 9-inch unbaked pastry shell at 375°, 10 minutes. Fill pastry shell with cheese, then egg mixture. Bake 40 minutes or until quiche tests done and pastry is golden.
Makes about 7 servings.

Freezing/Reheating Directions: Mini quiches can be baked, then frozen. Simply wrap in heavy-duty aluminum foil; freeze. To reheat, unwrap and bake at 350°, 15 minutes or until heated through. **OR,** place 12 quiches on plate and microwave at HIGH (Full Power) 4 minutes or until heated through, turning plate once.

"Philly" Stuffed Mushrooms

- 2 pounds medium mushrooms
- 6 tablespoons PARKAY Margarine
- 1 8-ounce package PHILADELPHIA BRAND Cream Cheese, softened
- ½ cup (2 ounces) crumbled KRAFT Natural Blue Cheese
- 2 tablespoons chopped onion

Remove mushroom stems; chop enough stems to measure ½ cup. Cook half of mushroom caps in 3 tablespoons margarine over medium heat 5 minutes; drain. Repeat with remaining mushroom caps and margarine. Combine cream cheese and blue cheese, mixing until well blended. Stir in chopped stems and onions; fill mushroom caps. Place on cookie sheet; broil until golden brown.
Approximately 2½ dozen.

Chicken-Stuffed Mushrooms

1 package (16 ounces) CAMPBELL'S FRESH® Mushrooms
2 tablespoons finely chopped celery
2 tablespoons finely chopped onion
1 tablespoon butter or margarine
½ cup soft bread crumbs
½ cup shredded Monterey Jack cheese (2 ounces)
Generous dash salt
Generous dash pepper
1 can (5 ounces) SWANSON® Premium Chunk White Chicken, drained

To Microwave:
1. Remove mushroom stems. Chop enough stems to measure ½ cup; reserve remaining stems for another use.
2. Arrange mushroom caps, stem side down, on 10-inch microwave-safe plate lined with paper towels, placing large caps around outside. Microwave, uncovered, on HIGH 2 minutes or until most mushrooms are tender.
3. In 1-quart microwave-safe bowl, combine the ½ cup mushroom stems, celery, onion and butter. Cover with vented plastic wrap; microwave on HIGH 3 minutes or until vegetables are tender, stirring once during cooking.
4. Stir in crumbs, cheese, salt and pepper. Add chicken; toss gently to mix.
5. Spoon chicken mixture into mushroom caps. Arrange stuffed caps on same 10-inch plate lined with clean paper towels, placing less-tender mushrooms around outside. Microwave, uncovered, on HIGH 2½ minutes or until mushrooms are tender.
Makes about 20 appetizers.

Cantonese Meatballs

1 can (20 oz.) pineapple chunks in syrup
3 tablespoons brown sugar, packed
5 tablespoons KIKKOMAN Teriyaki Sauce, divided
1 tablespoon vinegar
1 tablespoon tomato catsup
1 pound lean ground beef
2 tablespoons instant minced onion
2 tablespoons cornstarch
¼ cup water

Drain pineapple; reserve syrup. Combine syrup, brown sugar, 3 tablespoons teriyaki sauce, vinegar and catsup; set aside. Mix beef with remaining 2 tablespoons teriyaki sauce and onion; shape into 20 meatballs. Brown meatballs in large skillet; drain off excess fat. Pour syrup mixture over meatballs; simmer 10 minutes, stirring occasionally. Dissolve cornstarch in water; stir into skillet with pineapple. Cook and stir until sauce thickens and pineapple is heated through.
Makes 6 to 8 appetizer servings.

Spring Rolls

½ pound ground pork
1 teaspoon KIKKOMAN Soy Sauce
1 teaspoon dry sherry
½ teaspoon garlic salt
2 tablespoons vegetable oil
3 cups fresh bean sprouts
½ cup sliced onion
1 tablespoon KIKKOMAN Soy Sauce
1 tablespoon cornstarch
¾ cup water, divided
8 sheets egg roll skins
½ cup prepared biscuit mix
1 egg, beaten
Vegetable oil for frying
Hot mustard, tomato catsup and KIKKOMAN Soy Sauce

Combine pork, 1 teaspoon soy sauce, sherry and garlic salt; mix well. Let stand 15 minutes. Heat 2 tablespoons oil in hot wok or large skillet over medium-high heat; brown pork mixture in hot oil. Add bean sprouts, onion and 1 tablespoon soy sauce. Stir-fry until vegetables are tender-crisp; drain and cool. Dissolve cornstarch in ¼ cup water. Place about ⅓ cupful pork mixture on lower half of egg roll skin. Moisten left and right edges with cornstarch mixture. Fold bottom edge up to just cover filling. Fold left and right edges ½ inch over; roll up jelly-roll fashion. Moisten top edge with cornstarch mixture and seal. Complete all rolls. Combine biscuit mix, egg and remaining ½ cup water in small bowl; dip each roll in batter. Heat oil for frying in wok or large saucepan over medium-high heat, to 370°F. Deep fry rolls, a few at a time, in hot oil 5 to 7 minutes, or until golden brown, turning often. Drain on paper towels. Slice each roll into 4 pieces. Serve with mustard, catsup and soy sauce as desired.
Makes 8 appetizer servings.

Grilled Oysters

12 to 16 fresh oysters in shells
½ cup butter or margarine
2 tablespoons lemon juice
2 tablespoons chopped parsley

Thoroughly scrub oysters. Arrange oysters on grill grid; do not open shells. Grill oysters, on uncovered grill, over medium-hot KINGS-FORD® Charcoal Briquets 12 to 15 minutes or until shells steam open. (Discard any oysters that do not open.)

Meanwhile, in saucepan, combine butter, lemon juice and parsley. Heat butter mixture on edge of grill until butter is melted, stirring frequently.

Carefully remove cooked oysters from grill and serve hot with lemon-butter mixture spooned over.
Makes 4 appetizer servings.

Salmon Canapes

1 (6½-ounce) can salmon,
    drained and flaked
1 tablespoon low-calorie
    mayonnaise
1 tablespoon REALEMON®
    Lemon Juice from
    Concentrate
⅛ teaspoon dill weed
24 Melba rounds
6 slices LITE-LINE® Process
    Cheese Product,* any flavor,
    quartered
24 thin slices cucumber
    Parsley

In small bowl, combine salmon, mayonnaise, ReaLemon® brand and dill; mix well. On each Melba round, place a Lite-line piece, cucumber slice, 2 teaspoons salmon mixture and parsley. Serve immediately. Refrigerate leftovers.
Makes 24 appetizers; 36 calories per appetizer.
*"½ the calories"—8% milk fat version.
Calories by product analyses and recipe calculation.

Empress Chicken Wings

1½ pounds chicken wings (about
    8 wings)
3 tablespoons KIKKOMAN Soy
    Sauce
1 tablespoon dry sherry
1 tablespoon minced fresh
    ginger root
1 clove garlic, minced
2 tablespoons vegetable oil
¼ to ⅓ cup cornstarch
⅔ cup water
2 green onions and tops, cut
    diagonally into thin slices
1 teaspoon slivered fresh ginger
    root

Disjoint chicken wings; discard tips (or save for stock). Combine soy sauce, sherry, minced ginger and garlic in large bowl; stir in chicken. Cover and refrigerate 1 hour, stirring occasionally. Remove chicken; reserve marinade. Heat oil in large skillet over medium heat. Lightly coat chicken pieces with cornstarch; add to skillet and brown slowly on all sides. Remove chicken; drain off fat. Stir water and reserved marinade into same skillet. Add chicken; sprinkle green onions and slivered ginger evenly over chicken. Cover and simmer 5 minutes, or until chicken is tender.
Makes 4 to 6 appetizer servings.

Cajun-Style Chicken Nuggets

1 envelope LIPTON® Onion or
    Onion-Mushroom Recipe
    Soup Mix
½ cup plain dry bread crumbs
1½ teaspoons chili powder
1 teaspoon ground cumin
1 teaspoon thyme leaves
¼ teaspoon red pepper
2 pounds boneless chicken
    breasts, cut into 1-inch
    pieces
    Oil

In large bowl, combine onion recipe soup mix, bread crumbs, chili powder, cumin, thyme and pepper. Dip chicken in bread crumb mixture, coating well.
In large skillet, heat ½ inch oil and cook chicken over medium heat, turning once, until done; drain on paper towels. Serve warm and, if desired, with assorted mustards.
Makes about 5 dozen nuggets.
Microwave Directions: Prepare chicken as above. In 13×9-inch baking dish, arrange chicken, then drizzle with 2 to 3 tablespoons oil. Heat uncovered at HIGH (Full Power) 6 minutes or until chicken is done, rearranging chicken once; drain on paper towels. Serve as above.

Flaky Ham Puffs

1 recipe Mustard Sauce (see
    Index)
Pastry:
1⅔ cups all-purpose flour
⅓ cup yellow cornmeal
¼ cup grated Parmesan cheese
¼ teaspoon salt
½ cup CRISCO® Oil
3 tablespoons ice water
Filling:
¾ cup ground fully cooked ham
    (about 4 ounces)
¼ cup dairy sour cream
½ teaspoon prepared mustard
⅛ teaspoon onion powder
⅛ teaspoon pepper

Prepare Mustard Sauce as directed. Cover and refrigerate.
For pastry, combine flour, cornmeal, Parmesan cheese and salt in medium mixing bowl. Add Crisco® Oil. Stir with fork until moistened. Add water. Mix well. Divide dough in half. Form each half into a ball. Place 1 ball between 2 large sheets waxed paper. Roll dough ⅛ inch thick. Remove top sheet waxed paper. Cut dough into 2-inch circles. Repeat with remaining dough.
For filling, mix all ingredients in small mixing bowl. Preheat oven to 375°F.
To assemble puffs, place one pastry circle on ungreased baking sheet. Place 1 scant teaspoon filling in center of circle. Top with another pastry circle. Press edges of circles together with fork. Repeat with remaining pastry circles and filling.
Bake puffs at 375°F, 10 to 15 minutes, or until light golden brown. Remove to wire rack. Serve hot with Mustard Sauce.
About 2½ dozen appetizers.
Variation: Flaky Crab Puffs. Follow recipe above, substituting crab filling for ham filling. For crab filling, mix 1 can (6 to 6½ ounces) crab meat (rinsed and drained), 2 tablespoons grated Parmesan cheese, 1 tablespoon mayonnaise or salad dressing, 1 tablespoon minced green onion and ⅛ teaspoon hot pepper sauce in small mixing bowl.

Mini Cocktail Meatballs

1 envelope LIPTON® Onion, Onion-Mushroom, Beefy Mushroom or Beefy Onion Recipe Soup Mix
1 pound ground beef
½ cup plain dry bread crumbs
¼ cup dry red wine or water
2 eggs, slightly beaten

Preheat oven to 375°
In medium bowl, combine all ingredients; shape into 1-inch meatballs.
In shallow baking pan, arrange meatballs and bake 18 minutes or until done. Serve, if desired, with assorted mustards or tomato sauce.
Makes about 4 dozen meatballs.

Curried Chicken Puffs

½ cup water
⅓ cup PARKAY Margarine
⅔ cup flour
  Dash of salt
2 eggs
1 8-ounce package PHILADELPHIA BRAND Cream Cheese, softened
¼ cup milk
¼ teaspoon salt
  Dash of curry powder
  Dash of pepper
1½ cups chopped cooked chicken
⅓ cup slivered almonds, toasted
2 tablespoons green onion slices

Bring water and margarine to boil. Add flour and salt; stir vigorously over low heat until mixture forms ball. Remove from heat; add eggs, one at a time, beating until smooth after each addition. Place level measuring tablespoonfuls of batter on ungreased cookie sheet. Bake at 400°, 25 minutes. Cool.

Combine cream cheese, milk, salt, curry powder and pepper, mixing until well blended. Add chicken, almonds and onions; mix lightly. Cut tops from cream puffs; fill with chicken mixture. Replace tops. Place puffs on cookie sheet. Bake at 375°, 5 minutes or until warm.
Approximately 1½ dozen.
Note: Unfilled cream puffs can be prepared several weeks in advance and frozen. Place puffs on a jelly roll pan and wrap securely in plastic wrap.

Crispy Wontons

¾ pound ground pork
8 water chestnuts, finely chopped
¼ cup finely chopped green onions and tops
1 tablespoon KIKKOMAN Soy Sauce
½ teaspoon salt
1 teaspoon cornstarch
½ teaspoon grated fresh ginger root
1 package (1 lb.) wonton skins
  Vegetable oil for frying
  Tomato catsup and hot mustard or KIKKOMAN Sweet & Sour Sauce

Combine pork, water chestnuts, green onions, soy sauce, salt, cornstarch and ginger in medium bowl; mix well. Place ½ teaspoonful pork mixture in center of each wonton skin. Fold wonton skin over filling to form a triangle. Turn top of triangle down to meet fold. Turn over; moisten 1 corner with water. Overlap opposite corner over moistened corner; press firmly. Heat oil in wok or large saucepan over medium-high heat to 375°F. Deep fry wontons, a few at a time, 2 to 3 minutes, or until brown and crispy. Drain on paper towels. Serve warm with catsup and mustard or sweet & sour sauce, as desired.
Makes 10 appetizer servings.

Hot Sausage Bites

½ pound bulk sausage, browned and drained
1½ cups biscuit baking mix
1 cup (4 ounces) shredded mild Cheddar cheese
⅓ cup water
1 teaspoon WYLER'S® or STEERO® Beef-Flavor Instant Bouillon

Preheat oven to 400°. In medium bowl, combine ingredients; mix well. Shape into small balls. Place 1 inch apart on lightly greased baking sheets. Bake 12 to 15 minutes or until edges are lightly browned. Remove from baking sheets immediately. Serve hot. Refrigerate leftovers.
Makes about 3 dozen.

Petite "Philly" Pinwheels

1 8-ounce can PILLSBURY Refrigerated Quick Crescent Dinner Rolls
  Soft PHILADELPHIA BRAND Cream Cheese
½ cup finely chopped ham
2 tablespoons finely chopped stuffed green olives

Separate dough into four rectangles; firmly press perforations to seal. Spread with cream cheese; sprinkle with ham and olives, pressing lightly. Roll up, starting at short end; seal edges. Cut each roll into four slices. Place, cut-side down, on ungreased cookie sheet; flatten slightly. Bake at 375°, 15 to 17 minutes or until golden brown.
16 appetizers.
Variation: Substitute dried apricots and green pepper for ham and olives.

Herbed Mussels in Wine

3 pounds mussels (about 5 to 6 dozen)
2 tablespoons butter or margarine
1/3 cup chopped green onions
1 large clove garlic, minced
1/4 teaspoon dried Italian seasoning, crushed
3/4 cup V8® Vegetable Juice
1/4 cup Chablis or other dry white wine
Generous dash pepper

1. Discard any open mussels that do not close when tapped with fingers. Scrub mussels; clip off beards with kitchen shears.
2. In 4-quart saucepan over low heat, in hot butter, cook onions with garlic and Italian seasoning until onions are tender, stirring often. Add mussels, V8 juice, wine and pepper. Heat to boiling; reduce heat to low. Cover; simmer 6 to 8 minutes or until mussels open, stirring occasionally. Discard any mussels that do not open.
3. With slotted spoon, remove mussels from pan; remove and discard top halves of shells. Arrange mussels on serving platter; pour sauce over mussels.
Makes about 5 dozen appetizers.
   Note: To make sure raw mussels are safe to eat, tap on any open shells. If the mussel closes its shell, it will be safe to eat after cooking. Discard those that remain open. After cooking, discard any mussels with closed shells, because they were not alive before cooking and are not safe to eat.

Per appetizer: 10 calories, 1 g protein, 1 g fat, 1 g carbohydrate, 34 mg sodium, 3 mg cholesterol.

Spinach Rice Balls

1 1/2 cups cooked rice
1 package (10 ounces) frozen chopped spinach, cooked and well drained
1/2 cup shredded mozzarella cheese (about 1 1/2 ounces)
1/3 cup plain dry bread crumbs
2 eggs, slightly beaten
1/4 cup grated Parmesan cheese
1/4 cup milk
1 teaspoon Dijon-style prepared mustard
1 envelope LIPTON® Golden Onion Recipe Soup Mix

Preheat oven to 375°.
   In medium bowl, combine all ingredients; shape into 1-inch balls. On well-greased baking sheet, arrange rice balls and bake 20 minutes or until golden. Serve warm and, if desired, with assorted mustards.
Makes about 2 dozen rice balls.

Seafood Cocktails with Watercress Sauce

1 large bunch watercress, stems removed (about 2 cups loosely packed)*
1 small bunch parsley, stems removed (about 1 cup loosely packed)*
1 medium clove garlic, finely chopped
1 envelope LIPTON® Golden Onion Recipe Soup Mix
1/2 pint (8 ounces) sour cream
1/4 cup mayonnaise
1/8 teaspoon pepper
Suggested Seafood**

In food processor or blender, combine watercress, parsley and garlic until blended. Add golden onion recipe soup mix, sour cream, mayonnaise and pepper; process until smooth. Chill at least 2 hours. Serve with Suggested Seafood. Garnish as desired.
Makes about 2 cups sauce or about 8 appetizer servings.
   ***Variation:** Omit watercress. Use 2 small bunches parsley, stems removed (about 2 cups loosely packed).
   ****Suggested Seafood:** Use about 2 pounds cooked and chilled butterflied shrimp, scallops, crab claws and legs, lobster meat or clams.

Party Quiche Squares

1 (11-ounce) package pie crust mix
1 (10-ounce) package frozen chopped broccoli, thawed and well drained
1 1/2 cups shredded Swiss cheese (6 ounces)
2 tablespoons all-purpose flour
1 cup COLLEGE INN® Chicken Broth
3/4 cup heavy cream
5 eggs
2 tablespoons GREY POUPON® Dijon Mustard

Prepare pie crust mix according to package directions; roll out on floured surface to 16×11-inch rectangle. Arrange on bottom of ungreased 15 1/2×10 1/2×1-inch baking pan, trimming to fit.
   Combine broccoli, cheese and flour; arrange evenly over pastry. Blend chicken broth, cream, eggs and mustard; pour evenly over broccoli mixture. Bake at 350°F for 35 to 40 minutes or until knife inserted in center comes out clean. Cool slightly. To serve, cut into squares. Garnish as desired.
Makes 60 appetizers.

Beef Gems

- 10 ounces thinly sliced PETER ECKRICH DELI® Roast Beef
- 1 package (8 ounces) cream cheese, softened
- ¼ cup minced carrot
- ¼ cup minced green bell pepper
- ¼ cup minced radish
- ¼ cup minced cucumber
- 1½ teaspoons lemon juice
- ⅛ teaspoon onion powder
- Dash ground white pepper
- Crackers (about 3×2 inches)

Combine cream cheese, vegetables, lemon juice, onion powder and pepper in small bowl. Fold each slice of roast beef to fit crackers, cutting roast beef if necessary. Spread cream cheese mixture over center of roast beef.
Makes about 14 to 16 open-faced crackers.

Zesty Smoked Sausages

- 1 can (11 ounces) CAMPBELL'S® Condensed Zesty Tomato Soup/Sauce
- ½ cup orange marmalade or apricot preserves
- 2 tablespoons vinegar
- 1 teaspoon dry mustard
- 1 pound tiny smoked sausage links or kielbasa, cut into bite-size pieces

To Microwave:
1. In 2-quart microwave-safe casserole, stir together soup, marmalade, vinegar and mustard until well blended.
2. Stir in sausages. Cover with lid; microwave on HIGH 7 minutes or until hot and bubbling, stirring once during cooking. To serve, spear with cocktail picks.
Makes about 30 appetizers.

Beer-Batter Shrimp

- 1 cup flour
- 1 tablespoon paprika
- ½ teaspoon salt
- 1 (12-ounce) can or bottle beer
- ½ teaspoon Worcestershire sauce
- ¼ teaspoon TABASCO® pepper sauce
- Vegetable oil
- 2 pounds shrimp, peeled, deveined
- Flour for dredging
- Creole Tartar Sauce (recipe follows)

In medium bowl combine 1 cup flour, paprika and salt. Whisk in beer, Worcestershire sauce and Tabasco® sauce. Cover; let stand at room temperature at least 1 hour. In large heavy saucepot or deep-fat fryer, heat about 3 inches oil over medium-high heat to 375°F. Dredge shrimp in flour, then dip in batter. Fry shrimp, a few at a time, 2 to 3 minutes or until golden. Drain on paper towels. Serve immediately with Creole Tartar Sauce.
Makes 8 servings.

Creole Tartar Sauce

- ¼ cup finely chopped green onions
- ¼ cup finely chopped celery
- ¼ cup finely chopped parsley
- 3 tablespoons tomato paste
- 2 tablespoons Dijon-style mustard
- 2 tablespoons olive or vegetable oil
- 1 tablespoon white wine vinegar
- ¾ teaspoon TABASCO® pepper sauce
- ½ teaspoon paprika

In small bowl combine all ingredients until well blended.
Makes about 1 cup.

Sausage Antipasto Platter

- Pesto Spread (recipe follows)
- 1 large tomato
- 6 ounces thinly sliced Genoa salami
- 6 ounces thinly sliced ham cappicola
- 6 ounces thinly sliced pepperoni
- 1 loaf (8 ounces) French bread, cut into ¼-inch slices
- 1 pound unpared cooked new potatoes, cut into ¼-inch slices
- 4 ounces pea pods, trimmed, strings removed
- 1 red bell pepper, cut into strips
- 1 small zucchini, cut diagonally into ¼-inch slices
- 4 ounces mushrooms, sliced
- ½ cup dry cured olives (optional)

Prepare Pesto Spread. Cut ½-inch slice from top of tomato; zigzag edge. Scoop out pulp. Fill tomato with Pesto Spread; place in center of large serving platter. Arrange remaining ingredients around tomato. To serve, spread slices of bread or potatoes with Pesto Spread and top with sliced meat and vegetables.
Makes 8 servings.
PESTO SPREAD: Combine ¾ cup tightly packed fresh basil leaves, 2 teaspoons crushed fresh rosemary or ¾ teaspoon dried rosemary, crushed, ¼ cup tightly packed Italian parsley and 2 quartered garlic cloves in food processor. Cover and process until blended. Add ⅓ cup French bread crumbs, ¼ cup grated Parmesan cheese, 1 teaspoon lemon juice, ½ teaspoon salt, and dash pepper. With motor running, slowly pour in ⅓ cup light cream and ¼ cup olive oil through feed tube. Process until blended. Pour into small bowl. Refrigerate, covered, 1½ to 2 hours to blend flavors.
Makes about 1 cup.

*Favorite recipe from **National Live Stock and Meat Board***

Mongolian Almonds

1 cup whole natural almonds
2 tablespoons KIKKOMAN Teriyaki Sauce
1 teaspoon brown sugar
1/8 to 1/4 teaspoon TABASCO® pepper sauce
1 tablespoon water
1/2 teaspoon vegetable oil

Toast almonds on ungreased baking sheet in preheated 350°F oven 10 minutes without stirring. Remove pan from oven and cool almonds in pan on wire rack. *Reduce oven temperature to 250°F.* Combine teriyaki sauce, brown sugar, pepper sauce and water in narrow 1-quart saucepan. Bring to boil over medium-low heat. Stir in almonds and boil about 5 minutes, or until sauce is absorbed by almonds, stirring frequently. Add oil and toss almonds until coated; turn out onto baking sheet, separating almonds. Bake 5 minutes; stir and turn almonds over. Bake 5 minutes longer. Remove almonds from pan to large plate; cool in single layer. Store in loose-fitting container or plastic bag. *Makes 1 cup.*

Spiced Apple Party Mix

1/2 teaspoon ground cinnamon
1/4 teaspoon ground nutmeg
1 cup SUN-MAID® Raisins
3/4 cup coarsely chopped dried apples
1 cup DIAMOND® Walnut pieces

In medium bowl, combine cinnamon and nutmeg. Add raisins and apples; toss to coat with spices. Add walnuts; toss. Store in airtight container. *Makes 2 1/2 cups.*

Toasty Onion Sticks

1/3 cup LIPTON® Onion Butter (see recipe below right)
12 slices white bread

Prepare Lipton® Onion Butter. Trim crust from bread. Spread onion butter on bread; cut each slice into 5 strips. Arrange strips on ungreased baking sheet. Bake in preheated 375°F oven 10 minutes or until golden. *Makes 5 dozen appetizers.*

Sesame Cheese Crackers

1 cup all-purpose flour
1/2 teaspoon salt
1/8 teaspoon ground red pepper (cayenne)
6 tablespoons cold butter or margarine
1 cup (4 oz.) finely grated Cheddar cheese
1/4 cup sesame seed, toasted
1/2 teaspoon KIKKOMAN Soy Sauce
4 1/2 to 7 1/2 teaspoons ice-cold water

Combine flour, salt and pepper in medium bowl; cut in butter until mixture resembles coarse crumbs. Stir in cheese and sesame seed. Combine soy sauce and 3 teaspoons water; stir into dry ingredients. Add more water, a little at a time, mixing lightly until dough begins to stick together. Turn out dough and press together on lightly floured board or pastry cloth; roll out to 1/8-inch thickness. Cut dough into 2×1-inch rectangles with pastry wheel or knife. Place on lightly greased baking sheets and bake at 400°F 8 to 10 minutes, or until lightly browned. Remove crackers to rack to cool. *Makes 8 appetizer servings.*

Curried Popcorn Mix

6 cups unseasoned popped corn
2 cups pretzel sticks
1 1/2 cups DIAMOND® Walnut pieces
1/4 cup butter or margarine, melted
2 teaspoons curry powder
1/4 teaspoon hot pepper sauce
Salt to taste
1 1/2 cups SUN-MAID® Golden Raisins

In large, deep baking or roasting pan, combine popped corn, pretzels and walnuts. In small bowl, mix butter, curry powder and pepper sauce; drizzle over popcorn mixture and toss to coat evenly. Bake in 300°F oven about 30 minutes, tossing twice. Remove from oven. Mix in salt. Cool completely. Store in airtight container. Mix in raisins before serving. *Makes about 2 quarts.*

Onion Party Puffs

1/3 cup LIPTON® Onion Butter (recipe follows)
1 package (8 ounces) refrigerator biscuits

Prepare Lipton® Onion Butter. Cut each biscuit into 4 sections. Arrange on ungreased baking sheet; dot with onion butter. Bake in preheated 400°F oven 8 minutes or until golden. *Makes 40 puffs.*
LIPTON® ONION BUTTER: Thoroughly blend 1 envelope **LIPTON® Onion Soup Mix** with 1/2 pound butter or margarine in medium bowl. Refrigerate, covered, any unused portion. Use on baked potatoes and cooked vegetables. *Makes 1 1/4 cups.*

Onion-Buttered Popcorn

In large bowl, combine **1 pouch CAMPBELL'S® Onion Soup and Recipe Mix** with ½ **cup melted butter or margarine.** Toss with **4 quarts hot popped popcorn** to coat well. Serve immediately.
Makes 4 quarts.

Golden Snacking Granola

2 cups oats
1½ cups slivered almonds or coarsely chopped walnuts
1 (3½-ounce) can flaked coconut (1⅓ cups)
½ cup sunflower meats
½ cup wheat germ
2 tablespoons sesame seeds
1 teaspoon ground cinnamon
1 teaspoon salt
1 (14-ounce) can EAGLE® Brand Sweetened Condensed Milk (NOT evaporated milk)
¼ cup vegetable oil
1 cup banana chips, optional
1 cup raisins

Preheat oven to 300°. In large mixing bowl, combine all ingredients except banana chips and raisins; mix well. Spread evenly in aluminum foil-lined 15×10-inch jellyroll pan or baking sheet. Bake 55 to 60 minutes, stirring every 15 minutes. Remove from oven; stir in banana chips if desired and raisins. Cool thoroughly. Store tightly covered at room temperature.
Makes about 2½ quarts.

Peppered Pecans

3 tablespoons butter or margarine
3 cloves garlic, minced
1½ teaspoons TABASCO® pepper sauce
½ teaspoon salt
3 cups pecan halves

Preheat oven to 250°F. In small skillet melt butter. Add garlic, Tabasco® sauce and salt; cook 1 minute. Toss pecans with butter mixture; spread in single layer on baking sheet. Bake 1 hour or until pecans are crisp; stir occasionally.
Makes 3 cups.

Party Scramble

½ cup butter or margarine, cut up
1 pouch CAMPBELL'S® Onion Soup and Recipe Mix
1 cup bite-size wheat cereal squares
1 cup bite-size corn cereal squares
1 bag (6 ounces) PEPPERIDGE FARM® Cheddar Cheese Goldfish® Crackers
1 bag (5½ ounces) PEPPERIDGE FARM® Pretzel Goldfish® Crackers
2 cups unsalted peanuts

To Microwave:
1. Place butter in 2-cup glass measure. Cover with waxed paper; microwave on HIGH 45 seconds or until melted. Stir in soup mix.
2. In 4-quart microwave-safe bowl, combine remaining ingredients. Pour butter mixture over cracker mixture; toss to coat well. Microwave, uncovered, on HIGH 5 minutes or until hot, stirring twice during heating.
3. Cool. Store mixture in airtight container.
Makes about 10 cups.

Crispy Bagel Chips

1 envelope LIPTON® Golden Onion Recipe Soup Mix
½ cup butter or margarine, melted
1 teaspoon basil leaves
½ teaspoon oregano
¼ teaspoon garlic powder
4 to 5 plain bagels, cut into ⅛-inch slices

Preheat oven to 250°.
In small bowl, thoroughly blend all ingredients except bagels; generously brush on both sides of bagel slices. On two ungreased baking sheets, arrange bagel slices and bake 50 minutes or until crisp and golden. Store in airtight container up to 1 week.
Makes about 28 chips.

Hell-Fire Crispy Balls

1 cup flour
2 teaspoons baking powder
¼ teaspoon salt
1 egg
⅓ cup tomato juice, heated
1 small onion, finely chopped
1 teaspoon TABASCO® pepper sauce
Vegetable oil

In medium bowl combine flour, baking powder and salt. Stir in egg, tomato juice, onion and Tabasco® sauce. In large skillet over medium-high heat bring 1 inch oil to 350°F. Drop batter by teaspoonfuls into oil; fry, a few at a time, 5 to 7 minutes or until golden brown on all sides. Drain on paper towels. Serve immediately.
Makes 2 dozen balls.

BEVERAGES

A plentiful collection of drinks for all occasions. You'll find favorite standbys and new ideas for festive punches and party drinks, midday pick-me-ups, cool refreshers to soothe a summer thirst, and bracing hot mugs for a winter evening.

Mexicali Sipper

4 cups V8® Vegetable Juice *or* No Salt Added V8® Vegetable Juice
1 canned VLASIC® Hot Jalapeno Pepper, seeded
2 sprigs fresh cilantro
1 tablespoon lemon juice
1 small ripe avocado, halved, seeded, peeled and sliced
Sweet red pepper rings for garnish
Green onion brushes for garnish

1. In covered blender or food processor, blend V8 juice, jalapeno pepper, cilantro, lemon juice and avocado until smooth.
2. To serve: Pour over ice cubes in 10-ounce glasses. Garnish with red pepper rings and green onion brushes.
Makes 4½ cups or 6 servings.

Per serving: 75 calories, 0 g protein, 4 g fat, 9 g carbohydrate, 653 mg sodium (No Salt Added V8® Juice: 153 mg sodium), 0 mg cholesterol.

Beefy Mary

2 (10-ounce) cans tomato and chile cocktail
1 (13¾-fluid ounce) can COLLEGE INN® Beef Broth
¼ cup lemon juice
Ice
Celery or cucumber sticks

Combine tomato and chile cocktail, beef broth and lemon juice. Serve over ice; garnish with celery or cucumber sticks.
Makes 6 servings.

The Rattlesnake

3 cups DOLE® Pineapple Juice
⅓ cup tomato juice
1 tablespoon powdered sugar
½ to 1 teaspoon liquid hot pepper sauce
8 pineapple juice cubes (see page 34) or ice cubes
Lime wedges or slices, optional
Dried red pepper, ripe olive and lime peel for garnish

In pitcher, combine pineapple juice, tomato juice, sugar and hot pepper sauce; blend well. Pour over juice cubes in glass. Squeeze lime juice into each drink, if desired. Garnish with dried red pepper, ripe olive and lime peel.
Makes 4 servings.

Pizza Mocktail

5¾ cups V8® Vegetable Juice *or* No Salt Added V8® Vegetable Juice
½ teaspoon dried oregano leaves, crushed
Dash garlic powder
Dash pepper

In large pitcher, stir together all ingredients. Refrigerate until serving time, at least 1 hour. To serve: Strain into glasses filled with ice.
Makes 5¾ cups or 8 servings.

Per serving: 34 calories, 1 g protein, 0 g fat, 8 g carbohydrate, 595 mg sodium (No Salt Added V8® Juice: 44 mg sodium), 0 mg cholesterol.

Banana Shake

2 ripe bananas, cut up (about 2 cups)
⅓ cup REALEMON® Lemon Juice from Concentrate
1 cup cold water
1 (14-ounce) can EAGLE® Brand Sweetened Condensed Milk (NOT evaporated milk)
2 cups ice cubes

In blender container, combine all ingredients except ice; blend well. Gradually add ice, blending until smooth. Garnish as desired. Refrigerate leftovers. (Mixture stays thick and creamy in refrigerator.)
Makes about 5 cups.
Mixer Method: Omit ice cubes. In large mixer bowl, mash bananas; gradually beat in ReaLemon® brand, sweetened condensed milk and 2½ cups cold water. Chill before serving.
Strawberry-Banana Shake: Reduce bananas to ½ cup; add 1½ cups fresh strawberries *or* 1 cup frozen unsweetened strawberries, partially thawed.
Banana-Orange Shake: Reduce bananas to 1 cup; use 1 cup orange juice instead of water.

Classic Bloody Mary

1 quart tomato juice
1 cup vodka
1 tablespoon Worcestershire sauce
1 tablespoon fresh lime juice
¼ teaspoon TABASCO® pepper sauce
Lime slices (optional)
Celery stalks (optional)

In 2-quart pitcher combine all ingredients except garnishes; stir well. Serve over ice. Garnish with lime slices or celery stalks, if desired.
Makes 6 (6-ounce) servings.

Hot Tomato Sipper

1 tablespoon WYLER's® or STEERO® Beef-Flavor Instant Bouillon *or* 3 Beef-Flavor Bouillon Cubes
1 (46-ounce) can tomato juice
2 teaspoons prepared horseradish
4 drops hot pepper sauce

In large saucepan, combine all ingredients; over low heat, simmer 10 minutes or until bouillon dissolves. Serve hot.
Makes about 1½ quarts.
Microwave: In 2-quart glass measure, combine ingredients. Microwave on full power (high) 12 to 14 minutes or until hot and bouillon dissolves, stirring after 6 minutes.

Toro

½ cup Spicy Hot V8® Vegetable Juice *or* No Salt Added V8® Vegetable Juice
½ cup prepared CAMPBELL'S® Condensed Consommé
½ cup ice cubes
Green onion brushes for garnish (see Note below)

1. In covered blender or food processor, blend all ingredients except green onion brushes until smooth.
2. To serve: Pour into chilled 8-ounce glasses. Garnish with green onion brushes.
Makes 1½ cups or 2 servings.
Note: To make green onion brushes, slice off the roots and tops of green onions. Leaving at least 3 inches in the center, make lengthwise cuts from center to one or both ends to make a fringe. Place the green onions in ice water for a few hours. The ends will curl to look like brushes.

Per serving: 25 calories, 2 g protein, 0 g fat, 4 g carbohydrate, 592 mg sodium (No Salt Added V8® Juice: 400 mg sodium), 0 mg cholesterol.

Southwest Refresher

1½ cups V8® Vegetable Juice *or* No Salt Added V8® Vegetable Juice, chilled
½ cup chopped, seeded and peeled cucumber
1 tablespoon lime juice
¼ teaspoon chili powder
6 ice cubes (1 cup)
Lime slices for garnish

1. In covered blender or food processor, blend V8 juice, cucumber, lime juice and chili powder until smooth. Add ice cubes, one at a time, blending until ice is finely crushed.
2. To serve: Pour immediately into chilled 8-ounce glasses. Garnish with lime slices.
Makes 2½ cups or 3 servings.

Per serving: 29 calories, 0 g protein, 0 g fat, 6 g carbohydrate, 409 mg sodium (No Salt Added V8® Juice: 35 mg sodium), 0 mg cholesterol.

Hot Spiced V8

3 cups V8® Vegetable Juice *or* No Salt Added V8® Vegetable Juice
1 tablespoon brown sugar
1 teaspoon lemon juice
Generous dash ground allspice
Generous dash ground cinnamon

1. In 1-quart saucepan, combine all ingredients. Over medium heat, heat until hot but not boiling, stirring occasionally.
2. To serve: Ladle into punch cups or heat-safe glasses.
Makes 3 cups or 4 servings.

Per serving: 50 calories, 0 g protein, 0 g fat, 11 g carbohydrate, 608 mg sodium (No Salt Added V8® Juice: 47 mg sodium), 0 mg cholesterol.

Fresh Pineapple Daiquiri

1 large DOLE™ Fresh Pineapple
3/4 cup DOLE® Pineapple Juice
1/2 cup light rum
3 ounces frozen limeade concentrate
1 cup crushed ice

Twist crown from pineapple. Cut pineapple lengthwise into quarters. Remove fruit from shells with curved knife. Trim off core and cut fruit into chunks. Freeze half the pineapple until firm. (Refrigerate remaining pineapple for another use.) Combine half the frozen pineapple with pineapple juice, rum and limeade concentrate in blender. Blend until smooth. Add remaining frozen pineapple and ice; blend until frothy.
Makes 1 quart.

Checkmate

3 cups DOLE® Pineapple Juice
1 1/2 cups carrot pieces
1 1/2 teaspoons minced fresh ginger root
6 pineapple juice cubes (see recipe at right) or ice cubes
1 tablespoon frozen orange juice concentrate

Puree pineapple juice, carrots and ginger in blender. Strain through a sieve. Pour strained juice back into blender; add juice cubes and juice concentrate. Blend until smooth.
Makes 4 servings.

Island Fruit Cooler

3/4 cup DOLE® Pineapple Juice
1/2 cup guava, papaya or mango juice
1/4 cup lemon-lime soda
Ice cubes
Fresh fruit for garnish

In pitcher, combine pineapple and guava juices and soda. Pour over ice cubes in glass. Garnish with fresh fruit.
Makes 2 servings.

Pineapple Passion

2 cups DOLE® Pineapple Juice
8 pineapple juice cubes

Combine pineapple juice and juice cubes in blender; blend until slushy. Garnish as desired.
Makes 2 servings.
PINEAPPLE JUICE CUBES: Pour unsweetened, canned pineapple juice into your ice cube trays. Freeze and use just like regular ice cubes. Juice cubes add an intriguing tart-sweet flavor to iced tea, mineral water, lemonade, wine coolers (especially sangria), fruit juices and punch.

Pineapple Mint Tulip

1 cup DOLE® Pineapple Juice
2 tablespoons powdered sugar
1 tablespoon grenadine syrup
1 sprig fresh mint
Ice cubes or pineapple juice cubes (see recipe above)

In 1-quart measure, combine pineapple juice, sugar and grenadine; stir well. Rub mint sprig around inside of tall glass. Partially fill glass with ice cubes; pour in juice mixture.
Makes 1 serving.

Lemon Tea Sparkler

2 cups brewed tea
1/2 cup REALEMON® Lemon Juice from Concentrate
1/2 cup sugar
1 (32-ounce) bottle ginger ale, chilled
Ice

In pitcher, combine tea, ReaLemon® brand and sugar; stir until sugar dissolves. Just before serving, add ginger ale. Serve over ice.
Makes about 7 cups.

Low Calorie Lemonade

3 1/4 cups cold water
1/2 cup REALEMON® Lemon Juice from Concentrate
4 to 8 envelopes sugar substitute or 1 1/2 teaspoons liquid sugar substitute

Combine ingredients; mix well. Serve over ice. Garnish as desired.
Makes about 1 quart.
To make 1 serving: Combine 3/4 cup cold water, 2 tablespoons ReaLemon® brand and 1 to 2 envelopes sugar substitute or 1/2 teaspoon liquid sugar substitute.

Zesty V8

3 cups V8® Vegetable Juice *or* No Salt Added V8® Vegetable Juice, chilled
½ teaspoon prepared horseradish
½ teaspoon Worcestershire sauce

In small pitcher, combine all ingredients. To serve: Pour into chilled 8-ounce glasses.
Makes 3 cups or 4 servings.

Per serving: 36 calories, 1 g protein, 0 g fat, 9 g carbohydrate, 628 mg sodium (No Salt Added V8® Juice: 53 mg sodium), 0 mg cholesterol.

Quick Banana Malt

1 ripe, medium DOLE™ Banana, frozen*
¾ cup milk
3 tablespoons chocolate malted milk powder

Slice banana; puree with remaining ingredients in blender.
Makes 1 serving.
*Peel banana and freeze overnight in airtight plastic bag.

Tonic Thyme

1½ cups V8® Vegetable Juice *or* No Salt Added V8® Vegetable Juice
1 tablespoon lime juice
⅛ teaspoon dried thyme leaves, crushed
¼ cup tonic water, chilled
Fresh thyme sprigs or lime wedges for garnish

1. In small pitcher, stir together V8 juice, lime juice and dried thyme. Add tonic water; stir.
2. To serve: Pour over ice cubes in 10-ounce glasses. Garnish with fresh thyme.
Makes 1¾ cups or 2 servings.

Per serving: 49 calories, 0 g protein, 0 g fat, 11 g carbohydrate, 609 mg sodium (No Salt Added V8® Juice: 48 mg sodium), 0 mg cholesterol.

Sparkling V8

3 cups V8® Vegetable Juice *or* No Salt Added V8® Vegetable Juice
2 bottles (6½ ounces each) sparkling mineral water, chilled
Mint leaves for garnish

1. In small pitcher, mix V8 juice and sparkling mineral water.
2. To serve: Pour over ice cubes in 10-ounce glasses. Garnish with mint leaves.
Makes 4¾ cups or 6 servings.

Per serving: 24 calories, 0 g protein, 0 g fat, 6 g carbohydrate, 414 mg sodium (No Salt Added V8® Juice: 30 mg sodium), 0 mg cholesterol.

City Slicker

¾ cup DOLE® Pineapple Juice
Pineapple juice cubes (see page 34) *or* ice cubes
Ginger ale
Dash ground ginger
Cucumber slice, cherry tomato and lemon slice for garnish

Pour pineapple juice over juice cubes in glass. Fill with ginger ale. Add ginger and stir. Garnish with cucumber slice, cherry tomato and lemon slice.
Makes 1 serving.

Quick Wink Breakfast Drink

1 ripe, medium DOLE™ Banana, frozen*
¾ cup milk
1 tablespoon wheat germ
2 teaspoons honey
¼ teaspoon ground cinnamon

Slice banana; puree with remaining ingredients in blender.
Makes 1 to 2 servings.
*Peel banana and freeze overnight in airtight plastic bag.

Lemonade Syrup Base

2 cups sugar
½ cup water
2 cups REALEMON® Lemon Juice from Concentrate

In medium saucepan, combine sugar and water. Over low heat, cook until sugar dissolves, stirring occasionally; add ReaLemon® brand. Cool. Store covered in refrigerator.
Makes about 3⅔ cups.
For 1 (8-ounce) serving: Pour ⅓ cup lemonade syrup into glass; add ⅔ cup cold water. Stir; add ice.
For 1 quart: In pitcher, combine 1⅓ cups lemonade syrup and 2⅔ cups cold water; stir. Add ice.

Frosty Chocolate Shake

- 1 teaspoon KNOX® Unflavored Gelatine
- ½ cup skim milk
- 2 tablespoons chocolate syrup
- 2 packets aspartame sweetener
- ¼ teaspoon vanilla extract
- 1 cup ice cubes (6 to 8)

In small saucepan, sprinkle unflavored gelatine over ¼ cup milk; let stand 1 minute. Stir over low heat until gelatine is completely dissolved, about 5 minutes.

In blender, process remaining ¼ cup milk, syrup, sweetener and vanilla until blended. While processing, through feed cap, gradually add gelatine mixture and process until blended. Add ice cubes, 1 at a time; process at high speed until ice is melted.
Makes 2 servings; 77 calories per serving

Orange Tea Punch

- 4 cups brewed tea
- 2 cups orange juice, chilled
- 1 cup REALEMON® Lemon Juice from Concentrate
- 1 cup sugar
- 1 quart orange sherbet
- 1 (32-ounce) bottle ginger ale, chilled

In pitcher, combine tea, orange juice, ReaLemon® brand and sugar; stir until sugar dissolves. Chill. Just before serving, pour tea mixture into large punch bowl; add scoops of sherbet and ginger ale.
Makes about 4 quarts.

Sparkling Harvest Cider

- 2 quarts apple cider, chilled
- 1 cup REALEMON® Lemon Juice from Concentrate
- ½ cup sugar
- 1 (32-ounce) bottle ginger ale, chilled
- Apple slices or cinnamon sticks, optional
- Ice

In punch bowl, combine apple cider, ReaLemon® brand and sugar; stir until sugar dissolves. Just before serving, add ginger ale. Garnish with apple and cinnamon sticks if desired. Serve over ice.
Makes about 3 quarts.

Christmas Carol Punch

- 2 medium red apples
- 2 quarts clear apple cider
- 8 cinnamon sticks
- 2 teaspoons whole cloves
- ½ cup SUN-MAID® Raisins
- Orange slices
- Lemon slices
- ¼ cup lemon juice

Core apples; slice into ½-inch rings. In Dutch oven, combine cider, cinnamon, cloves, apple rings and raisins. Bring to boil over high heat; reduce heat to low and simmer 5 to 8 minutes or until apples are just tender. Remove cloves; add orange and lemon slices and lemon juice. Pour into punch bowl. Ladle into large mugs, including an apple ring, some raisins and citrus slices in each serving. Serve with spoons.
Makes about 2 quarts.

Volcano Punch

- 3 quarts DOLE® Pineapple Juice
- 2 cans (6 ounces each) frozen limeade concentrate
- 2 quarts ginger ale
- 2 pints orange or lemon sherbet
- Fresh fruit for garnish

In punch bowl, combine pineapple juice and limeade concentrate. Just before serving, stir in ginger ale and add scoops of sherbet. Garnish with fresh fruit.
Makes about 6 quarts.

Pineapple Orange Slush

- 3 cups DOLE® Pineapple Orange Juice, chilled
- 1 pint orange sherbet
- 1 cup crushed ice

Combine pineapple orange juice and sherbet in blender. Add ice; blend until slushy.
Makes 6 servings.

Fruit Punch

- 5½ cups DOLE® Pineapple Juice, chilled
- 1 quart apple juice, chilled
- 1 package (10 ounces) frozen strawberries, thawed
- 1 quart ginger ale, chilled
- Fresh strawberry slices, lime slices and fresh mint for garnish

In punch bowl, combine pineapple and apple juices. Puree undrained strawberries in blender; stir pureed strawberries into pineapple juice mixture. Pour in ginger ale. Garnish with strawberry slices, lime slices and fresh mint.
Makes 3 quarts.

Tropical Cream Punch

1 (14-ounce) can EAGLE® Brand Sweetened Condensed Milk (NOT evaporated milk)
1 (6-ounce) can frozen orange juice concentrate, thawed
1 (6-ounce) can frozen pineapple juice concentrate, thawed
2 (32-ounce) bottles club soda, chilled
Orange slices

In punch bowl, combine sweetened condensed milk and juice concentrates; mix well. Gradually add club soda; stir. Garnish with orange slices. Serve over ice.
Makes about 3 quarts.

Tip: Omit orange juice concentrate and pineapple juice concentrate. Add 1 (12-ounce) can frozen pineapple orange juice drink concentrate, thawed. Proceed as above.

Hot Cocoa Mix

1 cup CREMORA® Non-Dairy Creamer*
1 cup nonfat dry milk
3/4 to 1 cup sugar
1/2 cup unsweetened cocoa

In medium bowl, combine ingredients; mix well. Store in airtight container. To serve, spoon 3 heaping tablespoons mix into mug; add 3/4 cup boiling water. Stir.
Makes about 3 cups.

Mocha: Add 1/4 cup instant coffee.
Mexican: Add 1 teaspoon ground cinnamon.
Low-calorie: Omit sugar. Add 15 envelopes low-calorie sweetener with NUTRASWEET® *or* 2 teaspoons (5 envelopes) low-calorie granulated sugar substitute. To serve, spoon 2 heaping tablespoons into mug; add 3/4 cup boiling water. Stir.

*Cremora® non-dairy creamer is a coffee whitener and should not be used as a milk replacement.

Bullshot

1 cup V8® Vegetable Juice
1 cup SWANSON® Clear Ready to Serve Beef Broth
2 teaspoons lemon juice
1/4 teaspoon prepared horseradish

To Microwave: In 4-cup glass measure, stir together all ingredients. Cover with vented plastic wrap; microwave on HIGH 3 minutes or until boiling.
Makes about 2 cups or 2 servings.

Hot Mulled Pineapple Juice

5 1/2 cups DOLE® Pineapple Juice
1 apple, cored and cubed
1/2 cup DOLE™ Raisins
1/2 cup brown sugar, packed
2 cinnamon sticks, broken
1 tablespoon grated orange peel
1/2 teaspoon whole cloves
Quartered orange slices for garnish

In saucepan, combine all ingredients; simmer 15 minutes. Strain before serving. Garnish with quartered orange slices.
Makes 6 servings.

Microwave Hot Cocoa

5 tablespoons sugar
3 tablespoons HERSHEY'S Cocoa
Dash salt
3 tablespoons hot water
2 cups milk
1/4 teaspoon vanilla

Combine sugar, cocoa, salt and hot water in 1-quart micro-proof measuring cup. Microwave at HIGH (100%) for 1 to 1 1/2 minutes or until boiling. Add milk; stir and microwave an additional 1 1/2 to 2 minutes or until hot. Stir in vanilla; blend well.
4 servings.

One serving: Place 2 heaping teaspoons sugar, 1 heaping teaspoon HERSHEY'S Cocoa and dash salt in micro-proof cup. Add 2 teaspoons cold milk; stir until smooth. Fill cup with milk; microwave at HIGH (100%) for 1 to 1 1/2 minutes or until hot. Stir to blend.

Creamy Hot Chocolate

1 (14-ounce) can EAGLE® Brand Sweetened Condensed Milk (NOT evaporated milk)
1/2 cup unsweetened cocoa
1 1/2 teaspoons vanilla extract
1/8 teaspoon salt
6 1/2 cups hot water
CAMPFIRE® Marshmallows, optional

In large saucepan, combine sweetened condensed milk, cocoa, vanilla and salt; mix well. Over medium heat, slowly stir in water; heat through, stirring occasionally. Top with marshmallows if desired.
Makes about 2 quarts.

Tip: Chocolate can be stored in refrigerator up to 5 days. Mix well and reheat before serving.

Microwave: In 2-quart glass measure, combine all ingredients except marshmallows. Microwave on full power (high) 8 to 10 minutes, stirring every 3 minutes. Top with marshmallows if desired.

Spicy Warmer

2 cups V8® Vegetable Juice
1 teaspoon Worcestershire
  sauce
1/2 teaspoon prepared
  horseradish
1/4 teaspoon hot pepper sauce

To Microwave: In 4-cup glass measure, stir together all ingredients. Cover with vented plastic wrap; microwave on HIGH 3 minutes or until boiling.
Makes about 2 cups or 3 servings.

Hot Buttered Pineapple Smoothie

5 1/2 cups DOLE® Pineapple Juice
1/4 cup brown sugar, packed
2 tablespoons butter or
  margarine
10 whole cloves
3 cinnamon sticks
1 DOLE™ Lemon, sliced

In large saucepan, combine pineapple juice, brown sugar, butter, cloves and cinnamon sticks. Bring to a boil; simmer 5 minutes. Add lemon slices. Serve hot in mugs.
Makes 1 1/2 quarts.

Piña Colada

1/2 cup DOLE® Pineapple Juice
3 ounces rum
1/4 cup canned cream of coconut
2 cups crushed ice

Combine pineapple juice, rum and cream of coconut in blender. Add ice; blend until slushy.
Makes 2 servings.

Hot Cranberry Cider

1 quart apple cider or apple
  juice
1 (32-ounce) bottle cranberry
  juice cocktail
1/2 cup REALEMON® Lemon Juice
  from Concentrate
1/3 cup firmly packed light brown
  sugar
8 whole cloves
2 cinnamon sticks

In large saucepan, combine ingredients; bring to a boil. Reduce heat; simmer uncovered 10 minutes. Remove spices. Serve warm.
Makes about 2 quarts.

Pineapple Margarita

1/3 cup DOLE® Pineapple Juice
1 1/2 ounces tequila
1 ounce triple sec
  Juice of 1 lemon
  Crushed ice

Combine pineapple juice, tequila, triple sec and lemon juice in blender. Add ice; blend until slushy. Serve in frosted glass. (Do not put salt on rim.)
Makes 1 serving.

Spiced Tea

6 cups water
1 cup firmly packed light brown
  sugar
6 cinnamon sticks
8 whole cloves
8 tea bags
1 cup orange juice
1/2 cup REALEMON® Lemon Juice
  from Concentrate

In large saucepan, combine water, sugar, cinnamon and cloves; bring to a boil. Reduce heat; simmer uncovered 10 minutes. Remove spices. Pour over tea bags; steep 5 minutes. Remove tea bags; add fruit juices. Serve hot or cold.
Makes about 1 1/2 quarts.

Party Mai Tais

3 cups pineapple juice, chilled
1 cup light rum
1 (6-ounce) can frozen orange
  juice concentrate, thawed
1/2 cup REALEMON® Lemon Juice
  from Concentrate
  Ice
  Orange slices and maraschino
  cherries for garnish,
  optional

In pitcher, combine all ingredients except ice and garnish; stir to dissolve orange juice concentrate. Serve over ice; garnish with orange and cherries if desired.
Makes about 5 cups.

Bourbon Slush

2 cups brewed tea
1 (6-ounce) can frozen orange
  juice concentrate, thawed
1/3 cup sugar
2 cups cold water
1 cup bourbon
1/3 cup REALEMON® Lemon Juice
  from Concentrate

In large bowl, combine tea, juice concentrate and sugar; stir until sugar dissolves. Add remaining ingredients. Freeze. About 1 hour before serving, remove from freezer; when mixture is slushy, spoon into cocktail glasses. Garnish as desired.
Makes about 6 cups.

Bloody Mary

3 cups tomato juice, chilled
¾ cup vodka
4 teaspoons REALEMON®
   Lemon Juice from
   Concentrate
2 teaspoons Worcestershire
   sauce
½ teaspoon celery salt
⅛ teaspoon hot pepper sauce
   Dash pepper

In pitcher, combine ingredients; stir. Serve over ice; garnish as desired. *Makes about 1 quart.*
   Tip: For non-alcoholic Bloody Mary, omit vodka. Proceed as above.
BLOODY MARY GARNISHES
   Onion & Olive Pick: Dip cocktail onions in chopped parsley; alternate on toothpick with pimiento-stuffed olives.
   Green Onion Firecracker: With small scissors or very sharp knife, cut tips of green onion to end of dark green onion portion. Chill in ice water until curled.

Melon Citrus Cooler

2 cups orange juice, chilled
½ cup REALEMON® Lemon Juice
   from Concentrate
⅓ cup sugar
2 cups fresh or frozen melon
   balls
½ to 1 cup vodka, optional
2 (12-ounce) cans lemon-lime
   carbonated beverage, chilled
   Ice

In pitcher, combine orange juice, ReaLemon® brand and sugar; stir until sugar dissolves. Just before serving, add melon balls, vodka if desired and lemon-lime carbonated beverage. Serve over ice.
Makes about 2 quarts.

Devilish Daiquiri

2 ripe, medium DOLE™
   Bananas*
   Grated peel and juice from 1
   lemon
⅓ cup light rum
¼ cup creme de banana liqueur
2 tablespoons powdered sugar
2 cups crushed ice

Slice bananas; combine bananas, lemon peel and juice, rum, liqueur and sugar in blender. Add ice; blend until slushy.
Makes 2 to 4 servings.
   *Frozen bananas can be used. Peel bananas and freeze overnight in airtight plastic bag.

Seaside Mary

2 cups tomato juice, chilled
1 (8-ounce) bottle DOXSEE® or
   SNOW'S® Clam Juice, chilled
⅓ cup vodka, optional
1 tablespoon REALEMON®
   Lemon Juice from
   Concentrate
1 teaspoon Worcestershire
   sauce
¼ teaspoon celery salt
8 drops hot pepper sauce

In small pitcher, combine ingredients; stir. Serve over ice. Garnish as desired. Refrigerate leftovers.
Makes about 3½ cups.

Hot Spiced Lemonade

3 cups water
⅔ cup firmly packed light brown
   sugar
½ cup REALEMON® Lemon Juice
   from Concentrate
8 whole cloves
2 cinnamon sticks
   Additional cinnamon sticks for
   garnish, optional

In medium saucepan, combine all ingredients except garnish. Simmer uncovered 20 minutes to blend flavors; remove spices. Serve hot in mugs with cinnamon sticks if desired.
Makes about 4 cups.
   Microwave: In 1-quart glass measure, combine ingredients as above. Microwave on full power (high) 4 to 5 minutes or until heated through. Serve as above.

The Death Mix

   Fresh lime wedge
   Celery salt (optional)
   Ice
6 ounces tomato juice
1¼ ounces vodka
2 tablespoons lemon juice
½ beef bouillon cube, crushed
½ teaspoon horseradish
10 drops TABASCO® pepper
   sauce
4 drops Worcestershire sauce
   Pinch each of salt, pepper,
   celery salt
   Lemon slice (optional)

Wet rim of 12-ounce glass with lime wedge; dip into celery salt. Fill glass with ice. Add remaining ingredients except garnish; stir. Garnish with lemon slice, if desired.
Makes 1 serving.

White Sangria

½ to ¾ cup sugar
½ cup REALEMON® Lemon Juice from Concentrate, chilled
¼ cup REALIME® Lime Juice from Concentrate, chilled
1 (750 mL) bottle sauterne, chilled
¼ cup orange-flavored liqueur
1 (32-ounce) bottle club soda, chilled
Orange, plum or nectarine slices, green grapes or other fresh fruit
Ice

In pitcher, combine sugar and juices; stir until sugar dissolves. Add sauterne and orange-flavored liqueur. Just before serving, add club soda, fruit and ice.
Makes about 2 quarts.

Pina Colada Punch

Ice Ring, optional, or block of ice
1 (20-ounce) can crushed pineapple, undrained
2 (15-ounce) cans COCO LOPEZ® Cream of Coconut
1 (46-ounce) can pineapple juice, chilled
2 cups light rum, optional
1 (32-ounce) bottle club soda, chilled

Prepare ice ring in advance. In blender container, combine crushed pineapple and cream of coconut; blend until smooth. In large punch bowl, combine pineapple mixture, pineapple juice and rum if desired. Just before serving, add club soda and ice.
Makes about 4 quarts.
ICE RING: Fill ring mold with water to within 1 inch of top rim; freeze. Arrange pineapple chunks and maraschino cherries on top of ice. Carefully pour small amount of cold water over fruits; freeze.

Frozen Margaritas

½ cup REALIME® Lime Juice from Concentrate
½ cup tequila
¼ cup triple sec or other orange-flavored liqueur
1 cup confectioners' sugar
4 cups ice cubes

In blender container, combine all ingredients except ice; blend well. Gradually add ice, blending until smooth. Serve immediately.
Makes about 1 quart.

Lemony Light Cooler

3 cups dry white wine *or* white grape juice, chilled
½ to ¾ cup sugar
½ cup REALEMON® Lemon Juice from Concentrate
1 (32-ounce) bottle club soda, chilled
Strawberries, plum, peach or orange slices or other fresh fruit

In pitcher, combine wine, sugar and ReaLemon® brand; stir until sugar dissolves. Just before serving, add club soda and fruit; serve over ice.
Makes about 7 cups.
Tip: Recipe can be doubled.

Champagne Sherbet Punch

3 cups pineapple juice, chilled
¼ cup REALEMON® Lemon Juice from Concentrate
1 quart BORDEN® or MEADOW GOLD® Pineapple Sherbet
1 (750 mL) bottle champagne, chilled

In punch bowl, combine pineapple juice and ReaLemon® brand. Just before serving, scoop sherbet into punch bowl; add champagne. Stir gently.
Makes about 2½ quarts.
Tip: For rosy champagne punch, use raspberry sherbet and pink champagne.

Rosé Wine Cooler

Berry Mint Ice Ring, optional, or block of ice
1½ cups sugar
1 cup REALEMON® Lemon Juice from Concentrate
2 (750 mL) bottles rosé wine, chilled
1 (32-ounce) bottle club soda, chilled

Prepare ice ring in advance. In large punch bowl, combine sugar and ReaLemon® brand; stir until sugar dissolves. Just before serving, add wine, club soda and ice.
Makes about 3½ quarts.
BERRY MINT ICE RING: Combine 3 cups water, 1 cup ReaLemon® brand and ¾ cup sugar; stir until sugar dissolves. Pour 3 cups mixture into 6-cup ring mold; freeze. Arrange strawberries and mint leaves on top of ice. Slowly pour remaining ReaLemon® brand mixture over fruit; freeze.

Planter's Punch

4 cups orange juice, chilled
4 cups pineapple juice, chilled
¾ cup REALIME® Lime Juice from Concentrate
½ cup grenadine syrup
1½ cups dark rum
Ice

In punch bowl or large pitcher, combine all ingredients except ice; stir. Serve over ice.
Makes about 2½ quarts.

Spirited Coffee Lopez

4 cups hot coffee
1/2 cup COCO LOPEZ® Cream of Coconut
1/2 cup Irish whiskey
1 teaspoon vanilla extract
   Whipped cream

In heatproof pitcher, combine all ingredients except whipped cream; mix well. Pour into mugs; top with whipped cream. Serve immediately.
Makes 5 cups.

Lemon Toddy

1/3 cup water
1/4 cup REALEMON® Lemon Juice from Concentrate
3 tablespoons honey
3 tablespoons whiskey

In small saucepan, combine ingredients. Over low heat, simmer to blend flavors, stirring occasionally to dissolve honey. Serve hot.
Makes 1 serving.
   Microwave: In 2-cup glass measure, combine ingredients. Heat on 100% power (high) for 1 to 1½ minutes or until hot.

Syllabub

1 quart BORDEN® or MEADOW GOLD® Half-and-Half
1/2 cup sugar
1/3 cup REALEMON® Lemon Juice from Concentrate
1/3 cup brandy
3 tablespoons dry or cocktail sherry
   Candy lemon sticks, optional

In large mixer bowl, on low speed, beat half-and-half until frothy; gradually beat in sugar then ReaLemon® brand, brandy and sherry. Chill; stir before serving. Garnish with lemon sticks if desired.
Makes about 5 cups.

Spirited Egg Nog

1 (32-ounce) can BORDEN® Egg Nog, chilled
1/2 cup rum, brandy *or* bourbon
   Whipped cream
   Ground nutmeg

In pitcher, combine egg nog and liquor. Garnish with whipped cream and nutmeg. Refrigerate leftovers.
Makes about 1 quart.

Simmered Sherry Bouillon

8 cups water
3 tablespoons WYLER'S® or STEERO® Beef-Flavor Instant Bouillon *or* 9 Beef-Flavor Bouillon Cubes
1/3 cup dry or cocktail sherry
   Lemon slices, optional

In large saucepan, bring water and bouillon to a boil; stir until bouillon dissolves. Remove from heat; stir in sherry. Serve hot. Garnish with lemon slices if desired.
Makes about 2 quarts.
   Microwave: In 2-quart glass measure, heat water and bouillon on 100% power (high) 10 to 14 minutes or until boiling. Stir until bouillon dissolves. Proceed as above.

Mulled Cider

2 quarts apple cider
3/4 to 1 cup REALEMON® Lemon Juice from Concentrate
1 cup firmly packed light brown sugar
8 whole cloves
2 cinnamon sticks
3/4 cup rum, optional
   Additional cinnamon sticks, optional

In large saucepan, combine all ingredients except rum and additional cinnamon sticks; bring to a boil. Reduce heat; simmer uncovered 10 minutes. Remove spices; add rum just before serving if desired. Serve hot with cinnamon sticks if desired.
Makes about 2 quarts.
   Tip: Can be served cold.
   Microwave: In deep 3-quart round baking dish, combine ingredients as above. Heat on 100% power (high) 13 to 14 minutes or until hot. Serve as above.

Hot Maple Toddy

1 to 1¼ cups whiskey
1 (8-ounce) bottle CARY'S® Pure Maple Syrup
3/4 cup REALEMON® Lemon Juice from Concentrate
   Butter and cinnamon sticks, optional

In medium saucepan, combine all ingredients except butter and cinnamon sticks. Over low heat, simmer uncovered 10 minutes. Serve hot with butter and cinnamon sticks if desired.
Makes about 3 cups.
Microwave: In 1-quart glass measure, combine ingredients as above. Heat on 100% power (high) 4 to 5 minutes or until heated through. Serve as above.

SOUPS

For satisfying lunches and simple, informal suppers, nothing beats a hearty bowl of soup. Try robust soups, rich with meat and vegetables, or refreshing clear soups that whet the appetite. Along with traditional, long-simmering soups with their wonderful flavor and aroma, you'll discover tasty fuss-free creations prepared with convenience foods.

Black Bean Soup

4 quarts water
1 pound dried black beans, rinsed and drained
1 envelope LIPTON® Onion Recipe Soup Mix
1 small ham hock or bone
2 stalks celery, chopped
2 cloves garlic, chopped
1 teaspoon lemon juice
1 whole clove
1 bay leaf
Few sprigs parsley
3 tablespoons sherry
1 teaspoon pepper

In large saucepan or stockpot, bring 2 quarts water to a boil; add beans and boil 2 minutes. Remove from heat, then let stand covered 1 hour; drain.

In large saucepan or stockpot, combine beans, remaining water, onion recipe soup mix, ham hock, celery, garlic, lemon juice, clove, bay leaf and parsley. Bring to a boil, then simmer covered, stirring occasionally, 3 hours or until beans are tender.

Remove ham hock and bay leaf. In food processor or blender, puree hot soup mixture, adding water if mixture is too thick, then return to saucepan. Bring to a boil, then stir in sherry and pepper. Garnish, if desired, with sour cream, lemon slices or hard-cooked egg.
Makes about 4 (2-cup) servings.

Hearty Borscht

2 tablespoons butter or margarine
½ cup chopped onion
1 can (16 ounces) whole beets, drained and coarsely chopped
2 cups coarsely chopped cabbage
1 can (10¾ ounces) CAMPBELL'S® Home Cookin'® Old Fashioned Vegetable Beef Soup
1 can (10½ ounces) CAMPBELL'S® Condensed Beef Broth (Bouillon)
1 cup water
1 tablespoon lemon juice
1 teaspoon sugar
¼ teaspoon pepper
½ cup sour cream for garnish
2 tablespoons chopped fresh chives or green onion for garnish

To Microwave:
1. In 3-quart microwave-safe casserole, combine butter and onion. Cover with lid; microwave on HIGH 3 minutes or until tender, stirring once during cooking.
2. Stir in beets, cabbage, soup, broth, water, lemon juice, sugar and pepper. Cover; microwave on HIGH 12 minutes or until boiling, stirring once during cooking. Let stand, covered, 5 minutes.
3. Meanwhile, in small bowl, stir together sour cream and chives. Ladle soup into bowls and garnish with sour cream mixture.
Makes about 6½ cups or 6 servings.

Lentil and Brown Rice Soup

1 envelope LIPTON® Onion, Beefy Onion or Beefy Mushroom Recipe Soup Mix
4 cups water
3/4 cup lentils, rinsed and drained
1/2 cup uncooked brown or regular rice
1 can (14 1/2 ounces) whole peeled tomatoes, undrained and coarsely chopped
1 medium carrot, coarsely chopped
1 large stalk celery, coarsely chopped
1/2 teaspoon basil leaves
1/2 teaspoon oregano
1/4 teaspoon thyme leaves (optional)
1 tablespoon finely chopped parsley
1 tablespoon apple cider vinegar
1/4 teaspoon pepper

In large saucepan or stockpot, combine onion recipe soup mix, water, lentils, uncooked rice, tomatoes, carrot, celery, basil, oregano and thyme. Bring to a boil, then simmer covered, stirring occasionally, 45 minutes or until lentils and rice are tender. Stir in remaining ingredients.
Makes about 3 (2-cup) servings.
Microwave Directions: In 3-quart casserole, combine onion recipe soup mix, water, tomatoes, carrot, celery, basil, oregano and thyme. Heat covered at HIGH (Full Power) 12 minutes or until boiling. Stir in lentils and uncooked brown rice* and heat covered at MEDIUM (50% Full Power), stirring occasionally, 60 minutes or until lentils and rice are tender. Stir in remaining ingredients. Let stand covered 5 minutes.

*If using uncooked regular rice, decrease 60-minute cooking time to 30 minutes.

Spinach-Rice Soup

1 can (13 3/4 oz.) ready-to-serve chicken broth
1 package (11 oz.) BIRDS EYE® Creamed Spinach, thawed
1/4 cup MINUTE® Rice
Dash of pepper
Dash of nutmeg

Bring broth and spinach to a full boil in medium saucepan. Stir in rice. Cover; remove from heat. Let stand 5 minutes. Season with pepper and nutmeg.
Makes 3 servings.
Note: Recipe may be doubled.

Fresh Spinach Soup

1 tablespoon butter or margarine
2 cups loosely packed chopped spinach leaves
1 can (10 3/4 ounces) CAMPBELL'S® Condensed Cream of Potato Soup
1 soup can milk
2 tablespoons dry sherry or vermouth
Dash ground nutmeg

To Microwave:
1. In 2-quart microwave-safe casserole, combine butter and spinach. Cover with lid; microwave on HIGH 2 minutes or until spinach is wilted.
2. Stir in soup until smooth; stir in milk, sherry and nutmeg until well blended. Cover; microwave on HIGH 6 minutes or until hot and bubbling, stirring once during cooking.
Makes about 3 cups or 3 servings.

Harvest Bowl Soup

1 tablespoon olive oil
2 cups chopped onions
1 1/2 cups thinly sliced carrots
1 cup thinly sliced celery
4 cloves garlic, minced
2 teaspoons dried Italian seasoning, crushed
3 cans (14 1/2 ounces each) SWANSON® Clear Ready to Serve Chicken Broth or 4 cans (10 1/2 ounces each) CAMPBELL'S® Ready to Serve Low Sodium Chicken Broth*
3 cups V8® Vegetable Juice or No Salt Added V8® Vegetable Juice
1/4 pound green beans, cut into pieces
1 bay leaf
1/8 teaspoon pepper
2 cans (16 ounces each) red or white kidney beans, drained
2 cups coarsely chopped zucchini or yellow squash

1. In 6-quart Dutch oven over medium heat, in hot oil, cook onions, carrots, celery, garlic and Italian seasoning until vegetables are tender, stirring often.
2. Stir in remaining ingredients, except kidney beans and zucchini. Heat to boiling; reduce heat to low. Cover; simmer 30 minutes.
3. Stir in kidney beans and zucchini. Cover; simmer 5 minutes or until zucchini is tender. Discard bay leaf.
Makes 14 cups or 14 side-dish servings.
*Note: To use Campbell's® Ready to Serve Low Sodium Chicken Broth and No Salt Added V8® Juice for the soup, add 1 tablespoon lemon juice with the kidney beans and zucchini.

Per serving: 107 calories, 5 g protein, 3 g fat, 18 g carbohydrate, 809 mg sodium (No Salt Added V8® Juice and Campbell's® Ready to Serve Low Sodium Chicken Broth: 275 mg sodium), 0 mg cholesterol.

Extra-Good Mushroom Cream Soup

    2 tablespoons butter or
      margarine
  1/2 cup chopped onion
    1 cup sliced CAMPBELL'S
      FRESH® Mushrooms
  1/2 teaspoon dried thyme leaves,
      crushed
    1 can (10³/4 ounces)
      CAMPBELL'S® Condensed
      Cream of Mushroom Soup
  1/2 cup light cream
  3/4 cup milk
      PEPPERIDGE FARM® Goldfish®
      Crackers

1. In 2-quart saucepan over medium heat, in hot butter, cook onion, mushrooms and thyme until mushrooms are tender, stirring occasionally.
2. Stir in soup, cream and milk. Heat through, stirring occasionally. Ladle into bowls; serve with crackers.
Makes about 3 1/2 cups or 4 servings.
To Microwave: In 2-quart microwave-safe casserole, combine butter, onion, mushrooms and thyme. Cover with lid; microwave on HIGH 7 to 9 minutes until vegetables are tender, stirring once. Stir in soup, cream and milk. Cover; microwave on HIGH 5 to 7 minutes until heated through, stirring occasionally. Ladle into bowls; serve with crackers.

Creamed Corn Chowder

    6 slices bacon, cut in 1/2-inch
      pieces
  1/2 cup chopped onion
  1/3 cup chopped green pepper
    2 (17-ounce) cans cream style
      sweet corn
    2 (13³/4-fluid ounce) cans
      COLLEGE INN® Chicken
      Broth
  1/8 teaspoon ground black pepper

In large saucepan, over medium-high heat, cook bacon until crisp; remove and crumble bacon. Pour off all but 2 tablespoons drippings. Cook onion and green pepper in reserved drippings 2 to 3 minutes. Add corn, chicken broth and pepper. Heat to a boil; reduce heat. Cover and simmer 15 minutes. Serve garnished with bacon.
Makes 6 servings.

California Bisque

    1 tablespoon butter or
      margarine
  1/4 cup thinly sliced celery
  1/2 teaspoon chili powder
      Generous dash ground
      cinnamon
    1 can (11 ounces) CAMPBELL'S®
      Condensed Tomato Bisque
    1 soup can water
    2 teaspoons lemon juice
  1/2 cup chopped avocado

To Microwave:
1. In 1 1/2-quart microwave-safe casserole, combine butter, celery, chili powder and cinnamon. Cover with lid; microwave on HIGH 3 minutes or until celery is tender, stirring once during cooking.
2. Stir in soup, water and lemon juice. Cover; microwave on HIGH 3 minutes or until hot and bubbling. Stir in avocado.
Makes about 3 cups or 3 servings.

Oriental Vegetable Soup

    2 cans (14 1/2 ounces each)
      SWANSON® Clear Ready to
      Serve Chicken Broth
    1 tablespoon soy sauce
    1 tablespoon dry sherry
  1/8 teaspoon grated fresh ginger
  1/2 cup fresh or frozen cut green
      beans
  1/4 cup thinly sliced carrot
  1/4 cup cubed tofu

To Microwave:
1. In 2-quart microwave-safe casserole, stir together broth, soy sauce, sherry and ginger. Stir in beans and carrot. Cover with lid; microwave on HIGH 10 minutes or until soup is boiling and vegetables are tender-crisp.
2. Stir in tofu. Let stand, covered, 2 minutes.
Makes about 5 cups or 6 servings.

Cucumber-Leek Soup

    2 cans (10³/4 ounces each)
      CAMPBELL'S® Condensed
      Chicken Broth
  1/2 cup water
    1 large cucumber, peeled,
      seeded and sliced
    1 large leek, sliced (white part
      only)
    2 tablespoons chopped fresh
      parsley
    1 teaspoon fresh dill weed or
  1/2 teaspoon dried dill weed,
      crushed
  1/8 teaspoon pepper
  1/4 cup plain yogurt

To Microwave:

1. In 2-quart microwave-safe casserole, combine broth, water, cucumber and leek. Cover with lid; microwave on HIGH 8 minutes or until boiling.
2. With slotted spoon, transfer vegetables to blender or food processor. Add ½ cup of the broth mixture, parsley, dill and pepper. Cover; blend until smooth. Return mixture to broth. Cover; microwave on HIGH 4 minutes or until hot and bubbling.
3. Ladle soup into bowls; top with yogurt and garnish with additional dill weed.

Makes about 4 cups or 4 servings.

Double Onion Soup Gratinée

1 tablespoon butter or
    margarine
2 green onions, thinly sliced
1 can (10½ ounces)
    CAMPBELL'S® Condensed
    French Onion Soup
1 soup can water
2 tablespoons dry vermouth
1 cup PEPPERIDGE FARM®
    Onion & Garlic Croutons
1 cup shredded Swiss cheese
    (4 ounces)

To Microwave:

1. In 4-cup glass measure, combine butter and onions. Microwave, uncovered, on HIGH 1 minute or until onions are wilted.
2. Stir in soup, water and vermouth. Microwave, uncovered, on HIGH 5 minutes or until boiling, stirring once during cooking.
3. Ladle soup into three 10-ounce bowls. Sprinkle croutons over soup; sprinkle with cheese. Let stand, uncovered, 1 minute or until cheese is melted.

Makes about 3 cups or 3 servings.

Chilled Carrot Soup

2 tablespoons vegetable oil
1 large onion, chopped
1½ teaspoons curry powder
3½ cups chicken broth
1 pound carrots, sliced
2 stalks celery, sliced
1 bay leaf
½ teaspoon ground cumin
½ teaspoon TABASCO® pepper
    sauce
1 cup milk
1 cup cottage cheese

In large saucepan heat oil; cook onion and curry 3 to 5 minutes. Add broth, carrots, celery, bay leaf, cumin and Tabasco® sauce; mix well. Cover; simmer 25 minutes or until vegetables are tender. Remove bay leaf.

Spoon carrot mixture, milk and cottage cheese in several batches into container of blender or food processor. Cover; process until smooth. Pour into serving bowl. Cover; refrigerate until chilled. Serve with additional Tabasco® sauce, if desired.

Makes 8 servings.

Blushing Onion Soup

4 cups thinly sliced onions
1 clove garlic, finely chopped
¼ cup margarine or butter
1 (46-ounce) can tomato juice
1 cup water
2 teaspoons WYLER'S® or
    STEERO® Beef-Flavor
    Instant Bouillon *or* 2 Beef-
    Flavor Bouillon Cubes
2 teaspoons parsley flakes
8 slices French bread, toasted
2 cups (8 ounces) shredded
    Mozzarella cheese

In large kettle or Dutch oven, cook onions and garlic in margarine until tender. Stir in tomato juice, water, bouillon and parsley. Bring to a boil; reduce heat. Simmer uncovered 20 to 30 minutes, stirring occasionally. Ladle into 8 ovenproof soup bowls. Top with bread slices and sprinkle generously with cheese. Broil 2 to 3 minutes or until cheese melts. Serve immediately.

Makes 8 servings.

   Microwave: In 2-quart glass measure, melt margarine on 100% power (high) 1 minute. Add onions and garlic; cook covered on 100% power (high) 5 to 6 minutes or until onions are tender. Add tomato juice, water, *instant* bouillon and parsley. Cook covered on 100% power (high) 15 to 17 minutes or until boiling. Proceed as above.

Clear Japanese Soup

1½ quarts chicken broth
⅓ cup dry sherry
4½ teaspoons KIKKOMAN Soy
    Sauce
1 lemon, thinly sliced
Garnishes:
5 to 6 fresh mushrooms, sliced
2 green onions and tops, sliced
    diagonally
1 carrot, very thinly sliced

Bring broth to simmer in large saucepan. Add sherry and soy sauce; simmer 2 to 3 minutes. Ladle soup into small bowls; float a lemon slice in each bowl. Arrange garnishes on tray and add to soup as desired.

Makes about 6 cups.

Broccoli Cheese Soup

½ cup chopped onion
¼ cup margarine or butter
¼ cup unsifted flour
3 cups water
2 (10-ounce) packages frozen chopped broccoli, thawed and well drained
4 teaspoons WYLER'S® or STEERO® Chicken-Flavor Instant Bouillon or 4 Chicken-Flavor Bouillon Cubes
1 teaspoon Worcestershire sauce
3 cups (12 ounces) shredded Cheddar cheese
2 cups (1 pint) BORDEN® or MEADOW GOLD® Coffee Cream or Half-and-Half

In large saucepan or Dutch oven, cook onion in margarine until tender; stir in flour. Gradually stir in water then broccoli, bouillon and Worcestershire. Over medium heat, cook and stir until thickened and broccoli is tender, about 10 minutes. Add cheese and cream. Cook and stir until cheese melts and soup is hot (do not boil). Garnish as desired. Refrigerate leftovers.
Makes about 2 quarts.

Norwegian Pea Soup

3½ quarts water, divided
1 package (1 pound) whole dry yellow peas or split yellow peas, rinsed
1½ cups finely chopped carrots
1½ cups finely chopped onions
¼ teaspoon ground cumin
2½ pound shank end fully cooked ham
KAVLI Croutons (recipe follows)
1 cup thinly sliced celery
2 tablespoons olive oil

Place 7 cups of the water and the peas in heavy, large saucepan. Bring to a boil over high heat; boil 2 minutes. Remove from heat. Cover and let soak 1 hour. Drain peas; discard water. (If using split peas, omit this step.)

Return peas to heavy, large saucepan. Add remaining 7 cups water, the carrots, onions and cumin. Bring to a boil over high heat. Reduce heat to low. Cover and simmer 1 hour, stirring occasionally. Add ham; cook 1 hour more, stirring occasionally. Meanwhile, prepare Kavli Croutons. Add celery to soup mixture and cook until peas mash easily, stirring occasionally. Remove ham; cut into cubes. Brown ham in hot oil in large skillet over medium-high heat. Return to soup; heat through. Serve topped with Kavli Croutons.
Makes about 6 servings.

KAVLI CROUTONS: Melt ⅓ cup butter or margarine in large skillet over medium heat. Add 1 small garlic clove. Cook and stir several minutes. Add 1½ cups coarsely broken KAVLI Norwegian Thick-Style Crispbreads. Cook and stir until croutons are lightly browned. Stir in 2 tablespoons chopped parsley.

Southern Tomato-Bean Soup

1 tablespoon vegetable oil or bacon drippings
½ cup chopped celery
½ cup chopped onion
1 clove garlic, minced
¼ teaspoon dried thyme leaves, crushed
1 can (16 ounces) CAMPBELL'S® Pork & Beans in Tomato Sauce
1 can (14½ ounces) tomatoes, undrained, cut up
⅛ teaspoon black pepper
⅛ teaspoon ground red pepper (cayenne)

To Microwave:
1. In 2-quart microwave-safe casserole, combine oil, celery, onion, garlic and thyme. Cover with lid; microwave on HIGH 3 minutes or until vegetables are tender, stirring once during cooking.
2. Stir in pork and beans, tomatoes with their liquid, black pepper and red pepper. Cover; microwave on HIGH 8 minutes or until hot and bubbling, stirring once during cooking.
Makes about 4 cups or 4 servings.

Italian Vegetable Soup

1 pound bulk Italian sausage
2 cups chopped onion
2 cloves garlic, finely chopped
7 cups water
4 medium carrots, pared and sliced
1 (28-ounce) can tomatoes, undrained and broken up
2 tablespoons WYLER'S® or STEERO® Beef-Flavor Instant Bouillon or 6 Beef-Flavor Bouillon Cubes
1 teaspoon Italian seasoning
¼ teaspoon pepper
1½ cups coarsely chopped zucchini
1 (15-ounce) can garbanzo beans, drained
1 cup uncooked CREAMETTE® Rotini or Elbow Macaroni

In large kettle or Dutch oven, brown sausage, onion and garlic; pour off fat. Add water, carrots, tomatoes, bouillon, Italian seasoning and pepper; bring to a boil. Reduce heat; cover and simmer 30 minutes. Add zucchini, beans and rotini. Cover; cook 15 to 20 minutes or until rotini is tender. Garnish as desired. Refrigerate leftovers.
Makes about 2½ quarts.

Turkey Split Pea Soup

BUTTERBALL® turkey carcass
Water
2 cups cubed cooked
 BUTTERBALL® turkey
 (3/4 pound)
1 package (16 ounces) green
 split peas, washed
2 large carrots, sliced
1 cup chopped onion
2 cubes chicken bouillon
1/2 teaspoon salt
1/2 teaspoon ground black pepper
1 bay leaf

Place turkey carcass in Dutch oven. Add 8 cups water. Bring to boil over high heat; reduce heat to low. Cover and simmer 1 hour. Remove carcass. Strip turkey from bones; reserve turkey. Discard carcass. Strain broth. Measure broth and add water to make 8 cups. Combine broth, turkey and remaining ingredients in Dutch oven. Bring mixture to boil over high heat; reduce heat to low. Cover and simmer 1 hour, stirring occasionally.
Yield: 8 servings (10 cups).

Borscht

3 cups chopped cabbage
1/4 cup BLUE BONNET® Margarine
1 (16-ounce) can sliced beets
1 (46-fluid ounce) can COLLEGE
 INN® Beef Broth
2 tablespoons lemon juice
1/2 teaspoon ground black pepper
1 cup dairy sour cream

In large saucepan, over medium-high heat, cook cabbage in margarine until tender. Drain beets, reserving liquid; chop beets. Stir in beef broth, beets with liquid, lemon juice and pepper. Heat to a boil; reduce heat. Simmer 15 minutes. Serve with dollop of sour cream.
Makes 8 servings.

Lentil-Pasta Soup

1 tablespoon olive or vegetable
 oil
1 cup chopped onion
2 cloves garlic, minced
1 can (19 ounces) CAMPBELL'S®
 Home Cookin'® Hearty Lentil
 Soup
1 can (14 1/2 ounces) SWANSON®
 Clear Ready to Serve Beef
 Broth
1/2 cup chopped fresh parsley
1/2 teaspoon dried basil leaves,
 crushed
1/2 teaspoon dried oregano
 leaves, crushed
1/2 cup small shell pasta,
 uncooked

To Microwave:
1. In 3-quart microwave-safe casserole, combine oil, onion and garlic. Cover with lid; microwave on HIGH 3 minutes or until onion is tender, stirring once during cooking.
2. Stir in soup and broth. Cover; microwave on HIGH 8 minutes or until very hot. Stir in parsley, basil, oregano and pasta. Cover; microwave on HIGH 13 minutes or until pasta is tender, stirring twice during cooking. Let stand, covered, 5 minutes.
Makes about 4 cups or 4 servings.

Minestrone

3 medium carrots
3 stalks celery
2 medium onions
1 large potato
1/4 pound green beans
2 medium zucchini
1/2 pound cabbage
1 medium clove garlic
1/3 cup olive oil
3 tablespoons butter
3 1/2 cups beef broth
1 1/2 cups water
1 can (28 ounces) Italian plum
 tomatoes
1/2 teaspoon salt
1/2 teaspoon dried basil,
 crumbled
1/4 teaspoon dried rosemary,
 crumbled
1/4 teaspoon pepper
1 bay leaf
1 can (1 pound) cannellini beans

1. Pare carrots; chop coarsely. Chop celery coarsely. Chop onions. Pare potato; cut into 3/4-inch cubes. Trim green beans; cut into 1-inch pieces. Trim zucchini; cut into 1/2-inch cubes. Coarsely shred cabbage. Mince garlic.
2. Heat oil and butter in 5-quart Dutch oven over medium heat. Add onions; sauté, stirring occasionally, until soft and golden but not brown, 6 to 8 minutes. Stir in carrots and potato; sauté 5 minutes. Stir in celery and green beans; sauté 5 minutes. Stir in zucchini; sauté 3 minutes. Stir in cabbage and garlic; cook 1 minute.
3. Add broth, water and liquid from tomatoes to pan. Chop tomatoes coarsely; add to pan. Stir in salt, basil, rosemary, pepper and bay leaf. Heat to boiling; reduce heat to low. Simmer, covered, stirring occasionally, 1 1/2 hours.
4. Rinse and drain cannellini beans; add beans to soup. Cook, uncovered, over medium-low heat, stirring occasionally, until soup is thick, 30 to 40 minutes longer. Remove bay leaf.
Makes about 12 cups; 8 to 10 servings.
 Note: Serve sprinkled with grated Parmesan cheese, if desired.

Gazpacho

- 1 (14½-ounce) can stewed tomatoes
- 1 (13¾-fluid ounce) can COLLEGE INN® Chicken or Beef Broth
- 1 medium cucumber, coarsely chopped
- ½ cup sliced scallions
- ¼ cup red wine vinegar
- ¼ teaspoon liquid hot pepper seasoning

Drain tomatoes, reserving liquid; coarsely chop tomatoes. In medium bowl, combine chopped tomatoes, reserved liquid, broth, cucumber, scallions, vinegar and liquid hot pepper seasoning. Refrigerate 2 to 3 hours. Serve cold.
Makes 4 servings.

Turkey Barley Chowder

- 2 cups diced cooked BUTTERBALL® turkey (¾ pound)
- 2 cans (13¾ ounces each) chicken broth
- 1 can (15 ounces) tomato sauce with tomato bits
- ¼ cup medium pearl barley
- 1 medium onion, sliced thin
- 1 cup water
- 1½ tablespoons sugar
- ¼ teaspoon ground cloves
- ½ cup half and half
- 1 tablespoon sherry
- Chopped fresh parsley

Combine turkey, broth, tomato sauce, barley, onion, water, sugar and cloves in large saucepan. Bring to boil over high heat; reduce heat to low. Cover and simmer, stirring occasionally, 1 hour or until barley is tender. Stir in half and half and sherry. Heat to serving temperature; do not boil. Sprinkle with parsley.
Yield: 6 to 7 servings (8 cups).

Creamy Tomato Bisque

- 2 cups water
- 1 (14½-ounce) can tomatoes, undrained
- ½ cup chopped celery
- 2 tablespoons chopped onion
- 5 teaspoons WYLER'S® or STEERO® Chicken-Flavor Instant Bouillon *or* 5 Chicken-Flavor Bouillon Cubes
- 2 medium tomatoes, pared and diced
- ¼ cup margarine or butter
- 3 tablespoons flour
- 2 cups (1 pint) BORDEN® or MEADOW GOLD® Light or Coffee Cream
- 1 tablespoon sugar

In large saucepan, combine water, canned tomatoes, celery, onion and bouillon; cover and simmer 20 minutes. Place in blender container; blend until smooth. In same pan, cook fresh tomatoes in *2 tablespoons* margarine about 5 minutes; remove from pan. In same pan, melt remaining *2 tablespoons* margarine; stir in flour. Add cream; over low heat, cook and stir until thickened. Stir in bouillon mixture, tomatoes and sugar; heat through *(do not boil)*. Garnish as desired. Refrigerate leftovers.
Makes about 2½ quarts.

Tortellini Soup

- 2 cloves garlic, crushed
- 1 tablespoon BLUE BONNET® Margarine
- 2 (13¾-fluid ounce) cans COLLEGE INN® Chicken or Beef Broth
- 8 ounces frozen or fresh cheese tortellini
- 1 (15-ounce) can chopped spinach, undrained
- 1 (14½-ounce) can stewed tomatoes, undrained and cut up
- Grated Parmesan cheese

In large saucepan, over medium-high heat, cook garlic in margarine for 2 to 3 minutes. Add broth and tortellini. Heat to a boil; reduce heat; simmer 10 minutes. Add spinach and tomatoes; simmer 5 minutes more. Serve with cheese.
Makes 6 servings.

Wisconsin Cheese 'n Beer Soup

- 2 tablespoons butter or margarine
- 2 tablespoons all-purpose flour
- 1 envelope LIPTON® Golden Onion Recipe Soup Mix
- 3 cups milk
- 1 teaspoon Worcestershire sauce
- 1 cup shredded Cheddar cheese (about 4 ounces)
- ½ cup beer
- 1 teaspoon prepared mustard

In medium saucepan, melt butter and cook flour over medium heat, stirring constantly, 3 minutes or until bubbling. Stir in golden onion recipe soup mix thoroughly blended with milk and Worcestershire sauce. Bring just to the boiling point, then simmer, stirring occasionally, 10 minutes. Stir in remaining ingredients and simmer, stirring constantly, 5 minutes or until cheese is melted. Garnish, if desired, with additional cheese, chopped red pepper and parsley.
Makes about 4 (1-cup) servings.

Golden Cauliflower Soup

2 (10-ounce) packages frozen cauliflower *or* 1 small head fresh cauliflower, separated into small flowerets (about 4 cups)
2 cups water
½ cup chopped onion
⅓ cup margarine or butter
⅓ to ½ cup unsifted flour
2 cups BORDEN® or MEADOW GOLD® Milk
1 tablespoon WYLER'S® or STEERO® Chicken-Flavor Instant Bouillon *or* 3 Chicken-Flavor Bouillon Cubes
2 cups (8 ounces) shredded mild Cheddar cheese
⅛ to ¼ teaspoon ground nutmeg
Chopped green onion or parsley

In medium saucepan, cook cauliflower in *1 cup* water until tender. Reserve *1 cup* cooked flowerets. In blender or food processor, blend remaining cauliflower and liquid; set aside. In large heavy saucepan, cook onion in margarine until tender; stir in flour. Gradually add remaining *1 cup* water, milk and bouillon; cook and stir until well blended and slightly thickened. Add cheese, pureed cauliflower, reserved flowerets and nutmeg; cook and stir until cheese melts and mixture is hot (do not boil). Garnish with green onion. Refrigerate leftovers.
Makes 1½ to 2 quarts.

Clear Vegetable Soup

1 can (10¾ ounces) CAMPBELL'S® Condensed Chicken Broth
1 soup can water
½ cup sliced carrot
½ cup sliced celery
¼ cup rotelle or other macaroni
1 teaspoon chopped fresh parsley

1. In 2-quart saucepan over high heat, heat chicken broth, water, carrot and celery to boiling. Add rotelle. Reduce heat to low. Cover; simmer until macaroni is done, about 20 minutes.
2. Ladle soup into bowls; top with parsley.
Makes about 3 cups or 3 servings.

Two-Bean Soup

1 tablespoon olive oil
½ cup chopped onion
2 large cloves garlic, minced
1 teaspoon dried basil leaves, crushed
4 cups V8® Vegetable Juice *or* No Salt Added V8® Vegetable Juice
1 can (16 ounces) chick peas, drained
1 cup thinly sliced carrots
1 cup green beans, cut into 1-inch pieces
1 cup sliced CAMPBELL'S FRESH® Mushrooms (4 ounces)
1 large bay leaf

1. In 4-quart saucepan over medium heat, in hot oil, cook onion, garlic and basil until onion is tender, stirring frequently.
2. Stir in remaining ingredients. Heat to boiling. Reduce heat to low. Simmer 30 minutes or until vegetables are tender. Discard bay leaf.
Makes 6½ cups or 8 side-dish servings.

Per serving: 126 calories, 4 g protein, 3 g fat, 23 g carbohydrate, 591 mg sodium (No Salt Added V8® Juice: 208 mg sodium), 0 mg cholesterol.

Tortilla Soup

1 (4-ounce) jar sliced or diced pimientos
½ cup chopped onion
½ teaspoon ground cumin
1 tablespoon BLUE BONNET® Margarine
2 (13¾-fluid ounce) cans COLLEGE INN® Chicken or Beef Broth
1 (8¾-ounce) can whole kernel sweet corn, undrained
2 tablespoons chopped parsley
2 cups coarsely broken tortilla chips
1 cup shredded Monterey Jack, Cheddar or Monterey Jack with jalapeño pepper cheese (4 ounces)

Drain pimientos, reserving liquid. In medium saucepan, over medium-high heat, cook onion and cumin in margarine for 2 to 3 minutes, stirring occasionally. Stir in reserved pimiento liquid, broth, corn and parsley. Heat to a boil; reduce heat. Cover; simmer 10 minutes.

Meanwhile, arrange tortilla chips, cheese and pimientos in individual serving bowls. Ladle hot soup into bowls. Serve immediately.
Makes 6 to 8 servings.

White Gazpacho

4 teaspoons WYLER'S® or STEERO® Chicken-Flavor Instant Bouillon *or* 4 Chicken-Flavor Bouillon cubes
2 cups boiling water
3 medium cucumbers, pared, seeded and cut into cubes (about 3 cups)
1 (16-ounce) container BORDEN® or MEADOW GOLD® Sour Cream
2 tablespoons REALEMON® Lemon Juice from Concentrate
¼ teaspoon garlic powder
¼ teaspoon pepper

In small saucepan, dissolve bouillon in water. Cool completely. In blender or food processor, blend cucumber with *½ cup* bouillon liquid until smooth. In medium bowl, combine cucumber mixture, remaining bouillon liquid, sour cream, ReaLemon® brand, garlic powder and pepper; mix well. Chill thoroughly. Garnish as desired. Serve with condiments. Refrigerate leftovers.
Makes about 1½ quarts.
Suggested Condiments: Chopped fresh tomato, chopped green onions, chopped green pepper, toasted slivered almonds and toasted croutons.

Greek Lemon Soup

2 cans (14½ ounces each) SWANSON® Clear Ready to Serve Chicken Broth
¼ cup orzo or regular long-grain rice, uncooked
2 eggs
2 tablespoons lemon juice
Thin lemon slices for garnish

To Microwave:
1. In 2-quart microwave-safe casserole, combine broth and orzo. Cover with lid; microwave on HIGH 8 minutes or until boiling. Stir soup.
2. Reduce power to 50%. Cover; microwave 18 minutes or until orzo is tender, stirring once during cooking.
3. In small bowl, beat eggs with lemon juice. Slowly beat ½ cup hot soup into egg mixture. Return egg mixture to broth, stirring constantly until soup is slightly thickened. Garnish with lemon slices.
Makes about 4 cups or 4 servings.
Note: Orzo is a small rice-shaped pasta that is traditional in this classic soup.

Curried Zucchini Soup

1 tablespoon butter or margarine
2 cups coarsely chopped zucchini
2 tablespoons sliced green onion
1 teaspoon curry powder
1 can (10¾ ounces) CAMPBELL'S® Condensed Cream of Potato Soup
1¾ cups milk
PEPPERIDGE FARM® Croutons for garnish

To Microwave:
1. In 2-quart microwave-safe casserole, combine butter, zucchini, onion and curry powder. Cover with lid; microwave on HIGH 7 minutes or until zucchini is very tender, stirring once during cooking.
2. Stir soup into zucchini mixture. In covered blender or food processor, blend soup mixture until smooth. Return to casserole. Stir in milk.
3. Cover; refrigerate until serving time, at least 4 hours. Thin chilled soup to desired consistency with additional milk. Ladle into bowls and garnish with croutons.
Makes about 4 cups or 4 servings.
Note: To serve this soup hot, prepare as above through step 2. Cover; microwave on HIGH 4 minutes or until hot and bubbling.

Spinach-Potato Soup

2 tablespoons butter or margarine
1 cup sliced leeks
1½ pounds potatoes, peeled and cubed (4 cups)
2 cans (14½ ounces each) SWANSON® Clear Ready to Serve Chicken Broth or 3 cans (10½ ounces each) CAMPBELL'S® Ready to Serve Low Sodium Chicken Broth
¼ cup water
4 cups coarsely chopped spinach leaves
1 teaspoon lemon juice
⅛ teaspoon pepper
Sour cream or plain low-fat yogurt for garnish

1. In 3-quart saucepan over medium heat, in hot butter, cook leeks until tender, stirring often.
2. Add potatoes, broth and water. Heat to boiling; reduce heat to low. Cover; simmer 25 minutes or until potatoes are tender, stirring occasionally.
3. Stir in spinach, lemon juice and pepper; simmer 5 minutes. Garnish with sour cream.
Makes 6½ cups or 7 side-dish servings.

Per serving: 121 calories, 3 g protein, 5 g fat, 18 g carbohydrate, 587 mg sodium (Low Sodium Chicken Broth: 97 mg sodium), 9 mg cholesterol.

Black Bean Soup with Rice and Sherry

1 cup dry black beans, rinsed
4 cups beef broth
4 cups chicken broth
½ pound smoked ham hock
1 large yellow onion, sliced
1 carrot, sliced
4 sprigs parsley
2 cloves garlic
1 teaspoon ground thyme
  Salt
  Pepper
3 cups hot cooked rice
½ cup dry sherry
1 small red onion, chopped

Place beans in large bowl. Cover with water; soak overnight. Drain beans; discard water. Place beans in large stockpot. Add broths, ham hock, yellow onion, carrot, parsley, garlic and thyme. Bring to a boil over high heat. Reduce heat to low. Cover and simmer 6 to 8 hours, stirring occasionally. Strain soup into large saucepan, reserving bean mixture and discarding ham hock. Puree bean mixture, in batches, in blender or food processor. Stir bean mixture into broth. Cook over low heat 2 hours more, stirring occasionally. Season to taste with salt and pepper. Ladle soup into bowls. Top with rice, sherry and red onion.
Makes 6 servings.

Favorite recipe from Rice Council

Bavarian Pea Soup

1 tablespoon butter or margarine
½ cup shredded cabbage
¼ teaspoon caraway seed
1 can (19 ounces) CAMPBELL'S® Home Cookin'® Split Pea with Ham or Chunky Split Pea 'n Ham Soup
  Pumpernickel bread, torn into pieces for garnish
  Shredded Swiss cheese for garnish

To Microwave:
1. In 1-quart microwave-safe casserole, combine butter, cabbage and caraway. Cover with lid; microwave on HIGH 3 minutes or until cabbage is tender, stirring once during cooking.
2. Stir in soup. Cover with lid; microwave on HIGH 4 minutes or until heated through, stirring once during cooking.
3. Pour soup into 2 microwave-safe soup bowls; top with bread and cheese. Microwave, uncovered, on HIGH 1 minute or until cheese is melted.
Makes 2 servings.

Egg Drop Soup

2 cans (14½ ounces each) SWANSON® Clear Ready to Serve Chicken Broth
1 tablespoon cornstarch
1 tablespoon rice vinegar or dry sherry
2 teaspoons soy sauce
½ cup cooked ham cut into thin strips
½ cup snow peas
3 green onions, sliced
2 eggs, beaten

To Microwave:
1. In 2-quart microwave-safe casserole, stir together broth, cornstarch, vinegar and soy sauce until smooth; stir in ham, snow peas and onions. Cover with lid; microwave on HIGH 10 minutes or until boiling, stirring twice during cooking.
2. With fork, stir broth in swirling motion. Without stirring, slowly pour eggs into swirling broth; then stir just until eggs are set in long strands.
Makes about 4 cups or 4 servings.

Hot & Sour Soup

1 can (10½ oz.) condensed chicken broth
2 soup cans water
1 can (4 oz.) sliced mushrooms
2 tablespoons cornstarch
2 tablespoons KIKKOMAN Soy Sauce
2 tablespoons distilled white vinegar
½ teaspoon TABASCO® pepper sauce
1 egg, beaten
2 green onions and tops, chopped

Combine chicken broth, water, mushrooms, cornstarch, soy sauce, vinegar and pepper sauce in medium saucepan. Bring to boil over high heat, stirring constantly, until slightly thickened. Gradually pour egg into boiling soup, stirring constantly in 1 direction. Remove from heat; stir in green onions. Garnish with additional chopped green onions or cilantro, as desired. Serve immediately.
Makes about 5 cups.

Chicken & Rice Gumbo

1 (46-fluid ounce) can COLLEGE INN® Chicken Broth
1 pound boneless chicken, cut in bite-size pieces
1 (17-ounce) can whole kernel sweet corn, drained
1 (14½-ounce) can stewed tomatoes, undrained and chopped
1 (10-ounce) package frozen okra, thawed and chopped
½ cup uncooked rice
1 teaspoon ground black pepper

In large saucepan, over medium-high heat, heat chicken broth, chicken, corn, tomatoes, okra, rice and pepper to a boil. Reduce heat; simmer, uncovered, 20 minutes or until rice is cooked.
Makes 10 servings.

Chicken-Vegetable Soup

2½ cups water
1 pouch CAMPBELL'S® Chicken Rice Soup Mix
1 cup frozen mixed vegetables
Generous dash dried thyme leaves, crushed

1. In 2-quart saucepan, stir together all ingredients. Over medium-high heat, heat to boiling, stirring occasionally.
2. Reduce heat to low; simmer 5 minutes or until chicken and vegetables are tender.
Makes 2 servings.

Chicken-Corn Soup Santa Fe

1 tablespoon butter or margarine
1 clove garlic, minced
1 can (10¾ ounces) CAMPBELL'S® Condensed Chicken Broth
1 soup can water
1 can (8 ounces) cream-style golden corn
1 can (5 ounces) SWANSON® Premium Chunk White Chicken, undrained
½ teaspoon finely chopped VLASIC® Hot Jalapeno Peppers
¼ teaspoon ground cumin
Tortilla chips

To Microwave:
1. In 2-quart microwave-safe casserole, combine butter and garlic. Cover with lid; microwave on HIGH 30 seconds or until butter is melted.
2. Stir in broth, water, corn, chicken, peppers and cumin. Cover; microwave on HIGH 5 minutes or until hot and bubbling. Place a few tortilla chips in each of four 10-ounce soup bowls. Ladle hot soup over chips.
Makes about 4 cups or 4 servings.

Lettuce and Chicken Soup

2½ cups water
1 pouch CAMPBELL'S Chicken Noodle Soup Mix
½ cup shredded carrot
¼ cup sliced green onions
2 teaspoons lemon juice
1 cup shredded lettuce

To Microwave:
1. Pour water into 2-quart microwave-safe casserole. Cover with lid; microwave on HIGH 6 minutes or until boiling.
2. Stir in soup mix, carrot, onions and lemon juice. Microwave, uncovered, on HIGH 4 minutes or until chicken is tender. Stir in lettuce. Let stand, covered, 5 minutes.
Makes about 3 cups or 3 servings.

Chicken Noodle Chowder

1 pouch CAMPBELL'S® Chicken Noodle Soup Mix
2 cups water
½ cup shredded zucchini
1 can (about 8 ounces) whole kernel corn, drained
¼ cup chopped onion
¼ teaspoon dried rosemary leaves, crushed
1 cup milk
½ cup shredded Swiss cheese (2 ounces)

1. In 2-quart saucepan, stir together soup mix, water, zucchini, corn, onion and rosemary. Over high heat, heat to boiling.
2. Reduce heat to low. Cover; simmer 8 to 10 minutes until chicken in soup is tender, stirring occasionally.
3. Stir in milk and cheese; cook until cheese is melted and soup is heated through, stirring often. Serve at once.
Makes 3 servings.

Chicken and Pasta Soup

1 (2½-pound) chicken, cut up
1 (46-fluid ounce) can COLLEGE INN® Chicken Broth
1 (16-ounce) can cut green beans
1 (6-ounce) can tomato paste
1 cup uncooked small shell macaroni
1 teaspoon dried basil leaves

In large saucepan, over medium-high heat, heat chicken and chicken broth to a boil; reduce heat. Cover; simmer 25 minutes or until chicken is tender. Remove chicken; cool slightly. Add remaining ingredients to broth. Heat to a boil; reduce heat. Cover; simmer 20 minutes or until macaroni is cooked. Meanwhile, remove chicken from bones and cut into bite-size pieces. Add to soup; cook 5 minutes more.
Makes 6 servings.

Turkey Vegetable Soup

BUTTERBALL® turkey carcass
1 large onion, sliced
3 ribs celery, coarsely chopped
2 teaspoons salt
1 teaspoon dried rosemary leaves
½ teaspoon ground white pepper
2 bay leaves
6 sprigs fresh parsley
12 cups water
3 cubes chicken bouillon
2 cups sliced carrots
½ cup uncooked rice
1 package (10 ounces) frozen peas

Place turkey carcass, onion, celery, salt, rosemary, pepper, bay leaves and parsley in water in Dutch oven. Bring to boil over high heat; reduce heat to low. Cover and simmer 2 hours. Remove carcass. Strip turkey from bones; reserve turkey. Discard carcass. Strain broth and discard vegetables. Bring broth to boil over high heat; add bouillon cubes, carrots and rice. Reduce heat to low; simmer 10 to 12 minutes. Add peas and reserved turkey. Continue to cook 5 to 10 minutes or until vegetables and rice are tender, stirring occasionally.
Yield: 6 to 8 servings (10 cups).

New England Style Turkey Chowder

2 cups diced cooked BUTTERBALL® turkey (³/4 pound)
2 cans (17 ounces each) cream-style corn
2½ cups milk
1 cup chicken broth
1 cup diced potato
½ cup finely shredded carrot
½ cup finely chopped onion
1 teaspoon salt
¼ teaspoon ground black pepper

Combine all ingredients in large saucepan. Bring to boil over high heat; reduce heat to low. Cover and simmer 20 minutes, stirring occasionally.
Yield: 6 to 8 servings (9 cups).

Chicken Noodle Soup

1 (46-fluid ounce) can COLLEGE INN® Chicken Broth
½ pound boneless chicken, cut in bite-size pieces
1½ cups uncooked medium egg noodles
1 cup sliced carrots
½ cup chopped onion
⅓ cup sliced celery
1 teaspoon dried dill weed
¼ teaspoon ground black pepper

In large saucepan, over medium-high heat, heat chicken broth, chicken, noodles, carrots, onion, celery, dill and pepper to a boil. Reduce heat; simmer 20 minutes or until chicken and noodles are cooked.
Makes 8 servings.

Quick Deli Turkey Soup

½ pound BUTTERBALL® Deli Turkey Breast, cubed
1 can (13³/4 ounces) ready-to-serve chicken broth
1 can (14½ ounces) stewed tomatoes, undrained
1 small zucchini, cut up (about 1 cup)
¼ teaspoon dried basil leaves
½ cup cooked chili-mac pasta or macaroni

Combine broth, tomatoes with juice, zucchini and basil in large saucepan. Bring to a boil over high heat. Reduce heat to medium; simmer 10 minutes or until zucchini is tender. Stir in turkey and pasta. Continue heating until turkey is hot.
Makes 4 servings.

Apple-Cheese Soup

2 apples, peeled and chopped
1 tablespoon water
¼ teaspoon ground nutmeg
¼ teaspoon cinnamon
1 can (11 ounces) CAMPBELL'S® Condensed Cheddar Cheese Soup/Sauce
¾ cup milk
Sour cream or plain yogurt for garnish

To Microwave:
1. In 2-quart microwave-safe casserole, combine apples, water, nutmeg and cinnamon. Cover with lid; microwave on HIGH 5 minutes or until apples are very tender, stirring once during cooking.
2. Stir soup into apple mixture. In covered blender or food processor, blend soup mixture until smooth. Return to casserole. Stir in milk. Cover; microwave on HIGH 3 minutes or until hot and bubbling. Garnish with sour cream and additional nutmeg.
Makes about 3 cups or 3 servings.
Note: This soup is equally delicious served hot or cold.

Turkey-Barley Soup

2 quarts chicken or turkey stock
2 medium onions, chopped
½ cup sliced carrots
½ cup sliced celery
⅓ cup uncooked barley, rinsed
4 sprigs parsley
1 bay leaf
1 teaspoon salt
½ teaspoon poultry seasoning
1 can (16 ounces) tomatoes, undrained, chopped
2 cups cubed cooked turkey
¼ teaspoon TABASCO® pepper sauce
2 tablespoons chopped parsley (optional)

In large saucepot combine chicken stock, onions, carrots, celery, barley, parsley sprigs, bay leaf, salt and poultry seasoning. Cover; bring to a boil. Reduce heat; simmer 45 minutes or until barley is tender. Add tomatoes, turkey and Tabasco® sauce. Cook until heated through. Remove bay leaf. Garnish with chopped parsley, if desired.
Makes 8 servings.

Scandinavian Raspberry Soup

2 (10-ounce) packages frozen red raspberries in syrup, thawed
½ cup orange juice
¼ cup REALEMON® Lemon Juice from Concentrate
1 tablespoon cornstarch
¾ cup chablis or other dry white wine
Fresh orange sections
Raspberries, orange rind twists or mint leaves for garnish
Sour cream

In blender container, puree *1 package* raspberries; strain to remove seeds. In medium saucepan, combine pureed raspberries, orange juice, ReaLemon® brand and cornstarch; mix well. Over medium heat, cook and stir until slightly thickened and clear; cool. Stir in remaining package raspberries and chablis. Chill. To serve, place several orange sections in each bowl; add soup. Garnish as desired; serve with sour cream. Refrigerate leftovers.
Makes 8 to 10 servings.

Light and Lively Turkey Soup

2 cups cubed cooked BUTTERBALL® turkey (¾ pound)
1 cup uncooked instant rice
½ cup chopped celery
¼ cup minced fresh parsley
½ stick (¼ cup) butter or margarine
1 can (46 ounces) chicken broth
1 teaspoon finely shredded lemon peel
1 tablespoon lemon juice

Cook and stir rice, celery and parsley in butter in large saucepan over medium heat until celery is tender. Stir in remaining ingredients. Bring soup to boil over high heat. Reduce heat to low and simmer 15 minutes, stirring occasionally.
Yield: 5 to 6 servings (7 cups).

Egg Flower Soup with Corn

1 can (10½ oz.) condensed chicken broth
2 soup cans water
2 slices fresh ginger root, each ¼ inch thick
2 tablespoons plus 2 teaspoons cornstarch
¼ cup water
½ cup whole kernel corn
1 egg, beaten
2 tablespoons chopped green onions and tops
4 teaspoons KIKKOMAN Soy Sauce

Combine chicken broth, 2 soup cans water and ginger in medium saucepan. Bring to boil over high heat; reduce heat, cover and simmer 5 minutes. Discard ginger. Combine cornstarch and ¼ cup water; stir into saucepan with corn. Cook over high heat, stirring constantly, until mixture boils and is slightly thickened. Gradually pour egg into boiling soup, stirring constantly, but gently, in 1 direction. Remove from heat; stir in green onions and soy sauce. Serve immediately.
Makes about 4½ cups.

Shrimp Creole Soup

½ cup sliced celery
½ cup sliced green onions
1 clove garlic, minced
1 tablespoon vegetable oil
1 pouch CAMPBELL'S® Chicken Rice Soup Mix
1 can (about 15 ounces) tomatoes, undrained, cut up
1 cup water
1 small bay leaf
¼ teaspoon sugar
⅛ teaspoon dried thyme leaves, crushed
⅛ teaspoon pepper
    Generous dash hot pepper sauce
½ pound medium shrimp, peeled and deveined

1. In 2-quart saucepan over medium-high heat, cook celery, green onions and garlic in oil until celery is tender, stirring often.
2. Stir in soup mix, tomatoes with their liquid, water, bay leaf, sugar, thyme, pepper and hot pepper sauce. Heat to boiling, stirring occasionally.
3. Reduce heat to low. Cover; simmer 5 minutes. Stir in shrimp. Cover; simmer 5 minutes more or until shrimp are opaque. Remove bay leaf before serving.
Makes 3 servings.

Fish Soup Florentine

1 pouch CAMPBELL'S® Noodle Soup and Recipe Mix
2½ cups water
1 cup chopped fresh spinach
¼ teaspoon dried oregano leaves, crushed
    Dash crushed red pepper
½ pound flounder or other fish fillets, cut into ½-inch pieces
2 tablespoons Chablis or other dry white wine

1. In 2-quart saucepan, stir together soup mix, water, spinach, oregano and red pepper. Over high heat, heat to boiling. Reduce heat to low. Cover; simmer 5 minutes.
2. Stir in fish and wine. Cover; simmer 5 minutes more or until fish flakes easily when tested with a fork. Serve at once.
Makes 4 servings.

Skillet Seafood Bisque

¼ cup butter or margarine
1 cup sliced CAMPBELL'S FRESH® Mushrooms
2 tablespoons chopped fresh chives
1 clove garlic, minced
3 tablespoons all-purpose flour
1 can (10¾ ounces) CAMPBELL'S® Condensed Chicken Broth
1 pound medium shrimp, shelled and deveined
½ cup Chablis or other dry white wine
½ cup heavy cream
1 tablespoon chopped fresh parsley
    Fresh dill sprigs

1. In 10-inch skillet over medium heat, in hot butter, cook mushrooms, chives and garlic until tender, stirring occasionally. Stir in flour until smooth. .Gradually stir in chicken broth. Heat to boiling, stirring constantly.
2. Add shrimp. Reduce heat to low. Cover; simmer about 5 minutes or until shrimp are done. Stir in wine, cream and parsley; heat through. Ladle into bowls; top with dill sprigs.
Makes about 4½ cups or 6 servings.

Shrimp Bisque Orleans

¼ cup butter or margarine
1 large onion, chopped
½ cup chopped celery
2 cloves garlic, minced
2 tablespoons flour
2 tablespoons tomato paste
3 cups milk
2 cups clam or fish broth
1 bay leaf
½ teaspoon dried basil leaves
½ teaspoon TABASCO® pepper sauce
¼ teaspoon salt
1 pound shrimp, peeled, deveined
¼ cup sliced green onions

In large saucepot melt butter; add chopped onion, celery and garlic. Cook 5 minutes or until tender. Stir in flour and tomato paste; cook 1 minute. Remove from heat. Gradually stir in milk and broth; add bay leaf, basil, Tabasco® sauce and salt. Bring to a boil. Reduce heat; simmer 10 minutes. Add shrimp and green onions; simmer 5 minutes longer or until shrimp turn pink. Remove bay leaf.
Makes 6 servings.

Seafood Bisque

½ pound shrimp, shelled, deveined and cut in half crosswise
½ pound sea scallops, coarsely chopped
1 (16-ounce) can whole new potatoes, drained and diced
1 clove garlic, crushed
¼ cup BLUE BONNET® Margarine
⅔ cup all-purpose flour
2 (13¾-fluid ounce) cans COLLEGE INN® Chicken Broth
½ teaspoon ground white pepper
1 cup light cream or half-and-half

In large saucepan, over medium heat, cook shrimp, scallops, potatoes and garlic in margarine until seafood is done. Stir in flour until blended. Gradually add chicken broth and pepper. Heat to a boil, stirring constantly. Boil 1 minute. Stir in light cream; heat through. (Do not boil.)
Makes 6 servings.

Mussel Rice Soup

1 cup coarsely chopped onion
1 tablespoon butter or margarine
3 ribs celery, sliced
5 cups chicken broth
½ cup uncooked rice
½ teaspoon salt
½ teaspoon dried basil, crushed
¼ teaspoon pepper
2 medium tomatoes, peeled, seeded, chopped
2 cans (4 ounces each) mussels,* drained
2 cups torn spinach

Cook and stir onion in melted butter in Dutch oven over medium-high heat until crisp-tender. Add celery; cook 1 minute more. Add broth, rice and seasonings. Bring to a boil over high heat. Reduce heat to low. Cover and simmer 10 minutes. Stir in tomatoes and mussels; simmer 5 minutes more or until rice is tender. Add spinach. Serve immediately.
Substitution: Use 1 can (10 ounces) whole clams, drained, for the mussels.

*Favorite recipe from **Rice Council***

Fisherman's Bouillabaisse

¼ cup olive or vegetable oil
2 cloves garlic, finely chopped
1 cup water
½ cup dry white wine
1 envelope LIPTON® Onion or Onion-Mushroom Recipe Soup Mix
1 tablespoon finely chopped parsley
1 teaspoon thyme leaves
1 can (14½ ounces) whole peeled tomatoes, undrained and chopped
3 lobster tails (about 1½ pounds), cut into 3-inch pieces
1 pound red snapper, cod, halibut or haddock, cut into pieces
6 clams, well scrubbed
6 mussels, well scrubbed

In large saucepan or stockpot, heat oil and cook garlic over medium heat until golden. Add water, wine, onion recipe soup mix, parsley and thyme; blend thoroughly. Stir in tomatoes. Bring to a boil, then simmer covered 15 minutes. Add lobster and snapper and simmer 10 minutes. Add clams and mussels and simmer an additional 5 minutes or until shells open. (Discard any unopened shells.) Serve, if desired, with bread or rolls.
Makes about 4 (2-cup) servings.

Tomato-Shrimp Soup

2 tablespoons butter or margarine
½ cup thinly sliced onion
¼ cup chopped green pepper
1 medium clove garlic, minced
3 cups V8® Vegetable Juice
1 small bay leaf
¾ pound medium shrimp, shelled and deveined
½ pound flounder or other whitefish fillets, cut into 2-inch pieces
Toasted PEPPERIDGE FARM® Fully Baked French-Style Bread slices

1. In 2-quart saucepan over medium heat, in hot butter, cook onion, green pepper and garlic until vegetables are tender.
2. Stir in V8 juice and bay leaf. Heat to boiling. Reduce heat to low; simmer, uncovered, 10 minutes.
3. Add shrimp and fish. Cook until shrimp are pink and opaque and fish flakes easily with fork. Discard bay leaf. To serve: Ladle soup over toasted bread in bowls.
Makes 5 cups or 5 main-dish servings.

Per serving: 177 calories, 21 g protein, 7 g fat, 9 g carbohydrate, 663 mg sodium, 119 mg cholesterol.

Golden Broccoli Soup

2 cups broccoli flowerets
½ cup shredded carrot
½ cup chopped onion
¼ cup water
1 can (10¾ ounces) CAMPBELL'S® Condensed Creamy Natural Potato Soup
1 soup can milk
1 cup shredded Cheddar cheese (4 ounces)
¼ teaspoon pepper

To Microwave:

1. In 3-quart microwave-safe casserole, combine broccoli, carrot, onion and water. Cover with lid; microwave on HIGH 5 minutes or until vegetables are tender.

2. In small bowl, stir soup until smooth. Stir in milk, cheese and pepper; mix well. Stir into vegetables. Cover; microwave on HIGH 8 minutes or until hot and bubbling, stirring twice during cooking. Let stand, covered, 5 minutes.

Makes 4 cups or 4 servings.

Split Pea and Meatball Soup

1 cup dry green split peas, rinsed and drained
1 can (10½ ounces) CAMPBELL'S® Condensed Beef Broth
2 cups water
1 cup chopped onion
½ teaspoon summer savory leaves, crushed
⅛ teaspoon pepper
½ pound ground beef
¼ cup soft bread crumbs
1 egg
1 tablespoon chopped fresh parsley
1 clove garlic, minced
1 cup chopped carrots
1 cup sliced celery
1 can (14½ ounces) stewed tomatoes

1. In 4-quart Dutch oven over high heat, combine peas, beef broth, water, onion, savory and pepper. Heat to boiling; reduce heat to low. Cover; simmer 1 hour.

2. Meanwhile, for meatballs, in medium bowl, combine ground beef, bread crumbs, egg, parsley and garlic. Mix lightly, but well. Shape into 36 balls, using 1 rounded teaspoonful for each. Set aside.

3. Add carrots, celery and tomatoes to soup mixture. Over high heat, heat to boiling. Add meatballs; reduce heat to low. Cover; simmer 30 minutes until vegetables are tender and meat is done.

Makes about 8 cups or 6 servings.

Sausage Corn Chowder

1 package (8 ounces) SWIFT PREMIUM® BROWN 'N SERVE™ Microwave Sausage Links, thawed, cut into ½-inch slices
2 cups cubed potatoes
¾ cup chopped onion
½ cup chopped celery
¼ cup water
1 can (12 ounces) corn with red and green bell peppers
1 can (17 ounces) cream-style corn
2 cups milk
1 teaspoon salt
⅛ teaspoon ground thyme
Dash ground white pepper

Microwave Directions: Place potatoes, onion, celery and water in 2-quart microwave-safe bowl. Cover with vented plastic wrap and *microwave* on High (100%) 9 to 10 minutes or until vegetables are tender, stirring twice. Stir in sausage, corn, cream-style corn, milk, salt, thyme and pepper. Cover and *microwave* on High 7 to 8 minutes or until hot, stirring twice.

Makes 6 servings.

Creamy Clam Bisque

¼ cup chopped onion
2 tablespoons margarine or butter
3 tablespoons flour
Dash pepper
½ cup dry white wine
2 (6½-ounce) cans SNOW'S® or DOXSEE® Chopped Clams, drained, reserving liquid
2 cups (1 pint) BORDEN® or MEADOW GOLD® Half-and-Half
1 egg yolk
Paprika, optional

In medium saucepan, cook onion in margarine until tender. Gradually stir in flour and pepper; add wine and reserved clam liquid. Cook and stir until thickened; remove from heat. Blend half-and-half with egg yolk; stir into wine mixture along with clams. Heat through *(do not boil).* Garnish with paprika if desired. Refrigerate leftovers.

Makes about 1 quart.

Hearty Vegetable Soup

3 pounds beef shanks, cracked
8 cups water
3 tablespoons WYLER'S® or STEERO® Beef-Flavor Instant Bouillon *or* 9 Beef-Flavor Bouillon Cubes
2 bay leaves
1 (28-ounce) can whole tomatoes, undrained
1 cup pared, sliced carrots
½ cup chopped celery
½ cup chopped onion
1 teaspoon thyme leaves
1 cup uncooked CREAMETTES® Elbow Macaroni
2 cups sliced zucchini (2 small)

In large kettle or Dutch oven, combine shanks, water, bouillon and bay leaves. Bring to a boil; simmer covered 1½ hours or until meat is tender. Remove shanks and bay leaves; cut meat into cubes. Discard bones. Cool stock; skim fat from surface. Add meat, tomatoes, carrots, celery, onion and thyme; simmer covered 20 minutes. Add macaroni and zucchini. Cook 10 minutes longer or until tender. Refrigerate leftovers.

Makes about 3 quarts.

Frank and Vegetable Soup

1 package (16 ounces)
  ECKRICH® Franks, cut into
  1/4-inch slices
1 1/2 cups chopped onions
1 cup sliced carrots
1/2 cup sliced celery
1 tablespoon butter or
  margarine
1 can (14 1/2 ounces) whole
  tomatoes, undrained
1 package (10 ounces) frozen
  cut green beans, thawed
5 cups beef broth or bouillon
Grated Parmesan cheese

Saute onions, carrots and celery in butter in large saucepan over medium heat 5 minutes. Add tomatoes with juice; break up tomatoes. Mix in beans and broth. Bring to a boil over high heat. Reduce heat to low; simmer 15 minutes. Add franks and simmer 5 minutes more. Top each serving with cheese.
Makes 8 servings.

Tomato-Corn Soup

1 tablespoon butter or
  margarine
1 medium onion, chopped
2 cups fresh or frozen whole
  kernel corn
1 can (14 1/2 ounces) SWANSON®
  Clear Ready to Serve
  Chicken Broth
1 cup V8® Vegetable Juice
1 bay leaf
1/8 teaspoon pepper
1/2 cup milk
1 tablespoon chopped fresh
  parsley

1. In 2-quart saucepan over medium heat, in hot butter, cook onion until tender, stirring occasionally.
2. Stir in corn, broth, V8 juice, bay leaf and pepper. Heat to boiling. Reduce heat to low. Cover; simmer 25 minutes. Discard bay leaf. Gradually stir in milk and parsley; heat through.
Makes 4 1/2 cups or 6 side-dish servings.

Per serving: 97 calories, 3 g protein, 4 g fat, 15 g carbohydrate, 479 mg sodium, 8 mg cholesterol.

Hot and Sour Soup

1 ounce dried Oriental
  mushrooms
2 cans (13 3/4 ounces each)
  chicken broth or 3 1/3 cups
  chicken stock
2 cups orange juice
3/4 pound boneless pork, cut into
  julienne strips
1 cup carrots, cut into julienne
  strips
1 can (8 ounces) sliced water
  chestnuts, drained
1 tablespoon soy sauce
1/4 teaspoon salt
1/2 pound tofu, drained and cut
  into 1/2-inch cubes
3 tablespoons white wine
  vinegar
3/4 teaspoon TABASCO® pepper
  sauce
1/4 cup cornstarch
1/3 cup water

In small bowl pour enough boiling water over mushrooms to cover. Let stand 30 minutes; drain. In large saucepot combine mushrooms, broth, orange juice, pork, carrots, water chestnuts, soy sauce and salt. Bring to a boil. Reduce heat; simmer 3 minutes or until pork is cooked. Add tofu, vinegar and Tabasco® sauce. Combine cornstarch and water until smooth; add to soup. Stir constantly, bring to a boil over medium heat and boil for 1 minute.
Makes 8 servings.

Corned Beef & Cabbage Chowder

2 tablespoons butter or
  margarine
1/2 cup thinly sliced celery
1/2 cup finely chopped onion
2 cups water
2 cups coarsely shredded
  cabbage
1 cup thinly sliced carrots
1 envelope LIPTON® Noodle
  Soup Mix with Real Chicken
  Broth
1 teaspoon dry mustard
1 1/2 tablespoons all-purpose flour
2 cups milk
1/4 pound thinly sliced cooked
  corned beef, cut into thin
  strips

In large saucepan or stockpot, melt butter and cook celery and onion over medium heat until tender. Stir in water, cabbage and carrots. Bring to a boil, then simmer covered, stirring occasionally, 15 minutes or until vegetables are almost tender. Stir in noodle soup mix, then mustard and flour blended with milk. Bring just to the boiling point, then simmer, stirring constantly, until chowder is thickened, about 5 minutes. Stir in corned beef and heat through, but do not boil.
Makes about 3 (1 3/4-cup) servings.
Microwave Directions: In 3-quart casserole, heat butter at HIGH (Full Power) 1 minute. Add celery and onion and heat 5 minutes or until vegetables are tender, stirring once. Add water, cabbage and carrots. Heat covered, stirring occasionally, 15 minutes or until vegetables are tender. Stir in noodle soup mix, then mustard and flour blended with milk. Heat covered, stirring occasionally, 7 minutes or until chowder is thickened. Stir in corned beef. Let stand covered 5 minutes.

Sopa de Sonora

7½ cups water, divided
1 cup dry pinto beans, rinsed
1 pound boneless lean pork shoulder, trimmed, cut into 1-inch cubes
1 tablespoon vegetable oil
1 can (14½ ounces) ready-to-serve beef broth
1½ tablespoons LAWRY'S® Minced Onion with Green Onion Flakes
¼ teaspoon LAWRY'S® Garlic Powder with Parsley
1 package (1⅝ ounces) LAWRY'S® Chili Seasoning Mix
2 cups thinly sliced carrots
LAWRY'S® Seasoned Salt
Condiments*

Place 3 cups of the water and the beans in 3-quart saucepan. Bring to a boil over high heat; boil 2 minutes. Remove from heat. Cover and let soak 1 hour. Drain beans; discard water.

Brown pork in hot oil in Dutch oven over medium-high heat. Add beans, remaining 4½ cups water, the broth, minced onion, garlic powder and chili seasoning mix. Bring to a boil over high heat. Reduce heat to low. Cover and simmer 1½ hours. Add carrots; simmer, covered, about 30 minutes or until carrots are tender. Season to taste with seasoned salt. Ladle into bowls. Serve with condiments.
Makes 6 to 8 servings.
*Condiments: Cherry tomato quarters, sliced green onions, chopped cilantro, lime wedges, sour cream or LAWRY'S® Chunky Taco Sauce.

Albóndingas Soup

1 pound ground beef
¼ cup seasoned dry bread crumbs
2 tablespoons minced onion
2 tablespoons water
1 egg
½ teaspoon salt
¾ teaspoon TABASCO® pepper sauce, divided
1 large green pepper
2 tablespoons olive or vegetable oil
1 medium onion, chopped
1 clove garlic, minced
4 cups beef broth
1 can (16 ounces) tomatoes, undrained
¼ teaspoon saffron threads, crumbled

In medium bowl combine beef, crumbs, minced onion, water, egg, salt and ¼ teaspoon Tabasco® sauce; mix well. Shape into 1-inch meatballs. Cover; refrigerate. Coarsely chop enough green pepper to yield ½ cup; cut remainder into thin strips for garnish.

In large saucepot heat oil; cook ½ cup chopped green pepper, chopped onion and garlic 3 minutes or until tender. Stir in broth, tomatoes, saffron and remaining ½ teaspoon Tabasco® sauce. Bring to a boil, reduce heat and simmer uncovered 30 minutes; stir occasionally. Add meatballs; simmer covered 20 minutes longer or until meatballs are cooked. Garnish with green pepper strips.
Makes 6 servings.
Microwave Directions: Prepare meatballs as directed above. Chop and cut green pepper as directed above. In 3-quart microwave-safe casserole place *1 tablespoon* oil, chopped green pepper, chopped onion and garlic. Cover loosely with plastic wrap; cook on High 2 to 4 minutes or until vegetables are softened. Stir in broth, *drained* canned tomatoes, saffron and remaining ½ teaspoon Tabasco® sauce. Cook uncovered on High 10 minutes. Add meatballs and continue to cook uncovered on High 15 to 18 minutes or until meatballs are cooked; stir twice during cooking. Garnish with green pepper strips.

Beefy Vegetable Soup

1 tablespoon vegetable oil
2 pounds boneless beef chuck, cut into 1-inch cubes
2 medium onions, chopped
1 can (16 ounces) tomatoes, undrained
½ cup uncooked barley, rinsed
10 cups water
⅓ cup soy sauce
2 teaspoons dried thyme leaves
½ teaspoon salt
¼ pound fresh spinach leaves
4 large carrots, shredded
2 medium potatoes, pared, cubed
2 large celery stalks, sliced
¼ pound green beans, cut into pieces
½ teaspoon TABASCO® pepper sauce

In large heavy saucepot or Dutch oven heat oil over medium-high heat; add beef and brown on all sides. Remove and set aside. In same pot over medium heat, cook onions 3 minutes or until tender. Return meat to pot; add tomatoes, barley, water, soy sauce, thyme and salt. Cover. Bring to a boil. Reduce heat; simmer 1 hour. Add spinach, carrots, potatoes, celery, beans and Tabasco® sauce. Simmer covered 45 minutes longer or until meat and vegetables are tender.
Makes 10 to 12 servings.

BLT Soup

**6 slices bacon, cut in ¹/₂-inch
    pieces
1 medium onion, sliced
2 (13³/₄-fluid ounce) cans
    COLLEGE INN® Chicken or
    Beef Broth
1 (14¹/₂-ounce) can peeled
    tomatoes, undrained and cut
    up
2 tablespoons A.1.® Steak Sauce
2 cups shredded iceberg lettuce**

In large saucepan, cook bacon until
crisp; remove and crumble bacon.
Pour off all but 2 tablespoons drippings. Cook onion in reserved drippings for 2 to 3 minutes. Add broth,
tomatoes and steak sauce. Heat to a
boil; reduce heat. Cover and simmer
10 minutes. Add lettuce; simmer 2
minutes. Stir in bacon.
Makes 4 to 6 servings.

Octoberfest
Sausage Soup

**¹/₂ pound ECKRICH® Smoked
    Sausage
1 cup beef broth
1 cup chicken broth
¹/₄ cup coarsely chopped celery
¹/₄ cup coarsely chopped onion
¹/₄ cup coarsely chopped green
    bell pepper
1 medium potato, pared, diced
2 tablespoons cornstarch,
    dissolved in 2 tablespoons
    water
1 cup (4 ounces) shredded
    Swiss cheese
1 can (8 ounces) sauerkraut,
    drained
2 cups half and half
¹/₄ teaspoon ground white pepper
2 green onions, sliced**

Combine broths, celery, onion, green
pepper and potato in large saucepan;
bring to a boil over high heat. Reduce
heat to low; simmer until vegetables
are crisp-tender, about 15 minutes.
Add dissolved cornstarch; cook and
stir until soup thickens. Cut sausage
into quarters lengthwise, then cut
crosswise into ¹/₄-inch pieces. Add sausage, cheese, sauerkraut, half and
half and white pepper. Stir. Continue
heating until mixture is hot. DO NOT
BOIL. Serve immediately. Garnish
with green onions.
Makes 4 to 6 servings.

Vermont
Vegetable
Stew

**1 pound ECKRICH® Smoked
    Sausage, sliced thin
1 medium onion, chopped
1 tablespoon vegetable oil
3 cups water
2 teaspoons beef bouillon
    granules
1 bay leaf
¹/₂ teaspoon dried thyme leaves
3 carrots, sliced
3 ribs celery, sliced
¹/₄ head green cabbage, cut into
    1-inch pieces
2 tablespoons uncooked rice
1 can (8 ounces) tomato sauce
1 can (14¹/₂ ounces) red kidney
    beans
1 can (28 ounces) whole
    tomatoes, undrained, cut up**

Saute onion in oil in Dutch oven until
tender. Add remaining ingredients.
Bring to a boil over high heat. Reduce
heat to low; cover and simmer 30 minutes or until vegetables are tender.
Makes 8 servings.

Ham and Pea
Noodle Soup

**1 cup diced cooked ham
    (6 ounces)
1 tablespoon butter or
    margarine
1 pouch CAMPBELL'S® Noodle
    Soup and Recipe Mix
2¹/₂ cups water
¹/₂ cup frozen peas**

1. In 2-quart saucepan over medium
heat, cook ham in butter until
browned.
2. Stir in soup mix, water and peas.
Heat to boiling. Reduce heat to low.
Cover; simmer 7 to 10 minutes until
noodles and peas are tender, stirring
occasionally. Serve at once.
Makes 2 servings.

Chili Soup
Jarlsberg

**1 pound beef round steak, diced
2 tablespoons vegetable oil
2 cans (14¹/₂ ounces each)
    ready-to-serve beef broth
1 can (15 ounces) dark red
    kidney beans
1 can (14¹/₂ ounces) tomatoes,
    chopped, undrained
1 medium green bell pepper,
    chopped
1 medium red bell pepper,
    chopped
1 large onion, chopped
1 large clove garlic, minced
3¹/₄ teaspoons chili powder,
    divided
¹/₄ teaspoon ground cumin
1¹/₂ cups (6 ounces) shredded
    JARLSBERG cheese, divided
¹/₄ cup butter or margarine,
    softened
1 small clove garlic, minced
12 KAVLI Norwegian Thick-Style
    Crispbreads**

Brown beef in hot oil in large, deep saucepan over medium-high heat. Add broth. Bring to a boil over high heat. Reduce heat to low. Cover and simmer 1 hour. Add beans, tomatoes, peppers, onion, large garlic clove, 3 teaspoons of the chili powder and the cumin. Simmer, covered, 30 minutes. Gradually blend in 1/2 cup of the cheese. Heat just until cheese melts.

Blend butter, small garlic clove and remaining 1/4 teaspoon chili powder in small bowl. Spread on crispbreads; arrange on cookie sheet. Bake in preheated 375°F oven several minutes or until butter is melted. Sprinkle with 1/2 cup of the cheese. Bake just until cheese is melted.

Ladle soup into bowls. Garnish with remaining 1/2 cup cheese. Serve with crispbreads.
Makes 6 servings.

Favorite recipe from Norseland Foods, Inc.

Sausage and Lentil Soup

- 1 package (10 ounces) ECKRICH® SMOK-Y-LINKS® Sausages, cut into 1/2-inch slices
- 1/2 cup chopped onion
- 1/2 cup sliced carrot
- 1/2 cup sliced celery
- 1 clove garlic, minced
- 2 tablespoons vegetable oil
- 1 cup lentils, sorted, rinsed
- 6 cups water
- 3 teaspoons beef bouillon granules
- 1 can (14 1/2 ounces) whole tomatoes, undrained, cut up
  Dash ground black pepper
- 2 teaspoons lemon juice

Cook onion, carrot, celery and garlic in oil in Dutch oven over medium heat 5 minutes. Add lentils, water and bouillon granules. Bring to a boil over high heat. Reduce heat to low; cover and simmer 30 minutes or until lentils are tender. Add sausage, tomatoes with juice and pepper to lentil mixture. Simmer 10 minutes. Stir in lemon juice.
Makes 6 to 8 servings.

Chunky Beef Barley Soup

- 1 1/2 pounds beef stew meat, cut into 1/2-inch cubes
- 2 tablespoons all-purpose flour
- 2 cloves garlic, minced
- 1/4 cup vegetable oil
- 2 quarts water
- 1 can (14 1/2 ounces) tomatoes, coarsely chopped, undrained
- 1 cup coarsely chopped onion
- 1/2 cup QUAKER® Scotch® Brand Pearled Barley*
- 1 tablespoon salt (optional)
- 1 teaspoon dried basil, crushed
- 1/8 teaspoon pepper
- 1 package (16 ounces) frozen vegetable medley

Dredge meat in flour. Brown meat with garlic in hot oil in 4-quart Dutch oven over medium-high heat. Add water, tomatoes, onion, barley, salt, basil and pepper. Bring to a boil over high heat. Reduce heat to low. Cover and simmer 1 hour or until meat and barley are tender. Add frozen vegetables. Return to a boil over high heat. Reduce heat to low. Simmer 5 minutes or until vegetables are tender. Additional water may be added if soup becomes too thick upon standing.
Makes about 12 servings.

*Substitution: Use 3/4 cup Quaker® Scotch® Quick Barley for the pearled barley. Add quick barley with frozen vegetables. Return to a boil; cover and simmer 10 to 12 minutes or until barley is tender.

Monterey Cheese Soup

- 1 14 1/2-oz. can tomatoes
- 6 6-inch corn tortillas, cut into 1/4-inch strips
  Oil
- 1/2 cup chopped onion
- 2 garlic cloves, minced
- 1 lb. VELVEETA Pasteurized Process Cheese Spread, cubed
- 1 13 3/4-oz. can chicken broth
- 2 tablespoons chopped cilantro

Drain tomatoes, reserving 1/2 cup liquid. Chop tomatoes. Fry tortillas in large skillet in 1/4 inch hot oil until crisp but not brown. Drain oil, reserving 2 tablespoons. Saute onions and garlic in reserved oil until onions are tender. Reduce heat to low. Add tomatoes, reserved liquid, process cheese spread, broth and cilantro. Stir until process cheese spread is melted. Divide tortillas among five soup bowls; top with process cheese spread mixture.
Five 1-cup servings.

Preparation time: 10 minutes
Cooking time: 15 minutes

Variations: Substitute parsley for cilantro.
Substitute VELVEETA Mexican Pasteurized Process Cheese Spread with Jalapeño Pepper for Process Cheese Spread.
Microwave: Prepare tortillas as directed. Drain tomatoes, reserving 1/4 cup liquid. Chop tomatoes. Combine onions, garlic and 1 tablespoon oil in 2 1/2-quart microwave-safe bowl. Microwave on High 2 to 3 minutes or until onions are tender. Add tomatoes, reserved liquid, process cheese spread, broth and cilantro. Microwave on High 6 to 8 minutes or until process cheese spread is melted, stirring every 3 minutes. Divide tortillas among five soup bowls; top with process cheese spread mixture.

SALADS

Crisp vegetables, luscious fruits, substantial potatoes or pasta—along with meats, poultry or fish—combine to make salads of dazzling variety. Add to your salad repertoire with creations that complement a main course or make satisfying meals by themselves.

Lentil, Chick Pea & Cucumber Salad

1 quart water
1 cup uncooked lentils
3/4 cup WISH-BONE® Italian Dressing
1/2 cup chopped celery
1 tablespoon Dijon-style mustard
1 teaspoon lemon juice
1/8 teaspoon pepper
1 medium red onion, chopped
2 cups chick peas or garbanzos, rinsed and drained
1 large cucumber, peeled, seeded, sliced and quartered
1/2 cup chopped carrot
2 tablespoons finely chopped parsley

In large saucepan, combine water and lentils. Bring to a boil, then simmer covered 15 minutes or until tender. Drain and rinse with cold water until completely cool.

In food processor or blender, process Italian dressing, celery, mustard, lemon juice and pepper. In large salad bowl, toss dressing mixture with lentils, red onion, chick peas, cucumber, carrot and parsley. Garnish, if desired, with additional sliced cucumber and red onion.

Makes about 12 side-dish servings.

Note: Also terrific with Wish-Bone® Robusto Italian, Blended Italian, Herbal Italian or Lite Italian Dressing.

Winter Vegetable Toss

2 quarts mixed salad greens
1 medium cucumber, sliced
1 medium red or green pepper, cut into strips
1 cup cauliflowerets
1 cup pitted ripe olives, sliced
2 tablespoons grated Parmesan cheese
2/3 cup WISH-BONE® Italian Dressing

In large salad bowl, combine all ingredients except Italian dressing; cover and chill. Just before serving, toss with dressing.

Makes about 8 side-dish servings.

Note: Also terrific with Wish-Bone® Lite Italian or Herbal Italian Dressing.

Avocado-Tomato Salad

2 ripe large avocados, seeded and peeled
Lemon juice
2 or 3 medium tomatoes
Lettuce leaves
Prepared HIDDEN VALLEY RANCH® ORIGINAL RANCH® Salad Dressing

Slice avocados and sprinkle with lemon juice to prevent browning. Cut tomatoes into wedges. Arrange avocado slices and tomato wedges on individual lettuce-lined salad plates. Drizzle with salad dressing.

Makes 8 servings.

Cheese and Red Bean Salad

1 (16-ounce) container BORDEN® or MEADOW GOLD® Cottage Cheese
1 (15½-ounce) can kidney beans, drained
½ cup chopped green pepper
½ cup sliced pimiento-stuffed olives
½ cup chopped onion
¼ teaspoon seasoned pepper
Lettuce leaves

In large bowl, combine all ingredients except lettuce; mix well. Chill. Serve on lettuce. Refrigerate leftovers.
Makes 6 to 8 servings.

Classic Spinach Salad

½ pound fresh spinach leaves (about 10 cups)
1 cup sliced mushrooms
1 medium tomato, cut into wedges
⅓ cup seasoned croutons
¼ cup chopped red onion
4 slices bacon, crisp-cooked and crumbled
½ cup WISH-BONE® Classic Dijon Vinaigrette or Lite Classic Dijon Vinaigrette Dressing
1 hard-cooked egg, sliced

In large salad bowl, combine spinach, mushrooms, tomato, croutons, red onion and bacon. Add classic Dijon vinaigrette dressing and toss gently. Garnish with egg.
Makes about 6 side-dish servings.

Tomato and Onion Salad

6 tablespoons vegetable oil
3 tablespoons tarragon or cider vinegar
1 clove garlic, halved
1 tablespoon chopped parsley
¼ teaspoon dry mustard
¼ teaspoon dried oregano leaves
¼ teaspoon salt
¼ teaspoon TABASCO® pepper sauce
3 tomatoes, sliced
1 large onion, sliced

In small bowl combine oil, vinegar, garlic, parsley, mustard, oregano, salt and Tabasco® sauce; mix well. Cover; let stand at least 30 minutes. Remove garlic. Arrange tomato slices alternately with onion rings on serving platter. Top with salad dressing.
Makes 6 servings.

Firecracker Salad

1 tablespoon sesame seed, toasted
2 tablespoons distilled white vinegar
2 teaspoons sugar
1 teaspoon minced fresh ginger root
4 teaspoons KIKKOMAN Soy Sauce
1 cup julienne-stripped radishes
1 cup julienne-stripped cucumber
4 cups finely shredded iceberg lettuce
1½ teaspoons minced fresh cilantro or parsley

Measure sesame seed, vinegar, sugar, ginger and soy sauce into jar with screw-top lid; cover and shake well until sugar dissolves. Combine radishes, cucumber and 3 tablespoons dressing; cover and refrigerate 30 minutes, stirring occasionally. Toss lettuce with cilantro in large bowl. Pour radish mixture and remaining dressing over lettuce. Toss lightly to combine.
Makes 6 servings.

Marinated Vegetable Salad

2 cups broccoli flowerets
1 cup carrots cut into ½-inch diagonal slices
1 medium green pepper, cut into strips
1 medium zucchini, sliced
1½ cups V8® Vegetable Juice
⅓ cup red wine vinegar
2 tablespoons Dijon-style mustard
½ teaspoon dried basil leaves, crushed
2 cups sliced CAMPBELL'S FRESH® Mushrooms (8 ounces)

1. In 2-quart saucepan over high heat, in 1 inch boiling water, cook broccoli and carrots 3 minutes. Add green pepper and zucchini; cook 3 minutes or until vegetables are tender-crisp. Drain.
2. To make marinade: In small bowl, stir together V8 juice, vinegar, mustard and basil.
3. In 13- by 9-inch baking dish, place cooked vegetables and mushrooms. Pour marinade over vegetables. Cover; refrigerate until serving time, at least 6 hours, stirring occasionally.
Makes 5 cups or 8 side-dish servings.

Per serving: 45 calories, 2 g protein, 1 g fat, 9 g carbohydrate, 279 mg sodium, 0 mg cholesterol.

Pennsylvania Dutch Chow Chow

- 1 cup cauliflowerets
- 1 cup whole kernel corn
- 1 cup green beans cut into 1½-inch pieces
- 1 jar (16 ounces) VLASIC® Country Classic Sweet Chunky Relish
- ½ cup cooked or canned kidney beans, drained
- ¼ cup thinly sliced celery

1. In 2-quart saucepan over medium heat, in boiling water, cook cauliflower, corn and green beans 4 minutes or until tender-crisp. Drain.
2. In medium bowl, combine cooked vegetables, relish, kidney beans and celery. Cover; refrigerate until serving time, at least 4 hours, stirring occasionally.
Makes 5 cups or 10 servings.
To Microwave: In 1-quart microwave-safe casserole, combine cauliflower, corn, green beans and 2 tablespoons water. Microwave, covered, on HIGH 5 minutes or until vegetables are tender-crisp, stirring twice. Proceed as above.

Fresh Vegetable Salad

- ½ cup WISH-BONE® Italian Dressing
- 1 tablespoon chopped fresh tarragon leaves*
- 1 teaspoon lemon juice
- ¼ teaspoon pepper
  Assorted Fresh Vegetables**
- ½ cup sliced green onions
  Salt to taste

In large salad bowl, blend Italian dressing, tarragon, lemon juice and pepper. Toss with Assorted Fresh Vegetables and green onions; add salt. Cover and marinate in refrigerator, stirring occasionally, 3 hours.
Makes about 6 side-dish servings.
Substitution: Use 1 teaspoon dried tarragon leaves.
****Assorted Fresh Vegetables:** Use any combination of the following to equal 6 cups—broccoli florets, cauliflowerets, sliced red, green or yellow pepper, carrots, yellow squash, zucchini or snow peas.
Hint: For crisp-tender vegetables, cook vegetables in boiling water about 1 minute, then immediately drain and rinse with very cold water until completely cool.
Note: Also terrific with Wish-Bone® Robusto Italian, Herbal Italian, Italian & Cheese, Blended Italian or Classic Dijon Vinaigrette Dressing.

Marinated Tomatoes & Cucumbers

- 2 large tomatoes, sliced
- 1 small cucumber, sliced
- 1 small onion, sliced
- ⅓ cup vegetable oil
- ⅓ cup REALEMON® Lemon Juice from Concentrate
- 1 tablespoon sugar
- ¼ teaspoon basil leaves
- ½ teaspoon salt
- 1 clove garlic, finely chopped
  Lettuce leaves
  Imitation bacon or cooked crumbled bacon

In 2-quart shallow baking dish, arrange tomatoes, cucumber and onion. In small bowl, combine remaining ingredients except lettuce and imitation bacon; pour over tomatoes. Chill several hours. Line platter with lettuce; arrange tomatoes, cucumbers and onion on top and sprinkle with imitation bacon.
Makes 4 to 6 servings.

Lynn's Salad

- 1 head DOLE™ Cauliflower, cut into flowerets
- 1 bunch DOLE™ Broccoli, cut into flowerets
- 1 jar (6 ounces) marinated artichoke hearts, drained
- 8 ounces mozzarella cheese, cubed
- 2 cups pitted ripe olives
  Dash garlic salt
- 1 bottle (8 ounces) Italian salad dressing

In large bowl, combine cauliflower, broccoli, artichokes, cheese, olives and garlic salt. Pour salad dressing over vegetable mixture. Refrigerate, covered, overnight. Drain salad dressing (save for another use, if desired).
Makes 6 servings.

Corn Relish Salad

- ¾ cup sugar
- ½ cup CRISCO® Oil
- ¼ cup white vinegar
- ½ teaspoon celery seed
- ¼ teaspoon whole mustard seed
- 1 can (17 ounces) whole kernel corn, drained
- 1 can (16 ounces) sauerkraut, pressed to remove excess liquid
- ½ cup chopped green pepper
- ⅓ cup chopped onion
- 1 jar (2 ounces) diced pimiento, drained

Combine sugar, Crisco® Oil, vinegar, celery seed and mustard seed in medium serving bowl. Stir until sugar dissolves. Add remaining ingredients. Mix well. Cover and refrigerate at least 8 hours or overnight. Drain and stir before serving.
6 to 8 servings.

Dilly Bean Salad

1 envelope LIPTON® Onion
   Recipe Soup Mix
3/4 cup water
1/4 cup red wine vinegar
1/4 cup oil
1/4 cup snipped fresh dill*
1 tablespoon finely chopped
   parsley
1 small clove garlic, finely
   chopped
1 pound green beans, cooked**
1 can (16 ounces) chick peas
   (garbanzos) or red kidney
   beans, rinsed and drained
   (optional)
2 cups fresh or canned sliced
   mushrooms

In medium bowl, blend onion recipe
soup mix, water and vinegar. Stir in
oil, dill, parsley and garlic. Toss with
remaining ingredients; chill.
Makes about 6 cups salad.
   ***Substitution:** Use 1 tablespoon
dried dill weed.
   ****Substitution:** Use 2 cans (16
ounces each) cut green beans,
drained.

Bean Sprout & Spinach Salad

   Boiling water
1 pound fresh spinach, washed
1/2 pound fresh bean sprouts
1 tablespoon sugar
4 teaspoons distilled white
   vinegar
1 tablespoon KIKKOMAN Soy
   Sauce
1 teaspoon sesame seed,
   toasted

Pour boiling water over spinach in colander; rinse immediately with cold
water. Drain thoroughly and place in
medium serving bowl. Repeat procedure with bean sprouts and place in
same bowl. Combine sugar, vinegar,
soy sauce and sesame seed; pour over
vegetables and toss to combine. Cover
and refrigerate at least 1 hour before
serving.
Makes 4 servings.

Sunflower Seed Cole Slaw

1 can (20 ounces) DOLE®
   Pineapple Tidbits
1/2 pound DOLE™ Carrots,
   shredded
1/4 pound DOLE™ Green Cabbage,
   shredded
1/4 pound red cabbage, shredded
1/2 cup sunflower seeds, lightly
   toasted
1/2 cup mayonnaise
2 tablespoons DOLE® Frozen
   Pineapple Orange Juice
   Concentrate
1/4 teaspoon salt
   Pinch white pepper

Drain pineapple; reserve 2 tablespoons juice. In bowl, combine pineapple, carrots, green and red cabbage
and sunflower seeds. To make dressing, in 1-quart measure, combine
mayonnaise, juice concentrate, reserved pineapple juice, salt and pepper. Pour over salad mixture and toss.
Refrigerate, covered, until ready to
serve.
Makes 8 servings.

Dole's Summer Vegetable Salad

1 head DOLE™ Lettuce
2 DOLE™ Tomatoes
1 cucumber
1/2 DOLE™ Red Bell Pepper
1/4 red onion
1 cup sliced DOLE™ Celery
1 cup snow peas, ends and
   strings removed
1 cup sliced DOLE™ Cauliflower
   Dill Dressing (recipe follows)

Tear lettuce into bite-size pieces. Cut
tomatoes into wedges. Slice cucumber,
red pepper and red onion. Place all
vegetables in salad bowl; toss with
Dill Dressing.
Makes 4 servings.
DILL DRESSING: In 1-quart measure,
combine 1/2 cup *each* dairy sour cream
and mayonnaise, 1 tablespoon vinegar, 1 teaspoon *each* dried dill weed
and onion powder, 1 teaspoon Dijon
mustard, 3/4 teaspoon garlic salt and
cracked pepper to taste. Refrigerate,
covered, until ready to serve.

Simple Salad Élégante

1/4 cup WISH-BONE® Italian or
   Lite Italian Dressing
10 small snow peas (about 1 1/2
   ounces)
1/2 cup sliced mushrooms
1/2 small red pepper, cut into
   rings
2 cups mixed salad greens

In small bowl, combine all ingredients except salad greens. Cover and
marinate in refrigerator, stirring occasionally, 4 hours or overnight. To
serve, arrange marinated vegetables
on salad greens.
Makes about 2 side-dish servings.

Citrus, Avocado & Bacon Salad

3 tablespoons orange juice
    concentrate, thawed
2 tablespoons vegetable oil
1 tablespoon lime juice
1 tablespoon honey
1 tablespoon white vinegar
3 cups mixed salad greens,
    washed and drained
½ avocado, peeled, pitted and
    sliced
6 slices ARMOUR® Lower Salt
    Bacon, cut in half and
    cooked crisp
1 (11-ounce) can mandarin
    oranges, drained

Combine orange juice concentrate, oil, lime juice, honey and vinegar in small bowl; set aside. Divide mixed salad greens evenly between 2 individual salad plates. Arrange avocado and bacon spoke-fashion over greens. Arrange mandarin oranges on top of greens. Drizzle with dressing. Garnish with chopped unsalted peanuts, if desired.
Makes 2 servings.

Nutrition Information Per Serving: 496 calories, 9.4 g protein, 30.6 g fat, 51.5 g carbohydrates, 18 mg cholesterol, 398 mg sodium.

Watercress-Carrot Salad

2 medium bunches watercress
6 medium carrots
¾ cup CRISCO® Oil
¼ cup lemon juice
1 tablespoon sugar
¾ teaspoon salt
¼ teaspoon paprika
¼ teaspoon dry mustard
⅛ teaspoon pepper

Remove and discard tough ends and bruised leaves from watercress. Tear remaining watercress into bite-size pieces. Cut carrots in half lengthwise and crosswise. With a vegetable peeler, cut carrot pieces into ribbon-like strips. Combine watercress and carrots in salad bowl.

Blend remaining ingredients in small mixing bowl. Pour over vegetables. Toss to coat. Serve immediately. *6 to 8 servings.*

Spinach Salad with Raspberry Dressing

½ cup plain nonfat yogurt
¼ cup fresh or frozen red
    raspberries, thawed if frozen
1 tablespoon skim milk
1½ teaspoons chopped fresh mint
    or ½ teaspoon dried mint,
    crushed
4 to 6 cups fresh spinach,
    washed, drained and
    trimmed
2 large fresh mushrooms, sliced
1 tablespoon sesame seeds,
    toasted
4 to 6 red onion rings
6 slices ARMOUR® Lower Salt
    Bacon, cooked crisp and
    crumbled

Carefully combine yogurt, raspberries, milk and mint in small bowl; set aside. Combine spinach, mushrooms and sesame seeds in medium bowl; mix well. Arrange spinach mixture evenly on 2 individual salad plates; top with red onion rings. Drizzle yogurt dressing over salads; sprinkle with bacon. Garnish with fresh raspberries and mint sprig, if desired.
Makes 2 servings.

Nutrition Information Per Serving: 200 calories, 15.8 g protein, 10.1 g fat, 14.1 g carbohydrates, 19.1 mg cholesterol, 556 mg sodium.

Cauliflower-Avocado Salad

4 cups water
1¼ teaspoons salt, divided
1 medium head cauliflower,
    rinsed and trimmed
⅓ cup CRISCO® Oil
3 tablespoons plus 2 teaspoons
    lemon juice, divided
    Dash pepper
3 medium avocados
1 small onion, quartered
    Lettuce leaves
    Radish roses
    Cucumber slices

Combine water and ½ teaspoon salt in 3-quart saucepan. Heat to boiling. Add cauliflower. Cover. Simmer until cauliflower is tender. Drain; rinse under cold water. Place cauliflower, stem up, in large mixing bowl.

Blend Crisco Oil, 3 tablespoons lemon juice, pepper and ½ teaspoon salt in small mixing bowl. Pour over cauliflower. Cover and refrigerate at least 8 hours or overnight, spooning marinade over cauliflower occasionally.

Just before serving, peel avocados and cut into small pieces. Place in blender pitcher. Add onion, remaining ¼ teaspoon salt and remaining 2 teaspoons lemon juice. Blend at medium speed until puréed.

Line serving plate with lettuce leaves. Drain cauliflower and place, stem down, in center of plate. Spread avocado mixture on cauliflower. Spear radish roses on wooden picks and arrange on cauliflower. Arrange cucumber slices around edge of plate. Cut cauliflower into wedges to serve.
6 to 8 servings.

Eggplant Salad

1/3 cup CRISCO® Oil
1 tablespoon lemon juice
1/2 teaspoon dried oregano leaves
2 cloves garlic, minced
1 medium eggplant (about
   1 pound), peeled and cut
   into 1/2-inch cubes
1 medium onion, thinly sliced
   and separated into rings
1 medium zucchini, halved
   lengthwise and thinly sliced
1 cup sliced fresh mushrooms
1 medium tomato, peeled,
   seeded and chopped
1/4 teaspoon salt

Combine Crisco® Oil, lemon juice, oregano and garlic in large skillet. Cook over moderate heat, stirring occasionally, until garlic is lightly browned. Add eggplant and onion. Stir to coat. Cook, stirring occasionally, about 10 minutes, or until eggplant is tender. Remove from heat. Transfer to medium serving bowl. Stir in zucchini, mushrooms, tomato and salt. Cover and refrigerate at least 8 hours or overnight. Stir before serving. Sprinkle with *grated Parmesan cheese,* if desired.
6 to 8 servings.

Sprout-Green Bean Salad

3 packages (9 ounces each)
   frozen French-cut green
   beans
1/2 cup CRISCO® Oil
1/4 cup white vinegar
2 teaspoons sugar
1/2 teaspoon salt
1/4 teaspoon pepper
1 can (16 ounces) bean sprouts,
   rinsed and drained
1 cup thinly sliced celery
3/4 cup chopped green onion
1 jar (2 ounces) diced pimiento,
   drained

Cook beans in 3-quart saucepan according to package directions. Drain and cool. Blend Crisco® Oil, vinegar, sugar, salt and pepper in small mixing bowl. Set aside.

Mix green beans, bean sprouts, celery, onion and pimiento in large serving bowl. Stir dressing. Pour over bean mixture. Toss to coat. Cover and refrigerate at least 3 hours. Stir before serving. Garnish with *cherry tomatoes,* if desired.
10 to 12 servings.

Italian-Style Cauliflower Salad

1 head DOLE™ Cauliflower, cut
   into flowerets
1/2 cup olive or vegetable oil
1/4 cup vinegar
1 clove garlic, pressed
1/2 teaspoon salt
1/2 teaspoon cracked black
   pepper
1/4 teaspoon dried basil,
   crumbled
1 cup sliced DOLE™ Green or
   Red Bell Pepper
1 cup sliced DOLE™ Celery
1 cup sliced DOLE™ Carrots
1/2 cup sliced pimento-stuffed
   olives
1/4 cup chopped parsley

In large saucepan, cook cauliflower in steamer basket over boiling water 8 minutes or until tender-crisp. Drain; transfer to large bowl. To make dressing, in 1-quart measure, combine oil, vinegar, garlic, salt, pepper and basil. Pour dressing over warm cauliflower. Add remaining ingredients; toss to coat. Refrigerate, covered, overnight.
Makes 6 servings.

Zesty Mushroom Salad

1 cup vegetable oil
1/3 cup wine vinegar
1 tablespoon lemon juice
1 tablespoon chopped chives
1/2 teaspoon salt
1/4 teaspoon TABASCO® pepper
   sauce
1 small clove garlic, minced
6 cups torn iceberg lettuce
2 cups torn spinach leaves
1/4 pound mushrooms, sliced
1/3 cup sliced pitted ripe olives

In jar with tightly fitting lid combine oil, vinegar, lemon juice, chives, salt, Tabasco® sauce and garlic; shake well. In large bowl combine lettuce, spinach, mushrooms and olives. Add 3/4 cup dressing and toss lightly to mix well. Refrigerate remaining dressing in covered jar for later use.
Makes 8 servings.

Cucumber Dill Salad

1 envelope LIPTON® Vegetable
   Recipe Soup Mix
1/2 pint (8 ounces) sour cream
2 teaspoons red wine vinegar
2 teaspoons Dijon-style or
   yellow prepared mustard
1 teaspoon dill weed
1/8 teaspoon pepper
3 medium cucumbers, peeled
   and thinly sliced (about
   5 cups)

In medium bowl, blend all ingredients except cucumbers. Toss with cucumbers; chill at least 2 hours.
Makes about 4 cups salad.

Country Pineapple Slaw

1 can (20 ounces) DOLE®
   Pineapple Chunks
1 package (16 ounces) DOLE®
   Cole Slaw Mix
1/2 cup sunflower seeds
   Zesty Dressing (recipe follows)

Drain pineapple. In large bowl, combine pineapple with cole slaw mix and sunflower seeds. Toss with Zesty Dressing. Refrigerate, covered, until ready to serve.
Makes 6 servings.
ZESTY DRESSING: In 1-quart measure, combine 1/2 cup *each* mayonnaise and dairy sour cream, 2 tablespoons lemon juice, 1 tablespoon Dijon mustard and 1/2 teaspoon caraway seeds. Blend well.

Spinach Salad

1/4 pound sliced bacon
1/2 cup sliced scallions
2 tablespoons all-purpose flour
1 cup COLLEGE INN® Beef or
   Chicken Broth
1/3 cup red wine vinegar
8 cups spinach leaves, torn
2 cups sliced fresh mushrooms

In large skillet, over medium-high heat, cook bacon until crisp. Drain, reserving 1/4 cup drippings. Crumble bacon; set aside. In reserved drippings, over medium heat, cook scallions until tender. Stir in flour; cook 1 minute. Stir in broth and vinegar; heat to a boil. Reduce heat; cook until slightly thickened.

In large bowl, mix spinach leaves and mushrooms. Pour hot dressing over salad, tossing to coat well. Sprinkle with reserved bacon pieces. Serve immediately.
Makes 8 servings.

Warm Bean Salad

1 tablespoon vegetable oil
3/4 cup chopped celery
2 green onions, thinly sliced
1 can (16 ounces) CAMPBELL'S®
   Home Style Beans
1 tablespoon chopped fresh
   parsley
1 tablespoon red wine vinegar
1/8 teaspoon pepper
1 CAMPBELL'S FRESH® Tomato,
   chopped

To Microwave:
1. In 1 1/2-quart microwave-safe casserole, combine oil, celery and onions. Cover with lid; microwave on HIGH 1 1/2 minutes or until celery is tender-crisp.
2. Stir in beans, parsley, vinegar and pepper. Cover; microwave on HIGH 2 1/2 minutes or until heated through, stirring once during cooking. Stir in tomato.
Makes about 3 cups or 3 servings.

Mexican Tossed Salad

3 large ripe avocados, seeded,
   peeled and sliced
1/2 cup BORDEN® or MEADOW
   GOLD® Sour Cream
1/4 cup REALEMON® Lemon Juice
   from Concentrate
1 tablespoon finely chopped
   onion
1 tablespoon water
1/4 teaspoon salt
1/4 teaspoon hot pepper sauce
6 cups torn mixed salad greens
1 large tomato, seeded and
   chopped
1 cup (4 ounces) shredded mild
   Cheddar or Monterey Jack
   cheese
1/2 cup sliced pitted ripe olives
1 cup coarsely crushed tortilla
   chips

In medium bowl, mash *1 avocado;* stir in sour cream, *3 tablespoons* of the ReaLemon® brand, onion, water, salt and hot pepper sauce. Chill to blend flavors. In large salad bowl, sprinkle remaining *2 avocados* with remaining *1 tablespoon* ReaLemon® brand. Top with salad greens, tomato, cheese and olives; chill. Just before serving, toss with avocado dressing and tortilla chips.
Makes 8 servings.

Garden Gazpacho Salad

1 cup (8 ounces) WISH-BONE®
   Robusto Italian Dressing
1/4 cup tomato juice
6 dashes hot pepper sauce
   (optional)
2 medium cucumbers, chopped
2 medium tomatoes, chopped
2 medium green peppers,
   chopped
1 medium onion, chopped
1 loaf unsliced round bread
   (about 9-inch diameter)
Lettuce leaves

In large bowl, blend robusto Italian dressing, tomato juice and hot pepper sauce. Stir in vegetables. Cover and marinate in refrigerator, stirring occasionally, at least 2 hours.

Cut lengthwise slice off top of bread. Hollow out center, leaving 1/2-inch shell. Just before serving, line bread shell with lettuce and fill with vegetable mixture. To serve, spoon out vegetable mixture, then cut bread shell into wedges.
Makes about 8 side-dish servings.
  Note: Also terrific with Wish-Bone® Italian or Lite Italian Dressing.

Tangy Coleslaw

1 tablespoon BLUE BONNET®
  Margarine
2 tablespoons all-purpose flour
2 tablespoons sugar
¼ teaspoon ground black pepper
2 tablespoons GREY POUPON®
  Dijon Mustard
1½ cups COLLEGE INN® Chicken
  Broth
⅓ cup white wine vinegar
8 cups shredded red or green
  cabbage
½ cup chopped red onion

In medium saucepan, over medium heat, melt margarine. Blend in flour; cook 1 minute. Add sugar, pepper, mustard and chicken broth; cook until mixture thickens and boils. Stir in vinegar. Cover; refrigerate 1 hour.

In large bowl, mix together cabbage and onion. Pour dressing over salad, tossing to coat well. Refrigerate at least 1 hour to blend flavors.
Makes about 9 cups.

Piñata Salad

1 head DOLE™ Iceberg Lettuce,
  torn
1 avocado, diced
1 can (16 ounces) garbanzo
  beans, drained
1 cup diced DOLE™ Tomatoes
1 cup ripe olives, cut into
  wedges or sliced
1 cup sliced DOLE™ Celery
1 cup sliced jicama or radishes
4 ounces sharp Cheddar cheese,
  shredded
  Gazpacho Dressing (recipe
  follows)
  Chile Dressing (recipe follows)

Place lettuce in salad bowl. Place avocado, garbanzo beans, tomatoes, olives, celery, jicama and cheese in individual bowls for a choice of toppings. Serve with either Gazpacho or Chile Dressing.
Makes 6 to 8 servings.
GAZPACHO DRESSING: In screw-top jar, combine ½ cup olive or vegetable oil, ¼ cup vinegar, 3 sliced green onions, ¾ cup diced tomato, ¼ cup diced green bell pepper, 1 pressed garlic clove, 3 tablespoons chopped cilantro or parsley, 1 teaspoon salt and 6 drops liquid hot pepper seasoning. Shake well to combine.
CHILE DRESSING: Puree 7 ounces (1 can) diced green chiles, 1 cup mayonnaise and ¼ cup dairy sour cream in blender. Refrigerate, covered, until ready to serve.

Winter Fruit Bowl

2 packages (4-serving size) or
  1 package (8-serving size)
  JELL-O® Brand Lemon
  Flavor Gelatin
1½ cups boiling water
1 can (12 fluid ounces) lemon-
  lime carbonated beverage,
  chilled
  Ice cubes
3 cups diced or sliced fresh
  fruits* (bananas, oranges,
  apples, pears, grapes)

Dissolve gelatin in boiling water. Combine beverage and ice cubes to make 2½ cups. Add to gelatin, stirring until slightly thickened. Remove any unmelted ice. Chill until thickened, about 10 minutes. Fold in fruits. Pour into 8-cup serving bowl. Chill until set, about 3 hours. Garnish with whipped topping and orange sections, if desired.
Makes about 6½ cups or 12 servings.
  *Do not use fresh pineapple, kiwifruit, mango, papaya or figs.

Cucumber Salad

3 medium cucumbers, scored
  lengthwise with tines of fork
  and thinly sliced
¾ teaspoon salt, divided
⅓ cup chopped onion
⅓ cup cider vinegar
3 tablespoons CRISCO® Oil
2 tablespoons sugar
1½ teaspoons caraway seeds
½ teaspoon paprika
⅛ teaspoon pepper

Place cucumbers in medium mixing bowl. Sprinkle with ¼ teaspoon salt. Let stand about 1 hour. Drain.
  Blend remaining ingredients and remaining ½ teaspoon salt in small mixing bowl. Pour over cucumbers. Toss to coat. Cover and refrigerate at least 3 hours. Stir before serving.
6 to 8 servings.

Marinated Vegetables

4 cups assorted fresh
  vegetables*
¼ cup REALEMON® Lemon Juice
  from Concentrate
¼ cup vegetable oil
1 tablespoon sugar
1 teaspoon salt
½ teaspoon oregano or thyme
  leaves
⅛ teaspoon pepper

Place vegetables in 1½-quart shallow baking dish. In small bowl or jar, combine remaining ingredients; mix well. Pour over vegetables. Cover; refrigerate 6 hours or overnight, stirring occasionally. Serve as appetizer or on lettuce leaves as salad.
Makes 4 cups.
  Suggested Vegetables: Cauliflowerets, carrots, mushrooms, cherry tomatoes, broccoli flowerets, zucchini, onion or cucumber.
  Tip: Recipe can be doubled.

Golden Salad

1 package (4-serving size)
   JELL-O® Brand Lemon or
   Orange Flavor Gelatin
½ teaspoon salt
1¼ cups boiling water
1 can (8¼ ounces) crushed
   pineapple in juice
1 tablespoon lemon juice or
   vinegar
1½ cups shredded carrots
⅓ cup chopped pecans

Dissolve gelatin and salt in boiling
water. Stir in undrained pineapple
and lemon juice. Chill until thickened. Stir in carrots and nuts and
pour into individual molds. Chill until firm, about 3 hours. Unmold. Serve
with crisp salad greens and mayonnaise, if desired.
Makes about 3 cups or 6 servings.

Creamy Nectarine Mold with Strawberry Sauce

1 envelope unflavored gelatin
½ cup cold water
1 8-ounce package
   PHILADELPHIA BRAND
   Cream Cheese, softened
½ cup sugar
½ cup milk
2 tablespoons orange flavored
   liqueur
1 cup whipping cream, whipped
1 nectarine, sliced
1 pint strawberries, sliced
¼ cup sugar
1 tablespoon orange flavored
   liqueur

Soften gelatin in water; stir over low
heat until dissolved. Combine cream
cheese and sugar, mixing until well
blended. Gradually add gelatin, milk
and 2 tablespoons liqueur, mixing until blended. Fold in whipped cream.
Spoon ¼ cup cream cheese mixture
into lightly oiled 1-quart mold. Arrange nectarines on cream cheese
mixture; top with remaining cream
cheese mixture. Chill until firm. Unmold onto serving plate.
   Combine strawberries, sugar and
1 tablespoon liqueur; let stand 10
minutes. Serve with mold.
6 to 8 servings.
   Variation: Substitute orange juice
for orange flavored liqueur. Add 1 teaspoon grated orange peel to cream
cheese mixture.

Snack Cups

1 package (4-serving size)
   JELL-O® Brand Orange,
   Lemon or Lime Flavor Sugar
   Free Gelatin
¾ cup boiling water
½ cup cold water
   Ice cubes
1 tablespoon lemon juice
   (optional)
½ cup each sliced celery,
   chopped cabbage and
   shredded carrot*

Completely dissolve gelatin in boiling
water. Combine cold water and ice
cubes to make 1¼ cups. Add to gelatin
with lemon juice, stirring until
slightly thickened. Remove any unmelted ice. Fold in vegetables; spoon
into individual glasses. Chill until
set, about 30 minutes. Garnish with
parsley, if desired.
Makes about 3 cups or 6 servings.
   ***Additional Vegetable Combina-
tions:*** Use sliced celery with grated
carrots and golden raisins.
   Use sliced celery with chopped cabbage, chopped apple or sliced ripe or
green pitted olives.
   Use sliced celery with chopped cucumber and chopped pimiento.
   Use sliced celery with drained mandarin orange sections and chopped
green pepper.

Classic Tomato Aspic

3 envelopes KNOX® Unflavored
   Gelatine
3 cups cold tomato juice
2 cups tomato juice, heated to
   boiling
¼ cup lemon juice
2 tablespoons sugar
1½ teaspoons Worcestershire
   sauce
4 to 6 dashes hot pepper sauce

In large bowl, sprinkle unflavored gelatine over 1 cup cold juice; let stand 1
minute. Add hot juice and stir until
gelatine is completely dissolved,
about 5 minutes. Stir in remaining 2
cups cold juice, lemon juice, sugar,
Worcestershire sauce and hot pepper
sauce. Pour into 5½-cup ring mold or
bowl; chill until firm, about 4 hours.
To serve, unmold and fill, if desired,
with salad greens and your favorite
cut-up fresh vegetables.
Makes about 10 servings.

Neapolitan Vegetable Mold

2 packages (4-serving size) or
   1 package (8-serving size)
   JELL-O® Brand Lemon
   Flavor Gelatin
1 teaspoon salt
2 cups boiling water
1½ cups cold water
3 tablespoons vinegar
1½ cups shredded carrots
½ cup mayonnaise
1 cup finely chopped cabbage
1½ cups finely chopped spinach
1 teaspoon grated onion

Dissolve gelatin and salt in boiling water. Add cold water and vinegar. Measure 1⅓ cups of the gelatin into bowl. Place bowl in larger bowl of ice and water; stir until slightly thickened. Stir in carrots and pour into 6-cup ring mold or 9×5-inch loaf pan. Chill until set but not firm.

Measure 1 cup of the remaining gelatin; blend in mayonnaise. Chill over ice until thickened. Stir in cabbage; spoon over carrot layer in mold. Chill.

Chill remaining gelatin over ice until slightly thickened. Add spinach and onion. Spoon over mayonnaise layer in mold. Chill until firm, about 3 hours. Unmold. Garnish with chicory and carrot curls, if desired.
Makes 5½ cups or 10 servings.

Holiday Fruit Salad

3 packages (3 ounces each) strawberry flavor gelatin
3 cups boiling water
2 ripe DOLE™ Bananas
1 package (16 ounces) frozen strawberries
1 can (20 ounces) DOLE® Crushed Pineapple
1 package (8 ounces) cream cheese, softened
1 cup dairy sour cream or plain yogurt
¼ cup sugar
Crisp DOLE™ Lettuce leaves

In large bowl, dissolve gelatin in boiling water. Slice bananas into gelatin mixture. Add frozen strawberries and undrained pineapple. Pour half the mixture into 13×9-inch pan. Refrigerate 1 hour or until firm. In mixer bowl, beat cream cheese with sour cream and sugar; spread over chilled layer. Gently spoon remaining gelatin mixture on top. Refrigerate until firm, about 2 hours. Cut into squares; serve on lettuce-lined salad plates. Garnish with additional pineapple, if desired.
Makes 12 servings.

Cherry Waldorf Gelatin

2 cups boiling water
1 (6-ounce) package cherry flavor gelatin
1 cup cold water
¼ cup REALEMON® Lemon Juice from Concentrate
1½ cups chopped apples
1 cup chopped celery
½ cup chopped walnuts or pecans
Lettuce leaves
Apple slices and celery leaves, optional

In medium bowl, pour boiling water over gelatin; stir until dissolved. Add cold water and ReaLemon® brand; chill until partially set. Fold in apples, celery and nuts. Pour into lightly oiled 6-cup mold or 9-inch square baking pan. Chill until set, 4 to 6 hours or overnight. Serve on lettuce. Garnish with celery leaves and apple if desired.
Makes 8 to 10 servings.

Muffin Pan Snacks

1 package (4-serving size) JELL-O® Brand Lemon Flavor Gelatin
½ teaspoon salt
⅛ teaspoon garlic powder
1½ cups boiling water
2 teaspoons vinegar
1 teaspoon vegetable oil
⅛ teaspoon black pepper
⅛ teaspoon dried oregano, crumbled
Snack combinations*

Dissolve gelatin, salt and garlic powder in boiling water. Add vinegar, oil, pepper and oregano. Place aluminum-foil baking cups in muffin pans. Place different snack combinations in each cup, filling each about ⅔ full. Then fill with gelatin mixture. Chill until firm, about 2 hours. Unmold carefully from foil cups. Serve with crisp salad greens, if desired.
Makes 4 cups or 8 to 10 servings.
   Snack Combinations: Use cauliflower florets with diced pimiento.
   Use cucumber slices with tomato slices.
   Use chopped hard-cooked egg with chopped cucumber and pickle.
   Use shredded carrot with raisins.
   Use drained canned button or sliced mushrooms with pimiento strips.
   Use diced apple with chopped nuts.
   Use sliced hard-cooked egg with anchovies.
   Use cubed cream cheese with chopped nuts.
   Use diced pimiento with diced green pepper and tomato.
   Use sliced celery with sliced ripe or stuffed green olives.

Melon Wedges

1 cantaloupe or honeydew melon
1 package (4-serving size) JELL-O® Brand Apricot or Orange Flavor Sugar Free Gelatin
1 cup boiling water
¾ cup cold water
1 banana, sliced, ½ cup sliced strawberries or 1 can (8¼ ounces) crushed pineapple in juice, well drained

Cut melon in half lengthwise; scoop out seeds and drain well. Dissolve gelatin in boiling water. Add cold water. Chill until slightly thickened. Stir in fruit. Pour into melon halves. Chill until firm, about 3 hours. Cut in wedges. Serve with additional fresh fruit, cottage cheese and crisp greens, if desired.
Makes 6 servings.
   Note: Chill any excess fruited gelatin in dessert dishes.

Clam & Tomato Molded Salad

4 envelopes unflavored gelatine
4 cups tomato juice
1/2 cup chopped celery
1/4 cup chopped green onions
2 (6 1/2-ounce) cans SNOW'S® or DOXSEE® Minced Clams, drained, reserving 1/2 cup liquid
1 (4-serving size) package lemon flavor gelatin
1 (16-ounce) container BORDEN® or MEADOW GOLD® Cottage Cheese
Lettuce leaves

In medium saucepan, sprinkle unflavored gelatine over *1 1/2 cups* tomato juice; let stand 1 minute. Over low heat, stir until gelatine dissolves. Remove from heat; add celery, *2 tablespoons* onions and remaining *2 1/2 cups* tomato juice. Chill until partially set, about 45 minutes; stir in drained clams. Meanwhile, in small saucepan, heat reserved clam liquid; add lemon gelatin, stirring until dissolved. Remove from heat; add cheese and remaining *2 tablespoons* onions. Chill until partially set, about 30 minutes; stir. In lightly oiled 9×5-inch loaf pan, spoon half the tomato mixture; spread cheese mixture evenly over tomato layer. Top with remaining tomato mixture. Chill 6 hours or until set. Unmold onto lettuce. Garnish as desired. Refrigerate leftovers.
Makes 10 to 12 servings.

Buffet Slaw

2 cans (8 1/4 ounces each) crushed pineapple in juice
2 packages (4-serving size) or 1 package (8-serving size) JELL-O® Brand Lemon Flavor Gelatin
1 1/2 cups boiling water
Ice cubes
3 tablespoons vinegar
1/2 teaspoon celery salt
1 cup each finely shredded green and red cabbage
1/4 cup chopped parsley
1 tablespoon finely chopped onion

Drain pineapple, reserving juice. Add water to juice to make 1 cup; set aside. Completely dissolve gelatin in boiling water. Combine measured liquid and ice cubes to make 2 1/2 cups. Add to gelatin with vinegar and celery salt, stirring until slightly thickened. Remove any unmelted ice. Chill until thickened, about 10 minutes. Fold in pineapple, cabbage, parsley and onion. Pour into 8-cup bowl. Chill until set, about 3 hours. Garnish with cabbage leaves, parsley and onion rings, if desired.
Makes 6 cups or 12 servings.

Mediterranean Orange and Red Onion Salad

2 envelopes KNOX® Unflavored Gelatine
1 cup cold water
2 1/2 cups orange juice
2 tablespoons sugar
1 tablespoon lemon juice
2 teaspoons red wine vinegar
4 medium oranges, peeled, sectioned and chopped (about 1 cup)
1/2 cup finely chopped celery
1/4 cup finely chopped red onion

In medium saucepan, sprinkle unflavored gelatine over cold water; let stand 1 minute. Stir over low heat until gelatine is completely dissolved, about 5 minutes.

In large bowl, blend gelatine mixture, orange juice, sugar, lemon juice and vinegar. Chill, stirring occasionally, until mixture is consistency of unbeaten egg whites, about 40 minutes. Fold in remaining ingredients. Pour into 6-cup ring mold or bowl; chill until firm, about 4 hours. Unmold and garnish, if desired, with celery leaves.
Makes about 8 servings.

Sparkling Berry Salad

2 envelopes KNOX® Unflavored Gelatine
2 cups cranberry-raspberry juice*
1/3 cup sugar
1 cup club soda
1/4 cup creme de cassis (black currant) liqueur (optional)
1 teaspoon lemon juice
1 teaspoon fresh grated orange peel (optional)
3 cups assorted blueberries, raspberries or strawberries

In medium saucepan, sprinkle unflavored gelatine over 1 cup cranberry-raspberry juice; let stand 1 minute. Stir over low heat until gelatin is completely dissolved, about 5 minutes. Stir in sugar until dissolved.

In large bowl, blend remaining 1 cup cranberry-raspberry juice, soda, gelatine mixture, liqueur, lemon juice and orange peel. Chill, stirring occasionally, until mixture is consistency of unbeaten egg whites, about 60 minutes. Fold in berries. Pour into 6-cup mold or bowl; chill until firm, about 3 hours. Unmold and serve, if desired, with sour cream.
Makes about 8 servings.
***Substitution:** Use 2 cups cranberry juice cocktail and increase sugar to 1/2 cup.

Layered Peach Salad

1 can (8 ounces) sliced peaches, drained
1/4 cup sliced celery
3/4 cup boiling water
1 package (4-serving size) JELL-O® Brand Gelatin, any red flavor
1/2 cup cold water
Ice cubes

Arrange peach slices and celery in 8×4-inch loaf pan. Pour boiling water into blender. Add gelatin. Cover and blend at low speed until gelatin is completely dissolved, about 30 seconds. Combine cold water and ice cubes to make 1 cup. Add to gelatin and stir until ice is partially melted; then blend at high speed for 30 seconds. Pour into pan. Chill until firm, about 3 hours. Salad layers as it chills. Unmold. Garnish with celery leaves and additional peach slices, if desired.
Makes about 4 cups or 8 servings.

Layered Pear-Cucumber Salad: Prepare Layered Peach Salad as directed, substituting 1 can (8½ ounces) pear halves, drained and sliced, ¼ cup shredded peeled cucumber and lime or lemon flavor gelatin for peaches, celery and red flavor gelatin. Garnish with parsley and additional pear slices, if desired.

Layered Carrot-Pineapple Salad: Prepare Layered Peach Salad as directed, substituting 1 can (8¼ ounces) pineapple slices, drained and cut in half, ¼ cup shredded carrot and orange flavor gelatin for the peaches, celery and red flavor gelatin. Garnish with chicory and carrot curls, if desired.

Layered Grapefruit-Cabbage Salad: Prepare Layered Peach Salad as directed, substituting ¾ cup grapefruit sections, ¼ cup shredded cabbage and strawberry flavor gelatin for the peaches, celery and red flavor gelatin. Garnish with endive and additional grapefruit sections, if desired.

Ginger Pineapple Mold

1 can (20 ounces) pineapple slices in juice
2 packages (4-serving size) or 1 package (8-serving size) JELL-O® Brand Lime or Apricot Flavor Gelatin
1½ cups boiling water
1 cup ginger ale or cold water
1/4 teaspoon ginger

Drain pineapple, reserving juice. Cut 4 pineapple slices in half; set aside. Cut remaining pineapple slices into chunks. Dissolve gelatin in boiling water. Add reserved juice, ginger ale and ginger. Chill until slightly thickened. Measure 1 cup of the gelatin. Arrange some of the pineapple chunks in 6-cup ring mold; top with measured gelatin. Chill until set but not firm, about 10 minutes. Fold remaining pineapple chunks into remaining gelatin; spoon over gelatin in mold. Chill until firm, about 4 hours. Unmold. Garnish with halved pineapple slices, halved cherry tomatoes and crisp greens, if desired.
Makes 5 cups or 10 servings.

Minted Melon Mold

1½ cups boiling water
1 (3-ounce) package lemon flavor gelatin
1 (3-ounce) package lime flavor gelatin
3/4 cup REALIME® Lime Juice from Concentrate
1/2 cup cold water
1/8 teaspoon peppermint extract
2 cups melon balls (cantaloupe, honeydew, etc.)
Lettuce leaves
Coconut Cream Dressing
Mint leaves and additional melon balls, optional

In medium bowl, pour boiling water over gelatins; stir until dissolved. Add ReaLime® brand, cold water and extract; chill until partially set. Fold in melon. Pour into lightly oiled 5-cup ring mold. Chill until set, about 3 hours or overnight. Unmold onto lettuce. Serve with Coconut Cream Dressing; garnish with mint and melon balls if desired.
Makes 8 to 10 servings.

Coconut Cream Dressing

1/2 cup BORDEN® or MEADOW GOLD® Sour Cream
3 tablespoons flaked coconut
1 tablespoon honey
1 tablespoon REALIME® Lime Juice from Concentrate

In small bowl, combine all ingredients; mix well. Chill before serving. Refrigerate leftovers.
Makes about ½ cup.

California Fruit Salad Rosé

1 envelope KNOX® Unflavored Gelatine
3/4 cup cold water
2 tablespoons sugar
1¼ cups rosé wine
Suggested Fresh Fruit*

In medium saucepan, sprinkle unflavored gelatine over cold water; let stand 1 minute. Stir over low heat until gelatine is completely dissolved, about 5 minutes. Stir in sugar and wine until sugar is dissolved. Chill, stirring occasionally, until mixture is consistency of unbeaten egg whites, about 60 minutes. Fold in Suggested Fresh Fruit. Pour into wine glasses or 4-cup mold; chill until firm, about 3 hours. To serve, unmold onto platter.
Makes 8 servings at 62 calories per serving.

*Suggested Fresh Fruit:** Use any combination of the following to equal 2 cups—sliced bananas, peaches or strawberries; cut-up melon; blueberries, raspberries or grapes.

Creamy Garden Salad

2 envelopes unflavored gelatine
1½ cups water, divided
2 cups mayonnaise
⅓ cup lemon juice
¾ teaspoon TABASCO® pepper
   sauce
1½ cups diced cucumber
1 cup shredded carrot
½ cup thinly sliced radishes
½ cup thinly sliced green onions

In medium saucepan sprinkle gelatine over 1 cup water; let stand 1 minute. Stir over low heat until gelatine is completely dissolved. Add remaining ½ cup water, mayonnaise, lemon juice and Tabasco® sauce; mix well. Chill until slightly thickened. Stir in cucumber, carrot, radishes and green onions. Turn into 6-cup mold. Cover; refrigerate 3 hours or until firm. Unmold onto serving plate.
Makes 6 to 8 servings.

Tomato-Garden Aspic with Horseradish Cream

1 (13¾-fluid ounce) can
   COLLEGE INN® Beef or
   Chicken Broth
2 (3-ounce) or 1 (6-ounce)
   package ROYAL® Lemon
   Gelatin
2 cups tomato juice
1 tablespoon A.1.® Steak Sauce
½ cup finely chopped celery
½ cup finely chopped cucumber
⅓ cup finely chopped onion
   Lettuce
   Horseradish Cream (recipe
   follows)

Refrigerate broth; remove fat. In saucepan, over high heat, heat broth to a boil; stir in gelatin until dissolved. Stir in tomato juice and steak sauce. Refrigerate until slightly thickened. Stir in celery, cucumber and onion. Pour into 5- to 6-cup mold. Refrigerate until firm, about 3 hours. To serve, unmold onto lettuce-lined serving plate. Serve with Horseradish Cream. Garnish as desired.
Makes 6 to 8 servings.
HORSERADISH CREAM: In small bowl, beat together ½ cup prepared whipped topping, ¼ cup mayonnaise *or* salad dressing and 1 tablespoon horseradish. Refrigerate until serving time.

Autumn Pear 'n Apple Salad

2 envelopes KNOX® Unflavored
   Gelatine
2½ cups apple juice
¼ cup light brown sugar
1¼ cups pear nectar
¼ teaspoon ground cinnamon
⅛ teaspoon ground nutmeg
1 small pear, chopped
1 small apple, chopped
6 dried Calimyrna figs,
   quartered
¼ cup chopped pecans or
   walnuts (optional)

In medium saucepan, sprinkle unflavored gelatine over 1 cup apple juice; let stand 1 minute. Stir over low heat until gelatine is completely dissolved, about 5 minutes. Stir in sugar until dissolved.

In large bowl, blend remaining 1½ cups apple juice, pear nectar, gelatine mixture, cinnamon and nutmeg. Chill, stirring occasionally, until mixture is consistency of unbeaten egg whites, about 60 minutes. Fold in remaining ingredients. Pour into 6-cup mold; chill until firm, about 3 hours. Unmold onto serving platter.
Makes about 12 servings.

Cranberry-Apple Waldorf

2 envelopes KNOX® Unflavored
   Gelatine
⅓ cup sugar
½ cup boiling water
3½ cups cranberry juice cocktail
1 cup chopped apple
½ cup chopped celery
⅓ cup chopped walnuts

In large bowl, mix unflavored gelatine with sugar; add boiling water and stir until gelatine is completely dissolved, about 5 minutes. Stir in cranberry juice. Chill, stirring occasionally, until mixture is consistency of unbeaten egg whites, about 45 minutes. Fold in remaining ingredients. Pour into 8-inch square baking pan; chill until firm, about 3 hours. To serve, cut into 4-inch squares and serve, if desired, on lettuce-lined plates.
Makes about 4 servings.

Minted Fruit Salad

½ cup sugar
⅓ cup orange juice
⅓ cup REALEMON® Lemon Juice
   from Concentrate
⅓ cup water
¼ teaspoon peppermint extract
8 cups assorted fresh fruits
   Sherbet

In medium bowl, combine sugar, orange juice, ReaLemon® brand, water and peppermint extract; stir until sugar dissolves. Place fruit in 3-quart shallow baking dish; pour juice mixture over. Cover; chill 3 to 4 hours to blend flavors. Arrange drained fruit on platter; top with sherbet and garnish as desired.
Makes 4 servings.

Rainbow Fruit Salad

2 peaches, peeled, pitted and sliced
2 DOLE™ Oranges, peeled and sliced
2 cups DOLE™ Strawberries, hulled and sliced
1 cup DOLE™ Seedless Grapes
1 cup melon balls
Pineapple Lime Dressing (recipe follows)

In large bowl, combine fruit. Add Pineapple Lime Dressing; stir gently to coat.
Makes 8 servings.
PINEAPPLE LIME DRESSING: In small bowl, combine ½ cup Dole® Pineapple Juice, ½ teaspoon grated lime peel, 3 tablespoons *each* lime juice and honey and 1 tablespoon chopped crystallized ginger. Whisk until blended.

Ambrosia

1 can (20 ounces) DOLE® Pineapple Chunks
1 can (11 ounces) DOLE® Mandarin Orange Segments in Syrup
1 firm, large DOLE™ Banana, sliced, optional
1½ cups DOLE™ Seedless Grapes
1 cup miniature marshmallows
1 cup flaked coconut
½ cup pecan halves or coarsely chopped nuts
1 cup dairy sour cream or plain yogurt
1 tablespoon brown sugar

Drain pineapple and orange segments. In large bowl, combine pineapple, mandarin oranges, banana, grapes, marshmallows, coconut and nuts. In 1-quart measure, combine sour cream and brown sugar. Stir into fruit mixture. Refrigerate, covered, 1 hour or overnight.
Makes 4 servings.

Mai Tai Compote

1 medium DOLE™ Fresh Pineapple
1 DOLE™ Orange, peeled and sliced
1 kiwifruit, peeled and sliced
1 cup halved DOLE™ Strawberries
½ cup DOLE™ Seedless Red Grapes
¼ cup fresh lime juice
3 tablespoons honey
1 tablespoon light rum
1 tablespoon orange-flavored liqueur
½ teaspoon grated lime peel
1 firm DOLE™ Banana

Cut pineapple in half lengthwise through crown. Remove fruit with curved knife, leaving shells intact. Trim off core and cut fruit into chunks. In large bowl, combine pineapple, orange, kiwi, strawberries and grapes. To make dressing, in 1-quart measure, combine remaining ingredients, except banana. Pour dressing over fruit. Toss gently to coat. Refrigerate, covered, 1 hour. Just before serving, slice banana into fruit salad. Toss gently. Spoon salad into pineapple shells and serve.
Makes 6 to 8 servings.

Carrot Pineapple Salad

1 DOLE™ Fresh Pineapple
1 honeydew melon
3 large DOLE™ Carrots, thinly sliced
½ cup thinly sliced DOLE™ Pitted Dates
Honey-Lime Vinaigrette (recipe follows)

Twist crown from pineapple. Cut pineapple lengthwise into quarters. Remove fruit from shells with curved knife. Trim off core and cut fruit into chunks. Cut melon in half; scoop out seeds and cut fruit into 1-inch pieces. In salad bowl, combine pineapple, melon, carrots and dates. Toss with Honey-Lime Vinaigrette; garnish with lime slices, if desired.
Makes 6 servings.
HONEY-LIME VINAIGRETTE: In small bowl, combine ¼ cup honey, 2 tablespoons *each* white wine vinegar and lime juice, 1 tablespoon vegetable oil, and 2 teaspoons grated lime peel. Whisk until blended.

Creamy Topped Fruit Salad

1 8-ounce package *Light* PHILADELPHIA BRAND Neufchâtel Cheese, softened
2 tablespoons lemon juice
1 teaspoon grated lemon peel
½ cup whipping cream
¼ cup powdered sugar
2 cups peach slices
2 cups blueberries
2 cups strawberry slices
2 cups grapes

Combine neufchâtel cheese, juice and peel, mixing until well blended. Beat whipping cream until soft peaks form; gradually add sugar, beating until stiff peaks form. Fold into neufchâtel cheese mixture; chill. Layer fruit in 2½-quart glass serving bowl. Top with neufchâtel cheese mixture. Sprinkle with nuts, if desired. Chill.
8 servings.
Variation: Substitute PHILADELPHIA BRAND Cream Cheese for Neufchâtel Cheese.

Luau Fruit Salad

1 can (20 ounces) DOLE®
  Pineapple Chunks
3 DOLE™ Oranges, peeled and
  sectioned
2 apples, cored and chopped
1 papaya, peeled, seeded and
  cut into chunks
1 teaspoon cornstarch
¼ cup vegetable oil
2 tablespoons sugar
2 tablespoons white vinegar
1 tablespoon poppy seeds
1 teaspoon grated orange peel
½ teaspoon paprika
¼ teaspoon salt
5 quarts torn DOLE™ Romaine
  Lettuce
½ cup DOLE™ Blanched Slivered
  Almonds, toasted

Drain pineapple; reserve juice. In large bowl, combine pineapple, oranges, apples and papaya. For dressing, in saucepan, combine reserved pineapple juice and cornstarch. Cook, stirring, until mixture boils and thickens. Cool. Combine pineapple mixture with oil, sugar, vinegar, poppy seeds, orange peel, paprika and salt in blender. Blend until smooth. Pour dressing over fruit and toss; refrigerate, covered. Just before serving, toss with lettuce and sprinkle with almonds.
Makes 12 servings.

Fruit Salad with Poppy Seed Dressing

1 pear, cored and sliced
1 apple, cored and sliced
1 banana, peeled and sliced
1 orange, peeled and sectioned
⅓ cup CRISCO® Oil
2 tablespoons lime juice
2 tablespoons honey
½ teaspoon soy sauce
½ teaspoon poppy seed
¼ teaspoon ground ginger
¼ teaspoon dry mustard
  Dash salt

Combine pear, apple, banana and orange in medium serving bowl. Blend remaining ingredients in small mixing bowl. Pour over fruit. Toss to coat. Serve immediately.
Tip: Toss your own combination of fresh fruits with poppy seed dressing. Create a refreshing summertime salad with seasonal fruits like grapes, strawberries, peaches and melon. Add variety to this tangy salad with any of your favorites.
4 to 6 servings.

Indian Fruit Salad

1 DOLE™ Fresh Pineapple
2 firm DOLE™ Bananas
1 head DOLE™ Iceberg Lettuce,
  torn
1 DOLE™ Orange, peeled and
  sliced
2 cups melon balls or diced
  melon
½ cup cashew nuts
1 cup mayonnaise
¼ cup dairy sour cream
1 tablespoon fresh lime juice
1 tablespoon sugar
1 teaspoon curry powder
½ teaspoon grated lime peel
½ teaspoon salt

Twist crown from pineapple. Cut pineapple lengthwise into quarters. Remove fruit from shells with curved knife. Trim off core and dice fruit. Slice bananas into large bowl. Add 2½ cups pineapple (reserve remaining pineapple for another use), lettuce, orange, melon and nuts. To make dressing, in 1-quart measure, combine remaining ingredients; refrigerate, covered, until ready to serve. Pour dressing over salad and toss.
Makes 6 to 8 servings.

Fruit Salad with Orange Almond Dressing

1 head DOLE™ Leaf Lettuce
1 DOLE™ Orange, peeled and
  sectioned
1 peach, sliced
½ cantaloupe, cut into chunks
2 cups DOLE™ Fresh Pineapple
  chunks
1 cup sliced DOLE™
  Strawberries
1 cup DOLE™ Grapes
½ cup DOLE™ Whole Natural
  Almonds, toasted
  Orange Almond Dressing
  (recipe follows)

Line large salad bowl with lettuce leaves. Arrange fruit on top; sprinkle with almonds. Serve with Orange Almond Dressing.
Makes 6 to 8 servings.
ORANGE ALMOND DRESSING: In 1-quart measure, combine 1 cup dairy sour cream, ½ cup mayonnaise, ¼ cup toasted Dole™ Chopped Natural Almonds, 2 tablespoons lemon juice and 2 teaspoons grated orange peel. Refrigerate, covered, until ready to serve.

Hot Potato Salad

7 to 8 SIZZLEAN® Breakfast
    Strips, cut into ½-inch
    pieces
2 medium onions, chopped fine
1 tablespoon all-purpose flour
4 teaspoons sugar
1½ teaspoons salt
1 teaspoon paprika
½ cup vinegar
1 cup water
6 medium potatoes, pared,
    cooked, sliced thin

Cook Sizzlean® pieces in medium skillet over medium-low heat until they begin to look crisp. Add onions; cook and stir until tender. Combine flour, sugar, salt and paprika in small cup. Add to Sizzlean® pieces, mixing well. Pour in vinegar and water. Cook and stir until mixture thickens. Add potatoes; reduce heat to low. Heat 10 to 15 minutes or until hot.
Makes 6 servings.

Fresh and Creamy Potato Salad

4 cups cubed cooked potato
½ cup celery slices
¼ cup chopped green pepper
2 tablespoons green onion
    slices
1 teaspoon salt
1 8-ounce package
    PHILADELPHIA BRAND
    Cream Cheese, softened
½ cup sour cream
2 tablespoons milk

Combine potatoes, celery, green peppers, onions and salt; mix lightly. Combine cream cheese, sour cream and milk, mixing until well blended. Add to potato mixture; mix lightly. Chill.
6 to 8 servings.

Bacon & Egg Potato Salad

5 cups cooked, peeled and
    cubed potatoes (about
    2 pounds)
¼ cup chopped green onions
⅓ cup REALEMON® Lemon Juice
    from Concentrate
⅓ cup water
¼ cup vegetable oil
1½ teaspoons celery salt
1 teaspoon Worcestershire
    sauce
½ teaspoon dry mustard
¼ teaspoon pepper
4 slices bacon, cooked and
    crumbled
3 hard-cooked eggs, chopped
¼ cup grated Parmesan cheese
3 tablespoons chopped parsley

In large bowl, combine potatoes and onions. In small saucepan, combine ReaLemon® brand, water, oil, celery salt, Worcestershire, mustard and pepper; bring to a boil. Pour over potato mixture; mix well. Cover; chill overnight to blend flavors. Remove from refrigerator 30 minutes before serving; stir in bacon, eggs, Parmesan cheese and parsley. Refrigerate leftovers.
Makes 10 to 12 servings.

Creamy Red Potato Salad

½ cup WISH-BONE® Italian
    Dressing
¾ cup mayonnaise
½ cup sliced green onions
2 tablespoons snipped fresh
    dill*
1 teaspoon Dijon-style mustard
1 teaspoon lemon juice
⅛ teaspoon pepper
3 pounds red bliss or new
    potatoes, cooked and cut
    into large chunks

In large salad bowl, thoroughly combine all ingredients except potatoes. Toss with warm potatoes; cover and chill.
Makes about 10 side-dish servings.
    Substitution: Use 1 teaspoon dried dill weed.
    Notes: Recipe can be halved.
    Also terrific with Wish-Bone® Herbal Italian, Italian & Cheese, Robusto Italian or Blended Italian Dressing.

Marinated Potato and Mushroom Salad

1½ pounds new potatoes, cooked
    and cubed (about 4 cups)
1 cup sliced fresh mushrooms
    (about 4 ounces)
⅓ cup sliced celery
¼ cup sliced green onions
⅓ cup vegetable oil
¼ cup REALEMON® Lemon Juice
    from Concentrate
1½ teaspoons Dijon-style mustard
1 teaspoon sugar
1 teaspoon WYLER'S® or
    STEERO® Chicken-Flavor
    Instant Bouillon
Cracked black pepper, optional

In shallow baking dish, combine potatoes, mushrooms, celery and onions. In 1-pint jar with tight-fitting lid or cruet, combine remaining ingredients, except pepper; shake well. Pour over potato mixture; mix well. Cover; chill 3 to 4 hours to blend flavors. Serve with pepper if desired. Refrigerate leftovers.
Makes 6 to 8 servings.

Zesty Potato Salad

4 large potatoes
1 pouch CAMPBELL'S® Onion Soup and Recipe Mix
¾ cup mayonnaise
¼ cup VLASIC® Sweet Relish
2 teaspoons prepared mustard
¼ teaspoon pepper
1½ cups chopped celery
2 hard-cooked eggs, diced
2 tablespoons chopped pimento (optional)

1. Place potatoes in large saucepan; add enough water to cover potatoes. Over high heat, heat to boiling. Reduce heat to medium-low. Cover; simmer 30 to 40 minutes until potatoes are tender.
2. Drain potatoes; cool, peel and cut into cubes.
3. In large bowl, stir together soup mix, mayonnaise, relish, mustard and pepper. Stir in potatoes, celery, eggs and pimento.
4. Cover; chill until serving time, at least 2 hours.
Makes 8 servings.

Potluck Pasta Salad

8 ounces spiral pasta
½ cup vegetable oil
¼ cup white vinegar
1 large clove garlic, pressed or minced
2 tablespoons lemon juice
2 teaspoons prepared mustard
2 teaspoons Worcestershire sauce
1 teaspoon salt
Dash pepper
¼ pound snow peas, ends and strings removed
2 cups DOLE™ Broccoli flowerets
2 cups sliced fresh mushrooms
1 cup DOLE™ Cauliflower flowerets
1 cup halved cherry tomatoes

Cook pasta according to package directions. Drain. Meanwhile, in screw-top jar, combine oil, vinegar, garlic, lemon juice, mustard, Worcestershire, salt and pepper. Shake well. In large bowl, combine hot pasta with dressing. Mix well. Add vegetables; toss to coat. Refrigerate, covered.
Makes 8 servings.

Chilled Rigatoni Salad

1 clove garlic, halved
1½ to 2 cups cooked rigatoni
1 can (14 ounces) artichoke hearts, drained and cut into bite-size pieces
½ cup chopped sweet red pepper or green pepper
½ cup bite-size cubes mozzarella cheese
1 medium carrot, cut into julienne strips
¼ cup sliced pitted black olives
2 ounces salami, cut into thin strips
¼ cup CRISCO® Oil
2 tablespoons white wine vinegar
1 tablespoon olive oil
½ teaspoon salt
½ teaspoon sugar
½ teaspoon dry mustard
¼ to ½ teaspoon dried oregano leaves
¼ to ½ teaspoon dried basil leaves

Rub inside of medium serving bowl with cut sides of garlic. Discard garlic. Mix rigatoni, artichoke hearts, red pepper, mozzarella cheese, carrot, olives and salami in prepared bowl.

Blend remaining ingredients in small bowl. Pour over rigatoni mixture. Toss to coat. Cover and refrigerate 2 to 3 hours. Stir before serving.
4 to 6 servings.

Pasta Vegetable Medley

1 package (12 ounces) bows egg noodles
1¼ cups WISH-BONE® Italian or Robusto Italian Dressing
½ cup mayonnaise
½ teaspoon basil leaves
Assorted Fresh Vegetables*

Cook noodles according to package directions; drain and rinse with cold water until completely cool.

In large salad bowl, blend Italian dressing, mayonnaise and basil; stir in Assorted Fresh Vegetables. Add noodles and toss well; cover and chill.
Makes about 8 side-dish servings.

Assorted Fresh Vegetables: Use any combination of the following to equal 5 cups—chopped cucumber, tomato, celery and red, green or yellow pepper; sliced mushrooms and carrots.

German-Style Potato Salad

2 pounds small new potatoes
2 hard-cooked eggs, sliced
½ teaspoon dill weed, crushed
2 tablespoons vegetable oil
½ pound kielbasa, diced
½ cup chopped onion
2 tablespoons all-purpose flour
2 tablespoons sugar
⅓ cup cider vinegar
1 can (10¾ ounces) CAMPBELL'S® Condensed Chicken Broth
⅓ cup water
Dash pepper
VLASIC® or EARLY CALIFORNIA® Sliced Pimento-Stuffed Olives

1. In 4-quart saucepan, place potatoes; add water to cover. Over high heat, heat to boiling. Reduce heat to low. Cover; simmer 20 to 30 minutes until fork-tender. Drain. Cool slightly; cut potatoes into slices.

2. In large bowl, combine potatoes, eggs and dill weed; set aside.

3. In 10-inch skillet over medium heat, in hot oil, cook kielbasa and onion until meat is well browned, stirring occasionally. Remove meat and onion with slotted spoon; add to potato mixture. Reserve drippings in skillet.

4. Stir flour into drippings. Cook 1 minute, stirring constantly. Add sugar, vinegar, broth, water and pepper. Cook until mixture boils, stirring constantly. Pour over potato mixture; toss gently to mix well. Sprinkle with olives. Serve warm.

Makes about 6 cups or 8 servings.

Three Bean Rice Salad

1 can (16 oz.) cut wax beans, drained
1 can (16 oz.) French-style green beans, drained
1 can (8¾ oz.) red kidney beans, drained
½ cup prepared GOOD SEASONS® Italian Salad Dressing
¼ cup thinly sliced onion rings
1 teaspoon salt
⅛ teaspoon pepper
1½ cups water
1½ cups MINUTE® Rice

Mix beans, salad dressing, onion, ½ teaspoon of the salt and the pepper in large bowl; set aside to allow flavors to blend.

Meanwhile, bring water and remaining ½ teaspoon salt to a full boil in medium saucepan. Stir in rice. Cover; remove from heat. Let stand 5 minutes. Fold rice into bean mixture. Cover and chill thoroughly. Serve on lettuce.

Makes 6 servings.

Italian Pasta Salad

8 ounces uncooked mostaccioli or ziti macaroni
2 large tomatoes, coarsely chopped
1½ cups broccoli florets, cooked
1 medium green pepper, chopped
1 cup (8 ounces) WISH-BONE® Robusto Italian Dressing
1 tablespoon chopped fresh basil leaves*
1 package (8 ounces) mozzarella cheese, diced
¼ cup grated Parmesan cheese

Cook macaroni according to package directions; drain and rinse with cold water until completely cool.

In large salad bowl, combine tomatoes, broccoli, green pepper, robusto Italian dressing and basil. Add cheeses and macaroni, then toss lightly; cover and chill.

Makes about 10 side-dish servings.

***Substitution:** Use 1 teaspoon dried basil leaves.

Garden Macaroni Salad

¼ cup KRAFT Real Mayonnaise
1 8-ounce package PHILADELPHIA BRAND Cream Cheese, softened
¼ cup sweet pickle relish, drained
1 tablespoon KRAFT Pure Prepared Mustard
2 cups (7 ounces) elbow macaroni, cooked, drained
1 cup chopped cucumber
½ cup chopped green pepper
½ cup radish slices
2 tablespoons chopped onion
½ teaspoon salt

Gradually add mayonnaise to cream cheese, mixing until well blended. Stir in relish and mustard. Add remaining ingredients; mix lightly. Spoon into lightly oiled 9-inch springform pan with ring insert. Chill several hours or overnight. Unmold. Garnish with cucumber slices and radish roses, if desired.

6 to 8 servings.

Variation: Add ½ cup (2 ounces) KRAFT Grated Parmesan Cheese to cream cheese mixture.

Barley Salad

2 tablespoons butter or margarine
½ cup barley, uncooked
½ cup chopped onion
1 clove garlic, minced
¼ teaspoon dried thyme leaves, crushed
1 can (14½ ounces) SWANSON® Clear Ready to Serve Chicken Broth
1 medium zucchini, shredded
½ cup chopped CAMPBELL'S FRESH® Tomato
¼ cup chopped green onions
2 tablespoons chopped fresh parsley
1 tablespoon rice vinegar
1 tablespoon chopped capers
¼ teaspoon pepper

To Microwave:

1. In 2-quart microwave-safe casserole, combine butter, barley, onion, garlic and thyme. Cover with lid; microwave on HIGH 4 minutes or until onion is tender, stirring once during cooking.

2. Stir in broth. Cover; microwave on HIGH 5 minutes or until bubbling, stirring once during cooking. Reduce power to 50%. Microwave 25 minutes or until barley is tender and liquid is absorbed, stirring twice during cooking.

3. Cool slightly. Stir in remaining ingredients. Cover; refrigerate until serving time, at least 4 hours.

Makes about 4 cups or 8 servings.

South-of-the-Border Salad

1½ cups V8® Vegetable Juice *or* No Salt Added V8® Vegetable Juice
2 tablespoons wine vinegar
2 tablespoons chopped fresh parsley
1 clove garlic, minced
3 cups cooked rice (1 cup uncooked)
1 can (4 ounces) chopped chilies
½ cup frozen whole kernel corn, thawed and drained
3 tablespoons chopped pimento

1. In medium bowl, stir together V8 juice, vinegar, parsley and garlic.
2. Add rice, chilies, corn and pimento; mix well. Cover; refrigerate until serving time, at least 4 hours.
Makes 5 cups or 6 side-dish servings.

Per serving: 143 calories, 3 g protein, 1 g fat, 32 g carbohydrate, 327 mg sodium (No Salt Added V8® Juice: 136 mg sodium), 0 mg cholesterol.

Japanese Rice Salad

2 cups water
3 tablespoons KIKKOMAN Lite Soy Sauce, divided
1 cup uncooked long-grain rice, washed and drained
½ pound cooked baby shrimp
1 carrot, peeled and shredded
½ cup frozen green peas, thawed and drained
½ cup chopped green onions and tops
1 tablespoon minced fresh ginger root
¼ cup distilled white vinegar
2 tablespoons sugar
2 teaspoons sesame seed, toasted
2 teaspoons water
Lettuce leaves

Combine 2 cups water and 2 tablespoons lite soy sauce in medium saucepan. Bring to boil; stir in rice. Reduce heat and simmer, covered, 20 minutes, or until water is absorbed. Remove from heat and cool in pan. Rinse shrimp; drain thoroughly. Remove and reserve ½ cup. Combine remaining shrimp, carrot, peas, green onions and ginger in large bowl. Fluff rice with fork; fold into shrimp mixture. Cover and refrigerate until chilled. Meanwhile, measure vinegar, sugar, remaining 1 tablespoon lite soy sauce, sesame seed and 2 teaspoons water into jar with screw-top lid. Cover and shake until blended and sugar dissolves. Pour over rice mixture; toss to coat all ingredients well. Spoon over lettuce leaves on serving plates; sprinkle with reserved shrimp. Garnish as desired.
Makes 6 servings.

Tabbouleh

¾ cup bulgur, rinsed and drained
Boiling water
2 cups seeded, chopped cucumber
1 large tomato, seeded and chopped
1 cup snipped fresh parsley
⅓ cup CRISCO® Oil
⅓ cup chopped green onion
2 tablespoons lemon juice
1 teaspoon dried mint leaves
2 cloves garlic, minced
½ teaspoon salt
⅛ teaspoon white pepper
⅛ teaspoon cayenne

Place bulgur in medium mixing bowl. Add enough boiling water to just cover bulgur. Let stand about 1 hour, or until bulgur is rehydrated. Drain.

Combine bulgur, cucumber, tomato and parsley in large serving bowl. Set aside. Blend remaining ingredients in small mixing bowl. Pour over bulgur mixture. Toss to coat. Cover and refrigerate at least 3 hours. Stir before serving.
10 to 12 servings.

Wild Rice Salad

1 (13¾-fluid ounce) can COLLEGE INN® Beef or Chicken Broth
1 (6-ounce) package long-grain and wild rice
1 (11-ounce) can mandarin oranges, drained
1 (8-ounce) can CHUN KING® Sliced Water Chestnuts, drained
¼ cup sliced scallions
⅓ cup mayonnaise
Lettuce leaves

Reserve 2 tablespoons broth. Add enough water to remaining broth to substitute for water in rice package directions. Cook rice according to directions omitting butter or margarine; cool. Stir in oranges, water chestnuts and scallions. Blend reserved broth and mayonnaise; stir into rice mixture. Cover and refrigerate 2 to 3 hours. Serve on lettuce leaves.
Makes 6 to 8 servings.

Vegetable-Rice Salad

3 cups cooked long grain rice
1¾ cups prepared HIDDEN VALLEY RANCH® ORIGINAL RANCH® Salad Dressing
2 medium tomatoes, chopped
Milk
Lettuce
Cooked green beans (optional)

In bowl, combine rice and salad dressing. Toss gently to coat. Cover; refrigerate. Just before serving, stir in tomatoes. Stir in 2 to 3 tablespoons milk if rice mixture seems dry. Turn into lettuce-lined salad bowl. Garnish with green beans and additional chopped tomato, if desired.
Makes 8 servings.

Rice Pilaf Salad

1 package (6 ounces) ECKRICH®
   Ham, cut into thin strips
1 package (9 ounces) rice pilaf
   mix
3 tablespoons vegetable oil
1 tablespoon vinegar
1 cup chopped zucchini
½ cup cooked peas
¼ cup chopped fresh parsley
½ cup cherry tomato halves
6 lemon wedges
⅓ cup plain yogurt

Cook rice pilaf according to package directions, omitting butter. Combine oil and vinegar; pour over warm rice pilaf in large bowl. Mix in ham, zucchini, peas and parsley. Cool to room temperature. Garnish each serving with tomatoes and lemon wedges; top with about 1 tablespoon yogurt.
Makes 6 servings.

Chicken Salad Supreme

1 cup mayonnaise or salad
   dressing
¼ cup REALIME® Lime Juice
   from Concentrate
1 teaspoon salt
¼ teaspoon ground nutmeg
4 cups cubed cooked chicken or
   turkey
1 (11-ounce) can mandarin
   orange segments, drained
1 cup seedless green grape
   halves
¾ cup chopped celery
½ cup slivered almonds, toasted

In large bowl, combine mayonnaise, ReaLime® brand, salt and nutmeg. Add remaining ingredients; mix well. Chill. Serve on lettuce. Refrigerate leftovers.
Makes 4 to 6 servings.

Cobb Salad

½ cup vegetable oil
¼ cup REALEMON® Lemon Juice
   from Concentrate
1 tablespoon red wine vinegar
2 teaspoons sugar
½ teaspoon dry mustard
½ teaspoon salt
½ teaspoon Worcestershire
   sauce
¼ teaspoon garlic powder
¼ teaspoon pepper
6 cups finely shredded lettuce
2 cups finely chopped cooked
   chicken
3 hard-cooked eggs, finely
   chopped
2 medium tomatoes, seeded and
   chopped
1 ripe avocado, seeded, peeled
   and chopped
¼ cup (1 ounce) blue cheese,
   crumbled
¼ cup imitation bacon or cooked
   crumbled bacon

In 1-pint jar with tight-fitting lid or cruet, combine oil, ReaLemon® brand, vinegar, sugar and seasonings; shake well. Chill to blend flavors. In large salad bowl, arrange remaining ingredients; chill. Just before serving, toss with dressing. Refrigerate leftovers.
Makes 4 servings.

Cantonese Chicken Salad

3 chicken breast halves
2 cups water
5 tablespoons KIKKOMAN Soy
   Sauce, divided
4 cups shredded iceberg lettuce
1 medium carrot, peeled and
   shredded
½ cup finely chopped green
   onions and tops
⅓ cup distilled white vinegar
2 tablespoons sesame seed,
   toasted
2 teaspoons sugar
½ teaspoon ground ginger
2 tablespoons minced fresh
   cilantro or parsley

Simmer chicken in mixture of water and 1 tablespoon soy sauce in covered saucepan 15 minutes, or until chicken is tender. Remove chicken and cool. (Refrigerate stock for another use, if desired.) Skin and bone chicken; shred meat with fingers into large mixing bowl. Add lettuce, carrot and green onions. Combine vinegar, remaining 4 tablespoons soy sauce, sesame seed, sugar and ginger; stir until sugar dissolves. Pour over chicken and vegetables; toss to coat all ingredients. Cover and refrigerate 1 hour. Just before serving, add cilantro and toss to combine. Garnish as desired.
Makes 6 servings.

Hot Chicken Salad

2 cups cubed cooked chicken or
   turkey
1 cup chopped celery
1 (8-ounce) can water chestnuts,
   drained and coarsely
   chopped
2 tablespoons finely chopped
   onion
1 cup mayonnaise or salad
   dressing
3 tablespoons REALEMON®
   Lemon Juice from
   Concentrate
1 teaspoon WYLER'S® or
   STEERO® Chicken-Flavor
   Instant Bouillon
2 tablespoons sliced almonds,
   toasted
2 tablespoons chopped parsley

Preheat oven to 350°. In large bowl, combine all ingredients except almonds and parsley. Turn into 1½-quart baking dish; top with almonds. Bake 20 minutes or until hot. Garnish with parsley. Refrigerate leftovers.
Makes 4 to 6 servings.
Microwave: Prepare salad as above in 1½-quart baking dish. Microwave on full power (high) 5 to 6 minutes or until hot. Stir before serving. Garnish with parsley.

Stay Slim Salad

2 cups shredded DOLE™ Iceberg Lettuce
¼ cup chopped green onion
½ pound sliced cooked chicken
2 small DOLE™ Bananas, sliced
1 large DOLE™ Pink Grapefruit, peeled and sectioned
1 cup halved cherry tomatoes
½ cup sliced DOLE™ Celery
Low-Calorie Dressing (recipe follows)

In medium bowl, combine lettuce and onion. Arrange on 2 salad plates. Arrange chicken in center of each. Arrange bananas, grapefruit, tomatoes and celery around chicken. Serve with Low-Calorie Dressing.
Makes 2 servings.
LOW-CALORIE DRESSING: In screw-top jar, combine ¼ cup lime juice, 2 tablespoons vegetable oil, 2 teaspoons sugar, ½ teaspoon paprika and ¼ teaspoon *each* salt and dry mustard. Shake until well blended.

Deluxe Chicken Walnut Salad

½ cup WISH-BONE® Chunky Blue Cheese or Lite Chunky Blue Cheese Dressing
2 cups cut-up cooked chicken (about 12 ounces)
½ cup green or red seedless grapes
½ cup chopped walnuts
2 tablespoons sliced green onion

In medium bowl, combine all ingredients and toss well; cover and chill. Serve, if desired, on croissants.
Makes about 2 main-dish servings.

Waldorf Chicken Salad

1 cup uncooked CREAMETTE® Medium Macaroni Shells, cooked as package directs, rinsed and drained
2 cups cubed cooked chicken or turkey
2 cups coarsely chopped apple
1 cup (4 ounces) cubed mild Cheddar cheese
¾ cup sliced celery
½ cup mayonnaise or salad dressing
¼ cup applesauce
2 teaspoons WYLER'S® or STEERO® Chicken-Flavor Instant Bouillon
½ cup chopped pecans

In large bowl, combine ingredients; mix well. Chill thoroughly. Garnish as desired. Refrigerate leftovers.
Makes about 7½ cups.

Turkey Pineapple Salad

1½ cups (½ pound) cubed BUTTERBALL® SLICE 'N SERVE® Oven Prepared Breast of Turkey
1½ cups (½ pound) thin strips BUTTERBALL® SLICE 'N SERVE® Turkey Ham
2 cups fresh or canned pineapple chunks
1 cup diced unpared red apple
½ cup sliced celery
¾ cup pecan halves
¼ cup sour cream
¼ cup mayonnaise
½ teaspoon sugar
¼ teaspoon ground ginger
¾ teaspoon prepared mustard
Lettuce leaves or pineapple shells

Combine turkey breast, turkey ham, pineapple, apple, celery and pecans in medium bowl. Stir together sour cream, mayonnaise, sugar, ginger and mustard in small bowl. Spoon dressing over salad and toss to blend. Serve immediately on lettuce leaves or pineapple shells.
Makes 6 servings.
To Make Pineapple Shells: Cut pineapple lengthwise into quarters keeping top attached. Core and remove fruit from each quarter.

Festive Chicken Salad

1 8¼-ounce can crushed pineapple, undrained
1 8-ounce container Soft PHILADELPHIA BRAND Cream Cheese
2 cups chopped cooked chicken
1 8-ounce can water chestnuts, drained, sliced
½ cup celery slices
½ cup slivered almonds, toasted
¼ cup green onion slices
¼ teaspoon salt
Dash of pepper
4 medium tomatoes
Lettuce

Drain pineapple, reserving ¼ cup liquid. Combine reserved liquid and cream cheese, mixing until well blended. Add pineapple, chicken, water chestnuts, celery, ¼ cup almonds, onions, salt and pepper; mix lightly. Chill. Cut each tomato into six wedges, almost to stem end. Fill with chicken mixture. Sprinkle with remaining almonds. Serve on lettuce-lined plates.
4 servings.
Variations: Omit tomatoes; serve salad over honeydew or cantaloupe wedges or in lettuce cups.

Substitute chopped pecans for almonds.

Layered Chicken Salad

1 8-ounce package *Light*
   PHILADELPHIA BRAND
   Neufchâtel Cheese, softened
2 medium avocados, peeled,
   mashed
¼ cup milk
1 tablespoon lemon juice
1 tablespoon chopped onion
½ teaspoon salt
4 cups shredded lettuce
1 cup chopped red or green
   pepper
2 cups chopped cooked chicken
1 11-ounce can mandarin orange
   segments, drained
4 crisply cooked bacon slices,
   crumbled

Combine neufchâtel cheese, avocados, milk and juice, mixing until well blended. Add onions and salt; mix well. In 2½-quart glass serving bowl, layer lettuce, peppers, chicken and oranges. Spread neufchâtel cheese mixture over oranges to cover. Chill. Top with bacon just before serving.
6 to 8 servings.

Lemony Chicken Mold

1 (13¾-fluid ounce) can
   COLLEGE INN® Chicken
   Broth
2 (3-ounce) or 1 (6-ounce)
   package ROYAL® Lemon
   Gelatin
1 cup cold water
2 tablespoons white wine
   vinegar
1 (8-ounce) can crushed
   pineapple in its own juice,
   undrained
2 cups chopped cooked chicken
⅓ cup sliced celery
1 (2-ounce) jar diced pimientos,
   well drained

Refrigerate chicken broth; remove fat. In small saucepan, over high heat, heat broth to a boil; stir in gelatin until dissolved. Stir in water, vinegar and pineapple. Refrigerate until slightly thickened. Stir in chicken, celery and pimientos. Pour into 6-cup mold. Refrigerate until firm, about 3 hours. To serve, unmold onto serving plate. Garnish as desired.
Makes 6 to 8 servings.

Mandarin Chicken Salad

1 whole chicken breast, split
2 cups water
4 tablespoons KIKKOMAN Soy
   Sauce, divided
   Boiling water
¾ pound fresh bean sprouts
1 carrot, peeled and shredded
½ cup slivered green onions and
   tops
2 tablespoons minced fresh
   cilantro or parsley
¼ cup distilled white vinegar
2 teaspoons sugar
½ cup blanched slivered
   almonds, toasted

Simmer chicken in mixture of 2 cups water and 1 tablespoon soy sauce in covered saucepan 15 minutes, or until chicken is tender. Meanwhile, pour boiling water over bean sprouts. Drain; cool under cold water and drain thoroughly. Remove chicken and cool. (Refrigerate stock for another use, if desired.) Skin and bone chicken; shred meat with fingers into large mixing bowl. Add bean sprouts, carrot, green onions and cilantro. Blend vinegar, sugar and remaining 3 tablespoons soy sauce, stirring until sugar dissolves. Pour over chicken and vegetables; toss to coat all ingredients. Cover and refrigerate 1 hour. Just before serving, add almonds and toss to combine.
Makes 4 servings.

Apple & Tarragon Salad with Watercress

2 envelopes KNOX® Unflavored
   Gelatine
2 cups white grape juice
1½ cups apple juice
1 tablespoon lemon juice
1 medium apple, thinly sliced
1 cup loosely packed watercress
   leaves, chopped
1 cup seedless green grapes,
   halved
¼ cup chopped green onions
   (about 2 medium)
1 tablespoon chopped fresh
   tarragon*
   Grilled or broiled boneless
   chicken breasts, cut into
   strips

In medium saucepan, sprinkle unflavored gelatine over 1 cup grape juice; let stand 1 minute. Stir over low heat until gelatine is completely dissolved, about 5 minutes.

In large bowl, blend remaining 1 cup grape juice, apple juice, gelatine mixture and lemon juice. Chill, stirring occasionally, until mixture is consistency of unbeaten egg whites, about 30 minutes. Into 6-cup ring mold, spoon 1 cup gelatine mixture. Arrange apple slices, slightly overlapping, in bottom of mold. Fold watercress, grapes, green onions and tarragon into remaining gelatine mixture; carefully spoon over apple slices. Chill until firm, about 4 hours. To serve, unmold onto serving platter, then fill center with chicken and, if desired, additional watercress leaves. Serve, if desired, with WISH-BONE® Chunky Blue Cheese Dressing.
Makes about 8 servings.
   Substitution: Use ½ teaspoon dried tarragon leaves.

Shaved Ham Salad

8 ounces shaved fully cooked ham, coarsely chopped
1½ cups coarsely chopped fresh mushrooms
¾ cup bite-size cubes mozzarella cheese
½ cup quartered pimiento-stuffed olives
⅓ cup chopped green onion
1 medium tomato, seeded and chopped
⅓ cup CRISCO® Oil
2 tablespoons red wine vinegar
¼ teaspoon pepper

Mix ham, mushrooms, mozzarella cheese, olives, onion and tomato in medium serving bowl. Blend remaining ingredients in small mixing bowl. Pour over ham mixture. Toss to coat. Serve immediately, or refrigerate and stir before serving.
6 to 8 servings.

Confetti Beef Salad

½ pound PETER ECKRICH DELI® Roast Beef, cut into julienne strips
3 ounces uncooked thin spaghetti (about 2 cups cooked)
1 medium zucchini, cut into pieces
1 small yellow squash, cut into pieces
½ red bell pepper, cut into strips
½ cup coarsely shredded carrot
⅓ cup vinaigrette dressing with Dijon mustard
¼ teaspoon coarsely ground black pepper

Break spaghetti in half. Cook according to package directions. Rinse with cold water; drain. Combine all ingredients in large bowl. Cover and refrigerate at least 1 hour.
Makes 5 servings.

Marinated Beef Salad

½ pound sliced PETER ECKRICH DELI® Roast Beef, cut into strips
½ cup picante salsa
2 tablespoons vegetable oil
3 teaspoons vinegar
¼ cup chopped red onion
1 avocado, peeled, cubed
4 lettuce leaves
1 tomato, cut into wedges
Tortilla chips, optional

Combine salsa, oil, vinegar and red onion in medium bowl. Add roast beef; stir to coat meat with salsa mixture. Cover and refrigerate 1 hour. Just before serving, add avocado and toss. To serve, place beef mixture on lettuce leaves and garnish with tomato. Serve with tortilla chips.
Makes 4 servings.

Garden Chicken Salad

½ cup olive or vegetable oil
¼ cup red wine vinegar
1 tablespoon Dijon-style mustard
1 tablespoon finely chopped onion
1 tablespoon chopped fresh parsley
¼ teaspoon salt
¼ teaspoon pepper
½ pound small potatoes
¼ pound green beans, trimmed
¼ cup water
2 cans (5 ounces each) SWANSON® Premium Chunk White Chicken, drained
CAMPBELL'S FRESH® Butterhead Lettuce Leaves
2 hard-cooked eggs, sliced
1 CAMPBELL'S FRESH® tomato, cut into wedges
VLASIC® or EARLY CALIFORNIA® Pitted Ripe Olives for garnish

To Microwave:
1. To prepare dressing: In small bowl or shaker jar, combine first 7 ingredients; shake or stir until well blended. Set aside.
2. Pierce potatoes with fork in several places. Arrange potatoes in corners of 8- by 8-inch microwave-safe baking dish; arrange green beans in center. Add water. Cover with vented plastic wrap; microwave on HIGH 6 minutes or until vegetables are nearly tender, rearranging vegetables once during cooking. Let stand, covered, 5 minutes. Drain.
3. Cut potatoes into slices. In medium bowl, toss potatoes and beans with ¼ cup of the dressing. In another small bowl, toss chicken with 2 tablespoons of the dressing. Cover; chill if desired.
4. Arrange lettuce on platter. Mound chicken in center and arrange potatoes, beans, eggs and tomato wedges around chicken. Garnish with olives. Serve with remaining dressing.
Makes 4 servings.

Turkey Salad with Pita Bread

3 cups cubed cooked BUTTERBALL® turkey (1 pound)
1 cup sour cream
3 green onions, sliced
1 tablespoon dried dill weed
1 teaspoon seasoned salt
1 medium cucumber, sliced thin
1 small red onion, sliced thin
12 small cherry tomatoes, cut into halves
12 small fresh mushrooms, sliced thin
Lettuce leaves
6 pita breads, 6½-inch diameter, cut into halves

Blend sour cream, green onions, dill weed and salt in medium bowl. Add turkey and vegetables except lettuce; toss to combine. Serve on lettuce with pita bread. Or fill pita bread halves with turkey mixture and serve as sandwiches.
Yield: 6 servings.

Curried Pineapple Pasta Salad

1 can (20 ounces) DOLE®
    Pineapple Chunks
2 cups cooked, shredded
    chicken
8 ounces macaroni or other
    small pasta, cooked
2 cups sliced DOLE™ Celery
1/2 cup sliced green onion
1/2 cup julienne-cut DOLE™ Red
    Bell Pepper
1/2 cup sliced ripe olives
3/4 cup mayonnaise
1/3 cup chopped chutney
1/4 cup dairy sour cream
2 teaspoons curry powder
1 teaspoon salt

Drain pineapple. In salad bowl, combine pineapple, chicken, pasta, celery, onion, red pepper and olives. To make dressing, in 1-quart measure, combine remaining ingredients; toss with salad. Refrigerate, covered, until ready to serve.
Makes 8 servings.

French Quarter Rice Salad

1 package (6 ounces) long grain
    and wild rice mix
2/3 cup vegetable oil
1/3 cup white wine vinegar
1 tablespoon Dijon-style
    mustard
1 clove garlic, minced
1/2 teaspoon TABASCO® pepper
    sauce
2 cups diced cooked chicken or
    turkey
1 large carrot, shredded
1/2 cup raisins
1/3 cup chopped green onions
1/2 cup pecans, toasted

Cook rice according to package directions. Cool slightly. In large bowl combine oil, vinegar, mustard, garlic and Tabasco® sauce. Add rice, chicken, carrot, raisins and green onions; mix well. Cover; refrigerate 2 to 4 hours to blend flavors. Just before serving, stir in pecans.
Makes 4 servings.

Curried Smoked Turkey Salad

1/2 cup mayonnaise
1/4 cup WISH-BONE® Italian
    Dressing
2 tablespoons milk
1 teaspoon curry powder
1/4 teaspoon ground ginger
1/8 teaspoon pepper
2 cups cut-up cooked smoked or
    unsmoked turkey breast
    (about 12 ounces)
2 cups broccoli florets
1/2 cup chopped red pepper
1/4 cup sliced green onions

In large bowl, thoroughly blend mayonnaise, Italian dressing, milk, curry, ginger and pepper. Stir in remaining ingredients; cover and chill. Serve, if desired, over fresh spinach leaves.
Makes about 4 main-dish servings.
Notes: Recipe can be doubled.
    Also terrific with Wish-Bone® Robusto Italian, Herbal Italian, Blended Italian, Lite Italian, Classic Dijon Vinaigrette or Lite Classic Dijon Vinaigrette Dressing.

Dieter's Turkey Citrus Salad

1 cup cubed cooked
    BUTTERBALL® turkey
1 cup fresh grapefruit sections
1/2 cup fresh orange sections
1/2 small head lettuce, broken into
    bite-sized pieces
Low-calorie dressing
Leaf lettuce or endive

Place turkey, fruit and lettuce in medium bowl. Toss lightly with enough dressing to coat. Serve on lettuce.
Yield: 2 to 3 servings.

Pineapple and Ham Pasta Salad

1 can (20 ounces) DOLE®
    Pineapple Tidbits
1 pound cooked ham, diced
1 DOLE™ Red or Green Bell
    Pepper, seeded and diced
2 cups frozen peas, thawed
2 cups diced DOLE™ Celery
8 ounces elbow macaroni,
    cooked
1 1/4 cups mayonnaise
1 tablespoon vinegar
1 teaspoon onion powder
1/4 teaspoon pepper
1/4 teaspoon dried dill weed

Drain pineapple. In large bowl, combine pineapple, ham, red pepper, peas, celery and macaroni. To make dressing, in 1-quart measure, combine mayonnaise, vinegar, onion powder, pepper and dill weed. Stir dressing into pineapple mixture. Refrigerate 3 to 4 hours before serving to allow flavors to blend.
Makes 8 servings.

East Meets West Salad

6 cups shredded iceberg lettuce
1 large carrot, peeled and shredded
1 tablespoon minced fresh cilantro or parsley
2 tablespoons distilled white vinegar
4 teaspoons KIKKOMAN Soy Sauce
1 tablespoon sesame seed, toasted
1 tablespoon water
2 teaspoons sugar

Toss lettuce with carrot and cilantro. Measure vinegar, soy sauce, sesame seed, water and sugar into jar with screw-top lid; cover and shake well until sugar dissolves. Pour over lettuce mixture and toss lightly to combine. Serve immediately.
Makes 6 to 8 servings.

Ham-Pasta Salad Vinaigrette

1 cup V8® Vegetable Juice
1 tablespoon vegetable oil
1 tablespoon wine vinegar
1 teaspoon dried basil leaves, crushed
1 large clove garlic, minced
1½ cups corkscrew macaroni, cooked and drained (2 cups cooked)
¾ cup cooked ham cut into matchstick-thin strips (4 ounces)
½ cup cubed part-skim mozzarella cheese
2 tablespoons VLASIC® or EARLY CALIFORNIA® Sliced Pitted Ripe Olives
4 green onions, sliced

1. In medium bowl, stir together V8 juice, oil, vinegar, basil and garlic until well blended.
2. Add macaroni, ham, cheese, olives and onions; toss to coat well.
3. Cover; refrigerate until serving time, at least 2 hours.
Makes 4½ cups or 4 main-dish servings.

Per serving: 221 calories, 13 g protein, 10 g fat, 21 g carbohydrate, 732 mg sodium, 25 mg cholesterol.

Steak Salad in Red-Wine Dressing

½ cup WISH-BONE® Italian Dressing
½ cup dry red wine
1 tablespoon Worcestershire sauce
1 tablespoon rosemary leaves
2 teaspoons Dijon-style mustard
½ pound beef flank or round steak, thinly sliced
1 medium red onion, sliced
1 large tomato, coarsely chopped
1 cup sliced carrots
1 cup sliced zucchini

In large shallow baking dish, thoroughly blend Italian dressing, wine, Worcestershire sauce, rosemary and mustard. Add beef and red onion; turn to coat. Cover and marinate in refrigerator, stirring occasionally, at least 3 hours.

Remove beef, onion and marinade to large shallow heavy-duty aluminum-foil-lined baking pan or broiler rack. Broil beef with marinade, turning occasionally, 3 minutes or until done; cover and chill. To serve, toss beef mixture with tomato, then arrange on serving platter with carrots, zucchini and, if desired, watercress.
Makes about 4 main-dish servings.
Note: Also terrific with Wish-Bone® Robusto Italian, Italian & Cheese, Herbal Italian, Blended Italian, Lite Italian or Classic Dijon Vinaigrette Dressing.

Individual Taco Salads

⅓ cup French Dressing (see page 93)
CRISCO® Oil for frying
4 to 6 eight-inch flour tortillas
1 pound ground beef
¼ cup chopped onion
1 can (15½ ounces) kidney beans, rinsed and drained
1½ teaspoons chili powder
1 teaspoon cumin
½ teaspoon salt
⅛ teaspoon pepper
4 to 6 cups shredded lettuce
1 cup shredded Cheddar cheese (about 4 ounces)

Prepare French Dressing as directed. Cover and refrigerate.

Heat 3 inches Crisco® Oil in deep-fryer or heavy saucepan to 375°F. Place 1 tortilla in oil. Let float 5 to 10 seconds. Press center of tortilla into oil with metal ladle (tortilla will form a bowl shape). While pressing with metal ladle, fry 1 to 2 minutes longer, or until golden brown. Drain on paper towels. Repeat with remaining tortillas.

Combine ground beef and onion in large skillet. Brown over medium-high heat. Drain. Add beans, chili powder, cumin, salt and pepper. Cook over moderate heat, stirring constantly, for 5 minutes, or until flavors are blended. Stir in ⅓ cup French Dressing.

Divide shredded lettuce equally among fried tortillas. Top with meat mixture. Sprinkle with Cheddar cheese. Serve with *dairy sour cream, chopped tomato, chopped black olives or taco sauce,* if desired.
4 to 6 servings.

Layered Salad Extraordinaire

1 8-ounce package *Light*
    PHILADELPHIA BRAND
    Neufchâtel Cheese, softened
3/4 cup (3 ounces) crumbled
    KRAFT Natural Blue Cheese
1/4 cup KRAFT Light Reduced
    Calorie Mayonnaise
1/4 cup milk
2 tablespoons lemon juice
1 tablespoon chopped chives
2 quarts torn assorted greens
1 cup shredded carrot
2 1/2 cups ham cubes
1 cup chopped green pepper
2 cups chopped tomato

Combine neufchâtel cheese and blue cheese, mixing until well blended. Add mayonnaise, milk, juice and chives; mix well.

Combine greens and carrots. Combine meat and green peppers. In 3-quart bowl, layer greens mixture, tomatoes and meat mixture. Spread neufchâtel cheese mixture over meat mixture to seal. Cover; chill several hours.
8 servings.

Summer Kielbasa Salad

1/2 pound ECKRICH® Polska
    Kielbasa, cut into 1/8-inch
    slices
1 cup shredded red cabbage
1 medium cucumber, sliced thin
4 red radishes, sliced thin
1/2 cup mayonnaise
1/2 cup sour cream
2 tablespoons Dijon mustard
1 tablespoon prepared
    horseradish
1/2 teaspoon dried dill weed
1/2 teaspoon garlic salt
1/4 cup crumbled feta cheese
1 teaspoon chopped fresh
    parsley

Saute kielbasa in 10-inch skillet over medium heat until lightly browned. Drain on paper towels. Cool. Place kielbasa, cabbage, cucumber and radishes in large bowl. Combine mayonnaise, sour cream, mustard, horseradish, dill weed and garlic salt in small bowl. Whisk to blend; stir in cheese. Pour dressing over kielbasa and vegetables. Cover and refrigerate 20 minutes. Sprinkle with parsley and serve.
Makes 4 to 6 servings.

Marinated Oriental Beef Salad

1 (1- to 1 1/4-pound) flank steak
1/3 cup REALEMON® Lemon Juice
    from Concentrate
1/4 cup catsup
1/4 cup vegetable oil
1 tablespoon brown sugar
1/4 teaspoon garlic powder
1/4 teaspoon ground ginger
1/4 teaspoon pepper
8 ounces fresh mushrooms,
    sliced (about 2 cups)
1 (8-ounce) can sliced water
    chestnuts, drained
1 medium sweet onion, sliced
    and separated into rings
1 (6-ounce) package frozen pea
    pods, thawed, or 4 ounces
    fresh pea pods
Lettuce leaves
Tomato wedges

Broil meat 5 minutes on each side or until desired doneness; slice diagonally into thin strips. Meanwhile, in large bowl, combine ReaLemon® brand, catsup, oil, sugar, garlic powder, ginger and pepper; mix well. Add sliced meat, mushrooms, water chestnuts and onion; mix well. Cover; refrigerate 8 hours or overnight, stirring occasionally. Before serving, add pea pods. Serve on lettuce; garnish with tomato. Refrigerate leftovers.
Makes 4 servings.

Stir-Fried Beef & Eggplant Salad

1/2 pound boneless tender beef
    steak (sirloin, rib eye or top
    loin)
1/3 cup KIKKOMAN Stir-Fry Sauce
1 teaspoon distilled white
    vinegar
1/4 to 1/2 teaspoon crushed red
    pepper
1 clove garlic, pressed
    Lettuce leaves (optional)
3 cups finely shredded iceberg
    lettuce
3 tablespoons vegetable oil,
    divided
1 medium eggplant, cut into
    julienne strips
1 medium carrot, cut into
    julienne strips
6 green onions, cut into 1 1/2-inch
    lengths, separating whites
    from tops

Cut beef across grain into thin slices, then into strips. Combine stir-fry sauce, vinegar, red pepper and garlic. Coat beef with 1 tablespoon of the stir-fry sauce mixture; set aside remaining mixture. Line edge of large shallow bowl or large platter with lettuce leaves; arrange shredded lettuce in center. Heat 1 tablespoon oil in hot wok or large skillet over high heat. Add beef and stir-fry 1 minute; remove. Heat remaining 2 tablespoons oil in same pan; add eggplant and stir-fry 6 minutes. Add carrot and white parts of green onions; stir-fry 3 minutes. Add green onion tops; stir-fry 2 minutes longer. Add remaining stir-fry sauce mixture and beef. Cook and stir just until beef and vegetables are coated with sauce. Spoon mixture over shredded lettuce; toss well to combine before serving. Serve immediately.
Makes 2 to 3 servings.

Salada di Antipasto

- 2 quarts mixed salad greens
- 1/2 pound salami, cut into strips
- 1 package (8 ounces) mozzarella cheese, cut into strips
- 1 package (10 ounces) frozen artichoke hearts, cooked and drained
- 1 cup pitted ripe olives
- 1 medium tomato, cut into wedges
- 1/3 cup roasted red peppers, cut into strips
- 1 cup (8 ounces) WISH-BONE® Robusto Italian Dressing

In large salad bowl, arrange all ingredients except robusto Italian dressing; cover and chill. Just before serving, toss with dressing. Serve, if desired, with Italian bread.
Makes about 4 main-dish servings.
Note: Also terrific with Wish-Bone® Italian, Italian & Cheese, or Lite Italian Dressing.

Salad Taverna

- 1/3 cup olive or vegetable oil
- 3 tablespoons lemon juice
- 1 clove garlic, minced
- 1/2 teaspoon TABASCO® pepper sauce
- 1/2 teaspoon anise seed
- 1/4 teaspoon salt
- 8 ounces spinach egg noodles, cooked, drained
- 1/2 pound feta cheese, crumbled or 1 cup ricotta or cottage cheese
- 2 tomatoes, coarsely chopped
- 1/2 cup sliced pitted ripe olives
- 1/4 cup chopped parsley (optional)
- 1/4 cup pine nuts (optional)

In large bowl combine oil, lemon juice, garlic, Tabasco® sauce, anise seed and salt; mix well. Add noodles, cheese, tomatoes, olives, parsley and pine nuts; toss to coat evenly. Cover; refrigerate at least 1 hour. Serve with additional Tabasco® sauce, if desired.
Makes 4 to 6 servings.

Garden Patch Salad

- 6 ounces SWIFT PREMIUM® Deli Hard Salami, cut into julienne strips
- 1/3 cup olive oil
- 2 tablespoons fresh lemon juice
- 1 tablespoon minced fresh parsley
- 1 tablespoon grated Parmesan cheese
- 1 clove garlic, minced
- 6 ounces mozzarella cheese, cubed
- 1 pint cherry tomatoes, cut into halves
- 1 medium zucchini, cut lengthwise into halves, sliced thin
- 1 small onion, cut into quarters, sliced thin

Place oil, lemon juice, parsley, Parmesan cheese and garlic in jar with tight-fitting lid. Shake ingredients together and let stand 1 hour for flavors to blend. Combine salami, mozzarella cheese, tomatoes, zucchini and onion in salad bowl. Pour dressing over salad and toss to blend before serving.
Makes 6 servings.

Chef's Salad

- 6 cups torn lettuce
- 6 ounces spinach, rinsed, drained, trimmed and torn into bite-size pieces
- 8 ounces cooked turkey, cut into thin strips
- 8 ounces fully cooked ham, cut into thin strips
- 6 ounces Swiss cheese, cut into thin strips
- 1 cup broken melba cracker rounds
- 8 cherry tomatoes, halved
- 8 pitted black or green olives, halved
- 3 green onions, chopped

Combine all ingredients in large salad bowl or divide ingredients among individual salad bowls. Garnish with *hard-cooked egg slices,* if desired. Serve with desired dressing. (see pages 92–93).
6 to 8 servings.

Favorite recipe from CRISCO® Oil/Procter & Gamble

Soy-Spinach Salad

- 1 pound fresh spinach, washed and drained
- 4 medium-size fresh mushrooms, sliced
- 2 tablespoons vinegar
- 2 tablespoons water
- 1 tablespoon KIKKOMAN Soy Sauce
- 1 tablespoon vegetable oil
- 1 1/2 teaspoons sugar

Tear spinach into bite-size pieces; place in large salad bowl and top with mushrooms. Combine vinegar, water, soy sauce, oil and sugar in small saucepan; bring to boil. Pour hot dressing over vegetables and quickly toss until spinach wilts. Serve immediately.
Makes 4 servings.

Dilly Cucumber Salad

1 (8-ounce) container BORDEN® or MEADOW GOLD® Sour Cream
¼ cup REALEMON® Lemon Juice from Concentrate
3 tablespoons sugar
1 teaspoon salt
½ teaspoon dill weed
1 medium cucumber, sliced
1 medium sweet white onion, sliced and separated into rings

In medium bowl, combine sour cream, ReaLemon® brand, sugar, salt and dill weed; mix well. Add cucumber and onion. Cover; chill to blend flavors. *Makes 4 servings.*

Potato-Tuna Salad

½ cup olive or vegetable oil
¼ cup white wine vinegar
2 tablespoons lemon juice
1 clove garlic, minced
¾ teaspoon TABASCO® pepper sauce
¼ teaspoon salt
2 pounds cooked small red potatoes, cubed
2 cans (6½ or 7 ounces each) tuna, drained, separated into large chunks
1 cup sliced celery
⅓ cup sliced green onions
Fresh spinach leaves (optional)

In large bowl combine oil, vinegar, lemon juice, garlic, Tabasco® sauce and salt; mix well. Add potatoes, tuna, celery and green onions; toss lightly. Cover; refrigerate at least 1 hour. Serve over fresh spinach leaves, if desired. *Makes 6 to 8 servings.*

Sea Salad

1 bunch DOLE™ Broccoli, cut into flowerets (2 cups)
4 ounces snow peas, ends and strings removed
8 ounces shell-shaped pasta
2 cups sliced DOLE™ Celery
2 cups sliced fresh mushrooms
½ cup sliced DOLE™ Red Bell Pepper
8 ounces cooked, shelled shrimp
Lemon-Mustard Dressing (recipe follows)

To blanch vegetables, cover broccoli and snow peas with boiling water. Let stand 5 minutes. Rinse under cold water to stop cooking; drain. Cook pasta according to package directions; drain. In large bowl, combine vegetables, pasta and shrimp; toss with Lemon-Mustard Dressing. Refrigerate, covered, at least 2 hours before serving.
Makes 4 servings.
LEMON-MUSTARD DRESSING: In 1-quart measure, combine ½ cup olive or vegetable oil, 3 tablespoons lemon juice, 1 tablespoon wine vinegar, 2 teaspoons Dijon mustard, 1 teaspoon dried dill weed, ¼ teaspoon pepper and salt to taste. Blend well.

Wild Rice and Seafood Salad

½ cup WISH-BONE® Lite Classic Creamy Dijon Dressing
1 pound medium shrimp, cleaned, cooked and coarsely chopped*
2 cups cooked wild or regular white rice
1 small red or green pepper, chopped
½ cup halved seedless grapes
¼ cup sliced almonds, toasted
1 teaspoon lemon juice
3 dashes hot pepper sauce
Lettuce leaves

In large bowl, combine all ingredients except lettuce; cover and chill. To serve, line bowl or individual serving dishes with lettuce; fill with shrimp mixture. Garnish, if desired, with lemon slices.
Makes about 6 main-dish servings.
***Substitution:** Use 2 packages (6 ounces each) frozen crabmeat, thawed and drained. Increase dressing to ¾ cup.
Note: Also terrific with Wish-Bone® Creamy Italian or Lite Creamy Italian Dressing.

Dilled Crab Salad Mold

1 envelope unflavored gelatin
1 cup water
½ cup MARIE'S® Refrigerated Sour Cream and Dill Salad Dressing
1 tablespoon finely chopped onion
Dash hot pepper sauce
2 cups crabmeat, flaked
½ cup chopped VLASIC® Mild Banana Pepper Rings
1 cup heavy cream, whipped
CAMPBELL'S FRESH® Butterhead Lettuce Leaves

1. In medium saucepan, sprinkle gelatin over water to soften; let stand 1 minute. Over low heat, heat until gelatin is dissolved, stirring constantly. Do not boil.
2. In medium bowl, combine salad dressing, onion and hot pepper sauce. Gradually stir in gelatin mixture. Cover; refrigerate about 40 minutes or until mixture mounds slightly when dropped from spoon.
3. Gently fold crabmeat and peppers into gelatin mixture. Fold in whipped cream. Pour into 4-cup mold. Cover; refrigerate until set, at least 2 hours.
4. To serve: Unmold onto lettuce-lined serving platter. Serve with crackers.
Makes 4 cups.

Tuna & Cracked Wheat Salad

2½ cups water
1 package (8 ounces) wheat pilaf mix
¼ cup lemon juice
¼ cup vegetable oil
2 cans (6½ or 7 ounces each) tuna, drained, separated into chunks
1 cucumber, pared, seeded and diced
1 medium carrot, chopped
⅓ cup sliced green onions
¼ pound mushrooms, sliced
1 tomato, chopped
½ cup sliced pitted ripe olives
½ cup chopped parsley
½ teaspoon salt
½ teaspoon TABASCO® pepper sauce
Lettuce leaves
Yogurt Dressing (recipe follows)

In medium saucepan bring water to a boil. Add pilaf mix; reduce heat, cover and simmer 15 minutes. Remove from heat; stir in lemon juice and oil. Let stand at room temperature until cool. Stir in remaining ingredients except lettuce leaves and Yogurt Dressing. Cover; refrigerate 4 hours. Turn into lettuce-lined serving dish. Serve with Yogurt Dressing.
Makes 6 to 8 servings.

Yogurt Dressing

2 containers (8 ounces each) plain yogurt
4 teaspoons chopped fresh mint or ¼ teaspoon dried dill weed
⅛ teaspoon TABASCO® pepper sauce

In small bowl combine yogurt, mint and Tabasco® sauce; mix well. Cover; refrigerate.
Makes 2 cups.

Marinated Shrimp & Vegetables

1 pound medium raw shrimp, deveined and cooked
1 cup fresh cauliflowerets
4 ounces small whole fresh mushrooms
1 cup sliced zucchini
1 large red or green pepper, cut into squares
¾ cup REALEMON® Lemon Juice from Concentrate
1 tablespoon chopped green onion
2 teaspoons sugar
1 teaspoon salt
¼ to ½ teaspoon dill weed
5 drops hot pepper sauce
¾ cup vegetable oil

Place shrimp and vegetables in shallow dish. In small bowl or jar, combine remaining ingredients except oil; mix well. Add oil; mix well. Pour over shrimp and vegetables. Cover; refrigerate 6 hours or overnight, stirring occasionally. Refrigerate leftovers.
Makes about 5 cups.

Linguine Tuna Salad

½ (1-pound) package CREAMETTE® Linguine, broken in half
¼ cup REALEMON® Lemon Juice from Concentrate
¼ cup vegetable oil
¼ cup chopped green onions
2 teaspoons sugar
1 teaspoon Italian seasoning
1 teaspoon seasoned salt
1 (12½-ounce) can tuna, drained
1 (10-ounce) package frozen green peas, thawed
2 firm medium tomatoes, chopped

Cook linguine according to package directions; drain. Meanwhile, in large bowl, combine ReaLemon® brand, oil, onions, sugar, Italian seasoning and salt; mix well. Add *hot* linguine; toss. Add remaining ingredients; mix well. Cover; chill to blend flavors. Serve on lettuce; garnish as desired. Refrigerate leftovers.
Makes 6 servings.

Cashew-Shrimp Salad

¾ cup V8® Vegetable Juice
1 tablespoon soy sauce
1 teaspoon vegetable oil
½ teaspoon grated lemon peel
½ teaspoon grated fresh ginger
¾ pound medium shrimp, cooked, shelled and deveined
1½ cups cucumber slices cut in half
1 large carrot, cut into matchstick-thin strips (1¼ cups)
3 green onions, sliced (½ cup)
¼ cup coarsely chopped dry roasted unsalted cashews (1 ounce)
CAMPBELL'S FRESH® Butterhead Lettuce Leaves
4 slices PEPPERIDGE FARM® Fully Baked French-Style Bread

1. In medium bowl, combine V8 juice, soy sauce, oil, lemon peel and ginger.
2. Add shrimp, cucumbers, carrot and onions; toss to coat well. Cover; refrigerate until serving time, at least 2 hours.
3. Before serving, add cashews; toss to coat well. To serve: On 4 lettuce-lined salad plates, arrange shrimp mixture. Serve with French bread.
Makes 4 cups or 4 servings.

Per serving: 268 calories, 19 g protein, 7 g fat, 32 g carbohydrate, 739 mg sodium, 107 mg cholesterol.

Pacific Salad

1 pouch CAMPBELL'S® Onion
   Soup and Recipe Mix
1 cup mayonnaise
3/4 cup ketchup
1/4 cup VLASIC® Sweet Relish
   CAMPBELL'S FRESH®
   Butterhead Lettuce Leaves
1/2 pound asparagus spears,
   cooked and drained
1/2 pound whole green beans,
   cooked and drained
1 pound shrimp, cooked and
   peeled
2 hard-cooked eggs, cut into
   wedges
1 can (about 16 ounces) beets,
   drained and diced

1. To make dressing: In medium bowl, combine soup mix, mayonnaise, ketchup and relish; mix well. Cover; chill until serving time, at least 2 hours.
2. Arrange lettuce on 4 salad plates. Arrange asparagus, green beans, shrimp, eggs and beets in rows on greens.
3. Stir dressing and spoon over salad; reserve any remaining dressing for use on tossed salads.
Makes 4 servings.

Calypso Shrimp Salad

1 cantaloupe, peeled and sliced
   into 4 rings
   Crisp DOLE™ Lettuce leaves
1 pound frozen salad shrimp,
   thawed
2 firm DOLE™ Bananas, sliced
1 DOLE™ Orange, peeled and
   sliced
1 pound DOLE™ Red Grapes, cut
   into clusters
   Banana Chutney Dressing
   (recipe follows)

Arrange each cantaloupe ring on lettuce-lined salad plate. Fill centers with shrimp. Arrange banana slices, orange slices and grapes around cantaloupe. Serve with Banana Chutney Dressing.
Makes 4 servings.
BANANA CHUTNEY DRESSING: Puree 1 ripe Dole™ Banana in blender. Add 1/2 cup mayonnaise, 2 tablespoons chutney and 1 tablespoon lemon juice. Process until blended. Refrigerate, covered, until ready to serve.

Fisherman's Favorite Cioppino Salad

1 cup WISH-BONE® Italian
   Dressing
1/4 cup dry white wine
1 teaspoon chopped fresh basil
   leaves*
2 cups cooked crabmeat or sea
   legs (about 3/4 pound)
3/4 pound large shrimp, cleaned
   and cooked
2 quarts mixed salad greens
3 medium tomatoes, coarsely
   chopped
10 artichoke hearts, halved**
1 medium red onion, cut into
   rings

In large shallow baking dish, blend Italian dressing, wine and basil; add crabmeat and shrimp. Cover and marinate in refrigerator, stirring occasionally, at least 2 hours.

Meanwhile, in large salad bowl, arrange salad greens, tomatoes, artichoke hearts and onion; cover and chill. Just before serving, add seafood with marinade and toss. Garnish, if desired, with chopped parsley.
Makes about 6 main-dish servings.
   ***Substitution:** Use 1/4 teaspoon dried basil leaves.
   ****Substitution:** Use 1 can (15 ounces) artichoke hearts, drained and halved.
   Note: Also terrific with Wish-Bone® Robusto Italian or Lite Italian Dressing.

Creamy Shrimp 'n Yogurt Salad with Dill

1 envelope KNOX® Unflavored
   Gelatine
1/2 cup cold water
1/2 pint (8 ounces) plain yogurt
1/2 cup mayonnaise
1 pound shrimp, cleaned,
   cooked and coarsely
   chopped (about 2 1/2 cups)
1/2 cup chopped celery
1/4 cup grated Parmesan cheese
2 tablespoons snipped fresh
   dill*
1 tablespoon snipped chives
   (optional)
1 tablespoon Dijon-style
   prepared mustard
1/2 teaspoon salt
1/4 teaspoon pepper

In small saucepan, sprinkle unflavored gelatine over cold water; let stand 1 minute. Stir over low heat until gelatine is completely dissolved, about 3 minutes.

In large bowl, with wire whisk or rotary beater, thoroughly blend gelatine mixture, yogurt and mayonnaise. Stir in remaining ingredients. Turn into 4-cup mold or bowl; chill until firm, about 3 hours. Unmold and garnish, if desired, with additional fresh dill.
Makes about 4 main-dish servings.
   ***Substitution:** Use 1 1/2 teaspoons dried dill weed.

Rosy Blue Cheese Dressing

3/4 cup V8® Vegetable Juice
3 tablespoons vegetable oil
2 tablespoons crumbled blue cheese
1 tablespoon lemon juice
1 tablespoon finely chopped onion
1 small clove garlic, minced

In covered jar, combine all ingredients. Shake until well blended. Cover; refrigerate until serving time, at least 2 hours. Shake again before using. Serve over salad greens or vegetable salads.
Makes 1 cup.

Per tablespoon: 29 calories, 0 g protein, 3 g fat, 1 g carbohydrate, 54 mg sodium, 1 mg cholesterol.

Ginger-Soy Dressing

3/4 cup V8® Vegetable Juice
1/3 cup vegetable oil
2 tablespoons soy sauce
2 tablespoons red wine vinegar
1 tablespoon sugar
1 tablespoon grated fresh ginger
1 tablespoon dry sherry

In covered jar, combine all ingredients. Shake until well blended. Cover; refrigerate until serving time, at least 2 hours. Shake again just before using. Serve over salad greens or pasta salads.
Makes 1 1/2 cups.

Per tablespoon: 33 calories, 0 g protein, 3 g fat, 2 g carbohydrate, 112 mg sodium, 0 mg cholesterol.

Celery Seed Dressing

1/2 cup sugar
1/4 cup REALEMON® Lemon Juice from Concentrate
2 teaspoons cider vinegar
1 teaspoon dry mustard
1/2 teaspoon salt
1/2 cup vegetable oil
1 teaspoon celery seed or poppy seed

In blender container, combine all ingredients except oil and celery seed; blend until smooth. On low speed, continue blending, slowly adding oil. Stir in celery seed. Chill to blend flavors. Refrigerate leftovers.
Makes about 1 cup.

Golden Fruit Dressing

1/2 cup sugar
1 tablespoon cornstarch
1/4 teaspoon salt
2/3 cup orange juice
1/4 cup REALEMON® Lemon Juice from Concentrate
1 teaspoon grated orange rind
2 eggs, beaten
1 (8-ounce) container BORDEN® LITE-LINE® or VIVA® Plain Lowfat Yogurt

In small saucepan, combine sugar, cornstarch and salt; stir in juices and orange rind. Over medium heat, cook and stir until thickened and clear; remove from heat. Gradually stir about 1/4 cup hot mixture into eggs; stir into remaining juice mixture. Over low heat, cook and stir until slightly thickened. Cool. Fold in yogurt. Chill. Serve with fresh fruit. Refrigerate leftovers.
Makes about 2 cups.

Creamy V8 Dressing

1 package (8 ounces) Neufchâtel or reduced-calorie cream cheese, softened
1 cup reduced-calorie mayonnaise
1 cup V8® Vegetable Juice
3 cloves garlic, minced
1 teaspoon lemon juice

1. In medium bowl, blend Neufchâtel until smooth. Gradually stir in mayonnaise until well blended.
2. Stir in V8 juice, garlic and lemon juice. Cover; refrigerate until serving time, at least 2 hours. Use as a salad dressing, for dipping or as a sandwich spread.
Makes 2 1/2 cups.

Per tablespoon: 34 calories, 0 g protein, 3 g fat, 1 g carbohydrate, 89 mg sodium, 7 mg cholesterol.

Herbed Buttermilk Dressing

1 cup BORDEN® or MEADOW GOLD® Buttermilk
1 cup mayonnaise or salad dressing
1 teaspoon basil leaves
1/2 teaspoon garlic salt
1/2 teaspoon thyme leaves
1/4 teaspoon pepper
1/4 teaspoon onion powder

In small bowl, combine ingredients; mix well. Chill to blend flavors. Serve with salads or as a vegetable dip. Refrigerate leftovers.
Makes about 2 cups.

Onion Green Goddess Dressing

1 pouch CAMPBELL'S® Onion
   Soup and Recipe Mix
1½ cups mayonnaise
¾ cup chopped fresh parsley
⅓ cup milk
1 tablespoon lemon juice
1 tablespoon anchovy paste
2 teaspoons dried basil leaves,
   crushed
½ teaspoon dried tarragon
   leaves, crushed

1. In medium bowl, combine all ingredients. Stir until well blended. Cover; chill until serving time, at least 2 hours. Thin with additional milk to desired consistency.
2. Serve over salad greens or as a dip for raw vegetables.
Makes 2 cups.

Garlic Dressing

7 cloves garlic, divided
¾ cup CRISCO® Oil, divided
3 tablespoons white wine
   vinegar
½ teaspoon salt
½ teaspoon freeze-dried chives
¼ teaspoon dry mustard
⅛ teaspoon pepper

Cut 6 garlic cloves in half. Mince remaining clove and set aside.

Heat ¼ cup Crisco® Oil in small skillet. Add halved garlic cloves. Cook over low heat, stirring occasionally, about 5 minutes, or until garlic is golden brown. Remove from heat. Cool. Remove and discard garlic.

Transfer garlic-flavored oil to jar. Add remaining ingredients, including remaining ½ cup Crisco® Oil and minced garlic. Cover tightly and shake until blended. Refrigerate at least 2 hours. Shake before serving. Store covered in refrigerator.
About 1 cup.

Vinaigrette Dressing

¾ cup CRISCO® Oil
⅓ cup red wine vinegar
1 tablespoon snipped fresh
   parsley
1 teaspoon Worcestershire
   sauce
½ teaspoon salt
¼ teaspoon dry mustard
¼ teaspoon pepper
1 clove garlic, minced

Combine all ingredients in jar. Cover tightly and shake until blended.

Store covered in refrigerator. Shake before serving.
About 1 cup.

Lemony Low Cal Dressing

¼ cup REALEMON® Lemon Juice
   from Concentrate
⅔ cup plus 2 tablespoons water
1 (1.3-ounce) package low
   calorie Italian salad dressing
   mix

In 1-pint jar with tight-fitting lid or cruet, combine ingredients; shake well. Chill to blend flavors.
Makes about 1 cup: 8 calories per tablespoon.

Blue Cheese Dressing

1 pouch CAMPBELL'S® Onion
   Soup and Recipe Mix
1 cup sour cream
½ cup mayonnaise
½ cup crumbled blue cheese
½ cup milk

1. In medium bowl, combine all ingredients. Stir until well blended. Cover; chill until serving time, at least 2 hours. Thin with additional milk to desired consistency.
2. Serve over salad greens or as a dip for raw vegetables.
Makes 2 cups.

French Dressing

⅔ cup CRISCO® Oil
½ cup catsup
2 tablespoons white wine
   vinegar
1 tablespoon sugar
1 teaspoon paprika
½ teaspoon dry mustard

Combine all ingredients in blender pitcher. Blend at medium to high speed until smooth (at least 2 minutes), stopping to scrape pitcher, if necessary.

Cover and store in refrigerator. Stir before serving.
1¼ cups.

Parmesan Dressing

1 pouch CAMPBELL'S® Onion
   Soup and Recipe Mix
1½ cups mayonnaise
½ cup grated Parmesan cheese
⅓ cup milk
1 tablespoon anchovy paste
½ teaspoon curry powder
1 clove garlic, minced

1. In medium bowl, combine all ingredients. Stir until well blended. Cover; chill until serving time, at least 2 hours. Thin with additional milk to desired consistency.
2. Serve over salad greens or as a dip for raw vegetables.
Makes 2 cups.

MEATS

Hearty main dishes of beef, pork, lamb or veal are always favorites. Try new ideas for appetizing family meals or sophisticated entrees for a memorable evening. Serve steaks and chops hot from the grill, or sample the zesty flavors of international specialties.

Rouladen

6 slices bacon, partially cooked, reserving 2 tablespoons drippings
4 cups sliced onions
6 beef tip steaks (about ¼ pound each), pounded
Dijon-style mustard
6 dill pickle spears
Flour
2 tablespoons vegetable oil
1⅓ cups plus 2 tablespoons water
2 teaspoons WYLER'S® or STEERO® Beef-Flavor Instant Bouillon *or* 2 Beef-Flavor Bouillon Cubes
1 teaspoon thyme leaves
1 bay leaf
1 tablespoon flour
Hot cooked noodles

In large skillet, cook onions in reserved drippings until tender. Remove onions from skillet. On each steak, spread mustard; top with 1 slice bacon, about ½ cup onions and 1 pickle spear. Roll up. Secure with wooden picks. Coat with flour. In same skillet, brown meat in oil. Add *1⅓ cups* water, bouillon, thyme and bay leaf; bring to a boil. Cover and simmer 30 minutes or until tender. Remove meat from skillet; remove bay leaf. Mix remaining *2 tablespoons* water and *1 tablespoon* flour; stir into liquid in skillet. Cook and stir until slightly thickened. Remove picks; serve meat and gravy with noodles. Garnish as desired. Refrigerate leftovers.
Makes 6 servings.

Beef & Napa with Noodles

1 small head napa (Chinese cabbage)
Boiling water
½ pound boneless tender beef steak (sirloin, rib eye or top loin)
6 tablespoons KIKKOMAN Stir-Fry Sauce, divided
⅛ to ¼ teaspoon crushed red pepper
2 tablespoons vegetable oil, divided
¼ pound green onions, cut into 2-inch lengths, separating whites from tops
1 large red bell pepper, cut into strips
Hot cooked vermicelli or thin spaghetti

Separate and rinse napa; pat dry. Thinly slice enough leaves crosswise to measure 8 cups; place in colander or large strainer. Pour boiling water over cabbage just until leaves wilt. Cool under cold water; drain thoroughly. Cut beef across grain into thin slices, then into strips. Combine 1 tablespoon stir-fry sauce and crushed red pepper in small bowl; stir in beef to coat. Heat 1 tablespoon oil in hot wok or large skillet over high heat. Add beef and stir-fry 1 minute; remove. Heat remaining 1 tablespoon oil in same pan; add white parts of green onions and stir-fry 1 minute. Add red bell pepper; stir-fry 2 minutes. Add green onion tops; stir-fry 2 minutes longer. Add beef, cabbage and remaining 5 tablespoons stir-fry sauce; cook and stir until vegetables are coated with sauce. Serve immediately over vermicelli.
Makes 4 servings.

Beef & Vegetable Skillet Dinner

2 tablespoons oil
1 pound boneless sirloin steak, cut into thin strips
1 cup frozen sliced carrots
1 envelope LIPTON® Beefy Mushroom, Onion or Onion-Mushroom Recipe Soup Mix
1 cup water
2 tablespoons soy sauce
2 tablespoons ketchup
1/2 teaspoon garlic powder
1/4 teaspoon ground ginger
1 can (8 ounces) bamboo shoots, drained
1 package (6 ounces) frozen snow peas, thawed
Hot cooked rice

In large skillet, heat oil and brown beef, in two batches, over medium-high heat. Remove beef. Add carrots, then beefy mushroom recipe soup mix blended with water, soy sauce, ketchup, garlic powder and ginger. Bring to a boil, then simmer, stirring occasionally, 5 minutes or until carrots are crisp-tender. Add beef, bamboo shoots and snow peas; simmer 3 minutes or until heated through. To serve, arrange beef mixture over hot rice.
Makes about 4 servings.

Dragon Beef Kabobs

1 1/4 pounds boneless beef sirloin steak, 1 1/2 inches thick
1/4 cup KIKKOMAN Teriyaki Sauce
1 tablespoon peanut butter
1 teaspoon brown sugar
1 teaspoon garlic powder
1/2 teaspoon TABASCO® pepper sauce
1 can (8 1/4 oz.) pineapple chunks, drained

Microwave Directions: Cut beef into 1 1/2-inch cubes; place in medium bowl. Blend teriyaki sauce, peanut butter, brown sugar, garlic powder and pepper sauce. Pour mixture over beef, turning pieces over to coat thoroughly. Marinate 1 hour, turning pieces over occasionally. Reserving marinade, remove beef and thread alternately with pineapple chunks on 4 wooden or bamboo skewers. Arrange skewers in single layer on 12-inch round microwave-safe platter. Brush with reserved marinade. Microwave on High 2 minutes. Turn skewers over and rotate positions on platter, moving center skewers to edge. Brush with marinade. Microwave on High 2 minutes longer, or to desired degree of doneness.
Makes 4 servings.

Beef Tenderloin Dijon

1 beef tenderloin roast (about 2 pounds)
1 1/2 teaspoons salt, divided
3/4 teaspoon pepper, divided
2 tablespoons olive oil
2 cloves garlic, minced
4 cups water
2 cans (10 3/4 ounces each) condensed beef broth
1 bay leaf
1/2 teaspoon dried thyme leaves
2 whole cloves
1 tablespoon *each* cornstarch and Dijon-style mustard

Tie beef tenderloin roast with heavy string at 2-inch intervals. Combine 1 teaspoon of the salt and 1/2 teaspoon of the pepper; rub on surface of roast. Heat oil in Dutch oven over medium-high heat. Add roast and garlic; cook until evenly browned, about 6 minutes. Remove roast from pan; pour off drippings. Add water, broth, bay leaf, thyme and cloves; bring to a boil. Add roast; reduce heat to medium-low. Cover and simmer about 20 minutes. Check temperature with instant-read thermometer; temperature should register 130°F for rare. Do not overcook. Remove roast to serving platter. Cover tightly with plastic wrap or foil and allow to stand 10 minutes before carving. (Roast will continue to rise about 10°F in temperature to 140°F for rare.)

Strain cooking liquid; reserve 2 cups. Remove Dutch oven from heat; add cornstarch and mustard, mixing to form a thick paste. Gradually add reserved cooking liquid, stirring constantly. Place Dutch oven over medium heat; add remaining 1/2 teaspoon salt and 1/4 teaspoon pepper. Cook until slightly thickened, about 7 minutes. Remove strings from roast. Carve into thin slices. Serve with sauce and steamed vegetables, if desired.

Note: A beef tenderloin roast will yield four 3-ounce cooked servings per pound.

Nutrient data per 3-ounce cooked, trimmed serving: 213 calories; 11 g fat; 70 mg cholesterol; 841 mg sodium; 3.4 mg iron.

*Favorite recipe from **National Live Stock and Meat Board***

Steak Kabobs

2 pounds beef top round steak
1 bottle (8 ounces) French salad dressing
2 tablespoons lemon juice
1 can (16 ounces) white whole onions, drained
18 cherry tomatoes

Place steak in freezer 30 minutes to firm; slice into 1/4-inch-thick strips. Place strips in shallow glass dish. Drizzle with salad dressing and lemon juice. Cover and refrigerate at least 4 hours. Drain beef strips; reserve marinade. Thread beef, onions and tomatoes alternately on 6 skewers. Brush with marinade. Grill kabobs, on uncovered grill, over medium-hot **MATCH LIGHT® Charcoal Briquets** 7 to 10 minutes, turning and basting often, until beef is cooked to desired doneness.
Makes 6 servings.

Standing Rib Roast with Madeira Sauce

2 large cloves garlic, finely chopped
1 teaspoon marjoram leaves (optional)
1 teaspoon thyme leaves
1 teaspoon salt
1/4 teaspoon pepper
5-pound standing rib roast (about 3 ribs)
1/4 cup butter or margarine
2 cups thinly sliced mushrooms
1/4 cup Madeira or dry red wine
1 tablespoon tomato paste
1 envelope LIPTON® Onion, Onion-Mushroom or Beefy Mushroom Recipe Soup Mix
1 tablespoon all-purpose flour
1 1/2 cups water
1 tablespoon finely chopped parsley
Pepper to taste

Preheat oven to 500°. In small bowl, combine garlic, marjoram, thyme, salt and pepper; set aside.

Trim fat from roast. In roasting pan, on rack, place roast; rub with garlic mixture. Roast 10 minutes, then decrease heat to 350° and continue roasting 1 1/2 hours or until meat thermometer reaches 130° (rare) or 150° (medium).

Remove roast to serving platter and keep warm. Skim fat from pan drippings. In medium saucepan, combine pan juices with butter; stir in mushrooms. Cook 5 minutes or until mushrooms are tender. Stir in wine and tomato paste, then onion recipe soup mix and flour blended with water. Bring to a boil, then simmer, stirring frequently, 5 minutes or until sauce is thickened. Stir in parsley and pepper. Serve sauce with roast.
Makes about 6 servings.

Souper Pot Roast

2 tablespoons all-purpose flour
2 1/2- to 3-pound beef chuck roast
1 can (10 3/4 ounces) CAMPBELL'S® Condensed Cream of Mushroom Soup
1 bay leaf
4 carrots, peeled and cut into 2-inch lengths
2 large potatoes, cut into quarters

To Microwave:
1. Place flour in 3-quart microwave-safe casserole. Add roast, turning to coat with flour on all sides; discard excess flour. Spread soup over meat; add bay leaf. Cover with lid; microwave on HIGH 20 minutes.
2. Turn roast over, spooning soup over roast. Reduce power to 50%. Cover; microwave 20 minutes.
3. Add carrots and potatoes to casserole. Cover; microwave at 50% power 40 minutes or until meat and vegetables are tender, rotating dish once during cooking. Let stand, covered, 10 minutes. Remove bay leaf.
Makes 6 servings.

Note: The shape of a pot roast can make a big difference in the time needed for cooking it (this is also true for conventional cooking methods). Choose a flatter roast for quicker, more even cooking; a cube-shaped roast will require more time.

Old-Fashioned Pot Roast

3- to 3 1/2-pound boneless pot roast (rump, chuck or round)
1 envelope LIPTON® Onion, Beefy Onion, Beefy Mushroom or Onion-Mushroom Recipe Soup Mix
2 1/4 cups water

In Dutch oven, brown roast over medium heat. Add onion recipe soup mix blended with water. Simmer covered, turning occasionally, 2 1/2 hours or until tender. If desired, thicken gravy.
Makes about 6 servings.

Try some of these delicious international variations!

French-Style Pot Roast: Decrease water to 1 1/4 cups. Add 1 cup dry red wine and 1 teaspoon thyme leaves.

German-Style Pot Roast: Decrease water to 3/4 cup. Add 1 1/2 cups beer, 1 teaspoon brown sugar and 1/2 teaspoon caraway seeds.

Italian-Style Pot Roast: Decrease water to 1 cup. Add 1 can (14 1/2 ounces) whole peeled tomatoes, undrained and chopped, 1 teaspoon basil leaves and 1 bay leaf. (Remove bay leaf before serving.)

Microwave Directions: Decrease water to 1 1/4 cups. In 3-quart casserole, blend onion recipe soup mix with water and heat at HIGH (Full Power) 5 minutes. Add roast and heat uncovered 10 minutes, turning once. Heat covered at DEFROST (30% Full Power), turning occasionally, 50 minutes or until tender. Let stand covered 10 minutes.

Islander's Beef Barbecue

1 boneless beef chuck roast (3 to 3 1/2 pounds)
3/4 cup apricot-pineapple jam
2 tablespoons soy sauce
1 teaspoon ground ginger
1 teaspoon grated lemon peel

Slice roast across grain into 1/4-inch-thick slices. In bowl, combine remaining ingredients. Grill beef slices, on uncovered grill, over medium-hot KINGSFORD® Charcoal Briquets 8 to 10 minutes. Turn and baste often with jam mixture.
Makes 4 to 6 servings.

Pot Roast with Zucchini Sauce

1 (3- to 4-pound) beef rump
   roast
2 cloves garlic, crushed
2 tablespoons BLUE BONNET®
   Margarine
1 (46-fluid ounce) can COLLEGE
   INN® Beef Broth
1 (6-ounce) can tomato paste
1 teaspoon Italian seasoning
3 small zucchini, sliced
1 (12-ounce) package spiral
   macaroni

In large heavy pot, over medium-high heat, brown beef and cook garlic in margarine. Stir in 1 cup beef broth, tomato paste and Italian seasoning. Heat to a boil; reduce heat. Cover; simmer 2½ hours or until meat is tender. Add zucchini; cover and cook 10 minutes. During last 15 minutes cooking time, cook macaroni in remaining broth according to package directions omitting salt; drain. Serve zucchini sauce over sliced meat and macaroni.
Makes 6 to 8 servings.

Eight Flavors Pot Roast

1 can (20 ounces) DOLE®
   Pineapple Chunks
2½ pounds boneless beef chuck
1 tablespoon vegetable oil
1 small yellow onion, chopped
2 cloves garlic, pressed
1½ cups water
½ cup soy sauce
¼ cup dry sherry
2½ tablespoons brown sugar
2 cinnamon sticks
1 tablespoon minced fresh
   ginger root
1 teaspoon allspice
1 head Chinese cabbage, cut
   into quarters*
4 teaspoons cornstarch
2 tablespoons water

Drain pineapple; reserve juice. Trim excess fat from beef. Heat large pot until hot. Add oil, swirling to coat sides. Cook onion and garlic in hot oil, stirring, 1 minute. Add beef; brown 2 minutes on each side.

In medium bowl, combine reserved pineapple juice, 1½ cups water, soy sauce, sherry, sugar, cinnamon, ginger and allspice; pour over beef. Bring to boil; reduce heat and simmer, covered, turning meat occasionally, 1¼ hours. Add cabbage; cook 30 minutes longer, adding pineapple last 5 minutes.

Remove meat, cabbage and pineapple from pot. Slice meat and arrange on serving platter with cabbage and pineapple. Strain remaining broth. Pour 1 cup into saucepan. Dissolve cornstarch in 2 tablespoons water; add to broth. Cook, stirring, until sauce boils and thickens. Pour over beef to serve.
Makes 6 servings.
*Or use green cabbage (about 2 pounds).

Chuckwagon Roast and Vegetables

1 (3-pound) boneless beef chuck
   roast
3 tablespoons vegetable oil
3 tablespoons flour
1 cup BORDEN® or MEADOW
   GOLD® Buttermilk
1 cup water
4 teaspoons WYLER'S® or
   STEERO® Beef-Flavor
   Instant Bouillon *or* 4 Beef-
   Flavor Bouillon Cubes
½ teaspoon thyme leaves
¼ teaspoon pepper
4 medium carrots, cut into 1-
   inch pieces
2 medium onions, cut into
   wedges
1 (10-ounce) package frozen
   broccoli spears, thawed and
   cut into pieces
1 (10-ounce) package frozen
   cauliflower, thawed

Preheat oven to 350°. In large skillet, brown roast in oil. Place in 3-quart roasting or baking pan. Add flour to drippings in skillet; cook and stir until browned. Add buttermilk, water, bouillon, thyme and pepper. Cook and stir until bouillon dissolves and mixture thickens slightly, about 10 minutes. Place carrots and onions around meat; spoon sauce over meat. Cover; bake 1 hour and 45 minutes or until meat is tender. Add remaining vegetables; bake 10 minutes longer or until tender. Refrigerate leftovers.
Makes 6 to 8 servings.

German Beef Roulade

1½ pounds flank steak
4 teaspoons GREY POUPON®
   Dijon Mustard
6 slices bacon, diced
¾ cup chopped onion
⅓ cup chopped dill pickle
¼ cup all-purpose flour
1 (13¾-fluid ounce) can
   COLLEGE INN® Beef Broth

With meat mallet or rolling pin, flatten meat to approximately a 10×8-inch rectangle. Spread mustard over meat.

In large skillet, over medium-high heat, cook bacon and onion until bacon is crisp; pour off fat, reserving ¼ cup. Spread bacon mixture over meat; sprinkle with pickle. Roll up meat from short end; secure with string.

In large skillet, over medium-high heat, brown beef roll in reserved fat; place in 13×9×2-inch baking dish. Stir flour into fat in skillet until smooth; gradually stir in beef broth. Cook and stir over medium heat until thickened. Pour sauce over beef roll. Cover; bake at 325°F for 1½ hours or until done. Let stand 10 minutes before slicing. Skim fat from sauce; strain and serve with meat.
Makes 6 servings.

Steak with Hearty Mustard Marinade

½ cup Dijon-style mustard
3 tablespoons soy sauce
3 tablespoons dry sherry wine
2 tablespoons brown sugar
1 tablespoon vegetable oil
1 clove garlic, minced
½ teaspoon TABASCO® pepper sauce
2 pounds round steak, 1½ inches thick

In medium bowl combine mustard, soy sauce, wine, sugar, oil, garlic and Tabasco® sauce; mix well. Place steak in large shallow dish or plastic bag; add marinade. Cover; refrigerate at least 5 hours; turn meat occasionally.

Remove meat from marinade; place on grill about 5 inches from source of heat. Brush with marinade. Grill 15 minutes; turn meat and brush with marinade. Grill 10 minutes longer or until desired doneness.
Makes 8 servings.

Grilled Tenderloin with Cognac

1 beef tenderloin roast (2 pounds)
¼ cup whole green, white or black peppercorns
Garlic Mushrooms (recipe follows)
⅓ cup cognac or other brandy
1 cup whipping cream
2 tablespoons Dijon-style mustard
1 tablespoon Worcestershire sauce
2 teaspoons lemon juice

Trim excess fat from roast. Crack peppercorns coarsely with mortar and pestle; sprinkle on roast and press into surface.

In grill, arrange medium-hot **KINGSFORD® Charcoal Briquets** around drip pan. Place roast over drip pan. Cover grill and cook, turning once, until meat thermometer registers 140°F for rare (about 45 minutes), 150°F for medium-rare (about 55 minutes), or 170°F for well-done (about 60 minutes). While roast is cooking, prepare Garlic Mushrooms. About 15 minutes before meat is done, place mushrooms next to meat.

When roast is grilled to desired doneness, warm cognac in skillet on range-top. Remove from heat. Place roast in heated skillet. Carefully ignite cognac with match; allow flames to subside, carefully spooning cognac over meat. Remove roast to serving platter; reserve juices.

In saucepan, combine cream, mustard and Worcestershire sauce. Bring to boil. Cook and stir, over medium-low heat, 3 minutes or until slightly thickened. Remove from heat; stir in lemon juice and reserved cognac juices. Carve roast and arrange with Garlic Mushrooms. Pour cream sauce over sliced roast and mushrooms.
Makes 8 servings.

Garlic Mushrooms

32 large fresh mushrooms
½ cup olive or vegetable oil
2 cloves garlic, minced

Remove stems from mushrooms; reserve caps. In bowl, combine oil and garlic; add mushroom caps. Gently toss to coat. Remove mushrooms with slotted spoon; place mushroom caps on piece of heavy-duty foil. Seal edges tightly. Grill at side of roast over medium-hot **KINGSFORD® Charcoal Briquets** 10 to 15 minutes or until tender.
Makes 8 servings.

Peppery Rib Steaks

⅓ cup lemon juice
2 tablespoons vegetable oil
1 clove garlic, crushed
1 teaspoon chili powder
1 teaspoon seasoned salt
½ teaspoon seasoned or cracked pepper
4 beef rib eye steaks, cut ¾ to 1 inch thick (about 6 ounces each)

In shallow glass dish, combine all ingredients except steaks. Add steaks; turn to coat with marinade. Cover and refrigerate at least 2 hours or overnight. Drain steaks; reserve marinade. Grill steaks, on uncovered grill, over medium-hot **MATCH LIGHT® Charcoal Briquets** about 15 minutes or until cooked, turning and basting often with marinade.
Makes 4 servings.

California-Style Steak

1 beef sirloin steak, cut 1 to 1½ inches thin (2 pounds)
½ teaspoon olive or vegetable oil
1 teaspoon Beau Monde seasoning
½ teaspoon dried orange peel
½ teaspoon dried lemon peel
1 teaspoon pepper
1½ teaspoons seasoned salt

Rub both sides of steak with oil. Rub Beau Monde, orange and lemon peels, pepper and seasoned salt thoroughly into both sides of steak. Grill steak, on uncovered grill, over medium-hot **MATCH LIGHT® Charcoal Briquets** 4 minutes on each side or to desired doneness.
Makes 4 to 6 servings.

Pepper-Stuffed Flank Steak

2 beef flank steaks (about 1 pound each)
1¼ teaspoons garlic powder
¼ teaspoon black pepper
1 green pepper, cut into strips
1 red pepper, cut into strips
1 onion, cut into thin slices
1 can (15 ounces) tomato sauce
½ cup finely chopped onion
¼ cup soy sauce
1 tablespoon sugar
1 teaspoon dry mustard
⅛ teaspoon cayenne pepper
¼ cup vegetable oil

With meat mallet, pound each steak to ¼-inch thickness. Sprinkle steaks with ¼ teaspoon of the garlic powder and the pepper. Arrange green and red pepper strips horizontally on steaks. Cover with onion slices. Starting at narrow end of each steak, roll up jelly-roll fashion; tie with kitchen twine. Set aside. In large jar with screw-top lid, combine remaining ingredients except oil. Shake to blend. Brush outsides of beef rolls with oil. Lightly oil grid. Grill steaks, on covered grill, over hot **KINGSFORD® Charcoal Briquets** about 30 minutes, turning often, until done. Brush steaks with tomato-soy mixture during last 10 minutes of grilling.
Makes 6 to 8 servings.

Grilled Flank Steak Sangrita

1 beef flank steak (2½ to 3 pounds)
1 teaspoon salt
¼ teaspoon pepper
1 teaspoon dried thyme, crushed
¼ cup orange juice concentrate, thawed and undiluted
3 tablespoons vegetable oil
Fruity Wine Sauce (recipe follows)

Lightly score steak and rub with salt, pepper and thyme. In shallow glass dish, combine orange juice concentrate and oil. Add steak; turn to coat with marinade. Cover and refrigerate at least 30 minutes. Drain meat; reserve marinade. Grill steak, on covered grill, over medium-hot **KINGSFORD® Charcoal Briquets** 8 to 10 minutes on each side, turning once and basting often with marinade, until done. Cut meat across grain into diagonal slices. Serve with Fruity Wine Sauce.
Makes 6 servings.

Fruity Wine Sauce

1½ cups red wine
1 orange, thinly sliced
1 lime, thinly sliced
1 apple, thinly sliced
¾ cup chopped green onion with tops
½ cup butter or margarine
2 tablespoons chopped parsley

In small saucepan, combine red wine, fruit and green onion; bring to boil. Stir in butter and parsley; cook and stir until butter is melted and sauce is hot.
Makes about 2 cups.

Mongolian Beef

¾ pound boneless tender beef steak (sirloin, rib eye or top loin)
3 tablespoons cornstarch, divided
4 tablespoons KIKKOMAN Teriyaki Sauce, divided
1 tablespoon dry sherry
1 clove garlic, minced
1 cup water
1 teaspoon distilled white vinegar
¼ to ½ teaspoon crushed red pepper
2 tablespoons vegetable oil, divided
2 carrots, cut diagonally into thin slices
1 onion, chunked and separated
1 green pepper, chunked

Cut beef across grain into strips, then into 1½-inch squares. Combine 2 tablespoons cornstarch, 1 tablespoon teriyaki sauce, sherry and garlic in medium bowl; stir in beef. Let stand 30 minutes. Meanwhile, combine water, remaining 1 tablespoon cornstarch, 3 tablespoons teriyaki sauce, vinegar and red pepper; set aside. Heat 1 tablespoon oil in hot wok or large skillet over high heat. Add beef and stir-fry 1 minute; remove. Heat remaining 1 tablespoon oil in same pan. Add carrots, onion and green pepper; stir-fry 4 minutes. Add beef and teriyaki sauce mixture; cook and stir until sauce boils and thickens.
Makes 4 servings.

Stuffed Flank Steak

1 (1½-pound) flank steak, pounded
2 cups herb-seasoned stuffing mix
2 teaspoons WYLER'S® or STEERO® Beef-Flavor Instant Bouillon or 2 Beef-Flavor Bouillon Cubes
Flour
3 tablespoons vegetable oil
1 cup chopped onion
1 clove garlic, chopped
2 (10¾-ounce) cans condensed tomato soup
½ teaspoon basil leaves
Hot cooked noodles
Parsley

Preheat oven to 350°. Prepare stuffing mix according to package directions, dissolving bouillon in liquid. Spread stuffing evenly on top of steak to within 1 inch of edges. Roll up, tucking in ends; tie with string. Coat roll with flour. In large skillet, brown in oil. Place in shallow baking dish. In same skillet, cook onion and garlic until tender. Add soup and basil; cook and stir until smooth. Pour over meat. Cover; bake 1 hour, basting occasionally. Serve with noodles; garnish with parsley. Refrigerate leftovers.
Makes 6 servings.

Flank Steak Bearnaise

1 8-ounce package
  PHILADELPHIA BRAND
  Cream Cheese, cubed
¼ cup milk
1 tablespoon green onion slices
½ teaspoon dried tarragon
  leaves, crushed
2 egg yolks, beaten
2 tablespoons dry white wine
1 tablespoon lemon juice
1 1½-pound beef flank steak

In saucepan, combine cream cheese, milk, green onions and tarragon; stir over low heat until cream cheese is melted. Stir small amount of hot cream cheese mixture into egg yolks; return to hot mixture. Stir in wine and juice. Cook, stirring constantly, over low heat 1 minute or until thickened. Score steak on both sides. Place on rack of broiler pan. Broil on both sides to desired doneness. With knife slanted, carve steak across grain into thin slices. Serve with cream cheese mixture.
6 servings.

Stir-Fried Beef and Vegetables

½ pound boneless beef sirloin
  steak
1 can (10½ ounces)
  CAMPBELL'S® Condensed
  Beef Broth (Bouillon)
1 tablespoon cornstarch
1 tablespoon soy sauce
3 tablespoons vegetable oil
1 clove garlic, minced
4 green onions, cut into 1-inch
  pieces
1 cup fresh or frozen cut
  broccoli
1 can (8 ounces) sliced bamboo
  shoots, drained
Shredded lettuce

1. Freeze steak 1 hour to make slicing easier. Trim and discard excess fat from steak. Cut steak into very thin slices; set aside.
2. In small bowl, combine soup, cornstarch and soy sauce; stir to blend. Set aside.
3. In 10-inch skillet or wok over medium-high heat, in 2 tablespoons hot oil, stir-fry beef strips and garlic until meat is browned; remove from skillet.
4. Add remaining 1 tablespoon oil to skillet. Add green onions and broccoli; stir-fry 1 minute. Add bamboo shoots; stir-fry 30 seconds more.
5. Return beef to skillet. Stir soup mixture; stir into skillet. Heat to boiling; cook 1 minute more. Spoon over shredded lettuce.
Makes about 2½ cups or 2 servings.

Savory Steak

1½ cups V8® Vegetable Juice
¼ cup Burgundy or other dry red
  wine
2 large cloves garlic, minced
¼ teaspoon coarsely ground
  pepper
2 pounds top round steak

1. To make marinade: In 12- by 8-inch baking dish, stir together V8 juice, wine, garlic and pepper. Add steak to marinade, turning to coat. Cover; refrigerate at least 4 hours, turning steak occasionally.
2. Remove steak from marinade, reserving marinade. Place steak on grill or on rack in broiler pan. Grill or broil steak 4 inches from heat 15 minutes on each side or until desired doneness, basting occasionally with marinade.
3. Meanwhile, in small saucepan over medium-high heat, heat remaining marinade to boiling. Serve with steak.
Makes 8 servings.

Per serving: 166 calories, 27 g protein, 5 g fat, 3 g carbohydrate, 215 mg sodium, 65 mg cholesterol.

Vegetable-Stuffed Flank Steak

1 tablespoon olive or vegetable
  oil
1 cup chopped CAMPBELL'S
  FRESH® Mushrooms
1 package (10 ounces) frozen
  chopped spinach, thawed
  and drained
½ cup chopped onion
1 clove garlic, minced
1 cup shredded carrots
½ cup shredded Muenster or
  Swiss cheese (2 ounces)
½ teaspoon dried basil leaves,
  crushed
⅛ teaspoon pepper
1½ pounds beef flank steak,
  pounded to ¼-inch
  thickness
1 can (10¾ ounces)
  CAMPBELL'S® Condensed
  Cream of Mushroom Soup
2 tablespoons dry sherry

To Microwave:
1. In 1½-quart microwave-safe casserole, combine oil, mushrooms, spinach, onion and garlic. Cover with lid; microwave on HIGH 5 minutes or until vegetables are tender, stirring once during cooking. Drain. Stir in carrots, cheese, basil and pepper; mix well.
2. Spread vegetable mixture over steak to within 1 inch of edges. Roll up from long end, jelly-roll fashion, tucking ends of steak into roll. Secure with wooden toothpicks or tie with cotton string. Place rolls, seam side down, in 12- by 8-inch microwave-safe baking dish.
3. In small bowl, stir soup until smooth; stir in sherry. Pour over meat. Cover with vented plastic wrap; microwave on HIGH 10 minutes, rotating dish once during cooking.
4. Spoon pan juices over meat. Reduce power to 50%. Cover; microwave 20 minutes or until meat is tender, rotating dish twice during cooking. Let stand, covered, 10 minutes.
Makes 6 servings.

Beer Marinated Steak

1 large onion, thinly sliced
2 cloves garlic, finely chopped
1/2 cup vegetable oil
1 cup beer
1/2 cup REALEMON® Lemon Juice from Concentrate
2 tablespoons light brown sugar
1 tablespoon Worcestershire sauce
1 (1- to 1½-pound) flank steak, scored

In medium skillet, cook onion and garlic in ¼ cup oil until tender; remove from heat. Add remaining ingredients except meat. Place meat in shallow baking dish; pour beer marinade over. Cover; refrigerate 6 hours or overnight, turning occasionally. Remove meat from marinade; grill or broil as desired, basting frequently with marinade. Refrigerate leftovers.
Makes 4 to 6 servings.

Grilled Steak with Mushroom-Wine Sauce

4 beef loin T-bone, porterhouse or filet mignon steaks, cut 1 inch thick (8 ounces each)
3 tablespoons butter or margarine
1/2 pound mushrooms, sliced (about 2 cups)
1/4 cup white wine
2 tablespoons minced parsley
1/2 teaspoon dried tarragon, crushed
1 teaspoon instant beef bouillon granules

Slash any fat around edge of steaks every 4 inches. Lightly oil grid. Grill steaks on covered grill, over medium-hot **KINGSFORD® with Mesquite Charcoal Briquets** 8 to 10 minutes on each side for medium-rare, or to desired doneness. While steak is grilling, heat butter in large skillet until hot. Add mushrooms and saute 1 minute or until tender. Add wine, parsley, tarragon and beef bouillon granules; simmer 4 minutes, stirring often. Serve sauce over steak.
Makes 4 servings.

Liver and Onions

1/2 cup all-purpose flour
1 teaspoon ground sage
3/4 teaspoon salt
1/2 teaspoon paprika
1/8 teaspoon cayenne
1 pound beef liver, membrane removed, cut into 4×1×1/4-inch strips
1/4 cup CRISCO® Oil
1 large onion, thinly sliced and separated into rings
1/8 teaspoon instant minced garlic
2 tablespoons snipped fresh parsley
1/4 cup dry white wine or chicken broth
1 tablespoon lemon juice

Mix flour, sage, salt, paprika and cayenne in large plastic food storage bag. Add liver. Shake to coat. Remove liver from bag; set aside.

Heat Crisco® Oil in medium skillet. Add onion and garlic. Sauté over moderate heat until onion is tender. Push to one side of skillet. Add liver. Fry 6 to 8 minutes, or until no longer pink, turning over 1 or 2 times.

Stir together liver and onion. Sprinkle with parsley. Add wine and lemon juice. Cook, stirring constantly, 1 or 2 minutes longer.
4 servings.

Smothered Liver and Onions

2 tablespoons butter or margarine
1 large onion, thinly sliced
1 pound beef liver, 1/4 inch thick
1 can (10³/4 ounces) CAMPBELL'S® Condensed Cream of Mushroom Soup
1/4 cup milk or half-and-half
1/8 teaspoon pepper

To Microwave:
1. In 12- by 8-inch microwave-safe baking dish, combine butter and onion. Cover with vented plastic wrap; microwave on HIGH 5 minutes or until onion is tender, stirring once during cooking.
2. Cut liver into 4 portions. Arrange liver over onions, placing thicker portions toward edges of dish. In small bowl, stir soup until smooth; stir in milk and pepper. Pour over liver. Cover; microwave on HIGH 10 minutes or until liver is no longer pink in center, rearranging liver twice during cooking. Let stand, covered, 5 minutes before serving.
Makes 4 servings.

Marinated Steak

1/2 cup WISH-BONE® Italian or Robusto Italian Dressing
1 (2-pound) flank, London broil, sirloin or chuck steak

In large shallow baking dish, pour Italian dressing over steak. Cover and marinate in refrigerator, turning occasionally, at least 4 hours. Remove steak, reserving marinade.

Grill or broil steak, basting frequently with reserved marinade, until done.
Makes about 8 servings.

Marinated Flank Steak

1 envelope LIPTON® Onion or
    Onion-Mushroom Recipe
    Soup Mix
1/2 cup water
1/2 cup dry red wine
1/4 cup olive or vegetable oil
1 tablespoon finely chopped
    parsley
1 teaspoon oregano
1/8 teaspoon pepper
2-pound beef flank steak

In large shallow baking dish, thoroughly blend all ingredients except steak; add steak and turn to coat. Cover and marinate in refrigerator, turning steak and piercing with fork occasionally, at least 4 hours. Remove steak, reserving marinade.

Grill or broil steak, turning once, until done. Meanwhile, in small saucepan, bring remaining marinade to a boil, then simmer 5 minutes. If necessary, skim fat from marinade. Serve hot marinade with steak.
Makes about 8 servings.

Sirloin Steak Monte Carlo

1 3/4 pounds top sirloin steak
2 tablespoons olive oil
1/2 cup sliced onion
1 crushed large garlic clove
1/4 cup pine nuts
1 3/4 cups (14 1/2-ounce can)
    CONTADINA® Whole Peeled
    Tomatoes and juice
2 tablespoons rinsed capers
1/2 teaspoon dried oregano leaves
1/2 teaspoon dried basil leaves
1/4 teaspoon red pepper flakes

Saute steak in olive oil in 10-inch skillet over high heat, 3 to 4 minutes on each side for rare, 4 to 5 minutes on each side for medium rare. Remove to platter; keep warm. Saute onion, garlic, and pine nuts in pan drippings. Cut up tomatoes. Add tomatoes and juice with remaining ingredients; simmer 5 minutes. Serve over steak. *Makes 6 servings.*

Nutrients per serving: 280 calories; 30 g protein; 90 mg cholesterol; 7 g carbohydrate; 15 g fat; 280 mg sodium.

Steak with Mushroom and Wine Sauce

4 tenderloin, sirloin, T-bone or
    minute steaks (about
    1 pound)
1/4 cup WISH-BONE® Italian
    Dressing
2 tablespoons butter or
    margarine
2 cups thinly sliced mushrooms
1 medium red pepper, chopped
1/4 cup finely chopped shallots or
    onions
1/2 cup dry red wine
2 tablespoons finely chopped
    parsley
1/8 teaspoon pepper

Broil or pan-fry steaks until done; keep warm.

Meanwhile, in large skillet, heat Italian dressing with butter and cook mushrooms, red pepper and shallots over medium heat, stirring occasionally, 5 minutes or until tender. Add remaining ingredients and cook 2 minutes or until liquid is partially absorbed. Serve over steaks.
Makes about 4 servings.
Note: Also terrific with Wish-Bone® Robusto Italian, Blended Italian, Lite Italian or Italian & Cheese Dressing.

Burgundy Beef Stroganoff

2 pounds round steak, cut into
    1/4-inch strips
2 tablespoons BLUE BONNET®
    Margarine
4 medium onions, sliced (about
    3 cups)
1/4 cup all-purpose flour
1 cup COLLEGE INN® Beef Broth
1/2 cup Burgundy or other dry red
    wine
3 tablespoons tomato paste
1/2 teaspoon ground thyme
3/4 cup dairy sour cream
    Hot buttered noodles

In large skillet, over medium heat, brown meat in margarine. Stir in onions and cook for 3 minutes; remove from heat. Sprinkle flour over meat and stir until well blended. Stir in beef broth, Burgundy, tomato paste and thyme until smooth. Cook and stir over medium heat until sauce is thickened and begins to boil. Cover; cook over low heat for 40 to 45 minutes or until tender. Stir sour cream into sauce. (Do not boil.) Serve over hot buttered noodles.
Makes 6 to 8 servings.
Microwave: In 3-quart microwave-proof bowl, place margarine. Microwave, uncovered, on HIGH (100% power) for 1 minute until margarine melts. Toss beef strips with flour; add to margarine. Microwave, uncovered, on HIGH for 6 to 7 minutes, stirring every 2 minutes. Add onions. Microwave, uncovered, on HIGH for 2 to 3 minutes.

Stir in broth, Burgundy, tomato paste and thyme. Cover with plastic wrap; vent. Microwave on HIGH 10 to 12 minutes until sauce is thickened and bubbling. Stir in sour cream. Microwave, uncovered, on HIGH for 1 minute. Let stand 5 minutes before serving. Serve over noodles.

Sauerbraten

1 cup cider vinegar
½ cup dry red wine or beef broth
½ cup water
2 medium onions, thinly sliced
1 carrot, sliced
1 stalk celery, chopped
1 tablespoon salt
12 whole peppercorns
4 whole cloves
2 whole allspice
4-pound boneless beef rump roast
4 tablespoons all-purpose flour, divided
¼ cup CRISCO® Oil
⅓ cup cold water
1 tablespoon sugar
½ cup crushed gingersnap cookies

Mix vinegar, wine, ½ cup water, onions, carrot, celery, salt, peppercorns, cloves and allspice in large bowl or large plastic food storage bag. Add roast. Cover bowl or seal bag. Refrigerate 2 to 3 days, turning roast over each day.

Remove roast from marinade, reserving marinade. Pat roast dry with paper towels. Coat with 2 tablespoons flour. Heat Crisco® Oil in Dutch oven. Add roast. Brown over medium-high heat. Pour reserved marinade over roast. Cover. Reduce heat. Simmer 2½ to 3 hours, or until meat is tender, turning roast over after half the time. Transfer roast to serving platter, reserving liquid and vegetables in Dutch oven.

Strain vegetables and liquid through wire sieve into large bowl, pressing vegetables to remove liquid. Discard vegetables. Skim and discard fat from liquid. Pour 3 cups liquid into saucepan. Discard remaining liquid. Heat liquid to boiling. Meanwhile, place ⅓ cup cold water in small bowl. Blend in sugar and remaining 2 tablespoons flour. Add to boiling liquid. Cook, stirring constantly, until mixture is thickened. Stir in gingersnaps. Cook 1 to 2 minutes longer, or until heated through. Serve with roast.
8 to 10 servings.

Beef Goulash

¼ cup vegetable oil, divided
2 pounds boneless rump or chuck, cut into 1-inch cubes
3 medium onions, sliced
2 cloves garlic, minced
1 can (16 ounces) tomatoes, undrained, cut into pieces
4 teaspoons paprika
2 beef bouillon cubes
1 teaspoon dried marjoram leaves
1 teaspoon dried thyme leaves
¼ teaspoon TABASCO® pepper sauce
1 bay leaf

In large heavy saucepot or Dutch oven heat 2 tablespoons oil; brown meat in 2 batches. Remove; reserve. In same pot heat remaining 2 tablespoons oil; cook onions and garlic 5 minutes or until lightly browned. Stir in tomatoes, paprika, bouillon cubes, marjoram, thyme, Tabasco® sauce and bay leaf. Return meat to pot. Cover; simmer 1½ to 2 hours or until meat is tender; stir occasionally. Remove bay leaf. Serve over noodles, spaetzle, mashed potatoes or rice.
Makes 8 servings.

Beef Stew

2 pounds beef for stew, cut into 1-inch cubes
¼ cup all-purpose flour
4 tablespoons vegetable oil
2 medium onions, sliced
2 cloves garlic, minced
1 teaspoon dried thyme leaves, crushed
1 bay leaf
1 can (10¾ ounces) CAMPBELL'S® Condensed Beefy Mushroom Soup
½ cup water
3 medium potatoes, peeled and cubed
2 medium carrots, cut into 2- by ½-inch strips
1 cup fresh or frozen cut green beans

1. Coat beef cubes with flour; reserve remaining flour.
2. In 4-quart Dutch oven over medium-high heat, in 2 tablespoons hot oil, cook beef, a few pieces at a time, until browned on all sides. Remove beef as it browns. Reduce heat to medium.
3. Add remaining 2 tablespoons oil to skillet. In hot oil, cook onions, garlic, thyme and bay leaf until onions are tender, stirring occasionally. Stir in reserved flour. Gradually add soup and water; heat to boiling. Return meat to pan. Reduce heat to low. Cover; simmer 1 hour, stirring occasionally.
4. Add potatoes, carrots and green beans. Cover; simmer 25 minutes or until vegetables are tender. Discard bay leaf.
Makes about 6 cups or 8 servings.

Beef Stroganoff

1 pound boneless beef sirloin steak
½ cup chopped onion
1 can (10¾ ounces) CAMPBELL'S® Condensed Cream of Mushroom Soup
½ cup sour cream
½ teaspoon paprika
Hot cooked noodles

To Microwave:
1. Freeze steak 1 hour to make slicing easier. Cut steak into very thin slices across the grain.
2. In 2-quart microwave-safe casserole, combine beef and onion. Cover with lid; microwave on HIGH 5 minutes or until beef is no longer pink, stirring once during cooking.
3. In small bowl, stir soup until smooth; stir in sour cream and paprika. Add to beef, stirring to coat. Cover; microwave at 50% power 3 minutes or until heated through. Serve over noodles.
Makes about 3½ cups or 4 servings.

Oven-Baked Bourguignonne

2 pounds boneless beef chuck, cut into 1-inch cubes
¼ cup all-purpose flour
1⅓ cups sliced carrots
1 can (14½ ounces) whole peeled tomatoes, undrained and chopped
1 bay leaf
1 envelope LIPTON® Beefy Onion or Onion Recipe Soup Mix
½ cup dry red wine
1 cup fresh or canned sliced mushrooms
1 package (8 ounces) medium or broad egg noodles

Preheat oven to 400°.

In 2-quart casserole, toss beef with flour, then bake uncovered 20 minutes. Add carrots, tomatoes and bay leaf, then beefy onion recipe soup mix blended with wine. Bake covered 1½ hours or until beef is tender. Add mushrooms and bake covered an additional 10 minutes. Remove bay leaf.

Meanwhile, cook noodles according to package directions. To serve, arrange bourguignonne over noodles.
Makes about 8 servings.

Microwave Directions: Toss beef with flour; set aside. In 2-quart casserole, combine tomatoes, bay leaf and beefy onion recipe soup mix blended with wine. Heat covered at HIGH (Full Power) 7 minutes, stirring once. Add beef and carrots. Heat covered at DEFROST (30% Full Power), stirring occasionally, 1¼ hours. Add mushrooms and heat covered at DEFROST 30 minutes or until beef is tender. Remove bay leaf. Let stand covered 5 minutes. Cook noodles and serve as above.

Freezing/Reheating Directions: Bourguignonne can be baked, then frozen. Simply wrap covered casserole in heavy-duty aluminum foil; freeze. To reheat, unwrap and bake covered at 400°, stirring occasionally to separate beef and vegetables, 1 hour. **OR,** microwave at HIGH (Full Power), stirring occasionally, 20 minutes or until heated through. Let stand covered 5 minutes.

Mexican Beef Stew

2 tablespoons CRISCO® Oil
2 pounds beef stew meat, cut into 1-inch cubes
1 medium onion, chopped
1 clove garlic, minced
1 can (16 ounces) whole tomatoes, undrained, cut up
1 jar (4 ounces) pimiento, drained and mashed
½ to 1 teaspoon ground cumin
½ teaspoon salt
¼ teaspoon pepper

Heat Crisco® Oil in large skillet. Add beef. Brown over medium-high heat. Remove beef with slotted spoon; set aside. Add onion and garlic to skillet. Sauté over moderate heat until onion is tender. Stir in beef and remaining ingredients. Heat to boiling. Cover. Reduce heat. Simmer, stirring occasionally, about 2 hours, or until beef is tender. Add water during cooking, if necessary.
6 to 8 servings.

Szechuan Beef Stew

2 pounds boneless beef chuck
2 cloves garlic, pressed
4 tablespoons KIKKOMAN Soy Sauce, divided
3 teaspoons sugar, divided
1 cup water
½ to ¾ teaspoon crushed red pepper
¾ teaspoon fennel seed, crushed
¼ teaspoon black pepper
¼ teaspoon ground cloves
¼ teaspoon ground ginger
1 tablespoon vegetable oil
2 tablespoons cornstarch
2 tablespoons water

Cut beef into 2-inch cubes. Combine garlic, 2 tablespoons soy sauce and 1 teaspoon sugar in large bowl; stir in beef cubes until well coated. Let stand 15 minutes. Meanwhile, combine 1 cup water, remaining 2 tablespoons soy sauce, 2 teaspoons sugar, red pepper, fennel, black pepper, cloves and ginger; set aside. Heat oil in Dutch oven or large skillet over high heat. Brown beef on all sides in hot oil. Stir in soy sauce mixture. Bring to boil; reduce heat and simmer, covered, 2 hours, or until beef is very tender. Combine cornstarch with 2 tablespoons water; stir into beef mixture. Cook and stir until mixture boils and thickens, about 1 minute.
Makes 6 servings.

Stroganoff Superb

1 pound beef sirloin steak, cut into thin strips
3 tablespoons PARKAY Margarine
½ cup chopped onion
1 4-ounce can mushrooms, drained
½ teaspoon salt
¼ teaspoon dry mustard
¼ teaspoon pepper
1 8-ounce package PHILADELPHIA BRAND Cream Cheese, cubed
¾ cup milk
Hot parsleyed noodles

Brown steak in margarine in large skillet. Add onions, mushrooms and seasonings; cook until vegetables are tender. Add cream cheese and milk; stir over low heat until cream cheese is melted. Serve over noodles.
4 to 6 servings.

Beef Burgundy

½ cup all-purpose flour
¾ teaspoon salt
¼ teaspoon pepper
1½ pounds beef round steak, cut into 1-inch pieces
5 tablespoons CRISCO® Oil, divided
1½ cups water
1 cup Burgundy wine
1 medium onion, thinly sliced
½ cup snipped fresh parsley
2 cloves garlic, halved
2 bay leaves
1½ teaspoons instant beef bouillon granules
1 teaspoon dried thyme leaves
8 ounces fresh mushrooms, sliced
¼ cup sliced almonds
Hot cooked rice or noodles

Mix flour, salt and pepper in large plastic food storage bag. Add beef. Shake to coat. Heat 4 tablespoons Crisco® Oil in Dutch oven. Add beef and any remaining flour mixture. Brown over medium-high heat. Stir in water, wine, onion, parsley, garlic, bay leaves, bouillon granules and thyme. Heat to boiling. Cover. Reduce heat. Simmer 1½ to 2 hours, or until beef is tender, stirring occasionally. Stir in mushrooms; re-cover. Simmer 20 to 30 minutes longer, or until mushrooms are tender. Remove and discard garlic cloves and bay leaves.

Meanwhile, heat remaining 1 tablespoon Crisco® Oil in small skillet. Add almonds. Cook over moderate heat, stirring constantly, until almonds are lightly browned. Stir into beef mixture just before serving. Serve with rice or noodles.
4 to 6 servings.

Wine-Simmered Beef and Vegetables

1½ to 2 pounds beef round steak
6 tablespoons all-purpose flour, divided
½ teaspoon salt
¼ teaspoon pepper
3 tablespoons CRISCO® Oil
1 medium onion, thinly sliced and separated into rings
1 medium green pepper, cored, seeded and sliced into rings
⅔ cup julienne carrot strips
½ teaspoon dried basil leaves
½ teaspoon dried marjoram leaves
⅔ cup dry white wine
⅔ cup cold water
½ teaspoon instant beef bouillon granules

Trim bone and fat from beef. Pound trimmed beef with meat mallet. Cut into serving-size pieces. Set aside. Mix 4 tablespoons flour, salt and pepper in large plastic food storage bag. Add beef. Shake to coat.

Heat Crisco® Oil in large skillet. Add beef and any remaining flour mixture. Brown over medium-high heat. Layer onion, green pepper and carrots over beef. Sprinkle with basil and marjoram. Add wine. Heat to boiling. Cover. Reduce heat. Simmer about 1 hour, or until beef is tender. Transfer beef and vegetables to serving platter, reserving drippings in skillet.

Place cold water in 1-cup measure or small bowl. Blend in remaining 2 tablespoons flour. Stir flour mixture into drippings in skillet. Stir in bouillon granules. Cook over medium-high heat, stirring constantly, until thickened and bubbly. Serve with meat and vegetables.
4 to 6 servings.

Variation: Simmered Beef and Vegetables. Follow recipe above, substituting ⅔ cup water and ¾ teaspoon instant beef bouillon granules for wine.

Country French Beef Stew

2 pounds boneless beef, cut into 1-inch cubes
¼ cup all-purpose flour
2 slices bacon, cut into 1-inch pieces
3 tablespoons oil
¼ cup Cognac (optional)
1 envelope LIPTON® Onion, Beefy Onion, Onion-Mushroom or Beefy Mushroom Recipe Soup Mix
2 cups water
½ cup dry red wine
2 tablespoons Dijon-style prepared mustard
3 carrots, thinly sliced
½ pound mushrooms, halved
1 package (8 ounces) broad egg noodles

Lightly toss beef with flour; set aside.

In Dutch oven, cook bacon until crisp; remove. Reserve drippings. Heat oil with reserved drippings and brown beef, in three batches, over medium-high heat; remove beef and set aside. Into Dutch oven, add Cognac and cook 1 minute or until only a thin glaze of liquid remains. Stir in onion recipe soup mix blended with water, wine and mustard; bring to a boil. Add beef and bacon and simmer covered, stirring occasionally, 1½ hours or until beef is almost tender. Stir in carrots and simmer covered 25 minutes. Add mushrooms and simmer covered an additional 5 minutes or until beef and vegetables are tender.

Meanwhile, cook noodles according to package directions. To serve, arrange stew over noodles. Garnish, if desired, with chopped parsley.
Makes about 8 servings.

Beef Stew with Dumplings

4 pounds lean boneless beef
   chuck, cut into 2-inch cubes
¼ cup plus 2 tablespoons
   FILIPPO BERIO Olive Oil,
   divided
2½ teaspoons salt, divided
¼ teaspoon pepper
3 cups dry red wine
2 cups water
2 tablespoons tomato paste
1 large clove garlic, minced
½ teaspoon dried thyme,
   crushed
12 small white onions
4 carrots, cut into quarters
4 ribs celery, cut into 2-inch
   pieces
3 white turnips, cut into
   quarters
¼ pound small mushrooms
¼ cup chopped parsley
1 cup all-purpose flour
2 teaspoons baking powder
½ teaspoon sugar
1 egg, well beaten
½ cup milk

Brown beef in ¼ cup of the oil in Dutch oven over medium-high heat. Season with 2 teaspoons of the salt and the pepper. Add wine, water, tomato paste, garlic and thyme. Bring to a boil over high heat. Reduce heat to low. Cover and simmer 1 hour, stirring occasionally. Add onions, carrots, celery, turnips, mushrooms and parsley. Simmer, covered, 20 minutes more.*

Meanwhile, prepare dumplings. Combine flour, baking powder, remaining ½ teaspoon salt and the sugar in small bowl. Add egg, milk and remaining 2 tablespoons oil. Stir to blend. Drop dumplings by tablespoonfuls onto hot stew. Cook, uncovered, 10 minutes.
Makes 8 servings.

*If stew is too thin, thicken sauce before cooking dumplings. To thicken, blend 3 tablespoons all-purpose flour and ½ cup water in small bowl until smooth. Gradually stir mixture into stew. Continue cooking until thickened and smooth, stirring constantly.

Classic Chinese Pepper Steak

1 pound boneless beef sirloin
   steak
1 tablespoon KIKKOMAN Stir-Fry
   Sauce
2 tablespoons vegetable oil,
   divided
2 medium-size green, red or
   yellow bell peppers, cut into
   1-inch squares
2 medium onions, cut into 1-inch
   squares
¼ cup KIKKOMAN Stir-Fry Sauce
   Hot cooked rice (optional)

Cut beef across grain into thin strips, then into 1-inch squares; coat with 1 tablespoon stir-fry sauce. Heat 1 tablespoon oil in hot wok or large skillet over high heat. Add beef and stir-fry 1 minute; remove. Heat remaining 1 tablespoon oil in same pan. Add peppers and onions; stir-fry 5 minutes. Stir in beef and ¼ cup stir-fry sauce; cook and stir just until beef and vegetables are coated with sauce. Serve immediately with rice.
Makes 4 servings.

Orange-Flavor Grilled Beef

1 orange
3 tablespoons soy sauce
2 tablespoons brown sugar
2 tablespoons cider vinegar
½ teaspoon pepper
½ teaspoon chili powder
1 clove garlic, minced
1 teaspoon grated fresh ginger
2 pounds beef round tip roast,
   cut into 3-inch cubes

Grate peel from orange to equal 1 tablespoon. Squeeze juice from orange into large bowl. Stir in remaining ingredients except beef. Add beef cubes; toss to coat with marinade. Cover and refrigerate 8 hours or overnight. Drain meat cubes; reserve marinade. Grill beef cubes, on covered grill, over medium-hot KINGSFORD® Charcoal Briquets 3 minutes. Turn beef cubes, brush with marinade and cook 5 minutes longer or until done.
Makes 4 servings.

Beef Ragoût

1 tablespoon butter or
   margarine
½ cup chopped onion
1 large clove garlic, minced
1 pound beef for stew, cut into
   1-inch pieces
1 cup thinly sliced carrots
1 can (10¼ ounces) FRANCO-
   AMERICAN® Beef Gravy
¼ cup Burgundy or other dry red
   wine
¼ cup tomato paste
   Hot cooked noodles

To Microwave:
1. In 2-quart microwave-safe casserole, combine butter, onion and garlic. Cover with lid; microwave on HIGH 3 minutes or until onion is tender, stirring once during cooking.
2. Stir in beef. Cover; microwave on HIGH 5 minutes or until beef is no longer pink, stirring once during cooking.
3. Stir in carrots, gravy, wine and tomato paste. Cover; microwave on HIGH 5 minutes or until boiling. Stir again.
4. Reduce power to 50%. Cover; microwave 30 minutes or until meat is tender, stirring twice during cooking. Let stand, covered, 5 minutes. Serve over noodles.
Makes about 3 cups or 4 servings.

Note: It's often more economical to buy a chuck steak or roast and cut your own stew meat than to buy "beef for stew." You usually have to trim the market-cut meat anyway, and you can control the size of the pieces better when you cut it yourself.

Red-Cooked Short Ribs

3 pounds beef short ribs
1/3 to 1/2 cup all-purpose flour
2 tablespoons vegetable oil
1 3/4 cups water, divided
1/2 cup KIKKOMAN Teriyaki Sauce
1 clove garlic, pressed
1/2 teaspoon ground ginger
1/8 teaspoon ground cloves

Coat ribs thoroughly with flour; reserve 1/4 cup excess flour. Heat oil in Dutch oven or large saucepan over medium heat. Add ribs and brown slowly on all sides; drain off excess oil. Combine 1 1/4 cups water, teriyaki sauce, garlic, ginger and cloves; pour over ribs. Cover; simmer 2 hours, or until ribs are tender. Meanwhile, blend reserved flour and remaining 1/2 cup water. Remove ribs to serving platter; keep warm. Pour pan drippings into large measuring cup; skim off fat. Add enough water to measure 2 1/2 cups; return to pan and bring to boil. Gradually stir in flour mixture. Cook and stir until thickened; serve with ribs.
Makes 4 servings.

Chinese-Style Beef & Vegetables

1/3 cup WISH-BONE® Italian Dressing
1 tablespoon soy sauce
1/4 teaspoon ground ginger
1 cup thinly sliced carrots
1 cup sliced mushrooms
1 cup sliced zucchini
1 (1 1/2-pound) boneless sirloin steak, cut into thin strips
4 cups hot cooked buttered rice

In small bowl, blend Italian dressing, soy sauce and ginger; reserve 2 tablespoons. In large skillet, heat remaining dressing mixture and cook carrots, covered, over medium heat, stirring occasionally, 10 minutes. Add mushrooms and zucchini and cook covered an additional 5 minutes. Remove vegetables and keep warm. Add reserved dressing mixture to skillet, then add beef. Cook uncovered over high heat, stirring constantly, 5 minutes or until beef is done. Return vegetables to skillet and heat through. To serve, arrange beef and vegetables over hot rice.
Makes about 6 servings.
Note: Also terrific with Wish-Bone® Robusto Italian, Blended Italian, Herbal Italian, Lite Italian, Classic Dijon Vinaigrette or Lite Classic Dijon Vinaigrette Dressing.

Oriental Steak Kabobs

1 cup (8 ounces) WISH-BONE® Italian Dressing
1/4 cup soy sauce
2 tablespoons brown sugar
1/2 teaspoon ground ginger
1 green onion, thinly sliced
1 pound boneless beef round, cut into 1-inch pieces
12 large mushrooms
2 cups broccoli florets
1 medium red pepper, cut into chunks

In large shallow baking dish, combine Italian dressing, soy sauce, brown sugar, ginger and onion. Add beef and vegetables; turn to coat. Cover and marinate in refrigerator, stirring occasionally, 4 hours or overnight. Remove beef and vegetables, reserving marinade.
Onto large skewers, alternately thread beef with vegetables. Grill or broil, turning and basting frequently with reserved marinade, 10 minutes or until beef is done.
Makes about 4 servings.
Note: Also terrific with Wish-Bone® Robusto Italian or Lite Italian Dressing.

Broccoli & Beef Stir-Fry

1/2 pound boneless tender beef steak (sirloin, rib eye or top loin)
1 tablespoon cornstarch
4 tablespoons KIKKOMAN Soy Sauce, divided
1 teaspoon sugar
1 teaspoon minced fresh ginger root
1 clove garlic, minced
1 pound fresh broccoli
1 1/4 cups water
4 teaspoons cornstarch
3 tablespoons vegetable oil, divided
1 onion, chunked
Hot cooked rice

Cut beef across grain into thin slices. Combine 1 tablespoon *each* cornstarch and soy sauce with sugar, ginger and garlic in small bowl; stir in beef. Let stand 15 minutes. Meanwhile, remove flowerets from broccoli; cut in half lengthwise. Peel stalks; cut crosswise into 1/8-inch slices. Combine water, 4 teaspoons cornstarch and remaining 3 tablespoons soy sauce; set aside. Heat 1 tablespoon oil in hot wok or large skillet over high heat. Add beef and stir-fry 1 minute; remove. Heat remaining 2 tablespoons oil in same pan. Add broccoli and onion; stir-fry 4 minutes. Stir in beef and soy sauce mixture. Cook and stir until mixture boils and thickens. Serve immediately over rice.
Makes 2 to 3 servings.

Beef with Leafy Greens

3/4 pound romaine lettuce
1/2 pound boneless tender beef steak (sirloin, rib eye or top loin)
4 tablespoons KIKKOMAN Stir-Fry Sauce, divided
1 clove garlic, minced
2 tablespoons vegetable oil, divided
1 medium onion, chunked
1 teaspoon minced fresh ginger root
8 cherry tomatoes, halved or 1 medium tomato, chunked
2 tablespoons chopped unsalted peanuts

Separate and rinse lettuce; pat dry. Cut leaves crosswise into 1-inch strips; set aside. Cut beef across grain into thin slices. Combine 1 tablespoon stir-fry sauce and garlic in small bowl; stir in beef to coat. Heat 1 tablespoon oil in hot wok or large skillet over high heat. Add beef and stir-fry 1 minute; remove. Heat remaining 1 tablespoon oil in same pan. Add onion and ginger; stir-fry 2 minutes. Add lettuce; stir-fry 2 minutes longer. Add beef, tomatoes and remaining 3 tablespoons stir-fry sauce; cook and stir until vegetables are coated with sauce and tomatoes are just heated through. Serve immediately with peanuts.
Makes 2 to 3 servings.

Lime Kabobs Polynesian

1/2 cup REALIME® Lime Juice from Concentrate
1/2 cup vegetable oil
3 tablespoons sugar
1 tablespoon BENNETT'S® Chili Sauce
1/2 to 1 teaspoon curry powder
1/4 teaspoon garlic powder
1 (1 1/2-pound) sirloin steak (about 1 inch thick), cut into cubes
1 (8-ounce) can pineapple chunks, drained
1 large green pepper, cut into squares
2 medium onions, quartered
8 ounces fresh whole mushrooms (about 2 cups)
1/2 pint cherry tomatoes

In small bowl, combine ReaLime® brand, oil, sugar, chili sauce and seasonings; pour over meat. Cover; refrigerate 6 hours or overnight, stirring occasionally. Skewer meat with pineapple and vegetables. Grill or broil as desired, turning and basting frequently with marinade. Serve with rice if desired. Refrigerate leftovers.
Makes 6 servings.

Honey-Mustard Beef Ribs

1 cup butter or margarine
1 bunch green onions with tops, finely chopped
1 small yellow onion, finely chopped
4 cloves garlic, minced
4 tablespoons prepared mustard
4 tablespoons honey
1/2 teaspoon liquid smoke, optional
1 teaspoon lemon pepper
1 teaspoon brown sugar
5 pounds beef back ribs

In saucepan, combine butter, green onions, yellow onion and garlic. Cook over low heat 15 minutes or until onions are tender. Remove from heat and add remaining ingredients except ribs. Grill ribs, on covered grill, over medium-hot **KINGSFORD® Charcoal Briquets** 30 to 35 minutes, brushing ribs generously with mustard-honey mixture, until meat is tender.
Makes 4 servings.

Ginger Beef

3/4 pound beef flank steak
1 can (11 ounces) CAMPBELL'S® Condensed Zesty Tomato Soup/Sauce
1/3 cup water
2 tablespoons peanut or vegetable oil
1 tablespoon soy sauce
2 teaspoons grated fresh ginger or 1/2 teaspoon ground ginger
1 clove garlic, minced
1 medium green pepper, cut into 1-inch squares
1 cup broccoli flowerets
Hot cooked rice

To Microwave:
1. Freeze steak 1 hour to make slicing easier. Cut steak across the grain into very thin slices.
2. In 12- by 8-inch microwave-safe baking dish, stir together soup, water, oil, soy sauce, ginger and garlic. Add beef slices; toss to coat well. Cover; refrigerate at least 1 hour.
3. Cover with vented plastic wrap; microwave on HIGH 6 minutes or until beef is no longer pink, stirring twice during cooking.
4. Add green pepper and broccoli. Cover; microwave on HIGH 5 minutes or until vegetables are tender, stirring twice during cooking. Serve over rice.
Makes about 3 1/2 cups or 4 servings.

Fiery Beef Stir-Fry

½ pound boneless tender beef steak (sirloin, rib eye or top loin)
1 tablespoon cornstarch
4 tablespoons KIKKOMAN Soy Sauce, divided
½ teaspoon sugar
1 clove garlic, minced
1¼ cups water
4 teaspoons cornstarch
1½ teaspoons distilled white vinegar
⅛ to ¼ teaspoon ground red pepper (cayenne)
3 tablespoons vegetable oil, divided
3 cups bite-size cauliflowerets Salt
1 onion, chunked and separated
1 green pepper, chunked

Cut beef across grain into thin strips. Combine 1 tablespoon *each* cornstarch and soy sauce with sugar and garlic in small bowl; stir in beef. Let stand 15 minutes. Meanwhile, combine water, remaining 3 tablespoons soy sauce, 4 teaspoons cornstarch, vinegar and red pepper; set aside. Heat 1 tablespoon oil in hot wok or large skillet over high heat. Add beef and stir-fry 1 minute; remove. Heat remaining 2 tablespoons oil in same pan. Add cauliflowerets; lightly sprinkle with salt and stir-fry 2 minutes. Add onion and green pepper; stir-fry 4 minutes. Stir in beef and soy sauce mixture; cook and stir until sauce boils and thickens.
Makes 2 to 3 servings.

Beef and Bean Sprout Stir-Fry

1 egg white, slightly beaten
5 teaspoons soy sauce, divided
3 teaspoons cornstarch, divided
⅛ teaspoon ground ginger
⅛ teaspoon garlic powder
⅛ teaspoon salt
Dash white pepper
¾ to 1 pound boneless beef sirloin, cut into thin strips
½ cup cold water
1 tablespoon oyster sauce (optional)*
½ teaspoon instant chicken bouillon granules
4 tablespoons CRISCO® Oil, divided
1 cup sliced fresh mushrooms
½ cup green onion slices (1-inch slices)
1 can (14 ounces) bean sprouts, drained
½ cup sliced water chestnuts

Blend egg white, 2 teaspoons soy sauce, 1 teaspoon cornstarch, ginger, garlic powder, salt and pepper in medium mixing bowl. Add beef. Stir to coat. Cover; refrigerate 30 minutes.

Combine cold water, oyster sauce (optional), remaining 3 teaspoons soy sauce, remaining 2 teaspoons cornstarch and bouillon granules in small mixing bowl. Mix well. Set aside.

Heat 2 tablespoons Crisco® Oil in large skillet or wok. Add beef mixture. Stir-fry over medium-high heat until beef is browned. Remove mixture from skillet; set aside. Heat remaining 2 tablespoons Crisco® Oil in large skillet. Add mushrooms and onion. Stir-fry over medium-high heat 1 minute. Add bean sprouts and water chestnuts. Stir-fry 1 minute. Add cornstarch mixture and beef. Cook until thickened and bubbly. Serve with *rice* and additional *soy sauce,* if desired.
4 to 6 servings.
*Available in Oriental foods section of supermarket.

Szechuan Beef & Snow Peas

½ pound boneless tender beef steak (sirloin, rib eye or top loin)
2 tablespoons cornstarch, divided
3 tablespoons KIKKOMAN Soy Sauce, divided
1 tablespoon dry sherry
1 clove garlic, minced
¾ cup water
¼ to ½ teaspoon crushed red pepper
2 tablespoons vegetable oil, divided
6 ounces fresh snow peas, trimmed
1 medium onion, chunked Salt
1 medium tomato, chunked Hot cooked rice

Slice beef across grain into thin strips. Combine 1 tablespoon *each* cornstarch and soy sauce with sherry and garlic in small bowl; stir in beef. Let stand 15 minutes. Meanwhile, combine water, remaining 1 tablespoon cornstarch, 2 tablespoons soy sauce and red pepper; set aside. Heat 1 tablespoon oil in hot wok or large skillet over high heat. Add beef and stir-fry 1 minute; remove. Heat remaining 1 tablespoon oil in same pan. Add snow peas and onion; lightly sprinkle with salt and stir-fry 3 minutes. Add beef, soy sauce mixture and tomato. Cook and stir until sauce boils and thickens and tomato is heated through. Serve immediately with rice.
Makes 2 to 3 servings.

Two-Bean Chili

1 pound sweet Italian sausage,
    removed from casing
1 pound ground beef
2 medium onions, chopped
1 large green pepper, chopped
3 cloves garlic, minced
1/4 cup flour
3 tablespoons chili powder
2 teaspoons ground cumin
2 teaspoons dried basil leaves
2 teaspoons dried oregano
    leaves
1 teaspoon salt
2 cans (28 ounces each) Italian-
    style tomatoes, undrained
3 tablespoons Worcestershire
    sauce
1 1/4 teaspoons TABASCO® pepper
    sauce
1 can (20 ounces) chick peas,
    drained
1 can (15 1/2 ounces) red kidney
    beans, drained
    Sliced ripe olives, chopped
    onion, chopped green
    pepper, chopped tomato,
    shredded cheese and
    cooked rice (optional)

In large heavy saucepot or Dutch oven
cook sausage, beef, onions, green pepper and garlic about 20 minutes or
until meats are browned and vegetables are tender; drain off fat. Stir in
flour, chili powder, cumin, basil, oregano and salt; cook 1 minute. Add tomatoes; break up with fork. Stir in
Worcestershire sauce and Tabasco®
sauce. Cover and simmer 1 hour, adding water if necessary; stir occasionally. Stir in chick peas and kidney
beans. Cook until heated through.
Serve with sliced olives, chopped onion, chopped green pepper, chopped tomato, shredded cheese and rice, if
desired.
Makes 8 servings.

Cincinnati Chili

1 1/2 pounds lean ground beef
2 cups chopped onions
2 large cloves garlic, minced
2 teaspoons chili powder
1/4 teaspoon ground cinnamon
    Dash ground cloves
4 cups V8® Vegetable Juice
2 cans (16 ounces each) kidney
    beans, drained
    Hot cooked spaghetti

1. In 6-quart Dutch oven over medium
heat, cook ground beef, onions and
garlic until beef is browned and onions are tender, stirring to separate
meat. Spoon off fat.
2. Stir in chili powder, cinnamon and
ground cloves; cook 2 minutes. Stir in
V8 juice. Heat to boiling; reduce heat
to low. Cover; simmer 30 minutes.
3. Stir in beans. Cover; simmer 15
minutes, stirring occasionally. Serve
over spaghetti.
Makes 8 3/4 cups or 11 servings.
    Note: Unlike Southwestern-style
chili, Cincinnati Chili is spiced with
cinnamon and cloves, then served over
spaghetti.

Per serving: 225 calories, 15 g protein, 10 g fat, 19 g carbohydrate, 628
mg sodium, 38 mg cholesterol.

Fast 'n Easy Chili

1 1/2 pounds ground beef
1 1/2 cups water
1 can (8 ounces) tomato sauce
1 envelope LIPTON® Onion,
    Onion-Mushroom, Beefy
    Mushroom or Beefy Onion
    Recipe Soup Mix
1 tablespoon chili powder*
1 can (16 ounces) red kidney
    beans, drained

In large skillet, brown ground beef
over medium-high heat; drain. Stir in
remaining ingredients. Simmer covered, stirring occasionally, 20 minutes.
Makes about 6 servings.
    Variations: First Alarm Chili—Add
4 teaspoons chili powder.
    Second Alarm Chili—Add 2 table-
spoons chili powder.
    Third Alarm Chili—Add chili powder
at your own risk.
    Microwave Directions: In 2-quart
casserole, heat ground beef at HIGH
(Full Power) 4 minutes; drain. Stir in
remaining ingredients. Heat covered,
stirring occasionally, 10 minutes or
until heated through. Let stand covered 5 minutes.

Texas-Style Chili

3 pounds boneless stew beef,
    cut into 1/2-inch cubes *or*
3 pounds lean ground beef
1 1/2 cups chopped onion
1 cup chopped green pepper
3 cloves garlic, chopped
2 (28-ounce) cans tomatoes,
    undrained and broken up
2 cups water
1 (6-ounce) can tomato paste
8 teaspoons WYLER'S® or
    STEERO® Beef-Flavor
    Instant Bouillon *or* 8 Beef-
    Flavor Bouillon Cubes
2 tablespoons chili powder
1 tablespoon ground cumin
2 teaspoons oregano leaves
2 teaspoons sugar

In large kettle or Dutch oven, brown
beef (if using ground beef, pour off
fat). Add onion, green pepper and garlic; cook and stir until tender. Add remaining ingredients. Cover; bring to
a boil. Reduce heat; simmer 1 1/2 hours
(1 hour for ground beef) or until meat
is tender. Serve with corn chips and
shredded cheese if desired. Refrigerate leftovers.
Makes about 4 quarts.

Meat Loaf Italiano

1 egg, beaten
1½ lbs. ground beef
1 8-oz. can pizza sauce
¾ cup (3 ozs.) VELVEETA Shredded Pasteurized Process Cheese Food
¾ cup old fashioned or quick oats, uncooked
¼ cup cold water
½ teaspoon dried oregano leaves, crushed

In large bowl, combine all ingredients except ¼ cup pizza sauce; mix lightly. Shape into loaf in 10×6-inch baking dish. Bake at 350°, 1 hour. Top with remaining sauce. Let stand 10 minutes before serving.
6 servings.

Preparation time: 10 minutes
Baking time: 60 minutes plus standing

Chili in Tortilla Cups

Tortilla Cups (recipe follows)
¾ pound lean ground beef
½ cup chopped onion
1 tablespoon chili powder
1 teaspoon ground cumin
1½ cups V8® Vegetable Juice
1 can (16 ounces) kidney beans, drained
Dash hot pepper sauce
1 cup shredded Colby or Monterey Jack cheese (4 ounces)
½ cup diced green pepper
¾ cup diced CAMPBELL'S FRESH® Tomato
2½ cups shredded iceberg lettuce
Chopped green pepper for garnish
Chopped CAMPBELL'S FRESH® Tomato for garnish
Shredded cheese for garnish

1. Prepare Tortilla Cups.
2. In 10-inch nonstick skillet over medium-high heat, cook beef, onion, chili powder and cumin until beef is browned and onion is tender, stirring to separate meat. Spoon off fat.
3. Stir in V8 juice, kidney beans and hot pepper sauce. Heat to boiling. Reduce heat to low; simmer, uncovered, 15 minutes, stirring occasionally.
4. In large bowl, toss cheese, green pepper and tomato with meat mixture.
5. To serve: Divide lettuce among Tortilla Cups. Fill each with about ¾ cup meat mixture. Garnish with additional green pepper, tomato and cheese.
Makes 6 servings.
TORTILLA CUPS: Preheat oven to 400°F. On baking sheet, place 6 balls of foil (4-inch diameter). Spray 10-inch nonstick skillet with vegetable cooking spray. Over high heat, heat one (8-inch) flour tortilla 5 seconds on each side until tortilla is softened. Drain on paper towels. Immediately drape tortilla over foil ball on baking sheet. Repeat with 5 additional tortillas. Bake 5 minutes or until golden. Remove from oven and cool on foil.

Per serving: 388 calories, 21 g protein, 19 g fat, 36 g carbohydrate, 635 mg sodium, 53 mg cholesterol.

Italian-Style Salisbury Steaks

1 pound ground beef
¼ cup seasoned dry bread crumbs
¼ cup water
1 egg, slightly beaten
½ teaspoon salt
¼ teaspoon pepper
¼ cup WISH-BONE® Italian or Robusto Italian Dressing
2 cups thinly sliced onions
2 cups thinly sliced mushrooms
1 can (8 ounces) tomato sauce
½ teaspoon basil leaves

Preheat oven to 350°.

In medium bowl, thoroughly combine ground beef, bread crumbs, water, egg, salt and pepper. Shape into 4 oval patties, then place in 1½-quart oblong baking pan; set aside.

In medium skillet, heat Italian dressing and cook onions with mushrooms over medium heat, stirring occasionally, 5 minutes or until tender. Stir in tomato sauce and basil. Spoon tomato mixture over patties and bake 30 minutes or until done.
Makes 4 servings.

Zesty Meat Loaf

1½ pounds lean ground beef
1 can (11 ounces) CAMPBELL'S® Condensed Zesty Tomato Soup/Sauce
2 eggs, beaten
¾ cup finely crushed saltine crackers
1 tablespoon Worcestershire sauce
2 tablespoons grated Parmesan cheese

To Microwave:
1. In large bowl, thoroughly blend beef, ½ cup of the soup, eggs, crumbs and Worcestershire.
2. In 12- by 8-inch microwave-safe baking dish, firmly shape meat mixture into 8- by 4-inch loaf. Cover with waxed paper; microwave on HIGH 15 minutes or until loaf is firm in center, rotating dish twice during cooking.
3. Spread remaining soup over meat. Microwave, uncovered, on HIGH 2 minutes or until soup is hot. Top with cheese. Let stand, uncovered, 5 minutes before serving.
Makes 6 servings.
Note: If you are using a temperature probe, cook meat loaf to an internal temperature of 170°F.

Meatza Pizzas

2 pounds lean ground beef
½ cup finely chopped onion
½ cup fresh bread crumbs
   (1 slice bread)
2 eggs
4 teaspoons WYLER'S® or
   STEERO® Beef-Flavor
   Instant Bouillon
¼ teaspoon garlic powder
1 (6-ounce) can tomato paste
½ teaspoon oregano leaves
½ teaspoon sugar
Toppings:
   Sliced mushrooms
   Chopped green pepper
   Sliced pepperoni
   Cooked crumbled bacon
   Shredded Mozzarella cheese

In large bowl, combine meat, onion, crumbs, eggs, bouillon and garlic powder; mix well. Shape into 8 or 10 patties (about 3½ inches each), flattening centers and forming a ½-inch rim around edges. Arrange on broiler pan rack; broil 6 inches from heat 5 to 8 minutes. Meanwhile, stir together tomato paste, oregano and sugar. Spread equal portions in center of each patty. Top with your favorite toppings and cheese. Broil 1 to 2 minutes or until hot and bubbly. Serve immediately or cool completely, wrap tightly and freeze. To serve, thaw and reheat in 300° oven 15 to 20 minutes. Refrigerate leftovers.
Makes 8 to 10 servings.
Microwave: Prepare meat patties; top with sauce and desired toppings. Arrange half the patties on a microwave roasting rack in shallow baking dish *or* on a bacon rack. Microwave uncovered on full power (high) 7½ to 8½ minutes or to desired doneness, rotating dish once. Let stand 3 minutes before serving.

Easy Cheesy Meat Loaf

1½ pounds lean ground beef
2 cups fresh bread crumbs
   (4 slices bread)
1 cup tomato juice
⅓ cup chopped onion
2 eggs
2 teaspoons WYLER'S® or
   STEERO® Beef-Flavor
   Instant Bouillon
¼ teaspoon pepper
6 slices BORDEN® Process
   American Cheese Food

Preheat oven to 350°. In large bowl, combine all ingredients except cheese food; mix well. In shallow baking dish, shape half the mixture into loaf. Cut *4 slices* cheese food into strips; arrange on meat. Top with remaining meat; press edges together to seal. Bake 1 hour; pour off fat. Top with remaining cheese food slices. Refrigerate leftovers.
Makes 6 to 8 servings.

Brazilian Beans and Rice

3 green-tip, medium DOLE™
   Bananas
1 large onion, chopped
1 large clove garlic, pressed
2 tablespoons minced fresh
   ginger root
1 tablespoon vegetable oil
½ pound ground beef
½ pound bulk pork sausage
1 teaspoon ground cumin
¼ teaspoon cayenne pepper
1 can (15¼ ounces) kidney
   beans
1 can (11 ounces) black bean
   soup
1 can (8 ounces) stewed
   tomatoes
2 teaspoons minced cilantro or
   parsley
4 to 6 cups shredded lettuce
3 to 4 cups hot cooked rice

Cut bananas in half crosswise, then lengthwise. In large skillet, saute onion, garlic and ginger in oil; push to side of skillet. Add bananas; saute 30 to 45 seconds. Remove bananas to plate. Add beef, sausage, cumin and cayenne; brown, stirring in onion mixture. Add undrained beans, soup and tomatoes. Cover; simmer 30 minutes, stirring occasionally. Remove from heat. Stir in cilantro. Place bananas on top. Cover; cook 1 minute. Mound 1 cup lettuce on each plate. Top with ½ cup rice, then bean mixture, spooning bananas to side.
Makes 4 to 6 servings.

Meat Loaf Supreme

1 can (10¾ ounces)
   CAMPBELL'S® Condensed
   Cream of Mushroom Soup
1½ pounds ground beef
½ cup chopped onion
½ cup fine dry bread crumbs
1 egg
1 package (8 ounces)
   refrigerated crescent rolls
⅓ cup milk
1 teaspoon honey
¼ teaspoon dill weed, crushed
2 teaspoons Dijon-style mustard

1. In large bowl, thoroughly mix ½ cup of the soup, beef, onion, crumbs and egg. In 12- by 8-inch baking dish, firmly shape mixture into 8- by 4-inch loaf. Bake at 350°F. 1 hour. Remove meat loaf from oven; pour off fat.
2. Unroll and separate crescent roll dough into triangles. Place triangles crosswise over top and down sides of meat loaf, overlapping triangles. Bake 15 minutes or until browned.
3. Meanwhile, prepare sauce: In 1-quart saucepan, stir together remaining soup, milk, honey, dill weed and mustard. Over medium heat, heat to boiling, stirring constantly. Serve with meat loaf.
Makes 6 servings.

Mexican Meatloaf Roll

1½ pounds ground beef
¼ cup old fashioned or quick oats, uncooked
2 eggs, beaten
1 tablespoon worcestershire sauce
1 teaspoon pepper
1 8-ounce package PHILADELPHIA BRAND Cream Cheese, softened
1 4-ounce can chopped green chilies, drained
¾ cup salsa

Combine meat, oats, eggs, worcestershire sauce and pepper; mix well. On wax paper, press meat mixture into 20×10½-inch rectangle. Combine cream cheese and chilies; mix well. Spread cream cheese mixture over meat mixture to within 1 inch of outer edge. Roll, jelly roll fashion, starting at narrow end. Place in 12×8-inch baking dish. Bake at 350°, 40 minutes. Top with salsa; continue baking 10 minutes. Let stand 10 minutes before serving.
6 to 8 servings.

Picadillo-Stuffed Peppers

4 medium green or sweet red peppers
1 tablespoon water
1 pound lean ground beef
½ cup chopped onion
1 clove garlic, minced
½ teaspoon ground cinnamon
½ teaspoon ground cumin
⅛ teaspoon ground cloves
1 can (11 ounces) CAMPBELL'S® Condensed Zesty Tomato Soup/Sauce
1 small apple, chopped
¼ cup raisins
¼ cup toasted sliced almonds
1 tablespoon vinegar

To Microwave:
1. Cut thin slice from top of each pepper. Chop enough pepper tops to make ⅓ cup; set aside. Remove and discard inner membranes and seeds from peppers. Place pepper shells in 2-quart microwave-safe casserole; add water. Cover with lid; microwave on HIGH 5 minutes or until tender-crisp. Drain and set aside.
2. Crumble beef into same casserole; add onion, garlic, cinnamon, cumin, cloves and chopped pepper tops. Cover; microwave on HIGH 5 minutes or until beef is no longer pink, stirring once during cooking to break up meat. Spoon off fat.
3. Stir in soup, apple, raisins, almonds and vinegar. Divide mixture among peppers. Arrange in 2-quart microwave-safe casserole. Cover; microwave on HIGH 5 minutes or until hot.
Makes 4 servings.

Mini Meat Loaves

1 pouch CAMPBELL'S® Onion Soup and Recipe Mix
1½ pounds ground beef
½ pound bulk pork sausage
½ cup fine dry bread crumbs
1 egg
½ cup OPEN PIT® Original Flavor Barbecue Sauce
3 small VLASIC® Sweet Pickles, halved lengthwise
2 ounces Cheddar cheese, cut into thin strips

1. Preheat oven to 350°F. In large bowl, combine soup mix, beef, sausage, bread crumbs, egg and ¼ cup of the barbecue sauce; mix well.
2. Divide meat mixture into 6 equal portions. Flatten each to a 4-inch patty. Place a pickle half on each; fold meat over to enclose pickle. Shape each into a small loaf. Place loaves in large shallow baking pan.
3. Bake 30 minutes. Remove from oven; spoon fat from pan. Spread remaining ¼ cup barbecue sauce over loaves; top with cheese strips. Bake 2 minutes more or until cheese melts.
Makes 6 servings.

Souperior Meat Loaf

1 envelope LIPTON® Beefy Onion, Onion, Onion-Mushroom or Beefy Mushroom Recipe Soup Mix
2 pounds ground beef
1½ cups fresh bread crumbs
2 eggs
¾ cup water
⅓ cup ketchup

Preheat oven to 350°.
In large bowl, combine all ingredients. In large shallow baking pan, shape into loaf. Bake 1 hour or until done.
Makes about 8 servings.
Microwave Directions: Combine as above. In 2-quart oblong baking dish, shape into loaf. Heat uncovered at HIGH (Full Power), turning dish occasionally, 25 minutes or until done; drain. Let stand covered 5 minutes.

All-American Meat Loaf

8 slices BORDEN® Process American Cheese Food
2 pounds lean ground beef
1¼ cups dry bread crumbs
¾ cup catsup
2 eggs
1 (1.5 ounce) package MRS. GRASS® Onion Recipe, Soup & Dip Mix

Preheat oven to 350° (325° for glass dish). Cut *6 slices* cheese food into small pieces; combine with remaining ingredients. Mix well. In shallow baking pan, shape into loaf. Bake 1 hour. Remove from oven; arrange remaining cheese food slices on top. Return to oven 5 minutes or until cheese food begins to melt. Refrigerate leftovers.
Makes 8 servings.

Pork Chops with Browned Garlic-Butter Sauce

1 tablespoon salt
1 teaspoon onion powder
³/₄ teaspoon garlic powder
½ teaspoon white pepper
½ teaspoon dry mustard
½ teaspoon rubbed sage
½ teaspoon ground cumin
½ teaspoon dried thyme leaves
12 pork chops, ½ inch thick
1¼ cups flour
   Vegetable oil
   Browned Garlic-Butter Sauce
   (recipe follows)

In small bowl combine salt, onion powder, garlic powder, white pepper, dry mustard, sage, cumin and thyme; mix well. Sprinkle pork chops with 2 tablespoons seasoning mix; pat in with hand. On waxed paper combine remaining mix and flour.

In large skillet over medium-high heat bring ¼ inch oil to 375°F. Dredge chops in seasoned flour; shake off excess. Fry in oil 4 to 5 minutes per side or until chops are done. (Change oil if sediment starts to burn.) Drain on paper towels. Drizzle Browned Garlic-Butter Sauce over pork chops. *Makes 6 to 8 servings.*

Browned Garlic-Butter Sauce

³/₄ cup butter or margarine
2 cloves garlic, minced
2 tablespoons minced parsley
1 tablespoon TABASCO® pepper
   sauce

In small saucepan heat butter until half melted; shake pan constantly. Add garlic and cook 2 to 3 minutes or until butter is melted and foam on surface is barely browned; shake pan occasionally. Stir in parsley and Tabasco® sauce; cook 1 to 2 minutes or until sauce is lightly browned and very foamy. Remove from heat. *Makes ³/₄ cup sauce.*

Caribbean Pork Chops

1 green-tip, large DOLE™
   Banana
1 tablespoon vegetable oil
2 boneless loin pork chops,
   1 inch thick
1 large clove garlic, pressed
2 tablespoons slivered fresh
   ginger root
½ cup canned coconut milk
¼ cup water
2 tablespoons chutney
⅛ teaspoon cayenne pepper
1 tablespoon lime juice
   Shredded lettuce or hot
   cooked rice, optional

Cut banana in half crosswise, then lengthwise. In skillet, saute banana in oil 30 to 45 seconds, shaking skillet. Remove banana. Add more oil to skillet if necessary. Brown pork chops on each side 2 to 3 minutes. Stir in garlic and ginger; saute lightly. Stir in coconut milk, water, chutney and cayenne. Spoon over pork chops. Cover; simmer 8 to 10 minutes. Stir in lime juice. Remove from heat. Serve over shredded lettuce or with rice, if desired. Generously spoon sauce over pork chops and bananas. *Makes 2 servings.*

Harvest Pork Chops

1 cup shredded carrots
1 small apple, cored and
   chopped
¼ cup fine dry bread crumbs
¼ teaspoon dried thyme leaves,
   crushed
1 pouch CAMPBELL'S® Onion
   Soup and Recipe Mix
4 pork loin rib chops, each cut
   1 inch thick
1 tablespoon vegetable oil
³/₄ cup water
1 tablespoon all-purpose flour
³/₄ cup apple juice

1. To make filling: In medium bowl, stir together carrots, apple, bread crumbs, thyme and 2 tablespoons of the soup mix; mix well.
2. With knife, trim and discard excess fat from edges of pork chops. Make a pocket in each chop by cutting horizontally through each chop almost to the bone. Stuff filling into pockets; secure with toothpicks if needed.
3. In 10-inch ovensafe skillet over medium-high heat, cook pork chops in oil until browned on both sides.
4. Cover skillet; bake at 350°F. 45 minutes or until chops are fork-tender. Transfer chops to serving platter; keep warm. Skim fat from liquid in skillet.
5. In small bowl, whisk water into flour until smooth; stir into skillet along with apple juice and remaining soup mix. Over medium-high heat, heat to boiling, stirring constantly.
6. Reduce heat to low; simmer, uncovered, 5 minutes, stirring occasionally. Serve over pork chops.
Makes 4 servings.

Onion-Baked Pork Chops

1 envelope LIPTON® Golden
   Onion or Onion Recipe Soup
   Mix
²/₃ cup plain dry bread crumbs
8 pork chops, ½ inch thick
2 eggs, well beaten

Preheat oven to 350°.
Combine golden onion recipe soup mix with bread crumbs. Dip chops in eggs, then bread crumb mixture, coating well. In lightly greased large shallow baking pan, arrange chops, then drizzle, if desired, with melted butter. Bake, turning once, 1 hour or until done.
Makes 8 servings.
Microwave Directions: Dip chops in eggs and bread crumb mixture as above. In lightly greased 3-quart oblong baking dish, heat chops, uncovered, at MEDIUM (50% Full Power) 40 minutes or until chops are done, rearranging chops once. Let stand covered 10 minutes.

Pork Chops Roma

½ cup WISH-BONE® Italian or
  Robusto Italian Dressing
6 pork chops, ½ inch thick
  (about 2 pounds)
2 medium green peppers, sliced
¼ pound mushrooms, sliced

In large shallow baking dish, pour Italian dressing over pork chops. Cover and marinate in refrigerator, turning occasionally, at least 3 hours. Remove chops, reserving marinade.

In large skillet, heat 2 tablespoons reserved marinade and cook peppers and mushrooms over medium heat, stirring occasionally, until tender; remove. Brown pork chops; drain. Add remaining marinade and simmer covered 15 minutes. Return peppers and mushrooms to skillet and simmer covered an additional 10 minutes or until chops are tender.
Makes about 6 servings.

Fruit-Stuffed Pork Chops

1 can (16 ounces) pitted tart
  cherries, drained
½ cup chopped apple
¼ cup raisins
¼ cup chopped dried apricots
1 teaspoon ground cinnamon
½ teaspoon instant chicken
  bouillon granules
½ teaspoon salt
⅛ teaspoon ground allspice
⅛ teaspoon ground cloves
⅛ teaspoon pepper
5 tablespoons CRISCO® Oil,
  divided
⅓ cup chopped onion
1 cup herb-seasoned stuffing
  mix
¼ cup packed brown sugar
4 pork chops with pocket, 1 inch
  thick

Preheat oven to 350°F. Mix cherries, apple, raisins, apricots, cinnamon, bouillon granules, salt, allspice, cloves and pepper in medium mixing bowl. Set aside.

Heat 1 tablespoon Crisco® Oil in small saucepan. Add onion. Sauté over moderate heat until tender. Stir in stuffing mix, brown sugar and cherry mixture. Remove from heat. Fill each chop pocket with one fourth of stuffing. Secure edges with wooden picks.

Heat remaining 4 tablespoons Crisco® Oil in large skillet. Add chops. Brown over medium-high heat. Place chops in 8-inch square baking dish. Cover dish with aluminum foil. Bake at 350°F, about 40 minutes, or until pork is no longer pink. Remove wooden picks before serving.
4 servings.

Sweet and Sour Pork Chops

6 center-cut pork chops (about
  1¾ pounds)
Vegetable oil
½ cup REALEMON® Lemon Juice
  from Concentrate
3 tablespoons cornstarch
½ cup firmly packed brown sugar
¼ cup chopped onion
1 tablespoon soy sauce
1 teaspoon WYLER'S® or
  STEERO® Chicken-Flavor
  Instant Bouillon or 1
  Chicken-Flavor Bouillon
  Cube
1 (20-ounce) can pineapple
  chunks in heavy syrup,
  drained, reserving syrup
1 cup thinly sliced carrots
  Green pepper rings

Preheat oven to 350°. In large oven-proof skillet, brown chops in oil. Remove chops from skillet; pour off fat. In skillet, combine ReaLemon® brand and cornstarch; mix well. Add sugar, onion, soy sauce, bouillon and reserved syrup; cook and stir until slightly thickened and bouillon is dissolved. Add pork chops and carrots. Cover; bake 1 hour or until tender. Add pineapple; cover and bake 10 minutes longer. Garnish with green pepper; serve with rice if desired. Refrigerate leftovers.
Makes 6 servings.

Meatball Stew

1 pound ground beef
½ cup soft bread crumbs
½ teaspoon dried thyme leaves,
  crushed
1 egg
1 clove garlic, minced
2 tablespoons vegetable oil
1 can (10½ ounces)
  CAMPBELL'S® Condensed
  French Onion Soup
¼ cup water
3 medium potatoes, peeled and
  quartered
3 medium carrots, cut into
  1-inch chunks
1 medium onion, cut into thin
  wedges
1 tablespoon chopped fresh
  parsley

1. In medium bowl, combine ground beef, bread crumbs, thyme, egg and garlic; mix thoroughly. Shape into 20 meatballs.
2. In 10-inch skillet over medium heat, in hot oil, cook meatballs until browned on all sides. Pour off fat.
3. Stir soup and water into skillet; stir in potatoes, carrots and onion. Heat to boiling. Reduce heat to low. Cover; simmer 30 minutes or until vegetables are tender, adding more water if needed. Garnish with parsley.
Makes 4 servings.

Dijon Breaded Pork Chops

3/4 cup finely crushed saltine crackers
1/2 teaspoon salt
1/2 teaspoon ground thyme
1/4 teaspoon pepper
1/8 to 1/4 teaspoon ground sage
1 egg
1 tablespoon Dijon mustard
4 pork chops, 1/2 inch thick
1/4 cup CRISCO® Oil

Mix cracker crumbs, salt, thyme, pepper and sage in shallow dish or on sheet of waxed paper. Set aside. Blend egg and mustard in shallow dish. Dip each chop in egg mixture, then in cracker mixture to coat.

Heat Crisco® Oil in large skillet. Add chops. Fry over moderate heat 16 to 20 minutes, or until pork is no longer pink, turning over once.
2 to 4 servings.

Oriental Pork Chops

2 tablespoons vegetable oil
1 clove garlic, minced
4 teaspoons minced ginger root
1/2 cup dry sherry wine
1/2 cup soy sauce
1/4 cup honey
1 tablespoon grated orange peel
1 tablespoon sesame seeds
3/4 teaspoon TABASCO® pepper sauce
4 pork chops, 1 inch thick
1 teaspoon cornstarch
2 tablespoons water
 Orange slices, cut into quarters

In medium saucepan heat oil. Add garlic and ginger; cook 1 minute. Remove from heat; add sherry, soy sauce, honey, orange peel, sesame seeds and Tabasco® sauce. Place chops in large shallow dish or plastic bag; add marinade. Cover; refrigerate 1 hour; turn chops occasionally.

Remove chops from marinade; pour marinade into small saucepan. Place chops on grill about 5 inches from source of heat. Grill 10 minutes on each side. Meanwhile, in small bowl combine cornstarch and water; stir into marinade. Stir constantly, bring to a boil over medium heat and boil 1 minute. Brush chops with marinade. Grill 5 to 10 minutes longer or until chops are done; turn and brush frequently with marinade. Serve remaining marinade with chops. Garnish with orange slices.
Makes 4 servings.

Mandarin Pork Chops

4 center-cut pork chops (about 1 pound)
1 tablespoon vegetable oil
1/2 cup orange juice
1/4 cup water
3 tablespoons brown sugar
2 tablespoons REALEMON® Lemon Juice from Concentrate
1 tablespoon cornstarch
2 teaspoons WYLER'S® or STEERO® Chicken-Flavor Instant Bouillon
1 (11-ounce) can mandarin orange segments, drained
1 medium green pepper, sliced

In large skillet, brown chops in oil on both sides; remove from pan. In skillet, add remaining ingredients except orange segments and green pepper; cook and stir until slightly thickened. Add pork chops; cover and simmer 20 minutes or until tender. Add orange segments and green pepper; heat through. Garnish as desired. Refrigerate leftovers.
Makes 4 servings.

Barbecued Pork Leg

1 boneless pork leg roast, rolled and tied (8 to 10 pounds)
Sam's Mop Sauce (recipe follows)
K.C. MASTERPIECE® Hickory Barbecue Sauce

In grill, arrange medium-hot KINGSFORD® Charcoal Briquets around drip pan. Place prepared pork leg over drip pan; cover grill and cook pork 4 to 4 1/2 hours (adding additional briquets as necessary) or until meat thermometer inserted in thickest portion registers 170°F. Baste pork with Sam's Mop Sauce every 30 minutes, patting a thin coating of sauce on meat with cotton swab mop or pastry brush. Let stand, covered with foil, 10 minutes before serving.

Meanwhile, in saucepan, combine remaining Mop Sauce with an equal amount of barbecue sauce; bring to boil. Slice pork and serve with sauce mixture.
Makes about 20 servings.

Sam's Mop Sauce

1 lemon
1 cup water
1 cup cider vinegar
1 tablespoon butter or margarine
1 tablespoon olive or vegetable oil
1/2 teaspoon cayenne pepper
1 1/2 to 3 teaspoons hot pepper sauce
1 1/2 to 3 teaspoons Worcestershire sauce
1 1/2 teaspoons black pepper

With vegetable peeler, remove peel from lemon; squeeze juice from lemon. In heavy saucepan, combine lemon peel, juice and remaining ingredients. Bring to boil. Place saucepan on grill to keep warm, if space permits.
Makes 2 1/4 cups.

Pork Chops with Sweet Red Peppers

1 cup dry red wine
1/4 cup orange juice
1 clove garlic, minced
1 bay leaf, crumbled
1 teaspoon dried savory leaves
1 teaspoon dried marjoram leaves
1/2 teaspoon salt
1/2 teaspoon TABASCO® pepper sauce
4 pork chops, about 3/4 inch thick
2 tablespoons vegetable oil
2 medium red peppers, cut into strips
1/2 cup orange sections

In large shallow dish combine wine, orange juice, garlic, bay leaf, savory, marjoram, salt and Tabasco® sauce. Add pork chops. Cover; refrigerate 1 1/2 hours; turn occasionally. Remove chops and pat dry; reserve marinade.

In large skillet heat oil over medium heat. Add chops and brown well on both sides; remove from skillet. Add peppers to skillet; cook 5 minutes or until tender. Return chops to skillet. Add reserved marinade and bring to a boil. Cover. Reduce heat; simmer 20 to 25 minutes or until chops are done. Remove chops and peppers to serving dish. Increase heat to high; boil sauce about 3 minutes or until slightly thickened. Pour sauce over chops; garnish with orange sections. *Makes 4 servings.*

Teriyaki Pork Chops

1/4 cup soy sauce
1/4 cup peanut or vegetable oil
1/4 cup minced onion
3 tablespoons honey
3 tablespoons dry sherry
2 teaspoons grated fresh ginger *or* 3/4 teaspoon ground ginger
1 clove garlic, minced
4 pork loin chops, cut 1 inch thick

In shallow glass dish, combine all ingredients except pork chops. Add pork chops; turn to coat with marinade. Cover and refrigerate several hours or overnight, basting occasionally. Drain chops; reserve marinade. Arrange medium-hot **KINGSFORD® Charcoal Briquets** to one side of grill with drip pan next to briquets. Place chops over drip pan. Cover grill and cook 30 to 40 minutes or until chops are tender and cooked through, turning once and basting often with marinade. *Makes 4 servings.*

Mushroom & Pepper Stuffed Chops

2 tablespoons butter or margarine
1/2 pound mushrooms, sliced
1 small red or green pepper, chopped
1/2 cup sliced almonds
1 envelope LIPTON® Onion or Onion-Mushroom Recipe Soup Mix
1 cup fresh bread crumbs
1/8 teaspoon pepper
4 double loin pork or veal chops, 2 inches thick (about 2 1/2 pounds)

Preheat oven to 350°.

In medium skillet, heat butter and cook mushrooms, red pepper and almonds over medium-high heat 5 minutes or until vegetables are tender. Remove from heat, then stir in onion recipe soup mix combined with bread crumbs and pepper; set aside.

With knife parallel to cutting board, make a deep cut in meaty side of each chop. Evenly stuff each cut with mushroom mixture; secure, if desired, with skewers.

In shallow baking pan, arrange chops and bake 1 hour or until done. *Makes about 4 servings.*

Pork Chops and Sauerkraut

2 slices bacon, chopped
1/2 cup chopped onion
1 jar (32 ounces) VLASIC® Polish Sauerkraut, rinsed and drained
2 apples, peeled and chopped
1/4 teaspoon pepper
4 medium pork chops (about 1 1/2 pounds)

To Microwave:
1. In 3-quart microwave-safe casserole, combine bacon and onion. Cover with lid; microwave on HIGH 3 1/2 minutes or until bacon is crisp and onion is tender, stirring once during cooking.
2. Stir in sauerkraut, apples and pepper. Arrange pork chops over sauerkraut, placing thicker portions toward edge of dish. Cover; microwave on HIGH 8 minutes or until very hot. Rearrange pork chops.
3. Reduce power to 50%. Cover; microwave 20 minutes or until pork is no longer pink in center, rearranging chops once during cooking. Let stand, covered, 5 minutes.
Makes 4 servings.

Tasty Pork Ragout

½ pound boneless pork loin
1 small onion, chopped
1 large clove garlic, pressed
½ teaspoon dried rosemary, crumbled
2 tablespoons butter or margarine
   Salt and pepper
½ cup water
1 head DOLE™ Cauliflower, cut into flowerets (2 cups)
1 cup sliced DOLE™ Carrots
   Hot buttered noodles

Cut pork into 1-inch cubes. In large skillet, brown pork with onion, garlic and rosemary in butter. Sprinkle with salt and pepper to taste. Stir in water. Cover; simmer 20 minutes. Add cauliflower and carrots. Cover; simmer 5 minutes longer or until vegetables are tender-crisp. Serve over noodles. *Makes 2 servings.*

Peanut Pork Saté

1 cup (8 ounces) WISH-BONE® Sweet 'n Spicy French or Lite Sweet 'n Spicy French Dressing
¼ cup peanut butter
1 tablespoon dry sherry
2 teaspoons soy sauce
½ to 1 teaspoon crushed red pepper
1 (1-inch) piece fresh ginger, peeled and cut into pieces*
1 medium clove garlic
¼ cup water
1½ pounds pork tenderloin, sliced diagonally into ¼-inch strips**

In blender or food processor, blend sweet 'n spicy French dressing, peanut butter, sherry, soy sauce, pepper, ginger and garlic until smooth.

In large shallow baking dish, blend ½ cup dressing mixture with water; add pork and turn to coat. Cover and marinate in refrigerator, stirring occasionally, 4 hours or overnight. Cover and refrigerate remaining dressing mixture for use as a basting sauce. Remove pork from marinade.

Onto 12-inch skewers, thread pork strips, weaving back and forth. Grill or broil, turning and basting occasionally with reserved dressing mixture, 12 minutes or until pork is done. *Makes about 6 servings.*

  Substitution: Use ½ teaspoon ground ginger.

  ****Variation:*** Use 1½ pounds boneless flank or round steak, sliced diagonally into ¼-inch strips.

Herb-Marinated Pork Roast

3½- to 4-pound bone-in pork loin roast
1 small onion, chopped
½ cup CRISCO® Oil
3 tablespoons cider vinegar
1 tablespoon lemon juice
1 teaspoon dried oregano leaves
2 cloves garlic, minced
½ teaspoon dried rosemary leaves
¼ teaspoon dried dill weed
¼ teaspoon salt
¼ teaspoon pepper

Place roast in large bowl or large heavy plastic food storage bag. Blend remaining ingredients. Pour over roast. Cover dish or seal bag. Refrigerate 8 hours or overnight, turning roast over occasionally.

Preheat oven to 325°F. Remove roast from marinade. Discard marinade. Place roast in roasting pan. Roast at 325°F, 2 to 3 hours, or until internal temperature registers 170°F. Let stand 15 minutes before carving. *6 to 8 servings.*

Pork Roast with Corn Bread & Oyster Stuffing

1 (5- to 7-pound) pork loin roast*
2 tablespoons butter or margarine
½ cup chopped onion
½ cup chopped celery
2 cloves garlic, minced
½ teaspoon fennel seeds, crushed
1 teaspoon TABASCO® pepper sauce
½ teaspoon salt
2 cups packaged corn bread stuffing mix
1 can (8 ounces) oysters, undrained, chopped

Preheat oven to 325°F. Make a deep slit in back of each chop on pork loin. In large saucepan melt butter; add onion, celery, garlic and fennel. Cook 5 minutes or until vegetables are tender; stir in Tabasco® sauce and salt. Add corn bread, oysters and oyster liquid; toss to mix well.

Stuff corn bread mixture into slits in pork. (Any leftover stuffing may be baked in covered baking dish during last 30 minutes of roasting.) Place meat in shallow roasting pan. Cook 30 to 35 minutes per pound or until meat thermometer inserted into meat registers 170°F. Remove to heated serving platter. Allow meat to stand 15 minutes before serving. *Makes 10 to 12 servings.*

  *Have butcher crack backbone of pork loin roast.

Cranberry Glazed Pork Roast

1 (3½- to 4-pound) boneless pork loin roast
Salt and pepper
1 (16-ounce) can whole berry cranberry sauce
¼ cup REALEMON® Lemon Juice from Concentrate
3 tablespoons brown sugar
1 teaspoon cornstarch

Preheat oven to 450°. Place meat in shallow baking dish; season with salt and pepper. Roast 20 minutes. Reduce oven temperature to 325°; continue roasting. Meanwhile, in small saucepan, combine remaining ingredients. Over medium heat, cook and stir until slightly thickened, about 5 minutes. After meat has cooked 1 hour, drain off fat; spoon half of the sauce over meat. Continue roasting 1 to 1½ hours or until meat thermometer reaches 170°, basting occasionally. Spoon remaining sauce over meat; return to oven 10 to 15 minutes. Let stand 10 minutes before slicing. Refrigerate leftovers.

To Make Gravy: In small saucepan, combine meat drippings and 2 tablespoons cornstarch. Over medium heat, cook and stir until thickened, about 5 minutes.
Makes about 2 cups.

Cider-Glazed Pork Roast

½ cup apple cider
¼ cup Dijon-style mustard
¼ cup vegetable oil
¼ cup soy sauce
1 boneless pork loin roast (4 to 5 pounds), tied

In small bowl, combine apple cider, mustard, oil and soy sauce. Insert meat thermometer in center of thickest part of roast. Arrange medium-hot **KINGSFORD® Charcoal Briquets** around drip pan. Place roast over drip pan. Cover grill and cook 2½ to 3 hours or until meat thermometer registers 170°F, adding more briquets as necessary. Brush roast with cider mixture 3 or 4 times during last 30 minutes of cooking.
Makes 6 servings.

Glazed Pork Roast

1 (3-pound) boneless pork shoulder roast (Boston Butt)
1 cup KIKKOMAN Teriyaki Sauce
3 tablespoons brown sugar, packed
3 tablespoons dry sherry
1 teaspoon minced fresh ginger root
1 clove garlic, minced
¼ cup water
2 tablespoons sugar
1 tablespoon cornstarch

Microwave Directions: Pierce meaty parts of roast with fork; place in large plastic bag. Combine teriyaki sauce, brown sugar, sherry, ginger and garlic; pour over roast. Press air out of bag; tie top securely. Refrigerate 8 hours or overnight, turning bag over occasionally. Reserving marinade, remove roast and place, fat side down, in 8×8-inch shallow microwave-safe dish. Brush thoroughly with reserved marinade. Cover roast loosely with waxed paper. Microwave on Medium-high (70%) 30 minutes, or until meat thermometer inserted into thickest part registers 165°F., rotating dish once and brushing with marinade. Remove roast; let stand 10 minutes before slicing. Meanwhile, combine reserved marinade, water, sugar and cornstarch in 2-cup microwave-safe measuring cup. Microwave on High 3 minutes, until mixture boils and thickens, stirring occasionally. Serve teriyaki glaze with roast.
Makes 6 servings.

Pork Roast with Sausage & Spinach Stuffing

1 envelope LIPTON® Onion, Onion-Mushroom or Beefy Mushroom Recipe Soup Mix
1 package (10 ounces) frozen chopped spinach, cooked and drained
½ pound sweet Italian sausage links, removed from casing
½ cup fresh bread crumbs
½ cup slivered almonds, toasted
2 eggs, slightly beaten
2 tablespoons finely chopped parsley
2 teaspoons thyme leaves
1 teaspoon finely chopped garlic (about 1 medium clove)
⅛ teaspoon pepper
2½- pound boneless center cut pork loin roast
1 to 2 tablespoons oil

Preheat oven to 350°
In large bowl, thoroughly combine onion recipe soup mix, spinach, sausage, bread crumbs, almonds, eggs, parsley, 1 teaspoon thyme, ½ teaspoon garlic and pepper; set aside.

Butterfly roast as directed. Spread spinach mixture evenly on cut side of roast. Roll, starting at long end, jelly-roll style; tie securely with string. In roasting pan, on rack, place pork seam side down. Rub roast with oil, then top with remaining garlic and thyme. Roast for 1½ hours or until meat thermometer reaches 165° (medium) or 180° (well done).
Makes about 8 servings.

How to Butterfly a Pork Loin Roast:
1. Place the boneless roast fat side down. Starting at the thickest edge, slice horizontally through the meat, stopping 1 inch from the opposite edge so that the roast can open like a book.
2. Lightly pound the opened roast and remove any fat thicker than ¼ inch.

Tofu & Vegetable Stir-Fry

½ block tofu
1 pound napa (Chinese cabbage) or romaine lettuce*
½ cup water
2 tablespoons cornstarch, divided
4 tablespoons KIKKOMAN Soy Sauce, divided
¼ pound boneless lean pork
2 teaspoons minced fresh ginger root
1 clove garlic, minced
½ teaspoon sugar
2 tablespoons vegetable oil, divided
1 medium onion, chunked
2 medium tomatoes, chunked

Cut tofu into ½-inch cubes; drain well on several layers of paper towels. Separate and rinse cabbage; pat dry. Cut leaves crosswise into 1-inch strips; set aside. Blend water, 1 tablespoon cornstarch and 3 tablespoons soy sauce; set aside. Cut pork into thin slices, then into thin strips. Combine remaining 1 tablespoon cornstarch and 1 tablespoon soy sauce, ginger, garlic and sugar in small bowl; stir in pork. Heat 1 tablespoon oil in hot wok or large skillet over high heat. Add pork and stir-fry 2 minutes; remove. Heat remaining 1 tablespoon oil in same pan. Add onion; stir-fry 2 minutes. Add cabbage; stir-fry 1 minute. Add tomatoes, pork and soy sauce mixture. Cook and stir gently until sauce boils and thickens. Gently fold in tofu; heat through.
Makes 4 servings.
   *If using romaine, increase water to ⅔ cup.

Crispy Fried Pork and Apples

6 butterflied pork chops, ½ inch thick
1 large apple, peeled and cored
2 eggs
2 tablespoons half-and-half
1 cup unseasoned dry bread crumbs
1 teaspoon ground ginger
¾ teaspoon salt
½ teaspoon ground coriander (optional)
¼ teaspoon ground allspice
CRISCO® Oil for frying

Pound each chop with meat mallet. Slice apple into 6 rings. Blend eggs and half-and-half in small mixing bowl. Mix bread crumbs, ginger, salt, coriander (optional) and allspice in shallow dish or on sheet of waxed paper. Set aside.
Heat 2 to 3 inches Crisco® Oil in deep-fryer or large saucepan to 350°F. Dip pork and apple rings in egg mixture, then in bread crumb mixture to coat. Fry 2 pieces of pork at a time, 5 to 7 minutes, or until crust is deep golden brown and pork is no longer pink in center. Drain on paper towels. Fry apple rings 2 to 3 minutes, or until deep golden brown. Drain on paper towels.
6 servings.

Hawaiian Roast Pork

1 (3-pound) boneless pork shoulder roast (Boston butt)
½ cup KIKKOMAN Soy Sauce
1½ teaspoons liquid smoke seasoning

Cut pork in half lengthwise. Place halves in large plastic bag. Combine soy sauce and liquid smoke; pour over pork. Press air out of bag; tie top securely. Turn over several times to coat pieces well. Refrigerate 8 hours or overnight, turning bag over occasionally. Remove pork from marinade and place in shallow baking pan; cover with aluminum foil. Bake at 350°F. 30 minutes. Discard foil; turn pieces over. Bake 1 hour longer, or until meat thermometer inserted into thickest part registers 170°F. To serve, cut across grain into thin slices. *Makes 6 servings.*

Hunan Pork Stir-Fry

½ pound boneless lean pork
2 teaspoons cornstarch
6 teaspoons KIKKOMAN Lite Soy Sauce, divided
2 cloves garlic, minced and divided
¾ cup water
1 tablespoon cornstarch
⅛ to ¼ teaspoon crushed red pepper
3 tablespoons vegetable oil, divided
3 cups bite-size cauliflowerets
1 medium-size green pepper, chunked
2 medium tomatoes, cut into eighths
Hot cooked rice

Cut pork across grain into thin slices, then into strips. Combine 2 teaspoons *each* cornstarch and lite soy sauce with ½ of the garlic in small bowl; stir in pork. Let stand 30 minutes. Meanwhile, combine water, 1 tablespoon cornstarch, remaining 4 teaspoons lite soy sauce and red pepper; set aside. Heat 1 tablespoon oil in hot wok or large skillet over high heat. Add pork and stir-fry 2 minutes; remove. Heat remaining 2 tablespoons oil in same pan over medium-high heat. Add cauliflowerets and remaining garlic; stir-fry 2 minutes. Add green pepper; stir-fry 3 minutes. Stir in tomatoes, pork and soy sauce mixture. Cook and stir gently until sauce boils and thickens. Serve with rice. *Makes 2 to 3 servings.*

Colorful Stir-Fried Pork

- ⅓ cup KIKKOMAN Stir-Fry Sauce
- 1 teaspoon distilled white vinegar
- ¼ to ½ teaspoon crushed red pepper
- ¾ pound boneless lean pork
- 1 tablespoon KIKKOMAN Stir-Fry Sauce
- 3 tablespoons vegetable oil, divided
- 2 medium carrots, cut into julienne strips
- 1 medium onion, halved and sliced
- ¼ pound fresh snow peas, trimmed and cut lengthwise in half

Combine ⅓ cup stir-fry sauce, vinegar and red pepper; set aside. Cut pork across grain into thin slices, then into strips; coat with 1 tablespoon stir-fry sauce. Heat 1 tablespoon oil in hot wok or large skillet over high heat. Add pork and stir-fry 2 minutes; remove. Heat remaining 2 tablespoons oil in same pan. Add carrots, onion and snow peas; stir-fry 4 minutes. Stir in pork and stir-fry sauce mixture. Cook and stir just until pork and vegetables are coated with sauce. Serve immediately. *Makes 4 servings.*

Crown Roast of Pork with Cognac Glaze

- 1 cup orange juice
- 1 jar (12 ounces) red currant or grape jelly
- 1 envelope LIPTON® Onion or Onion-Mushroom Recipe Soup Mix
- ½ cup Cognac or brandy
- ½ teaspoon ground ginger
- 8- to 9-pound crown roast of pork (about 22 ribs)
- Warm Dried Fruit Compote (recipe follows)

Preheat oven to 200°.

In medium saucepan, heat orange juice, jelly, onion recipe soup mix, Cognac and ginger over low heat, stirring occasionally, 5 minutes or until jelly is melted.

In roasting pan, place crown roast; brush with jelly glaze, then pour remaining glaze over roast. Loosely cover with heavy-duty aluminum foil; roast 2 hours. Increase heat to 350° and continue roasting, basting occasionally, an additional 1½ hours or until meat thermometer reaches 175°. Remove foil and continue roasting, basting occasionally and adding water if needed, 20 minutes or until thermometer reaches 180°.

Remove roast to serving platter and keep warm. Skim fat from pan drippings and serve pan juices with roast. Spoon Warm Dried Fruit Compote into center cavity and around roast. *Makes about 12 servings.*

WARM DRIED FRUIT COMPOTE: In large saucepan, combine 2 cups dried apricots, 2 cups pitted dried prunes, 12 dried figs, halved,* 2 cups orange juice, 2 tablespoons fresh squeezed lemon juice, 3 cinnamon sticks and 1 teaspoon whole cloves. Bring to a boil, then simmer 5 minutes. Stir in 1 cup green or red seedless grapes and simmer 2 minutes or until heated through. Remove cinnamon. *Makes about 8 cups.*

***Substitution:** Use 2 packages (11 ounces each) pitted mixed dried fruit instead of apricots, prunes and figs.

Make-Ahead Directions for Compote: Compote can be prepared up to 2 days ahead. Simply combine as above; bring to a boil, then simmer 5 minutes. Cover and refrigerate. Just before serving, heat through; stir in grapes, then continue as above.

Pineapple Citrus Glazed Pork Roast

- 1 boneless pork loin roast (3 to 4 pounds)
- Garlic salt
- Pepper
- 1 can (20 ounces) DOLE® Crushed Pineapple
- 1 cup orange juice
- ½ cup lemon juice
- ¼ cup sugar
- 2 tablespoons cornstarch
- 1 tablespoon grated orange peel
- 1 tablespoon grated lemon peel
- 2 teaspoons dried mint, crushed

Preheat oven to 400°F. Place pork on rack in shallow roasting pan, fat side up. Sprinkle pork with garlic salt and pepper to taste. Insert meat thermometer. Roast in preheated oven, uncovered, 30 minutes. Reduce oven to 325°F and roast 30 minutes longer.

In saucepan, combine undrained pineapple, orange and lemon juices, sugar and cornstarch. Cook, stirring, until mixture boils and thickens. Stir in orange peel, lemon peel and mint. Spread half of glaze over pork after 1 hour of roasting. Continue roasting and baste with glaze every 30 minutes until thermometer reaches 170°F (about 2 hours total cooking time). Remove pork to serving platter. Let stand 15 minutes before slicing. Serve with remaining glaze. *Makes 8 servings.*

Sweet-and-Sour Pork

½ cup all-purpose flour
1 teaspoon salt
½ teaspoon baking powder
½ cup cold water
1 pound lean boneless pork, cut into 1-inch cubes
1 can (20 ounces) pineapple chunks
2 tablespoons white vinegar
1 tablespoon cornstarch
CRISCO® Oil for frying
3 carrots, cut into thin diagonal slices
1 green pepper, seeded, cored and cut into 1-inch pieces
3 tablespoons packed brown sugar
Hot cooked rice

Mix flour, salt and baking powder in medium mixing bowl. Blend in cold water. Add pork. Stir to coat. Set aside. Drain pineapple chunks, reserving juice. Set aside pineapple chunks. Blend reserved pineapple juice, vinegar and cornstarch in small bowl. Set aside.

Heat 1 inch Crisco® Oil in Dutch oven to 375°F. Remove half the pork from batter with slotted spoon; add to Crisco® Oil. Fry 3 to 5 minutes, or until golden brown. Drain on paper towels. Repeat with remaining pork. Pour off all but 1 tablespoon drippings from Dutch oven. Add carrots. Stir-fry over moderate heat 2 to 3 minutes, or until tender-crisp. Add green pepper. Stir-fry 2 to 3 minutes longer. Add pineapple juice mixture, pineapple chunks and brown sugar. Heat to boiling, stirring constantly. Cook and stir until mixture is clear and thickened. Stir in pork. Cook about 3 minutes, or until hot. Serve with rice.
4 to 6 servings.

Cashew Pork Stir-Fry

¾ pound boneless lean pork
1 tablespoon KIKKOMAN Stir-Fry Sauce
3 tablespoons vegetable oil, divided
2 stalks celery, cut diagonally into ½-inch slices
1 onion, chunked
1 large green pepper, chunked
¼ pound fresh mushrooms, sliced
2 medium tomatoes, chunked
¼ cup KIKKOMAN Stir-Fry Sauce
¼ cup roasted cashews

Cut pork across grain into thin slices; coat with 1 tablespoon stir-fry sauce. Heat 1 tablespoon oil in hot wok or large skillet over medium-high heat. Add pork and stir-fry 3 minutes; remove. Wipe out pan with paper towel. Heat remaining 2 tablespoons oil in same pan over high heat. Add celery, onion and green pepper; stir-fry 2 minutes. Add mushrooms and stir-fry 2 minutes longer. Add pork, tomatoes and ¼ cup stir-fry sauce. Cook and stir only until tomatoes are heated through. Just before serving, sprinkle cashews over pork and vegetables.
Makes 4 servings.

Sweet & Sour Pork Loin

½ cup chicken broth or water
½ cup catsup
2 tablespoons brown sugar
2 tablespoons cider vinegar
2 tablespoons Worcestershire sauce
1 clove garlic, crushed
½ teaspoon salt
¼ teaspoon black pepper
⅛ teaspoon cayenne pepper
1 boneless pork loin roast (2 pounds), tied

In saucepan, combine all ingredients except roast. Heat to boiling. Cut roast crosswise into 4 pieces; arrange in shallow glass dish. Pour sweet and sour mixture over pork. Cover and refrigerate overnight. Drain pork; reserve sweet and sour mixture. Grill pork, on uncovered grill, over medium-hot **MATCH LIGHT® Charcoal Briquets** 20 to 25 minutes or until pork is cooked through, turning 3 to 4 times and basting often with sweet and sour mixture.
Makes 4 servings.

Oriental Pork

1 teaspoon sesame oil
1 teaspoon vegetable oil
1 teaspoon grated fresh ginger
1 tablespoon soy sauce
1 tablespoon dry sherry
1 clove garlic, minced
1 pound boneless pork, cut into 2- by ¼-inch strips
1 can (10½ ounces) CAMPBELL'S® Condensed Beef Broth (Bouillon)
2 tablespoons cornstarch
1 cup fresh snow peas
1 sweet red pepper, cut into thin strips
1 cup sliced CAMPBELL'S FRESH® Mushrooms
Hot cooked rice

To Microwave:
1. In 3-quart microwave-safe casserole, stir together oils, ginger, soy sauce, sherry and garlic. Stir in pork to coat. Cover with lid; refrigerate 1 hour.
2. Microwave, covered, on HIGH 5 minutes or until pork is no longer pink, stirring once during cooking.
3. In small bowl, stir together broth and cornstarch; add to pork mixture along with peas, pepper and mushrooms. Cover; microwave on HIGH 7 minutes or until hot and bubbling, stirring 3 times during cooking. Serve over rice.
Makes about 5 cups or 5 servings.

Curried Pork

- 1 pound boneless pork, cut into ¾-inch cubes
- 2 tablespoons all-purpose flour
- 2 tablespoons butter or margarine, divided
- 1 large onion, chopped
- 1 medium apple, chopped
- 2 cloves garlic, minced
- 2 teaspoons curry powder
- 1½ cups V8® Vegetable Juice
- 2 tablespoons raisins
  Hot cooked rice

1. In medium bowl, toss pork with flour to coat.
2. In 10-inch nonstick skillet over medium heat, in 1 tablespoon hot butter, cook half of the pork until browned on all sides; remove with slotted spoon. Repeat with remaining butter and pork; remove from skillet.
3. In same skillet over medium heat, cook onion, apple, garlic and curry until onion is nearly tender, stirring often. Stir in V8 juice, raisins and pork. Heat to boiling, stirring occasionally; reduce heat to low. Cover; simmer until pork is no longer pink, about 10 minutes. Serve over rice.
Makes 4 cups or 4 servings.

Per serving: 317 calories, 26 g protein, 15 g fat, 20 g carbohydrate, 446 mg sodium, 87 mg cholesterol.

Satay Pork

- ½ cup peanut or vegetable oil
- ¼ cup soy sauce
- 2 tablespoons chopped peanuts
- 1 tablespoon Worcestershire sauce
- 1 tablespoon chopped onion
- 2 cloves garlic, crushed
- 2 teaspoons brown sugar
- ¼ teaspoon curry powder
- ⅛ teaspoon coriander
- 3 pounds boneless pork, cut into ½-inch cubes

In shallow glass dish, combine all ingredients except pork. Add pork, turning to coat with marinade. Cover and refrigerate 1 to 2 hours, stirring occasionally. Drain pork; reserve marinade. Thread pork on skewers. Grill kabobs, on uncovered grill, over hot **KINGSFORD® Charcoal Briquets** 5 to 6 minutes or until cooked through, turning often and basting with marinade.
Makes 4 to 6 servings.

Pork and Peanut Stir-Fry

- ¼ pound boneless lean pork
- 4 teaspoons cornstarch, divided
- 3 tablespoons KIKKOMAN Lite Soy Sauce, divided
- 1 teaspoon minced fresh ginger root
- ½ cup water
- 2 teaspoons distilled white vinegar
- ¼ teaspoon garlic powder
- 2 tablespoons vegetable oil, divided
- 1 medium onion, sliced
- 1 medium carrot, cut diagonally into ⅛-inch-thick slices
- 2 medium zucchini, cut diagonally into ⅛-inch-thick slices
- ⅓ cup unsalted roasted peanuts
  Hot cooked rice (optional)

Cut pork across grain into thin slices, then into strips. Combine 2 teaspoons *each* cornstarch and lite soy sauce with ginger in small bowl; stir in pork. Let stand 15 minutes. Meanwhile, combine water, remaining 2 teaspoons cornstarch, 2 tablespoons plus 1 teaspoon lite soy sauce, vinegar and garlic powder; set aside. Heat 1 tablespoon oil in hot wok or large skillet over high heat. Add pork and stir-fry 2 minutes; remove. Heat remaining 1 tablespoon oil in same pan. Add onion and carrot; stir-fry 2 minutes. Add zucchini; stir-fry 2 minutes. Stir in pork and soy sauce mixture. Cook and stir until mixture boils and thickens. Stir in peanuts; serve immediately with rice.
Makes 2 to 3 servings.

Roast Loin of Pork Oriental-Style

- ½ cup WISH-BONE® Italian or Robusto Italian Dressing
- ½ cup honey
- 1 tablespoon finely chopped fresh ginger*
- 1 tablespoon hoisin sauce (optional)
- 2 teaspoons soy sauce
- 1 teaspoon Dijon-style mustard
- 1 (3- to 3½-pound) boneless pork loin roast, tied for roasting

Preheat oven to 375°.
In small bowl, combine all ingredients except pork. In roasting pan, on rack, place pork and roast 45 minutes. Brush pork with ½ of the dressing mixture, then continue roasting, basting occasionally, 35 minutes or until meat thermometer reaches 165° (medium) or 180° (well done). Heat remaining dressing mixture and serve with pork.
Makes about 10 servings.
Substitution: Use 1 teaspoon ground ginger.

Pork Spareribs

- 4 pounds pork spareribs or pork back ribs
- 1¼ cups K.C. MASTERPIECE® Barbecue Sauce

Remove breast section from ribs, if desired. Cut ribs into 4 or 5 rib portions. Arrange medium-hot **KINGSFORD® Charcoal Briquets** around drip pan. Place ribs over drip pan; cover grill and cook 1¼ hours. Turn; brush with barbecue sauce. Cook, on covered grill, 10 to 15 minutes longer or until ribs are thoroughly cooked, brushing once or twice with barbecue sauce. Bring remaining sauce to boil and serve with ribs, if desired.
Makes 4 servings.

Zesty Barbecued Ribs

6 pounds spareribs
  Water
2 cups catsup
½ cup REALEMON® Lemon Juice
  from Concentrate
½ cup firmly packed brown sugar
1 tablespoon prepared mustard
½ cup finely chopped onion
¼ cup margarine or butter
¼ cup Worcestershire sauce
1 clove garlic, finely chopped
¼ teaspoon salt
⅛ teaspoon hot pepper sauce

In large pan, cook ribs in boiling water 45 to 60 minutes or until tender. Meanwhile, in medium saucepan, combine remaining ingredients; simmer uncovered 20 minutes, stirring occasionally. Grill or broil ribs as desired, turning and basting frequently with sauce. Refrigerate leftovers.
Makes 6 to 8 servings.
Microwave: To pre-cook ribs, place 1½ pounds ribs in 12×7-inch shallow baking dish. Add ¼ cup water; cover with vented plastic wrap. Microwave on full power (high) 5 minutes. Reduce to ½ power (medium); continue cooking 7 minutes. Turn ribs over; cook covered on ½ power (medium) 7 minutes longer. Repeat with remaining ribs. Proceed as above.

Glazed Pork Tenderloin

2 pork tenderloins, about
    ¾ pound each
½ cup KIKKOMAN Teriyaki Baste
    & Glaze
¼ teaspoon anise seed, crushed
¼ teaspoon pepper
⅛ teaspoon ground cloves
    Mustard-Soy Dipping Sauce
    (recipe follows)

Place tenderloins on rack in shallow foil-lined baking pan; tuck under thin ends of each tenderloin. Combine teriyaki baste & glaze, anise, pepper and cloves; brush each tenderloin thoroughly with baste & glaze mixture. Bake in 325°F. oven 1 hour, or until meat thermometer inserted into thickest part registers 170°F. Brush occasionally with baste & glaze mixture during baking. Remove from oven and let stand 15 minutes. Cut across grain into thin slices and serve with Mustard-Soy Dipping Sauce.
Makes 4 to 6 servings.
MUSTARD-SOY DIPPING SAUCE: Blend *2 tablespoons dry mustard* with *1 teaspoon each distilled white vinegar* and *water* to make a smooth paste. Cover and let stand 10 minutes. Thin with enough *KIKKOMAN Soy Sauce* to dipping consistency.

Barbecued Pork Chops

6 pork loin chops, cut 1 inch
    thick
½ teaspoon seasoned salt
6 slices orange
6 thin slices onion
6 thin slices lemon
⅓ cup K.C. MASTERPIECE®
    Barbecue Sauce

Arrange medium-hot **KINGSFORD® Charcoal Briquets** to one side of grill with drip pan next to briquets. Sprinkle chops with seasoned salt. Place chops over drip pan; cover grill and cook 40 minutes or until nearly done, turning once after 25 minutes.

Top each chop with slices of orange, onion and lemon and about 1 tablespoon barbecue sauce. Cover grill and cook 5 to 10 minutes longer or until chops are tender and thoroughly cooked.
Makes 6 servings.

Spicy Country Ribs

1 medium onion, finely chopped
3 cloves garlic, crushed
2 tablespoons vegetable oil
1 can (15 ounces) tomato sauce
½ cup red wine
¼ cup packed brown sugar
¾ teaspoon salt
½ teaspoon dry mustard
½ teaspoon chili powder
½ teaspoon hot pepper sauce
⅛ teaspoon pepper
5 pounds country-style
    spareribs

In medium skillet, saute onion and garlic in oil until onion is soft but not brown. Stir in remaining ingredients except spareribs. Bring to boil; reduce heat and simmer, covered, 20 minutes. Trim any excess fat from ribs. Arrange ribs in shallow glass dish. Cover with plastic wrap, vented. Microwave at 50% power 20 minutes, rearranging ribs once. Remove from oven. Brush ribs with sauce. Lightly oil grid. Grill ribs, on covered grill, over medium-hot **KINGSFORD® Charcoal Briquets** 30 minutes or until cooked through, turning often and basting with sauce.
Makes 6 servings.

Barbecued Spareribs

1 pouch CAMPBELL'S® Onion
    Soup and Recipe Mix
½ cup water
½ cup ketchup
¼ cup packed brown sugar
2 tablespoons vinegar
1 teaspoon chili powder
¼ teaspoon hot pepper sauce
2½ pounds pork spareribs, cut
    into individual ribs

To Microwave:

1. To prepare sauce, in small bowl, stir together soup mix, water, ketchup, brown sugar, vinegar, chili powder and hot pepper sauce. Arrange ribs in 12- by 8-inch microwave-safe baking dish, placing thicker portions toward edges of dish. Pour sauce over ribs. Cover with vented plastic wrap; microwave on HIGH 5 minutes. Rearrange ribs.

2. Reduce power to 50%. Cover; microwave 40 minutes or until ribs are tender, rearranging ribs and spooning off fat twice during cooking. Let stand, covered, 5 minutes. Spoon off fat.

Makes 4 servings.

Chinese-Style Spareribs

½ cup butter or margarine
1 medium clove garlic, finely chopped
1 envelope LIPTON® Onion, Onion-Mushroom, Beefy Mushroom or Beefy Onion Recipe Soup Mix
1 can (16 ounces) tomato puree
½ cup brown sugar
¼ cup soy sauce
¼ cup white vinegar
¼ cup chili sauce
5 pounds spareribs, country-style ribs or baby back ribs

Preheat oven to 375°.

In large saucepan, melt butter and cook garlic with onion recipe soup mix over medium heat until garlic is golden. Stir in tomato puree, sugar, soy sauce, vinegar and chili sauce. Bring to a boil, then simmer, stirring occasionally, 15 minutes.

Meanwhile, in large aluminum-foil-lined baking pan or on broiler rack, arrange spareribs meaty side up and bake 20 minutes. Brush spareribs generously with sauce, then continue baking, meaty side up, brushing occasionally with remaining sauce, 50 minutes or until spareribs are done.

Makes about 7 main-dish or 12 appetizer servings.

Kamaaina Spareribs

4 pounds lean pork spareribs
Salt and pepper
1 can (20 ounces) DOLE® Crushed Pineapple, drained
1 cup catsup
½ cup brown sugar, packed
⅓ cup red wine vinegar
¼ cup soy sauce
1 teaspoon ground ginger
½ teaspoon dry mustard
¼ teaspoon garlic powder

Have butcher cut across rib bones to make strips 1½ inches wide. Preheat oven to 350°F. Place ribs close together in single layer in baking pan. Sprinkle with salt and pepper to taste. Cover tightly with aluminum foil. Bake in preheated oven 1 hour. Uncover; pour off and discard drippings. In bowl, combine remaining ingredients. Spoon sauce over ribs. Grill over hot coals 15 minutes or bake, uncovered, 30 minutes longer or until ribs are tender and glazed.

Makes 6 servings.

Sweet Jalapeno Ribs

1½ cups OPEN PIT® Original Flavor Barbecue Sauce
½ cup jalapeno jelly
¼ cup cider vinegar
2 tablespoons seeded and chopped VLASIC® Hot Jalapeno Peppers
2 teaspoons garlic powder
6 pounds pork spareribs (2 slabs)

1. To make sauce: In 1-quart saucepan, combine barbecue sauce, jelly, vinegar, peppers and garlic. Over medium heat, heat until jelly melts, stirring often.

2. In covered grill, arrange preheated coals around drip pan; test for medium heat above pan.

3. On grill rack, place ribs, fat side up, over pan but not over coals. Grill, covered, 1½ to 2 hours or until well-done. Adjust vents and add more charcoal as necessary. Turn and brush often with sauce during the last 30 minutes.

Makes 6 servings.

To roast: Place ribs, fat side up, on rack in roasting pan. Roast, uncovered, at 350°F. 1½ to 2 hours or until well-done. Turn and brush often with sauce during the last 30 minutes.

Note: You'll find jalapeno jelly in the Mexican or condiment section of your grocery store. Serve leftover jelly with cream cheese and crackers.

Bake & Glaze Teri Ribs

3 pounds pork spareribs
½ teaspoon garlic powder
½ teaspoon pepper
⅔ cup KIKKOMAN Teriyaki Baste & Glaze
½ teaspoon grated lemon peel

Cut ribs into serving pieces; place, meaty side up, in shallow foil-lined baking pan. Sprinkle garlic powder and pepper evenly over ribs; cover pan loosely with foil. Bake in 350°F. oven 45 minutes. Meanwhile, combine teriyaki baste & glaze and lemon peel. Remove foil and brush both sides of ribs with baste & glaze mixture. Cover and bake 40 minutes longer, or until ribs are tender, brushing with baste & glaze mixture occasionally.

Makes 4 servings.

Stuffed Cabbage Leaves

1 pound ground pork or beef
½ cup chopped onion
1 can (10½ ounces)
    CAMPBELL'S® Condensed
    Beef Broth (Bouillon)
½ cup regular rice, uncooked
½ teaspoon grated lemon peel
½ cup chopped apple
¼ cup chopped walnuts
¼ cup chopped fresh parsley
½ teaspoon dried mint leaves,
    crushed (optional)
1 medium head cabbage
1 can (10¾ ounces)
    CAMPBELL'S® Condensed
    Tomato Soup
1 tablespoon lemon juice
¼ teaspoon ground cinnamon

1. In 10-inch skillet over medium heat, cook pork and onion until pork is well browned, stirring occasionally to break up meat. Pour off fat.
2. Add beef broth, rice and lemon peel. Heat to boiling. Reduce heat to low. Cover; simmer 20 to 25 minutes or until rice is tender (add a little water during cooking if mixture becomes dry). Remove from heat. Stir in apple, walnuts, parsley and mint.
3. Meanwhile, in 4-quart saucepan over high heat, heat about 6 cups water to boiling. Add whole head of cabbage to boiling water. Reduce heat to low. Cover; simmer 1 to 2 minutes or until outer leaves are softened. Remove cabbage from water. Carefully remove 6 outer leaves. Reserve remaining cabbage for another use.
4. Drain cabbage leaves on paper towels. Lay leaves flat on cutting board and cut out any tough stems. Spoon about ¾ cup pork filling into center of one leaf. Fold in sides, then roll up from stem end to form a bundle. Repeat procedure with remaining leaves and filling.
5. In medium bowl, stir together tomato soup, lemon juice and cinnamon. Pour ½ of the soup mixture into 12-by 8-inch baking dish. Place cabbage rolls, seam side down, in prepared dish. Pour remaining soup mixture over all. Cover with foil. Bake at 350°F. 35 minutes or until heated through.
Makes 6 servings.

Herbed Pork Sauté

¼ cup all-purpose flour
½ teaspoon dried basil leaves
½ teaspoon dried marjoram
    leaves
½ teaspoon salt
¼ teaspoon pepper
1 to 1½ pounds butterflied pork
    chops, cut into thin strips
4 tablespoons CRISCO® Oil,
    divided
1 teaspoon instant chicken
    bouillon granules
1 teaspoon instant beef bouillon
    granules
1 cup hot water
½ cup coarsely chopped onion
½ cup chopped carrot
1 package (10 ounces) frozen
    Brussels sprouts

Mix flour, basil, marjoram, salt and pepper in large plastic food storage bag. Add pork. Shake to coat.

Heat 3 tablespoons Crisco® Oil in large skillet. Add pork and any remaining flour mixture. Brown over medium-high heat. Remove pork and drippings from skillet; set aside.

Dissolve chicken and beef bouillon granules in hot water. Set aside. Heat remaining 1 tablespoon Crisco® Oil in large skillet. Add onion and carrot. Sauté over moderate heat until tender. Stir in pork, bouillon mixture and Brussels sprouts. Heat to boiling. Cover. Cook over moderate heat, stirring occasionally, about 10 minutes, or until Brussels sprouts are tender and pork is no longer pink. Serve with *hot mashed potatoes,* if desired.
4 to 6 servings.

Fire and Ice Chili

1 can (20 ounces) DOLE®
    Pineapple Chunks
1 can (28 ounces) whole
    tomatoes
1 can (6 ounces) tomato paste
1 can (4 ounces) diced green
    chiles
2 medium yellow onions,
    chopped
1 DOLE™ Green Bell Pepper,
    seeded and chopped
3 cloves garlic, pressed or
    minced
¼ cup chili powder
4 teaspoons ground cumin
1 tablespoon diced jalapeño
    chiles*
2 teaspoons salt
2 tablespoons olive oil
2 pounds lean boneless pork
    butt, cut into 1-inch cubes
Condiments: small bowls of
    sliced green onions,
    shredded Cheddar cheese
    and dairy sour cream

Drain pineapple; reserve juice. Drain and chop tomatoes; reserve juice. In large bowl, combine reserved juices, tomatoes, tomato paste, green chiles, 1 onion, green pepper, 2 cloves garlic, chili powder, cumin, jalapeño chiles and salt.

In Dutch oven, heat oil until very hot. Brown ¼ of the pork in oil. Remove from pot. Repeat with remaining pork. Return browned pork to pot; add remaining 1 onion and 1 clove garlic. Cook until onion is soft. Add tomato mixture to pork mixture. Cover and simmer 2½ hours, stirring occasionally. Stir in pineapple; cover and simmer 30 minutes longer. Serve with condiments.
Makes 8 to 10 servings.
*For more fire, add 2 tablespoons jalapeño chiles.

Tangy Coconut Ham Glaze

¾ cup COCO LOPEZ® Cream of
   Coconut
2 tablespoons prepared mustard
1½ teaspoons cornstarch

In small saucepan, combine ingredients; bring to a boil. Cook and stir 2 to 3 minutes or until thickened. Use to glaze ham during last 30 minutes of baking.
Makes about ¾ cup, enough to glaze a 10- to 12-pound ham.
Microwave: In 2-cup glass measure, combine ingredients. Microwave on ⅔ power (medium-high) 4 to 6 minutes or until thickened, stirring every 2 minutes. Let stand 5 minutes. Proceed as above.

Pineapple-Glazed Ham and Sweets

1 can (8 ounces) pineapple
   slices in juice, undrained
1 package (12 ounces) MRS.
   PAUL'S® Frozen Candied
   Sweet Potatoes
1 tablespoon Dijon-style
   mustard
¾ pound cooked ham, cut into
   3 slices

To Microwave:
1. To make sauce: Drain pineapple, reserving 2 tablespoons juice; set pineapple aside. To prepare sauce, in small bowl, stir together reserved pineapple juice, contents of sauce packet from sweet potatoes and mustard.

2. Arrange ham slices in center of 10-inch microwave-safe pie plate. Cut pineapple slices in half; arrange pineapple and sweet potatoes around edge of dish. Spoon sauce over.
3. Cover with vented plastic wrap; microwave on HIGH 10 minutes or until potatoes are tender, rotating dish once during cooking. Spoon sauce over ham and sweet potatoes before serving.
Makes 3 servings.

Hawaiian Pork Stew

2 pounds boneless pork
   shoulder (Boston butt)
¼ cup all-purpose flour
1 teaspoon ground ginger
2 tablespoons vegetable oil
1 can (8 oz.) pineapple chunks
   in juice
1¾ cups water, divided
⅓ cup KIKKOMAN Teriyaki Sauce
1 pound fresh yams or sweet
   potatoes, peeled and cut
   into 2-inch chunks
1 large onion, cut into eighths
   Hot cooked rice

Cut pork into 1½-inch cubes. Coat in mixture of flour and ginger; reserve 2 tablespoons flour mixture. Heat oil in Dutch oven or large pan; brown pork on all sides in hot oil. Drain pineapple; reserve juice. Add juice, 1 cup water and teriyaki sauce to pork. Cover pan; bring to boil. Reduce heat and simmer 1 hour, stirring occasionally. Add yams to pork; simmer, covered, 10 minutes. Stir in onion; simmer, covered, 20 minutes longer, or until pork and yams are tender. Meanwhile, combine reserved flour mixture and remaining ¾ cup water; stir into pork mixture and cook until slightly thickened. Stir in pineapple; cook only until heated through. Serve with rice.
Makes 6 servings.

Golden Glazed Ham Loaf

1 pound lean ground ham
1 pound ground pork
1 cup soft bread crumbs
   (2 slices bread)
⅓ cup chopped onion
¼ cup BORDEN® or MEADOW
   GOLD® Milk
1 egg
   Dash pepper
1 cup BAMA® Peach Preserves
   or Orange Marmalade
2 tablespoons REALEMON®
   Lemon Juice from
   Concentrate
1 tablespoon prepared mustard

Preheat oven to 350°. In large bowl, combine all ingredients except preserves, ReaLemon® brand and mustard; mix well. In shallow baking dish, shape into loaf. Bake 1½ hours. Meanwhile, stir together preserves, ReaLemon® brand and mustard. Use ⅓ to ½ cup sauce to glaze loaf during last 30 minutes of baking. Heat remaining glaze and serve with loaf. Garnish as desired. Refrigerate leftovers.
Makes 8 servings.
Microwave: Prepare loaf as above. Cover loosely; microwave on full power (high) 5 minutes. Rotate dish; microwave on ½ power (medium) 20 to 23 minutes or until center is set. Spread with glaze as above; microwave uncovered on ½ power (medium) 3 to 5 minutes. Let stand 5 minutes before serving. Meanwhile, microwave remaining glaze on full power (high) 1 to 2 minutes or until hot, stirring after 1 minute. Serve as above.

Asparagus-Ham Roll-Ups

- 1 pound fresh asparagus
- 2 tablespoons water
- 8 slices (1 ounce each) boiled ham
- 1 can (10¾ ounces) CAMPBELL'S® Condensed Cream of Celery Soup
- ½ cup sour cream
- ¼ cup milk
- 2 tablespoons chopped fresh parsley
- 1 teaspoon prepared mustard Hot cooked rice

To Microwave:

1. Arrange asparagus with tips toward center in 12- by 8-inch microwave-safe baking dish; add water. Cover with vented plastic wrap; microwave on HIGH 4 minutes or until asparagus is tender, rotating dish once during cooking. Drain well.

2. Divide asparagus spears among ham slices; roll ham around asparagus. Secure with wooden toothpicks if necessary. Arrange rolls in same baking dish.

3. In small bowl, stir soup until smooth; stir in sour cream, milk, parsley and mustard until well blended. Pour over ham rolls. Cover with vented plastic wrap; microwave at 50% power 13 minutes or until heated through. Let stand, covered, 5 minutes. Serve over rice.
Makes 4 servings.

Note: Substitute 1 package (10 ounces) frozen asparagus spears for fresh asparagus. Cook frozen asparagus according to package directions. Drain well, then proceed as above in steps 2 and 3.

Pineapple-Orange Glazed Ham

- 1 ARMOUR® Lower Salt Ham Nugget (about 1¾ pounds)
- ⅔ cup orange marmalade
- 1 (8-ounce) can pineapple chunks, drained and juice reserved

Preheat oven to 350°F. Spray roasting pan with nonstick cooking spray; place ham in pan. Combine orange marmalade, 2 tablespoons reserved pineapple juice and pineapple chunks in small bowl. Spoon a third over ham; brush to cover entire surface. Bake, uncovered, for 1 hour and 10 minutes, or until ham reaches an internal temperature of 145°F. Baste with pineapple-marmalade sauce every 10 minutes. Serve with remaining sauce. Garnish with fresh mint leaves or parsley, if desired.
Makes 8 to 10 servings.

Note: Try apricot-pineapple jam in place of orange marmalade for a different flavor combination.

Nutrition Information Per Serving: 185 calories, 14.1 g protein, 3.9 g fat, 17.2 carbohydrates, 39.2 mg cholesterol, 672 mg sodium.

Holiday Baked Ham

- 1 bone-in smoked ham (8½ pounds)
- 1 can (20 ounces) DOLE® Sliced Pineapple in Syrup
- 1 cup apricot preserves
- 1 teaspoon dry mustard
- ½ teaspoon ground allspice Whole cloves Maraschino cherries

Preheat oven to 325°F. Remove rind from ham. Place ham on rack in open roasting pan, fat side up. Insert meat thermometer with bulb in thickest part away from fat or bone. Roast ham in preheated oven about 3 hours.

Drain pineapple; reserve syrup. In small saucepan, combine syrup, preserves, mustard and allspice. Bring to boil; boil, stirring occasionally, 10 minutes. Remove ham from oven, but keep oven hot. Stud ham with cloves; brush with glaze. Using wooden picks, secure pineapple and cherries to ham. Brush again with glaze. Return ham to oven. Roast 30 minutes longer or until thermometer registers 160°F (about 25 minutes per pound total cooking time). Brush with glaze 15 minutes before done. Let ham stand 20 minutes before slicing.
Makes 8 to 10 servings.

Ham-Sauced Sweet Potatoes

- 3 sweet potatoes (about 8 ounces each)
- 1 can (10¾ ounces) CAMPBELL'S® Condensed Golden Mushroom Soup
- 1 cup cooked ham cut into thin strips
- ½ teaspoon grated orange peel
- ⅓ cup orange juice
- ¼ cup raisins

To Microwave:

1. Pierce potatoes with fork in several places; arrange in circular pattern on microwave-safe plate. Microwave, uncovered, on HIGH 8 minutes or until tender, rearranging potatoes once during cooking. Let stand, uncovered, while preparing sauce.

2. In medium microwave-safe bowl, combine remaining ingredients. Cover with vented plastic wrap; microwave on HIGH 4 minutes or until hot, stirring once during cooking. Split potatoes; spoon sauce over each.
Makes 3 servings.

Glazed Ham Steak

1 (8-ounce) can crushed
   pineapple, well drained
½ cup BAMA® Peach or Apricot
   Preserves
2 tablespoons REALEMON®
   Lemon Juice from
   Concentrate
1 teaspoon cornstarch
1 (1- to 1½-pound) center cut
   ham slice

In small saucepan, combine pineapple, preserves, ReaLemon® brand and cornstarch; mix well and bring to a boil. Reduce heat; simmer uncovered 10 to 15 minutes to blend flavors. Broil ham to desired doneness on both sides. Spoon pineapple mixture on top; heat until hot and bubbly. Refrigerate leftovers.
Makes 4 servings.

Baked Ham with Wine & Onion Glaze

1 envelope LIPTON® Onion or
   Onion-Mushroom Recipe
   Soup Mix
1 cup water
⅓ cup brown sugar
¼ cup Madeira wine or sherry
2 tablespoons butter or
   margarine, melted
1 tablespoon finely chopped
   parsley
5- to 6-pound fully cooked ham
   butt end
1 pound shallots or small
   onions, peeled and
   quartered

Preheat oven to 375°.
In small bowl, blend onion recipe soup mix, water, sugar, wine, butter and parsley; set aside.
In roasting pan, place ham. With knife, score (lightly cut) fat in diamond pattern; top with soup mixture. Arrange shallots around ham. Bake, stirring shallots and basting ham occasionally, 60 minutes or until golden brown.
Makes about 8 servings.

Ham-Stuffed Peppers

1½ cups cooked unsalted regular
   rice (½ cup uncooked)
1 cup (5 ounces) diced cooked
   ham
1 can (16 ounces) whole kernel
   corn, drained
1 jar (15½ ounces) spaghetti
   sauce
1 cup (4 ounces) shredded
   Cheddar cheese
1 can (2.8 ounces) DURKEE
   French Fried Onions
¼ teaspoon DURKEE Seasoned
   Salt
¼ teaspoon DURKEE Ground
   Black Pepper
4 medium green peppers, cut
   into halves lengthwise and
   seeded
¼ cup water

Preheat oven to 350°. To hot rice in saucepan, add ham, corn, *1 cup* spaghetti sauce, *½ cup* cheese, *½ can* French Fried Onions and the seasonings; stir well. Spoon rice filling into green pepper halves. Arrange stuffed peppers in 8×12-inch baking dish. In small bowl, combine remaining spaghetti sauce and the water; pour over peppers. Bake, covered, at 350° for 30 minutes or until peppers are done. Top with remaining cheese and onions; bake, uncovered, 5 minutes or until onions are golden brown.
Makes 4 servings.

Baked Ham with Glazed Vegetables

1 cup apricot nectar
1 cup dried apricot halves
1 cup (8 ounces) WISH-BONE®
   Deluxe French Dressing
¼ cup honey
¼ teaspoon ground cinnamon
⅛ teaspoon ground nutmeg
½ cup sliced almonds (optional)
1 (5- to 6-pound) fully cooked
   ham butt end with bone
2 pounds sweet potatoes or
   yams, peeled and cut into
   large chunks
1 pound pearl onions, peeled

Preheat oven to 375°.
In medium saucepan, bring nectar to a boil. Add apricots, then remove from heat. Let stand 10 minutes. Stir in deluxe French dressing, honey, cinnamon, nutmeg, then almonds.
On aluminum-foil-lined roasting pan, place ham. With knife, score (lightly cut) fat in diamond pattern. Arrange potatoes and onions around ham. Spoon dressing mixture over ham and vegetables. Loosely cover with heavy-duty aluminum foil and bake, turning vegetables and basting occasionally, 1 hour or until ham is golden and vegetables are tender.
Makes about 10 servings.
Note: Also terrific with Wish-Bone® Lite French Style, Sweet 'n Spicy French or Lite Sweet 'n Spicy French Dressing.

Grandpa Snub's Chili

2 tablespoons vegetable oil
2 pounds boneless pork shoulder, cut into 1-inch cubes
1 medium onion, chopped
1 small green pepper, chopped
2 cloves garlic, minced
3 tablespoons chili powder
1 teaspoon paprika
1/2 teaspoon celery seed
1/2 teaspoon salt
1/2 cup sliced pimiento-stuffed green olives
3 tablespoons olive juice (from jar)
2 cans (16 ounces each) pinto beans, undrained
1 cup water
1 teaspoon TABASCO® pepper sauce
Accompaniments: Cooked rice, chopped tomatoes, shredded cheese, chopped green peppers, chopped onion and crackers (optional)

In large heavy saucepot or Dutch oven heat oil. Add pork; cook over medium-high heat until browned. Add onion, green pepper, garlic, chili powder, paprika, celery seed and salt. Cook 15 minutes or until vegetables are tender. Stir in olives and olive juice. Cover. Simmer 1 hour or until meat is tender; stir occasionally. Stir in beans, water and Tabasco® sauce. Cover. Simmer 30 minutes; add more water if necessary to prevent sticking. Serve with suggested accompaniments, if desired.
Makes 8 servings.
Note: This chili is equally delicious made with beef.

Two-Bean Franks

1/2 cup chopped onion
1/2 cup chopped celery
1 clove garlic, minced
2 cans (16 ounces each) CAMPBELL'S® Pork & Beans in Tomato Sauce
1 can (about 15 ounces) kidney beans, drained
5 frankfurters, sliced
1/4 teaspoon dry mustard

To Microwave:
1. In 3-quart microwave-safe casserole, combine onion, celery and garlic. Cover with lid; microwave on HIGH 3 minutes or until vegetables are tender, stirring once during cooking.
2. Stir in remaining ingredients. Cover; microwave on HIGH 10 minutes or until hot and bubbling, stirring twice during cooking. Let stand, covered, 5 minutes.
Makes about 6 cups or 5 servings.

Barbecued Sausage Kabobs

1 pound ECKRICH® Smoked Sausage, cut into 1-inch pieces
1 cup dried apricots
1 can (12 ounces) beer
1/2 red bell pepper
1/2 green bell pepper
1 Spanish onion, cut into wedges
1/4 pound fresh medium mushrooms, sliced
3/4 cup apricot preserves
1 tablespoon prepared mustard
2 tablespoons chili sauce
1 teaspoon Worcestershire sauce

Simmer sausage and apricots in beer in large saucepan over low heat 10 minutes. Cut peppers into 1 1/4-inch squares. Add peppers to sausage mixture; let stand off heat 10 minutes. Assemble kabobs on skewers, alternately threading sausage with onion, red and green peppers, mushrooms and apricots. Combine apricot preserves, mustard, chili sauce and Worcestershire sauce in small saucepan. Heat over medium heat, stirring until blended. Brush kabobs with sauce. Grill or broil, 4 inches from heat, 10 minutes, turning and brushing with more sauce after 5 minutes. Brush with remaining sauce and serve.
Makes 4 servings.

Bean and Kraut Franks

1 jar (16 ounces) VLASIC® Old Fashioned Sauerkraut, rinsed and drained
1 can (16 ounces) CAMPBELL'S® Pork & Beans in Tomato Sauce
1 small onion, chopped
2 tablespoons brown sugar
1/2 teaspoon caraway seed
1 pound frankfurters or knockwurst

To Microwave:
1. In 12- by 8-inch microwave-safe baking dish, stir together sauerkraut, pork and beans, onion, brown sugar and caraway. Cover with vented plastic wrap; microwave on HIGH 5 minutes or until hot, stirring once during cooking.
2. Arrange frankfurters over sauerkraut mixture. Cover; microwave on HIGH 5 minutes or until heated through, rotating dish once during cooking. Let stand, covered, for 2 minutes.
Makes 4 servings.

Grilled Sausage with Apples & Onions

1 pound smoked sausage, cut into 1-inch chunks
2 small apples, cored and cut into quarters
2 small onions, cut into quarters
2 tablespoons apple jelly
1 tablespoon butter or margarine

Thread sausage, apples and onions alternately on 4 skewers. In small saucepan, combine jelly and butter; heat until melted. Brush jelly mixture on sausage kabobs. Grill kabobs, on uncovered grill, over medium-hot **MATCH LIGHT®** Charcoal Briquets 10 to 15 minutes or until cooked through, turning often and basting with jelly mixture.
Makes 4 servings.

Corn-Pepper-Sausage Skillet

12 ounces Italian or bulk pork sausage
1 cup chopped green or red pepper
1 cup chopped onion
3 cups fresh whole kernel corn *or* 1 package (16 ounces) frozen whole kernel corn, thawed
1/2 teaspoon garlic salt
1/4 teaspoon pepper
1/4 teaspoon chili powder
1/4 teaspoon ground cumin
Halved cherry tomatoes (optional)
Herbed cream cheese, softened (optional)
Sprig parsley (optional)

Crumble sausage into heavy 10-inch skillet or heavy foil pan. Add green pepper and onion. Place skillet, on covered grill, over medium-hot **KINGSFORD®** Charcoal Briquets about 15 minutes or until meat is browned, stirring once or twice. Remove from grill; drain off fat.

Stir in corn, garlic salt, pepper, chili powder and cumin; mix well. Cover skillet with foil. Grill, on covered grill, over medium-hot coals, 10 minutes longer or until heated through. Garnish with tomato halves spread with cream cheese; top with parsley sprig.
Makes 6 servings.

Sausage and Peppers

1 pound Italian sausage, cut into 2-inch chunks
2 tablespoons water
2 large green peppers, cut into 1/2-inch-wide strips
1 medium onion, sliced and separated into rings
2 cloves garlic, minced
1 can (11 ounces) CAMPBELL'S® Condensed Tomato Bisque
1/2 cup water
1/2 teaspoon dried basil leaves, crushed
Polenta (recipe follows)

1. In 10-inch covered skillet over medium heat, cook sausage and 2 tablespoons water 5 minutes. Uncover; cook until sausage is browned on all sides.
2. Add green peppers, onion and garlic; cook until vegetables are tender, stirring frequently.
3. Stir in soup, 1/2 cup water and basil; reduce heat to low. Cover; simmer 10 minutes. Serve with polenta.
Makes 4 servings.
POLENTA: In heavy 4-quart saucepan, heat 4 cups water to boiling. With wire whisk, gradually stir in 1 cup cornmeal. Reduce heat to low. Simmer 20 to 25 minutes, stirring often. Pour into buttered 9-inch pie plate. Let stand 10 minutes; cut into wedges.

Mustard Glazed Sausage with Sauteed Cabbage

1 pound ECKRICH® Smoked Sausage
2 tablespoons packed brown sugar
1 tablespoon catsup
1 tablespoon prepared mustard
3 tablespoons butter or margarine
1/2 cup chopped onion
8 cups coarsely chopped green cabbage
3/4 teaspoon salt
Dash coarsely ground black pepper

Preheat oven to 350°F. Place sausage in 12×8×2-inch baking dish. Make several diagonal cuts about 1/4 inch deep in sausage. Combine brown sugar, catsup and mustard in small bowl. Spoon over sausage. Bake 20 minutes or until sausage is hot. Meanwhile, melt butter in large skillet over medium-high heat. Add onion and saute until tender. Add cabbage, salt and pepper. Cook, stirring often, until cabbage is crisp-tender. Cut sausage into pieces and serve with cabbage.
Makes 4 to 5 servings.

Roasted Leg of Lamb with Lemon-Rosemary Glaze

5- to 6-pound leg of lamb
6 large cloves garlic, halved
4 large sprigs fresh rosemary, torn into pieces*
1/2 teaspoon pepper
1/4 cup butter or margarine, melted
1 can (6 ounces) frozen lemonade concentrate, partially thawed and undiluted
1 envelope LIPTON® Onion or Onion-Mushroom Recipe Soup Mix

Preheat oven to 325°.

In roasting pan, place lamb fat side up. With knife, make several 1-inch-deep cuts in lamb; stuff cuts with garlic and 1/2 of the rosemary. Sprinkle with pepper, then drizzle with butter. Roast 1 hour or until meat thermometer reaches 140°.

Meanwhile, in small bowl, blend lemonade concentrate, onion recipe soup mix and remaining rosemary. Pour over lamb, then continue roasting, basting occasionally, 30 minutes or until thermometer reaches 145°.

Remove lamb to serving platter and keep warm. Skim fat from pan drippings and serve pan juices with lamb. Garnish, if desired, with additional rosemary and lemon slices.
Makes about 10 servings.
   ***Substitution:** Use 1 tablespoon dried rosemary leaves.

Western Lamb Riblets

5 pounds lamb riblets, cut into serving-size pieces
3/4 cup chili sauce
1/2 cup honey
1/2 cup beer
1/4 cup Worcestershire sauce
1/4 cup finely chopped onion
1 clove garlic, minced
1/2 teaspoon red pepper flakes

Trim excess fat from riblets. In saucepan, combine chili sauce, honey, beer, Worcestershire sauce, onion, garlic and red pepper flakes. Heat mixture to boiling. Reduce heat; simmer, covered, 10 minutes. Remove from heat; cool.

Place riblets in plastic bag; set bag in large bowl. Pour marinade over riblets in bag. Close bag securely and refrigerate about 2 hours, turning bag occasionally to distribute marinade evenly.

Drain riblets; reserve marinade. In grill, arrange medium-hot **KINGS-FORD® Charcoal Briquets** around drip pan. Place riblets over drip pan. Cover grill and cook 45 minutes, turning riblets and brushing with marinade twice. Bring remaining marinade to boil and serve with riblets.
Makes 6 servings.

Lamb Stew

1 1/2 pounds boneless lamb, cut into 1/2-inch pieces
1 can (10 1/2 ounces) FRANCO-AMERICAN® Mushroom Gravy
4 small potatoes, cut into quarters
1 tablespoon chopped fresh mint leaves or 1 teaspoon dried mint leaves, crushed
1 cup frozen peas
1 cup quartered CAMPBELL'S FRESH® Mushrooms
1 tablespoon lemon juice

To Microwave:
1. Place lamb in 3-quart microwave-safe casserole. Cover with lid; microwave on HIGH 6 minutes or until lamb is no longer pink, stirring once during cooking. Spoon off fat.
2. Stir in gravy, potatoes and mint. Cover; microwave on HIGH 5 minutes or until bubbling. Stir again.
3. Reduce power to 50%. Cover; microwave 20 minutes or until meat is nearly tender, stirring twice during cooking.
4. Stir in peas, mushrooms and lemon juice. Cover; microwave at 50% power 10 minutes or until vegetables and meat are tender, stirring once during cooking. Let stand, covered, 5 minutes before serving.
Makes about 6 cups or 6 servings.

Pork Steaks with Peppers

2 tablespoons olive or vegetable oil
1 1/2 pounds pork blade steaks, 1/2 inch thick (about 4 to 5)
3 medium red, green or yellow peppers, cut into thin strips
1 clove garlic, finely chopped
1 medium tomato, coarsely chopped
1 envelope LIPTON® Onion, Onion-Mushroom or Beefy Mushroom Recipe Soup Mix
1 cup water
1/2 teaspoon thyme leaves
1/8 teaspoon pepper

In large skillet, heat oil and brown steaks over medium-high heat. Remove steaks. Reduce heat to medium; into skillet, add peppers and garlic and cook 5 minutes or until peppers are crisp-tender. Stir in tomato, then onion recipe soup mix blended with water, thyme and pepper; bring to a boil. Return steaks to skillet and simmer uncovered, stirring sauce occasionally, 25 minutes or until steaks and vegetables are tender.
Makes about 4 servings.

Hunan Stir-Fry with Tofu

1 block tofu
½ pound ground pork
1 tablespoon dry sherry
1 teaspoon minced fresh ginger root
1 clove garlic, minced
½ cup regular-strength chicken broth
1 tablespoon cornstarch
3 tablespoons KIKKOMAN Soy Sauce
1 tablespoon vinegar
½ teaspoon crushed red pepper
1 tablespoon vegetable oil
1 onion, cut into ¾-inch pieces
1 green pepper, cut into ¾-inch pieces
Hot cooked rice

Cut tofu into ½-inch cubes; drain well on several layers of paper towels. Meanwhile, combine pork, sherry, ginger and garlic in small bowl; let stand 10 minutes. Blend broth, cornstarch, soy sauce, vinegar and red pepper; set aside. Heat wok or large skillet over medium-high heat; add pork. Cook, stirring to separate pork, about 3 minutes, or until lightly browned; remove. Heat oil in same pan. Add onion and green pepper; stir-fry 4 minutes. Add pork and soy sauce mixture. Cook and stir until mixture boils and thickens. Gently fold in tofu; heat through. Serve immediately over rice.
Makes 4 servings.

Grilled Smoked Sausage

1 cup apricot or pineapple preserves
1 tablespoon lemon juice
1½ pounds smoked sausage

In small suacepan, heat preserves. Strain; reserve fruit pieces. Combine strained preserve liquid with lemon juice. Grill whole sausage, on uncovered grill, over low **KINGSFORD® Charcoal Briquets** 5 minutes. Brush with glaze; grill sausage about 5 minutes longer, turning and brushing with glaze occasionally. Garnish with fruit pieces.
Makes 6 servings.

Lamb Curry

1 tablespoon butter or margarine
1 cup chopped onion
2 tablespoons curry powder
1½ pounds boneless lamb, cut into ½-inch pieces
¼ cup all-purpose flour
1 cup SWANSON® Clear Ready to Serve Chicken Broth
2 apples, peeled and chopped
1 can (8 ounces) tomatoes, drained and cut up (optional)
¼ cup chutney
½ cup sour cream or plain yogurt
Chopped peanuts for garnish
Hot cooked rice

To Microwave:
1. In 3-quart microwave-safe casserole, combine butter, onion and curry. Cover with lid; microwave on HIGH 4 minutes or until onion is tender, stirring once during cooking.
2. In large bowl, toss lamb with flour. Stir lamb and flour into casserole. Cover; microwave on HIGH 6 minutes or until meat is no longer pink, stirring once during cooking.
3. Stir in broth, apples, tomatoes and chutney. Cover; microwave on HIGH 7 minutes or until boiling, stirring once during cooking. Stir again.
4. Reduce power to 50%. Microwave 30 minutes or until meat is tender, stirring 3 times during cooking. Let stand, covered, 5 minutes.
5. Stir in sour cream. Garnish with peanuts; serve over rice.
Makes about 5 cups or 6 servings.
   Note: Add tomatoes for a more robust flavor and color; leave them out for creamier curry.

Apricot-Stuffed Lamb Chops

4 double loin lamb chops, 2 inches thick (about 2 pounds)
4 dried apricots, halved
1 envelope LIPTON® Onion or Onion-Mushroom Recipe Soup Mix
1 cup water
¼ cup olive or vegetable oil
¼ cup honey
2 tablespoons Dijon-style prepared mustard
2 teaspoons rosemary leaves
½ teaspoon ground ginger

With knife parallel to cutting board, make a 1-inch-wide by 1-inch-deep cut in meaty side of each chop. Stuff each cut with 2 apricot halves; press firmly to close.

In shallow glass baking dish, combine remaining ingredients; add chops and turn to coat. Cover and marinate in refrigerator, turning occasionally, at least 2 hours.

Preheat oven to 425°. Bake chops with marinade, basting and turning chops occasionally, 35 minutes or until meat thermometer reaches 145° (rare), 155° (medium) or 165° (well done).
Makes about 4 servings.

Lamb Chops with Lemony Apple Glaze

½ cup BAMA® Apple Jelly
¼ cup REALEMON® Lemon Juice from Concentrate
¼ cup steak sauce
8 loin lamb chops, 1 inch thick

In small saucepan, melt jelly; stir in ReaLemon® brand and steak sauce. Heat through. Grill or broil chops as desired, basting frequently with sauce. Refrigerate leftovers.
Makes 4 servings.

Lamb Pilaf

3 tablespoons CRISCO® Oil
1 pound boneless leg of lamb or lamb shoulder, cut into ¾-inch cubes
½ cup chopped onion
⅓ cup chopped green pepper
2½ cups hot water
1½ cups uncooked long grain rice
2 teaspoons dried parsley flakes
2 teaspoons instant chicken bouillon granules
1½ teaspoons curry powder
1 bay leaf
¼ teaspoon pepper
¼ teaspoon salt

Heat Crisco® Oil in medium skillet. Add lamb. Brown over medium-high heat. Remove with slotted spoon; set aside. Add onion and green pepper to drippings in skillet. Cook over moderate heat, stirring occasionally, until tender. Stir in lamb and remaining ingredients. Heat to boiling. Cover. Reduce heat. Simmer 20 to 25 minutes, or until lamb and rice are tender and liquid is absorbed. Fluff with fork and remove bay leaf before serving.
4 to 6 servings.

Lemon and Garlic Lamb Chops

1 tablespoon all-purpose flour
1 tablespoon grated lemon peel
½ teaspoon garlic powder
¼ teaspoon salt
⅛ teaspoon pepper
4 lamb shoulder chops
¼ cup CRISCO® Oil

Mix flour, lemon peel, garlic powder, salt and pepper in large plastic food storage bag. Add chops. Shake to coat. Set aside.

Heat Crisco® Oil in large skillet. Add chops and any remaining flour mixture. Fry over medium-high heat about 10 minutes, or until chops are golden brown, turning over once. Drain on paper towels.
4 servings.

Lamb Patties

3 tablespoons CRISCO® Oil, divided
¼ cup chopped onion
¼ cup snipped fresh parsley
1 clove garlic, minced
¾ pound ground lamb
¼ pound ground beef
½ teaspoon dried dill weed
½ teaspoon salt
¼ teaspoon dried rosemary leaves, crushed
¼ teaspoon pepper

Heat 1 tablespoon Crisco® Oil in large skillet. Add onion, parsley and garlic. Sauté over moderate heat until onion is tender. Transfer mixture to medium mixing bowl. Add remaining ingredients. Mix well. Shape into four ½-inch thick patties.

Heat remaining 2 tablespoons Crisco® Oil in large skillet. Add patties. Fry over moderate heat, 8 to 10 minutes, or until desired doneness, turning over once.
4 servings.

Marinated Kabobs

1 pouch CAMPBELL'S® Onion Soup and Recipe Mix
1½ cups water
¼ cup Burgundy or other dry red wine
2 tablespoons vegetable oil
1 large clove garlic, minced
1 teaspoon dried basil leaves, crushed
2 small bay leaves
¼ teaspoon black pepper
1 pound boneless lamb, cut into 1-inch pieces
1 green pepper, cut into 1-inch squares
1 sweet red pepper, cut into 1-inch squares
1 yellow pepper, cut into 1-inch squares
2 tablespoons chutney
Hot cooked rice

1. To make marinade: In 2-cup measure, combine soup mix, ½ cup of the water, wine, oil, garlic, basil, bay leaves and black pepper; mix well with a fork.
2. Place lamb in shallow dish or bowl; pour marinade over lamb. Cover; refrigerate several hours or overnight.
3. Drain meat, reserving marinade. On each of four 8-inch skewers, alternately thread meat and pepper squares. Arrange skewers on rack in broiler pan. Broil 6 inches from heat 10 minutes or until meat is desired doneness, turning occasionally and brushing with reserved marinade.
4. To make sauce: Pour remaining marinade into 1-quart saucepan. Add remaining 1 cup water and chutney. Over medium-high heat, heat to boiling, stirring often. Reduce heat to low; simmer, uncovered, 5 minutes. Remove bay leaves.
5. Serve kabobs on rice with sauce.
Makes 4 servings.
Note: You can use boneless beef sirloin instead of lamb.

Basque Lamb

3/4 cup fresh lemon juice
1 cup dry sherry
1/2 cup olive or vegetable oil
1 clove garlic, crushed
1 boneless lamb shoulder
    (3 pounds), left untied
1 bunch chives, chopped
1 clove garlic, chopped
1 bunch parsley, chopped
    Salt and pepper

In small bowl, combine lemon juice, sherry, oil and crushed garlic. Let stand 1 hour. Sprinkle inside of roast with an even layer of chives, chopped garlic and parsley. Season with salt and pepper to taste. Roll up meat and tie securely with kitchen twine. In grill, arrange medium-hot **KINGS-FORD® Charcoal Briquets** around drip pan. Fill pan with water. Add hickory chips to coals, if desired. Place roast over drip pan. Cover grill and cook 45 to 60 minutes or until medium-rare, basting often with lemon juice mixture. Remove roast from grill; let stand 15 minutes. Carve into 1-inch-thick slices.
Makes 4 to 6 servings.

Lamb Curry

1 cup diced onions
1 large tart cooking apple, cored
    and diced
2 to 3 teaspoons curry powder
1/4 teaspoon ground ginger
1/4 teaspoon ground black pepper
3 tablespoons BLUE BONNET®
    Margarine
3 tablespoons all-purpose flour
1 (13 3/4-fluid ounce) can
    COLLEGE INN® Chicken
    Broth
1/4 cup heavy cream
3 1/2 cups diced cooked lamb or
    other cooked meat
    Curry Accompaniments*

In large saucepan, over medium heat, cook onions, apple, curry powder, ginger and pepper in margarine until tender, about 5 minutes. Blend in flour; gradually stir in chicken broth until smooth. Cook and stir until sauce is thickened and begins to boil. Stir in cream and lamb; cook until heated through. (Do not boil.) Serve with Curry Accompaniments. Garnish as desired.
Makes 6 servings.

Curry Accompaniments: If desired, this curry can be served over hot cooked rice with a selection of the following: chutney, raisins, flaked coconut, salted peanuts, crumbled cooked bacon, hard-cooked eggs, sliced avocado and grated orange peel.

Microwave: In 2-quart microwave-proof bowl, combine onions, apple, curry powder, ginger, pepper and margarine. Microwave, uncovered, on HIGH (100% power) for 4 to 5 minutes, stirring every 2 minutes. Blend in flour; gradually stir in broth until smooth. Microwave, uncovered, on HIGH for 6 to 7 minutes until thickened and bubbling, stirring every 2 minutes. Stir in cream and meat. Microwave on MEDIUM (50% power) for 6 to 7 minutes until heated through, stirring after 3 minutes. Let stand 5 minutes before serving. Serve as above.

Apple and Veal Scallop

2 large all-purpose apples,
    peeled, cored and sliced
1/4 cup REALEMON® Lemon Juice
    from Concentrate
1/2 cup unsifted flour
1 teaspoon salt
    Fresh ground pepper
8 veal scallops (about
    12 ounces)
1/4 cup margarine or butter
1/2 cup apple cider or apple juice
1 cup (1/2 pint) BORDEN® or
    MEADOW GOLD® whipping
    cream, unwhipped

In medium bowl, combine apples and ReaLemon® brand; set aside. In paper or plastic bag, combine flour, salt and pepper. Add veal, a few pieces at a time; shake to coat. In large skillet, brown veal on both sides in margarine; remove from skillet and set aside. Stir in apple mixture and cider, scraping bottom of skillet. Cook 3 to 5 minutes. Slowly add cream, stirring constantly. Simmer 5 to 10 minutes or until slightly thickened. Add veal; heat through. Refrigerate leftovers.
Makes 4 servings.

Aegean Lamb Stew

1 tablespoon vegetable oil
2 pounds lamb with bones for
    stew, cut into large pieces
1 large onion, sliced
2 cloves garlic, minced
1 can (28 ounces) tomatoes,
    undrained
1/2 teaspoon ground cinnamon
1/2 teaspoon turmeric
1/2 teaspoon TABASCO® pepper
    sauce
1/4 teaspoon salt
    Pinch ground cloves
6 new potatoes, cut into chunks
1 small eggplant, cut into 1-inch
    pieces
1 zucchini, cut into 3/4-inch
    pieces

Preheat oven to 350°F. In large skillet heat oil over medium-high heat. Add lamb, a few pieces at a time; brown on all sides. Arrange lamb in 3-quart casserole. Drain off all but 1 tablespoon fat from skillet; cook onion and garlic 5 minutes or until tender. Add tomatoes; stir up bits from bottom of skillet. Stir in cinnamon, turmeric, Tabasco® sauce, salt and cloves. Pour mixture over lamb. Stir in potatoes. Cover; bake 30 minutes. Stir in eggplant and zucchini. Cover; cook 45 minutes longer or until meat and vegetables are tender.
Makes 6 servings.

Veal Parmesan

2 tablespoons CRISCO® Oil
1 small onion, thinly sliced and separated into rings
½ cup chopped green pepper
1 clove garlic, minced
1 can (15 ounces) tomato sauce
2 tablespoons dry white wine
¾ teaspoon dried basil leaves
½ teaspoon sugar
¼ teaspoon fennel seed
¼ teaspoon salt
⅛ teaspoon pepper
1 cup seasoned dry bread crumbs
¾ cup grated Parmesan cheese, divided
¼ teaspoon pepper
2 eggs
1 pound veal cutlets, ¼ inch thick
CRISCO® Oil for frying

For sauce, heat 2 tablespoons Crisco® Oil in medium saucepan. Add onion, green pepper and garlic. Sauté over moderate heat until tender. Stir in tomato sauce, wine, basil, sugar, fennel, salt and ⅛ teaspoon pepper. Heat to boiling. Reduce heat. Simmer, uncovered, for 30 minutes, or until sauce is thickened.

Mix bread crumbs, ¼ cup Parmesan cheese and ¼ teaspoon pepper in shallow dish. Beat eggs slightly in another shallow dish. Dip veal into eggs, then in bread crumb mixture to coat.

Preheat oven to 350°F. Heat ¼ inch Crisco® Oil in large skillet. Add veal. Fry over moderate heat, 3 to 4 minutes, or until golden brown, turning over once. Drain on paper towels. Arrange cutlets in 13×9-inch baking dish. Pour sauce over veal. Sprinkle with remaining ½ cup Parmesan cheese. Bake at 350°F, 15 to 20 minutes or until cheese melts.
4 to 6 servings.

Stuffed Veal Cutlets

1 package (3 ounces) cream cheese, softened
2 teaspoons grated Parmesan cheese
1 teaspoon Dijon mustard
½ teaspoon dried parsley flakes
⅛ teaspoon garlic powder
½ cup all-purpose flour
¼ teaspoon salt
⅛ teaspoon pepper
1 cup seasoned dry bread crumbs
2 eggs
8 thin slices fully cooked ham
8 veal cutlets, pounded thin
8 thin slices Swiss cheese (each about 4 inches square), halved
CRISCO® Oil for frying

Combine cream cheese, Parmesan cheese, mustard, parsley flakes and garlic powder in small mixing bowl. Mix well. Set aside. Mix flour, salt and pepper in shallow dish. Place bread crumbs on sheet of waxed paper. Beat eggs slightly in another shallow dish. Set aside.

Place ham slice on top of each cutlet. Trim ham to within ½ inch of cutlet edge. Spread each ham slice with one-eighth of cream cheese mixture (a scant tablespoon). Top each with 2 pieces Swiss cheese. Brush top edges of cutlets with egg. Fold in half. Press and pound edges of cutlets together with meat mallet to seal. Carefully coat both sides with flour mixture. Dip stuffed cutlets in egg, and then in bread crumbs, pressing to coat thoroughly. Cover and refrigerate about 1 hour.

Heat 2 inches Crisco® Oil in deep-fryer or large saucepan to 350°F. Fry 1 stuffed cutlet at a time, about 2½ minutes, or until deep golden brown, turning over once. Drain on paper towels.
4 to 8 servings.

Country-Style Veal

¼ cup all-purpose flour
3 tablespoons water
2 tablespoons dry white wine
1½ teaspoons instant beef bouillon granules
½ teaspoon dried basil leaves
½ teaspoon dried thyme leaves
¼ teaspoon dried marjoram leaves
¼ teaspoon salt
⅛ teaspoon pepper
⅛ teaspoon garlic powder
3 tablespoons CRISCO® Oil
1 to 1½ pounds veal round steak, cut into serving-size pieces
1 medium onion, halved and thinly sliced
8 ounces whole fresh mushrooms
2 tomatoes, peeled, seeded and cut into chunks
2 slices lemon
1 bay leaf

Mix flour, water, wine, bouillon granules, basil, thyme, marjoram, salt, pepper and garlic powder in small mixing bowl. Set aside. Heat Crisco® Oil in large skillet. Add veal. Fry over medium-high heat until no longer pink. Remove veal from skillet; set aside.

Add onion to drippings in skillet. Sauté over moderate heat until tender. Reduce heat to low. Stir in remaining ingredients and the veal. Add flour mixture. Stir. Cover. Simmer, stirring once, 25 to 30 minutes, or until mushrooms are tender. Remove and discard bay leaf.
4 to 6 servings.

Veal Chops Stuffed with Fontina

**4 loin veal chops, 1 inch thick
(about 3 pounds)
2 ounces thinly sliced fontina or
Swiss cheese
2 ounces thinly sliced prosciutto
or ham
4 tablespoons all-purpose flour
1/2 cup WISH-BONE® Italian or
Robusto Italian Dressing
1/2 cup finely chopped onion
3/4 cup water
3/4 cup beef broth
1/4 cup Marsala wine
1 tablespoon fresh or dried
rosemary leaves, crumbled
1/8 teaspoon pepper
1/4 cup whipping or heavy cream**

With knife parallel to cutting board, make a 2-inch-wide by 2-inch-deep cut in meaty side of each chop. Evenly stuff each cut with cheese and prosciutto; secure, if desired, with skewers. Lightly coat chops with 2 tablespoons flour, then dip in 1/4 cup Italian dressing. On aluminum-foil-lined broiler rack or in large shallow baking pan, arrange chops and broil, turning once, 10 minutes or until done. Remove to serving platter and keep warm.

Meanwhile, in medium skillet, heat remaining 1/4 cup Italian dressing and cook onion over medium heat, stirring occasionally, 5 minutes or until tender. Add water, broth and wine thoroughly blended with rosemary, pepper and remaining 2 tablespoons flour. Bring to a boil, then simmer, stirring occasionally, 3 minutes or until thickened. Stir in cream; heat through. Serve over chops.
Makes about 4 servings.

Veal Stew

**1 pound veal for stew, cut into
1/2-inch pieces
1 tablespoon all-purpose flour
1 can (10 1/2 ounces)
CAMPBELL'S® Chunky
Creamy Mushroom Soup
1 cup frozen baby carrots or
fresh carrots cut into sticks
1/2 cup fresh or frozen pearl
onions
1/4 teaspoon dried thyme leaves,
crushed
1 teaspoon lemon juice**

To Microwave:
1. In 3-quart microwave-safe casserole, stir together veal and flour. Cover with lid; microwave on HIGH 5 minutes or until veal is no longer pink, stirring once during cooking.
2. Stir soup into meat mixture until smooth. Stir in carrots, onions and thyme. Cover; microwave at 50% power 25 minutes or until veal is tender, stirring 3 times during cooking. Stir in lemon juice. Let stand, covered, 5 minutes.
Makes about 3 1/2 cups or 4 servings.

Veal Scallopini with Brandy Cream Sauce

**1 pound veal scallopini,
pounded 1/4 inch thick
(about 4 cutlets)
1/4 cup all-purpose flour
3 tablespoons butter or
margarine
1 medium apple, thinly sliced
1 envelope LIPTON® Golden
Onion Recipe Soup Mix
1 1/2 cups water
2 tablespoons brandy
1/2 cup light cream or half and
half
1 tablespoon light brown sugar**

Lightly coat veal with flour.

In large skillet, melt butter and cook veal over medium heat until tender. Remove veal to serving platter and keep warm. Reserve 1 tablespoon drippings. Add apple, then golden onion recipe soup mix thoroughly blended with water and brandy to reserved drippings. Bring to a boil, then simmer, stirring occasionally, 10 minutes. Stir in cream and sugar and heat through. Serve sauce over veal.
Makes about 4 servings.

Veal Marengo

**1 tablespoon olive or vegetable
oil
1 1/2 pounds veal for stew, cut into
1 1/2-inch cubes
1/2 pound small mushrooms
2 medium onions, chopped
2 cloves garlic, minced
2 tablespoons flour
1 cup dry white wine
1/2 cup orange juice
1/4 cup tomato paste
1/2 teaspoon dried basil leaves
1/2 teaspoon dried thyme leaves
1/4 teaspoon TABASCO® pepper
sauce
1 chicken bouillon cube
Hot cooked rice or noodles**

In large heavy saucepot or Dutch oven, heat oil; brown meat in 2 batches. Remove; reserve. In same pot cook mushrooms, onions and garlic 5 minutes or until tender. Return meat to pot; sprinkle with flour. Stir constantly; cook 3 minutes. Stir in wine, orange juice, tomato paste, basil, thyme, Tabasco® sauce and bouillon cube. Cover; simmer 1 hour or until meat is tender; stir occasionally. Serve over rice or noodles.
Makes 6 servings.

POULTRY

Versatile, economical poultry can be prepared in so many different ways that you can enjoy it often. For a quick meal, try any one of the tasty stir-fry recipes; when more time is available, choose a slow-simmering stew. And you'll discover new ideas for serving turkey all year round.

Chicken Paprika

2½- to 3-pound broiler-fryer chicken, cut up
1 teaspoon salt, divided
¼ teaspoon pepper, divided
¼ cup CRISCO® Oil
1 medium onion, chopped
1 can (8 ounces) tomato sauce
½ cup water, divided
1½ to 2 tablespoons paprika
1 cup dairy sour cream
¼ cup all-purpose flour
   Hot cooked narrow egg noodles

Sprinkle chicken with ½ teaspoon salt and ⅛ teaspoon pepper. Heat Crisco® Oil in large skillet. Add chicken pieces. Brown over medium-high heat. Remove chicken from skillet; set aside.

Pour off all but 1 tablespoon drippings. Add onion. Sauté over moderate heat until tender. Stir in tomato sauce, ¼ cup water, paprika, remaining ½ teaspoon salt and remaining ⅛ teaspoon pepper. Add chicken. Heat to boiling. Cover. Reduce heat. Simmer, stirring occasionally, 35 to 40 minutes, or until chicken is tender and meat near bone is no longer pink. Remove chicken from skillet; keep warm.

Blend sour cream, remaining ¼ cup water and flour in small mixing bowl. Blend into mixture in skillet. Cook over low heat, stirring constantly, until thickened. Serve with chicken and egg noodles. Garnish with *fresh parsley sprigs,* if desired.
4 servings.

Chicken Dijon with Vegetables

1 pound boneless chicken breasts, halved
½ cup WISH-BONE® Classic Dijon Vinaigrette or Lite Classic Dijon Vinaigrette Dressing
½ cup plain dry bread crumbs*
1 cup chopped onions
2 cups sliced mushrooms
1 cup chopped tomato
1 tablespoon chopped parsley

Preheat oven to 350°.

Dip chicken in ¼ cup classic Dijon vinaigrette dressing, then bread crumbs, coating well. In large shallow baking pan, arrange chicken. Bake uncovered, turning once, 15 minutes or until done. Remove to serving platter and keep warm.

Meanwhile, in large skillet, heat remaining ¼ cup dressing and cook onions over medium-high heat, stirring occasionally, 5 minutes. Add mushrooms and tomato and cook, stirring occasionally, 5 minutes or until vegetables are tender. To serve, arrange vegetable mixture over chicken and sprinkle with parsley.
Makes about 4 servings.

*Substitution: Use 1 cup fresh bread crumbs.

Grilled Deviled Chicken

¼ cup catsup
¼ cup CRISCO® Oil
2 tablespoons lemon juice
1 tablespoon chili powder
1 teaspoon lemon pepper seasoning
½ teaspoon ground oregano
½ teaspoon onion powder
⅛ teaspoon cayenne
2½- to 3-pound broiler-fryer chicken, cut up

Combine all ingredients except chicken in small bowl. Mix well. Set aside.

Place chicken on seasoned cooking grids over medium coals. Grill, turning over frequently, 45 to 60 minutes, or until juices run clear and meat near bone is no longer pink. Brush with sauce during last 15 minutes.
4 servings.

Beijing Chicken

3 pounds frying chicken pieces
½ cup KIKKOMAN Teriyaki Sauce
1 tablespoon dry sherry
2 teaspoons minced fresh ginger root
½ teaspoon fennel seed, crushed
½ teaspoon grated orange peel
½ teaspoon honey

Rinse chicken pieces and pat dry with paper towels; place in large plastic bag. Combine teriyaki sauce, sherry, ginger, fennel, orange peel and honey; pour over chicken. Press air out of bag; tie top securely. Refrigerate 8 hours or overnight, turning bag over occasionally. Reserving marinade, remove chicken and place on rack of broiler pan. Broil 5 to 7 inches from heat source about 40 minutes, or until chicken is tender, turning pieces over and basting occasionally with reserved marinade.
Makes 4 servings.

Oven-Baked Buttermilk Chicken

1 envelope LIPTON® Golden Onion Recipe Soup Mix
1 cup all-purpose flour
2 eggs
½ cup buttermilk*
2½- to 3-pound chicken, cut into serving pieces
¼ cup butter or margarine, melted

Preheat oven to 425°.

Combine golden onion recipe soup mix with flour; set aside.

Beat eggs with buttermilk. Dip chicken in buttermilk mixture, then flour mixture, coating well. Place in large shallow baking pan, on rack, and chill 30 minutes. Drizzle with butter, then bake 45 minutes or until done.
Makes about 4 servings.

Substitution: Blend 1½ teaspoons lemon juice with enough milk to equal ½ cup; let stand 5 minutes.

Chicken in Wine Sauce

4 slices bacon, chopped
1 cup carrots cut into matchstick-thin strips
1 pouch CAMPBELL'S® Onion Soup and Recipe Mix
1 cup water
½ cup Chablis or other dry white wine
⅛ teaspoon pepper
4 skinless boneless chicken breast halves (about 1 pound)

To Microwave:

1. Place bacon in 3-quart microwave-safe casserole. Cover with paper towel; microwave on HIGH 3 minutes or until crisp, stirring once during cooking. Remove bacon to paper towels, reserving drippings in casserole.
2. Add carrots to drippings. Cover with lid; microwave on HIGH 3 minutes or until carrots are tender. Stir in soup mix, water, wine and pepper until well blended.
3. Add chicken breasts, placing thicker portions toward edge of dish. Cover; microwave on HIGH 10 minutes or until chicken is nearly done, rearranging chicken once during cooking. Let stand, covered, 5 minutes or until chicken is no longer pink in center. Sprinkle with reserved bacon.
Makes 4 servings.

Versatile Chicken

1 (2½- to 3-pound) broiler-fryer chicken, cut up
¾ cup BORDEN® or MEADOW GOLD® Buttermilk
1 tablespoon WYLER'S® or STEERO® Chicken-Flavor Instant Bouillon
½ teaspoon oregano leaves, optional
1 cup unsifted flour
1 teaspoon paprika
¼ cup margarine or butter, melted

In 1-cup measure, combine buttermilk, bouillon and oregano if desired; mix well. Let stand 10 minutes; stir. Place chicken in large bowl. Pour bouillon mixture over chicken; toss to coat. Let stand 30 minutes to blend flavors. In paper or plastic bag, combine flour and paprika. Add chicken, a few pieces at a time; shake to coat. Place in 13×9-inch baking dish. Drizzle with margarine. Bake uncovered in preheated 350° oven 1 hour or until golden. Refrigerate leftovers.
Makes 4 to 6 servings.

Tip: To fry chicken, omit melted margarine; fry in vegetable oil.

Creamy Chicken Tarragon

2 tablespoons oil
2¹/2- to 3-pound chicken, cut into
   serving pieces
1 envelope LIPTON® Onion,
   Onion-Mushroom or Golden
   Onion Recipe Soup Mix
¹/2 teaspoon tarragon leaves
1 cup water
¹/2 cup dry white wine
2 tablespoons all-purpose flour
¹/2 cup whipping or heavy cream

In large skillet, heat oil and brown chicken over medium-high heat; drain. Add onion recipe soup mix and tarragon blended with water and wine. Simmer covered 45 minutes or until chicken is done. Remove chicken to serving platter and keep warm. Into skillet, stir in flour blended with cream. Bring just to the boiling point, then simmer, stirring constantly, until sauce is thickened, about 5 minutes. Serve sauce over chicken.
Makes about 4 servings.
Microwave Directions: Omit oil. In 3-quart casserole, heat chicken, uncovered, at HIGH (Full Power) 12 minutes, rearranging chicken once; drain. Add onion recipe soup mix and tarragon blended with water and wine. Heat covered 14 minutes or until chicken is done, rearranging chicken once. Remove chicken to serving platter and keep warm. Into casserole, stir flour blended with cream and heat uncovered 4 minutes or until sauce is thickened, stirring once. Serve as above.

Baked Apricot Chicken

1 (10-ounce) jar BAMA® Apricot
   or Peach Preserves (1 cup)
¹/4 cup REALEMON® Lemon Juice
   from Concentrate
2 teaspoons soy sauce
¹/2 teaspoon salt
1 (2¹/2- to 3-pound) broiler-fryer
   chicken, cut up
1 cup dry bread crumbs
¹/4 cup margarine or butter,
   melted

Preheat oven to 350°. In shallow dish, combine preserves, ReaLemon® brand, soy sauce and salt. Coat chicken with apricot mixture; roll in bread crumbs. Set aside remaining apricot mixture. In greased 13×9-inch baking dish, arrange chicken; drizzle with margarine. Bake uncovered 1 hour or until tender. Heat remaining apricot mixture; serve with chicken. Refrigerate leftovers.
Makes 4 to 6 servings.

Chicken Livers in Wine Sauce

¹/4 cup CRISCO® Oil
1 medium onion, cut into
   8 pieces
¹/2 cup chopped celery
¹/4 cup snipped fresh parsley
1 clove garlic, minced
¹/3 cup all-purpose flour
³/4 teaspoon salt
¹/4 teaspoon pepper
1 pound chicken livers, drained
¹/2 cup water
¹/2 cup milk
3 tablespoons dry white wine
³/4 teaspoon instant chicken
   bouillon granules
¹/2 teaspoon dried rosemary
   leaves
Hot cooked egg noodles

Heat Crisco® Oil in large skillet. Add onion, celery, parsley and garlic. Sauté over moderate heat until onion is tender. Set aside.
Mix flour, salt and pepper in large plastic food storage bag. Add livers. Shake to coat. Add livers and any remaining flour mixture to onion mixture. Brown livers over medium-high heat, stirring occasionally. Stir in water, milk, wine, bouillon granules and rosemary. Heat to boiling, stirring constantly. Cover. Reduce heat. Simmer, stirring occasionally, 7 to 10 minutes, or until livers are no longer pink. Serve with noodles.
4 to 6 servings.

Grilled Curried Chicken

1 cup (8 ounces) WISH-BONE®
   Classic Dijon Vinaigrette
   Dressing
¹/2 cup finely ground unsalted
   peanuts
¹/2 cup orange marmalade
2 teaspoons curry powder
¹/2 teaspoon tarragon leaves
2 whole chicken breasts (about
   1 pound each), split and
   skinned

In large shallow baking dish, thoroughly blend all ingredients except chicken. Add chicken and turn to coat. Cover and marinate in refrigerator, turning occasionally, 4 hours or overnight. Remove chicken, reserving marinade.
Grill or broil chicken, turning and basting frequently with reserved marinade, until done. If chicken browns too quickly, loosely cover with aluminum foil.
Makes about 4 servings.
Note: Also terrific with Wish-Bone® Lite Classic Creamy Dijon, Blended Italian, Creamy Italian or Lite Creamy Italian Dressing.

Dan D's Chicken BBQ

⅓ cup white Zinfandel wine
⅓ cup olive or vegetable oil
1 tablespoon Dijon-style
    mustard
1 teaspoon dried rosemary,
    crushed
1 clove garlic, minced
    Salt and pepper
1 broiler-fryer chicken (2 to
    3 pounds), quartered

In shallow glass dish, combine all ingredients except chicken. Add chicken; turn to coat with marinade. Cover and refrigerate several hours or overnight, basting occasionally. Drain chicken; reserve marinade. Grill chicken, on covered grill, over medium-hot **KINGSFORD® Charcoal Briquets** about 15 minutes on each side or until fork-tender, basting often with marinade.
Makes 4 servings.

Chicken Cacciatore

⅓ cup all-purpose flour
2½- to 3-pound broiler-fryer
    chicken, cut up
¼ cup CRISCO® Oil
1 medium onion, thinly sliced
    and separated into rings
½ cup chopped green pepper
2 cloves garlic, minced
1 can (16 ounces) whole
    tomatoes, undrained
1 can (8 ounces) tomato sauce
1 can (4 ounces) sliced
    mushrooms, drained
¾ teaspoon salt
½ teaspoon dried oregano leaves
    Hot cooked noodles

Place flour in large plastic food storage bag. Add a few chicken pieces. Shake to coat. Remove chicken from bag. Repeat with remaining chicken. Heat Crisco® Oil in large skillet. Add chicken. Brown over medium-high heat. Remove chicken from skillet; set aside. Add onion, green pepper and garlic to skillet. Sauté over moderate heat until tender. Add tomatoes, tomato sauce, mushrooms, salt and oregano, stirring to break apart tomatoes. Place chicken pieces on top of tomato mixture. Cover. Reduce heat. Simmer 30 to 40 minutes, or until chicken is tender and meat near bone is no longer pink. Serve with noodles.
4 servings.

Spicy Orange Chicken

1 cup water
1 medium onion, chopped
1 can (6 ounces) frozen orange
    juice concentrate, thawed,
    undiluted
¼ cup catsup
3 medium cloves garlic, minced
1 teaspoon ground cinnamon
1 teaspoon TABASCO® pepper
    sauce
¼ teaspoon salt
2 (2½- to 3-pound) broiler-fryer
    chickens, cut up

In medium bowl combine water, onion, orange concentrate, catsup, garlic, cinnamon, Tabasco® sauce and salt; mix well. Place chicken in large shallow dish or plastic bag; add marinade. Cover; refrigerate at least 4 to 6 hours; turn chicken occasionally.

Remove chicken from marinade; place on grill 4 to 5 inches from source of heat. Grill 25 to 30 minutes or until done; turn frequently and brush each time with marinade. Heat any remaining marinade to a boil and serve with chicken.
Makes 8 servings.

Country Chicken and Peppers

1 (2½- to 3-pound) chicken, cut
    up
1 pound hot Italian sausage, cut
    in 1-inch pieces
4 medium potatoes, unpared,
    cut in bite-size pieces
4 red or green peppers, cut in
    bite-size pieces
4 medium onions, quartered
1 (13¾-fluid ounce) can
    COLLEGE INN® Chicken
    Broth
¼ cup red wine vinegar with
    garlic
2 teaspoons Italian seasoning
3 tablespoons cornstarch

Cut each chicken breast into 2 pieces. In large roasting pan, combine chicken, sausage and potatoes. Bake at 425°F for 20 minutes; stir in peppers and onions. In small bowl, combine 1 cup chicken broth, vinegar and Italian seasoning; pour over meat and vegetables in pan. Cover; bake for 40 to 45 minutes more or until chicken is done, stirring occasionally.

Spoon meat and vegetables into serving dish. In 1-quart measuring cup, combine cornstarch with remaining broth until smooth; add enough pan liquid to equal 3 cups. Discard any remaining pan liquid. Return cornstarch mixture to roasting pan; cook and stir over medium heat until mixture thickens and boils. Pour over meat and vegetables.
Makes 6 servings.

Country Captain

2½ pounds chicken parts (breasts, legs, wings), skinned
1 can (11 ounces) CAMPBELL'S® Condensed Zesty Tomato Soup/Sauce
1 green pepper, cut into ½-inch pieces
¼ cup raisins
1 teaspoon curry powder
¼ cup toasted slivered almonds
Hot cooked rice

To Microwave:
1. Arrange chicken in 12- by 8-inch microwave-safe baking dish, placing thicker portions toward edges of dish.
2. In small bowl, stir together soup, green pepper, raisins and curry powder. Spoon soup mixture over chicken.
3. Cover with waxed paper; microwave on HIGH 22 minutes or until chicken is no longer pink in center, rearranging chicken and basting with pan juices once during cooking. Let stand, covered, 5 minutes. Sprinkle with almonds; serve over rice.
Makes 6 servings.

Chicken Roma

2 tablespoons oil
2½- to 3-pound chicken, cut into serving pieces
1 can (14½ ounces) whole peeled tomatoes, undrained and chopped
½ cup sliced pitted ripe olives
1 clove garlic, finely chopped
1 envelope LIPTON® Onion, Onion-Mushroom, Beefy Mushroom or Beefy Onion Recipe Soup Mix
¼ cup dry red wine
1 package (8 ounces) broad egg noodles

In large skillet, heat oil and brown chicken over medium-high heat; drain. Add tomatoes, olives and garlic, then onion recipe soup mix blended with wine. Simmer covered 40 minutes or until chicken is done.

Meanwhile, cook noodles according to package directions. If necessary, skim fat from sauce. To serve, arrange chicken and sauce over hot noodles.
Makes about 4 servings.

Microwave Directions: Omit oil. In 2-quart casserole, heat chicken at HIGH (Full Power) 12 minutes, rearranging chicken once; drain. Add tomatoes, olives and garlic, then onion recipe soup mix blended with wine. Heat covered 14 minutes or until chicken is done, rearranging chicken once. Let stand covered 5 minutes. Serve as above.

Lemon Herbed Chicken

½ cup butter or margarine
½ cup vegetable oil
⅓ cup lemon juice
2 tablespoons finely chopped parsley
2 tablespoons garlic salt
1 teaspoon dried rosemary, crushed
1 teaspoon dried summer savory, crushed
½ teaspoon dried thyme, crushed
¼ teaspoon coarsely cracked black pepper
6 chicken breast quarters with wings attached

In saucepan, combine all ingredients except chicken. Heat until butter melts. Place chicken in shallow glass dish and brush with sauce; let stand 10 to 15 minutes before cooking. Lightly oil grid. Grill chicken, skin-side up, on uncovered grill, over medium-hot **KINGSFORD® Charcoal Briquets** 30 to 45 minutes or until fork-tender, turning and basting with sauce every 10 minutes.
Makes 6 servings.

Poulet à la Jardinière

2 whole boneless chicken breasts (about 1½ pounds), halved and lightly pounded
Pepper
2 tablespoons chopped parsley
8 pieces carrot, about 3×¼ inch each
2 tablespoons butter or margarine
1 bay leaf
1 envelope LIPTON® Onion-Mushroom Recipe Soup Mix*
1¼ cups water
¾ cup dry white wine
1 tablespoon cornstarch

Sprinkle each chicken breast half with pepper and ½ tablespoon parsley, then top with 2 carrot pieces; roll up and secure with wooden toothpicks.

In medium skillet, melt butter and brown chicken over medium heat. Add bay leaf, then onion-mushroom recipe soup mix blended with 1 cup water and wine. Simmer covered 15 minutes or until chicken is done. Stir in cornstarch blended with remaining water. Bring to a boil, then simmer, stirring constantly, until sauce is thickened, about 5 minutes. Remove bay leaf.
Makes about 4 servings.

***Variation:** Use Lipton® Beefy Mushroom Recipe Soup Mix and decrease cornstarch to 2 teaspoons.

Microwave Directions: Decrease water to ¾ cup. Roll chicken as above. In 2-quart oblong baking dish, heat butter at HIGH (Full Power) 2 minutes. Add chicken and heat covered 5 minutes. Add bay leaf, then onion-mushroom recipe soup mix blended with cornstarch, water and wine. Heat uncovered 8 minutes or until chicken is done, rearranging chicken once. Let stand covered 5 minutes. Remove bay leaf.

Elegant Chicken Piccata

1/3 cup plus 1 tablespoon unsifted flour
1/2 teaspoon paprika
4 skinned chicken breast halves
3 tablespoons margarine or butter
1/4 cup water
2 cups (1 pint) BORDEN® or MEADOW GOLD® Coffee Cream or Half-and-Half
1 tablespoon WYLER'S® or STEERO® Chicken-Flavor Instant Bouillon *or* 3 Chicken-Flavor Bouillon Cubes
2 tablespoons dry sherry
2 tablespoons REALEMON® Lemon Juice from Concentrate
1/2 to 3/4 cup shredded Swiss cheese
Hot cooked rice

Preheat oven to 350°. In paper or plastic bag, combine *1/3 cup* flour and paprika. Add chicken, a few pieces at a time; shake to coat. In large skillet, over medium heat, brown chicken in margarine on both sides until golden brown. Add water; cover and simmer 20 minutes. Remove chicken; arrange in 12×7-inch baking dish. Stir remaining *1 tablespoon* flour into drippings. Gradually add cream and bouillon. Over low heat, cook and stir until slightly thickened and bouillon is dissolved, about 5 to 10 minutes. Add sherry and ReaLemon® brand; pour over chicken. Bake covered 20 minutes. Uncover; top with cheese. Bake 5 minutes longer. Serve with rice. Refrigerate leftovers.
Makes 4 servings.

Orange-Honey Chicken

1 1/2 cups V8® Vegetable Juice
2 tablespoons lemon juice
4 teaspoons honey
1/2 teaspoon grated orange peel
1/4 teaspoon garlic powder
1/8 teaspoon pepper
2 1/2-to 3-pound broiler-fryer chicken, cut up

1. To make marinade: In 12- by 8-inch baking dish, stir together V8 juice, lemon juice, honey, orange peel, garlic powder and pepper. Add chicken to marinade, turning to coat. Cover; refrigerate at least 2 hours, turning chicken occasionally.
2. Remove chicken from marinade, reserving marinade. Arrange chicken on rack in broiler pan; broil 6 inches from heat 35 minutes or until chicken is fork-tender, basting chicken with marinade and turning occasionally.
Makes 6 servings.

Per serving: 233 calories, 25 g protein, 13 g fat, 4 g carbohydrate, 180 mg sodium, 81 mg cholesterol.

Chicken Marinated with Orange & Tarragon

1 envelope LIPTON® Onion or Onion-Mushroom Recipe Soup Mix
1 jar (12 ounces) orange marmalade
1 cup orange juice
1 teaspoon tarragon leaves
2 1/2- to 3-pound chicken, cut into serving pieces
Hot cooked rice

In 13×9-inch glass baking dish, thoroughly blend onion recipe soup mix, marmalade, orange juice and tarragon; add chicken and turn to coat. Cover and marinate in refrigerator, turning chicken occasionally, at least 4 hours.
Preheat oven to 400°. Bake chicken with marinade, basting and turning chicken occasionally, 1 hour or until done. To serve, arrange chicken over hot rice. If necessary, skim fat from sauce. Serve sauce with chicken.
Makes about 4 servings.
Microwave Directions: Marinate chicken as above. Remove chicken from marinade; reserve marinade. In 3-quart casserole, heat chicken, covered, at MEDIUM (50% Full Power) 15 minutes, rearranging chicken once; drain. Add reserved marinade and heat uncovered at HIGH (Full Power) 20 minutes or until chicken is done. Serve as above.

Fried Chicken

1/3 cup all-purpose flour
1/2 teaspoon salt
1/2 teaspoon paprika
1/4 teaspoon garlic powder
1/4 teaspoon pepper
1 can (5.3 ounces) evaporated milk
2 1/2- to 3-pound broiler-fryer chicken, cut up
1/4 cup CRISCO® Oil

Mix flour, salt, paprika, garlic powder and pepper in large plastic food storage bag. Set aside. Pour evaporated milk into bowl. Dip chicken in evaporated milk. Add a few chicken pieces to food storage bag. Shake to coat. Remove chicken from bag. Repeat with remaining chicken.
Heat Crisco® Oil in large skillet. Add chicken. Brown over medium-high heat. Cook over moderate heat about 25 minutes, or until meat near bone is no longer pink and juices run clear, turning pieces over frequently.
4 servings.

Chicken Adobo

3 pounds frying chicken pieces
1/2 cup KIKKOMAN Soy Sauce
1/2 cup distilled white vinegar
2 tablespoons sugar
1 teaspoon pepper
6 large cloves garlic, pressed

Microwave Directions: Rinse chicken pieces and pat dry with paper towels. Combine soy sauce, vinegar, sugar, pepper and garlic in large microwave-safe casserole with lid; add chicken pieces, skin side down. Cover and microwave on High 10 minutes. Turn chicken pieces over; rearrange in dish. Cover and microwave on High 13 minutes longer, or until chicken is tender, rearranging pieces once. Serve immediately.
Makes 4 servings.

Chicken Breasts in Wine Sauce

1/3 cup plus 2 tablespoons all-purpose flour, divided
1/2 teaspoon onion salt
1/4 teaspoon pepper
2 whole chicken breasts, skinned and halved lengthwise
3 tablespoons CRISCO® Oil
2 small onions, cut into thirds
2/3 cup dry white wine
1 teaspoon instant chicken bouillon granules
1/2 teaspoon dried tarragon leaves
3/4 cup half-and-half

Mix 1/3 cup flour, onion salt and pepper in large plastic food storage bag. Add chicken. Shake to coat.

Heat Crisco® Oil in large skillet. Add chicken. Brown over medium-high heat. Add onion, wine, bouillon granules and tarragon. Heat to boiling. Cover. Reduce heat. Simmer about 20 minutes, or until juices run clear and meat near bone is no longer pink. Transfer chicken to serving platter. Cover to keep warm. Remove and discard onion.

Place half-and-half in small bowl. Blend in remaining 2 tablespoons flour. Stir into drippings in large skillet. Cook over medium-low heat, stirring constantly, until thickened and bubbly. Serve with chicken.
4 servings.

Sauteed Chicken Livers

1/4 cup butter or margarine
1 pound chicken livers
1 medium onion, coarsely chopped
2 tablespoons all-purpose flour
1 can (10¾ ounces) CAMPBELL'S® Condensed Chicken Broth
1/2 cup water
Dash pepper
8 slices PEPPERIDGE FARM® Wheat Bread, toasted

1. In 10-inch skillet over medium-high heat, in hot butter, cook livers and onion 8 to 10 minutes or until livers are done, stirring frequently.
2. With slotted spoon, remove livers and onion from skillet. Into pan drippings, stir flour. Gradually add chicken broth, water and pepper, stirring constantly. Over medium heat, heat to boiling, stirring occasionally. Cook 1 minute more.
3. Add liver mixture; heat through. Serve over toast.
Makes about 3 cups or 4 servings.

Chicken with Potatoes & Peppers

1/4 cup WISH-BONE® Italian Dressing
1 (2½- to 3-pound) chicken, cut into serving pieces
1 can (28 ounces) whole peeled tomatoes, undrained and chopped
1 pound all-purpose potatoes, cut into chunks
2 medium onions, cut into quarters
2 medium red, green or yellow peppers, cut into thin strips
1 tablespoon fresh rosemary leaves*
1 teaspoon thyme leaves
1 teaspoon salt
1/4 teaspoon pepper

Preheat oven to 375°.

In large skillet, heat Italian dressing and brown chicken over medium-high heat; set aside.

In 13×9-inch baking pan, combine remaining ingredients; add chicken and turn to coat. Bake uncovered, stirring occasionally, 50 minutes or until chicken is done and vegetables are tender. Serve, if desired, with French or Italian bread.
Makes about 4 servings.

*Substitution: Use 1 teaspoon dried rosemary leaves.

Note: Also terrific with Wish-Bone® Robusto Italian, Blended Italian, Lite Italian, Herbal Italian, Italian & Cheese, Classic Dijon Vinaigrette or Lite Classic Dijon Vinaigrette Dressing.

Oven Barbecued Chicken

- 1 (2½- to 3-pound) broiler-fryer chicken, cut up
- 1 cup unsifted flour
- 1 teaspoon salt
- 6 tablespoons margarine or butter, melted
- ¼ cup chopped onion
- 1 clove garlic, finely chopped
- 1 cup catsup
- ¼ cup firmly packed light brown sugar
- ¼ cup REALEMON® Lemon Juice from Concentrate
- ¼ cup water
- 2 tablespoons Worcestershire sauce

Preheat oven to 350°. In paper or plastic bag, combine flour and salt. Add chicken, a few pieces at a time; shake to coat. Place in greased 13×9-inch baking dish; drizzle with ¼ cup margarine. Bake 30 minutes. Meanwhile, in small saucepan, cook onion and garlic in remaining *2 tablespoons* margarine until tender. Add remaining ingredients; simmer uncovered 10 minutes. Pour over chicken; bake 30 minutes longer or until tender. Refrigerate leftovers.
Makes 4 to 6 servings.

Honey-Mustard Chicken

- 1 package (32 ounces) SWANSON® Frozen Fried Plump & Juicy® Chicken
- 1 tablespoon butter or margarine
- ¼ cup finely chopped green onions
- 3 tablespoons honey
- 1 teaspoon Dijon-style mustard

To Microwave:
1. Prepare chicken according to package directions.
2. To make glaze: In small microwave-safe bowl, combine butter and onions. Cover with vented plastic wrap; microwave on HIGH 2 minutes or until onions are tender.
3. Stir in honey and mustard. Microwave, uncovered, on HIGH 1 minute or until hot. Drizzle glaze over chicken.
Makes 6 servings.

Brunswick Stew

- 1 (14½-ounce) can peeled tomatoes
- 1 (17-ounce) can green lima beans
- 1 (2½-pound) chicken, cut up
- 1 (13¾-fluid ounce) can COLLEGE INN® Chicken Broth
- 2 (6-ounce) cans tomato paste
- 2 tablespoons red wine vinegar
- 2 tablespoons Worcestershire sauce
- ¼ teaspoon ground red pepper
- 2 cups cubed cooked pork

Drain tomatoes and lima beans, reserving liquid; coarsely chop tomatoes. In large heavy pot, over medium-high heat, combine chicken, chicken broth, tomato paste, tomato liquid, lima bean liquid, red wine vinegar, Worcestershire sauce and pepper; heat to a boil. Reduce heat; cover and simmer 20 minutes. Add tomatoes, lima beans and pork; cover. Simmer 20 to 25 minutes more or until chicken is done.
Makes 6 servings.

Microwave: In 5-quart microwave-proof casserole, combine first 8 ingredients as above. Cover with waxed paper. Microwave on MEDIUM (50% power) for 28 to 30 minutes, stirring twice during cooking time. Add tomatoes, lima beans and pork; cover. Microwave on LOW (30% power) for 18 to 20 minutes. Let stand, covered, 10 minutes before serving.

Chicken Kyoto

- 1 cup apple cider
- ½ cup soy sauce
- ½ cup vegetable oil
- ¼ cup sugar
- 2 teaspoons ground ginger
- 1 broiler-fryer chicken (2 to 3 pounds), quartered

In small saucepan, combine all ingredients except chicken. Simmer over medium heat 5 to 8 minutes or until sugar is dissolved. Place chicken in shallow glass dish. Pour marinade over chicken; cover and refrigerate about 6 hours. Drain chicken; reserve marinade. Grill chicken, on uncovered grill, over medium-hot **KINGSFORD® Charcoal Briquets**, about 25 minutes on each side or until fork-tender, basting often with marinade.
Makes 4 servings.

Italian Chicken

- 2½ pounds chicken parts (breasts, legs, wings), skinned
- 1 cup sliced CAMPBELL'S FRESH® Mushrooms
- ½ cup chopped onion
- 1 jar (15½ ounces) PREGO® Spaghetti Sauce

To Microwave:
1. Arrange chicken in 12- by 8-inch microwave-safe baking dish, placing thicker portions toward edges of dish. Top with mushrooms and onion. Pour spaghetti sauce over chicken.
2. Cover with waxed paper; microwave on HIGH 22 minutes or until chicken is no longer pink in center, rearranging chicken parts once during cooking. Let stand, covered, 5 minutes.
Makes 6 servings.

Grilled Capon

1 capon or whole roasting
   chicken (6 to 7 pounds)
   Salt
¼ teaspoon poultry seasoning
1½ medium onions, quartered
1 tablespoon rubbed sage
2 stalks celery with leaves, cut
   into 1-inch pieces
2 medium carrots, cut into
   ½-inch pieces
2 tablespoons butter or
   margarine, melted
   K.C. MASTERPIECE® Barbecue
   Sauce

Wash capon thoroughly under cold running water; pat dry with paper toweling. Rub cavity lightly with salt and poultry seasoning. Insert a few onion quarters in neck and fold neck skin over onion. Fold wings across back with tips touching to secure neck skin. Sprinkle 1 teaspoon of the sage in body cavity and stuff with remaining onion quarters, the celery and carrots. Tie legs and tail together with kitchen twine. Insert meat thermometer in center of thigh muscle, not touching bone. Brush skin with melted butter. Rub with remaining 2 teaspoons sage.

Arrange medium-hot KINGS-FORD® Charcoal Briquets around drip pan. Place capon, breast-side up, over drip pan; cover grill and cook 1½ to 2 hours or until thermometer registers 185°F. Tent with heavy-duty foil to prevent overbrowning, if necessary. Brush capon with barbecue sauce during last 10 minutes of cooking. Garnish with parsley; serve with additional heated barbecue sauce, if desired.
Makes 6 servings.

Tequila-Orange Chicken

½ cup orange juice
¼ cup tequila
2 tablespoons seeded and finely
   chopped VLASIC® Hot
   Jalapeno Peppers
½ teaspoon grated orange peel
1 can (10½ ounces) FRANCO-
   AMERICAN® Chicken Gravy
3 whole chicken breasts, split

1. To make sauce: In 1-quart saucepan, combine juice, tequila, peppers and peel. Over high heat, heat to boiling. Reduce heat to low; simmer, uncovered, 10 minutes. Add gravy; heat through, stirring constantly.
2. On grill rack, place chicken, skin side up, directly above medium coals. Grill, uncovered, 1 hour or until tender and juices run clear, turning and brushing often with sauce during the last 30 minutes.
Makes 6 servings.

To broil: Arrange chicken, skin side up, on rack in broiler pan. Broil 6 inches from heat 40 minutes or until tender and juices run clear, turning and brushing often with sauce during the last 20 minutes.

Sweet and Spicy Chicken Barbecue

1½ cups DOLE® Pineapple Orange
   Juice
1 cup orange marmalade
⅔ cup teriyaki sauce
½ cup brown sugar, packed
½ teaspoon ground cloves
½ teaspoon ground ginger
4 frying chickens (about
   2 pounds each), halved or
   quartered
   Salt and pepper
   DOLE™ Pineapple slices
4 teaspoons cornstarch

In saucepan, combine juice, marmalade, teriyaki sauce, brown sugar, cloves and ginger. Heat until sugar dissolves; let cool. Sprinkle chicken with salt and pepper to taste. Place in glass baking pan. Pour juice mixture over chicken; turn to coat all sides. Marinate, covered, 2 hours in refrigerator, turning often.

Preheat oven to 350°F. Light charcoal grill. Drain chicken; reserve marinade. Bake chicken in preheated oven 20 minutes. Arrange chicken on lightly greased grill 4 to 6 inches above glowing coals. Grill, turning and basting often with reserved marinade, 20 to 25 minutes or until meat near bone is no longer pink. Grill pineapple slices 3 minutes or until heated through.

In small saucepan, dissolve cornstarch in remaining marinade. Cook over medium heat until sauce boils and thickens. Spoon over chicken.
Makes 8 servings.

Grilled Chicken Ribbons

¼ cup olive or vegetable oil
2 tablespoons lemon or lime
   juice
2 cloves garlic, minced
1 teaspoon honey
¾ teaspoon dried thyme,
   crushed
½ to 1 teaspoon red pepper
   flakes
   Salt and pepper
4 chicken breast halves, skinned
   and boned (about 6 ounces
   each)

In small bowl, combine all ingredients except chicken; mix well. Cut chicken lengthwise into strips about 1 inch wide. Thread chicken on 8 skewers; brush generously with sauce mixture. Grill chicken, on covered grill, over hot KINGSFORD® Charcoal Briquets 3 to 4 minutes on each side or until chicken is cooked through, basting with sauce once or twice.
Makes 4 servings.

Golden Glazed Stuffed Chicken

1 (3- to 4-pound) whole broiler-
   fryer chicken
Vegetable oil
Salt and pepper
4 cups prepared corn bread
   stuffing
½ cup BAMA® Peach *or* Apricot
   Preserves
1 tablespoon margarine or
   butter, melted
1 tablespoon REALEMON®
   Lemon Juice from
   Concentrate

Preheat oven to 375°. Brush chicken with oil; sprinkle lightly with salt and pepper. Stuff neck and body cavities loosely with stuffing. Place breast-side up on rack in shallow roasting pan. Bake 1 hour and 15 minutes. Turn remaining stuffing into greased 1-quart baking dish; bake 30 minutes. Meanwhile, stir together preserves, margarine and ReaLemon® brand. Spoon glaze over chicken; return to oven and bake 15 minutes longer. Refrigerate leftovers.
Makes 4 to 6 servings.

Microwave: Prepare chicken and stuffing as above. Place chicken breast-side down on microwave rack in 12×7-inch baking dish; cover loosely. Microwave on full power (high) 15 minutes. Turn chicken breast-side up; cover loosely. Microwave on full power (high) 10 to 15 minutes or until tender. Meanwhile, prepare glaze as above. Spoon glaze over chicken during last 5 minutes of cooking time. Turn remaining stuffing into 1-quart round baking dish. Cover; microwave on full power (high) 2 to 3 minutes or until hot.

Roasted Dill Chicken

½ cup WISH-BONE® Italian
   Dressing
1 cup loosely packed snipped
   fresh dill*
½ cup coarsely chopped shallots
   or onions
½ teaspoon salt
¼ teaspoon pepper
1 (5- to 5½-pound) roasting
   chicken
2 pounds all-purpose potatoes,
   cut into chunks

Preheat oven to 375°.

In food processor or blender, process Italian dressing, dill, shallots, salt and pepper until blended.

In roasting pan, on rack, place chicken; spread dill mixture inside cavity, then under and over skin. Close cavity with skewers or wooden toothpicks; tie legs together with string. Arrange potatoes around chicken. Loosely cover with heavy-duty aluminum foil, then roast 1½ hours, turning potatoes occasionally. Remove foil and continue roasting 15 minutes or until meat thermometer reaches 185° and potatoes are done.
Makes about 4 servings.

Substitution: Use 2 tablespoons dried dill weed.

Note: Also terrific with Wish-Bone® Robusto Italian, Herbal Italian, Italian & Cheese, Blended Italian or Lite Italian Dressing.

Mexican Chicken with Spicy Bacon

2 serrano chili peppers
2 cloves garlic
   Dash ground cloves
   Dash ground cinnamon
4 slices bacon, partially cooked
1 whole roasting chicken (3½ to
   4 pounds)

Remove stems from peppers. Slit open; remove seeds and ribs. Finely chop peppers and garlic. Place in small bowl. Stir in cloves and cinnamon. Cut bacon into 1-inch pieces.

Lift skin layer of chicken at neck cavity. Insert hand, lifting skin from meat along breast, thigh and drumstick. Using small metal spatula, spread pepper mixture evenly over meat under skin. Place layer of bacon pieces over pepper mixture. Skewer neck skin to back. Tie legs securely to tail with kitchen twine; twist wing tips under back of chicken. Insert meat thermometer in center of thigh muscle, not touching bone.

Arrange medium-hot KINGS-FORD® Charcoal Briquets around drip pan. Place chicken, breast-side up, over drip pan. Cover grill and cook about 1 hour or until meat thermometer registers 185°F. Garnish with grilled cherry tomatoes and additional serrano chili peppers, if desired.
Makes 4 servings.

Glorified Chicken

2½ pounds chicken parts (breasts,
   legs, wings), skinned
1 can (10¾ ounces)
   CAMPBELL'S® Condensed
   Cream of Chicken, Cream of
   Mushroom or Golden
   Mushroom Soup
2 tablespoons chopped fresh
   parsley

To Microwave:
1. Arrange chicken in 12- by 8-inch microwave-safe baking dish, placing thicker portions toward edges of dish.
2. In small bowl, stir soup until smooth; stir in parsley. Spread soup evenly over chicken.
3. Cover with waxed paper; microwave on HIGH 20 minutes or until chicken is no longer pink in center, rearranging chicken and basting with pan juices once during cooking. Let stand, covered, 5 minutes.
Makes 6 servings.

Herb-Roasted Chicken

2½- to 3-pound broiler-fryer
    chicken
2 cloves garlic, quartered
¼ cup CRISCO® Oil
1 tablespoon lime juice
1 teaspoon dried tarragon
    leaves
1 teaspoon dried chervil leaves
½ teaspoon dried thyme leaves
    Pepper

Preheat oven to 375°F. Lift skin from chicken breast and place 6 pieces garlic between skin and meat. Cut small slit in each drumstick. Insert a piece of garlic into each slit.

Blend Crisco® Oil and lime juice in small bowl. Brush on chicken. Mix tarragon, chervil and thyme in another small bowl. Rub onto chicken. Sprinkle chicken with pepper.

Place chicken, breast-side up, in roasting pan. Bake at 375°F, 1¼ to 1½ hours, or until juices run clear and meat near bone is no longer pink, brushing with lime juice mixture several times during roasting. Let stand 10 minutes before carving.
4 servings.

Special Lemony Chicken

¼ cup unsifted flour
1 teaspoon salt
¼ teaspoon pepper
6 skinned boneless chicken
    breast halves
¼ cup margarine or butter
¼ cup REALEMON® Lemon Juice
    from Concentrate
8 ounces fresh mushrooms,
    sliced (about 2 cups)
    Hot cooked rice
    Chopped parsley

In paper or plastic bag, combine flour, salt and pepper. Add chicken, a few pieces at a time; shake to coat. In large skillet, brown chicken in margarine on both sides until golden brown. Add ReaLemon® brand and mushrooms. Reduce heat; cover and simmer 20 minutes or until tender. Serve with rice; garnish with parsley. Refrigerate leftovers.
Makes 6 servings.

Shantung Chicken

1 whole chicken breast, skinned
    and boned
2 tablespoons cornstarch,
    divided
3 tablespoons KIKKOMAN Soy
    Sauce, divided
1 tablespoon dry sherry
1 clove garlic, minced
1 cup water
3 tablespoons vegetable oil,
    divided
½ pound fresh bean sprouts
¼ pound green onions and tops,
    cut into 1½-inch lengths,
    separating whites from tops
1 tablespoon slivered fresh
    ginger root
1 tablespoon sesame seed,
    toasted
    Hot cooked noodles

Cut chicken into narrow strips. Combine 1 tablespoon *each* cornstarch and soy sauce with sherry and garlic in small bowl; stir in chicken. Let stand 5 minutes. Meanwhile, blend water, remaining 1 tablespoon cornstarch and 2 tablespoons soy sauce; set aside. Heat 1 tablespoon oil in hot wok or large skillet over high heat. Add chicken and stir-fry 2 minutes; remove. Heat remaining 2 tablespoons oil in same pan; add bean sprouts, white parts of green onions and ginger; stir-fry 3 minutes. Stir in chicken, soy sauce mixture, green onion tops and sesame seed. Cook and stir until mixture boils and thickens. Serve immediately over noodles.
Makes 4 servings.

Corn-Stuffed Chicken

¼ cup butter or margarine
½ cup chopped onion
½ cup sliced celery
½ teaspoon dried thyme leaves,
    crushed
4 cups fresh bread cubes
1 cup whole kernel corn, cooked
2 cans (10½ ounces *each*)
    FRANCO-AMERICAN®
    Chicken Gravy
¼ teaspoon pepper
5-pound roasting chicken

1. To make stuffing: In 1½-quart saucepan over medium heat, in hot butter, cook onion, celery and thyme until vegetables are tender, stirring often. In large bowl, combine onion mixture, bread, corn, ¼ cup of the gravy and pepper; toss gently to coat.
2. Remove neck and giblets from inside bird. Remove excess fat. Cut off and discard neck skin. Rinse bird with cold running water; drain well. Spoon stuffing loosely into body cavity. Fold skin over stuffing; secure with skewer. With breast side up, lift wings toward neck, then fold tips under back of bird to balance. Tie legs.
3. In covered grill, arrange preheated coals around drip pan; test for medium heat above pan. Insert meat thermometer into thickest part of meat between breast and thigh, without touching fat or bone.
4. On grill rack, place chicken, breast side up, over pan but not over coals. Grill, covered, 2 to 2½ hours or until well-done or 180°F. Adjust vents and add more charcoal as necessary.
5. To make sauce: Remove chicken from grill, reserving 2 tablespoons drippings. In 1-quart saucepan, combine remaining gravy and reserved drippings. Over medium heat, heat through, stirring constantly. Serve sauce with chicken.
Makes 8 to 10 servings.

To roast: Place stuffed bird, breast side up, on rack in roasting pan. Roast, uncovered, at 325°F. 2½ to 3 hours or until well-done or 180°F.

Apple-Raisin Stuffed Chicken Breasts

1 (13¾-fluid ounce) can
   COLLEGE INN® Chicken
   Broth
⅓ cup BLUE BONNET® Margarine
1 cup herb-seasoned stuffing
   mix
⅓ cup chopped apple
¼ cup seedless raisins
2 whole boneless chicken
   breasts, split and pounded
   (1 pound)
3 tablespoons all-purpose flour
1 teaspoon dried tarragon
   leaves

In saucepan, over medium-high heat, heat ⅓ cup chicken broth and 2 tablespoons margarine until margarine melts. Stir in stuffing mix, apple and raisins. Divide mixture evenly among 4 chicken pieces. Roll up; secure with toothpicks.

In skillet, over medium-high heat, melt remaining margarine. Brown chicken on all sides; remove. Blend flour and tarragon into margarine in skillet. Gradually add remaining broth, stirring constantly until mixture thickens and boils. Return chicken to skillet; reduce heat. Cover; simmer 20 minutes or until done. Garnish as desired.
Makes 4 servings.

Microwave: In 1-quart microwave-proof bowl, place ⅓ cup broth and 2 tablespoons margarine. Microwave, uncovered, on HIGH (100% power) for 1 to 2 minutes until margarine melts. Stir in stuffing mix, apple and raisins. Stuff chicken breasts as above.

In 9-inch microwave-proof pie plate, place remaining margarine. Microwave on HIGH for 35 to 40 seconds until melted. Stir in flour and tarragon. Gradually add remaining broth. Microwave, uncovered, on HIGH for 4 to 5 minutes until mixture thickens and boils, stirring every 2 minutes. Place stuffed chicken in pie plate, turning to coat with sauce; cover with waxed paper. Microwave on HIGH for 8 to 9 minutes until done, rotating dish ¼ turn after 4 minutes. Let stand, covered, 5 minutes.

Chicken Colombia

2 green-tip, medium DOLE™
   Bananas
2 tablespoons vegetable oil
2 whole chicken breasts, split
   Salt and pepper
2 cloves garlic, pressed
2 tablespoons minced fresh
   ginger root
   Orange peel strips*
½ cup orange juice
½ cup water
2 tablespoons chopped chutney
2 teaspoons cornstarch
   Chopped parsley, optional

Cut bananas in half crosswise, then lengthwise. In large skillet, saute bananas in 1 tablespoon oil 30 to 45 seconds, shaking skillet. Remove bananas. Sprinkle chicken with salt and pepper to taste. Add remaining 1 tablespoon oil to skillet. Brown chicken on both sides in hot oil. Add garlic and ginger; saute. Stir in orange peel and juice, ¼ cup water and chutney. Cover; simmer 20 minutes. Dissolve cornstarch in remaining ¼ cup water; stir into pan juices. Cook until sauce boils and thickens. Arrange chicken and bananas on 4 plates. Generously spoon sauce over chicken. Sprinkle with parsley, if desired.
Makes 4 servings.

*Use vegetable peeler to cut thin strips from orange.

Spinach & Pesto Stuffed Chicken Breasts

¼ cup *plus* 2 tablespoons
   WISH-BONE® Italian
   Dressing
¼ cup chopped fresh basil
   leaves*
¼ cup grated Parmesan cheese
⅛ teaspoon pepper
1 package (10 ounces) frozen
   chopped spinach, cooked
   and squeezed dry**
1 cup fresh bread crumbs
4 whole boneless chicken
   breasts (about 2 pounds),
   halved

In food processor or blender, process ¼ cup Italian dressing with basil, cheese and pepper until blended. In medium bowl, thoroughly combine dressing mixture, spinach and bread crumbs.

With knife parallel to cutting board, make deep, 3-inch-long cut in center of each chicken breast half to form pocket. Evenly stuff pockets with spinach mixture.

In aluminum-foil-lined large shallow baking pan or on broiler rack, arrange chicken, then brush with remaining 2 tablespoons dressing. Broil, turning once, 7 minutes or until chicken is done.
Makes about 8 servings.

***Substitution:** Use 1 tablespoon dried basil leaves.

****Substitution:** Use 1 pound fresh spinach leaves, cooked, squeezed dry and chopped (about 1½ cups).

Note: Also terrific with Wish-Bone® Robusto Italian, Herbal Italian, Blended Italian, Italian & Cheese or Lite Italian Dressing.

Chicken-Vegetable Kabobs

½ cup WISH-BONE® Italian & Cheese Dressing
¼ cup dry white wine
1 pound boneless chicken breasts, cubed
1 medium zucchini, cut into ½-inch pieces
1 large green pepper, cut into chunks

In large shallow baking dish, blend Italian & cheese dressing with wine. Add chicken and vegetables and turn to coat. Cover and marinate in refrigerator, turning occasionally, at least 2 hours. Remove chicken and vegetables, reserving marinade.

Onto skewers, alternately thread chicken and vegetables. Grill or broil, turning and basting frequently with reserved marinade, until chicken is done.
Makes about 4 servings.

Quick Chicken Curry

3 cups cubed cooked chicken *or* turkey
1 cup chopped onion
1 clove garlic, finely chopped
¼ cup margarine or butter
¼ cup unsifted flour
2½ cups BORDEN® or MEADOW GOLD® Milk
¾ cup COCO LOPEZ® Cream of Coconut
1 tablespoon curry powder
1 tablespoon WYLER'S® or STEERO® Chicken-Flavor Instant Bouillon *or* 3 Chicken-Flavor Bouillon Cubes
¼ cup REALEMON® Lemon Juice from Concentrate
Hot cooked rice
Condiments

In large skillet, cook onion and garlic in margarine until tender; stir in flour. Gradually add milk; stir until smooth. Add cream of coconut, curry and bouillon. Over medium heat, cook and stir until thickened. Add ReaLemon® brand; reduce heat and simmer 10 minutes. Add chicken. Cook 10 minutes longer. Serve over rice with condiments. Refrigerate leftovers.
Makes 6 servings.

Suggested condiments: Toasted flaked coconut, cashews, pecans or peanuts, chopped green onion, chopped hard-cooked eggs, chutney, crumbled bacon, raisins or sunflower meats.

Microwave: Increase flour to ⅓ *cup;* reduce milk to *2 cups.* In 2-quart round baking dish, microwave margarine on full power (high) 45 seconds to 1 minute or until melted. Add onion and garlic. Cover; microwave on full power (high) 4 minutes or until onion is tender. Proceed as above to add flour, milk, cream of coconut, curry and bouillon. Microwave on ⅔ power (medium-high) 9 to 12 minutes or until slightly thickened, stirring every 2 minutes. Add ReaLemon® brand; microwave on ½ power (medium) 5 minutes. Add chicken; microwave on ½ power (medium) 5 minutes or until chicken is heated through. Let stand 5 minutes before serving. Proceed as above.

Spicy Chicken

2 whole chicken breasts, split
Salt and pepper
1 egg, lightly beaten
1 cup cornmeal
¼ cup olive or vegetable oil
1 onion, sliced
1 large clove garlic, pressed
1 can (14½ ounces) chicken broth
1 teaspoon chili powder
½ teaspoon ground coriander
¼ teaspoon ground cumin
3 green-tip, large DOLE™ Bananas
1 cup halved pimento-stuffed olives

Sprinkle chicken with salt and pepper to taste. Dip in egg and coat with cornmeal. In skillet, brown chicken in oil. Remove chicken. Stir in onion and garlic; saute. Stir in chicken broth, chili powder, coriander and cumin until blended. Return chicken to skillet. Cover; simmer 30 minutes. Slice bananas; add bananas and olives to skillet. Spoon juices over and heat through.
Makes 4 servings.

Chicken Breasts Florentine

2 pounds boneless chicken breasts
¼ cup all-purpose flour
2 eggs, well beaten
⅔ cup seasoned dry bread crumbs
¼ cup oil
1 medium clove garlic, finely chopped
½ cup dry white wine
1 envelope LIPTON® Golden Onion Recipe Soup Mix
1½ cups water
2 tablespoons finely chopped parsley
⅛ teaspoon pepper
Hot cooked rice pilaf or white rice
Hot cooked spinach

Dip chicken in flour, then eggs, then bread crumbs.

In large skillet, heat oil and cook chicken over medium heat until almost done. Remove chicken. Reserve 1 tablespoon drippings. Add garlic and wine to reserved drippings and cook over medium heat 5 minutes. Stir in golden onion recipe soup mix thoroughly blended with water; bring to a boil. Return chicken to skillet and simmer covered 10 minutes or until chicken is done and sauce is slightly thickened. Stir in parsley and pepper. To serve, arrange chicken over hot rice and spinach; garnish as desired.
Makes about 6 servings.

Microwave Directions: Omit oil and decrease wine to ¼ cup. Dip chicken in flour, eggs and bread crumbs as above. In 3-quart casserole, heat chicken, uncovered, at HIGH (Full Power) 4 minutes, rearranging chicken once. Stir in garlic, then golden onion recipe soup mix thoroughly blended with water and wine. Heat uncovered 5 minutes or until boiling, stirring once. Decrease heat to MEDIUM (50% Full Power) and heat uncovered, stirring occasionally, 7 minutes or until chicken is done and sauce is slightly thickened. Stir in parsley and pepper. Let stand covered 5 minutes. Serve as above.

Grilled Stuffed Chicken Breasts

- **6 chicken breast halves, skinned and boned**
- **6 tablespoons butter or margarine**
- **3 tablespoons Dijon-style mustard**
- **6 slices cooked ham**
- **1 cup shredded Swiss cheese (about 4 ounces)**
- **3 tablespoons vegetable oil**
- **1 tablespoon honey**
  Salt and pepper

With meat mallet, pound chicken breasts to ¼-inch thickness. In small bowl, blend butter with 2 tablespoons of the mustard; spread over one side of each chicken breast. Cut ham slices to fit chicken breasts. Place 1 ham slice on each breast; top with shredded cheese. Roll chicken pieces and skewer each to enclose ham and cheese. In small bowl, combine remaining 1 tablespoon mustard, the oil and honey; brush on all sides of each roll. Grill chicken, on covered grill, over medium-hot **KINGSFORD® Charcoal Briquets** 25 to 35 minutes or until chicken is tender, basting often with mustard-honey mixture.
Makes 6 servings.

Tandoori-Style Chicken Kabobs

- **½ pint (8 ounces) plain yogurt**
- **½ cup WISH-BONE® Italian Dressing**
- **1 tablespoon chopped fresh ginger***
- **1 teaspoon cumin seeds****
- **1 teaspoon coriander seeds (optional)**
- **½ teaspoon paprika**
- **1 pound boneless chicken breasts, cut into 1-inch pieces**

In food processor or blender, process all ingredients except chicken until blended. In large shallow baking dish, combine chicken with dressing mixture. Cover and marinate in refrigerator, stirring occasionally, at least 3 hours. Remove chicken, reserving marinade.

Onto skewers, thread chicken, then grill or broil, turning and basting occasionally with reserved marinade, 5 minutes or until chicken is done. Serve, if desired, with Tandoori Rice and assorted grilled vegetables.
Makes about 8 servings.

***Substitution:** Use ½ teaspoon ground ginger.

****Substitution:** Use ½ teaspoon ground cumin.

Note: Also terrific with Wish-Bone® Robusto Italian, Blended Italian, Herbal Italian, Lite Italian, Classic Dijon Vinaigrette or Lite Classic Dijon Vinaigrette Dressing.

Try this unusual side dish as an authentic tandoori accompaniment:
TANDOORI RICE: In medium saucepan, bring 2 cups water, ¼ cup chopped onion, 2 tablespoons butter or margarine, 2 tablespoons brown sugar, ½ teaspoon salt, ½ teaspoon ground cinnamon, ½ teaspoon coriander seeds (optional), ½ teaspoon cardamom and ¼ teaspoon ground cloves to a boil. Stir in 1 cup uncooked regular rice and simmer covered 20 minutes or until rice is tender.

Rolled Chicken Breasts Florentine

- **4 skinless boneless chicken breast halves (about 1 pound)**
- **4 thin slices (1 ounce each) cooked ham**
- **4 thin slices (1 ounce each) Swiss cheese**
- **1 package (10 ounces) frozen chopped spinach, thawed and well drained**
- **1 can (10¾ ounces) CAMPBELL'S® Condensed Golden Mushroom or Cream of Chicken Soup**
- **⅓ cup water**
- **¼ cup sliced green onions**
- **⅛ teaspoon dried thyme leaves, crushed**

To Microwave:
1. With flat side of meat mallet, pound chicken to ¼-inch thickness. Place a ham slice, cheese slice and ¼ of the spinach on each chicken piece. Roll up chicken from short end, jelly-roll fashion. Secure with wooden toothpicks if needed.
2. Place chicken, seam side down, in 12- by 8-inch microwave-safe baking dish. Cover with vented plastic wrap; microwave on HIGH 5 minutes.
3. In small bowl, stir soup until smooth; stir in water, onions and thyme. Pour over chicken. Cover; microwave on HIGH 10 minutes or until chicken is fork-tender, rotating dish once during cooking. Let stand, covered, 5 minutes.
Makes 4 servings.

Note: To thaw 1 package (10 ounces) frozen spinach: Place frozen spinach in 1½-quart microwave-safe casserole. Cover with lid; microwave on HIGH 5 minutes, stirring once during heating. Drain thoroughly.

Mongolian Pot

2 whole chicken breasts,
  skinned and boned
4 tablespoons KIKKOMAN Soy
  Sauce, divided
2 teaspoons minced fresh ginger
  root
1/2 teaspoon sugar
2 cans (10 1/4 oz. each)
  condensed chicken broth
4 soup cans water
1 large clove garlic, minced
1/2 pound cabbage, cut into
    3/4-inch chunks (about
    4 cups)
3/4 pound fresh spinach, trimmed,
    washed and drained
3 green onions and tops, cut
    into 1-inch lengths and
    slivered
4 ounces vermicelli or thin
    spaghetti, cooked and
    drained
1/4 pound fresh mushrooms,
    sliced

Cut chicken into thin strips. Combine 2 tablespoons soy sauce, ginger and sugar in medium dish; stir in chicken. Let stand 15 minutes. Meanwhile, combine chicken broth, water, remaining 2 tablespoons soy sauce and garlic in deep electric skillet or electric wok; bring to boil. Reduce heat; keep broth mixture hot. Arrange cabbage, spinach, green onions, vermicelli and mushrooms on platter. Using chopsticks or tongs, let individuals select and add chicken, vegetables and vermicelli to hot broth. Cook chicken until tender, vegetables to desired doneness and vermicelli until heated through. Serve in individual bowls with additional soy sauce, as desired. When all foods are cooked, serve broth as soup.
Makes 4 to 6 servings.

Jade & Ruby Stir-Fry

1 whole chicken breast, skinned
  and boned
1 pound fresh broccoli
2 tablespoons vegetable oil
1 medium onion, chunked
2 tablespoons water
2 medium-size red bell peppers,
  chunked
1/2 pound fresh mushrooms,
  quartered
1/3 cup KIKKOMAN Stir-Fry Sauce
1/4 teaspoon crushed red pepper

Cut chicken into 1-inch square pieces. Remove flowerets from broccoli; cut into bite-size pieces. Peel stalks; cut into thin slices. Heat oil in hot wok or large skillet over high heat. Add chicken; stir-fry 1 minute. Add broccoli and onion; stir-fry 1 minute. Add water; cover and cook 2 minutes, stirring once. Add bell peppers and mushrooms; stir-fry 2 minutes. Stir in stir-fry sauce and crushed red pepper. Cook and stir until chicken and vegetables are coated with sauce. Serve immediately.
Makes 4 servings.

Cashew Chicken

3/4 pound skinless boneless
    chicken breasts
2 tablespoons cornstarch
1 tablespoon dry sherry
1 tablespoon soy sauce
1 teaspoon grated fresh ginger
3 cups broccoli flowerets
3 tablespoons peanut or
  vegetable oil
1 cup snow peas, each cut in
  half
1 1/2 cups water
1 pouch CAMPBELL'S® Noodle
  Soup Mix
1 cup sliced radishes
1/2 cup roasted cashews

1. Cut chicken crosswise into 1/8-inch-wide strips. In medium bowl, combine cornstarch, sherry, soy sauce and ginger; mix well. Add chicken strips; stir to coat well.
2. In 10-inch skillet over high heat, stir-fry broccoli in 1 tablespoon of the oil 1 minute. Add snow peas; stir-fry 3 minutes or until vegetables are tender-crisp. Remove vegetables to plate.
3. In same skillet, stir-fry chicken in remaining 2 tablespoons oil until all pieces change color.
4. Stir in water and soup mix. Heat to boiling, stirring constantly. Reduce heat to low. Cover; simmer 5 minutes or until noodles are tender, stirring occasionally.
5. Return cooked vegetables to skillet; add radishes and cashews. Cook until heated through.
Makes 4 servings.

Sweet-and-Sour Chicken

1 can (16 ounces) whole
  tomatoes
1/2 cup plum jelly
1/4 cup cider vinegar
1 tablespoon sugar
1 tablespoon cornstarch
1 tablespoon soy sauce
1 teaspoon instant chicken
  bouillon granules
Batter:
1/2 cup water
1/3 cup all-purpose flour
1/3 cup cornstarch
1 teaspoon salt
1/8 teaspoon garlic powder
1/8 teaspoon pepper

1 whole boneless chicken
  breast, skinned, cut into
  1- to 1 1/2-inch pieces
CRISCO® Oil for frying
1 large green pepper, cored,
  seeded and cut into 1-inch
  pieces
4 green onions, cut into 1-inch
  pieces
1 can (8 ounces) pineapple
  chunks, drained
Hot cooked rice

Drain tomatoes, reserving ¼ cup juice. Cut up tomatoes and set aside. Blend reserved juice, plum jelly, vinegar, sugar, 1 tablespoon cornstarch, soy sauce and bouillon granules in small mixing bowl. Set aside.

For batter, blend all ingredients in small mixing bowl. Add chicken. Stir to coat. Heat 2 to 3 inches Crisco® Oil in large saucepan to 350°F. Remove several chicken pieces from batter with slotted spoon. Fry in hot Crisco® Oil 3 to 4 minutes, or until light golden brown. Drain on paper towels. Repeat with remaining chicken.

Discard Crisco® Oil, reserving 2 tablespoons in saucepan. Add green pepper and onions. Stir-fry over medium-high heat about 3 minutes, or until tender. Stir in tomato juice mixture. Heat to boiling, stirring constantly. Continue to boil 1 minute, stirring constantly. Stir in pineapple chunks, chicken and tomatoes. Cook 1 to 2 minutes longer. Serve with rice.
2 to 4 servings.

Moo Goo Gai Pan

2 tablespoons cornstarch
2 tablespoons water
3 whole boneless chicken
**   breasts, skinned, cut into**
**   1-inch pieces**
½ teaspoon salt
⅛ teaspoon pepper
¼ cup CRISCO® Oil
¼ cup chopped green onion
2 cups sliced fresh mushrooms
1 jar (2 ounces) sliced pimiento,
**   drained**
1 teaspoon ground ginger
1 can (14½ ounces) chicken
**   broth**
2 packages (6 to 7 ounces each)
**   frozen pea pods**
**   Hot cooked rice**

Blend cornstarch and water in small bowl until smooth. Set aside.

Sprinkle chicken with salt and pepper. Heat Crisco® Oil in large skillet or wok. Add chicken. Stir-fry over medium-high heat until no longer pink. Remove chicken from skillet. Add onion to skillet. Stir-fry over medium-high heat 1 minute. Stir in mushrooms, pimiento and ginger. Cook, stirring constantly, 2 to 3 minutes, or until mushrooms are tender. Add chicken broth and pea pods. Heat to boiling, stirring to break apart pea pods. Add cornstarch mixture. Heat to boiling, stirring constantly. Boil 1 minute. Remove from heat. Stir in chicken. Serve with rice. Sprinkle with *toasted almonds* and serve with *soy sauce,* if desired.
6 to 8 servings.

Baked Asian-Style Chicken

1 can (15 ounces) cream of
**   coconut**
1 cup (8 ounces) WISH-BONE®
**   Deluxe French Dressing**
1 medium onion, coarsely
**   chopped**
1 tablespoon lime juice
1 teaspoon ground ginger
1 teaspoon ground cumin
1 (2½- to 3-pound) chicken, cut
**   into serving pieces**

In large shallow baking dish, thoroughly blend all ingredients except chicken; add chicken and turn to coat. Cover and marinate in refrigerator, turning occasionally, at least 4 hours.

Preheat oven to 400°. Bake chicken with marinade, uncovered, turning and basting occasionally, 40 minutes or until chicken is done.
Makes about 4 servings.

Note: Also terrific with Wish-Bone® Lite French Style, Sweet 'n Spicy French or Lite Sweet 'n Spicy French Dressing.

Chicken Walnut Stir-Fry

5 tablespoons CRISCO® Oil,
**   divided**
5 teaspoons soy sauce, divided
3 teaspoons cornstarch, divided
2 whole boneless chicken
**   breasts, skinned, cut into**
**   1-inch pieces**
½ cup chicken broth
½ teaspoon ground ginger
½ teaspoon dried crushed red
**   pepper**
1 medium onion, cut into 1-inch
**   pieces**
1 clove garlic, minced
½ pound fresh broccoli, cut into
**   1-inch pieces**
½ cup coarsely chopped walnuts
**   Hot cooked rice**

Mix 1 tablespoon Crisco® Oil, 2 teaspoons soy sauce and 1 teaspoon cornstarch in small mixing bowl. Add chicken. Stir to coat. Cover and refrigerate about 30 minutes.

Mix chicken broth, ginger, remaining 3 teaspoons soy sauce and remaining 2 teaspoons cornstarch in small bowl. Set aside.

Heat remaining 4 tablespoons Crisco® Oil in large skillet or wok. Add refrigerated chicken mixture and red pepper. Stir-fry over medium-high heat until chicken is no longer pink. Remove chicken from skillet; set aside. Add onion and garlic to skillet. Stir-fry over medium-high heat until onion is tender. Add broccoli. Stir-fry until tender. Add chicken and chicken broth mixture. Cook, stirring constantly, until thickened. Stir in walnuts. Serve with rice.
4 servings.

Mushroom-Stuffed Chicken Breasts

4 tablespoons butter or margarine
1½ cups chopped CAMPBELL'S FRESH® Mushrooms
¼ cup chopped green onions
¼ cup finely chopped celery
¼ teaspoon dried marjoram leaves, crushed
2 cups PEPPERIDGE FARM® Herb Seasoned Stuffing Mix, coarsely crushed
4 skinless boneless chicken breast halves (about 1 pound)
1 egg
2 tablespoons milk
1 teaspoon paprika

To Microwave:
1. To make stuffing: In 2-quart microwave-safe casserole, combine 2 tablespoons of the butter, mushrooms, onions, celery and marjoram. Cover with lid; microwave on HIGH 4 minutes or until vegetables are tender, stirring once during cooking. Stir in ½ cup of the stuffing mix until blended; set aside.
2. With flat side of meat mallet, pound chicken to ¼-inch thickness. Divide stuffing among breast halves. Roll up chicken from short end, jelly-roll fashion. Secure with wooden toothpicks if needed.
3. In small bowl, beat egg and milk. In pie plate, combine remaining 1½ cups stuffing mix and paprika. Dip rolled breasts in egg mixture, then in paprika mixture. Place chicken, seam side down, in 12- by 8-inch microwave-safe baking dish.
4. Place remaining 2 tablespoons butter in small microwave-safe bowl. Microwave on HIGH 30 seconds or until melted. Drizzle over chicken.
5. Cover with waxed paper; microwave on HIGH 8 minutes or until chicken is no longer pink in center, rotating dish once during cooking. Let stand, covered, 5 minutes.
Makes 4 servings.
Note: For even crisper chicken, prepare as directed above. Transfer cooked chicken to broiler pan; broil 4 inches from heat 1 to 2 minutes or until top is browned.

Lemon Chicken

1¼ pounds boneless chicken breasts, skinned and cut into bite-size pieces
1 egg, slightly beaten
3 tablespoons cornstarch
2 tablespoons soy sauce
½ cup sugar
2 teaspoons WYLER'S® or STEERO® Chicken-Flavor Instant Bouillon
½ teaspoon garlic powder
1 cup water
½ cup REALEMON® Lemon Juice from Concentrate
2 tablespoons catsup
Additional cornstarch
Vegetable oil
Shredded lettuce or hot cooked rice

In medium bowl, combine egg, *1 tablespoon* cornstarch and soy sauce; mix well. Add chicken, stirring to coat; marinate 10 minutes. Meanwhile, in medium saucepan, combine remaining *2 tablespoons* cornstarch, sugar, bouillon and garlic powder. Gradually add water, ReaLemon® brand and catsup; mix well. Over high heat, cook and stir until mixture comes to a boil. Reduce heat; continue cooking and stirring until mixture thickens. Keep sauce warm. Coat chicken with additional cornstarch. In large skillet, cook chicken in ½ inch hot oil until tender and golden. Arrange chicken on shredded lettuce; pour warm sauce over chicken. Garnish as desired. Serve immediately. Refrigerate leftovers.
Makes 4 servings.

Golden Chicken Stir-Fry

1 whole chicken breast, skinned and boned
1 tablespoon cornstarch
5 tablespoons KIKKOMAN Teriyaki Sauce, divided
1 clove garlic, minced
1¼ cups regular-strength chicken broth
4 teaspoons cornstarch
Boiling water
½ pound fresh bean sprouts
2 cups finely shredded lettuce
2 tablespoons vegetable oil, divided
2 medium carrots, cut into julienne strips
1 onion, chunked
2 teaspoons slivered fresh ginger root

Cut chicken into thin strips. Combine 1 tablespoon *each* cornstarch and teriyaki sauce with garlic in small bowl; stir in chicken. Let stand 15 minutes. Meanwhile, combine chicken broth, remaining 4 tablespoons teriyaki sauce and 4 teaspoons cornstarch; set aside. Pour boiling water over bean sprouts in bowl; let stand 1 minute. Drain; rinse under cold water and drain thoroughly. Toss sprouts with lettuce. Line serving platter with mixture; set aside. Heat 1 tablespoon oil in hot wok or large skillet over high heat. Add chicken and stir-fry 2 minutes; remove. Heat remaining 1 tablespoon oil in same pan. Add carrots, onion and ginger; stir-fry 4 minutes. Add chicken and teriyaki sauce mixture. Cook and stir until sauce boils and thickens. Turn out onto lined platter; toss to combine before serving.
Makes 4 servings.

Baked Chicken Breasts with Rice & Vegetable Stuffing

- 1 envelope LIPTON® Vegetable Recipe Soup Mix
- 1½ cups water
- ½ cup uncooked regular rice
- 1 package (10 ounces) frozen chopped spinach, cooked and squeezed dry
- ½ medium tomato, coarsely chopped
- ½ cup shredded mozzarella cheese (about 1½ ounces)
- ¼ cup grated Parmesan cheese
- 1 small clove garlic, finely chopped
- 4 whole boneless chicken breasts (about 2 pounds), skinned and halved

In medium saucepan, blend vegetable recipe soup mix with water; bring to a boil. Stir in uncooked rice and simmer covered 20 minutes or until tender. Stir in spinach, tomato, cheeses and garlic; set aside.

Preheat oven to 350°. With knife parallel to cutting board, make deep, 3-inch-long cut in center of each chicken breast half to form pocket. Evenly stuff pockets with rice mixture.

In lightly greased baking dish, arrange chicken and bake uncovered, basting occasionally, 40 minutes or until done. Sprinkle, if desired, with paprika.
Makes about 8 servings.

Colorful Dragon Stir-Fry

- 1 whole chicken breast, skinned and boned
- 1 pound fresh broccoli
- 5 tablespoons KIKKOMAN Stir-Fry Sauce, divided
- 3 tablespoons vegetable oil, divided
- 1 medium onion, cut into thin wedges
- 1 medium carrot, cut diagonally into thin slices
- 2 tablespoons water

Cut chicken into ½-inch strips. Remove flowerets from broccoli; set aside. Peel stalks; cut into thin slices. Coat chicken with 1 tablespoon stir-fry sauce. Heat 1 tablespoon oil in hot wok or large skillet over high heat. Add chicken and stir-fry 3 minutes; remove. Heat remaining 2 tablespoons oil in same pan. Add onion; stir-fry 1 minute. Add broccoli and carrot; stir-fry 2 minutes longer. Pour water into pan. Reduce heat and simmer, covered, 3 minutes; stir once. Add remaining 4 tablespoons stir-fry sauce and chicken. Cook and stir just until chicken and vegetables are coated. Serve immediately.
Makes 4 servings.

Spicy Cashew Stir-Fry

- 3 chicken breast halves, skinned and boned
- 2 tablespoons vegetable oil
- 2 teaspoons minced fresh ginger root
- 6 to 8 whole red chili peppers
- 1 small onion, thinly sliced
- 1 small zucchini, thinly sliced
- 2 tablespoons chicken broth or water
- 1 tablespoon dry sherry
- 3 tablespoons KIKKOMAN Stir-Fry Sauce
- ½ cup unsalted roasted cashews

Cut chicken into thin slices. Place wok or large skillet over high heat until hot. Add oil, swirling to coat sides of pan. Add ginger and chili peppers; cook and stir until fragrant. Add chicken and stir-fry 3 minutes. Add onion, zucchini, broth, sherry and stir-fry sauce; cover and cook 1 minute, or until vegetables are tender-crisp. Stir in cashews; serve immediately.
Makes 4 servings.

Crunchy Almond Chicken Cutlets

- 1 cup fresh bread crumbs
- 1 cup blanched slivered almonds, toasted and finely chopped
- 2 tablespoons chopped parsley
- ½ teaspoon ground ginger
- ¼ teaspoon salt
- ⅛ teaspoon pepper
- 3 whole boneless chicken breasts (about 1½ pounds), halved
- 1 cup (8 ounces) WISH-BONE® Creamy Italian or Lite Creamy Italian Dressing

Preheat oven to 350°.

In medium bowl, combine bread crumbs, almonds, parsley, ginger, salt and pepper. Dip chicken in creamy Italian dressing, then bread crumb mixture, coating well. In large shallow baking pan, arrange chicken. Bake uncovered 20 minutes or until done.
Makes about 6 servings.

Chicken Parisian

1/4 cup unsifted flour
1/4 teaspoon *each* paprika and pepper
6 boneless chicken breast halves, skinned
3 tablespoons margarine or butter
8 ounces fresh mushrooms, sliced (about 2 cups)
1/2 cup water
1/4 cup dry white wine
2 teaspoons WYLER'S® or STEERO® Chicken-Flavor Instant Bouillon *or* 2 Chicken-Flavor Bouillon Cubes
2 teaspoons chopped parsley
1/4 teaspoon thyme leaves

In paper or plastic bag, combine flour, paprika and pepper. Add chicken, a few pieces at a time; shake to coat. In large skillet, brown chicken in margarine on both sides; remove from pan. In skillet, add remaining ingredients; simmer 3 minutes. Add chicken; simmer covered 20 minutes or until tender. Garnish as desired. Refrigerate leftovers.
Makes 6 servings.

Spicy Smoked Duck

1 (4- to 5-pound) frozen duckling, thawed
1/4 cup KIKKOMAN Lite Soy Sauce
1 teaspoon liquid smoke seasoning
1/2 teaspoon fennel seed, well crushed
1/4 teaspoon pepper
1/8 teaspoon ground cloves

Remove and discard giblets and neck from duckling cavity. Wash duckling; drain and gently pat dry with paper towels. Combine lite soy sauce, liquid smoke, fennel, pepper and cloves. Brush body cavity with sauce mixture. Place duckling, breast side up, on rack in roasting pan. Roast at 425°F. 1 hour. *Reduce oven temperature to 350°F.* Continue roasting 45 minutes, or until tender. Brush skin of duckling several times with sauce mixture during last 30 minutes of cooking time. Let stand 15 minutes before carving.
Makes 4 servings.

Chicken Breasts with Artichoke-Cheese Stuffing

4 whole boneless chicken breasts, skinned and halved lengthwise
1 1/2 cups shredded Monterey Jack cheese (about 6 ounces)
1/4 cup mayonnaise
1 tablespoon finely chopped onion
1 tablespoon dried parsley flakes
1 teaspoon Dijon mustard
1 jar (6 ounces) marinated artichoke hearts, drained
1/3 cup all-purpose flour
1/4 teaspoon salt
1/8 teaspoon pepper
1 egg
2 tablespoons water
1 cup seasoned dry bread crumbs
1/3 cup CRISCO® Oil

Pound chicken breasts to 1/4-inch thickness. Set aside. Mix cheese, mayonnaise, onion, parsley flakes and mustard in small mixing bowl. Cut artichoke hearts into bite-size pieces. Stir into cheese mixture. Spread about 1/4 cup cheese mixture down center of each piece of chicken. Roll up and secure ends with wooden picks. Mix flour, salt and pepper in shallow dish. Dip rolled chicken in flour mixture to coat. Set aside.

Mix egg and water in shallow dish. Place bread crumbs in another shallow dish or on sheet of waxed paper. Dip rolled chicken in egg mixture then in bread crumbs, pressing to coat thoroughly. Cover and refrigerate coated chicken about 1 hour.

Preheat oven to 350°F. Place Crisco® Oil in 13×9-inch baking pan. Place in oven 10 minutes. Remove from oven. Using tongs, roll coated chicken in hot Crisco Oil. Arrange chicken in pan. Bake at 350°F, 35 minutes, or until golden brown.
8 servings.

Grilled Game Hens, Texas-Style

1 can (8 ounces) tomato sauce
1/4 cup vegetable oil
1 1/2 teaspoons chili powder
1 teaspoon paprika
1/4 teaspoon garlic powder
1/4 teaspoon cayenne pepper
4 Cornish game hens (1 to 1 1/2 pounds each), cut into halves

In small bowl, combine all ingredients except game hens. Brush hens generously with tomato mixture. Grill hens, on covered grill, over medium-hot **KINGSFORD® with Mesquite Charcoal Briquets** 45 to 50 minutes or until fork-tender, brushing frequently with tomato mixture.
Makes 4 servings.

Chicken 'n Vegetable Stir Fry

3 tablespoons oil
1 pound boneless chicken breasts, cut into thin strips
½ cup broccoli florets
2 ounces snow peas (about ½ cup)
1 medium carrot, thinly sliced
½ medium red or green pepper, cut into thin strips
1 envelope LIPTON® Golden Onion Recipe Soup Mix
1 teaspoon cornstarch
½ teaspoon ground ginger
1½ cups water
2 teaspoons soy sauce
1 teaspoon white or rice vinegar
Hot cooked rice

In large skillet, heat oil and cook chicken with vegetables over medium-high heat, stirring constantly, 10 minutes or until chicken is golden and vegetables are crisp-tender. Thoroughly blend golden onion recipe soup mix, cornstarch, ginger, water, soy sauce and vinegar; stir into chicken mixture. Bring to a boil, then simmer uncovered 5 minutes or until sauce is thickened. Serve over hot rice and garnish, if desired, with sliced green onion and toasted sesame seeds.
Makes about 4 servings.

Microwave Directions: Omit oil and decrease ginger to ¼ teaspoon. In 2-quart casserole, heat chicken, uncovered, at HIGH (Full Power) 4 minutes or until almost done; remove chicken and drain. Add vegetables to casserole and heat uncovered 5 minutes. Thoroughly blend golden onion recipe soup mix, cornstarch, ginger, water, soy sauce and vinegar; stir into vegetables. Heat uncovered 5 minutes or until sauce is thickened, stirring once. Return chicken to casserole and heat 1 minute or until heated through. Let stand covered 5 minutes. Serve and garnish as above.

Chicken and Broccoli

1 pound skinned boneless chicken breasts, cut into bite-size pieces
3 cups broccoli flowerets, cooked
1 egg white, beaten
5 teaspoons soy sauce
2 teaspoons cornstarch
¼ cup vegetable oil
8 ounces fresh mushrooms, sliced (about 2 cups)
2 tablespoons REALEMON® Lemon Juice from Concentrate
2 tablespoons dry sherry
1 tablespoon chopped pimiento, optional
Hot cooked rice

In medium bowl, combine egg white, *3 teaspoons* soy sauce and cornstarch; mix well. Add chicken; stir to coat. Refrigerate 1 hour. In large skillet, over high heat, brown chicken in oil; remove. Add mushrooms; cook and stir until tender. Add chicken, broccoli and remaining ingredients except rice; heat through. Serve with rice. Refrigerate leftovers.
Makes 4 to 6 servings.

Orange-Cashew Chicken

1 pound boneless chicken breasts
½ cup KIKKOMAN Teriyaki Baste & Glaze
2 tablespoons orange juice
2 tablespoons dry white wine
2 tablespoons vegetable oil
1 green pepper, cut into thin strips
½ cup diagonally sliced celery
1 can (11 oz.) mandarin orange segments, drained
½ cup roasted cashews

Cut chicken into thin slices. Combine teriyaki baste & glaze, orange juice and wine; set aside. Heat oil in hot wok or large skillet over medium heat. Add chicken, green pepper and celery; stir-fry 3 to 4 minutes. Pour in baste & glaze mixture; cook and stir until chicken and vegetables are coated with sauce. Remove from heat; stir in orange segments and cashews. Serve immediately.
Makes 4 servings.

Chicken Cordon Bleu with Golden Cream Sauce

3 whole boneless chicken breasts (about 2½ pounds), halved and lightly pounded
6 slices Swiss cheese
6 slices cooked ham
2 tablespoons butter or margarine
¼ teaspoon ground nutmeg
⅛ teaspoon pepper
1 envelope LIPTON® Golden Onion Recipe Soup Mix
2 cups (1 pint) light cream or half and half
¼ cup water
Hot cooked noodles

Top each chicken breast half with slice of cheese and ham; roll up and secure with wooden toothpicks.

In large skillet, melt butter and brown chicken over medium heat; drain. Add nutmeg and pepper, then golden onion recipe soup mix blended with cream and water. Bring just to the boiling point, then simmer covered, basting occasionally, 20 minutes or until chicken is done. To serve, arrange chicken and sauce over hot noodles.
Makes about 6 servings.

Oriental Game Hens

4 Cornish game hens (1 to 1½ pounds each)
Salt
½ cup peanut or vegetable oil
½ cup soy sauce
2 tablespoons brown sugar
1 tablespoon wine vinegar
½ teaspoon grated fresh ginger
Dash ground cloves

Remove giblets from hens. Remove fatty portion from neck and tail area of hens. Rinse hens under cold running water. Pat hens dry with paper toweling. Sprinkle cavities with salt. Close neck and body openings with skewers. Tie legs together; tuck wings under back and tie with kitchen twine. Arrange hens in shallow microwaveable dish and cover with vented plastic wrap. Microwave at 50% power 10 minutes. For basting sauce, in small bowl, combine remaining ingredients. Lightly oil grid. Grill hens, on uncovered grill, over medium-hot **KINGSFORD® Charcoal Briquets** 20 minutes or until thigh moves easily and juices run clear, basting often with sauce.
Makes 4 servings.

Thai Hens

3 fresh or thawed Rock Cornish hens (1¼ to 1½ pounds each)
½ cup KIKKOMAN Teriyaki Sauce
1 tablespoon grated lemon peel
1 tablespoon lemon juice
2 cloves garlic, pressed
¼ to ½ teaspoon ground red pepper (cayenne)
1 tablespoon minced fresh cilantro

Remove and discard giblets and necks from hens. Split hens lengthwise. Rinse halves under cold running water; drain well and pat dry with paper towels. Place in large plastic bag. Combine teriyaki sauce, lemon peel and juice, garlic and red pepper; pour over hens. Press air out of bag; tie top securely. Turn bag over several times to coat halves. Refrigerate 8 hours or overnight, turning bag over occasionally. Reserving marinade, remove hens and place on rack of broiler pan. Broil about 7 inches from heat source 45 to 50 minutes, or until tender, turning over frequently and brushing with reserved marinade. Remove to serving platter and immediately sprinkle cilantro over hens.
Makes 4 to 6 servings.

Lemon Herb Cornish Hens

2 (1½-pound) Rock Cornish hens, split in half lengthwise
Salt and pepper
2 tablespoons finely chopped onion
1 clove garlic, finely chopped
¼ cup vegetable oil
¼ cup REALEMON® Lemon Juice from Concentrate
2 teaspoons WYLER'S® or STEERO® Chicken-Flavor Instant Bouillon or 2 Chicken-Flavor Bouillon Cubes
1 teaspoon chopped parsley
1 teaspoon rosemary leaves, crushed

Season hens lightly with salt and pepper. In small saucepan, cook onion and garlic in oil until tender. Add remaining ingredients; simmer 10 minutes. Grill hens until tender and crisp, about 1 hour, turning and basting frequently with sauce. Refrigerate leftovers.
Makes 4 servings.

Oven Method: Place hens on rack in roasting pan. Bake at 375° for 1 hour and 15 minutes; basting frequently.

Glazed Stuffed Cornish Hens

2 Cornish hens (1½ pounds each)
¼ cup butter or margarine
½ cup chopped onion
½ cup sweet red pepper cut into matchstick-thin strips
½ cup green pepper cut into matchstick-thin strips
1 package (8 ounces) PEPPERIDGE FARM® Herb Seasoned Stuffing Mix
1 cup SWANSON® Clear Ready to Serve Chicken Broth
½ cup apricot preserves

To Microwave:
1. Remove giblets and neck from inside hens (reserve for another use if desired). Rinse hens; pat dry. Split hens along backbone and breastbone; set aside.
2. In 3-quart microwave-safe casserole, combine butter, onion and peppers. Cover with lid; microwave on HIGH 3 minutes or until tender, stirring once during cooking. Add stuffing and broth; toss to mix well.
3. Pat stuffing mixture into bottom of 12- by 8-inch microwave-safe baking dish. Arrange hen halves, skin side up, over stuffing; set aside.
4. Place preserves in small microwave-safe bowl. Microwave, uncovered, on HIGH 45 seconds or until melted. Brush preserves over hens. Cover with waxed paper; microwave on HIGH 17 minutes or until hens are no longer pink in center, rotating dish twice and rearranging hens once during cooking. Let stand, covered, 5 minutes.
Makes 4 servings.

Roasted Duckling with Orange & Plum Sauce

1 (3-pound) duckling
1 medium orange, halved
1 medium onion, halved
1/2 cup WISH-BONE® Deluxe French or Lite French Style Dressing
1/2 cup orange juice
2 tablespoons brown sugar
1 teaspoon grated orange peel (optional)
1/4 teaspoon ground cinnamon
1/8 teaspoon ground cloves
1/8 teaspoon ground nutmeg
1 tablespoon butter or margarine
1/2 cup chopped onion
1 teaspoon finely chopped garlic
2 tablespoons brandy
2 medium plums, pitted and cut into wedges
2 small oranges, peeled, sectioned and seeded

Preheat oven to 400°.

Stuff duckling with orange and onion halves. Close cavity with skewers or wooden toothpicks; tie legs together with string. With pin or fork, pierce skin. In roasting pan, on rack, arrange duckling breast side up. Roast 40 minutes, turning duckling every 10 minutes.

Meanwhile, in small bowl, blend deluxe French dressing, orange juice, sugar, orange peel, cinnamon, cloves and nutmeg. Pour 1/2 of the dressing mixture over duckling; loosely cover with heavy-duty aluminum foil. Continue roasting, basting occasionally, 30 minutes or until meat thermometer reaches 185°. Remove to serving platter and keep warm.

Meanwhile, in medium saucepan, melt butter and cook onion with garlic over medium heat, stirring occasionally, 5 minutes or until onion is tender. Add brandy, the plums and orange sections and cook, stirring occasionally, 5 minutes. Stir in remaining dressing mixture and heat through. Serve with duckling.
Makes about 2 servings.

Braised Chinese Duckling

1 (4- to 5-pound) frozen duckling, thawed and quartered
3 tablespoons KIKKOMAN Lite Soy Sauce, divided
1 tablespoon vegetable oil
2 tablespoons dry sherry
1 clove garlic, minced
1 teaspoon ginger juice*
4 green onions and tops, cut into 2-inch lengths
1/3 cup water
2 teaspoons cornstarch

Wash duckling quarters; dry with paper towels. Rub thoroughly with 2 tablespoons lite soy sauce. Let stand 30 minutes. Heat oil in Dutch oven or large skillet over medium heat. Brown duckling slowly in hot oil; drain off fat. Add sherry and garlic. Cover and cook over low heat 45 minutes, or until tender, turning quarters over once. Remove from pan; keep warm. Spoon off and discard excess fat from pan juices; return 1/3 cup juices to pan. Add remaining 1 tablespoon lite soy sauce, ginger juice and green onions; cook 1 minute. Combine water with cornstarch; stir into pan. Cook and stir until sauce boils and thickens. To serve, spoon sauce over duckling quarters.
Makes 4 servings.

*Peel fresh ginger root, then squeeze through garlic press.

Pineapple Orange Crispy Chicken

1/3 cup sesame seeds
1 1/4 teaspoons dried tarragon, crumbled
1/4 teaspoon ground cloves
2 chicken breasts, split, skinned and boned
1 large clove garlic, pressed
1 egg, beaten
Salt
1/2 teaspoon coarsely ground pepper
1 tablespoon olive oil
1 can (8 1/4 ounces) DOLE® Pineapple Slices
1 DOLE™ Orange
1/2 cup orange juice
1 tablespoon sherry wine
1 to 2 teaspoons cornstarch

In pie plate, combine sesame seeds, 1 teaspoon tarragon and 1/8 teaspoon cloves. Rub chicken breasts with garlic, dip in egg, then sprinkle with salt and pepper. Coat chicken breasts with sesame seed mixture.

In large skillet, brown chicken in oil on both sides. Reduce heat to low, cover and cook 2 minutes. Turn chicken and cook 3 to 4 minutes longer or until cooked through. Remove chicken and keep warm. Drain pineapple; reserve syrup. With vegetable peeler, remove peel from orange in thin strips; reserve. Slice orange. In small bowl, combine reserved syrup, remaining 1/4 teaspoon tarragon and 1/8 teaspoon cloves, orange juice, sherry and cornstarch. Stir into skillet; add reserved orange peel. Cook, stirring, until sauce boils and thickens. Add pineapple and orange slices; heat through. Serve sauce over fruit and chicken.
Makes 4 servings.

Turkey with Garlic and Chili Pepper Stuffing

14- to 16-pound BUTTERBALL®
   Turkey, thawed if frozen
2 medium red bell peppers,
   chopped
1/2 cup chopped onion
4 to 5 large cloves garlic,
   minced
1/3 cup butter or margarine
2 cans (4 ounces each) diced
   green chili peppers, drained
1/4 cup chopped fresh parsley
1/4 teaspoon salt
1/4 teaspoon ground red pepper
8 cups unseasoned dried whole
   wheat or white bread cubes
1 1/2 cups (6 ounces) shredded
   Cheddar cheese
3/4 to 1 cup chicken broth

Preheat oven to 325°F. To make stuffing, saute red bell peppers, onion and garlic in butter in medium saucepan over medium-high heat until crisp-tender. Stir in chili peppers, parsley, salt and ground red pepper. Combine bread cubes, cheese and vegetable mixture in large bowl. Add enough broth to moisten. Toss to mix.

Prepare turkey for roasting, stuffing neck and body cavities lightly. Roast immediately according to package directions, or roast turkey unstuffed and place stuffing in greased 2 1/2-quart casserole. Cover casserole and bake alongside turkey 1 hour or until hot.
12 to 14 servings (10 cups stuffing).

Apple & Herb Stuffing

2 cups sliced celery
1 1/2 cups chopped onion
1/2 cup margarine or butter
1 3/4 cups hot water
1 tablespoon WYLER'S® or
   STEERO® Chicken-Flavor
   Instant Bouillon *or*
   3 Chicken-Flavor Bouillon
   Cubes
12 cups dry bread cubes (about
   16 slices bread)
3 cups coarsely chopped red
   apples
1 cup slivered almonds, toasted
1 tablespoon chopped parsley
2 teaspoons poultry seasoning
1/4 teaspoon rubbed sage

In large skillet, cook celery and onion in margarine until tender. Add water and bouillon; cook until bouillon dissolves. In large bowl, combine remaining ingredients; add bouillon mixture. Mix well. Loosely stuff turkey just before roasting. Place remaining stuffing in greased baking dish; bake at 350° for 30 minutes or until hot. Refrigerate leftovers.
Makes about 2 1/2 quarts.

Cornbread Pecan Stuffing

1 package (8 ounces) cornbread
   stuffing
3/4 cup chicken or turkey broth
1/2 stick (1/4 cup) butter or
   margarine, melted
1/2 to 3/4 cup chopped pecans
2 apples, pared, cored and
   chopped
1 tablespoon parsley flakes

Combine all ingredients in large bowl. Stuff neck and body cavities of turkey. Roast immediately.
Yield: 6 cups (enough for 10- to 12-pound turkey).

Favorite recipe from **Swift-Eckrich, Inc.**

Raisin-Stuffed Cornish Game Hens with Apples

1 envelope LIPTON® Onion
   Recipe Soup Mix
1 1/4 cups apple cider or juice
2 cups unseasoned cube
   stuffing mix
1/3 cup raisins
1/3 cup coarsely chopped walnuts
4 Cornish hens (1 to 1 1/2 pounds
   each)
2 large apples, cored and halved
1/4 cup brown sugar
1/2 teaspoon ground cinnamon

Preheat oven to 375°.

In medium bowl, blend onion recipe soup mix with cider. Pour 1/2 mixture into medium bowl; stir in stuffing mix, raisins and walnuts. Stuff hens with raisin mixture; secure cavities with poultry pins or skewers. In shallow baking pan, arrange hens and apples.

To remaining cider mixture, blend in sugar and cinnamon; brush hens and apples with 1/2 mixture. Bake, brushing occasionally with remaining glaze mixture, 1 hour or until hens are done. To serve, on large serving platter, arrange hens and apples, sliced.
Makes 4 servings.

Microwave Directions: Prepare hens and glaze mixture as above. Slice apples in quarters. In 3-quart oblong baking dish, arrange hens and apples; brush with 1/2 glaze. Heat at HIGH (Full Power), brushing occasionally with remaining glaze and turning dish occasionally, 45 minutes or until hens are done. Let stand covered 5 minutes. Serve as above.

Cornish Hens with Oyster Stuffing

3/4 cup butter or margarine, divided
1 large onion, chopped
1 cup chopped celery
1/2 cup chopped shallots
1 small red pepper, chopped
1 small green pepper, chopped
2 medium cloves garlic, minced
2 bay leaves
2 dozen fresh oysters, shucked, liquid reserved
3/4 teaspoon dried thyme leaves, divided
1/2 teaspoon dried oregano leaves
3/4 teaspoon TABASCO® pepper sauce, divided
5 cups cooked rice
6 Cornish game hens
1/4 teaspoon salt
1 tablespoon flour
1 cup chicken broth

Preheat oven to 350°F. In large skillet melt 1/2 cup butter. Add onion, celery, shallots, red and green peppers, garlic and bay leaves; cook 5 minutes or until tender. Cut up oysters; reserve liquid. Stir oysters into skillet with 1/2 teaspoon thyme, oregano and 1/2 teaspoon Tabasco® sauce. Cook 5 minutes longer. Remove bay leaves. Add rice and oyster liquid.

Wash Cornish hens; pat dry. Stuff cavity of each hen with oyster stuffing. (Bake remaining stuffing in greased, covered baking dish during last half hour of roasting time.) Arrange hens on rack in shallow roasting pan. Melt remaining 1/4 cup butter; stir in salt, remaining 1/4 teaspoon thyme and remaining 1/4 teaspoon Tabasco® sauce. Brush hens with butter mixture. Bake 1 1/2 hours or until hens are cooked; baste often with pan drippings.

To serve, spoon extra stuffing onto serving platter; arrange hens on stuffing. To make gravy, pour excess fat from roasting pan; add flour to pan and stir. Place pan on stove-top burner over medium heat; gradually add broth, scraping up bits from bottom of pan. Stir constantly, bring to a boil and boil 1 minute. Serve with hens.
Makes 6 servings.

Grilled Cornish Game Hens

2 Cornish game hens (1 to 1 1/2 pounds each)
3 tablespoons olive or vegetable oil
1/3 cup lemon juice
1 tablespoon black peppercorns, coarsely crushed
1/2 teaspoon salt
Sprig fresh rosemary

Split hens lengthwise. Rinse under cold running water; pat dry with paper toweling. Place hens in large plastic bag; set in bowl. In small bowl, combine oil, lemon juice, peppercorns and salt. Pour marinade over hens in bag. Close bag securely and refrigerate several hours or overnight, turning hens occasionally to coat with marinade.

Arrange medium-hot **KINGS-FORD® Charcoal Briquets** around drip pan. Just before grilling, add rosemary sprig to coals. Drain hens; reserve marinade. Place hens, skin-side up, over drip pan. Cover grill and cook 45 minutes or until thigh moves easily and juices run clear. Baste with marinade occasionally. Garnish with fresh rosemary, if desired.
Makes 4 servings.

Cornish Hens with Chestnut-Sausage Stuffing

1/4 cup WISH-BONE® Italian or Robusto Italian Dressing
1 medium onion, chopped
1 cup chopped celery
1 pound sweet Italian sausage links, removed from casing
1 cup cooked chestnuts, chopped
2 cups fresh bread crumbs
1/2 cup pine nuts or slivered almonds, toasted
1/2 teaspoon marjoram leaves
1/2 teaspoon thyme leaves
1/8 teaspoon pepper
4 Cornish hens (1 to 1 1/2 pounds each)*

Preheat oven to 350°.

In large skillet, heat Italian dressing and cook onion with celery over medium-high heat, stirring occasionally, 3 minutes or until tender. Add sausage and cook, stirring occasionally, 5 minutes or until lightly browned. Stir in chestnuts, bread crumbs, pine nuts, marjoram, thyme and pepper. Stuff hens with sausage mixture. Close cavities with skewers or wooden toothpicks; tie legs together with string. In roasting pan, on rack, place stuffed hens. Loosely cover with heavy-duty aluminum foil, then roast 1 hour. Remove foil and continue roasting 15 minutes or until meat thermometer reaches 185°. Serve, if desired, with cooked carrots and green beans.
Makes 4 servings.
***Substitution:** Use 1 (5- to 6-pound) roasting chicken. Adjust cooking temperature and times as needed.

Wild Rice Stuffing

1 (4-ounce) package wild rice, rinsed and drained
4 teaspoons WYLER'S® or STEERO® Chicken-Flavor Instant Bouillon *or* 4 Chicken-Flavor Bouillon Cubes
1 cup chopped celery
1/2 cup chopped green pepper
1/2 cup margarine or butter
1 cup boiling water
1 (8-ounce) package herb-seasoned stuffing mix
2 teaspoons poultry seasoning

Prepare rice as package directs, dissolving *3 teaspoons* bouillon in water before adding rice; cook as directed. Preheat oven to 325°. In medium skillet, cook celery and green pepper in margarine until tender. Dissolve remaining *1 teaspoon* bouillion in *1 cup* water. In large bowl, combine all ingredients; mix well. Use to stuff turkey or turn into greased 2-quart baking dish; bake at 375° for 30 to 40 minutes. Refrigerate leftovers.
Makes 12 servings.

Rich Turkey Gravy

1/4 to 1/3 cup unsifted flour
1/4 cup turkey pan drippings or margarine
2 cups hot water
2 teaspoons WYLER'S® or STEERO® Chicken-Flavor Instant Bouillon *or* 2 Chicken-Flavor Bouillon Cubes

In medium skillet, stir flour into drippings until smooth; cook and stir until dark brown. Add water and bouillon; cook and stir until thickened and bouillon is dissolved. Refrigerate leftovers.
Makes about 1 1/2 cups.

Traditional Gravy

Drippings
Fat
Turkey, chicken or giblet broth
1/2 cup all-purpose flour
Salt and ground black pepper, to taste
Cooked giblets, chopped fine, optional

Conventional Directions: Pour drippings from roasting pan into large measuring cup. Place 1/4 cup fat from drippings into medium saucepan or roasting pan. Discard any remaining fat from drippings. To drippings, add enough broth to make 4 cups. Stir flour into fat in saucepan. Gradually blend in drippings. Bring to boil over medium-high heat, stirring constantly. Reduce heat to low; continue cooking 3 to 5 minutes. Season with salt and pepper. Add cooked giblets, if desired.
Yield: 4 cups.

Microwave Directions: Pour drippings from roasting pan into large measuring cup. Place 1/4 cup fat from drippings into medium microwave-safe bowl. Discard any remaining fat from drippings. To drippings, add enough broth to make 4 cups. Stir flour into fat in bowl. Gradually blend in drippings. Microwave, uncovered, on HIGH 7 to 10 minutes or until mixture comes to boil and thickens, stirring every 2 minutes. Season with salt and pepper. Add cooked giblets, if desired.

Gravy Additions: Add 1 or 2 of the following: 2 tablespoons chopped fresh parsley, 2 tablespoons sherry, 1/2 cup sour cream or 1 jar (2 1/2 ounces) sliced mushrooms, drained.

*Favorite recipe from **Swift-Eckrich, Inc.***

Turkey with Sausage and Orange Corn Bread Stuffing

1/2 roll (8 ounces) ECKRICH® Country Sausage
12- to 14-pound BUTTERBALL® Turkey, thawed if frozen
Orange Corn Bread (recipe follows)
1 cup chopped onion
1/2 cup chopped green bell pepper
1/2 cup chopped celery
2 eggs, beaten
1 teaspoon dried thyme leaves
1/2 teaspoon salt
1 to 1 1/4 cups turkey or chicken broth

Prepare Orange Corn Bread. Cool and crumble; set aside. Preheat oven to 325°F. To make stuffing, cook sausage, onion, green pepper and celery in large skillet until meat is browned and vegetables are tender. Drain thoroughly. Combine sausage mixture, eggs, thyme and salt in large bowl. Add corn bread; toss to mix. Add enough broth to moisten; toss. Prepare turkey for roasting; stuff neck and body cavities lightly. Roast immediately according to package directions, or roast turkey unstuffed and place stuffing in greased 2 1/2-quart casserole. Cover casserole and bake alongside turkey 1 hour or until hot.
Makes 10 to 12 servings (8 cups stuffing).

ORANGE CORN BREAD: Preheat oven to 400°F. Combine 1 1/2 cups yellow cornmeal, 1/2 cup all-purpose flour, 2 tablespoons sugar, 4 teaspoons baking powder and 1/2 teaspoon salt in medium bowl. Stir in 1 cup milk, 1 beaten egg, 1/3 cup vegetable oil and 2 teaspoons finely shredded orange peel (zest) until just blended. (Do not overmix.) Pour into greased 9×9×2-inch baking pan. Bake 20 to 25 minutes or until wooden pick inserted near center comes out clean.
Makes 9 servings.

Harvest Sausage Stuffing

1 pound bulk sausage
2 cups chopped celery
8 ounces fresh mushrooms, sliced (about 2 cups)
1½ cups chopped onion
4 teaspoons WYLER'S® or STEERO® Chicken-Flavor Instant Bouillon or 4 Chicken-Flavor Bouillon Cubes
1 to 1½ cups boiling water
2 (7-ounce) packages herb-seasoned stuffing mix
1⅓ cups (one-half jar) NONE SUCH® Ready-to-Use Mincemeat
1 (8-ounce) can sliced water chestnuts, coarsely chopped
2 teaspoons poultry seasoning

In large skillet, brown sausage; pour off fat. Add celery, mushrooms and onion; cook until onion is tender. Add bouillon and water to sausage mixture; bring to a boil. In large bowl, combine remaining ingredients with sausage mixture; mix well. Use to loosely stuff turkey just before roasting; place remaining stuffing in 2-quart greased baking dish; cover. Bake at 350° for 45 minutes or until hot. Refrigerate leftovers.
Makes about 3 quarts.

Savory Corn Bread Stuffing

1 pound fresh mushrooms, sliced (about 4 cups)
1 cup chopped celery
¾ cup chopped onion
½ cup margarine or butter
4 teaspoons WYLER'S® or STEERO® Chicken-Flavor Instant Bouillon or 4 Chicken-Flavor Bouillon Cubes
1⅔ cups boiling water
1 pound bulk sausage, browned and drained
1 (16-ounce) package corn bread stuffing mix
1½ teaspoons poultry seasoning

In large skillet, cook mushrooms, celery and onion in margarine until tender. In large bowl, dissolve bouillon in water. Add sausage, mushroom mixture and remaining ingredients; mix well. Loosely stuff turkey just before roasting. Place remaining stuffing in greased baking dish; bake at 350° for 30 minutes or until hot. Refrigerate leftovers.
Makes about 3 quarts.

Turkey with American Stuffing

6- to 8-pound BUTTERBALL® Breast of Turkey
3 cups dried bread cubes
1 cup (4 ounces) crumbled fully cooked sausage
¾ cup diced red apple, unpared
½ cup chopped onion
½ cup chopped walnuts
1 teaspoon dried rosemary leaves, crushed
½ teaspoon rubbed sage
¾ cup water
⅓ cup butter or margarine

Roast turkey according to package directions. Meanwhile, prepare stuffing. Combine bread cubes, sausage, apple, onion, walnuts and seasonings in medium bowl. Heat water and butter in small saucepan over medium heat until butter melts. Toss with bread mixture. Spoon into 2-quart casserole. Cover and bake alongside turkey last 45 minutes of roasting time. Slice turkey and serve with stuffing.
Yield: 8 servings.

Old-Fashioned Bread Stuffing

1½ cups chopped onion
1½ cups diced celery
1 stick (½ cup) butter or margarine
1 teaspoon poultry seasoning
1 teaspoon rubbed sage
1 teaspoon salt
Dash ground black pepper
½ cup water or chicken broth
8 cups dried bread cubes (10 to 12 bread slices, cubed and dried overnight)

Cook and stir onion and celery in butter in medium skillet over medium heat until tender. Stir in seasonings. Add onion mixture and water to bread cubes in large bowl. Toss to mix. Stuff neck and body cavities of turkey. Roast immediately.
Yield: 8 cups (enough for 12- to 14-pound turkey).

Cranberry-Sausage: Cut 1 cup fresh cranberries into halves. Cut 1 package (8 ounces) fully cooked sausage links into pieces. Add to bread cubes.

Bacon and Green Pepper: Substitute 1½ cups chopped green bell pepper for celery. Substitute 1 teaspoon dried thyme leaves, crushed, for poultry seasoning and sage. Reduce salt to ½ teaspoon. Add 12 slices cooked diced bacon to bread cubes.

*Favorite recipe from **Swift-Eckrich, Inc.***

Oyster Stuffing

1 cup chopped cooked oysters
1 cup chopped celery
1 medium onion, chopped
½ stick (¼ cup) butter or
  margarine
8 cups fresh bread cubes
1 cup chicken or turkey broth
2 eggs, beaten
½ to 1 teaspoon dried tarragon
  leaves or parsley flakes
1 to 2 teaspoons lemon juice
½ teaspoon salt

Cook and stir oysters, celery and onion in butter in medium skillet over medium heat until tender. Add to bread cubes in large bowl. Combine remaining ingredients in small bowl. Pour over bread mixture and toss to mix. Stuff neck and body cavities of turkey. Roast immediately. Or, bake in covered 2-quart casserole in preheated 325°F oven 45 minutes or until hot.
Yield: 6 cups (enough for 10- to 12-pound turkey).

Favorite recipe from **Swift-Eckrich, Inc.**

Parmesan Seasoned Turkey

4 slices BUTTERBALL® SLICE'N
  SERVE® Breast of Turkey,
  cut ⅜ inch thick
2 tablespoons butter or
  margarine, melted
1½ teaspoons grated Parmesan
  cheese
  Dash coarsely ground black
  pepper
  Dash crushed red pepper
  Dash onion powder

Combine butter, cheese, peppers and onion powder in small dish. Brush both sides of turkey with seasoned butter. Grill over medium coals 6 to 8 minutes or until hot. Turn over halfway through heating.
Makes 4 servings.
   Note: Turkey may be heated under broiler. Place turkey on broiler pan. Broil, 4 inches from heat, 8 minutes or until hot. Turn turkey over and baste with seasoned butter halfway through heating.

Turkey Curry

3 cups cubed cooked
  BUTTERBALL® turkey
  (1 pound)
½ cup finely chopped onion
2 tablespoons butter or
  margarine
1 tablespoon curry powder
1 gravy packet (8 ounces)
  included with turkey
⅔ cup water
½ cup whipping cream or half
  and half
1½ teaspoons honey
½ teaspoon salt
¼ teaspoon ground black pepper
  Hot cooked rice
  Toasted almonds, shredded
  coconut and/or chopped
  dried fruit, optional

Cook and stir onion in butter in medium saucepan over low heat 5 minutes or until tender. Add curry powder and cook 2 minutes, stirring occasionally. Stir in contents of gravy packet and water. Bring to boil over high heat, stirring constantly. Reduce heat to low; simmer 3 to 5 minutes, stirring occasionally. Blend in cream, honey, salt and pepper. Stir turkey into sauce and heat 3 to 5 minutes or until heated through. Serve over rice with almonds, coconut and/or dried fruit as a garnish or accompaniment.
Yield: 4 servings.

Barbecued Turkey with Herbs

1 turkey (9 to 13 pounds), fresh
  or frozen, thawed
¾ cup vegetable oil
½ cup chopped fresh parsley
2 tablespoons chopped fresh
  sage *or* 2 teaspoons dried
  sage, crushed
2 tablespoons chopped fresh
  rosemary *or* 2 teaspoons
  dried rosemary, crushed
1 tablespoon chopped fresh
  thyme *or* 1 teaspoon dried
  thyme, crushed
  Salt and coarsely cracked
  black pepper

Remove neck and giblets from turkey. Rinse turkey under cold running water; drain and pat dry with paper toweling. In small bowl, combine remaining ingredients. Brush cavities and outer surface of turkey generously with herb mixture. Pull skin over neck and secure with skewer. Fold wings behind back and tie legs and tail together with kitchen twine. Insert meat thermometer into center of thickest part of thigh, not touching bone.
   Arrange medium-hot **KINGS-FORD® Charcoal Briquets** around large drip pan. Position turkey directly over drip pan. Cover grill and cook turkey 11 to 13 minutes per pound or until internal temperature reaches 185°F, basting occasionally with herb mixture. Add more briquets as necessary. Garnish with additional fresh herbs, if desired.
Makes 8 to 10 servings.

Clove Glazed Turkey

**3-pound BUTTERBALL®
   Boneless Turkey, thawed
20 whole cloves
3 tablespoons red currant jelly
1 pineapple slice, cut into halves
2 maraschino cherries
   Spiced Currant Sauce (recipe
   follows)**

Press cloves into turkey. Melt jelly in small saucepan over medium heat. Brush 1½ tablespoons jelly over turkey. Roast turkey according to package directions; omit brushing with oil. About 30 minutes before turkey is done, brush with remaining 1½ tablespoons jelly. Wrap turkey in foil and let stand 10 to 15 minutes. Remove netting from turkey. Garnish with pineapple and maraschino cherries. Slice turkey and serve with Spiced Currant Sauce.
Yield: 8 servings.

Spiced Currant Sauce

**½ cup red currant jelly
½ cup pineapple juice
1 tablespoon brown sugar
1 tablespoon cornstarch
¼ teaspoon ground cloves**

Combine all ingredients in small saucepan, stirring until cornstarch dissolves. Cook and stir over medium heat until sauce comes to boil and thickens. Cook and stir 1 minute more.
Yield: 1 cup.

Turkey à la Cordon Bleu

**6- to 8-pound BUTTERBALL®
   Breast of Turkey
   Cordon Bleu Rice (recipe
   follows)
   Cordon Bleu Sauce (recipe
   follows)**

Roast turkey according to package directions. Meanwhile, prepare Cordon Bleu Rice and Cordon Bleu Sauce. Slice turkey and serve with rice and sauce.
Yield: 8 to 10 servings.

Cordon Bleu Rice

**3 cups cooked rice
2 cups diced fully cooked ham
   or Canadian-style bacon
1½ cups (6 ounces) shredded
   aged Swiss cheese
3 tablespoons chopped fresh
   parsley
3 tablespoons butter or
   magarine, melted**

Combine rice, ham, cheese, parsley and butter in medium bowl. Spoon into 2-quart casserole. Cover and bake alongside turkey last 40 minutes of roasting time.
Yield: 5 cups.

Cordon Bleu Sauce

**½ stick (¼ cup) butter or
   margarine
¼ cup all-purpose flour
½ teaspoon salt
2½ cups milk
1 package (3 ounces) cream
   cheese, cut into small
   pieces
1½ cups (6 ounces) shredded
   aged Swiss cheese**

Melt butter in medium saucepan over medium heat. Blend in flour and salt. Gradually add milk. Bring to boil, stirring constantly. Cook and stir 1 minute more. Reduce heat to low. Add cream cheese and Swiss cheese; stir until melted.
Yield: 3⅓ cups.

Turkey Oscar

**4 slices cooked BUTTERBALL®
   turkey (1 pound)
2 tablespoons butter or
   margarine
1 can (6 ounces) crab meat,
   drained, warmed
8 hot cooked asparagus spears
   Bearnaise Sauce (recipe
   follows)
   Toast points, optional**

Heat turkey slices in butter in medium skillet over medium heat. Place slices on individual plates. Top each slice with crab meat, asparagus spears and Bearnaise Sauce. Serve with toast points.
Yield: 4 servings.

Bearnaise Sauce

**2 tablespoons tarragon vinegar
1 tablespoon dried tarragon
   leaves, crushed
2 tablespoons finely chopped
   shallots or green onions
   Dash freshly ground black
   pepper
2 egg yolks
2 tablespoons water
1 stick (½ cup) butter, melted
   and cooled to room
   temperature**

Combine vinegar, tarragon, shallots and pepper in small saucepan. Over medium heat, cook and stir until vinegar evaporates and shallots soften. Blend yolks and water in cup; add to shallots, stirring constantly over *low* heat until mixture thickens. Remove from heat. Add butter gradually, stirring briskly after each addition until blended.
Yield: ¾ cup.

Turkey Hash

2 cups cubed cooked
   BUTTERBALL® turkey
   (³/₄ pound)
½ cup chopped celery
⅓ cup chopped onion
⅓ cup chopped green bell
   pepper
½ stick (¼ cup) butter or
   margarine
3 cups diced cooked potatoes
½ teaspoon poultry seasoning
¼ teaspoon salt
⅛ teaspoon ground black pepper
½ to 1 cup turkey gravy

Cook and stir celery, onion and green
pepper in butter in heavy skillet over
medium heat until tender. Stir in potatoes, turkey and seasonings. Cook
over low heat, about 5 minutes, stirring frequently. Add gravy; cook and
stir until mixture is hot.
Yield: 4 servings (4½ cups).

Turkey Florentine

6- to 8-pound BUTTERBALL®
   Breast of Turkey
1 package (6 ounces) long grain
   and wild rice mix
1 package (10 ounces) frozen
   chopped spinach, thawed,
   drained
¾ cup diced fully cooked ham

Roast turkey according to package directions. Prepare rice according to
package directions. Stir in spinach
and ham. Place in buttered 1½-quart
casserole. Bake alongside turkey last
45 minutes of roasting time. Slice turkey and serve with Florentine rice.
Yield: 8 servings.

Kensington Crepes

Filling:
   2 cups finely diced cooked
      BUTTERBALL® turkey
      (³/₄ pound)
   ¼ cup chopped onion
   ½ stick (¼ cup) butter or
      margarine
   ¼ cup all-purpose flour
   ½ teaspoon salt
   2 cups milk
   1 cup chopped nuts
   ½ teaspoon curry powder
   1 egg, beaten
   3 tablespoons (³/₄ ounce)
      shredded Cheddar cheese
Crepes:
   6 eggs
   ¼ cup all-purpose flour
   2 tablespoons water
   ¼ teaspoon salt

To make filling: Cook and stir onion
in butter in small saucepan over medium heat until tender. Blend in flour
and salt. Remove from heat. Gradually add milk. Cook over medium heat
until mixture thickens, stirring constantly. Pour 1½ cups sauce into medium bowl. Add turkey, nuts and
curry powder. Combine well. Add egg
and cheese to remaining sauce in pan.
Bring to boil over medium-low heat,
stirring constantly until cheese
melts. Set aside.
   To make crepes: Combine eggs,
flour, water and salt in medium bowl.
Beat thoroughly. Spoon 2 tablespoons
batter into seasoned 6-inch crepe pan
or skillet. Cook over medium heat until lightly browned. Remove from pan
and stack between paper towels.
   To fill crepes: Preheat oven to
325°F. Spread about ¼ cup filling
across center of each crepe. Roll edges
over filling and place in 13×9-inch
baking dish. Spoon cheese sauce over
top. Heat in oven about 10 minutes.
For a golden top, place under broiler
about 2 to 3 minutes.
Yield: 6 servings, 2 crepes each.

Note: Or assemble crepes and refrigerate if not to be served immediately. Spoon sauce over crepes just
before heating. Allow 15 to 20 minutes to heat if taken directly from refrigerator.

Turkey Orloff

3-pound BUTTERBALL®
   Boneless Breast of Turkey
Orloff Rice (recipe follows)
Orloff Sauce (recipe follows)

Roast turkey according to package directions. Wrap in foil. Let stand 10 to
15 minutes. Meanwile, prepare Orloff
Rice and Orloff Sauce. Remove netting from turkey. Slice turkey and
place rice between slices. Spoon some
sauce over turkey. Serve remaining
sauce with turkey.
Yield: 8 servings.

Orloff Rice

⅓ cup long grain rice
8 cups water
½ stick (¼ cup) butter
1 medium onion, chopped fine
1 egg, beaten

Cook rice, uncovered, 5 minutes in
boiling water. Drain. Melt butter in 2-
quart baking dish. Stir in onion and
rice. Cover and bake alongside turkey
1 hour, stirring after 30 minutes.
Blend egg into cooked rice; keep
warm.
Yield: 1 cup.

Orloff Sauce

½ stick (¼ cup) butter or
   margarine
⅓ cup all-purpose flour
2 cups chicken broth
½ cup cottage cheese, pureed
2 egg yolks, beaten
½ cup (2 ounces) shredded
   Monterey Jack cheese

Melt butter in medium saucepan over
medium-low heat. Blend in flour and
cook 2 minutes, stirring frequently.
Gradually stir in broth. Bring to boil
over medium heat, stirring constantly. Cook 2 minutes more. Remove
from heat. Add cottage cheese, egg
yolks and Monterey Jack cheese, stirring until smooth.
Yield: 2½ cups.

Glazed Turkey Kabobs

16 cubes (1 inch each) cooked BUTTERBALL® turkey (1 pound)
Water
1 can (20 ounces) pineapple chunks, drained; reserve juice
½ cup packed brown sugar
2 tablespoons soy sauce
16 slices bacon, cut into halves
2 large red bell peppers, cut into 24 (1½-inch) triangles
3 large green bell peppers, cut into 32 (1½-inch) triangles
Hot cooked rice

Preheat broiler. Add water to pineapple juice to make 1 cup. Combine juice, brown sugar and soy sauce in small saucepan. Bring to boil over high heat. Reduce heat to low; simmer 2 to 3 minutes. Set glaze aside. Cook bacon in large skillet over medium-high heat until done, but not crisp. Dip turkey and pineapple into glaze. Assemble each kabob as follows: red pepper, green pepper, pineapple, bacon piece folded in half, turkey, bacon piece folded in half, pineapple and green pepper. Repeat. Complete kabob with additional red pepper. Brush kabobs with glaze. Broil 4 to 5 inches from heat 4 to 5 minutes. Turn kabobs, brush with glaze and broil 4 to 5 minutes more or until heated through. Serve kabobs on rice.
Yield: 4 servings, 2 kabobs each.

Turkey Parmigiana

4 to 6 slices (⅜ inch thick) cooked BUTTERBALL® turkey (1 pound)
2 eggs, slightly beaten
1 tablespoon water
2 teaspoons vegetable oil
½ cup seasoned dried bread crumbs
¾ cup grated Parmesan cheese, divided
Vegetable oil
2½ cups spaghetti or marinara sauce
2 teaspoons dried oregano leaves, crushed
¾ cup (3 ounces) shredded mozzarella cheese

Preheat oven to 350°F. Combine eggs, water and 2 teaspoons oil in shallow dish; set aside. Combine bread crumbs and ½ cup Parmesan cheese in another shallow dish. Dip turkey slices into egg mixture, then coat with bread crumb mixture. Heat oil in heavy skillet over medium heat. Brown turkey slices 2 to 4 minutes per side. Layer turkey in 11×7-inch baking dish. Combine spaghetti sauce and oregano; pour over turkey. Top each turkey slice with mozzarella cheese and remaining ¼ cup Parmesan cheese. Bake in oven 20 to 25 minutes or until cheese melts.
Yield: 4 servings.

Turkey Schnitzel

4 slices (¼ inch thick) cooked BUTTERBALL® turkey (¾ pound)
¼ cup lemon juice
1 egg
2 teaspoons milk
¾ cup seasoned dried bread crumbs
Butter or margarine
Hot cooked noodles
Lemon wedges

Marinate turkey slices in lemon juice in plastic bag in refrigerator 1 hour; drain. Blend egg and milk in shallow dish. Dip turkey slices into egg mixture; coat with bread crumbs. Brown turkey in butter in large skillet over medium heat 2 to 4 minutes per side. Serve with noodles and lemon wedges.
Yield: 4 servings.

Shanghai Turkey Stir-Fry

1 small turkey thigh, skinned and boned
3 tablespoons cornstarch, divided
4 tablespoons KIKKOMAN Soy Sauce, divided
1 tablespoon dry sherry
1 tablespoon minced fresh ginger root
1 clove garlic, minced
1 cup water
3 tablespoons vegetable oil, divided
1 large carrot, cut into julienne strips
1 onion, sliced
1 package (10 oz.) frozen French-style green beans, thawed and drained

Cut turkey into thin, narrow strips; set aside. Combine 2 tablespoons *each* cornstarch and soy sauce with sherry, ginger and garlic in medium bowl; stir in turkey. Let stand 30 minutes. Meanwhile, combine water, remaining 1 tablespoon cornstarch and 2 tablespoons soy sauce; set aside. Heat 2 tablespoons oil in hot wok or large skillet over high heat. Add turkey and stir-fry 3 minutes, or until tender; remove. Heat remaining 1 tablespoon oil in same pan. Add carrot and onion; stir-fry 2 minutes. Add green beans; stir-fry 1 minute longer. Stir in turkey and soy sauce mixture. Cook and stir until mixture boils and thickens. Serve immediately.
Makes 6 servings.

Turkey with Wine-Glazed Vegetables

3-pound BUTTERBALL®
   Boneless Breast of Turkey or
   Boneless Turkey, thawed if
   frozen
Vegetable oil
1 teaspoon dried rosemary
   leaves, divided
1 teaspoon dried thyme leaves,
   divided
8 carrots, cut into ½-inch slices
8 small red potatoes, unpared,
   cut into quarters
4 small onions, cut into halves
1 cup chicken broth
⅓ cup white wine
1 medium clove garlic, minced
2 bay leaves
4 ribs celery, cut into 1-inch
   pieces
4 teaspoons cornstarch,
   dissolved in 1 tablespoon
   white wine

Brush turkey with oil; sprinkle with ½ teaspoon of the rosemary and ¼ teaspoon of the thyme. Roast according to package directions.

Meanwhile, place carrots, potatoes and onions in 2-quart casserole. Combine broth, ⅓ cup wine, garlic, bay leaves, remaining ½ teaspoon rosemary and remaining ¾ teaspoon thyme in small saucepan. Bring to a boil over high heat. Reduce heat to low; simmer 3 minutes. Pour over vegetables; cover. Bake alongside turkey during last hour of roasting time. After 45 minutes, add celery.

When done, remove turkey from oven, wrap in foil and let stand 15 minutes before removing netting. Remove vegetables from oven and discard bay leaves. Drain broth into small saucepan. Add turkey pan drippings. Gradually stir dissolved cornstarch into broth mixture. Cook and stir over medium heat until clear and thickened. Pour over hot vegetables and serve with sliced turkey.
Makes 8 servings.

Turkey Fillets in Spicy Cilantro Marinade

1 cup chopped onion
1 large tomato, quartered
⅓ cup soy sauce
¼ cup chopped green pepper
3 tablespoons vegetable oil
3 tablespoons lime juice
2 tablespoons minced cilantro or
   parsley
2 cloves garlic, minced
¾ teaspoon pepper
4 turkey breast fillets (about
   ½ pound each)

Place all ingredients, except turkey, in blender; blend 30 seconds. Place turkey fillets in large plastic bag; place bag in bowl. Pour marinade over turkey in bag. Close bag securely; refrigerate 4 hours, turning occasionally. Drain turkey fillets; reserve marinade. Grill turkey, on uncovered grill, over hot **KINGSFORD® Charcoal Briquets** 5 minutes on each side or until tender, brushing often with marinade.
Makes 4 servings.

Oriental Turkey Terrine

2½ pounds ground turkey
2 eggs, beaten
¾ cup finely chopped onion
¼ cup chopped fresh cilantro or
   parsley
¼ cup KIKKOMAN Soy Sauce
1½ cups dry bread crumbs
½ teaspoon ground ginger
¼ teaspoon fennel seed, crushed
¼ teaspoon pepper
⅛ teaspoon ground cloves
   Dash ground cinnamon

Combine turkey, eggs, onion, cilantro and soy sauce in large bowl; set aside. Stir together bread crumbs, ginger, fennel, pepper, cloves and cinnamon. Sprinkle evenly over turkey mixture, mixing until thoroughly blended. Press firmly into greased 12-cup Bundt or tube pan. Bake at 375°F. 45 minutes, or until top is lightly browned and starts to pull away from side of pan. Turn out onto serving platter; let stand 5 minutes before cutting into thin slices.
Makes 6 to 8 servings.
   Note: If desired, press turkey mixture into greased 9¼×5¼-inch loaf pan; bake at 375°F. 1 hour, or to doneness described above.

Creamed Turkey Stack-Ups

2 cups cubed cooked turkey or
   chicken
¼ cup margarine or butter
¼ cup unsifted flour
2 cups BORDEN® or MEADOW
   GOLD® Milk
1 tablespoon WYLER'S® or
   STEERO® Chicken-Flavor
   Instant Bouillon *or* 3
   Chicken-Flavor Bouillon
   Cubes
1 (2½-ounce) jar sliced
   mushrooms, drained
¼ cup chopped green pepper
1 (2-ounce) jar sliced pimientos,
   drained
12 pancakes

In medium saucepan, melt margarine; stir in flour. Add milk and bouillon; cook and stir until bouillon dissolves and mixture thickens. Stir in remaining ingredients except pancakes; heat through. Serve over pancakes. Refrigerate leftovers.
Makes 4 to 6 servings.
   Tip: Turkey mixture can be served in patty shells or as a crepe filling.

Turkey Parmesan

- 1 teaspoon diet margarine
- 1 (2-ounce) slice raw turkey breast
- 3 tablespoons prepared spaghetti sauce
- 1 teaspoon grated Parmesan cheese
- 1 slice LITE-LINE® Mozzarella Flavor Process Cheese Product*

In small skillet, over medium heat, melt margarine. Add turkey breast slice. Cook 2 minutes; turn. Reduce heat to low; top turkey with remaining ingredients. Cover; cook 2 to 3 minutes longer. Garnish as desired.
Makes 1 serving; 198 calories.
*"½ the calories"—8% milkfat product. Caloric values by product analyses and recipe calculation.

Turkey Marengo

- 3-pound BUTTERBALL® Boneless Breast of Turkey, thawed
  Vegetable oil
- ½ teaspoon parsley flakes
- ¼ teaspoon ground black pepper
- ¼ cup white wine
- 1 jar (15½ ounces) spaghetti sauce
- ¼ cup water
- 1 jar (2½ ounces) sliced mushrooms, drained
- 1 can (2¼ ounces) sliced black olives, drained
- 2 tablespoons brandy
  Hot cooked rice

Brush turkey with oil. Combine parsley and pepper in cup; sprinkle over turkey. Roast turkey according to package directions. Remove turkey from pan. Wrap in foil and let stand 10 to 15 minutes. Pour wine into roasting pan, stirring to combine with pan juices. Cook juices down to half amount over medium heat. Add spaghetti sauce, water, mushrooms, olives and brandy. Simmer over low heat until heated through. Remove netting from turkey. Slice turkey and serve on rice with sauce.
Yield: 8 servings.

Turkey Cutlets with Ginger & Lime Sauce

- 1 pound boneless turkey cutlets
- ¾ cup all-purpose flour
- 3 eggs, slightly beaten
- ½ cup WISH-BONE® Italian Dressing
- ½ cup chopped green onions
- ½ cup chicken broth
- 1 tablespoon butter or margarine
- 1 teaspoon lime juice
- ¼ teaspoon ground ginger
- ⅛ teaspoon pepper

Dip turkey in flour, then eggs, then again in flour. In large skillet, heat ¼ cup Italian dressing and cook ½ of the turkey over medium heat, turning once, 5 minutes or until done; drain on paper towels and keep warm. Heat remaining ¼ cup Italian dressing and repeat with remaining turkey.

Into skillet, add green onions and cook 1 minute. Stir in remaining ingredients, then bring to a boil to heat through. Serve over turkey.
Makes about 4 servings.
Note: Also terrific with Wish-Bone® Robusto Italian, Herbal Italian or Blended Italian Dressing.

Turkey Paprikash

- 3-pound BUTTERBALL® Boneless Breast of Turkey
  Vegetable oil
- 5 teaspoons paprika, divided
  Dash salt and ground black pepper
- 2 tablespoons butter or margarine
- ¾ cup chopped onion
- 1 tablespoon all-purpose flour
- 1 cube chicken bouillon dissolved in 1 cup hot water
- 1 cup sour cream
  Hot cooked spaetzle or noodles

Brush turkey with oil. Combine 1 teaspoon paprika, salt and pepper in cup; sprinkle on turkey. Roast turkey according to package directions. Remove from pan. Wrap in foil and let stand 10 to 15 minutes. Melt butter in medium saucepan over medium heat. Add onion; cook and stir until tender. Stir in flour. Gradually add remaining 4 teaspoons paprika and bouillon. Bring to boil over high heat. Reduce heat to low; simmer and stir 3 minutes. Blend small amount of hot mixture into sour cream, then add to sauce. Heat gently over low heat to serving temperature. Do not boil. Remove netting from turkey. Slice turkey; serve with sauce and spaetzle.
Yield: 8 servings.

FISH & SHELLFISH

Increasingly popular for its nutritional value, seafood has always been prized for its flavor. Serve sole in a delicate sauce, or try a Creole specialty bursting with tomatoes and spices. For a special occasion, create a splendid lobster or swordfish dish. An added benefit—most seafood cooks quickly, so in very little time you can produce an impressive, delicious meal.

Shrimp & Mushroom Stuffed Sole

1/4 cup *plus* 2 tablespoons WISH-BONE® Italian Dressing
2 cups thinly sliced mushrooms
1/2 cup sliced green onions
3/4 pound uncooked medium shrimp, cleaned and coarsely chopped
2 tablespoons brandy or sherry
1/2 teaspoon thyme leaves
1/2 teaspoon salt (optional)
1/8 teaspoon pepper
2 cups fresh bread crumbs
4 sole or flounder fillets (1 to 1 1/2 pounds)

Preheat oven to 400°.

In large skillet, heat 1/4 cup Italian dressing and cook mushrooms with green onions over medium heat, stirring occasionally, 3 minutes. Add shrimp and cook, stirring constantly, 2 minutes or until shrimp turn pink. Stir in brandy, thyme, salt and pepper, then bread crumbs.

In large shallow baking pan, evenly divide shrimp mixture into 4 mounds. Place 1 fillet over each mound; brush fillets with remaining 2 tablespoons dressing. Bake 10 minutes or until fish flakes. Garnish, if desired, with chopped parsley and paprika.
Makes about 4 servings.

Note: Also terrific with Wish-Bone® Robusto Italian, Herbal Italian, Blended Italian or Classic Dijon Vinaigrette Dressing.

Salmon Steaks in Dill Sauce

1 tablespoon butter or margarine
1/2 cup chopped green onions
1 can (10 3/4 ounces) CAMPBELL'S® Condensed Cream of Celery Soup
1/2 cup half-and-half
1/4 cup Chablis or other dry white wine
2 tablespoons chopped fresh dill weed or 1 teaspoon dried dill weed, crushed
4 salmon steaks, 3/4 inch thick (about 6 ounces each)

To Microwave:
1. In 12- by 8-inch microwave-safe baking dish, combine butter and onions. Cover with vented plastic wrap; microwave on HIGH 2 minutes or until onions are tender, stirring once during cooking.
2. Stir in soup until smooth. Stir in half-and-half, wine and dill; blend well.
3. Arrange salmon steaks in sauce with thicker portions toward edges of dish. Cover; microwave on HIGH 9 minutes or until fish flakes easily when tested with fork, rotating dish twice during cooking. Let stand, covered, 5 minutes. Garnish with additional dill weed.
Makes 4 servings.

Crab-Stuffed Sole Fillets

1 package (10 ounces) MRS. PAUL'S® Frozen Au Naturel Sole Fillets
2 tablespoons butter or margarine
2 tablespoons chopped green onion
½ cup chopped CAMPBELL'S FRESH® Mushrooms
¼ cup chopped celery
1 can (6 ounces) crabmeat, drained and picked over
1 can (10¾ ounces) CAMPBELL'S® Condensed Cream of Chicken or Condensed Cream of Celery Soup
⅓ cup milk
2 tablespoons Chablis or other dry white wine
½ cup shredded Swiss cheese (2 ounces)

To Microwave:
1. Separate fish fillets, reserving seasoning packet. Arrange fish on microwave-safe plate. Microwave, uncovered, on HIGH 1 minute or until fish is pliable. Set aside.
2. To make stuffing: In small microwave-safe bowl, combine butter, onion, mushrooms and celery. Cover with vented plastic wrap; microwave on HIGH 2 minutes or until vegetables are tender. Stir in crabmeat and 2 tablespoons of the soup. Make 4 mounds of stuffing in 10-inch microwave-safe pie plate. Divide fillets into 4 parts and arrange over stuffing; set aside.
3. In small microwave-safe bowl, stir remaining soup until smooth; stir in milk, wine, cheese and contents of seasoning packet. Microwave, uncovered, on HIGH 3 minutes or until cheese melts, stirring once during cooking.
4. Pour soup mixture over fish. Cover with waxed paper; microwave on HIGH 6 minutes or until fish flakes easily when tested with fork, rotating dish once during cooking. Let stand, covered 5 minutes.
Makes 4 servings.

Bacon-Wrapped Tuna

3 pounds fresh tuna
½ cup olive or vegetable oil
¼ cup lime juice
1 cup dry white wine
2 cloves garlic, crushed
1 teaspoon grated fresh ginger
6 slices bacon

Cut tuna into 6 steaks, each about 1 inch thick. Remove any skin or bone. In shallow glass dish, combine oil, lime juice, wine, garlic and ginger. Add tuna; turn to coat with marinade. Cover and refrigerate 2 hours. Drain fish; reserve marinade. Wrap 1 slice of bacon around each steak and secure with wooden pick. Lightly oil grid. Grill fish steaks, on uncovered grill, over medium-hot **KINGSFORD® Charcoal Briquets** about 10 minutes or until fish flakes easily when tested with fork. Turn once halfway through cooking time; baste often with marinade.
Makes 6 servings.

Lively Lemon Roll-Ups

1 cup cooked rice
⅓ cup butter or margarine
⅓ cup REALEMON® Lemon Juice from Concentrate
2 teaspoons salt
¼ teaspoon pepper
1 (10-ounce) package frozen chopped broccoli, thawed and well drained
1 cup (4 ounces) shredded Cheddar cheese
8 fish fillets, fresh or frozen, thawed (about 2 pounds)
Paprika

Preheat oven to 375°. In small saucepan, melt margarine; add ReaLemon® brand, salt and pepper. In medium bowl, combine rice, broccoli, cheese and ¼ cup lemon sauce; mix well. Divide broccoli mixture equally among fillets. Roll up and place seam-side down in shallow 2-quart baking dish. Pour remaining lemon sauce over roll-ups. Bake 25 minutes or until fish flakes with fork. Spoon sauce over individual servings; garnish with paprika. Refrigerate leftovers.
Makes 8 servings.
Microwave: Prepare fish as above. Arrange in 12×7-inch baking dish; cover with plastic wrap. Microwave on full power (high) 10 to 12 minutes or until fish flakes with fork, rotating dish once. Serve as above.

Orange-Ginger Fish

1 package (10 ounces) MRS. PAUL'S® Frozen Au Naturel Haddock or Cod Fillets
1 tablespoon butter or margarine
½ teaspoon grated orange peel
2 tablespoons orange juice
1 teaspoon teriyaki sauce
1 teaspoon chopped fresh chives
⅛ teaspoon grated fresh ginger

To Microwave:
1. Arrange fish fillets in 12- by 8-inch microwave-safe baking dish, placing thicker portions toward edges of dish; reserve seasoning packet. Set aside.
2. Place butter in small microwave-safe bowl. Cover; microwave on HIGH 20 seconds or until melted. Stir in orange peel, orange juice, teriyaki sauce, chives and ginger; pour over fish. Sprinkle with contents of seasoning packet.
3. Cover with vented plastic wrap; microwave on HIGH 6 minutes or until fish flakes easily when tested with fork, rotating dish once during cooking. Let stand, covered, 5 minutes.
Makes 2 servings.

Chinese Trout

4 medium trout (about
    2 pounds), dressed
1/4 cup KIKKOMAN Soy Sauce
2 tablespoons vegetable oil,
    divided
1 cup water
4 teaspoons cornstarch
1 tablespoon sugar
2 tablespoons tomato catsup
1 tablespoon KIKKOMAN Soy
    Sauce
2 1/2 teaspoons distilled white
    vinegar
1/8 teaspoon crushed red pepper
1/2 cup sliced green onions and
    tops
2 teaspoons finely chopped
    garlic
2 teaspoons finely chopped
    fresh ginger root

Score both sides of trout with diagonal slashes 1/4 inch deep and 1 inch apart; place in large shallow pan. Combine 1/4 cup soy sauce and 1 tablespoon oil; pour over trout, turning to coat both sides well. Marinate 45 minutes, turning over once. Reserving marinade, remove trout and place on rack of broiler pan. Broil 3 inches from heat source 5 minutes on each side, or until fish flakes easily when tested with fork; brush occasionally with reserved marinade. Meanwhile, combine water, cornstarch, sugar, catsup, 1 tablespoon soy sauce, vinegar and red pepper; set aside. Heat remaining 1 tablespoon oil in saucepan over medium-high heat. Add green onions, garlic and ginger; stir-fry 2 minutes. Stir in catsup mixture. Cook and stir until sauce boils and thickens. Serve with trout.
Makes 4 servings.

Teriyaki Fish Fillets

1 can (20 ounces) DOLE®
    Pineapple Chunks
1 clove garlic, pressed
2 tablespoons slivered fresh
    ginger root
1 tablespoon minced green
    onion
5 teaspoons teriyaki sauce
1 teaspoon white vinegar
1 pound sole fillets
2 teaspoons cornstarch
1 teaspoon minced fresh ginger
    root
1 teaspoon sesame oil

Measure 2 tablespoons juice from pineapple can; mix with garlic, slivered ginger, onion, 3 teaspoons teriyaki sauce and vinegar. Arrange fish in shallow dish. Pour marinade over fish. Refrigerate 10 minutes. Arrange fish on greased broiler rack. Brush with marinade. Broil 6 inches from heat 5 to 6 minutes. In saucepan, combine remaining 2 teaspoons teriyaki sauce, undrained pineapple and remaining ingredients. Cook until sauce boils and thickens. Serve with fish.
Makes 4 servings.

Swordfish Steaks with Dill-Mustard Sauce

1/3 cup WISH-BONE® Italian
    Dressing
2 swordfish or shark steaks,
    1 inch thick (about 1 pound)
1/2 cup dry white wine
1/8 teaspoon pepper
1 tablespoon snipped fresh dill*
1 tablespoon Dijon-style
    mustard
1/2 cup whipping or heavy cream

In large skillet, heat Italian dressing and cook fish over medium heat, turning once, 8 minutes or until fish flakes. Remove to serving platter and keep warm. Into skillet, add wine, then pepper, dill and mustard. Bring to a boil, then simmer, stirring occasionally, 8 minutes. Stir in cream and heat 1 minute or until thickened. Serve over fish. Garnish, if desired, with baby vegetables.
Makes about 2 servings.
  Substitution: Use 1 teaspoon dried dill weed.
  Note: Also terrific with Wish-Bone® Robusto Italian, Blended Italian or Italian & Cheese Dressing.

Grilled Fish with Salsa

1/2 cup quartered cherry
    tomatoes
1/2 cup cubed mango or papaya
1/4 cup sliced green onion
1/4 cup cubed avocado
2 tablespoons chopped cilantro
    or parsley
1 tablespoon olive or vegetable
    oil
2 tablespoons lime juice
1 teaspoon minced jalapeño
    pepper
Salt and pepper
1 1/4 pounds white fish fillets (ling
    cod, red snapper or halibut)

In small bowl, combine tomatoes, mango, onion, avocado, cilantro, oil, 1 tablespoon of the lime juice and the jalapeño pepper. Season with salt and pepper to taste; set aside. Measure fish at its thickest part to determine cooking time. Sprinkle both sides of fish with remaining 1 tablespoon lime juice and additional pepper. Lightly oil grid. Grill fillets, on covered grill, over medium-hot **KINGSFORD® Charcoal Briquets** 10 minutes per inch of thickness or until fish flakes easily when tested with fork. Garnish with additional mango or papaya slices, if desired. Serve with salsa.
Makes 4 servings.

Lemony Fish Fillets

1¼ cups crushed cornflakes
2 teaspoons lemon pepper
    seasoning
¼ to ½ teaspoon dried dill weed
⅛ teaspoon garlic powder
¼ cup buttermilk
1 egg
1 pound fish fillets, ½ inch
    thick, cut into serving-size
    pieces
CRISCO® Oil for frying

Mix cornflake crumbs, lemon pepper seasoning, dill weed and garlic powder in shallow dish or on sheet of waxed paper. Set aside. Blend buttermilk and egg in medium mixing bowl. Dip fish in buttermilk mixture, then in cornflake mixture to coat.

Heat ⅛ inch Crisco® Oil in large skillet. Add fish. Fry 5 to 8 minutes, or until fish flakes easily with fork, turning over once. Drain on paper towels.

4 servings.

Saucy Fish Fillets

1 can (8 ounces) DOLE®
    Pineapple Tidbits
1 tablespoon cider vinegar
1 tablespoon sugar
1½ teaspoons cornstarch
½ teaspoon instant chicken
    bouillon granules
¼ teaspoon ground ginger
    Pinch cayenne pepper
¼ cup sliced green onions
¼ cup sliced water chestnuts
4 white fish fillets, about ½ inch
    thick
2 tablespoons butter or
    margarine, melted
½ cup flavored cracker crumbs
    Paprika

Microwave: Drain pineapple; reserve juice. To make sauce, add enough water to juice to make ⅔ cup liquid. In 1½-quart microwave-safe bowl, whisk together juice mixture, vinegar, sugar, cornstarch, bouillon, ginger and cayenne. Microwave on HIGH 4 to 5 minutes or until sauce is thickened and clear, whisking after 2 minutes to prevent lumps. Stir in onions, water chestnuts and pineapple. Set aside.

Arrange fish fillets in 12×8×2-inch microwave-safe dish with thickest areas to outside edges of dish. Drizzle with butter; sprinkle with cracker crumbs and paprika. Cover with waxed paper. Microwave on HIGH 5 to 9 minutes, rotating dish after 3 minutes. Fish is done when thin areas flake easily with fork and thick areas are fork-tender. Let fish stand 2 to 3 minutes; serve with sauce.
Makes 4 servings.

Cajun Pan-Fried Fish

2 tablespoons paprika
2 teaspoons thyme leaves
½ teaspoon salt
½ teaspoon crushed red pepper
¼ teaspoon black pepper
4 tilefish, swordfish, halibut,
    haddock or salmon steaks,
    1 inch thick (about
    2 pounds)
½ cup WISH-BONE® Italian
    Dressing

In medium bowl, combine paprika, thyme, salt and peppers. Dip fish in paprika mixture, coating well.

In large skillet, heat Italian dressing and cook fish over medium heat, turning once, 8 minutes or until fish flakes.
Makes about 4 servings.

Note: Also terrific with Wish-Bone® Robusto Italian, Herbal Italian, Italian & Cheese, Lite Italian, Classic Dijon Vinaigrette or Lite Classic Dijon Vinaigrette Dressing.

Crab-Stuffed Trout

⅓ cup butter or margarine,
    divided
2 cups chopped CAMPBELL'S
    FRESH® Mushrooms
½ cup finely chopped onion
½ cup shredded carrot
1 cup crabmeat, flaked
¼ cup fine dry bread crumbs
3 tablespoons chopped fresh
    parsley, divided
1 tablespoon white wine
    Worcestershire sauce
6 brook trout or salmon
    (8 ounces each), pan-
    dressed
2 teaspoons lemon juice
    Arugula for garnish
    Cherry tomatoes for garnish

1. To make filling: In 10-inch skillet over medium heat, in 3 tablespoons hot butter, cook mushrooms, onion and carrot until tender and liquid has evaporated, stirring occasionally. In medium bowl, combine onion mixture, crabmeat, crumbs, 2 tablespoons of the parsley and Worcestershire; toss gently to coat. Spoon ½ cup filling loosely into each fish cavity; secure with toothpicks.
2. Arrange fish in oiled grill basket. In covered grill, arrange preheated coals around drip pan; test for hot coals above pan. On grill rack, place grill basket over pan but not over coals. Cover; grill 16 to 20 minutes or until fish begins to flake when tested with fork, turning once.
3. To make sauce: In 1-quart saucepan, combine remaining butter, remaining parsley and juice. Over medium heat, heat until butter is melted, stirring occasionally.
4. To serve: Garnish with arugula and tomatoes. Serve with sauce.
Makes 6 servings.

To broil: Arrange fish on rack in broiler pan. Broil 6 inches from heat 16 to 20 minutes or until fish begins to flake when tested with fork, turning once.

Almondine Fish

1 pound fish fillets, fresh or frozen, thawed
Margarine or butter, melted
REALEMON® Lemon Juice from Concentrate
½ cup margarine or butter
3 tablespoons REALEMON® Lemon Juice from Concentrate
¼ cup sliced almonds, toasted

Preheat broiler. Place fish on oiled cold broiler pan. Brush fish with melted margarine and sprinkle with ReaLemon® brand. Broil 4 to 6 inches from heat 10 to 12 minutes per inch of fish thickness, turning halfway through cooking and basting frequently. Cook until fish flakes with fork. Meanwhile, in small saucepan, melt *½ cup* margarine; stir in *3 tablespoons* ReaLemon® brand and almonds. Serve warm over fish. Refrigerate leftovers.
Makes 4 servings.

Crispy Fried Catfish

½ cup white or yellow cornmeal
1 teaspoon salt
¼ to ½ teaspoon cayenne
1 can (5.3 ounces) evaporated milk
1½ to 2 pounds catfish fillets
CRISCO® Oil for frying

Mix cornmeal, salt and cayenne in shallow bowl or on sheet of waxed paper. Set aside. Place milk in another shallow dish. Dip fish in milk, then in cornmeal mixture to coat.

Heat 2 to 3 inches Crisco® Oil in deep-fryer or large saucepan to 375°F. Fry a few fish pieces at a time, 3 to 4 minutes, or until light golden brown. Drain on paper towels. Repeat with remaining fish. Serve immediately or keep warm in 175°F oven.
6 to 8 servings.

Vegetable-Stuffed Fish Rolls

½ cup chopped CAMPBELL'S FRESH® Tomato
½ cup chopped CAMPBELL'S FRESH® Mushrooms
¼ cup chopped green onions
1 can (10¾ ounces) CAMPBELL'S® Condensed Cream of Celery Soup
6 haddock fillets (1½ pounds)
¼ cup water
1 cup shredded Muenster cheese (4 ounces)

1. In medium bowl, combine tomato, mushrooms, green onions and ¼ cup of the soup. Place about 3 tablespoons of the mixture on each fish fillet and roll up. Secure with toothpicks if needed.
2. Place fish rolls, seam side down, in 10- by 6-inch baking dish. Bake at 350°F. 25 minutes or until fish flakes easily when tested with fork. Discard any liquid in baking dish.
3. Meanwhile, in 2-quart saucepan, combine remaining soup and water. Over medium heat, heat through. Pour sauce over fish rolls; sprinkle with cheese.
4. Bake 2 minutes more or until cheese is melted.
Makes 6 servings.

To Microwave: In medium bowl, combine tomato, mushrooms, green onions and ¼ cup of the soup. Fill and roll fish fillets as directed. Place fish rolls, seam side down, in 10- by 6-inch microwave-safe dish. Cover with vented plastic wrap; microwave on HIGH 8 to 14 minutes or until fish flakes easily when tested with fork, rotating dish twice during cooking. Discard any liquid in dish. Let stand, covered, 2 to 3 minutes. Meanwhile, in 2-cup glass measure, combine remaining soup and water. Microwave, uncovered, on HIGH 2 minutes or until hot. Pour sauce over fish rolls; top with cheese. Microwave, uncovered, on HIGH 1 minute more or until cheese melts.

Grilled Trout with Two Sauces

4 whole, cleaned trout or other small whole fish (about 12 ounces each)
Walnut Butter Sauce (recipe follows) *or*
Tarragon Cream Sauce (recipe follows)

Grill fish on well-oiled grid or in well-oiled wire grill basket, on covered grill, over medium-hot **KINGS-FORD® with Mesquite Charcoal Briquets** 3 to 5 minutes or until fish flakes easily when tested with fork; turn once. Serve with Walnut Butter Sauce or Tarragon Cream Sauce.
Makes 4 servings.

Walnut Butter Sauce

½ cup chopped walnuts
½ cup butter or margarine
3 tablespoons Madeira wine

In skillet, saute walnuts in 2 tablespoons of the butter until golden and fragrant. Reduce heat and add remaining 6 tablespoons butter; stir until melted. Stir in Madeira. Serve warm.
Makes about ½ cup.

Tarragon Cream Sauce

¼ cup olive or vegetable oil
¼ cup whipping cream
1 tablespoon red wine vinegar
1 tablespoon finely chopped parsley
1 garlic clove, minced
½ teaspoon dried tarragon, crushed
¼ teaspoon pepper

In medium bowl, combine all ingredients; mix well with wire whisk. Serve cool.
Makes about ½ cup.

Quick and Easy Tuna Rice with Peas

1 package (10 oz.) BIRDS EYE®
   Green Peas
1¼ cups water
1 can (11 oz.) condensed
   cheddar cheese soup
1 can (12½ oz.) tuna, drained
   and flaked
1 chicken bouillon cube
1½ cups MINUTE® Rice

Bring peas, water, soup, tuna and bouillon cube to a full boil in medium saucepan. Stir in rice. Cover; remove from heat. Let stand 5 minutes. Fluff with fork.
Makes 4 servings.

Pineapple-Tomato Salsa and Fish

1 DOLE™ Fresh Pineapple
1 cucumber, peeled, seeded and
   diced
1 DOLE™ Green Bell Pepper,
   seeded and diced
1 DOLE™ Tomato, chopped
½ red onion, finely chopped
¼ cup lemon juice
1 clove garlic, pressed
2 tablespoons finely chopped
   cilantro or parsley
2 tablespoons white wine
   vinegar
1 tablespoon vegetable oil
2 teaspoons sugar
1 teaspoon salt
1 teaspoon dried dill weed
4 white fish steaks (½ inch
   thick)
1 tablespoon butter or
   margarine

Twist crown from pineapple. Cut pineapple lengthwise into quarters. Remove fruit from shells with curved knife. Trim off core and cut fruit into bite-size pieces. In medium bowl, combine half of pineapple with next 12 ingredients (reserve remaining pineapple for another use). In skillet, saute fish in butter 2 to 3 minutes. Spread pineapple salsa over fish. Cover; simmer 10 minutes or until fish is tender and flakes with a fork.
Makes 4 servings.

Oriental Steamed Fish

4 white fish steaks, about
   ¾ inch thick
1 tablespoon slivered fresh
   ginger root
¼ cup orange juice
2 tablespoons KIKKOMAN Soy
   Sauce
1½ teaspoons distilled white
   vinegar
½ teaspoon brown sugar
1 teaspoon Oriental sesame oil
2 green onions and tops, minced

Place fish, in single layer, on oiled rack of bamboo steamer; sprinkle ginger evenly over fish. Set rack in large pot or wok of boiling water. (Do not allow water level to reach fish.) Cover and steam 8 to 10 minutes, or until fish flakes easily when tested with fork. Meanwhile, combine orange juice, soy sauce, vinegar and brown sugar in small saucepan; bring to boil. Remove from heat; stir in sesame oil. Arrange fish on serving platter; sprinkle green onions over fish and pour sauce over all.
Makes 4 servings.

Mexican Style Tuna Loaf

4 (6½-ounce) cans tuna, drained
3 cups fresh bread crumbs
   (6 slices bread)
2 eggs, slightly beaten
¼ cup chopped green pepper
¼ cup chopped onion
3 tablespoons REALEMON®
   Lemon Juice from
   Concentrate
2 teaspoons WYLER'S® or
   STEERO® Chicken-Flavor
   Instant Bouillon
Mexican Sauce

Preheat oven to 350°. In large bowl, combine all ingredients except Mexican Sauce. In greased shallow baking dish, shape into loaf. Bake 30 to 35 minutes. Let stand 10 minutes before serving. Serve with Mexican Sauce. Garnish as desired. Refrigerate leftovers.
Makes 6 to 8 servings.
MEXICAN SAUCE: In small saucepan, combine 1 (15-ounce) can tomato sauce with tomato bits and 2 teaspoons cornstarch; mix well. Stir in 3 tablespoons ReaLemon® Lemon Juice from Concentrate, 1 tablespoon sugar, 1½ teaspoons chili powder and 1 teaspoon Wyler's® or Steero® Chicken-Flavor Instant Bouillon. Over high heat, bring to a boil. Reduce heat; simmer 5 minutes.
Makes about 1½ cups.

Microwave
Tuna Loaf: Mix ingredients as above. Turn into 2½-quart microwave baking ring. Cook on 100% power (high) 12 to 13 minutes or until set and almost firm in center. Let stand 5 minutes. Serve as above.
Sauce: In 1-quart glass measure, combine tomato sauce and cornstarch. Add remaining ingredients. Cook on 100% power (high) 8 minutes or until thickened, stirring every 2 minutes.

Poached Red Snapper

2 quarts water
1 cup (8 ounces) WISH-BONE®
    Italian Dressing
1 cup dry white wine
2 medium carrots, finely
    chopped
1/2 cup chopped shallots or
    onions
1 tablespoon lemon juice
1 teaspoon grated lemon peel
    (optional)
3 whole cloves
1 teaspoon salt
1/4 teaspoon pepper
1 pound new or all-purpose
    potatoes, cut into large
    chunks
1 whole red snapper (about
    2 1/2 to 3 pounds)
1 pound fresh spinach leaves,
    stems trimmed

Place 13×9×2 1/2-inch baking pan on
2 stove burners; fill with water, Italian dressing, wine, carrots, shallots,
lemon juice, lemon peel, cloves, salt
and pepper. Bring to a boil, then
simmer uncovered 5 minutes. Add potatoes and simmer, stirring occasionally, 20 minutes. Add snapper and
simmer, basting occasionally, 25 minutes or until fish flakes and potatoes
are tender. Carefully remove snapper
and potatoes to serving platter and
keep warm. Add spinach to cooking
liquid and simmer 30 seconds; drain.
To serve, arrange potatoes and spinach around snapper.
Makes about 4 servings.
    Note: Also terrific with Wish-
Bone® Robusto Italian, Blended Italian, Herbal Italian, Italian & Cheese,
Lite Italian, Classic Dijon Vinaigrette or Lite Classic Dijon Vinaigrette Dressing.

Salmon and Spinach Pie

1 can (15 1/2 ounces) salmon,
    drained and flaked
1/3 cup fine dry bread crumbs
1 tablespoon lemon juice
1/8 teaspoon pepper
1 can (10 3/4 ounces)
    CAMPBELL'S® Condensed
    Cream of Celery Soup
3 eggs
1 package (10 ounces) frozen
    chopped spinach, thawed
    and well drained
1/4 teaspoon ground nutmeg

To Microwave:
1. In medium bowl, thoroughly mix
salmon, crumbs, lemon juice, pepper,
1/3 cup of the soup and 1 of the eggs.
Spread evenly in 9-inch microwave-
safe pie plate. Cover with waxed paper; microwave on HIGH 3 minutes or
until hot, rotating dish once during
cooking.
2. Meanwhile, in same bowl, stir remaining soup until smooth; stir in remaining 2 eggs, spinach and nutmeg.
Spread evenly over salmon mixture.
3. Microwave, uncovered, at 50%
power 20 minutes or until center is
set, rotating dish twice during cooking. Let stand, uncovered, 5 minutes.
Makes 6 servings.

Fish Rolls with Asparagus

1/2 pound fresh asparagus, cut
    into 4-inch spears, or 1
    package (10 ounces) frozen
    asparagus spears
1 1/2 pounds flounder fillets
2 cups sliced CAMPBELL'S
    FRESH® Mushrooms
1 cup V8® Vegetable Juice
1 tablespoon fresh dill weed or
    1/2 teaspoon dried dill weed,
    crushed
1 tablespoon cornstarch

1. Divide asparagus evenly among
fish fillets. Roll up fillets jelly-roll
fashion; secure with toothpicks, if necessary. Set aside.
2. Spray 10-inch nonstick skillet with
vegetable cooking spray. Over medium heat, cook mushrooms until
lightly browned.
3. In small bowl, stir together V8
juice, dill and cornstarch until
smooth. Gradually stir into skillet.
Cook over medium heat until mixture
boils and thickens.
4. Place fish rolls in sauce. Reduce
heat to low. Cover; simmer 15 minutes
or until fish flakes easily when tested
with fork. Before serving, remove
toothpicks.
Makes 6 servings.

Per serving: 127 calories, 23 g protein, 3 g fat, 5 g carbohydrate, 263 mg
sodium, 55 mg cholesterol.

Pacific Coast Barbecued Salmon

4 fresh or frozen salmon steaks,
    1 inch thick (about 8 ounces
    each)
1/2 cup butter or margarine
2 tablespoons fresh lemon juice
1 tablespoon Worcestershire
    sauce

Thaw salmon steaks, if frozen. In
saucepan, combine butter, lemon juice
and Worcestershire sauce; simmer 5
minutes, stirring frequently. Brush
salmon steaks with butter mixture.
Place steaks in well-greased wire grill
basket.
    Grill steaks, on uncovered grill, over
medium-hot KINGSFORD® Char-
coal Briquets 6 to 9 minutes or until
lightly browned. Baste steaks with
butter mixture and turn; grill 6 to 9
minutes longer, basting often, until
fish flakes easily when tested with
fork.
Makes 4 servings.

Grilled Oriental Fish Steaks

4 fish steaks (halibut, salmon or swordfish), about ³/₄ inch thick
¼ cup KIKKOMAN Lite Soy Sauce
3 tablespoons minced onion
1 tablespoon chopped fresh ginger root
1 tablespoon sesame seed, toasted
½ teaspoon sugar

Place fish in single layer in shallow baking pan. Measure lite soy sauce, onion, ginger, sesame seed and sugar into blender container; process on low speed 30 seconds, scraping sides down once. Pour sauce over fish; turn over to coat both sides. Marinate 30 minutes, turning fish over occasionally. Remove fish and broil or grill 4 inches from heat source or moderately hot coals 5 minutes on each side, or until fish flakes easily when tested with fork. Garnish as desired.
Makes 4 servings.

Seafood Creole

1 tablespoon vegetable oil
3 tomatoes, peeled, coarsely chopped
1 large onion, chopped
1 green pepper, chopped
1 celery stalk, chopped
3 cloves garlic, minced
1½ cups water
³/₄ cup uncooked rice
1 teaspoon ground cumin
½ teaspoon dried thyme leaves
½ teaspoon TABASCO® pepper sauce
1 bay leaf
1½ pounds red snapper fillets with skin, cut into 2-inch pieces
¼ cup chopped parsley

In large skillet heat oil; cook tomatoes, onion, green pepper, celery and garlic until crisp-tender. Add water, rice, cumin, thyme, Tabasco® sauce and bay leaf. Bring to a boil; reduce heat and simmer covered 10 minutes. Add fish and parsley. Cover; simmer 5 to 10 minutes longer or until liquid is absorbed and fish flakes easily when tested with fork. Remove bay leaf.
Makes 4 servings.

Microwave Directions: In 3-quart microwave-safe casserole place oil, onion, green pepper, celery and garlic. Cover loosely with plastic wrap; cook on High 3 to 4 minutes or until vegetables are crisp-tender. Stir in tomatoes, *1 cup* water, rice, cumin, thyme, Tabasco® sauce and bay leaf. Re-cover; cook on High 20 minutes; stir. Add fish and parsley. Re-cover; cook on High 5 to 7 minutes or until fish flakes easily when tested with fork. Let stand covered 10 minutes before serving. Remove bay leaf.

Salmon Steaks with Cucumber Sauce

4 salmon steaks, 1 inch thick
2 tablespoons CRISCO® Oil
³/₄ cup peeled, seeded and chopped cucumber
¼ cup finely chopped celery
2 tablespoons chopped green onion
2 tablespoons all-purpose flour
1 teaspoon instant chicken bouillon granules
⅛ teaspoon pepper
1 cup half-and-half
1 egg yolk, slightly beaten

Set oven to broil and/or 550°F. Place salmon steaks on broiler pan. Broil 3 to 4 inches from heat, 10 to 15 minutes, or until fish flakes easily with fork, turning over once.

Meanwhile, heat Crisco® Oil in small saucepan. Add cucumber and celery. Sauté over moderate heat until tender-crisp. Add onion. Sauté 30 seconds longer. Stir in flour, bouillon granules and pepper. Blend in half-and-half. Cook, stirring constantly, 5 to 7 minutes, or until thickened and bubbly. Blend small amount of hot mixture into egg yolk. Add back to hot mixture. Cook, stirring constantly, 1 minute. Serve with salmon.
4 servings.

Grilled Salmon Steaks with Watercress Sauce

1 cup (8 ounces) WISH-BONE® Italian Dressing
½ cup chopped watercress
4 salmon, tuna or swordfish steaks, 1 inch thick (about 2 pounds)
½ cup whipping or heavy cream
2 tablespoons dry vermouth
Pinch of sugar (optional)

In large shallow baking dish, combine Italian dressing with watercress. Add fish and turn to coat. Cover and marinate in refrigerator, turning fish occasionally, at least 4 hours. Remove fish, reserving marinade. Grill or broil, turning once and basting with reserved marinade, until fish flakes.

Meanwhile, in small saucepan, bring ¼ cup reserved marinade to a boil, then simmer uncovered 5 minutes. Stir in cream, vermouth and sugar. Cook, stirring occasionally, 3 minutes or until slightly thickened. Serve hot sauce over fish.
Makes about 4 servings.

Note: Also terrific with Wish-Bone® Robusto Italian, Lite Italian, Blended Italian, Herbal Italian, Classic Dijon Vinaigrette or Lite Classic Dijon Vinaigrette Dressing.

Grilled Fish Steaks with Vegetable Butter

1 envelope LIPTON® Vegetable Recipe Soup Mix
½ cup butter or margarine, softened
2 tablespoons brandy or sherry
½ teaspoon ground ginger
4 halibut, cod, swordfish, salmon or shark steaks (about 2 pounds), ½ inch thick
½ cup orange juice
¼ cup oil

In medium bowl, with electric mixer or rotary beater, thoroughly blend vegetable recipe soup mix, butter, brandy and ginger. Turn onto wax paper and shape into 8×2-inch log. Wrap in plastic wrap or wax paper, then chill until firm.

Meanwhile, in large baking dish, arrange fish; add orange juice and oil. Cover and marinate in refrigerator, turning occasionally, at least 1 hour. Remove fish from marinade. Grill or broil until fish flakes. To serve, top each steak with ½-inch slice butter mixture.
Makes 4 servings.
Microwave Directions: Prepare butter mixture and marinate fish as above. In 13×9-inch baking dish, arrange fish and heat uncovered at HIGH (Full Power), rearranging fish occasionally, 9 minutes or until fish flakes. Top with butter as above. Let stand covered 5 minutes.

Ginger Fish Fillets

1 pound fresh or thawed fish fillets
½ cup KIKKOMAN Teriyaki Sauce
1 tablespoon vegetable oil
1 teaspoon sugar
1 tablespoon slivered fresh ginger root
1 large green onion and top, cut into 1-inch lengths and slivered
⅓ cup water
1½ teaspoons cornstarch

Place fillets in single layer in shallow baking pan. Combine teriyaki sauce, oil and sugar; pour over fish. Turn fillets over to coat well. Marinate 20 minutes, turning fish over occasionally. (If fillets are very thin, marinate for only 10 minutes.) Sprinkle ginger and green onion evenly over each fillet. Bake in marinade at 350°F. 6 to 10 minutes, or until fish flakes easily when tested with fork. Remove to serving platter and keep warm; reserve ¼ cup pan juices. Blend water and cornstarch in small saucepan. Stir in reserved pan juices. Cook and stir until mixture boils and thickens. To serve, spoon sauce over fish.
Makes 4 servings.

Poached Sole with Dill Sauce

1 (13¾-fluid ounce) can COLLEGE INN® Chicken Broth
6 sole or flounder fillets (about 1½ pounds)
3 tablespoons lemon juice
1 tablespoon cornstarch
3 tablespoons snipped fresh dill or 1 tablespoon dried dill weed

In skillet, over medium-high heat, heat 1¼ cup chicken broth to a boil; reduce heat. Add fish; cover and simmer 2 to 3 minutes or until fish flakes easily with fork. Carefully remove fish with slotted spoon to heated serving platter.

Meanwhile, in small saucepan, blend remaining broth and lemon juice into cornstarch. Cook over medium-high heat, stirring, until mixture thickens and boils. Boil 1 minute; stir in dill. To serve, spoon sauce over fish. Garnish as desired.
Makes 6 servings.
Microwave: In 2-quart microwave-proof oblong dish, place fish and 1¼ cups broth; cover with plastic wrap. Microwave on HIGH (100% power) for 5 to 6 minutes until fish flakes easily with fork. Remove fish to warm serving platter.

In 1-quart microwave-proof bowl, mix ¼ cup broth, lemon juice and 2 tablespoons cornstarch. Microwave on HIGH for 4 to 5 minutes until mixture thickens and boils; stir in dill. Spoon sauce over fish; serve as above.

Fisherman's Light Fillets

½ cup WISH-BONE® Lite Italian or Italian Dressing
1 small green pepper, cut into strips
1 small onion, thinly sliced
1 pound fish fillets
1 medium tomato, coarsely chopped
Hot cooked rice

In large skillet, heat lite Italian dressing and cook green pepper and onion over medium heat, stirring occasionally, 5 minutes or until tender. Add fish and tomato, then simmer covered 10 minutes or until fish flakes. Serve over hot rice.
Makes about 4 servings.

Tangy Catfish

1½ pounds catfish fillets, fresh or frozen*
⅔ cup lemon juice
2 teaspoons TABASCO® pepper sauce
⅔ cup flour
⅔ cup yellow cornmeal
1 teaspoon salt
    Vegetable oil

Thaw fish if frozen. Cut fillets crosswise into ¾-inch strips. In shallow dish combine lemon juice and Tabasco® sauce; add fish. Cover; refrigerate 1 hour; turn fish occasionally. On waxed paper combine flour, cornmeal and salt. Coat fish with flour mixture.

In large skillet over medium-high heat bring 1 inch oil to 350°F. Fry fillet strips, a few at a time, 3 to 5 minutes or until golden brown on all sides. Drain on paper towels. Serve with additional Tabasco® sauce, if desired.

Makes 6 to 8 appetizer servings.

    *Haddock or halibut fillets may be substituted.

Fabulous Fish Terrine

½ cup dry white wine or fish broth
¼ teaspoon salt
2 pounds white fish fillets
2 tablespoons butter or margarine
⅓ cup chopped onion
1 clove garlic, minced
1 small red pepper, slivered
½ cup chopped celery
3 eggs, lightly beaten
⅔ cup dry bread crumbs
½ to ¾ teaspoon TABASCO® pepper sauce
    Lemon slices, parsley and red pepper rings for garnish

Preheat oven to 350°F. In medium skillet combine wine and salt; bring to a boil. Add fish; cover and cook over low heat 5 minutes or until fish flakes easily when tested with fork. Remove fish and liquid to large bowl; cool.

In same skillet melt butter; cook onion and garlic 5 minutes or until tender. Add red pepper slivers and celery; cook 5 minutes longer. Add cooked vegetables to fish and mix well, breaking up fish into large pieces. Add eggs, bread crumbs and Tabasco® sauce; mix well. Press mixture into greased 9×5×3-inch loaf pan. Bake 45 minutes or until center is firm. Cool 10 minutes. Loosen edges of loaf with spatula; turn onto serving platter. Garnish with lemon slices, parsley and red pepper rings.

Makes 8 servings.

Microwave Directions: In 2-quart microwave-safe baking dish place ¼ cup wine and fish fillets. Cover loosely with plastic wrap; cook on High 5 to 7 minutes or until fish flakes easily when tested with fork. Remove fish fillets to large bowl; discard liquid. In same baking dish place *1 tablespoon* butter, onion, garlic, red pepper slivers and celery. Cover loosely with plastic wrap; cook on High 5 to 8 minutes or until vegetables are tender. Add vegetables to bowl with fish. Add salt, eggs, bread crumbs and Tabasco® sauce; mix well. Press mixture into greased 9×5×3-inch microwave-safe loaf pan. Cover loosely with plastic wrap; cook on High 10 to 12 minutes or until mixture is slightly firm on top. Re-cover; let stand 10 minutes. Loosen edges of loaf with spatula; turn onto serving platter. Garnish with lemon slices, parsley and red pepper rings.

Fillets of Sole with Garden Vegetables

2 tablespoons olive or vegetable oil
1 envelope LIPTON® Golden Onion Recipe Soup Mix
1¾ cups water
¼ cup dry white wine
1 tablespoon lemon juice
2 cups shredded cabbage
2 cups shredded carrots
¼ teaspoon oregano
⅛ teaspoon pepper
1 pound sole or flounder fillets

In large skillet, heat oil and stir in golden onion recipe soup mix thoroughly blended with water, wine and lemon juice. Add cabbage, carrots, oregano and pepper. Cook over medium-high heat, stirring occasionally, 10 minutes or until vegetables are crisp-tender. Remove vegetables to serving platter and keep warm; reserve liquid. Into reserved liquid, add fish and cook 7 minutes or until fish flakes. To serve, arrange fish over vegetables and garnish, if desired, with parsley and lemon slices.

Makes about 4 servings.

Microwave Directions: Omit oil and decrease water to 1½ cups. In 1½-quart casserole, thoroughly blend golden onion recipe soup mix with water, wine and lemon juice. Add cabbage, carrots, oregano and pepper. Heat covered at HIGH (Full Power), stirring occasionally, 8 minutes or until vegetables are crisp-tender. Remove vegetables to serving platter and keep warm; reserve liquid. Into reserved liquid, add fish and heat uncovered 5 minutes or until fish flakes, turning casserole once. Serve and garnish as above.

Skillet Fish Italiano

1 small onion, sliced
2 tablespoons margarine or butter
1 pound fish fillets, fresh or frozen, thawed
1/4 cup REALEMON® Lemon Juice from Concentrate
1/2 teaspoon oregano leaves
2 cups sliced zucchini
1 cup sliced fresh mushrooms (about 4 ounces)
1/2 cup chopped tomato
1/2 cup (2 ounces) shredded Swiss cheese

In large skillet, cook onion in margarine until tender. Add fish fillets, ReaLemon® brand, oregano, zucchini and mushrooms; cover and simmer 10 minutes. Top with tomato and cheese; cover and simmer 2 minutes or until cheese melts. Serve immediately. Refrigerate leftovers.
Makes 4 servings.

Microwave: In 2-quart baking dish, melt margarine on full power (high) 45 seconds to 1 minute. Add onion; cover with plastic wrap and microwave on full power (high) 2 to 3 minutes or until tender. Add zucchini and mushrooms; cover and microwave on full power (high) 3 minutes or until zucchini is tender-crisp. Stir; add oregano, fish and ReaLemon® brand. Cover and microwave on full power (high) 5 to 6 minutes or until fish flakes with fork. Sprinkle with tomato and cheese. Microwave on full power (high) 1 to 1 1/2 minutes or until cheese begins to melt. Let stand until cheese melts.

Dilled Salmon Loaf

1/4 lb. VELVEETA Pasteurized Process Cheese Spread, cubed
1/4 cup milk
1 15 1/2-oz. can salmon, drained, skinned, boned, flaked
2 eggs, beaten
2/3 cup dry bread crumbs
1/2 cup finely chopped celery
1/2 cup chopped onion
1 tablespoon lemon juice
1/2 teaspoon dill weed

* * *

1/2 lb. VELVEETA Pasteurized Process Cheese Spread, cubed
1/4 cup milk
1 2 1/4-oz. can sliced ripe olives, drained

In large saucepan, combine process cheese spread and milk; stir over low heat until process cheese spread is melted. Add salmon, eggs, crumbs, celery, onions, juice and dill; mix well. Place in greased 8×4-inch loaf pan. Bake at 350°, 40 to 45 minutes or until golden brown.

Combine process cheese spread and milk in saucepan, stirring over low heat until process cheese spread is melted. Stir in olives. Serve over salmon.
6 servings.

Preparation time: 20 minutes
Baking time: 45 minutes

Microwave: Prepare and bake salmon loaf as directed. Microwave process cheese spread and milk in 2-cup microwave-safe measure on High 3 to 4 minutes or until process cheese spread is melted, stirring after 2 minutes. Stir in olives. Microwave on High 30 seconds to 1 minute or until thoroughly heated. Serve over salmon.

Spanish Stuffed Bell Peppers

9 medium green, red or yellow bell peppers
1 1/2 cups chopped onions
1 tablespoon extra virgin olive oil
1 tablespoon all-purpose flour
1 can (8 ounces) tomato sauce
1/2 cup PET® Evaporated or PET® Light Evaporated Skimmed Milk
1/4 teaspoon saffron
1/4 teaspoon ground fennel
1/4 teaspoon salt
1/4 teaspoon black pepper
1 cup tricolor corkscrew pasta, cooked, drained
1/2 cup frozen peas
1 can (6 1/2 ounces) STARKIST® Solid White or Solid Light Tuna in Springwater, drained, flaked

Remove top and seeds from peppers. Tops may be reserved for garnish, if desired. Chop 1 pepper; set 8 peppers aside. Cook and stir onions and chopped pepper in hot oil in medium skillet over low heat until vegetables are soft. Stir in flour. Cook 3 minutes, stirring constantly. Gradually stir in tomato sauce, milk and seasonings. Cook until mixture thickens and comes to a boil, stirring constantly. Remove from heat and stir in pasta, peas and tuna. Fill remaining 8 peppers with tuna mixture and arrange in baking pan. Cover with foil. Bake at 350°F 45 minutes. Garnish as desired.
Makes 8 servings.

Lemony Stuffed Flounder

5 tablespoons butter or
    margarine
1/2 cup water
2 cups PEPPERIDGE FARM®
    Herb Seasoned Stuffing Mix
1/2 teaspoon grated lemon peel
1/2 cup chopped onion
1/2 cup shredded carrot
1 pound flounder fillets
    Paprika for garnish
    Lemon slices for garnish

To Microwave:
1. In 4-cup glass measure, combine 4 tablespoons of the butter and water. Microwave, uncovered, on HIGH 1½ minutes or until butter is melted. Stir in stuffing mix and lemon peel; set aside.
2. In 10-inch microwave-safe pie plate, combine remaining 1 tablespoon butter, onion and carrot. Cover with waxed paper; microwave on HIGH 3 minutes or until vegetables are tender, stirring once during cooking. Stir into stuffing mixture.
3. Make 4 mounds of stuffing in same pie plate. Divide fish into 4 parts and arrange over stuffing. Sprinkle with paprika and top with lemon slices. Cover with waxed paper; microwave on HIGH 8 minutes or until fish flakes easily when tested with fork, rotating dish once during cooking. Let stand, covered, 5 minutes.
Makes 4 servings.

Halibut Provençale

6 tablespoons CRISCO® Oil,
    divided
1/2 cup chopped onion
1/2 cup chopped green pepper
2 cloves garlic, minced
1 cup sliced fresh mushrooms
1 large tomato, peeled, seeded
    and chopped
3 pounds halibut fillets, cut into
    serving-size pieces
3/4 cup dry white wine*
2 tablespoons snipped fresh
    parsley
2 small bay leaves

Heat 2 tablespoons Crisco® Oil in small skillet. Add onion, green pepper and garlic. Sauté over moderate heat until tender. Stir in mushrooms and tomato. Set aside.

Heat remaining 4 tablespoons Crisco® Oil in large skillet. Add fish. Fry over medium-high heat 4 minutes, turning over once. Remove from heat. Spread vegetable mixture over fish. Add wine, parsley and bay leaves. Cover. Cook over low heat, 10 to 15 minutes, or until fish flakes easily with fork. Remove and discard bay leaves.
12 servings.

*For milder flavor, substitute ½ cup water and ¼ cup dry white wine for 3/4 cup dry white wine.

Lemon Broiled Fish

1/2 cup margarine or butter,
    melted
1/4 cup REALEMON® Lemon Juice
    from Concentrate
2 cups fresh bread crumbs
    (about 4 slices)
1 tablespoon chopped parsley
1/2 teaspoon paprika
1 pound fish fillets, fresh or
    frozen, thawed

Combine margarine and ReaLemon® brand. In medium bowl, combine bread crumbs, parsley and 1/4 cup of the lemon mixture. Add paprika to remaining lemon mixture. Dip fish into paprika mixture; broil until fish flakes with fork. Top with bread crumb mixture. Return to broiler; heat through. Refrigerate leftovers.
Makes 4 servings.

Emperor's Sweet & Sour Fish

1½ pounds fresh or thawed fish
    fillets, ½ inch thick
1 can (6 oz.) unsweetened
    pineapple juice
1/4 cup KIKKOMAN Soy Sauce
1/4 cup water
1/4 cup sugar
2 tablespoons cornstarch
3 tablespoons vinegar
2 tablespoons tomato catsup
    Dash ground red pepper
    (cayenne)
1/4 cup minced green onions and
    tops

Microwave Directions: Place fish in single layer in large microwave-safe dish; set aside. Combine pineapple juice, soy sauce, water, sugar, cornstarch, vinegar, catsup and red pepper in 2-cup microwave-safe measuring cup. Microwave on High 5 minutes, or until mixture boils and thickens, stirring occasionally to prevent lumping. Remove 1/4 cup sauce and pour over fillets, turning each piece over to coat both sides. Keep remaining sauce warm. Cover fish with waxed paper; microwave on High 8 minutes, or until fish flakes easily when tested with fork, turning dish once. Remove fillets to serving platter with slotted spoon. To serve, drizzle warm sauce over fillets and sprinkle green onions over sauce. Pass remaining sauce.
Makes 4 to 6 servings.

Steamed Trout with Orange & Ginger

- ½ cup WISH-BONE® Italian or Robusto Italian Dressing
- 1 medium red onion, chopped
- ¼ cup orange juice
- 1 tablespoon finely chopped fresh ginger*
- 1 teaspoon grated orange peel (optional)
- ½ teaspoon ground cumin
- ⅛ teaspoon pepper
- 2 whole trout or fresh-water fish (about 1 pound each), boned
- 1 cup coarsely chopped green onions
- 1 cup thinly sliced carrots
- 1 cup thinly sliced yellow squash
- 1 cup thinly sliced snow peas (about 4 ounces)

In large shallow oblong baking dish, thoroughly combine Italian dressing, red onion, orange juice, ginger, orange peel, cumin and pepper. Add trout and turn to coat. Cover and marinate in refrigerator, turning occasionally, at least 3 hours. Remove trout, reserving marinade.

Preheat oven to 450°. For each serving, place 1 trout on 1 piece (18×18-inch) parchment paper or heavy-duty aluminum foil; equally top each with reserved marinade, green onions, carrots, squash and snow peas. Wrap parchment or foil loosely around trout and vegetables, sealing edges airtight with double fold. Bake 20 minutes or until trout flakes. Serve, if desired, with hot cooked wild rice.
Makes 2 servings.
*Substitution: Use 1 teaspoon ground ginger.

Steamed Mussels in White Wine

- ⅓ cup WISH-BONE® Italian Dressing
- ½ cup chopped shallots or onions
- 3 pounds mussels, well scrubbed
- ⅔ cup dry white wine
- ½ cup chopped parsley
- ¼ cup water
  Generous dash crushed red pepper

In large saucepan or stockpot, heat Italian dressing and cook shallots over medium heat, stirring occasionally, 2 minutes or until tender. Add remaining ingredients. Bring to a boil, then simmer covered 4 minutes or until mussel shells open. (Discard any unopened shells.) Serve, if desired, with Italian or French bread.
Makes about 3 main-dish or 6 appetizer servings.
Note: Also terrific with Wish-Bone® Robusto Italian or Blended Italian Dressing.

Lemon Swordfish

- 1 tablespoon grated lemon peel
- ¾ cup fresh lemon juice
- ¾ cup olive or vegetable oil
- ¼ to ½ cup parsley, chopped
- 2 tablespoons prepared horseradish
- 2 cloves garlic, minced
- 1 teaspoon dried thyme, crushed
- 1 teaspoon salt
- ¼ teaspoon pepper
- 1 bay leaf
- 1½ pounds swordfish steaks

In shallow glass dish, combine all ingredients except fish. Add swordfish; turn to coat with marinade. Cover and refrigerate at least 2 hours, turning fish occasionally. Drain fish; reserve marinade. Grill swordfish, on uncovered grill, over medium-hot **KINGSFORD® Charcoal Briquets** about 7 minutes, basting lightly with marinade. Carefully turn swordfish and grill 5 to 6 minutes longer or until fish flakes easily when tested with fork, basting lightly with marinade.
Makes 4 servings.

Salmon Cheese Puff Pies

- 1 (15½-ounce) can salmon, drained and flaked
- 1 cup BORDEN® or MEADOW GOLD® Cottage Cheese
- ¼ cup chopped green pepper
- ¼ cup chopped onion
- 3 tablespoons REALEMON® Lemon Juice from Concentrate
- 1 (2-ounce) jar pimientos, drained and chopped
- ¼ cup dill weed
- 1 (10-ounce) package frozen puff pastry patty shells, thawed in refrigerator overnight

Preheat oven to 450°. In large bowl, combine all ingredients except patty shells. On floured surface, roll each shell to an 8-inch circle. Place equal amounts of salmon mixture in center of each circle. Fold over; seal edges with water and press with fork. Place on ungreased baking sheet; cut slit near center of each turnover. Reduce oven temperature to 400°; bake 25 minutes or until golden brown. Refrigerate leftovers.
Makes 6 servings.

Salmon Loaf with Clam Cheese Sauce

1 (15½-ounce) can salmon, drained and flaked
2 cups fresh bread crumbs (4 slices bread)
2 eggs
¼ cup chopped onion
3 tablespoons butter or margarine, melted
2 tablespoons REALEMON® Lemon Juice from Concentrate
¼ teaspoon basil leaves
Clam Cheese Sauce

Preheat oven to 350°. In large bowl, combine all ingredients except Clam Cheese Sauce; mix well. In greased shallow baking pan, shape into loaf. Bake 35 to 40 minutes. Let stand 5 minutes before serving. Garnish as desired. Serve with Clam Cheese Sauce. Refrigerate leftovers.
Makes 4 to 6 servings.,
CLAM CHEESE SAUCE: Drain 1 (6½-ounce) can SNOW'S® or DOXSEE® Minced Clams, reserving ⅓ cup liquid. In small saucepan, over low heat, melt 1 tablespoon margarine or butter; stir in 1 tablespoon flour. Gradually stir in ⅔ cup BORDEN® or MEADOW GOLD® Milk and reserved ⅓ cup clam liquid. Over medium heat, cook and stir until thickened and bubbly. Remove from heat; add ¼ cup (1 ounce) shredded Cheddar cheese and clams, stirring until cheese melts.
Makes about 1⅓ cups.

Cajun Fish

1 cup butter or margarine
2 tablespoons paprika
2 teaspoons popcorn butter salt
2 teaspoons onion powder
2 teaspoons garlic powder
2 teaspoons cayenne pepper
1½ teaspoons white pepper
1½ teaspoons black pepper
1 teaspoon dried thyme, crushed
1 teaspoon dried oregano, crushed
2 pounds red snapper fillets

Heat iron skillet on grill directly over medium-hot **MATCH LIGHT® Charcoal Briquets** at least 15 minutes. Meanwhile, in small saucepan, melt butter. In small bowl, combine remaining ingredients except fish. Brush fillets with butter; sprinkle seasoning mix evenly on both sides of fillets. Place fillets in hot skillet and ladle melted butter over fillets.* Cook about 2 minutes on each side. Serve immediately with additional melted butter for dipping.
Makes 4 servings.
Note: This method of grilling produces heavy smoke.

Greek-Style Shrimp

2 tablespoons olive oil
1 cup sliced green onions
4 large cloves garlic, minced
1 pound large shrimp, shelled and deveined
¾ cup V8® Vegetable Juice *or* No Salt Added V8® Vegetable Juice
⅓ cup crumbled feta cheese (2 ounces)
2 tablespoons chopped fresh parsley
Dash pepper
8 slices PEPPERIDGE FARM® Fully Baked French-Style Bread

In 10-inch skillet over medium heat, in hot oil, cook onions and garlic until onions are tender. Add shrimp; cook until shrimp are pink and opaque, stirring constantly. Stir in V8 juice. Heat to boiling. Reduce heat to low; simmer 2 minutes. Sprinkle with cheese, parsley and pepper. Serve with bread.
Makes 4 servings.
Note: If desired, use oven-safe skillet. After sprinkling with cheese, broil 3 minutes or until cheese is lightly browned.

Per serving: 420 calories, 28 g protein, 14 g fat, 45 g carbohydrate, 858 mg sodium (No Salt Added V8® Juice: 714 mg sodium), 155 mg cholesterol.

Tuna Loaf

1 can (6½ ounces) STARKIST® Solid White Tuna in Springwater, drained
2 eggs, lightly beaten
1 cup PET® Evaporated or PET® Light Evaporated Skimmed Milk
½ cup whole wheat bread crumbs
2 tablespoons finely chopped green bell pepper
1 tablespoon finely chopped onion
2 tablespoons lemon juice
½ teaspoon salt
⅛ teaspoon white pepper
¼ teaspoon Worcestershire sauce

Combine all ingredients in medium bowl. Transfer to 8½×4½-inch glass loaf pan. Bake at 350°F 30 to 40 minutes or until firm. May be served hot or cold or used as spread for sandwiches or crackers. Garnish as desired.
Makes 4 servings.
Note: Recipe may be doubled. Bake in 8×8-inch baking dish.

Grilled Lobster with Spicy Sauce

4 whole, live lobsters* (1 to 1½ pounds each)
¼ cup dry sherry
3 tablespoons soy sauce
2 to 3 tablespoons sugar
2 teaspoons grated fresh ginger or ½ teaspoon ground ginger
1 teaspoon red pepper flakes
2 cloves garlic, minced
Butter or margarine, melted

Bring large kettle of water to boil. Plunge lobsters into water. Return water to boil; cover and simmer 3 minutes or just until lobsters turn pink. Remove lobsters; rinse under cold running water and drain. Turn lobsters, underside up, and cut through inner shell of tails to expose meat.

For spicy sauce, in small bowl, combine remaining ingredients except butter. Brush lobster shells and meaty underside with sauce, letting sauce soak into meat. Grill lobsters, meat-side up, on covered grill, over medium-hot **KINGSFORD® with Mesquite Charcoal Briquets** 13 to 15 minutes or until meat turns opaque, basting often with sauce. When lobsters are cooked, make a deep cut lengthwise in center of underside with sharp knife. Spread halves enough to remove stomach (near head) and black vein. Crack claw shells with hammer. Serve with melted butter and additional spicy sauce.
Makes 4 servings.

*2 pounds jumbo fresh shrimp can be substituted for lobster. Leave shell on and thread on skewers. Grill as above, reducing cooking time to 5 minutes or until shrimp turn pink.

Seafood Kabobs

2 dozen large sea scallops
1 dozen medium shrimp, shelled and deveined
1 can (8½ ounces) whole small artichoke hearts, drained
2 red or yellow peppers, cut into 2-inch pieces
¼ cup olive or vegetable oil
¼ cup lime juice

In large bowl, combine all ingredients and toss gently. Thread scallops, shrimp, artichoke hearts and peppers alternately on skewers; reserve marinade. Lightly oil grid. Grill kabobs, on uncovered grill, over low **KINGSFORD® Charcoal Briquets** 6 to 8 minutes or until scallops turn opaque and shrimp turn pink. Turn kabobs carefully at least twice during grilling and brush with marinade.
Makes 6 servings.

Shrimp Oriental

8 ounces fresh mushrooms, sliced (about 2 cups)
1 cup sliced celery
½ cup finely chopped onion
¼ cup margarine or butter
⅓ cup REALEMON® Lemon Juice from Concentrate
¼ cup water
2 tablespoons brown sugar
1 tablespoon soy sauce
¼ teaspoon ground ginger
2 teaspoons cornstarch
12 ounces small raw shrimp, peeled and deveined
1 (6-ounce) package frozen pea pods, thawed, or 4 ounces fresh pea pods
Hot cooked rice

In large skillet, cook mushrooms, celery and onion in margarine until the celery is tender-crisp. Mix together ReaLemon® brand, water, sugar, soy sauce, ginger and cornstarch; add to mushroom mixture. Over medium heat, cook and stir until thick and clear. Add shrimp; cook 3 to 5 minutes or until shrimp is pink. Add pea pods; heat through. Serve immediately over rice. Refrigerate leftovers.
Makes 4 servings.

Some-Like-It-Hot Shrimp

1 egg white, lightly beaten
2 tablespoons dry white wine
1 teaspoon cornstarch
¼ teaspoon salt
1½ pounds medium-size shrimp, peeled, deveined
Vegetable oil
½ cup plus 2 tablespoons chopped green onions, divided
1 tablespoon chopped ginger root
½ cup chicken broth
2 tablespoons catsup
¾ teaspoon TABASCO® pepper sauce
½ teaspoon salt
½ teaspoon sugar

In medium bowl combine egg white, wine, cornstarch and salt; mix well. Add shrimp. Cover; refrigerate 1 hour. Drain shrimp; reserve egg white mixture. Pour oil into heavy saucepan to depth of 3 inches; heat over medium-high heat to 350°F. Fry shrimp, a few at a time, just until they turn pink, about 1 minute. Drain on paper towels. Drain all but 2 tablespoons oil from pan.

Add 2 tablespoons chopped green onions and ginger to pan; stir-fry 1 minute. Stir in broth, catsup, Tabasco® sauce, salt and sugar. Bring to a boil. Stir in reserved egg white mixture, shrimp and remaining ½ cup chopped green onions. Add additional Tabasco® sauce, if desired. Serve in a chafing dish.
Makes 16 to 18 appetizer servings.

Beer-Batter Shrimp

½ cup beer
⅓ cup all-purpose flour
⅓ cup cornstarch
1 egg
2 tablespoons CRISCO® Oil
⅛ teaspoon cayenne
⅛ teaspoon garlic powder
CRISCO® Oil for frying
1 pound fresh medium shrimp, peeled, deveined and butterflied

Combine beer, flour, cornstarch, egg, 2 tablespoons Crisco® Oil, cayenne and garlic powder in medium mixing bowl. Mix well. Cover and refrigerate at least 1 hour.

Heat 2 to 3 inches Crisco® Oil in deep-fryer or large saucepan to 375°F. Dip shrimp in batter. Fry a few shrimp at a time, 1 to 1½ minutes, or until golden brown. Drain on paper towels. Serve immediately or keep warm in 175°F oven.
4 to 6 servings.

Festival Shrimp

1 DOLE™ Fresh Pineapple
1 large DOLE™ Tomato, cut into quarters
1 medium onion, cut into quarters
1 jar (4 ounces) pimentos
¼ cup canned diced green chilies
2 tablespoons lime juice
1½ teaspoons ground coriander
1 teaspoon garlic salt
1 teaspoon sugar
¼ cup butter or margarine
1 pound medium shrimp, cooked and shelled*
1 tablespoon chopped fresh cilantro or parsley
Hot cooked rice

Twist crown from pineapple. Cut pineapple lengthwise into quarters. Remove fruit from shell with curved knife. Trim off core and cut fruit into chunks. Set aside.

In food processor or blender, combine tomato, onion, pimentos, green chilies, lime juice, coriander, garlic salt and sugar. Process until pureed.

In large skillet, melt butter. Add pureed sauce and simmer 5 minutes. Stir in shrimp, pineapple and cilantro. Cook just until heated through. Serve immediately over hot rice.
Makes 4 servings.

*Cook shrimp in simmering water 2 to 3 minutes or until pink and firm. Drain; set aside until cool enough to handle. Remove shells; cut along curve of body with sharp knife to remove back vein.

Deep-Fried Clams

2 cups oyster crackers, finely crushed
½ teaspoon poultry seasoning
¼ teaspoon salt
¼ teaspoon cayenne
¼ teaspoon garlic powder
¼ teaspoon ground marjoram
2 eggs
1 can (10 ounces) whole baby clams, drained
CRISCO® Oil for frying

Mix cracker crumbs, poultry seasoning, salt, cayenne, garlic powder and marjoram in large plastic food storage bag. Set aside. Beat eggs slightly in small mixing bowl. Gently stir in clams. Remove a few clams with slotted spoon and add to cracker mixture. Shake to coat. Remove clams from cracker mixture; set aside. Repeat with remaining clams.

Heat 2 to 3 inches Crisco® Oil in deep-fryer or large saucepan to 375°F. Fry a few clams at a time, about 30 seconds, or until golden brown. Drain on paper towels. Serve immediately.
2 to 4 servings.

Seafood Cacciatore

1 pound shrimp, cleaned
1 small onion, chopped
2 garlic cloves, minced
2 tablespoons oil
1 can (14½ oz.) whole tomatoes in juice
1 can (8 oz.) tomato sauce
1½ cups water
1 medium green pepper, cut into thin strips
¾ teaspoon dried basil leaves
½ teaspoon dried oregano leaves
½ teaspoon salt
⅛ teaspoon ground red pepper
1 chicken bouillon cube
1½ cups MINUTE® Rice
8 clams, well scrubbed

Cook and stir shrimp with onion and garlic in hot oil in large skillet until shrimp turn pink. Stir in tomatoes with juice, tomato sauce, water, green pepper, seasonings and bouillon cube. Bring to a full boil, breaking up tomatoes with spoon. Stir in rice. Cover; remove from heat. Let stand 5 minutes.

Meanwhile, place clams on rack in pan with water below rack. Bring to a boil. Cover and steam 5 to 10 minutes or until clams open. Discard any unopened clams. Fluff rice mixture with fork and serve topped with clams.
Makes 4 servings.

Microwave Directions: Combine shrimp, onion, garlic and oil in microwavable dish. Cover and cook at HIGH 4 minutes. Stir in remaining ingredients, except clams. Break up tomatoes with spoon. Cover and cook at HIGH 7 to 8 minutes longer. Let stand 5 minutes.

Meanwhile, arrange clams in microwavable dish. Cover and cook at HIGH 5 to 7 minutes or until shells are open and meat is firm. Discard any unopened clams. Fluff rice mixture with fork and serve topped with clams.
Makes 4 servings.

Barbecued Shrimp on a Skewer

1 envelope LIPTON® Onion or Onion-Mushroom Recipe Soup Mix
1 can (14½ ounces) whole peeled tomatoes, undrained and chopped
½ cup vegetable or olive oil
¼ cup dry white wine or vermouth
¼ cup chopped fresh basil leaves*
1 tablespoon lemon juice
1 teaspoon cracked peppercorns
2 pounds uncooked large shrimp, cleaned
4 thin slices cooked ham, cut into strips
1 tablespoon finely chopped parsley

In large bowl, combine onion recipe soup mix, tomatoes, oil, wine, basil, lemon juice and peppercorns. Add shrimp. Cover and marinate in refrigerator, stirring occasionally, at least 2 hours. Remove shrimp, reserving marinade.

On skewers, alternately thread shrimp with ham strips, weaving ham around shrimp. Grill or broil, turning and basting frequently with reserved marinade, until shrimp are done. Bring remaining marinade to a boil, then simmer 2 minutes; stir in parsley. Serve as a dipping sauce or, if desired, arrange skewers over hot cooked rice and top with sauce.
Makes about 6 servings.
Substitution: Use 1½ teaspoons dried basil leaves.

Scallops with Golden Cream Sauce

2 tablespoons butter or margarine
1 medium red pepper, cut into thin strips
1 cup uncooked regular rice
1 envelope LIPTON® Golden Onion Recipe Soup Mix
2¼ cups water
1 tablespoon lime juice
¼ cup light cream or half and half
1 pound bay scallops
2 medium green onions, sliced

In medium skillet, melt butter and cook red pepper over medium heat until crisp-tender. Stir in uncooked rice, then golden onion recipe soup mix thoroughly blended with water and lime juice. Bring to a boil, then simmer covered 30 minutes or until rice is tender. Stir in remaining ingredients and cook covered 5 minutes or until scallops are tender. Serve, if desired, with freshly ground pepper.
Makes about 4 servings.

Shrimp Creole

½ cup WISH-BONE® Italian Dressing
1 medium green pepper, cut into chunks
1 medium onion, sliced
1 can (14½ ounces) whole peeled tomatoes, undrained and chopped
1 pound uncooked medium shrimp, cleaned
⅛ teaspoon crushed red pepper
2 cups hot cooked rice

In medium skillet, heat Italian dressing and cook green pepper and onion over medium heat, stirring occasionally, 5 minutes or until tender. Stir in tomatoes and simmer covered 15 minutes. Add shrimp and red pepper and simmer covered an additional 5 minutes or until shrimp turn pink. To serve, arrange shrimp mixture over hot rice.
Makes about 4 servings.
Note: Also terrific with Wish-Bone® Robusto Italian, Lite Italian, Italian & Cheese or Herbal Italian Dressing.

Lemon-Dill Lobster Tails

¾ cup MARIE'S® Refrigerated Sour Cream and Dill Salad Dressing
1 teaspoon grated lemon peel
1 clove garlic, minced
⅛ teaspoon pepper
4 frozen lobster tails (6 ounces each), thawed

1. To make sauce: In small bowl, combine salad dressing, peel, garlic and pepper.
2. With kitchen shears, cut membrane from underside of tails; discard. With sharp knife, loosen meat from shell, leaving meat and shell intact. To prevent tail from curling, bend backwards, breaking at joints.
3. Brush grill rack with oil. On grill rack, place lobster tails, shell side down, directly above medium coals. Grill, uncovered, 18 minutes or until opaque, turning twice and brushing tops with sauce.
4. To serve: With fork, loosen meat from shell, starting at end and pulling forward. Serve with any remaining sauce.
Makes 4 servings.

Tangy Cocktail Sauce

¾ cup BENNETT'S® Chili Sauce or catsup
3 tablespoons REALEMON® Lemon Juice from Concentrate
½ teaspoon prepared horseradish
½ teaspoon Worcestershire sauce

In small bowl, combine ingredients. Chill to blend flavors.
Makes about 1 cup.

Crab and Rice Primavera

1½ cups BIRDS EYE® FARM FRESH Broccoli, Green Beans, Pearl Onions and Red Peppers
¼ cup water
1⅓ cups milk
1 pound imitation crabmeat or crabmeat
2 tablespoons butter or margarine
1 teaspoon garlic salt
¾ teaspoon dried basil leaves
1½ cups MINUTE® Rice
½ cup grated Parmesan cheese

Bring vegetables and water to a boil in medium saucepan, stirring occasionally. Reduce heat; cover and simmer 3 minutes.

Add milk, imitation crabmeat, butter, garlic salt and basil. Bring to a full boil. Stir in rice and cheese. Cover; remove from heat. Let stand 5 minutes. Fluff with fork.
Makes 4 servings.

Saucy Shrimp over Chinese Noodle Cakes

Chinese Noodle Cakes (recipe follows)
1¼ cups water
2 tablespoons cornstarch, divided
4 tablespoons KIKKOMAN Soy Sauce, divided
1 teaspoon tomato catsup
½ pound medium-size raw shrimp, peeled and deveined
2 tablespoons vegetable oil, divided
1 clove garlic, minced
½ teaspoon minced fresh ginger root
1 green pepper, chunked
1 medium onion, chunked
2 stalks celery, cut diagonally into thin slices
2 tomatoes, chunked

Prepare Chinese Noodle Cakes. Combine water, 1 tablespoon cornstarch and 3 tablespoons soy sauce with catsup; set aside. Blend remaining 1 tablespoon cornstarch and 1 tablespoon soy sauce in small bowl; stir in shrimp until coated. Heat 1 tablespoon oil in hot wok or large skillet over high heat. Add shrimp and stir-fry 1 minute; remove. Heat remaining 1 tablespoon oil in same pan. Add garlic and ginger; stir-fry until fragrant. Add green pepper, onion and celery; stir-fry 4 minutes. Stir in soy sauce mixture, shrimp and tomatoes. Cook and stir until sauce boils and thickens. Cut Chinese Noodle Cakes into squares and serve with shrimp mixture.
Makes 4 servings.
CHINESE NOODLE CAKES: Cook *8 ounces capellini* (angel hair pasta) according to package directions. Drain; rinse under cold water and drain thoroughly. Heat *1 tablespoon vegetable oil* in large, nonstick skillet over medium-high heat. Add half the capellini; slightly spread to fill bottom of skillet to form noodle cake. Without stirring, cook 5 minutes, or until golden on bottom. Lift cake with wide spatula; add *1 tablespoon oil* to skillet and turn cake over. Cook 5 minutes longer, or until golden brown, shaking skillet occasionally to brown evenly; remove to rack and keep warm in 200°F. oven. Repeat with remaining capellini.

Shrimp Etouffée

½ cup butter or margarine
2 medium onions, chopped
1 cup chopped celery
1 cup chopped green onions
2 cloves garlic, minced
½ cup flour
4 cups water
2 cans (16 ounces each) tomatoes, drained
2 tablespoons lemon juice
1 teaspoon salt
2 bay leaves
¼ teaspoon dried thyme leaves
2 pounds shrimp, peeled, deveined
½ teaspoon TABASCO® pepper sauce
Hot cooked rice

In large saucepot or Dutch oven melt butter; add onions, celery, green onions and garlic. Cook 5 minutes or until tender. Add flour; stir until well blended. Stir in water, tomatoes, lemon juice, salt, bay leaves and thyme. Bring to a boil, reduce heat and simmer covered 30 minutes; stir occasionally. Add shrimp and Tabasco® sauce. Simmer 5 minutes longer or until shrimp turn pink. Remove bay leaves. Serve over rice.
Makes 8 servings.

Bacon-Wrapped Shrimp

1 pound fresh or frozen shrimp, shelled and deveined
1 small onion, finely chopped
½ cup olive or vegetable oil
½ teaspoon sugar
½ teaspoon cayenne pepper
¼ teaspoon salt
¼ teaspoon dried oregano, crushed
½ teaspoon garlic powder
½ pound bacon
Mexican Fried Rice (recipe follows)

Thaw shrimp, if frozen. Place shrimp in plastic bag; set in bowl. For marinade, in small bowl, combine onion, oil, sugar, cayenne pepper, salt, oregano and garlic powder. Pour marinade over shrimp; close bag. Marinate shrimp 3 hours in refrigerator, turning occasionally.

Cut bacon slices into halves lengthwise, then crosswise. In large skillet, partially cook bacon. Drain on paper toweling. Drain shrimp; reserve marinade. Wrap bacon strips around shrimp and secure with wooden picks. Place shrimp in wire grill basket or on 12×9-inch piece of heavy-duty foil. (If using foil, puncture foil in several places.)

Grill shrimp, on uncovered grill, over medium-hot **KINGSFORD® Charcoal Briquets** 6 minutes or until bacon and shrimp are done, turning basket or individual shrimp once and basting with marinade. Serve with Mexican Fried Rice.
Makes 6 servings.

Mexican Fried Rice

3 tablespoons vegetable oil
1 cup long grain rice
2 cups water
1 cup chili salsa
½ cup chopped green pepper
1 small onion, chopped
1 clove garlic, minced

In 12-inch skillet, heat oil. Add rice; cook until golden brown, stirring often. Stir in remaining ingredients. Bring mixture to boil; reduce heat. Cover; simmer 15 to 20 minutes or until rice is tender. Season to taste; serve with additional salsa, if desired.
Makes 6 servings.

Paella Olé

½ pound shrimp, cleaned
2 garlic cloves, crushed
2 tablespoons butter or margarine
1¼ cups chicken broth
1 tablespoon cornstarch
1 can (14½ oz.) stewed tomatoes
½ cup sliced pepperoni
1 package (10 oz.) BIRDS EYE® CLASSICS, Peas and Pearl Onions, thawed
¼ teaspoon ground red pepper
1½ cups MINUTE® Rice
⅛ teaspoon saffron (optional)

Cook and stir shrimp and garlic in hot butter in large skillet until shrimp turn pink. Mix broth and cornstarch in small bowl; stir into shrimp. Add tomatoes, pepperoni, vegetables and red pepper. Cook and stir until mixture thickens and comes to a full boil. Stir in rice and saffron. Cover; remove from heat. Let stand 5 minutes. Fluff with fork.
Makes 4 servings.

Microwave Directions: Reduce butter to 1 tablespoon. Cook garlic and butter in 2½-quart microwavable dish at HIGH 1 minute. Mix broth and cornstarch in small bowl; stir into garlic mixture. Add remaining ingredients. Cover and cook at HIGH 3 minutes. Stir; cover and cook at HIGH 3 minutes longer. Stir again; cover and cook at HIGH 2 to 4 minutes longer or until thickened. Fluff with fork.
Makes 4 servings.

Shrimp Scampi Italiano

⅓ cup WISH-BONE® Italian or Robusto Italian Dressing
1 pound uncooked medium shrimp, cleaned

In large shallow nonaluminum broiler-proof pan, pour Italian dressing over shrimp. Cover and marinate in refrigerator, turning occasionally, at least 2 hours. Broil shrimp with dressing, turning and basting frequently, until pink. Garnish, if desired, with chopped parsley. Serve, if desired, with hot cooked rice.
Makes about 4 servings.

Shanghai Shrimp

4 scallions, cut in 1-inch pieces
1 teaspoon minced ginger
2 tablespoons peanut oil
1 pound large shrimp, shelled and deveined
1 cup COLLEGE INN® Chicken Broth
1 tablespoon cornstarch
1 (11-ounce) can mandarin oranges, undrained
1 (8-ounce) can CHUN KING® Sliced Water Chestnuts, undrained
Hot cooked rice

In large skillet, over medium-high heat, cook scallions and ginger in oil for 2 to 3 minutes. Add shrimp; cook for 3 to 4 minutes. Blend chicken broth into cornstarch; stir into skillet with oranges and water chestnuts. Reduce heat; simmer, covered, until slightly thickened and heated through. Serve over rice. Garnish as desired.
Makes 6 servings.

Shanghai Chicken: Substitute 1 pound boneless chicken, cut in 2-inch strips, for shrimp.

Savory Seafood Stew

⅔ cup WISH-BONE® Italian Dressing
½ cup dry white wine
¼ cup sliced onion
6 clams, well scrubbed
1 lobster, cut into 2-inch pieces (about 1 pound)
½ pound fish fillets, cut into large pieces
¼ pound scallops
¼ pound uncooked medium shrimp, cleaned

In large saucepan, combine Italian dressing, wine, onion and clams. Bring to a boil, then simmer covered, stirring occasionally, 5 minutes. Add remaining ingredients, then simmer covered, stirring occasionally, 5 minutes or until seafood is done. (Discard any unopened clam shells.) Serve, if desired, with hot cooked rice or crusty French bread.
Makes about 4 servings.
Note: Also terrific with Wish-Bone® Robusto Italian, Blended Italian, Herbal Italian, Italian & Cheese or Lite Italian Dressing.

Shrimp-in-Shell

1 pound medium-size raw shrimp, unpeeled
½ cup regular-strength chicken broth
2 tablespoons cornstarch
3 tablespoons KIKKOMAN Soy Sauce
2 teaspoons sugar
3 tablespoons vegetable oil
1 tablespoon minced fresh ginger root
1 large clove garlic, minced
1 red bell pepper, cut into thin strips
¼ pound fresh snow peas, trimmed

Thoroughly rinse shrimp; devein. Let drain on several layers of paper towels. Combine chicken broth, cornstarch, soy sauce and sugar; set aside. Heat oil in hot wok or large skillet over high heat. Add ginger and garlic; stir-fry 30 seconds. Add shrimp; stir-fry 1 to 2 minutes, or until pink. Remove shrimp with slotted spoon, leaving oil in pan. Add red pepper and snow peas to same pan; stir-fry 1 minute. Stir in shrimp and soy sauce mixture. Cook and stir until mixture boils and thickens, about 1 minute.
Makes 4 to 6 servings.

Stir-Fried Scallops & Vegetables

1 pound scallops
¼ cup REALEMON® Lemon Juice from Concentrate
1 cup thinly sliced carrots
3 cloves garlic, finely chopped
⅓ cup margarine or butter
2 cups sliced fresh mushrooms (about 8 ounces)
¾ teaspoon thyme leaves
2 teaspoons cornstarch
½ teaspoon salt
¼ cup diagonally sliced green onions
1 (6-ounce) package frozen pea pods, thawed, or 4 ounces fresh pea pods
2 tablespoons dry sherry
Hot cooked rice

In shallow baking dish, marinate scallops in ReaLemon® brand 30 minutes, stirring occasionally. In large skillet, over high heat, cook and stir carrots and garlic in margarine until tender-crisp, about 3 minutes. Add mushrooms and thyme; cook and stir about 5 minutes. Stir cornstarch and salt into scallops mixture; add to vegetables. Cook and stir until scallops are opaque, about 4 minutes. Stir in onions, pea pods and sherry. Remove from heat. Serve immediately with hot cooked rice. Refrigerate leftovers.
Makes 4 servings.

Shrimp & Vegetable Stir-Fry

2 tablespoons cornstarch, divided
4 tablespoons KIKKOMAN Teriyaki Sauce, divided
1 tablespoon minced fresh ginger root
½ pound medium-size raw shrimp, peeled and deveined
¾ cup water
2 tablespoons vegetable oil, divided
2 stalks celery, cut diagonally into ¼-inch-thick slices
1 medium-size red bell pepper, cut into 1-inch squares
¼ pound green onions and tops, cut into 1-inch lengths, separating whites from tops

Combine 1 tablespoon *each* cornstarch and teriyaki sauce with ginger in small bowl; add shrimp and stir to coat evenly. Let stand 15 minutes. Meanwhile, combine water, remaining 1 tablespoon cornstarch and 3 tablespoons teriyaki sauce; set aside. Heat 1 tablespoon oil in hot wok or large skillet over high heat. Add shrimp and stir-fry 1 minute; remove. Heat remaining 1 tablespoon oil in same pan. Add celery, red pepper and white parts of green onions; stir-fry 2 minutes. Stir in shrimp, teriyaki sauce mixture and green onion tops. Cook and stir until mixture boils and thickens. Serve over rice, if desired.
Makes 4 servings.

MAIN-DISH CASSEROLES

Easy-to-serve casseroles are a mainstay for the busy cook—for a complete meal, just add a crisp green salad. Serve enchiladas or a hearty chicken pot pie for welcome family fare, and work magic with leftovers and pantry-shelf ingredients. For entertaining a group, grace the buffet table with a gourmet cassoulet—a perfect melding of flavors and textures in one dish.

Meat 'n' Tater Pie

2 cups KELLOGG'S CORN FLAKES® cereal, crushed to make 1 cup, divided
½ teaspoon salt
¼ teaspoon pepper
1 tablespoon prepared mustard
⅓ cup milk
1 pound ground beef
2 eggs
2 cups stiff mashed potatoes
¼ cup chopped onion
2 teaspoons parsley flakes
2 tablespoons butter or margarine, melted
½ cup shredded American cheese
Paprika

Combine ½ cup of the crushed cereal, the salt, pepper, mustard and milk in large bowl; beat well. Add ground beef, mixing until combined. Gently press meat mixture in bottom and up side of 9-inch pie pan. Beat eggs lightly in small bowl. Add potatoes, onion and parsley. Stir until combined. Spread potato mixture evenly in meat shell. Place pie pan on baking sheet. Bake at 350°F 35 minutes. Meanwhile, combine remaining ½ cup crushed cereal with melted butter in small bowl; set aside. Sprinkle cheese evenly over potato mixture. Top with cereal mixture. Bake 10 minutes more or until cheese melts. Sprinkle with paprika.
Makes 6 servings.

Smoked Sausage Noodle Bake

1 pound ECKRICH® Smoked Sausage
8 ounces uncooked medium egg noodles
2 tablespoons butter or margarine
½ cup chopped onion
½ cup chopped celery
1 can (17 ounces) cream-style corn
½ cup sour cream
½ teaspoon salt
Dash ground black pepper

Preheat oven to 350°F. Cook noodles according to package directions. Melt butter in small saucepan over medium-high heat. Saute onion and celery until crisp-tender. Combine noodles, onion, celery, corn, sour cream, salt and pepper in large bowl. Pour into buttered shallow 2-quart baking dish. Cut sausage into serving-size pieces. Arrange on top of noodles and push down partially into noodles. Bake 40 minutes or until hot.
Makes 4 to 6 servings.

Ham and Cheese Strata

12 white bread slices
1½ cups (6 ounces) shredded 100% Natural KRAFT Mild Cheddar Cheese
1 10-ounce package frozen chopped broccoli, thawed, well-drained
1 cup chopped ham
1 8-ounce package PHILADELPHIA BRAND Cream Cheese, softened
3 eggs
1 cup milk
½ teaspoon dry mustard

Place six bread slices on bottom of 12×8-inch baking dish. Cover with 1 cup cheddar cheese, broccoli, ham and remaining bread slices, cut in half diagonally. Beat cream cheese until light and fluffy. Add eggs, one at a time, mixing well after each addition. Blend in milk and mustard; pour over bread. Top with remaining cheddar cheese. Bake at 350°, 45 to 50 minutes or until set. Let stand 10 minutes before serving.
Makes 6 servings.

Casserole Primavera

2 cups (4 ounces) spinach noodles
4 ounces linguini
½ cup thinly sliced zucchini
1 can (2.8 ounces) DURKEE French Fried Onions
1 cup (4 ounces) shredded provolone cheese
½ cup (2 ounces) grated Parmesan cheese
2 tablespoons all-purpose flour
1 teaspoon DURKEE Garlic Salt
½ teaspoon DURKEE Italian Seasoning
2½ cups milk
1 cup chopped tomato
⅓ cup sliced pitted ripe olives

Preheat oven to 325°. In large saucepan, cook noodles and linguini according to package directions, omitting salt. Add zucchini during last 2 minutes of cooking. Drain. Return pasta and zucchini to saucepan. Toss lightly with ½ can French Fried Onions, the cheeses, flour, seasonings, milk, tomato and olives. Pour into 8×12-inch baking dish. Bake, covered, at 325° for 25 minutes or until heated through. Stir to blend sauce and noodles. Top with remaining onions; bake, uncovered, 5 minutes or until onions are golden brown.
Makes 6 main-dish servings.

Microwave Directions: Prepare pasta mixture as above; pour into 8×12-inch microwave-safe dish. Cook, covered, on HIGH 12 to 14 minutes or until heated through. Stir pasta mixture halfway through cooking time. Top with remaining onions; cook, uncovered, 1 minute. Let stand 5 minutes.

Bean and Ham Roll-Ups

1 can (28 ounces) B&M® Brick Oven Baked Beans
12 slices baked or boiled ham
2 tablespoons butter or margarine
¼ cup packed brown sugar
1½ tablespoons prepared mustard

Spoon beans in strip at narrow end of ham slices. Roll up ham slices, jellyroll style, beginning at narrow end; secure with wooden picks. Arrange ham rolls in shallow baking dish. Melt butter in small saucepan over medium heat. Stir in brown sugar and mustard. Reduce heat to low. Cook until well blended, stirring constantly. Baste tops of rolls with mustard glaze. Bake in preheated 350°F oven 25 minutes or until heated through, basting occasionally. Garnish as desired.
Makes 6 servings.

Chicken and Vegetable Pie

3⅓ cups water, divided
1½ cups cubed potatoes, ½-inch cubes
¾ teaspoon salt
3 tablespoons CRISCO® Oil
1 small onion, thinly sliced
2 tablespoons plus 1 teaspoon all-purpose flour
1 tablespoon instant chicken bouillon granules
1 teaspoon dried parsley flakes
¼ to ½ teaspoon dried thyme leaves
¼ teaspoon pepper
1 cup milk
1½ cups cut-up cooked chicken or turkey
½ cup frozen corn
½ cup frozen green peas
1 can (4 ounces) mushroom stems and pieces, drained
1 recipe Pastry for Two-Crust Pie (see Index)

Combine 3 cups water, potatoes and salt in 2-quart saucepan. Heat to boiling. Cover. Reduce heat. Simmer about 10 minutes, or until potatoes are tender. Drain. Set aside.

Heat Crisco® Oil in medium saucepan. Add onion. Sauté over moderate heat until tender. Stir in flour, bouillon granules, parsley flakes, thyme and pepper. Blend in milk and remaining ⅓ cup water. Cook over moderate heat, stirring constantly, until thickened and bubbly. Remove from heat. Add potatoes, chicken, corn, peas and mushrooms. Stir to break apart corn and peas. Set aside.

Preheat oven to 425°F. Prepare Pastry for Two-Crust Pie. Roll and fit into 9-inch pie plate as directed. Fill with chicken mixture. Top with remaining pastry; flute edges. Cut slits in top. Place in oven. Immediately reduce temperature to 325°F. Bake at 325°F, 45 to 60 minutes, or until filling is hot and crust is flaky.
4 to 6 servings.

Tortilla Lasagna

1 tablespoon vegetable oil
1 large onion, chopped
1 medium green pepper, chopped
1 large clove garlic, minced
1 pound ground beef
1 teaspoon dried oregano leaves
1 can (16 ounces) tomatoes, drained, chopped
1 can (8 ounces) tomato sauce
1 cup sour cream
3/4 teaspoon TABASCO® pepper sauce
10 corn tortillas, 5 inches in diameter
1 can (16 ounces) pinto beans, drained
2 cups (8 ounces) shredded Cheddar cheese

Preheat oven to 350°F. In large skillet heat oil; cook onion, green pepper and garlic 3 minutes or until tender. Add ground beef and oregano, breaking up meat with fork as it cooks; cook until browned. Drain off fat; remove from heat.

In medium bowl combine tomatoes, tomato sauce, sour cream and Tabasco® sauce; mix well. Cut each tortilla in half. Arrange 10 halves in shallow 11×7-inch baking dish. Spread half the meat mixture over tortillas. Top with half the pinto beans, half the tomato mixture and 1 cup shredded cheese. Repeat with remaining ingredients. Bake 30 minutes or until heated through. Let stand 10 minutes before serving.
Makes 4 servings.

Microwave Directions: *Omit oil.* In 2-quart microwave-safe casserole place onion, green pepper, garlic, ground beef and oregano. Cook uncovered on High 6 to 8 minutes or until meat is no longer pink; stir with fork to break up meat. Drain off fat. In medium bowl combine tomatoes, tomato sauce, sour cream and Tabasco® sauce; set aside. Cut each tortilla in half. Arrange 10 halves in 11×7-inch microwave-safe baking dish. Spread half the meat mixture over tortillas. Top with half the pinto beans, half the tomato mixture and 1 cup shredded cheese. Repeat with remaining ingredients. Cook uncovered on High 10 to 15 minutes or until heated through and bubbly; turn dish 1/2 turn halfway through cooking. Let stand 10 minutes before serving.

Country French Cassoulet

1/4 cup WISH-BONE® Italian Dressing
2 medium onions, chopped
2 medium carrots, chopped
1 pound kielbasa (Polish sausage), sliced diagonally
1/4 cup dry white wine
1 cup chicken broth
1 can (8 ounces) tomato puree
1 teaspoon thyme leaves
2 cups cut-up cooked pork or lamb (about 12 ounces)
1 can (16 ounces) cannellini beans, rinsed and drained
1/2 cup fresh bread crumbs
2 tablespoons butter or margarine, melted
2 tablespoons finely chopped parsley

Preheat oven to 350°.

In large skillet, heat Italian dressing and cook onions, carrots and kielbasa over medium heat, stirring occasionally, 10 minutes or until vegetables are tender and kielbasa is lightly browned. Stir in wine, then broth, tomato puree, thyme and pork.

In lightly greased deep 2-quart casserole, layer 1/2 of the tomato mixture, then 1/2 of the beans; repeat. Top with bread crumbs combined with butter and parsley. Bake 40 minutes or until heated through.
Makes about 8 servings.

Note: Also terrific with Wish-Bone® Robusto Italian, Blended Italian, Lite Italian, Classic Dijon Vinaigrette or Lite Classic Dijon Vinaigrette Dressing.

American-Style Cassoulet

4 1/2 quarts water, divided
1 package (1 pound) dry green peas, rinsed
2 large onions, cut into wedges
1 bay leaf
2 pounds boneless lamb, cut into 1 1/2-inch cubes
2 pounds boneless pork loin, partially frozen and cut into 1/2-inch slices
1 pound garlic-flavored sausage links
1/2 cup FILIPPO BERIO Olive Oil, divided
1 cup coarsely chopped carrots
1 cup chopped onion
1 large clove garlic, minced
1 1/2 cups dry white wine
1 can (14 1/2 ounces) tomatoes
1/4 cup tomato paste
1/3 cup chopped parsley
1/2 teaspoon dried thyme, crushed
Salt
Pepper
1/2 cup coarse fresh bread crumbs

Place 2 quarts of the water, the peas, onion wedges and bay leaf in large, deep saucepan. Bring to a boil over high heat; boil 2 minutes. Remove from heat. Cover and let soak 1 hour. Drain peas; discard water. Place peas and 2 quarts of the water in same saucepan. Bring to a boil over high heat. Reduce heat to low. Cover and simmer 1 hour or until peas are tender, stirring occasionally. Drain, reserving liquid. Discard bay leaf. Set peas aside; keep warm.

Brown meats, in batches, in 1/4 cup of the oil in Dutch oven over medium-high heat. Return meats to Dutch oven; add carrots, chopped onion and garlic. Cook and stir several minutes. Add remaining 2 cups water, the wine, tomatoes, tomato paste, parsley and thyme. Bring to a boil. Reduce heat to low. Cover and simmer 30 minutes, stirring occasionally. Season to taste

with salt and pepper. Alternately layer peas and meat mixture in large, deep casserole. Pour 1 cup of the reserved liquid over top. Sprinkle with bread crumbs and drizzle with remaining ¼ cup oil. Bake at 375°F 1 hour. Add additional reserved liquid if casserole becomes dry.
Makes 8 to 10 servings.

Cheesy Pork Chops 'n Potatoes

1 jar (8 ounces) pasteurized
    processed cheese spread
1 tablespoon vegetable oil
6 thin pork chops, ¼ to ½ inch
    thick
    DURKEE Seasoned Salt
½ cup milk
4 cups frozen cottage fries
1 can (2.8 ounces) DURKEE
    French Fried Onions
1 package (10 ounces) frozen
    broccoli spears,* thawed
    and drained

Preheat oven to 350°. Spoon cheese spread into 8×12-inch baking dish; place in oven just until cheese melts, 5 minutes. Meanwhile, in large skillet, heat oil. Brown pork chops on both sides; drain. Sprinkle chops with seasoned salt; set aside. Using fork, stir milk into melted cheese until well blended. Stir cottage fries and ½ *can* French Fried Onions into cheese mixture. Divide broccoli spears into 6 small bunches. Arrange bunches of spears over potato mixture with flowerets around edges of dish. Arrange chops over broccoli *stalks*. Bake, covered, at 350° for 35 to 40 minutes or until pork chops are done. Top chops with remaining onions; bake, uncovered, 5 minutes or until onions are golden brown.
Makes 4 to 6 servings.

Microwave Directions: Omit oil. Reduce milk to ¼ cup. In 8×12-inch microwave-safe dish, place cheese spread and milk. Cook, covered, on HIGH 3 minutes; stir to blend. Stir in cottage fries and ½ *can* onions. Cook, covered, 5 minutes; stir. Top with broccoli spears as above. Arrange *unbrowned* pork chops over broccoli *stalks* with meatiest parts toward edges of dish. Cook, covered, on MEDIUM (50-60%) 24 to 30 minutes or until pork chops are done. Turn chops over, sprinkle with seasoned salt and rotate dish halfway through cooking time. Top with remaining onions; cook, uncovered, on HIGH 1 minute. Let stand 5 minutes.

*1 small head fresh broccoli (about ½ pound) may be substituted for frozen spears. Divide into spears and cook 3 to 4 minutes before using.

Tex-Mex Bake

2 cups crushed corn chips
1 egg, beaten
2 tablespoons water
1 envelope LIPTON® Onion
    Recipe Soup Mix
1 pound lean ground beef
1 can (4 ounces) chopped green
    chilies, drained
1 cup shredded Monterey Jack
    cheese (about 3 ounces)
1 can (8 ounces) tomato sauce
1 medium green pepper,
    chopped

Preheat oven to 350°.
Combine corn chips, egg and water; press into 9-inch pie plate or casserole. Bake 10 minutes.

Meanwhile, in large bowl, combine onion recipe soup mix, ground beef, chilies and ½ cup cheese; evenly press into prepared crust. Top with tomato sauce, then green pepper and bake 30 minutes. Top with remaining cheese, then bake an additional 5 minutes or until cheese is melted and beef is done.
Makes about 6 servings.

Chili Beef and Corn Casserole

1 (13¾-fluid ounce) can
    COLLEGE INN® Beef Broth
1 (6-ounce) can tomato paste
1 (1¼-ounce) package ORTEGA®
    Taco Seasoning Mix
¾ cup uncooked rice
1 pound ground beef
1 cup chopped onion
1 (17-ounce) can whole kernel
    sweet corn, drained
    Corn chips, optional
    Diced fresh tomato, optional

In small bowl, blend 1 cup beef broth, tomato paste and taco seasoning mix; set aside. In saucepan, over high heat, combine remaining broth and enough water to equal 1¾ cups liquid; heat to a boil. Add rice and cook according to package directions.

In large skillet, over medium-high heat, brown beef and cook onion until done; pour off fat. In 2-quart casserole, layer ⅓ each of the rice, corn, meat mixture and reserved sauce; repeat layers twice, combining the last portion of meat and sauce for the top layer. Cover; bake at 375°F for 40 to 45 minutes or until hot. Garnish with corn chips and diced tomato, if desired.
Makes 4 to 6 servings.

Microwave: Combine first 3 ingredients as above. In 1½-quart microwave-proof bowl, combine remaining broth and enough water to equal 1¾ cups liquid. Stir in rice; cover. Microwave on HIGH (100% power) for 15 to 17 minutes, stirring after 7 minutes.

Crumble beef in 1½-quart microwave-proof bowl. Microwave, uncovered, on HIGH for 2 minutes; stir in onion. Microwave, uncovered, on HIGH for 2 to 3 minutes; pour off fat. In 2-quart microwave-proof casserole, layer as above; cover. Microwave on HIGH for 15 to 17 minutes, rotating casserole ½ turn after 7 minutes. Let stand, covered, for 5 minutes before serving.

Beef and Wild Rice Casserole

2²/₃ cups boiling water
²/₃ cup uncooked wild rice, rinsed and drained
4 teaspoons WYLER'S® or STEERO® Beef-Flavor Instant Bouillon or 4 Beef-Flavor Bouillon Cubes
1¹/₂ pounds lean ground beef
1 cup chopped celery
¹/₂ cup chopped onion
1 clove garlic, finely chopped
1 (10³/₄-ounce) can condensed cream of mushroom soup
¹/₂ cup uncooked long grain rice
¹/₈ teaspoon pepper

Preheat oven to 350°. In 2-quart baking dish, combine water, wild rice and bouillon; set aside. In large skillet, brown meat; pour off fat. Stir in celery, onion and garlic; cook until tender. Add soup, long grain rice and pepper. Add meat mixture to wild rice mixture; mix well. Cover. Bake 1 hour and 30 minutes. Serve hot. Refrigerate leftovers.
Makes 8 servings.

Cheese-Stuffed Beef Rolls

1 jar (15¹/₂ ounces) spaghetti sauce
1 egg, slightly beaten
¹/₄ teaspoon DURKEE Leaf Oregano
¹/₄ teaspoon DURKEE Garlic Powder
1 container (15 ounces) ricotta cheese
¹/₄ cup (1 ounce) grated Parmesan cheese
1 cup (4 ounces) shredded mozzarella cheese
1 can (2.8 ounces) DURKEE French Fried Onions
6 thin slices deli roast beef (about ¹/₂ pound)
2 medium zucchini, sliced (about 3 cups)

Preheat oven to 375°. Spread ¹/₂ cup spaghetti sauce in bottom of 8×12-inch baking dish. In large bowl, thoroughly combine egg, seasonings, ricotta cheese, Parmesan cheese, ¹/₂ cup mozzarella cheese and ¹/₂ can French Fried Onions. Spoon equal amounts of cheese mixture on 1 end of each beef slice. Roll up beef slices jelly-roll style and arrange, seam-side down, in baking dish. Place zucchini along both sides of dish. Pour remaining spaghetti sauce over beef rolls and zucchini. Bake, covered, at 375° for 40 minutes or until heated through. Top beef rolls with remaining mozzarella cheese and onions. Bake, uncovered, 3 minutes or until onions are gold ᵢ brown.
Makes 6 servings.

Microwave Directions: In large microwave-safe bowl, prepare cheese mixture as above. Cook, covered, on HIGH 2 to 4 minutes or until warmed through. Stir cheese mixture halfway through cooking time. Spread ¹/₂ cup spaghetti sauce in bottom of 8×12-inch microwave-safe dish. Prepare beef rolls and place in dish as above. Arrange zucchini along both sides of dish. Pour remaining spaghetti sauce over beef rolls and zucchini. Cook, loosely covered, 14 to 16 minutes or until heated through. Rotate dish halfway through cooking time. Top beef rolls with remaining mozzarella cheese and onions; cook, uncovered, 1 minute or until cheese melts. Let stand 5 minutes.

Turkey Divan

1 pound broccoli, cut into spears, or 1 package (16 ounces) frozen broccoli spears
¹/₄ cup water
1 can (10³/₄ ounces) CAMPBELL'S® Condensed Cream of Mushroom Soup
¹/₄ cup milk
1 tablespoon dry sherry Generous dash ground nutmeg
2 cups cubed cooked turkey or chicken
¹/₄ cup shredded Cheddar cheese (1 ounce)

To Microwave:
1. In 10- by 6-inch microwave-safe casserole, combine broccoli and water. Cover with vented plastic wrap; microwave on HIGH 6 minutes or until broccoli is almost tender, rotating dish once during cooking. Let stand, covered, 3 minutes. Drain.
2. In medium bowl, stir soup until smooth. Stir in milk, sherry and nutmeg; stir in turkey. Pour over broccoli. Sprinkle with cheese. Cover with waxed paper; microwave on HIGH 6 minutes or until heated through, rotating dish once during cooking. Let stand, covered, 5 minutes.
Makes 4 servings.

Cheeseburger Pie

1 (9-inch) unbaked pastry shell, pricked
8 slices BORDEN® Process American Cheese Food
1 pound lean ground beef
¹/₂ cup tomato sauce
¹/₃ cup chopped green pepper
¹/₃ cup chopped onion
1 teaspoon WYLER'S® or STEERO® Beef-Flavor Instant Bouillon or 1 Beef-Flavor Bouillon Cube
3 eggs, well beaten
2 tablespoons flour Chopped tomato and shredded lettuce, optional

Preheat oven to 425°. Bake pastry shell 8 minutes; remove from oven. Reduce oven temperature to 350°. Cut *6 slices* cheese food into pieces; set aside. In large skillet, brown meat; pour off fat. Add tomato sauce, green pepper, onion and bouillon; cook and stir until bouillon dissolves. Remove from heat; stir in eggs, flour and cheese food pieces. Turn into prepared shell. Bake 20 to 25 minutes or until hot. Arrange remaining cheese food slices on top. Return to oven 3 to 5 minutes or until cheese food begins to melt. Garnish with tomato and lettuce if desired. Refrigerate leftovers.
Makes one 9-inch pie.

Chicken Enchiladas

3 cups finely chopped cooked chicken
1 cup chopped onion
¼ cup margarine or butter
¼ cup unsifted flour
2½ cups hot water
1 tablespoon WYLER'S® or STEERO® Chicken-Flavor Instant Bouillon *or* 3 Chicken-Flavor Bouillon Cubes
1 (8-ounce) container BORDEN® or MEADOW GOLD® Sour Cream, at room temperature
2 cups (8 ounces) shredded Cheddar cheese
1 (4-ounce) can chopped mild green chilies, drained
1 teaspoon ground cumin
12 (6-inch) corn tortillas *or* 10 (8-inch) flour tortillas
Sour cream, chopped green onions and chopped tomato for garnish

Preheat oven to 350°. In medium saucepan, cook onion in margarine until tender. Stir in flour then water and bouillon; cook and stir until thickened and bouillon dissolves. Remove from heat; stir in sour cream. In large bowl, combine *1 cup* sauce, chicken, *1 cup* cheese, chilies and cumin; mix well. Dip each tortilla into remaining hot sauce to soften; fill each with equal portions of chicken mixture. Roll up. Arrange in greased 13×9-inch baking dish. Spoon remaining sauce over. Sprinkle with remaining cheese. Bake 25 minutes or until bubbly. Garnish as desired. Refrigerate leftovers.
Makes 6 to 8 servings.

Microwave: In 2-quart round baking dish, microwave margarine on full power (high) 1 minute or until melted. Add onion; microwave on full power (high) 3 to 5 minutes or until tender. Stir in flour, then water and bouillon; microwave on full power (high) 8 minutes, or until thickened and bouillon dissolves, stirring every 2 minutes. Stir in sour cream. Proceed as above. Arrange rolled tortillas in greased 12×7-inch baking dish. Microwave on ⅔ power (medium-high) 9 minutes or until bubbly. Let stand 5 minutes before serving.

Country-Style Chicken Dinner

3 cups frozen hash brown potatoes
1 can (2.8 ounces) DURKEE French Fried Onions
1 can (10¾ ounces) condensed cream of chicken soup
1 cup milk
6 slices (¾ ounce *each*) processed American cheese
2 to 2½ pounds chicken pieces, fat trimmed, skinned if desired
1 package (10 ounces) frozen mixed vegetables, thawed and drained

Preheat oven to 375°. In 9×13-inch baking dish, combine frozen potatoes and ½ can French Fried Onions. In small bowl, blend soup and milk; pour *half* over potato mixture. Arrange cheese slices over potato mixture; top with chicken, skin-side down. Pour remaining soup mixture over chicken. Bake, uncovered, at 375° for 35 minutes. Stir vegetables into potatoes and turn chicken pieces over. Bake, uncovered, 20 minutes or until chicken is done. Stir potato mixture and top chicken with remaining onions; bake, uncovered, 3 minutes or until onions are golden brown. Let stand 15 minutes before serving.
Makes 4 to 6 servings.

Chicken in French Onion Sauce

1 package (10 ounces) frozen baby carrots, thawed and drained or 4 medium carrots, cut into strips (about 2 cups)
2 cups sliced mushrooms
½ cup thinly sliced celery
1 can (2.8 ounces) DURKEE French Fried Onions
4 chicken breast halves, skinned and boned
½ cup white wine
¾ cup prepared HERB-OX Chicken Bouillon
½ teaspoon DURKEE Garlic Salt
¼ teaspoon DURKEE Ground Black Pepper
DURKEE Paprika

Preheat oven to 375°. In 8×12-inch baking dish, combine vegetables and *½ can* French Fried Onions. Arrange chicken breasts on vegetables. In small bowl, combine wine, bouillon, garlic salt and pepper; pour over chicken and vegetables. Sprinkle chicken with paprika. Bake, covered, at 375° for 35 minutes or until chicken is done. Baste chicken with wine sauce and top with remaining onions; bake, uncovered, 3 minutes or until onions are golden brown.
Makes 4 servings.

Microwave Directions: In 8×12-inch microwave-safe dish, combine vegetables and *½ can* onions. Arrange chicken breasts, skinned side down, along sides of dish. Prepare wine mixture as above, except reduce bouillon to ⅓ cup; pour over chicken and vegetables. Cook, covered, on HIGH 6 minutes. Turn chicken breasts over and sprinkle with paprika. Stir vegetables and rotate dish. Cook, covered, 7 to 9 minutes or until chicken is done. Baste chicken with wine sauce and top with remaining onions; cook, uncovered, 1 minute. Let stand for 5 minutes.

Turkey Cottage Pie

1/4 cup butter or margarine
1/4 cup all-purpose flour
1 envelope LIPTON® Golden Onion Recipe Soup Mix
2 cups water
2 cups cut-up cooked turkey or chicken
1 package (10 ounces) frozen mixed vegetables, thawed
1 1/4 cups shredded Swiss cheese (about 5 ounces)
1/8 teaspoon pepper
5 cups hot mashed potatoes

Preheat oven to 375°.

In large saucepan, melt butter and cook flour over medium-low heat, stirring constantly, 5 minutes or until golden. Stir in golden onion recipe soup mix thoroughly blended with water. Bring to a boil, then simmer 15 minutes or until thickened. Stir in turkey, vegetables, 1 cup cheese and pepper. Turn into lightly greased 2-quart casserole; top with hot potatoes, then remaining cheese. Bake 30 minutes or until bubbling.

Makes about 8 servings.

Microwave Directions: In 2-quart casserole, heat butter at HIGH (Full Power) 1 minute. Stir in flour and heat uncovered, stirring frequently, 2 minutes. Stir in golden onion recipe soup mix thoroughly blended with water. Heat uncovered, stirring occasionally, 4 minutes or until thickened. Stir in turkey, vegetables, 1 cup cheese and pepper. Top with hot potatoes, then remaining cheese. Heat uncovered, turning casserole occasionally, 5 minutes or until bubbling. Let stand uncovered 5 minutes. For additional color, sprinkle, if desired, with paprika.

Deep Dish Turkey Pie

3 cups cubed cooked turkey *or* chicken
1 cup sliced cooked carrots
1 cup cubed cooked potatoes
1 cup frozen green peas, thawed
6 tablespoons margarine or butter
1/3 cup unsifted flour
2 tablespoons WYLER'S® or STEERO® Chicken-Flavor Instant Bouillon *or* 6 Chicken-Flavor Bouillon Cubes
1/4 teaspoon pepper
4 cups BORDEN® or MEADOW GOLD® Milk
2 1/4 cups biscuit baking mix

Preheat oven to 375°. In large saucepan, melt margarine; stir in flour, bouillon and pepper. Over medium heat, gradually add milk; cook and stir until mixture thickens. Add remaining ingredients except biscuit mix; mix well. Pour into 2 1/2-quart baking dish. Prepare biscuit mix according to package directions for rolled biscuits. Roll out to cover dish; cut slashes in center of dough. Place on top of dish; crimp edges. Bake 40 minutes or until golden. Refrigerate leftovers.

Makes 6 servings.

Scalloped Turkey

2 cups diced cooked BUTTERBALL® turkey (3/4 pound)
1/2 cup chopped celery
1/4 cup chopped green bell pepper
3 tablespoons butter or margarine, divided
2 tablespoons all-purpose flour
1/4 teaspoon salt
1 1/2 cups milk
1 tablespoon chopped pimiento
4 cups potato chips, divided

Preheat oven to 350°F. Cook and stir celery and green pepper in 1 tablespoon butter in medium saucepan over medium heat. Remove from pan. Melt remaining 2 tablespoons butter in same saucepan over medium heat. Blend in flour and salt. Remove from heat. Gradually add milk. Cook over medium heat until mixture thickens, stirring constantly. Add turkey, celery, green pepper and pimiento. Crush potato chips lightly to make 2 cups. Put about 1 1/2 cups potato chips in bottom of buttered 1 to 1 1/2-quart baking dish. Add turkey mixture. Sprinkle remaining chips on top. Bake in oven 30 to 40 minutes or until sauce bubbles.

Yield: 4 servings.

California-Style Chicken

1 can (15 ounces) tomato sauce
3 tablespoons red wine vinegar
1/2 teaspoon DURKEE Sweet Basil
1/4 teaspoon DURKEE Garlic Powder
12 small red potatoes, thinly sliced (about 3 cups)
1 can (2.8 ounces) DURKEE French Fried Onions
2 1/2 pounds chicken pieces, fat trimmed, skinned if desired
1 package (10 ounces) frozen whole green beans, thawed and drained

Preheat oven to 375°. In small bowl, combine tomato sauce, vinegar and seasonings. Spread *1/2 cup* tomato mixture in bottom of 9×13-inch baking dish; top with potatoes and *1/2 can* French Fried Onions. Arrange chicken over potatoes and onions. Spoon *1 cup* tomato mixture over chicken and potatoes. Bake, covered, at 375° for 35 minutes. Stir green beans into potatoes. Spoon remaining tomato mixture over chicken. Bake, covered, 10 to 15 minutes or until chicken and beans are done. Top chicken with remaining onions; bake, uncovered, 3 minutes or until onions are golden brown.

Makes 4 to 6 servings.

Chicken and Ham Supreme

- 1 package (9 ounces) frozen artichoke hearts
- 1 can (10³/₄ ounces) CAMPBELL'S® Condensed Cream of Mushroom Soup
- ½ cup plain yogurt
- ½ cup shredded Swiss cheese (2 ounces)
- 1 teaspoon dried basil leaves, crushed
- ⅛ teaspoon ground red pepper (cayenne)
- 2 cups cooked rice
- 1½ cups cubed cooked chicken
- 1 cup cubed cooked ham
  Chopped fresh parsley for garnish

To Microwave:
1. Place artichoke hearts in small microwave-safe bowl. Cover with vented plastic wrap; microwave on HIGH 4 minutes or until heated through, stirring once during cooking. Drain; set aside.
2. In small bowl, stir soup until smooth; stir in yogurt, cheese, basil and pepper.
3. In 8- by 8-inch microwave-safe baking dish, combine rice and ½ cup of the soup mixture; spread evenly in dish. Top with chicken, ham and artichoke hearts. Spoon remaining soup mixture over.
4. Cover with vented plastic wrap; microwave on HIGH 8 minutes or until heated through, rotating dish once during cooking. Let stand, covered, 2 minutes. Garnish with parsley.
Makes 4 servings.

Note: You can substitute 1 package (about 10 ounces) frozen asparagus or broccoli spears for the artichoke hearts. Cook vegetables according to package directions; drain, then cut into bite-size pieces. Proceed as above in steps 2 through 4.

Old-Fashioned Chicken Pot Pie

- 6 tablespoons butter or margarine, divided
- 3 tablespoons flour
- 2 cups chicken broth
- 1¼ teaspoons dried rosemary leaves, divided
- ¼ teaspoon TABASCO® pepper sauce
- ½ pound cubed cooked chicken
- 2 medium carrots, sliced and cooked
- 1 cup frozen peas
- 1½ cups packaged dry biscuit mix
- ½ cup milk

Preheat oven to 400°F. In large saucepan melt 3 tablespoons butter. Stir in flour; cook 1 minute. Remove from heat. Gradually add broth. Stir constantly, bring to a boil over medium heat and boil 1 minute. Stir in ½ teaspoon rosemary, Tabasco® sauce, chicken, carrots and peas. Spoon mixture into greased 2-quart shallow baking dish.

In medium bowl combine biscuit mix and remaining ¾ teaspoon rosemary. Cut in remaining 3 tablespoons butter until mixture resembles coarse crumbs. Stir in milk. On heavily floured surface pat out biscuit dough ½ inch thick. Cut into 10 triangles. Arrange triangles on chicken mixture. Bake 25 minutes or until biscuits are browned.
Makes 4 servings.

Chicken Puff Bravo

- ³/₄ lb. VELVEETA Mexican Pasteurized Process Cheese Spread with Jalapeño Pepper, cubed
- ½ cup sour cream
- ¼ teaspoon garlic salt
- 2 eggs, separated
- 2 10-oz. pkgs. frozen chopped spinach, thawed, well-drained
- 3 cups chopped cooked chicken
- ¼ cup chopped red or green pepper
- 1 4-oz. can sliced mushrooms, drained
- 2 8-oz. cans PILLSBURY Refrigerated Quick Crescent Dinner Rolls

In 3-quart saucepan, combine process cheese spread, sour cream and garlic salt; stir over low heat until process cheese spread is melted. Remove from heat. Beat egg yolks thoroughly; reserve 1 tablespoon for glaze. Gradually stir remaining egg yolks into cheese mixture. Cool. Beat egg whites until stiff peaks form; fold into cheese mixture. Add remaining ingredients except dough; mix lightly. Unroll one can dough; press onto bottom and sides of greased 12-inch ovenproof skillet, pressing perforations together to seal. Spread spinach mixture over dough. Unroll second can dough; separate into eight triangles. Loosely twist each triangle at pointed end. Arrange dough triangles on spinach mixture, pointed ends towards center. Seal outer edges to crust. Brush dough with reserved egg yolk. Bake at 375°, 35 to 40 minutes or until egg mixture is set.
8 servings.

Preparation time: 20 minutes
Baking time: 40 minutes

Variation: Substitute 2-oz. jar sliced pimento, drained, for red or green pepper.

Recipe Tip: Substitute 12-inch deep-dish pizza pan for skillet.

Creamed Chicken in Patty Shells

½ cup chopped onion
1 can (11 ounces) CAMPBELL'S® Condensed Cheddar Cheese Soup/Sauce or Nacho Cheese Soup/Dip
1 cup shredded Swiss cheese (4 ounces)
½ cup milk
3 tablespoons chopped pimento
1 tablespoon dry sherry
2 cans (5 ounces each) SWANSON® Premium Chunk White Chicken, drained
4 PEPPERIDGE FARM® Frozen Puff Pastry Shells, baked

To Microwave:
1. Place onion in 2-quart microwave-safe casserole. Cover with lid; microwave on HIGH 1½ minutes or until tender.
2. Stir in soup until smooth. Stir in cheese, milk, pimento and sherry. Gently fold in chicken. Cover; microwave on HIGH 5 minutes or until hot and bubbling, stirring once during cooking. Serve over patty shells.
Makes about 3 cups or 4 servings.

Creamy Turkey & Broccoli

1 package (6 ounces) stuffing mix,* plus ingredients to prepare mix
1 can (2.8 ounces) DURKEE French Fried Onions
1 package (10 ounces) frozen broccoli spears, thawed and drained
1 package (1⅛ ounces) DURKEE Cheese Sauce Mix
1¼ cups milk
½ cup sour cream
2 cups (10 ounces) cubed cooked turkey or chicken

Preheat oven to 350°. In medium saucepan, prepare stuffing mix according to package directions; stir in ½ can French Fried Onions. Spread stuffing over bottom of greased 9-inch round baking dish. Arrange broccoli spears over stuffing with flowerets around edge of dish. In medium saucepan, prepare cheese sauce mix according to package directions using 1¼ cups milk. Remove from heat; stir in sour cream and turkey. Pour turkey mixture over broccoli *stalks*. Bake, covered, at 350° for 30 minutes or until heated through. Sprinkle remaining onions over turkey; bake, uncovered, 5 minutes or until onions are golden brown.
Makes 4 to 6 servings.

Microwave Directions: In 9-inch microwave-safe dish, prepare stuffing mix according to package microwave directions; stir in ½ can onions. Arrange stuffing and broccoli spears in dish as above; set aside. In medium microwave-safe bowl, prepare cheese sauce mix according to package microwave directions using 1¼ cups milk. Add turkey and cook, covered, 5 to 6 minutes, stirring turkey halfway through cooking time. Stir in sour cream. Pour turkey mixture over broccoli *stalks*. Cook, covered, 8 to 10 minutes or until heated through. Rotate dish halfway through cooking time. Top turkey with remaining onions; cook, uncovered, 1 minute. Let stand 5 minutes.

*3 cups leftover stuffing may be substituted for stuffing mix. If stuffing is dry, stir in water, 1 tablespoon at a time, until moist but not wet.

Cheesy Chicken Tetrazzini

2 boneless, skinless whole chicken breasts, cut into 1-inch pieces (about 1½ pounds)
2 tablespoons butter or margarine
1½ cups sliced mushrooms
1 small red bell pepper, cut into julienne strips
½ cup sliced green onions
¼ cup all-purpose flour
1¾ cups chicken broth
1 cup light cream or half-and-half
2 tablespoons dry sherry
½ teaspoon salt
¼ teaspoon black pepper
¼ teaspoon dried thyme, crushed
1 package (8 ounces) tricolor corkscrew pasta, cooked, drained
¼ cup grated Parmesan cheese
2 tablespoons chopped parsley
1 cup (4 ounces) shredded NOKKELOST or JARLSBERG cheese

Brown chicken in melted butter in large skillet over medium-high heat. Add mushrooms; cook and stir until tender. Add red pepper and green onions; cook several minutes, stirring occasionally. Stir in flour and cook several minutes over medium heat until blended. Gradually blend in broth, cream and sherry. Cook until thickened and smooth, stirring constantly. Stir in salt, pepper and thyme. Toss with pasta, Parmesan cheese and parsley. Spoon into 1½-quart baking dish. Bake at 350°F 30 minutes. Top with shredded cheese. Bake until cheese is melted.
Makes 6 servings.

*Favorite recipe from **Norseland Foods, Inc.***

Sausage-Chicken Creole

1 can (14½ ounces) whole
    tomatoes, undrained and cut
    up
½ cup uncooked regular rice
½ cup hot water
2 teaspoons DURKEE RedHot
    Cayenne Pepper Sauce
¼ teaspoon DURKEE Garlic
    Powder
¼ teaspoon DURKEE Leaf
    Oregano
1 bag (16 ounces) frozen
    vegetable combination
    (broccoli, corn, red pepper),
    thawed and drained
1 can (2.8 ounces) DURKEE
    French Fried Onions
4 chicken thighs, skinned
½ pound link Italian sausage,
    quartered and cooked*
1 can (8 ounces) tomato sauce

Preheat oven to 375°. In 8×12-inch baking dish, combine tomatoes, uncooked rice, hot water, cayenne pepper sauce and seasonings. Bake, covered, at 375° for 10 minutes. Stir vegetables and ½ can French Fried Onions into rice mixture; top with chicken and cooked sausage. Pour tomato sauce over chicken and sausage. Bake, covered, at 375° for 40 minutes or until chicken is done. Top chicken with remaining onions; bake, uncovered, 3 minutes or until onions are golden brown.
Makes 4 servings.

*To cook sausage, simmer in water to cover until done. Or, place in microwave-safe dish and cook, covered, on HIGH 3 minutes or until done.

Southwestern-Style Popover

½ pound ground beef
½ cup chopped onion
1 8-ounce package
    PHILADELPHIA BRAND
    Cream Cheese, cubed
¼ cup water
½ teaspoon salt
½ teaspoon dried oregano
    leaves, crushed
¼ teaspoon ground cumin
¾ cup flour
½ teaspoon salt
¾ cup milk
2 eggs, beaten
1 tablespoon cornmeal
1 medium tomato, chopped

Brown meat; drain. Add onions; cook until tender. Add cream cheese and water; stir over low heat until cream cheese is melted. Stir in seasonings.

Combine flour, salt, milk and eggs; beat until smooth. Pour into greased 9-inch pie plate; sprinkle with cornmeal. Spoon meat mixture over batter. Bake at 400°, 35 minutes. Top with tomato.
6 to 8 servings.

Variation: Add 4-ounce can chopped green chilies, drained, to meat mixture.

Turkey Cassoulet

3-pound BUTTERBALL®
    Boneless Turkey
2 cans (15½ ounces each) Great
    Northern beans, drained
1 can (15 ounces) tomato sauce
    special
½ pound fully cooked Polish
    smoked sausage, cut into
    ½-inch pieces
6 slices cooked bacon, cut into
    1-inch pieces
¼ cup chopped onion
2 cloves garlic, minced
1 teaspoon fennel seed
¼ teaspoon ground black pepper

Roast turkey according to package directions. Combine remaining ingredients in 2-quart casserole. Cover and bake alongside turkey last hour of roasting time. Wrap turkey in foil and let stand 10 to 15 minutes. Remove netting from turkey; slice turkey. To serve, arrange turkey on bean mixture, spooning some beans over turkey slices.
Yield: 8 servings.

Turkey Tetrazzini

6 slices cooked BUTTERBALL®
    turkey (1 pound)
⅔ cup sliced onion
½ stick (¼ cup) butter or
    margarine
¼ cup all-purpose flour
1 teaspoon salt
¼ teaspoon ground white pepper
½ teaspoon poultry seasoning
¼ teaspoon dry mustard
2 cups milk
1 cup (4 ounces) shredded
    sharp Cheddar cheese,
    divided
2 tablespoons chopped pimiento
2 tablespoons sherry
1 can (4 ounces) sliced
    mushrooms, undrained
1 package (7 ounces) spaghetti,
    cooked, drained

Preheat oven to 400°F. Cook and stir onion in butter in medium saucepan over medium heat until tender. Blend in flour and seasonings. Remove from heat. Gradually add milk. Stirring constantly, cook over medium heat until mixture thickens. Add ⅔ cup cheese and pimiento, stirring until cheese melts. Add sherry and undrained mushrooms to cheese sauce. Place layer of spaghetti in 12×8-inch baking dish. Cover with layer of turkey and layer of sauce. Repeat the layers. Sprinkle remaining ⅓ cup cheese over top. Bake about 25 minutes.
Yield: 6 servings.

Note: Casserole may be assembled in advance and frozen. To serve, heat, covered, in 350°F oven for 1½ hours or until hot.

Jambalaya

2 cloves garlic, crushed
1 tablespoon BLUE BONNET®
   Margarine
1 (14½-ounce) can stewed
   tomatoes, undrained and
   coarsely chopped
1½ cups cubed cooked ham
1 (13¾-fluid ounce) can
   COLLEGE INN® Chicken
   Broth
1 cup uncooked rice
½ teaspoon dried thyme leaves
12 ounces shrimp, shelled and
   deveined

In skillet, over medium-high heat, cook garlic in margarine for 1 to 2 minutes. Add remaining ingredients except shrimp; heat to a boil; reduce heat. Cover; simmer 25 minutes. Add shrimp; cook, covered, 5 to 10 minutes or until liquid is absorbed.
Makes 6 servings.

Creole Chicken Jambalaya

¼ cup vegetable oil
2 medium onions, chopped
6 green onions, chopped
2 medium green peppers,
   chopped
1 (2½- to 3-pound) broiler-fryer
   chicken, cut into 8 pieces
½ pound cooked ham, cubed
½ pound smoked or Polish
   sausage, cut into ½-inch
   slices
1 can (16 ounces) tomatoes, cut
   into pieces, undrained
1 can (6 ounces) tomato paste
1 teaspoon salt
1¾ cups uncooked rice
½ cup water
¾ teaspoon TABASCO® pepper
   sauce

In large saucepot or Dutch oven heat oil. Add onions, green onions and peppers; cook 10 minutes or until tender. Add chicken and brown on all sides, about 10 minutes. Add ham, sausage, tomatoes, tomato paste and salt. Cover; simmer 10 minutes; stir in rice. Add water. Cover. Simmer 1 hour or until chicken is done; stir frequently. Add additional water if rice begins to stick to bottom of pan. Before serving, stir in Tabasco® sauce.
Makes 8 servings.

Tuna-Pasta Casserole

1 cup frozen peas
1 can (10¾ ounces)
   CAMPBELL'S® Condensed
   Cream of Celery Soup
½ cup milk
½ cup shredded Swiss cheese
   (2 ounces)
1 can (6½ ounces) tuna, drained
   and flaked
2 cups cooked corkscrew or
   other macaroni (1 cup
   uncooked)
2 hard-cooked eggs, chopped
½ cup crushed potato chips

To Microwave:

1. Place peas in 1½-quart microwave-safe casserole. Cover with lid; microwave on HIGH 4 minutes or until tender. Drain; set aside.

2. In same casserole, stir soup until smooth; stir in milk and cheese. Fold tuna, macaroni, eggs and peas into soup mixture. Cover; microwave on HIGH 7 minutes or until hot and bubbling, stirring once during cooking. Let stand, covered, 5 minutes.

3. Sprinkle potato chips over casserole.
Makes 4 servings.

Clam Noodle Florentine

½ (1-pound) package
   CREAMETTE® Egg Noodles,
   cooked and drained
⅓ cup chopped onion
¼ cup margarine or butter
¼ cup unsifted flour
½ teaspoon salt
¼ teaspoon pepper
2 cups (1 pint) BORDEN® or
   MEADOW GOLD® Half-and-
   Half or Milk
2 (6½-ounce) cans SNOW'S® or
   DOXSEE® Minced or
   Chopped Clams, drained,
   reserving liquid
1 (10-ounce) package frozen
   chopped spinach, thawed
   and well drained
¼ cup grated Parmesan cheese
½ cup buttered bread crumbs

Preheat oven to 350°. In large saucepan, cook onion in margarine until tender. Stir in flour, salt and pepper. Gradually stir in half-and-half and reserved clam liquid. Over medium heat, cook and stir until thickened and bubbly, about 8 minutes. Remove from heat; add noodles, clams, spinach and cheese. Mix well. Turn into greased 2-quart baking dish. Top with crumbs. Bake 25 to 30 minutes or until hot. Refrigerate leftovers.
Makes 6 to 8 servings.

Microwave: In 3-quart round baking dish, combine onion and margarine. Microwave on full power (high) 2 to 3 minutes or until onion is tender. Stir in flour, salt and pepper. Gradually stir in half-and-half and reserved clam liquid. Microwave on full power (high) 5 to 6 minutes, stirring after each minute or until thickened. Add noodles, clams, spinach and cheese; mix well. Cover tightly; microwave on ⅔ power (medium-high) 6 to 7 minutes. Top with crumbs; microwave uncovered on ⅔ power (medium-high) 6 to 8 minutes. Let stand 5 minutes.
Makes 6 to 8 servings.

Layered Seafood Quiche

- **³/₄ cup finely chopped onion**
- **1 can (12½ ounces) or 2 cans (6½ ounces) STARKIST® Solid White or Solid Light Tuna in Springwater, drained, flaked**
- **2 cups (8 ounces) shredded Cheddar cheese**
- **3 eggs, lightly beaten**
- **1 can (12 ounces) PET® Evaporated or PET® Light Evaporated Skimmed Milk**
- **½ teaspoon salt**

Cook onion in medium saucepan, covered, over very low heat until soft, adding water if necessary to prevent scorching. Line bottom of 9-inch pie pan with tuna. Sprinkle with cooked onion; top with cheese. Combine eggs, milk and salt in small bowl; mix well. Pour over cheese. Bake in preheated 350°F oven 30 minutes or until set. Let stand at least 10 minutes before cutting. Garnish as desired.
Makes 8 servings.

So-Easy Fish Divan

- **1 package (1⅛ ounces) DURKEE Cheese Sauce Mix**
- **1⅓ cups milk**
- **1 bag (16 ounces) frozen vegetable combination (brussels sprouts, carrots, cauliflower), thawed and drained**
- **1 can (2.8 ounces) DURKEE French Fried Onions**
- **1 pound unbreaded fish fillets, thawed if frozen**
- **½ cup (2 ounces) shredded Cheddar cheese**

Preheat oven to 375°. In small saucepan, prepare cheese sauce mix according to package directions using 1⅓ cups milk. In 8×12-inch baking dish, combine vegetables and *½ can* French Fried Onions; top with fish fillets. Pour cheese sauce over fish and vegetables. Bake, covered, at 375° for 25 minutes or until fish flakes easily with fork. Top fish with Cheddar cheese and remaining onions; bake, uncovered, 3 minutes or until onions are golden brown.
Makes 3 to 4 servings.

Tuna-Swiss Pie

- **2 cups cooked unsalted regular rice (²/₃ cup uncooked)**
- **1 tablespoon butter or margarine**
- **¼ teaspoon DURKEE Garlic Powder**
- **3 eggs**
- **1 can (2.8 ounces) DURKEE French Fried Onions**
- **1 cup (4 ounces) shredded Swiss cheese**
- **1 can (9¼ ounces) water-packed tuna, drained and flaked**
- **1 cup milk**
- **¼ teaspoon salt**
- **¼ teaspoon DURKEE Ground Black Pepper**

Preheat oven to 400°. To hot rice in saucepan, add butter, garlic powder and *1 slightly beaten egg;* mix thoroughly. Spoon rice mixture into *ungreased* 9-inch pie plate. Press rice mixture firmly across bottom and up side of pie plate to form a crust. Layer *½ can* French Fried Onions, *½ cup* cheese and the tuna evenly over rice crust. In small bowl, combine milk, remaining eggs and the seasonings; pour over tuna filling. Bake, uncovered, at 400° for 30 to 35 minutes or until center is set. Top with remaining cheese and onions; bake, uncovered, 1 to 3 minutes or until onions are golden brown.
Makes 4 to 6 servings.

Herb-Baked Fish & Rice

- **1½ cups hot HERB-OX Chicken Bouillon**
- **½ cup uncooked regular rice**
- **¼ teaspoon DURKEE Italian Seasoning**
- **¼ teaspoon DURKEE Garlic Powder**
- **1 package (10 ounces) frozen chopped broccoli, thawed and drained**
- **1 can (2.8 ounces) DURKEE French Fried Onions**
- **1 tablespoon grated Parmesan cheese**
- **1 pound unbreaded fish fillets, thawed if frozen**
- **DURKEE Paprika (optional)**
- **½ cup (2 ounces) shredded Cheddar cheese**

Preheat oven to 375°. In 8×12-inch baking dish, combine hot bouillon, uncooked rice and seasonings. Bake, covered, at 375° for 10 minutes. Top with broccoli, *½ can* French Fried Onions and the Parmesan cheese. Place fish fillets diagonally down center of dish; sprinkle fish lightly with paprika. Bake, covered, at 375° for 20 to 25 minutes or until fish flakes easily with fork. Stir rice. Top fish with Cheddar cheese and remaining onions; bake, uncovered, 3 minutes or until onions are golden brown.
Makes 3 to 4 servings.

Microwave Directions: In 8×12-inch microwave-safe dish, prepare rice mixture as above, except reduce bouillon to 1¼ cups. Cook, covered, on HIGH 5 minutes, stirring halfway through cooking time. Stir in broccoli, *½ can* onions and the Parmesan cheese. Arrange fish fillets in single layer on top of rice mixture; sprinkle fish lightly with paprika. Cook, covered, on MEDIUM (50–60%) 18 to 20 minutes or until fish flakes easily with fork and rice is done. Rotate dish halfway through cooking time. Top fish with Cheddar cheese and remaining onions; cook, uncovered, on HIGH 1 minute or until cheese melts. Let stand 5 minutes.

Superb Fillet of Sole & Vegetables

1 can (10³/₄ ounces) condensed cream of celery soup
¹/₂ cup milk
1 cup (4 ounces) shredded Swiss cheese
¹/₂ teaspoon DURKEE Sweet Basil
¹/₄ teaspoon DURKEE Seasoned Salt
¹/₄ teaspoon DURKEE Ground Black Pepper
1 package (10 ounces) frozen baby carrots, thawed and drained
1 package (10 ounces) frozen asparagus cuts, thawed and drained
1 can (2.8 ounces) DURKEE French Fried Onions
1 pound unbreaded sole fillets, thawed if frozen

Preheat oven to 375°. In small bowl, combine soup, milk, ¹/₂ cup cheese and the seasonings; set aside. In 8×12-inch baking dish, combine carrots, asparagus and ¹/₂ can French Fried Onions. Roll up fish fillets. (If fillets are wide, fold in half lengthwise before rolling.) Place fish rolls upright along center of vegetable mixture. Pour soup mixture over fish and vegetables. Bake, covered, at 375° for 30 minutes or until fish flakes easily with fork. Stir vegetables; top fish with remaining cheese and onions. Bake, uncovered, 3 minutes or until onions are golden brown.
Makes 3 to 4 servings.

Microwave Directions: Prepare soup mixture as above; set aside. In 8×12-inch microwave-safe dish, combine vegetables as above. Roll up fish fillets as above; place upright around edges of dish. Pour soup mixture over fish and vegetables. Cook, covered, on HIGH 14 to 16 minutes or until fish flakes easily with fork. Stir vegetables and rotate dish halfway through cooking time. Top fish with remaining cheese and onions; cook, uncovered, 1 minute or until cheese melts. Let stand 5 minutes.

All-in-One Tuna Casserole

1 envelope LIPTON® Golden Onion Recipe Soup Mix
1¹/₂ cups milk
1 package (10 ounces) frozen peas and carrots, thawed
1 package (8 ounces) medium egg noodles, cooked and drained
1 can (6¹/₂ ounces) tuna, drained and flaked
¹/₂ cup shredded Cheddar cheese (about 2 ounces)

Preheat oven to 350°.
In large bowl, blend golden onion recipe soup mix with milk; stir in peas and carrots, cooked noodles and tuna. Turn into greased 2-quart oblong baking dish, then top with cheese. Bake 20 minutes or until bubbling.
Makes about 4 servings.

Hasty Shore Dinner

1 cup small shell pasta, cooked in unsalted water and drained
¹/₂ cup mayonnaise
¹/₂ cup milk
1 can (10³/₄ ounces) condensed cream of celery soup
1 package (8 ounces) frozen imitation crabmeat,* thawed, drained and cut into chunks
1 can (4 ounces) shrimp, drained
1 cup (4 ounces) shredded Swiss cheese
1 can (2.8 ounces) DURKEE French Fried Onions
¹/₂ teaspoon DURKEE Dill Weed
¹/₄ teaspoon DURKEE Seasoned Salt

Preheat oven to 350°. Return hot pasta to saucepan. Stir in mayonnaise, milk, soup, crabmeat, shrimp, ¹/₂ cup cheese, ¹/₂ can French Fried Onions and the seasonings; mix well. Pour into 1¹/₂-quart casserole. Bake, covered, at 350° for 35 minutes or until heated through. Top with remaining cheese and onions; bake, uncovered, 5 minutes or until onions are golden brown.
Makes 4 to 6 servings.

Microwave Directions: Prepare pasta mixture as above; pour into 1¹/₂-quart microwave-safe casserole. Cook, covered, on HIGH 12 to 15 minutes or until heated through. Stir casserole halfway through cooking time. Top with remaining cheese and onions; cook, uncovered, 1 minute or until cheese melts. Let stand 5 minutes.

*1 can (6 ounces) crabmeat, drained, may be substituted for imitation crabmeat.

Cheese-Mushroom Strata

4 eggs, lightly beaten
1 (13³/₄-fluid ounce) can COLLEGE INN® Chicken or Beef Broth
¹/₂ cup dairy sour cream
2 teaspoons GREY POUPON® Dijon Mustard
8 slices white bread, cubed (about 4 cups cubes)
2 cups shredded Cheddar cheese (8 ounces)
1 (4¹/₂-ounce) can sliced mushrooms, drained

In large bowl, beat together eggs, broth, sour cream and mustard. Stir in bread cubes, cheese and mushrooms. Pour into greased 2-quart oval or 12×8×2-inch baking dish. Cover; refrigerate overnight.
Uncover; bake at 350°F for 50 to 60 minutes or until set. Let stand 5 to 10 minutes before serving. Garnish as desired.
Makes 6 to 8 servings.

Broccoli-Cheese Pie

1 can (11 ounces) CAMPBELL'S® Condensed Cheddar Cheese Soup/Sauce
1½ cups cooked rice
4 eggs
1 package (10 ounces) frozen chopped broccoli, cooked and drained
1 cup ricotta cheese or creamed cottage cheese
1 sweet red pepper, cut into matchstick-thin strips
¼ teaspoon black pepper

To Microwave:

1. In medium bowl, stir ⅓ cup of the soup until smooth; stir in rice and 1 of the eggs. Press mixture onto bottom and side of 9-inch microwave-safe pie plate, forming a shell. Microwave, uncovered, on HIGH 2 minutes or until nearly set. Let stand, uncovered, while preparing filling.
2. In large bowl, stir remaining soup until smooth; stir in remaining 3 eggs, broccoli, ricotta, sweet red pepper and black pepper. Spoon into rice shell.
3. Microwave, uncovered, at 50% power 22 minutes or until center is set, rotating dish 3 times during cooking. Let stand, uncovered, 10 minutes.
Makes 6 servings.

Eggplant Parmesan

1 egg
2 tablespoons milk
1 cup Italian-seasoned fine dry bread crumbs
1 medium eggplant, peeled and cut into ¼-inch slices (1 pound)
1 jar (15½ ounces) PREGO® Spaghetti Sauce
2 cups shredded mozzarella cheese (8 ounces)
2 tablespoons grated Parmesan cheese

To Microwave:

1. In pie plate, beat together egg and milk. Place bread crumbs in another pie plate. Dip eggplant slices in egg mixture, then in crumbs to coat well.
2. Arrange ½ of the eggplant slices on a 10-inch microwave-safe plate lined with paper towels. Microwave, uncovered, on HIGH 4 minutes or until tender, rearranging slices once during cooking. Repeat with remaining eggplant.
3. Spread ¼ cup of the spaghetti sauce in 8- by 8-inch microwave-safe baking dish. Layer ½ of the eggplant, ½ of the mozzarella and ½ of the remaining spaghetti sauce in dish; repeat layers. Sprinkle with Parmesan cheese.
4. Cover with vented plastic wrap; microwave on HIGH 4 minutes or until hot. Rotate dish. Reduce power to 50%. Microwave, covered, 10 minutes or until hot and bubbling, rotating dish once during cooking. Let stand, covered, 5 minutes.
Makes 4 servings.

Smoky Macaroni and Cheese

1 can (10¾ ounces) CAMPBELL'S® Condensed Cream of Celery Soup
¾ cup milk
¼ teaspoon white pepper
¾ cup shredded mozzarella cheese (3 ounces)
½ cup shredded smoked mozzarella or smoked gouda cheese (2 ounces)
½ cup shredded white Cheddar cheese (2 ounces)
8 ounces ziti, cooked and drained (6 cups cooked)
2 tablespoons grated Parmesan cheese
2 tablespoons buttered bread crumbs

1. In 3-quart saucepan over medium heat, stir soup. Add milk, pepper, mozzarella, smoked mozzarella and Cheddar cheese; heat until cheeses melt, stirring often. Remove from heat. Add cooked ziti; toss to coat.
2. Spoon ziti mixture into 1½-quart casserole. Sprinkle top with Parmesan cheese. Bake at 350°F. 25 minutes. Sprinkle with bread crumbs. Bake 5 minutes more.
Makes 6 cups or 6 main-dish servings.

Per serving: 329 calories, 14 g protein, 14 g fat, 36 g carbohydrate, 601 mg sodium, 36 mg cholesterol.

Tortilla-Vegetable Bake

2 cups shredded carrots
1 cup shredded, peeled potato
½ teaspoon dried oregano leaves, crushed
½ teaspoon ground cumin
1½ cups V8® Vegetable Juice
1½ cups chopped zucchini
1 cup fresh or frozen whole kernel corn
1 can (4 ounces) chopped chilies
4 (6-inch) corn tortillas
2 cups shredded Monterey Jack cheese, divided (8 ounces)

1. Spray 10-inch nonstick skillet with vegetable cooking spray. Over medium heat, cook carrots and potato with oregano and cumin until vegetables are lightly browned, stirring occasionally.
2. Stir in V8 juice, zucchini, corn and chilies; heat through.
3. In 10- by 6-inch baking dish, arrange 2 corn tortillas; top with ½ of the vegetable mixture and ½ of the cheese. Repeat layers.
4. Bake at 350°F., uncovered, 25 minutes or until hot.
Makes 6 main-dish servings.

Per serving: 267 calories, 13 g protein, 13 g fat, 27 g carbohydrate, 580 mg sodium, 33 mg cholesterol.

PASTA

What can be more heartwarming than a steaming dish of pasta? Tangy tomato sauces enhanced by olives or capers, robust sausage dishes, seafood sauces with a Mediterranean ambience, or distinctly American creations— serve any of these pasta specialties for a friendly, convivial meal.

Vegetables Fromage

2 cups julienne-cut carrots
2 cups julienne-cut zucchini
1 medium green pepper, cut into strips
1 garlic clove, minced
3 tablespoons PARKAY Margarine
½ lb. VELVEETA Pasteurized Process Cheese Spread, cubed
¼ cup half and half
1 teaspoon dried basil leaves, crushed
1½ cups (6 ozs.) bow noodles, cooked, drained

In large skillet, stir-fry carrots, zucchini, peppers and garlic in margarine until crisp-tender. Reduce heat to low. Add process cheese spread, half and half and basil; stir until process cheese spread is melted. Add noodles; mix lightly. Heat thoroughly, stirring occasionally.
4 to 6 servings.

Preparation time: 20 minutes
Cooking time: 10 minutes

Variations: Substitute milk for half and half.
Substitute corkscrew noodles for bow noodles.
Substitute 2 tablespoons chopped fresh basil leaves for dried basil.
Microwave: In 2-quart microwave-safe bowl, microwave carrots, zucchini, peppers, garlic and margarine on High 3 to 4 minutes or until vegetables are crisp-tender. Add process cheese spread, half and half and basil. Microwave on High 2 minutes or until process cheese spread is melted. Add noodles; mix lightly.

Tortellini in Cream Sauce

1 teaspoon olive or vegetable oil
2 cloves garlic, minced
½ cup chopped sweet red pepper
¼ cup chopped onion
1 can (10¾ ounces) CAMPBELL'S® Condensed Cream of Mushroom Soup
½ cup half-and-half or milk
¼ cup Chablis or other dry white wine
¼ teaspoon dried tarragon leaves, crushed
8 ounces cheese tortellini, cooked and drained
½ cup crumbled feta or grated Parmesan cheese
¼ cup sliced green onions

To Microwave:
1. In 2-quart microwave-safe casserole, combine oil, garlic, red pepper and chopped onion. Cover with lid; microwave on HIGH 2 minutes or until vegetables are tender, stirring once during cooking.
2. Stir in soup until smooth. Stir in half-and-half, wine and tarragon. Cover; microwave on HIGH 5 minutes or until hot and bubbling, stirring once during cooking. Let stand, covered, 5 minutes.
3. Toss with hot tortellini. Sprinkle with cheese and green onions.
Makes 4 servings.

Lasagna Roll-Ups

1 pound Italian sausage, casings removed
1 cup chopped onion
2 cloves garlic, minced
1 tablespoon dried basil leaves, crushed
1 can (10³/4 ounces) CAMPBELL'S® Condensed Tomato Soup
1 cup water
1 can (6 ounces) tomato paste
1¹/2 pounds ricotta cheese
1 cup shredded mozzarella cheese (4 ounces)
2 tablespoons chopped fresh parsley
¹/4 teaspoon ground nutmeg
8 lasagna noodles, cooked and drained
¹/4 cup grated Parmesan cheese

1. To make sauce: In 4-quart Dutch oven over medium heat, cook sausage, onion, garlic and basil until meat is browned and onion is tender, stirring to break up meat. Pour off fat. Stir in soup, water and tomato paste. Heat to boiling; reduce heat to low. Simmer, uncovered, 30 minutes or until desired consistency, stirring occasionally.
2. To make filling: In large bowl, combine ricotta cheese, mozzarella cheese, parsley and nutmeg; set aside.
3. Pat drained noodles dry with paper towels. On each noodle, spread about ¹/3 cup filling. Fold over 1 inch and roll up each noodle jelly-roll fashion.
4. Spread 2 cups of the meat sauce in 13- by 9-inch baking dish. Place rolls, seam side down, in dish. Spoon remaining sauce over rolls. Sprinkle with Parmesan cheese. Bake at 350°F. 45 minutes or until hot. Let stand 5 minutes before serving.
Makes 8 servings.

Pasta with Vegetables

1 teaspoon olive or vegetable oil
2 medium zucchini, cut into 1¹/2-inch-long sticks
1 sweet red pepper, cut into ¹/2-inch squares
¹/2 cup chopped onion
2 cloves garlic, minced
1 can (11 ounces) CAMPBELL'S® Condensed Zesty Tomato Soup/Sauce
¹/2 cup water
¹/4 cup Chablis or other dry white wine
8 ounces thin spaghetti or other pasta, cooked and drained
Grated Parmesan cheese for garnish

To Microwave:
1. In 2-quart microwave-safe casserole, combine oil, zucchini, red pepper, onion and garlic. Cover with lid; microwave on HIGH 4 minutes or until vegetables are tender, stirring once during cooking.
2. Stir in soup, water and wine. Cover; microwave on HIGH 7 minutes or until hot and bubbling, stirring once during cooking. Let stand, covered, 5 minutes. Serve over hot pasta. Garnish with Parmesan cheese.
Makes 8 servings.

Pizzaiola Sauce

1 can (28 ounces) Italian plum tomatoes
2 cloves garlic
1 tablespoon olive oil
³/4 teaspoon dried marjoram, crumbled
¹/2 teaspoon salt
¹/8 teaspoon pepper
2 tablespoons minced fresh parsley
¹/2 pound spaghetti, cooked
¹/2 cup freshly grated Parmesan cheese, if desired

Press tomatoes and their liquid through sieve into bowl; discard seeds. Cut garlic cloves in half. Heat oil in 2-quart noncorrosive saucepan over medium heat. Add garlic; cook and stir until garlic is golden but not brown, 2 to 3 minutes. Remove and discard garlic. Add sieved tomatoes to oil; stir in marjoram, salt and pepper. Heat to boiling; reduce heat to medium-low. Cook, uncovered, stirring frequently, until sauce is reduced and measures 2 cups, 30 to 40 minutes. Stir in parsley. Toss sauce with spaghetti. Serve immediately with Parmesan cheese to sprinkle.
Makes 2 to 3 servings.

Ham Pasta Primavera

3 tablespoons unsalted margarine or butter, divided
1 cup pea pods
¹/2 cup shredded carrots
3 green onions, sliced
1 small red pepper, cut into strips
³/4 cup evaporated skim milk
3 cups (12 ounces) ARMOUR® Lower Salt Ham cut into small cubes
10 ounces uncooked spaghetti, cooked according to package directions omitting salt and drained

Melt 1 tablespoon of the margarine in medium skillet over medium heat. Add vegetables; sauté until tender. Add remaining 2 tablespoons margarine, milk and ham. Cook over medium-high heat about 3 to 4 minutes, or until mixture thickens slightly. Serve over warm spaghetti. Garnish with fresh basil, cilantro or freshly ground pepper, if desired.
Makes 4 to 6 servings.

Nutrition Information Per Serving: 347 calories, 19 g protein, 9.7 g fat, 43.5 g carbohydrates, 29.1 mg cholesterol, 521 mg sodium.

Creamy Fettucini Alfredo

1 8-ounce package
  PHILADELPHIA BRAND
  Cream Cheese, cubed
3/4 cup (3 ounces) KRAFT Grated
  Parmesan Cheese
1/2 cup PARKAY Margarine
1/2 cup milk
8 ounces fettucini, cooked,
  drained

In large saucepan, combine cream cheese, parmesan cheese, margarine and milk; stir over low heat until smooth. Add fettucini; toss lightly.
4 servings.

Smoked Sausage Stuffed Pasta Shells

3/4 pound ECKRICH® Smoked
  Sausage, chopped fine
18 large macaroni shells
1 pound ricotta cheese
1 egg, beaten
1 1/2 cups (6 ounces) shredded
  mozzarella cheese
1/2 cup chopped fresh parsley
1/4 cup grated Parmesan cheese
1/2 teaspoon dried basil leaves
1/2 teaspoon dried oregano leaves
1 jar (15 ounces) prepared
  spaghetti sauce with
  mushrooms and onions
1/3 cup water

Prepare shells according to package directions. Preheat oven to 375°F. Combine ricotta cheese and egg in medium bowl. Add mozzarella, parsley, Parmesan cheese, basil and oregano. Stir in sausage. Combine spaghetti sauce and water in small bowl. Put 3/4 cup of the sauce in bottom of 13×9×2-inch baking pan. Fill shells with sausage-cheese mixture and place in pan. Pour remaining sauce over top. Bake 35 minutes or until stuffed shells are heated through and cheese melts.
Makes 9 servings (2 shells each).

Fettuccine Alfredo

3/4 pound uncooked fettuccine
  Boiling salted water
6 tablespoons unsalted butter
2/3 cup whipping cream
1/2 teaspoon salt
  Large pinch ground white
  pepper
  Large pinch ground nutmeg
1 cup freshly grated Parmesan
  cheese (about 3 ounces)
2 tablespoons chopped fresh
  parsley

1. Cook fettuccine in large pot of boiling salted water just until al dente, 6 to 8 minutes; drain well. Return to dry pot.
2. While fettuccine is cooking, place butter and cream in 10-inch heavy skillet over medium-low heat. Cook, stirring constantly, until blended and mixture bubbles for 2 minutes. Stir in salt, pepper and nutmeg. Remove from heat. Gradually stir in Parmesan cheese until thoroughly blended and fairly smooth. Return skillet briefly to heat if necessary to completely blend cheese, but don't let sauce bubble or cheese will become lumpy and tough.
3. Pour sauce over fettuccine in pot. Place over low heat. Stir and toss with 2 forks until sauce is slightly thickened and fettuccine evenly coated, 2 to 3 minutes. Sprinkle with parsley. Serve immediately.
Makes 4 servings.

Linguine with Red Seafood Sauce

3 tablespoons olive or vegetable
  oil
1 large onion, finely chopped
2 cloves garlic, minced
1/2 cup dry white wine
2 cups (16 ounces) canned or
  homemade meatless
  spaghetti sauce
2 tablespoons chopped parsley
1 bay leaf, crumbled
2 teaspoons dried basil leaves
3/4 teaspoon TABASCO® pepper
  sauce
1/2 teaspoon salt
3/4 pound medium shrimp,
  peeled, deveined
3/4 pound sea scallops, quartered
  or bay scallops
12 ounces linguine, cooked,
  drained

In large heavy saucepot or Dutch oven heat oil; cook onion and garlic 5 minutes or until golden. Add wine; simmer until reduced by half. Stir in spaghetti sauce, parsley, bay leaf, basil, Tabasco® sauce and salt. Cover; simmer 10 minutes. Add shrimp and scallops. Cover; simmer 4 to 5 minutes or until seafood is done. Serve with linguine.
Makes 6 servings.

Microwave Directions: In 3-quart microwave-safe casserole place oil, onion, garlic and white wine. Cook uncovered on High 5 to 7 minutes or until onion is tender. Stir in spaghetti sauce, parsley, bay leaf, basil, Tabasco® sauce and salt. Cook uncovered on High 5 to 8 minutes or until bubbly. Stir in shrimp and scallops. Cook uncovered on High 7 to 9 minutes or until seafood is done. Serve with linguine.

Savory Cheese Tortellini

**½ lb. VELVEETA Pasteurized
   Process Cheese Spread,
   cubed
¼ cup milk
¼ teaspoon ground nutmeg
1 7-oz. pkg. cheese-filled
   tortellini, cooked, drained**

Combine process cheese spread, milk and nutmeg in saucepan. Stir over low heat until process cheese spread is melted. Add tortellini; mix lightly. Garnish with tomato rose and fresh basil, if desired.
4 servings.

Preparation time: 10 minutes
Cooking time: 10 minutes

Microwave: Combine process cheese spread, milk and nutmeg in 1-quart microwave-safe bowl. Microwave on High 2½ to 4½ minutes or until process cheese spread is melted, stirring after 2 minutes. Add tortellini; mix lightly. Garnish with tomato rose and fresh basil, if desired.

Pesto

**¼ cup plus 1 tablespoon olive oil
2 tablespoons pine nuts
1 cup tightly packed, rinsed,
   drained, stemmed fresh
   basil leaves (do not use
   dried basil)
2 medium cloves garlic
¼ teaspoon salt
¼ cup freshly grated Parmesan
   cheese
1½ tablespoons freshly grated
   Romano cheese**

1. Heat 1 tablespoon of the oil in small saucepan or skillet over medium-low heat. Add pine nuts; saute, stirring and shaking pan constantly, until nuts are light brown, 30 to 45 seconds. Transfer nuts immediately to paper-towel-lined plate to drain.

2. Combine pine nuts, basil leaves, garlic, salt and remaining ¼ cup oil in food processor or blender container. Process until mixture is evenly blended and pieces are very finely chopped.
3. Transfer basil mixture to small bowl. Stir in Parmesan and Romano cheeses. Pesto can be refrigerated, covered with thin layer of olive oil, up to 1 week, or pesto can be frozen for several months. Thaw and bring to room temperature before using.
Makes about ¾ cup pesto.

Serving Suggestions: Toss pesto with hot cooked buttered fettuccine or linguine; this recipe will dress ½ to ¾ pound pasta. Stir small amount of pesto into broth-based vegetable or meat soups. Whisk small amount of pesto into vinaigrette for tossed salads. Mix pesto with softened butter to be used on steamed vegetables, poached fish or omelets.

Santa Fe Pasta

**¾ lb. VELVEETA Pasteurized
   Process Cheese Spread
2 tablespoons milk
1 8¾-oz. can whole kernel corn,
   drained
1 8-oz. can kidney beans,
   drained
2 cups (8 ozs.) mostaccioli
   noodles, cooked, drained
1 4-oz. can chopped green
   chilies, drained
½ teaspoon chili powder
1 cup corn chips**

Cube ½ lb. process cheese spread. Combine with milk in saucepan; stir over low heat until process cheese spread is melted. Add corn, beans, noodles, chilies and chili powder; mix lightly. Spoon mixture into 1½-quart casserole. Bake at 350°, 20 minutes. Top with chips and remaining process cheese spread, sliced. Continue baking until process cheese spread begins to melt.
6 servings.

Preparation time: 15 minutes
Baking time: 25 minutes

Microwave: Cube ½ lb. process cheese spread. Combine with milk in 2-quart microwave-safe bowl. Microwave on High 2 to 3 minutes or until process cheese spread is melted, stirring after 2 minutes. Stir in corn, beans, noodles, chilies and chili powder; microwave on High 5 minutes, stirring every 2 minutes. Top with chips and remaining process cheese spread, sliced. Microwave on High 2 minutes or until process cheese spread begins to melt.

Fettuccine with Roasted Red Pepper Sauce

**3 large red peppers*
½ cup whipping or heavy cream
¼ cup WISH-BONE® Italian
   Dressing
2 tablespoons chopped fresh
   basil leaves**
   **Salt and pepper to taste
1 package (12 ounces)
   fettuccine or medium egg
   noodles, cooked and
   drained
   Grated Parmesan cheese**

In large aluminum-foil-lined baking pan or on broiler rack, place peppers. Broil, turning occasionally, 20 minutes or until peppers turn almost completely black. Immediately place in paper bag; close bag and let cool about 30 minutes. Under cold running water, peel off skin, then remove stems and seeds.

In food processor or blender, process prepared peppers, cream, Italian dressing, basil, salt and pepper until blended. Toss with hot fettuccine and serve with cheese.
Makes about 4 main-dish servings.
   ***Substitution:** Use 2 cups drained roasted red peppers.
   ****Substitution:** Use 2 teaspoons dried basil leaves.
   Note: Also terrific with Wish-Bone® Robusto Italian, Blended Italian, Herbal Italian, Lite Italian or Classic Dijon Vinaigrette Dressing.

Shrimp Milano

1 lb. frozen cleaned shrimp, cooked, drained
2 cups mushroom slices
1 cup green or red pepper strips
1 garlic clove, minced
¼ cup PARKAY Margarine
¾ lb. VELVEETA Pasteurized Process Cheese Spread, cubed
¾ cup whipping cream
½ teaspoon dill weed
⅓ cup (1½ ozs.) KRAFT 100% Grated Parmesan Cheese
8 ozs. fettucini, cooked, drained

In large skillet, saute shrimp, vegetables and garlic in margarine. Reduce heat to low. Add process cheese spread, cream and dill. Stir until process cheese spread is melted. Stir in parmesan cheese. Add fettucini; toss lightly.
4 to 6 servings.

Preparation time: 20 minutes
Cooking time: 15 minutes

Spinach and Noodles Parmesan

½ cup chopped onion
1 package (10 ounces) frozen chopped spinach
1 can (10¾ ounces) CAMPBELL'S® Condensed Cream of Celery Soup
½ cup sour cream
½ cup grated Parmesan cheese
⅛ teaspoon black pepper
⅛ teaspoon ground nutmeg Generous dash ground red pepper (cayenne)
2 cups cooked wide egg noodles (6 ounces uncooked)

To Microwave:
1. Place onion in 2-quart microwave-safe casserole. Cover with lid; microwave on HIGH 3 minutes or until tender, stirring once during cooking.
2. Add spinach. Cover; microwave on HIGH 5 minutes or until spinach is thawed, stirring twice during cooking. Stir in soup; stir in sour cream, cheese, black pepper, nutmeg and red pepper.
3. Cover; microwave at 50% power 8 minutes or until hot, stirring once during cooking. Add hot noodles; toss to coat.
Makes about 5 cups or 8 servings.

Tuna Lasagna

½ cup chopped onion
1 garlic clove, minced
1 tablespoon oil
2 6½-oz. cans tuna, drained, flaked
1 10¾-oz. can condensed cream of celery soup
½ cup milk
½ teaspoon dried oregano leaves, crushed
¼ teaspoon pepper
8 ozs. lasagna noodles, cooked, drained
1 6-oz. pkg. 100% Natural KRAFT Low Moisture Part-Skim Mozzarella Cheese Slices
½ lb. VELVEETA Pasteurized Process Cheese Spread, sliced
¼ cup (1 oz.) KRAFT 100% Grated Parmesan Cheese

Saute onions and garlic in oil. Stir in tuna, soup, milk and seasonings. In 12×8-inch baking dish, layer half of noodles, mozzarella cheese, tuna mixture, process cheese spread and parmesan cheese; repeat layers. Bake at 350°, 30 minutes. Let stand 10 minutes before serving.
6 to 8 servings.

Preparation time: 20 minutes
Baking time: 30 minutes plus standing

Seafood over Angel Hair Pasta

¼ cup WISH-BONE® Italian Dressing
¼ cup chopped shallots or onions
1 cup thinly sliced carrots
1 cup thinly sliced snow peas (about 4 ounces)
1 cup chicken broth
¼ cup sherry
8 mussels, well scrubbed
½ pound sea scallops
½ pound uncooked medium shrimp, cleaned (keep tails on)
¼ cup whipping or heavy cream
2 tablespoons all-purpose flour Salt and pepper to taste
8 ounces angel hair pasta or capellini, cooked and drained

In 12-inch skillet, heat Italian dressing and cook shallots over medium-high heat 2 minutes. Add carrots and snow peas and cook 2 minutes. Add broth, then sherry. Bring to a boil, then add mussels, scallops and shrimp. Simmer uncovered 3 minutes or until seafood is done and mussel shells open. (Discard any unopened shells). Stir in cream blended with flour and cook over medium heat, stirring occasionally, 2 minutes or until sauce is slightly thickened. Stir in salt and pepper. Serve over hot angel hair pasta and, if desired, with freshly ground pepper.
Makes about 4 main-dish servings.
Note: Also terrific with Wish-Bone® Robusto Italian, Italian & Cheese, Lite Italian, Herbal Italian, Blended Italian, Classic Dijon Vinaigrette or Lite Classic Dijon Vinaigrette Dressing.

Creamy Tortellini Primavera

3 tablespoons olive or vegetable oil
1 medium clove garlic, finely chopped
1 envelope LIPTON® Vegetable Recipe Soup Mix
2 cups (1 pint) light cream or half and half
1 pound egg or spinach tortellini, cooked and drained
1/4 cup grated Parmesan cheese
1/4 cup finely chopped parsley
1/4 teaspoon pepper

In large skillet, heat oil and cook garlic over medium heat until golden. Stir in vegetable recipe soup mix blended with cream, then hot tortellini. Bring just to the boiling point, then simmer, stirring occasionally, 5 minutes. Stir in remaining ingredients. Garnish, if desired, with additional parsley and cheese.
Makes about 4 appetizer or 2 main-dish servings.

Microwave Directions: In 2-quart casserole, heat oil with garlic at HIGH (Full Power) 2 minutes. Stir in vegetable recipe soup mix blended with cream and heat uncovered 4 minutes, stirring twice. Add hot tortellini and heat uncovered 3 minutes. Stir in remaining ingredients and heat 1 minute. Garnish and serve as above.

Nouvelle Fettucini

2 cups broccoli flowerets
1 cup carrot slices
1/4 cup PARKAY Margarine
2 cups summer squash slices
1/2 lb. asparagus spears, cut into 1-inch pieces
1 teaspoon dried oregano leaves, crushed
3/4 lb. VELVEETA Pasteurized Process Cheese Spread, cubed
3/4 cup half and half
1/4 lb. pepperoni, chopped
1/3 cup (1 1/2 ozs.) KRAFT 100% Grated Parmesan Cheese
8 ozs. fettucini, cooked, drained

In large skillet, stir-fry broccoli and carrots in margarine 3 minutes. Add squash, asparagus and oregano; stir-fry until crisp-tender. Reduce heat to low. Add process cheese spread, half and half, pepperoni and parmesan cheese; stir until process cheese spread is melted. Add fettucini; toss lightly.
6 servings.

Preparation time: 25 minutes
Cooking time: 15 minutes

Microwave: Reduce half and half to 1/2 cup. Microwave broccoli, carrots and margarine in 2 1/2-quart microwave-safe bowl on High 2 minutes, stirring after 1 minute. Stir in squash, asparagus and oregano; microwave on High 2 to 3 minutes or until crisp-tender, stirring after 2 minutes. Add process cheese spread and half and half; mix lightly. Microwave on High 4 to 6 minutes or until process cheese spread is melted, stirring every 2 minutes. Stir in pepperoni and parmesan cheese; microwave on High 2 to 4 minutes or until thoroughly heated, stirring after 2 minutes. Add fettucini; toss lightly.

Paradise Pasta

1/4 cup unsalted butter
1 can (28 ounces) Italian plum tomatoes
1/4 cup finely shredded carrot
1/4 cup finely chopped celery
1/4 cup finely chopped onion
1 tablespoon dried basil, crumbled
1/4 teaspoon sugar
6 tablespoons pine nuts (1 1/2 to 2 ounces), toasted
1 pound uncooked angel hair pasta
Boiling salted water
2 tablespoons unsalted butter, at room temperature
1 cup whipping cream
3/4 teaspoon salt
1/4 teaspoon ground white pepper
Fresh parsley sprigs, if desired

1. Melt 1/4 cup butter in 3-quart heavy noncorrosive saucepan over medium heat. Drain liquid from tomatoes into saucepan. Puree tomatoes in blender or food processor and press through sieve into saucepan; discard seeds.
2. Add carrot, celery, onion, basil and sugar to saucepan. Heat to boiling. Reduce heat to low; simmer, uncovered, stirring occasionally, 1 hour.
3. Coarsely chop 3 tablespoons of the pine nuts; keep remaining 3 tablespoons pine nuts whole.
4. Cook angel hair pasta in large kettle of boiling salted water just until al dente, 2 minutes; drain well. Transfer to heated serving bowl. Add 2 tablespoons butter; toss until melted.
5. Just before serving, stir cream, chopped pine nuts, salt and pepper into sauce. Cook over low heat just until sauce is hot; do not boil. Pour sauce over pasta; toss to mix. Sprinkle with remaining whole pine nuts; garnish with parsley. Serve immediately.
Makes 6 servings.

Spaghetti Mediterranean

1½ pounds fresh tomatoes (about 4 large)
12 pitted green olives
4 to 6 flat anchovy fillets
2 medium cloves garlic
½ pound uncooked spaghetti
    Boiling salted water
¼ cup olive oil
½ cup chopped fresh parsley
1 tablespoon drained capers
2 teaspoons chopped fresh basil or ½ teaspoon dried basil, crumbled
½ teaspoon dried oregano, crumbled
½ teaspoon salt
¼ teaspoon dried hot red pepper flakes

1. Place tomatoes in large saucepan with boiling water to cover 60 seconds to loosen skins. Immediately drain tomatoes and rinse under cold running water. Peel, seed and chop tomatoes coarsely. Slice olives. Chop anchovies. Mince garlic.
2. Cook spaghetti in large kettle of boiling salted water just until al dente, 8 to 12 minutes; drain well.
3. While spaghetti is cooking, heat oil in 10-inch noncorrosive skillet over medium-high heat. Add garlic; cook just until garlic begins to color, 45 to 60 seconds. Stir in tomatoes, parsley, capers, basil, oregano, salt and the pepper flakes.
4. Add olives and anchovies to skillet; cook over medium-high heat, stirring constantly until most of the visible liquid has evaporated and sauce is slightly thickened, about 10 minutes. Pour sauce over spaghetti in heated serving bowl. Toss lightly and serve immediately.
Makes 3 to 4 servings.

Spaghetti with Cream Sauce

2 cups mushroom slices
1 cup halved zucchini slices
1 garlic clove, minced
2 tablespoons PARKAY Margarine
⅓ cup half and half
½ lb. VELVEETA Pasteurized Process Cheese Spread, cubed
8 ozs. spaghetti, cooked, drained

Sauté vegetables and garlic in margarine until zucchini is crisp-tender. Reduce heat to low. Add half and half and process cheese spread; stir until process cheese spread is melted. Toss with hot spaghetti.
6 servings.

Preparation time: 15 minutes
Cooking time: 10 minutes

Creamy Spinach Fettucini

1 small green pepper, chopped
1 small red pepper, chopped
1 small onion, chopped
1 (8-ounce) carton plain nonfat yogurt
½ cup canned white sauce
2 tablespoons dried Italian seasoning
1½ cups (6 ounces) ARMOUR® Lower Salt Ham cut into ½-inch cubes
12 ounces uncooked spinach fettucini, cooked according to package directions omitting salt and drained
6 slices ARMOUR® Lower Salt Bacon, cooked crisp and crumbled

Spray large skillet with nonstick cooking spray; place over medium heat. Add vegetables; sauté until tender-crisp. Mix yogurt, white sauce and seasoning in small bowl. Add to vegetables and heat through. Add ham; continue cooking until hot. Spoon over warm fettucini; top with bacon. Garnish with parsley or fresh rosemary, if desired.
Makes 4 to 6 servings.

Nutrition Information Per Serving: 352 calories, 17.7 g protein, 9 g fat, 48 g carbohydrates, 20.6 mg cholesterol, 531 mg sodium.

Creamy Fettucini Toss

¼ cup margarine or butter
1 tablespoon flour
2 teaspoons WYLER'S® or STEERO® Chicken-Flavor Instant Bouillon
¾ teaspoon basil leaves
¼ teaspoon garlic powder
⅛ teaspoon pepper
1 cup (½ pint) BORDEN® or MEADOW GOLD® Light or Coffee Cream
1 cup BORDEN® or MEADOW GOLD® Milk
½ (1-pound) package CREAMETTE® Fettucini
¼ cup grated Parmesan cheese
    Chopped parsley, walnuts and cooked crumbled bacon

In medium saucepan, over medium heat, melt margarine; stir in flour, bouillon, basil, garlic powder and pepper. Gradually add cream and milk. Cook and stir until bouillon dissolves and sauce thickens slightly, about 15 minutes. Meanwhile, cook fettucini as package directs; drain. Remove sauce from heat; add cheese. In large bowl, pour sauce over *hot* fettucini; stir to coat. Garnish with parsley, walnuts and bacon. Serve immediately. Refrigerate leftovers.
Makes 6 to 8 servings.

Pasta Primavera

2 cups V8® Vegetable Juice
1 tablespoon all-purpose flour
1/8 teaspoon pepper
1 tablespoon olive oil
2 large stalks celery, thinly sliced
1 large onion, thinly sliced
2 medium cloves garlic, minced
1 teaspoon dried oregano leaves, crushed
1/2 teaspoon dried basil leaves, crushed
1 large sweet red pepper, cut into strips
1 medium zucchini, cut into quarters lengthwise and sliced
6 cups hot cooked linguini
Grated Parmesan cheese (optional)

1. In small bowl, stir together V8 juice, flour and pepper; set aside. In 10-inch skillet over medium heat, in hot oil, cook celery, onion, garlic, oregano and basil until vegetables are tender, stirring occasionally.
2. Add red pepper and zucchini. Cook until tender, stirring occasionally. Stir V8 mixture into skillet. Cook until mixture boils and thickens, stirring often. Reduce heat to low; simmer, uncovered, 3 minutes.
3. Serve over hot linguini. Top with Parmesan cheese, if desired.
Makes 4 cups sauce or 8 side-dish servings.

Per serving: 164 calories, 4 g protein, 3 g fat, 32 g carbohydrate, 221 mg sodium, 0 mg cholesterol.

Peanut Noodles

1 cup V8® Vegetable Juice
1/2 cup chopped green onions
1/2 cup chopped sweet red pepper
1/3 cup creamy peanut butter
1 clove garlic, minced
1 tablespoon soy sauce
1/2 teaspoon grated fresh ginger
Dash crushed red pepper
8 ounces spaghetti, cooked and drained
Chopped unsalted peanuts for garnish

In 1-quart saucepan, combine V8 juice, green onions, sweet red pepper, peanut butter, garlic, soy sauce, ginger and crushed red pepper. Over medium heat, heat until hot and smooth, stirring often. In large bowl, combine spaghetti and V8 mixture; toss to coat well. Garnish with peanuts.
Makes 5 cups or 4 main-dish servings.

Per serving: 357 calories, 14 g protein, 12 g fat, 51 g carbohydrate, 566 mg sodium, 0 mg cholesterol.

Summer Spaghetti

1 pound firm ripe fresh plum tomatoes
1 medium onion
6 pitted green olives
2 medium cloves garlic
1/3 cup chopped fresh parsley
2 tablespoons finely shredded fresh basil or 3/4 teaspoon dried basil, crumbled
2 teaspoons drained capers
1/2 teaspoon paprika
1/4 teaspoon dried oregano, crumbled
1 tablespoon red wine vinegar
1/2 cup olive oil
1 pound uncooked spaghetti
Boiling salted water

1. Chop tomatoes coarsely. Chop onion and olives. Mince garlic. Combine tomatoes, onion, olives, garlic, parsley, basil, capers, paprika and oregano in medium bowl; toss well. Drizzle vinegar over tomato mixture. Then pour oil over tomato mixture. Stir until thoroughly mixed. Refrigerate, covered, at least 6 hours or overnight.
2. Just before serving, cook spaghetti in large kettle of boiling salted water just until al dente, 8 to 12 minutes; drain well. Immediately toss hot pasta with cold marinated tomato sauce. Serve at once.
Makes 4 to 6 servings.

Mediterranean Pasta

1 roll (16 ounces) ECKRICH® Country Sausage
2 medium onions, sliced thin
1 small clove garlic, minced
1 tablespoon olive oil
2 medium zucchini, sliced thin
1/2 teaspoon dried basil leaves
1/4 teaspoon dried oregano leaves
1/4 teaspoon salt
Dash ground black pepper
2 large tomatoes, seeded, cut into large pieces
Hot cooked thin spaghetti
Grated Parmesan cheese, optional

Break sausage into pieces and cook in large skillet over medium heat until lightly browned. Drain and set aside. Place onions, garlic and oil in same skillet. Cook and stir over medium heat until onions are quite soft and lightly browned. Add zucchini, basil, oregano, salt and pepper; cook 5 minutes more. Add tomatoes; cover and simmer 10 minutes more, stirring occasionally. Serve over spaghetti with Parmesan cheese.
Makes 4 to 5 servings.

Pasta with Clam Sauce

1 can (10¾ ounces) CAMPBELL'S® Condensed Cream of Mushroom or Cream of Celery Soup
1 can (6½ ounces) minced clams, undrained
¼ cup milk
¼ cup Chablis or other dry white wine
2 tablespoons chopped fresh parsley
2 tablespoons grated Parmesan cheese
1 large clove garlic, minced
8 ounces linguini, cooked and drained

To Microwave:
1. In 1½-quart microwave-safe casserole, stir soup until smooth; stir in clams with their liquid, milk, wine, parsley, Parmesan and garlic. Cover with lid; microwave on HIGH 8 minutes or until hot and bubbling, stirring once during cooking.
2. Toss with linguini; serve with additional Parmesan.
Makes 4 servings.

Souper Quick "Lasagna"

1½ pounds ground beef
1 envelope LIPTON® Onion or Onion-Mushroom Recipe Soup Mix
3 cans (8 ounces each) tomato sauce
1 cup water
½ teaspoon oregano (optional)
1 package (8 ounces) broad egg noodles, cooked and drained
1 package (16 ounces) mozzarella cheese, shredded

Preheat oven to 375°.

In large skillet, brown ground beef over medium-high heat; drain. Stir in onion recipe soup mix, tomato sauce, water and oregano. Simmer covered, stirring occasionally, 15 minutes.

In 2-quart oblong baking dish, spoon enough sauce to cover bottom. Alternately layer noodles, ground beef mixture and cheese, ending with cheese. Bake 30 minutes or until bubbling.
Makes about 6 servings.

Microwave Directions: In 2-quart casserole, heat ground beef, uncovered, at HIGH (Full Power) 7 minutes, stirring once; drain. Stir in onion recipe soup mix, tomato sauce, water and oregano. Heat at MEDIUM (50% Full Power) 5 minutes, stirring once. In 2-quart oblong baking dish, spoon enough sauce to cover bottom. Alternately layer as above. Heat covered at MEDIUM, turning dish occasionally, 10 minutes or until bubbling. Let stand covered 5 minutes.

Neapolitan Sauce

1 can (28 ounces) Italian plum tomatoes
2 tablespoons butter
1 tablespoon olive oil
1 teaspoon dried basil, crumbled
½ teaspoon salt
⅛ teaspoon pepper
3 tablespoons chopped fresh parsley
½ pound spaghetti, cooked
½ cup freshly grated Parmesan cheese, if desired

Press tomatoes and their liquid through sieve into bowl; discard seeds. Heat butter and oil in 2-quart noncorrosive saucepan over medium heat. Stir in sieved tomatoes, basil, salt and pepper. Heat to boiling; reduce heat to medium-low. Cook, uncovered, stirring frequently, until sauce is reduced and measures 2 cups, 30 to 40 minutes. Stir in parsley. Toss with spaghetti. Serve immediately with Parmesan cheese to sprinkle.
Makes 2 to 3 servings.

Lasagna Deliciousa

½ of a 1-pound package uncooked CREAMETTE® Lasagna
1 pound bulk Italian sausage
½ pound ground beef
1 cup chopped onion
2 cloves garlic, minced
1 can (28 ounces) tomatoes, cut up, undrained
2 cans (6 ounces each) tomato paste
2 teaspoons sugar
2½ teaspoons salt, divided
1½ teaspoons dried basil, crushed
½ teaspoon fennel seeds
¼ teaspoon pepper
1 container (15 ounces) ricotta cheese
1 egg, beaten
1 tablespoon parsley flakes
1 cup sliced pitted ripe olives
4 cups (1 pound) shredded mozzarella cheese
¾ cup grated Parmesan cheese

Prepare lasagna according to package directions; drain. Cook sausage, ground beef, onion and garlic in large skillet over medium-high heat until sausage is no longer pink and onion is tender; drain. Stir in tomatoes, tomato paste, sugar, 2 teaspoons of the salt, the basil, fennel seeds and pepper. Bring to a boil over high heat. Reduce heat to low. Simmer, uncovered, 20 minutes.

In small bowl, blend ricotta, egg, parsley and remaining ½ teaspoon salt. Spoon 1½ cups of the meat sauce into 13×9-inch baking dish. Layer ⅓ *each* of the lasagna, remaining meat sauce, ricotta mixture, olives, mozzarella and Parmesan cheese into dish. Repeat layers. Cover with foil. Bake at 375°F 25 minutes. Uncover. Bake about 20 minutes more or until heated through. Let stand 10 minutes before cutting.
Makes 8 to 10 servings.

Lasagna with White and Red Sauces

Béchamel Sauce (recipe follows)
½ medium onion, sliced
1 clove garlic, minced
2 to 3 tablespoons vegetable oil
1 pound lean ground beef
1 can (28 ounces) crushed tomatoes or 1 can (28 ounces) whole tomatoes, chopped, undrained
½ cup thinly sliced celery
½ cup thinly sliced carrot
1 teaspoon dried basil, crushed
1 package (1 pound) lasagna noodles, cooked, drained
6 ounces BEL PAESE® cheese,* thinly sliced
6 hard-cooked eggs, sliced (optional)
2 tablespoons butter or margarine, cut into small pieces
1 cup (about 2 ounces) freshly grated GALBANI® Parmigiano-Reggiano or Grana Padano cheese

Prepare Béchamel Sauce; set aside. Cook and stir onion and garlic in hot oil in Dutch oven over medium-high heat until tender. Add ground beef and cook until no longer pink, stirring occasionally. Add tomatoes, celery, carrot and basil. Reduce heat to low. Cover and simmer 45 minutes. Remove cover and simmer 15 minutes more.

Arrange ⅓ of the lasagna noodles in bottom of buttered 13½×9-inch baking dish. Add ½ of the Bel Paese® and ½ of the eggs. Spread with meat sauce. Repeat layers of noodles, Bel Paese® and eggs. Spread with Béchamel Sauce. Top with layer of noodles. Dot with butter. Sprinkle with Parmigiano-Reggiano. Bake in preheated 350°F oven 30 to 40 minutes or until heated through. Let stand 10 minutes before cutting.
Makes 6 servings.

*Remove wax coating and moist, white crust from cheese.

BÉCHAMEL SAUCE: Melt 2 tablespoons butter or margarine in small saucepan over medium-low heat. Stir in 2 tablespoons all-purpose flour. Gradually blend in ¾ cup milk. Season to taste with white pepper. Cook until thick and bubbly, stirring constantly.
Makes ¾ cup sauce.

Creamy Lasagne

1 pound ground beef
½ cup chopped onion
1 14½-ounce can tomatoes, cut up
1 6-ounce can tomato paste
⅓ cup water
1 garlic clove, minced
1 teaspoon dried oregano leaves, crushed
½ teaspoon salt
¼ teaspoon pepper
1 8-ounce package PHILADELPHIA BRAND Cream Cheese, cubed
¼ cup milk
8 ounces lasagne noodles, cooked, drained
2 6-ounce packages 100% Natural KRAFT Low Moisture Part-Skim Mozzarella Cheese Slices
½ cup (2 ounces) KRAFT Grated Parmesan Cheese

Brown meat in large skillet; drain. Add onions; cook until tender. Stir in tomatoes, tomato paste, water, garlic and seasonings. Cover; simmer 30 minutes. Combine cream cheese and milk in saucepan; stir over low heat until smooth. In 13×9-inch baking pan, layer half of noodles, meat mixture, cream cheese mixture, mozzarella and parmesan cheese; repeat layers. Bake at 350°, 30 minutes. Let stand 10 minutes before serving.
6 to 8 servings.

Microwave: Crumble meat into 1½-quart casserole. Microwave on High 4 to 5 minutes or until meat loses pink color when stirred; drain. Add onions, tomatoes, tomato paste, water and seasonings. Cover; microwave 12 minutes, stirring every 3 minutes. Microwave cream cheese and milk in 1-quart measure 3 to 4 minutes or until sauce is hot and smooth, stirring after 1½ minutes. In 13×9-inch baking dish, layer half of noodles, meat mixture, cream cheese mixture, mozzarella and parmesan cheese; repeat with remaining noodles, meat mixture and cream cheese mixture. Microwave 12 minutes, turning dish every 4 minutes. Top with remaining mozzarella and parmesan cheese. Microwave 4 to 6 minutes or until thoroughly heated. Let stand 10 minutes before serving.

Tagliatelle with Creamy Sauce

7 to 8 ounces tagliatelle pasta, cooked, drained
1 cup GALBANI® Mascarpone cheese
1 package (10 ounces) frozen peas, cooked, drained
2 ounces (½ cup) finely chopped prosciutto
1½ cups (6 ounces) shredded mozzarella cheese
Butter or margarine

Layer ½ of the tagliatelle in buttered 9×9-inch baking dish. Spoon ½ of the Mascarpone onto tagliatelle. Sprinkle with ½ of the peas and ½ of the prosciutto. Top with ½ of the mozzarella. Repeat layers. Dot with butter. Bake in preheated 350°F oven 20 minutes or until heated through.
Makes 4 to 6 servings.

*Favorite recipe from **Bel Paese Sales Co., Inc.***

SIDE DISHES

Vegetable, rice, and potato dishes are sensational accompaniments when prepared with the great ideas you'll find here. Serve crisp green beans, carrots, broccoli, and asparagus that sparkle with flavor. Try rice dishes with an international touch or potatoes that are out of the ordinary. These side dishes are alluring enough to steal the limelight.

Homestyle Zucchini & Tomatoes

2 tablespoons oil
1 medium clove garlic, finely chopped*
3 medium zucchini, thinly sliced (about 4½ cups)
1 can (14½ ounces) whole peeled tomatoes, drained and chopped (reserve liquid)
1 envelope LIPTON® Golden Onion or Onion Recipe Soup Mix
½ teaspoon basil leaves

In large skillet, heat oil and cook garlic with zucchini over medium-high heat 3 minutes. Stir in tomatoes, then golden onion recipe soup mix thoroughly blended with reserved liquid and basil. Bring to a boil, then simmer, stirring occasionally, 10 minutes or until zucchini is tender and sauce is slightly thickened.
Makes about 4 servings.
   *Substitution: Use ¼ teaspoon garlic powder.
   Microwave Directions: In 2-quart casserole, combine zucchini with tomatoes. Stir in golden onion recipe soup mix thoroughly blended with reserved liquid, garlic and basil. Heat covered at HIGH (Full Power) 5 minutes, stirring once. Remove cover and heat 4 minutes or until zucchini is tender, stirring once. Let stand covered 2 minutes.

Buffet Bean Bake

6 slices bacon
1 cup packed brown sugar
½ cup vinegar
½ teaspoon salt
1 tablespoon FRENCH'S America's Favorite Mustard or DURKEE Famous Sauce
1 can (16 ounces) butter beans, drained
1 can (16 ounces) French-style green beans, drained
1 can (16 ounces) pork and beans, drained
1 can (16 ounces) lima beans, drained
1 can (15½ ounces) yellow wax beans, drained
1 can (15 ounces) kidney beans, drained
1 can (2.8 ounces) DURKEE French Fried Onions

Preheat oven to 350°. In medium skillet, fry bacon until crisp. Remove from skillet; crumble and set aside. Drain all but about 2 tablespoons drippings from skillet; add sugar, vinegar, salt and mustard. Simmer, uncovered, 10 minutes. In large bowl, combine drained beans, ½ can French Fried Onions and hot sugar mixture. Spoon bean mixture into 9×13-inch baking dish. Bake, covered, at 350° for 30 minutes or until heated through. Top with crumbled bacon and remaining onions; bake, uncovered, 5 minutes or until onions are golden brown.
Makes 12 to 14 servings.

Kasha-Stuffed Tomatoes

3/4 cup uncooked kasha (roasted buckwheat kernels), medium granulation
1 egg white
1/4 cup butter or margarine, divided
1 large onion, chopped
1 clove garlic, minced
1 1/2 cups chicken or beef broth
1 teaspoon Worcestershire sauce
1 teaspoon dried oregano leaves
1/2 teaspoon dried thyme leaves
1/4 teaspoon TABASCO® pepper sauce
4 large ripe tomatoes
1/2 cup shredded Jarlsberg cheese
2 tablespoons chopped parsley

Preheat oven to 375°F. In small bowl mix kasha and egg white. In large skillet melt 2 tablespoons butter; add kasha. Stir with fork or wooden spoon 2 to 3 minutes or until kernels are separated. Remove and reserve. In same skillet melt remaining 2 tablespoons butter; add onion and garlic. Cook 5 minutes or until tender. Return kasha to skillet. Add broth, Worcestershire sauce, oregano, thyme and Tabasco® sauce; mix well. Cover; simmer over low heat 10 minutes or until liquid has been absorbed and kasha is tender. Meanwhile, slice tops off tomatoes. Scoop out insides to form shells; discard seeds. Chop tomato pulp; add to cooked kasha. Stir in cheese and parsley. Fill tomato shells with kasha mixture. Arrange in shallow baking dish. Bake 20 minutes or until tomatoes are heated through.
Makes 4 servings.

Vegetable Bake

3 tomatoes, sliced 1/2 inch thick
2 small zucchini, sliced 1/4 inch thick
1/4 cup butter or margarine, divided
1 tablespoon flour
3/4 cup milk
1 cup shredded sharp Cheddar cheese
1/2 teaspoon salt
1/4 teaspoon TABASCO® pepper sauce
1/2 cup dry bread crumbs
1/4 cup grated Parmesan cheese

Preheat oven to 350°F. In shallow 8×8-inch baking dish arrange slices of tomato and zucchini. In small saucepan melt 2 tablespoons butter over medium heat; blend in flour until smooth. Remove from heat. Gradually stir in milk; return to heat. Stir constantly, bring to a boil over medium heat and boil 1 minute. Stir in Cheddar cheese, salt and Tabasco® sauce until smooth. Pour over vegetables.

Melt remaining 2 tablespoons butter; stir in crumbs until moistened. Stir in Parmesan cheese. Sprinkle crumb mixture over vegetables. Bake 35 to 40 minutes or until top is lightly browned and vegetables are tender.
Makes 4 servings.

Country Bean Barbecue

1 can (16 ounces) lima beans
6 slices bacon, diced
1/2 cup sliced onion
1/2 cup diced celery
1 clove garlic, minced
1 cup catsup
1 can (16 ounces) red kidney beans, drained
1/2 teaspoon TABASCO® pepper sauce

Drain lima beans; reserve 1/2 cup liquid. In large skillet cook bacon until browned. Drain all but 1 tablespoon bacon fat from skillet. Add onion, celery and garlic; cook 5 minutes or until tender. Stir in catsup, lima beans, reserved lima bean liquid and kidney beans; mix gently. Simmer uncovered 20 minutes; stir occasionally. Stir in Tabasco® sauce.
Makes 6 to 8 servings.

Marinated Vegetables

1 cup carrots cut into matchstick-thin strips
1/2 pound green beans, cut into 1-inch lengths
2 tablespoons finely chopped onion
1 large sweet red pepper, cut into matchstick-thin strips
1 large zucchini, cut into matchstick-thin strips
1 1/2 cups V8® Vegetable Juice
2 tablespoons vinegar
1 tablespoon vegetable oil
1 teaspoon chili powder
Salad greens

To Microwave:
1. In 12- by 8-inch microwave-safe baking dish, combine carrots, beans and onion. Cover with vented plastic wrap; microwave on HIGH 4 minutes or until vegetables are nearly tender, stirring once during cooking.
2. Stir in pepper and zucchini. Cover; microwave on HIGH 4 minutes or until vegetables are tender-crisp, stirring once during cooking.
3. In small bowl, stir together V8 juice, vinegar, oil and chili powder. Pour over warm vegetables. Cover; refrigerate until serving time, at least 4 hours. Serve on salad greens.
Makes about 5 cups or 8 servings.
Note: You can substitute 1 package (9 ounces) frozen cut green beans for fresh beans.

Asparagus in Anchovy Sauce

3/4 cup water
3/4 teaspoon salt, divided
2 packages (8 to 10 ounces each) frozen asparagus spears
1 cup CRISCO® Oil
3 tablespoons lemon juice
1 tablespoon anchovy paste
1 teaspoon onion powder
1 teaspoon dried chervil leaves
1/4 teaspoon garlic powder

Combine water and 1/2 teaspoon salt in large saucepan. Heat to boiling. Add asparagus. Return to boiling. Cover. Reduce heat to moderate. Cook 3 to 4 minutes, or until asparagus is thawed and warm. Drain. Spread asparagus in shallow baking dish.

Blend remaining ingredients, including remaining 1/4 teaspoon salt, in small mixing bowl. Pour over asparagus. Cover and refrigerate 3 to 4 hours, stirring occasionally. Serve chilled or at room temperature.
4 to 6 servings.

Broccoli and Rice with Walnuts

1/4 cup coarsely chopped walnuts or slivered almonds
1 tablespoon oil
1/2 package (2 1/4 cups) BIRDS EYE® Broccoli Cuts*
2 tablespoons sliced scallions
1 garlic clove, minced
1 cup chicken broth or water
2 tablespoons dry sherry (optional)
1 1/2 tablespoons soy sauce
1 cup MINUTE® Rice

Cook and stir walnuts in hot oil in large skillet until lightly browned; remove from skillet. Add broccoli, scallions and garlic to oil remaining in skillet. Cook and stir 2 to 3 minutes. Add broth, sherry and soy sauce. Bring to a full boil. Stir in rice. Cover; remove from heat. Let stand 5 minutes. Fluff with fork and sprinkle with walnuts.
Makes 4 servings.
*You may use 1 package (9 oz.) BIRDS EYE® Cut Green Beans for the broccoli.

Cheddar Broccoli Corn Bake

1/4 cup butter or margarine, divided
2 tablespoons all-purpose flour
1/4 teaspoon salt
1 1/2 cups milk
1 1/2 cups (6 ounces) shredded Cheddar cheese
1 can (12 ounces) whole kernel corn, drained
2 cups KELLOGG'S CORN FLAKES® cereal, crushed to make 1 cup, divided
2 packages (10 ounces each) frozen broccoli spears, cooked, drained

Melt 2 tablespoons of the butter in large saucepan over medium heat. Stir in flour and salt. Gradually stir in milk. Cook until thickened and bubbly, stirring constantly. Add cheese, stirring until melted. Stir in corn and 1/4 cup of the crushed cereal. Remove from heat.

Arrange broccoli in 12×8-inch glass baking dish with florets toward both long edges. Pour cheese sauce over broccoli stalks. Melt remaining 2 tablespoons butter in small saucepan over medium heat. Stir in remaining 3/4 cup cereal. Sprinkle over cheese sauce. Bake at 350°F 30 minutes or until heated through.
Makes 8 servings.

Brussels Sprouts Amandine

1 tablespoon CRISCO® Oil
1/4 cup sliced almonds
3/4 cup water
1 1/2 teaspoons instant beef bouillon granules
1 package (16 ounces) frozen Brussels sprouts
Dash pepper

Heat Crisco® Oil in medium saucepan. Add almonds. Sauté over moderate heat until light golden brown. Drain on paper towels.

Combine water and bouillon granules in medium saucepan. Heat to boiling. Add Brussels sprouts. Return to boiling. Cover. Reduce heat. Simmer, stirring once to break apart Brussels sprouts, 8 to 12 minutes, or until tender. Drain. Stir in almonds and pepper.
4 to 6 servings.

Country-Style Baked Beans

1 envelope LIPTON® Onion, Onion-Mushroom or Beefy Mushroom Recipe Soup Mix
1 can (24 ounces) pork and beans in tomato sauce
1 medium apple, chopped
1/4 cup brown sugar
1 tablespoon prepared mustard

In large saucepan, combine all ingredients. Cook uncovered over medium heat, stirring occasionally, 20 minutes.
Makes about 6 servings.
Microwave Directions: In 1 1/2-quart casserole, combine all ingredients. Heat covered at HIGH (Full Power), stirring occasionally, 12 minutes or until bubbling. Let stand covered 5 minutes.

Sesame Broccoli

½ bunch DOLE™ Broccoli, cut
    into flowerets
1 tablespoon butter or
    margarine, melted
2 teaspoons sesame seeds,
    toasted
2 teaspoons soy sauce
    Pinch garlic powder
    Pinch ground ginger

In large saucepan, cook broccoli in vegetable steamer basket over boiling water 5 minutes; drain. In small bowl, combine remaining ingredients. In serving bowl, toss broccoli with sesame mixture.
Makes 2 to 3 servings.

Vegetable Stir-Fry

1 8-ounce package *Light*
    PHILADELPHIA BRAND
    Neufchâtel Cheese, cubed
¼ cup sesame seed, toasted
2 cups diagonally cut carrot
    slices
2 cups diagonally cut celery
    slices
¾ cup thin green pepper strips
2 tablespoons PARKAY
    Margarine
¼ teaspoon salt
    Dash of pepper

Coat neufchâtel cheese cubes with sesame seed; chill. In large skillet or wok, stir-fry vegetables in margarine and seasonings until crisp-tender. Remove from heat. Add neufchâtel cheese to vegetables; mix lightly.
6 to 8 servings.
Variation: Substitute PHILADELPHIA BRAND Cream Cheese for Neufchâtel Cheese.

Savory Spinach Casserole

1 8-ounce package *Light*
    PHILADELPHIA BRAND
    Neufchâtel Cheese, softened
¼ cup milk
2 10-ounce packages frozen
    chopped spinach, cooked,
    drained
⅓ cup (1½ ounces) KRAFT
    Grated Parmesan Cheese

Combine neufchâtel cheese and milk, mixing until well blended. Spoon spinach into 1-quart casserole; top with neufchâtel cheese mixture. Sprinkle with parmesan cheese. Bake at 350°, 20 minutes.
4 to 6 servings.
Variation: Substitute PHILADELPHIA BRAND Cream Cheese for Neufchâtel Cheese.
Microwave: Prepare casserole as directed except for baking. Microwave on High 4½ to 5 minutes or until hot.

Barley with Corn and Red Pepper

½ cup WISH-BONE® Italian
    Dressing
1 medium red pepper, chopped
½ cup chopped onion
1 cup uncooked pearled barley
1¾ cups chicken broth
1¼ cups water
2 tablespoons finely chopped
    coriander (cilantro) or
    parsley
1 tablespoon lime juice
½ teaspoon ground cumin
⅛ teaspoon pepper
1 can (7 ounces) whole kernel
    corn, drained

In large saucepan, heat Italian dressing and cook red pepper with onion over medium heat, stirring occasionally, 5 minutes or until tender. Stir in barley and cook, stirring constantly, 1 minute. Stir in broth, water, coriander, lime juice, cumin and pepper. Simmer covered 50 minutes or until barley is done. (Do not stir while simmering.) Stir in corn.
Makes about 6 servings.
    Note: Also terrific with Wish-Bone® Robusto Italian, Herbal Italian, Lite Italian, Blended Italian, Classic Dijon Vinaigrette or Lite Classic Dijon Vinaigrette Dressing.

Red Cabbage 'n' Apples

¼ cup margarine or butter
⅓ cup REALEMON® Lemon Juice
    from Concentrate
¼ cup firmly packed light brown
    sugar
¼ cup water
½ teaspoon caraway seeds
½ teaspoon salt
4 cups shredded red cabbage
2 medium all-purpose apples,
    cored and coarsely chopped

In large saucepan, melt margarine; stir in ReaLemon® brand, sugar, water, caraway and salt. Add cabbage and apples; bring to a boil. Reduce heat; cover and simmer 25 to 30 minutes.
Makes 6 to 8 servings.
Microwave: In 2-quart round baking dish, melt margarine on 100% power (high) 45 seconds. Stir in ReaLemon® brand, sugar, water, caraway and salt; add cabbage and apples. Cook covered on 100% power (high) 15 to 20 minutes, stirring every 5 minutes. Let stand for 2 minutes before serving.

Vegetables in Cheese Sauce

1 can (11 ounces) CAMPBELL'S® Condensed Cheddar Cheese Soup/Sauce
⅓ cup milk
½ teaspoon dried basil leaves, crushed
1 clove garlic, minced
2 cups cauliflowerets
1 small onion, cut into thin wedges
1½ cups diagonally sliced carrots
1 package (10 ounces) frozen peas

To Microwave:
1. In 3-quart microwave-safe casserole, stir soup until smooth. Stir in milk, basil and garlic; mix well.
2. Add vegetables; stir to coat well. Cover with lid; microwave on HIGH 15 minutes or until vegetables are tender, stirring twice during cooking. Let stand, covered, 5 minutes.
Makes about 5½ cups or 8 servings.

Spiced Red Cabbage

¼ cup CRISCO® Oil
2-pound head red cabbage, cored and chopped
1 small onion, thinly sliced and separated into rings
1 small apple, cored and chopped
½ cup raisins
¼ teaspoon ground cloves
⅛ teaspoon ground allspice
1 tablespoon white wine vinegar
2 teaspoons sugar
1 teaspoon salt

Heat Crisco® Oil in Dutch oven or large saucepan. Add cabbage, onion, apple, raisins, cloves and allspice. Stir to coat. Cover. Cook over moderate heat, stirring occasionally, about 1 hour, or until cabbage is tender. Stir in vinegar, sugar and salt.
6 to 8 servings.

Broccoli and Pasta

1 package (10 ounces) frozen chopped broccoli
2 tablespoons CRISCO® Oil
2 tablespoons finely chopped onion
1 tablespoon snipped fresh parsley
1 teaspoon anchovy paste (optional)
1 small clove garlic, minced
¼ teaspoon salt
Dash pepper
1 cup cooked small shell macaroni
Grated Parmesan cheese

Cook broccoli according to package directions. Drain and set aside.

Heat Crisco® Oil in medium skillet. Add onion, parsley, anchovy paste (optional) and garlic. Cook over moderate heat, stirring constantly, about 3 minutes, or until onion is tender. Stir in broccoli, salt and pepper. Cook, stirring occasionally, 2 to 3 minutes longer, or until heated through. Remove from heat. Stir in macaroni. Sprinkle with Parmesan cheese. Serve immediately.
4 to 6 servings.

Carrot Saute

1 small clove garlic, pressed
2 tablespoons butter or margarine
1 tablespoon soy sauce
1½ teaspoons water
½ teaspoon sugar
1 cup sliced DOLE™ Carrots
½ onion, sliced into chunks
½ cup sliced DOLE™ Celery
¼ cup DOLE™ Blanched Slivered Almonds, toasted

In large skillet, saute garlic in butter. Stir in soy sauce, water and sugar; bring to a boil. Add carrots, onion and celery; saute until tender-crisp. Sprinkle with nuts.
Makes 2 servings.

Sweet 'n Sour Cabbage

1 can (11 ounces) DOLE® Mandarin Orange Segments
6 cups DOLE® Shredded Cabbage
1 medium onion, chopped
1 clove garlic, pressed
1 tablespoon vegetable oil
¼ cup white wine vinegar
1 teaspoon caraway seeds
1 teaspoon salt
1 cup DOLE™ Fresh Pineapple chunks

Drain oranges; reserve ⅓ cup syrup. In large skillet, saute cabbage, onion and garlic in oil until onion is soft. Stir in reserved syrup, vinegar, caraway seeds and salt. Cover and simmer 10 minutes. Stir in pineapple and oranges. Cover; cook 5 minutes longer.
Makes 4 servings.

Leeks with Bel Paese®

3 leeks
3 tablespoons butter or
   margarine
1 tablespoon olive oil
2 cups milk
4 ounces BEL PAESE® cheese,*
   thinly sliced
Pepper

Trim greens from leeks 2 inches above bulb; discard greens. Remove outer layer of bulb. Wash leeks thoroughly. Cut into large pieces. Melt butter in medium saucepan over medium-low heat. Add oil, milk and leeks. Cover and simmer 20 to 30 minutes or until leeks are tender; drain thoroughly. Place leeks in buttered 1-quart casserole. Cover with cheese. Bake in preheated 350°F oven 10 to 15 minutes or until cheese is melted. Season to taste with pepper. Serve immediately. *Makes 4 servings.*
   *Remove wax coating and moist, white crust from cheese.

Lemon Orange Carrots

3 cups pared, sliced carrots,
   cooked and drained
½ cup orange marmalade
2 tablespoons REALEMON®
   Lemon Juice from
   Concentrate
2 tablespoons margarine or
   butter

In medium saucepan, combine carrots, marmalade, ReaLemon® brand and margarine; stir to coat evenly. Heat through.
Makes 6 servings.

Broccoli and Celery Oriental

1 tablespoon vegetable oil
3 cups broccoli flowerets
1½ cups thinly sliced celery
¼ cup sliced green onions
2 tablespoons chopped pimento
1 can (10½ ounces) FRANCO-
   AMERICAN® Chicken Gravy
1 tablespoon soy sauce
   Cashews for garnish

To Microwave:
1. In 2-quart microwave-safe casserole, combine oil, broccoli, celery and green onions. Cover with lid; microwave on HIGH 4 minutes or until vegetables are tender-crisp, stirring once during cooking.
2. Stir in pimento, gravy and soy sauce. Cover; microwave on HIGH 3 minutes or until hot and bubbling. Garnish with cashews.
Makes about 3 cups or 4 servings.

Onion-Glazed Carrots

1 pound carrots
1 pouch CAMPBELL'S® Onion
   Soup and Recipe Mix
2 tablespoons butter or
   margarine
¼ cup packed brown sugar
¼ teaspoon grated orange peel
¼ cup orange juice
¼ teaspoon ground cinnamon
   Pecan halves for garnish

1. Cut carrots into 2-inch pieces, then cut each piece in half lengthwise.
2. Place carrots in 2-quart saucepan; add enough water to cover carrots. Over high heat, heat to boiling. Reduce heat to medium-low. Cover; simmer 10 minutes or until carrots are tender. Drain carrots in colander.
3. In same saucepan, combine soup mix, butter, brown sugar, orange peel, orange juice and cinnamon. Over medium heat, heat to boiling, stirring constantly.
4. Return carrots to saucepan. Cook 5 minutes more or until carrots are glazed, stirring often. Garnish with pecan halves.
Makes 4 servings.
   Note: Sweet potatoes may be prepared in the same way as these carrots. Peel sweet potatoes and cut into bite-size pieces before cooking.

Dilled Carrots and Parsnips

1 can (10¾ ounces)
   CAMPBELL'S® Condensed
   Cream of Celery Soup
½ cup milk
¼ teaspoon dried dill weed,
   crushed
2 cups carrots cut into 1-inch-
   long sticks
2 cups parsnips cut into 1-inch-
   long sticks

To Microwave:
1. In 3-quart microwave-safe casserole, stir soup until smooth. Add milk and dill weed; stir until well blended. Stir in carrots. Cover with lid; microwave on HIGH 6 minutes.
2. Stir in parsnips. Cover; microwave on HIGH 13 minutes or until vegetables are nearly tender, stirring twice during cooking. Let stand, covered, 5 minutes.
Makes 6 servings.
   Dilled Carrots: Prepare as above but use 4 cups carrots and omit parsnips. Microwave a total of 19 minutes, stirring twice during cooking.

Vegetable Couscous

1 tablespoon olive oil
1½ cups sliced CAMPBELL'S FRESH® Mushrooms (6 ounces)
1 cup chopped onions
¼ cup chopped sweet red pepper
4 cloves garlic, minced
¼ teaspoon dried thyme leaves, crushed
⅛ teaspoon pepper
1¼ cups V8® Vegetable Juice
1 cup shredded zucchini
1 cup quick-cooking couscous, uncooked

1. In 3-quart saucepan over medium heat, in hot oil, cook mushrooms, onions, red pepper, garlic, thyme and pepper until vegetables are tender-crisp, stirring often.
2. Stir in V8 juice and zucchini; heat to boiling. Remove from heat. Stir in couscous. Cover; let stand 5 minutes or until liquid is absorbed.
Makes 4½ cups or 9 side-dish servings.

Per serving: 105 calories, 3 g protein, 2 g fat, 19 g carbohydrate, 117 mg sodium, 0 mg cholesterol.

Corn Fritters

1 can (16 ounces) whole kernel corn, drained
1 cup all-purpose flour
1 cup dairy sour cream
2 eggs
2 tablespoons CRISCO® Oil
2 tablespoons finely chopped onion
1 teaspoon baking powder
1 teaspoon sugar
½ teaspoon salt
¼ teaspoon ground nutmeg
⅛ teaspoon white pepper
CRISCO® Oil for frying

Combine all ingredients except Crisco® Oil for frying in medium mixing bowl. Mix well. Let stand 1 hour.
Heat 2 to 3 inches Crisco® Oil in deep-fryer or large saucepan to 350°F. Drop batter by heaping tablespoonfuls into hot Crisco® Oil. Fry a few at a time 5 to 6 minutes, or until deep golden brown. Drain on paper towels. Repeat with remaining batter. Serve immediately or keep warm in 175°F oven.
14 to 16 fritters.

Cauliflower au Gratin

1 recipe Sesame Vegetable Topping (see Index)
1 cup water
¾ teaspoon salt, divided
2 packages (10 ounces each) frozen cauliflower
1 medium tomato, peeled, seeded and chopped
1 teaspoon dried parsley flakes
2 tablespoons CRISCO® Oil
2 tablespoons all-purpose flour
⅛ teaspoon pepper
1 cup milk
1 cup shredded Cheddar cheese (about 4 ounces)

Prepare Sesame Vegetable Topping as directed. Set aside.
Preheat oven to 350°F. Combine water and ½ teaspoon salt in large saucepan. Heat to boiling. Add cauliflower. Return to boiling. Cover. Reduce heat to moderate. Cook 3 minutes, or until cauliflower is thawed and warm. Drain. Place in 2-quart casserole. Stir in tomato and parsley flakes. Set aside.
Blend Crisco® Oil, flour, remaining ¼ teaspoon salt and pepper in small saucepan. Slowly stir in milk. Cook over moderate heat, stirring constantly, until thickened and bubbly. Add cheese. Stir until cheese melts. Pour over cauliflower mixture. Sprinkle with Sesame Vegetable Topping. Bake at 350°F, 25 to 30 minutes, or until bubbly.
6 to 8 servings.

Hot & Spicy Glazed Carrots

2 tablespoons vegetable oil
2 dried red chili peppers
1 pound carrots, peeled and cut diagonally into ⅛-inch slices
¼ cup KIKKOMAN Teriyaki Baste & Glaze

Heat oil in hot wok or large skillet over high heat. Add peppers and stir-fry until darkened; remove and discard. Add carrots; reduce heat to medium. Stir-fry 4 minutes, or until tender-crisp. Stir in teriyaki baste & glaze and cook until carrots are glazed. Serve immediately.
Makes 4 servings.

Carrot Nut Pudding

1 pound carrots, grated
1½ cups milk
½ teaspoon salt
½ cup whipping cream
1 tablespoon all-purpose flour
1 cup ground blanched almonds
½ cup firmly packed brown sugar
¼ cup CRISCO® Oil
¼ cup raisins
½ teaspoon ground turmeric
¼ teaspoon ground nutmeg

Combine carrots, milk and salt in medium saucepan. Blend cream and flour in small mixing bowl. Stir into carrot mixture. Heat to boiling, stirring constantly. Cook, uncovered, over moderate heat, stirring frequently, 40 to 45 minutes, or until liquid cooks away. Stir in remaining ingredients. Cook over low heat, stirring frequently, 10 minutes. Garnish with *slivered almonds*, if desired.
6 servings.

Barbecued Garlic

1 whole head of garlic
Olive or vegetable oil for basting

Peel loose, outermost skin from garlic; brush all over with oil. Grill garlic, on covered grill, not directly over medium-hot **KINGSFORD®** **Charcoal Briquets** 30 to 45 minutes or until garlic cloves are very tender, basting frequently with oil. Press individual cloves between thumb and forefinger to squeeze out garlic. Serve with grilled meats or as a spread for hot fresh bread.
Makes 4 servings.

Skillet Zucchini and Mushrooms

4 cups sliced zucchini (about 1 pound)
1 cup sliced fresh mushrooms (about 4 ounces)
¼ cup chopped onion
¼ cup margarine or butter
3 tablespoons REALEMON® Lemon Juice from Concentrate
¼ teaspoon Italian seasoning
¼ teaspoon salt

In large skillet, cook zucchini, mushrooms and onion in margarine until tender-crisp. Add remaining ingredients; heat through.
Makes 6 to 8 servings.

Crunchy Scalloped Celery

3 cups diagonally sliced celery
1 package (10 ounces) frozen peas, thawed and drained
1 can (8 ounces) sliced water chestnuts, drained
1 can (4 ounces) mushroom stems and pieces, drained
1 can (10¾ ounces) condensed cream of celery soup
¼ cup milk
½ teaspoon DURKEE Seasoned Salt
1 can (2.8 ounces) DURKEE French Fried Onions

Preheat oven to 350°. In large saucepan, simmer celery in small amount of boiling water until tender-crisp, about 5 minutes; drain. Stir in peas, water chestnuts, mushrooms, soup, milk, seasoned salt and *½ can* French Fried Onions. Pour into 1½-quart casserole. Bake, uncovered, at 350° for 20 minutes or until heated through. Top with remaining onions; bake, uncovered, 5 minutes or until onions are golden brown.
Makes 4 to 6 servings.

Baked Celery and Almonds

4 cups diagonally sliced celery
1 (13¾-fluid ounce) can COLLEGE INN® Chicken or Beef Broth
2 tablespoons all-purpose flour
½ cup dairy sour cream
1 (8-ounce) can CHUN KING® Sliced Water Chestnuts, drained
½ cup sliced almonds, toasted
2 tablespoons BLUE BONNET® Margarine
28 RITZ® Crackers, finely rolled (about 1 cup crumbs)

In large covered saucepan, over medium heat, cook celery in ¾ cup broth until tender-crisp, about 10 to 12 minutes; drain in colander. In same saucepan, blend flour into remaining broth until smooth. Cook and stir over medium heat until thickened; blend in sour cream. Stir in celery, water chestnuts and almonds. Pour into shallow 1½-quart baking dish. In small skillet, over medium heat, melt margarine; stir in cracker crumbs. Sprinkle over casserole. Bake at 350°F for 30 minutes or until hot.
Makes 6 servings.

Mushroom Risotto

1 tablespoon butter or margarine
½ cup finely chopped onion
1 can (10¾ ounces) CAMPBELL'S® Condensed Chicken Broth
½ cup water
¼ cup Chablis or other dry white wine
1 cup regular long-grain rice, uncooked
1 cup sliced CAMPBELL'S FRESH® Mushrooms
½ cup grated Parmesan cheese
Chopped fresh parsley for garnish

To Microwave:
1. In 2-quart microwave-safe casserole, combine butter and onion. Cover with lid; microwave on HIGH 3 minutes or until onion is tender, stirring once during cooking.
2. Stir in broth, water and wine. Cover; microwave on HIGH 2 minutes or until hot.
3. Stir in rice. Cover; microwave on HIGH 10 minutes or until bubbling. Stir in mushrooms. Cover; microwave at 50% power 10 minutes or until rice is nearly done. Stir in cheese. Let stand, covered, 5 minutes. Garnish with parsley.
Makes about 3 cups or 6 servings.

Creamy Green Beans Almondine

- 2 (9-ounce) packages frozen green beans, cooked and drained
- 2 tablespoons margarine or butter
- 2 tablespoons flour
- 2 teaspoons WYLER'S® or STEERO® Chicken-Flavor Instant Bouillon *or* 2 Chicken-Flavor Bouillon Cubes
- 3/4 cup BORDEN® or MEADOW GOLD® Milk
- 1/2 cup (2 ounces) shredded Mozzarella cheese
- 1/4 cup sliced almonds, toasted if desired

In medium saucepan, melt margarine; stir in flour and bouillon. Gradually stir in milk; cook and stir until thickened. Add cheese; stir until melted. Add beans; heat through. Stir in almonds. Serve immediately. Refrigerate leftovers.
Makes 6 servings.

Microwave: In 2-cup glass measure, microwave margarine on full power (high) 30 seconds or until melted. Stir in flour and bouillon. Gradually stir in milk. Microwave on full power (high) 3 to 3½ minutes, stirring after each minute, until thick and bubbly. Add cheese; stir until cheese melts. Add beans; microwave on full power (high) 1 to 2 minutes or until heated through. Stir in almonds.

Country Corn Bake

- 5 slices bacon, fried crisp
- 1 bag (20 ounces) frozen whole kernel corn, thawed and drained
- 1 can (10³/₄ ounces) condensed cream of potato soup
- 1/2 cup milk
- 1/2 cup thinly sliced celery
- 1 tablespoon diced pimiento (optional)
- 1/2 teaspoon DURKEE Seasoned Salt
- 1/2 cup (2 ounces) shredded Cheddar cheese
- 1 can (2.8 ounces) DURKEE French Fried Onions

Preheat oven to 375°. In large bowl, combine corn, soup, milk, celery, pimiento, seasoned salt, *1/4 cup* cheese and *1/2 can* French Fried Onions. Crumble 3 slices bacon; stir into corn mixture. Spoon corn mixture into 8-inch square baking dish. Bake, covered, at 375° for 40 to 45 minutes or until hot and bubbly. Top with remaining bacon slices, cheese and onions; bake, uncovered, 3 minutes or until onions are golden brown.
Makes 4 to 6 servings.

Fresh Corn Maque Choux

- 2 medium red peppers, halved lengthwise
- 6 ears fresh corn
- 2 tablespoons butter or margarine, divided
- 2 tablespoons vegetable oil
- 1 small onion, finely chopped
- 1 tablespoon sugar
- 1/2 teaspoon TABASCO® pepper sauce
- 1/2 cup chicken broth
- 1/3 cup heavy cream
- 1 egg, lightly beaten

In large saucepan over 1 inch boiling water steam pepper halves 8 minutes or until crisp-tender. Drain; reserve. With knife, cut kernels off corn cobs. (You should have about 2½ cups.) In medium skillet heat 1 tablespoon butter with oil. Add corn, onion, sugar and Tabasco® sauce. Cook until corn is almost tender and starts to form a crust on bottom of pan. Gradually stir in broth, scraping up bits on bottom of pan. Stir in remaining 1 tablespoon butter and cream. Cook 5 minutes longer or until almost all liquid evaporates; stir frequently. Remove skillet from heat. Add egg; stir 1 minute or until egg is cooked. Serve in red pepper halves.
Makes 4 servings.

Fried Eggplant

- 1 cup unseasoned dry bread crumbs
- 1/4 cup grated Parmesan cheese
- 1 teaspoon Italian seasoning
- 1/2 teaspoon salt
- 1/2 cup all-purpose flour
- 2 eggs
- 1/4 cup milk
- 1 pound eggplant, peeled and cut into 1/4-inch slices
  CRISCO® Oil for frying

Mix bread crumbs, Parmesan cheese, Italian seasoning and salt in shallow dish. Place flour on sheet of waxed paper. Blend eggs and milk in another shallow dish. Dip each slice of eggplant first in flour, then in egg mixture, then in bread crumb mixture to coat.

Heat 1/4 inch Crisco® Oil in medium skillet. Fry a few slices eggplant at a time, over moderate heat, 4 to 5 minutes, or until golden brown, turning over once. Drain on paper towels. Serve immediately or keep warm in 175°F oven. Garnish with *grated Parmesan cheese,* if desired.
4 to 6 servings.

Zesty Green Beans

1 cup water
½ teaspoon salt
⅛ to ¼ teaspoon dried crushed red pepper
1½ pounds fresh green beans, trimmed and cut into 1-inch pieces
3 tablespoons CRISCO® Oil
1 small onion, thinly sliced

Combine water, salt, and red pepper in large saucepan. Heat to boiling. Add green beans. Return to boiling. Cover. Reduce heat to moderate. Cook 10 to 15 minutes, or until tender-crisp. Drain.

Meanwhile, heat Crisco® Oil in large skillet. Add onion. Sauté over moderate heat until tender. Stir in green beans. Cover. Cook 1 to 2 minutes, or until heated through.
6 servings.

Corncakes

1⅓ cups all-purpose flour
3 tablespoons sugar
1 tablespoon DAVIS® Baking Powder
1 cup COLLEGE INN® Chicken Broth
1 egg, slightly beaten
¼ cup BLUE BONNET® Margarine, melted
1 (8¾-ounce) can whole kernel sweet corn, drained
Maple syrup

In medium bowl, combine flour, sugar and baking powder. Add chicken broth, egg and margarine, stirring just until blended. Stir in corn. Using ¼ cup batter for each pancake, cook on greased griddle or skillet, over medium heat, turning to brown on both sides. Serve with syrup.
Makes 10 (4-inch) pancakes.

Applecakes: Substitute ½ cup diced apple for corn.

Cajun-Style Green Beans

2 pounds green beans, trimmed
½ cup diced salt pork
1 clove garlic, minced
2 tablespoons white wine vinegar
1 tablespoon Dijon-style mustard
1 teaspoon sugar
½ teaspoon TABASCO® pepper sauce
¼ cup chopped celery leaves

In medium saucepan in 1 inch boiling salted water, cook beans covered 10 minutes or until crisp-tender. Drain. In small skillet over medium-high heat cook salt pork 2 to 3 minutes to render fat. Reduce heat; add garlic and cook 1 minute. Stir in vinegar, mustard, sugar and Tabasco® sauce. Remove from heat; stir in celery leaves. Toss with beans to coat.
Makes 8 servings.

Green Beans Napoli

¾ pound green beans, cut in half crosswise
2 tablespoons olive or vegetable oil
1 tablespoon butter or margarine
3 tablespoons pine nuts
1 large clove garlic, minced
1 tablespoon chopped fresh basil or ½ teaspoon dried basil leaves
¼ teaspoon TABASCO® pepper sauce
¼ teaspoon dried rosemary leaves
1 medium red pepper, cut into strips
½ teaspoon salt

In large skillet bring 1 inch water to a boil; add green beans. Cover; cook 8 to 10 minutes or until crisp-tender. Drain; set aside. In same skillet heat oil and butter; add pine nuts, garlic, basil, Tabasco® sauce and rosemary. Cook over medium heat until pine nuts are lightly browned; stir frequently. Add green beans, red pepper strips and salt to skillet. Stir-fry 2 minutes or until pepper strips are crisp-tender.
Makes 4 servings.

Original Green Bean Casserole

2 cans (16 ounces *each*) cut green beans, drained or 2 packages (9 ounces *each*) frozen cut green beans, cooked and drained
¾ cup milk
1 can (10¾ ounces) condensed cream of mushroom soup
⅛ teaspoon DURKEE Ground Black Pepper
1 can (2.8 ounces) DURKEE French Fried Onions

Preheat oven to 350°. In medium bowl, combine beans, milk, soup, pepper and ½ can French Fried Onions; pour into 1½-quart casserole. Bake, uncovered, at 350° for 30 minutes or until heated through. Top with remaining onions; bake, uncovered, 5 minutes or until onions are golden brown.
Makes 6 servings.

Microwave Directions: Prepare green bean mixture as above; pour into 1½-quart microwave-safe casserole. Cook, covered, on HIGH 8 to 10 minutes or until heated through. Stir beans halfway through cooking time. Top with remaining onions; cook, uncovered, 1 minute. Let stand for 5 minutes.

Spicy Bean Toss

1 9-oz. pkg. frozen Italian green beans, thawed, drained
1 cup red or green pepper strips
1 medium onion, sliced
3 tablespoons PARKAY Margarine
1 8³/₄-oz. can garbanzo beans, drained
¹/₃ cup pitted ripe olive slices
³/₄ teaspoon Italian seasoning
¹/₂ lb. VELVEETA Pasteurized Process Cheese Spread, cubed
¹/₄ cup milk

In large skillet, stir-fry Italian beans, peppers and onions in margarine until crisp-tender. Add garbanzo beans, olives and Italian seasoning; mix lightly. Reduce heat to low. Add process cheese spread and milk; stir until process cheese spread is melted.
4 to 6 servings.
Preparation time: 15 minutes
Cooking time: 15 minutes

Harvest Vegetable Scallop

4 medium carrots, thinly sliced (about 2 cups)
1 package (10 ounces) frozen chopped broccoli, thawed and drained
1 can (2.8 ounces) DURKEE French Fried Onions
5 small red potatoes, sliced ¹/₈ inch thick (about 2 cups)
1 jar (8 ounces) pasteurized processed cheese spread
¹/₄ cup milk
DURKEE Ground Black Pepper
DURKEE Seasoned Salt

Preheat oven to 375°. In 8×12-inch baking dish, combine carrots, broccoli and ¹/₂ can French Fried Onions. Tuck potato slices into vegetable mixture at an angle. Dot vegetables evenly with cheese spread. Pour milk over vegetables; sprinkle with seasonings as desired. Bake, covered, at 375° for 30 minutes or until vegetables are tender. Top with remaining onions; bake, uncovered, 3 minutes or until onions are golden brown.
Makes 6 servings.

Microwave Directions: In 8×12-inch microwave-safe dish, prepare vegetables as above. Top with cheese spread, milk and seasonings as above. Cook, covered, on HIGH 12 to 14 minutes or until vegetables are tender. Rotate dish halfway through cooking time. Top with remaining onions; cook, uncovered, 1 minute. Let stand 5 minutes.

French Green Peas

4 slices bacon, cooked and crumbled with 2 tablespoons drippings reserved
2 tablespoons CRISCO® Oil
¹/₂ cup all-purpose flour
2¹/₄ cups chicken broth
2 packages (10 ounces each) frozen green peas
2 small onions, thinly sliced
2 teaspoons dried parsley flakes
¹/₂ teaspoon salt
¹/₈ teaspoon pepper

Combine reserved bacon drippings and Crisco® Oil in large saucepan. Stir in flour. Cook over moderate heat, stirring constantly, 3 to 4 minutes, or until light brown. Gradually stir in broth. Heat to boiling. Add peas, onions, parsley flakes, salt and pepper. Return to boiling. Cover. Reduce heat. Simmer, stirring occasionally to break apart peas, 20 minutes, or until onion is tender. Sprinkle with crumbled bacon. Garnish with *sliced pimiento*, if desired.
8 servings.

Cajun Stuffed Eggplant

3 medium eggplants, split in half lengthwise
3 slices bacon
1 medium onion, chopped
1 small green pepper, chopped
¹/₂ cup chopped celery
2 cloves garlic, minced
¹/₂ pound ground pork
¹/₂ pound ground beef
1 can (16 ounces) whole tomatoes, drained, chopped
1 teaspoon TABASCO® pepper sauce
¹/₂ teaspoon dried thyme leaves
¹/₂ teaspoon dried oregano leaves
¹/₂ teaspoon salt
¹/₂ cup dry bread crumbs
³/₄ cup grated Parmesan cheese, divided

Place eggplant halves in large pot of boiling salted water; boil 20 to 30 minutes or until tender. Remove from water and drain cut-side-down on wire racks. Scoop out pulp being careful not to break skin. Reserve shells. Cut scooped-out portion into ¹/₂-inch cubes; set aside.

Preheat oven to 350°F. In large skillet cook bacon until crisp; remove to paper towel to cool, then crumble and reserve. In same skillet cook onion, green pepper, celery and garlic 5 minutes or until tender. Add pork and beef; cook 5 minutes longer or until meat is browned. Drain off fat. Stir in eggplant cubes, bacon, chopped tomatoes, Tabasco® sauce, thyme, oregano and salt; simmer 5 minutes. Remove from heat; stir in bread crumbs and ¹/₂ cup cheese. Spoon mixture into eggplant shells. Top with remaining ¹/₄ cup cheese. Bake 20 to 30 minutes or until eggplant is heated through and cheese is lightly browned.
Makes 6 servings.

Creamy Baked Onions

¼ cup butter or margarine
1½ pounds small whole white onions, peeled
1½ cups sliced celery
2 tablespoons flour
1¾ cups milk
2 tablespoons dry sherry wine
¼ to ½ teaspoon TABASCO® pepper sauce
¼ teaspoon salt
½ cup grated Parmesan cheese Paprika

Preheat oven to 350°F. In large skillet melt butter; add onions. Cook until lightly browned. Stir in celery; cook 1 minute longer. Remove vegetables with slotted spoon to 1½-quart casserole. In same skillet stir in flour; cook 1 minute. Remove from heat. Gradually add milk. Stir in sherry, Tabasco® sauce and salt. Return to heat. Stir constantly, bring to a boil over medium heat and boil 1 minute; stir in cheese. Pour sauce over vegetables. Bake 30 to 40 minutes or until onions are tender. Sprinkle with paprika before serving.
Makes 6 servings.

Okra-Bacon Casserole

1½ pounds young fresh okra
3 large tomatoes, chopped
1 medium onion, chopped
1 small green pepper, chopped
½ teaspoon TABASCO® pepper sauce
5 slices bacon

Preheat oven to 350°F. Slice okra into thin rounds. In greased 2½-quart casserole arrange okra, tomatoes, onion and green pepper. Season with Tabasco® sauce. Place bacon on top. Bake uncovered 1½ hours or until okra is tender.
Makes 6 to 8 servings.

Note: Two (10-ounce) packages frozen okra, thawed, may be substituted for fresh okra. Bake casserole 1 hour.
Microwave Directions: In 2½-quart microwave-safe casserole place bacon; cover with paper towel. Cook on High 4 to 5 minutes or until crisp; remove to paper towel to cool, then crumble and set aside. Into drippings in same casserole place okra, onion and green pepper; season with Tabasco® sauce. Cover loosely with plastic wrap; cook on High 15 to 18 minutes or until okra is just tender. Add tomatoes. Re-cover; cook on High 1 to 2 minutes or until tomatoes are tender. Sprinkle with reserved bacon before serving.

Onion Rings

Batter:
¾ cup all-purpose flour
½ cup water
½ cup milk
6 tablespoons white cornmeal
1 tablespoon CRISCO® Oil
¾ teaspoon seasoned salt
½ teaspoon sugar
5 or 6 drops hot red pepper sauce
Onion Rings:
CRISCO® Oil for frying
1 large onion, cut into ½-inch slices and separated into rings

Combine all batter ingredients in small mixing bowl. Stir until smooth.

Heat 2 to 3 inches Crisco® Oil in deep-fryer or large saucepan to 375°F. Dip a few onion rings in batter. Let excess batter drip back into bowl. Fry a few at a time, 2 to 3 minutes, or until golden brown. Drain on paper towels. Repeat with remaining onion rings. Serve immediately or keep warm in 175°F oven.
4 to 6 servings.

Blushing Onions

1 (16-ounce) package frozen small whole onions, cooked and drained
½ cup BAMA® Apple Jelly
¼ cup BENNETT'S® Chili Sauce
1 tablespoon margarine or butter
¼ teaspoon salt

In medium saucepan, combine ingredients; mix well. Over medium heat, bring mixture to a boil; reduce heat and simmer 10 to 15 minutes. Refrigerate leftovers.
Makes 6 servings.
Microwave: In 1½-quart baking dish, combine ingredients; mix well. Cook covered on 100% power (high) 3 to 4 minutes; stir.

Grill-Roasted Onions

4 medium yellow onions, unpeeled
1 tablespoon olive or vegetable oil
Salt and pepper
8 teaspoons butter or margarine

Cut unpeeled onion in halves lengthwise. Brush onions with oil. Place onion halves on 18×18-inch piece of heavy-duty foil. Season to taste with salt and pepper. Place 1 teaspoon butter on each onion half. Wrap loosely in foil; seal edges tightly.

Grill packet, on covered grill, over medium-hot **KINGSFORD® Charcoal Briquets** 20 minutes or until onions are tender, turning packet once. Unwrap packet and serve onions in skins.
Makes 8 servings.

Potato Pancakes

4 medium white potatoes, peeled and coarsely shredded
1 small onion, grated
1 egg
1/3 cup all-purpose flour
1 1/2 teaspoons salt
1/8 teaspoon pepper
2 tablespoons CRISCO® Oil

Combine potatoes, onion, egg, flour, salt and pepper in medium mixing bowl. Mix well. Heat Crisco® Oil in large skillet. Spoon 1/4 cup potato mixture into skillet for each of 4 pancakes. Flatten with spatula. Cook over moderate heat 10 to 15 minutes, or until golden brown, turning over once. Drain on paper towels. Add additional Crisco® Oil, if necessary. Repeat with remaining potato mixture.
6 to 8 servings.

Note: To keep shredded potatoes from turning brown, place in cold water until ready to use. Drain thoroughly and pat dry between paper towels before using.

Confetti Fried Rice

1 can (20 ounces) DOLE® Pineapple Chunks
3 1/2 teaspoons vegetable oil
1 egg, beaten
1 carrot, shredded
1 clove garlic, pressed
4 cups cooked rice
1 can (8 ounces) water chestnuts, chopped
4 ounces cooked ham, julienne-cut
1/2 cup frozen peas, thawed
1/3 cup chopped green onions
1/4 cup soy sauce
1/4 teaspoon ground ginger

Drain pineapple. Heat 1/2 teaspoon oil in wok or large skillet over low heat. Add egg and swirl around bottom of wok until egg sets in 6-inch pancake. Remove and cool. Cut into 1/8-inch strips. Heat remaining 3 teaspoons oil in wok over high heat. Stir-fry carrot and garlic about 1 minute or until tender. Add rice, stirring until grains separate. Reduce heat slightly. Stir in pineapple, water chestnuts, ham, peas, onions, soy sauce and ginger; increase heat and heat through. Gently stir in egg strips.
Makes 6 servings.

Italian-Style Roasted Peppers

6 large red, green or yellow peppers
1 cup (8 ounces) WISH-BONE® Italian Dressing
1/2 cup chopped fresh basil leaves*
1/8 teaspoon pepper

In large aluminum-foil-lined baking pan or on broiler rack, place red peppers. Broil, turning occasionally, 20 minutes or until peppers turn almost completely black. Immediately place in paper bag; close bag and let cool about 30 minutes. Under cold running water, peel off skin, then remove stems and seeds; slice into long thick strips.

In large bowl, combine peppers with remaining ingredients. Cover and marinate in refrigerator, stirring occasionally, at least 4 hours. For best flavor, serve peppers at room temperature and, if desired, with olives, mozzarella cheese and tomatoes.
Makes about 3 cups roasted peppers.

Substitution: Use 1 tablespoon dried basil leaves.

Note: Also terrific with Wish-Bone® Robusto Italian, Herbal Italian, Italian & Cheese or Lite Italian Dressing.

Homespun Scalloped Potatoes

1 8-ounce package PHILADELPHIA BRAND Cream Cheese, cubed
1 1/4 cups milk
1/2 teaspoon salt
1/8 teaspoon pepper
4 cups thin potato slices
2 tablespoons chopped chives

In large saucepan, combine cream cheese, milk, salt and pepper; stir over low heat until smooth. Add potatoes and chives; mix lightly. Spoon into 1 1/2-quart casserole; cover. Bake at 350°, 1 hour and 10 minutes or until potatoes are tender. Stir before serving.
6 servings.

Make Ahead: Prepare as directed except for baking. Cover; refrigerate overnight. When ready to serve, bake as directed.

New Year Fried Rice

3 strips bacon, diced
3/4 cup chopped green onions and tops
1/3 cup diced red bell pepper
1/4 cup frozen green peas, thawed
1 egg, beaten
4 cups cold, cooked rice
2 tablespoons KIKKOMAN Soy Sauce

Cook bacon in wok or large skillet over medium heat until crisp. Add green onions, red pepper and peas; stir-fry 1 minute. Add egg and scramble. Stir in rice and cook until heated, gently separating grains. Add soy sauce; cook and stir until heated through. Serve immediately.
Makes 6 to 8 servings.

Cajun Dirty Rice

1 package (8 ounces)
   SWANSON® Frozen Chicken
   Livers, thawed and chopped
½ cup chopped green pepper
½ cup chopped celery
1 large clove garlic, minced
¼ cup butter or margarine
1 pouch CAMPBELL'S® Onion
   Soup and Recipe Mix
2 cups water
½ teaspoon hot pepper sauce
1 cup regular rice, uncooked

1. In 10-inch skillet over medium-high heat, cook livers, green pepper, celery and garlic in butter until vegetables are tender, stirring often.
2. Stir soup mix, water and hot pepper sauce into skillet. Heat to boiling; stir in rice.
3. Reduce heat to low. Cover; simmer 20 minutes or until rice is tender.
Makes 6 servings.

Louisiana Beans and Rice

1 tablespoon vegetable oil
1 cup chopped onion
1 large green pepper, chopped
2 cloves garlic, minced
½ teaspoon dried thyme leaves,
   crushed
¼ teaspoon dried oregano
   leaves, crushed
2 cans (16 ounces each) red
   beans or pinto beans,
   drained
1 can (10¾ ounces)
   CAMPBELL'S® Condensed
   Tomato Soup
1 cup diced cooked ham or
   smoked sausage
¼ teaspoon ground red pepper
   (cayenne)
   Hot cooked rice

To Microwave:
1. In 2-quart microwave-safe casserole, combine oil, onion, green pepper, garlic, thyme and oregano. Cover with lid; microwave on HIGH 5 minutes or until vegetables are tender, stirring once during cooking.
2. Stir in beans, soup, ham and red pepper. Cover; microwave on HIGH 5 minutes or until hot. Stir.
3. Reduce power to 50%. Cover; microwave 15 minutes or until flavors are blended. Serve over rice.
Makes about 5 cups or 5 servings.
   Note: Serve as a side dish or in larger servings as a main dish.

Garden Medley Rice

1 can (13¾ oz.) ready-to-serve
   chicken broth
2 cups assorted vegetables
   (broccoli florets, sliced
   yellow squash, peas, grated
   carrot)
1 teaspoon onion flakes
2 teaspoons snipped fresh
   rosemary or 1 teaspoon
   dried rosemary leaves
¼ teaspoon garlic powder
1½ cups MINUTE® Rice
   Freshly ground pepper
   (optional)

Stir together broth, vegetables, onion flakes, rosemary and garlic powder in saucepan and bring to a full boil. Stir in rice. Cover; remove from heat. Let stand 5 minutes. Fluff with fork and sprinkle with pepper. Serve with chicken cutlets or your favorite main dish.
Makes 4 servings.
   Microwave Directions: Stir together all ingredients except pepper in microwavable bowl. Cover with plastic wrap and cook at HIGH 4 minutes. Stir; cover and cook at HIGH 3 to 5 minutes longer. Stir again; cover and cook at HIGH 3 minutes. Let stand 5 minutes. Fluff with fork and sprinkle with pepper. Serve with chicken cutlets or your favorite main dish.
Makes 4 servings.

Potato and Cheese Casserole

1 can (10¾ ounces)
   CAMPBELL'S® Condensed
   Cream of Celery Soup
1 cup shredded Cheddar cheese
   (4 ounces)
½ cup milk
   Generous dash pepper
1 large clove garlic, minced
4 cups thinly sliced potatoes
1 cup thinly sliced onions

To Microwave:
1. In medium bowl, stir soup until smooth. Add cheese, milk, pepper and garlic; stir until well blended.
2. In 2-quart microwave-safe casserole layer ½ of the potatoes, ½ of the onions and ½ of the soup mixture. Repeat layers.
3. Cover with lid; microwave on HIGH 23 minutes or until potatoes are tender, rotating dish 3 times during cooking. Let stand, covered, 5 minutes.
Makes 6 servings.

Grilled Potato Fans

¼ cup butter or margarine,
   softened
½ teaspoon salt
¼ teaspoon TABASCO® pepper
   sauce
¼ teaspoon dried oregano leaves
4 baking potatoes

In small bowl cream butter, salt, Tabasco® sauce and oregano. Without cutting all the way through, cut potatoes crosswise into slices. Spread butter mixture over potatoes. Wrap in heavy-duty aluminum foil. Place on grill over hot coals and roast 1 hour or until potatoes are tender; turn occasionally.
Makes 4 servings.

Classic Spanish Rice

1½ cups MINUTE® Rice
 1 onion, cut into thin wedges
 1 garlic clove, minced
¼ cup (½ stick) butter or
    margarine
1½ cups water
 1 can (8 oz.) tomato sauce
 1 small green pepper, diced
 1 teaspoon salt
½ teaspoon prepared mustard
    (optional)
   Sliced stuffed green olives

Cook and stir rice, onion and garlic in hot butter in large skillet over medium heat, stirring frequently until mixture is lightly browned. Stir in remaining ingredients except olives. Bring to a full boil. Cover; remove from heat. Let stand 5 minutes. Fluff with fork. Garnish with olives. Serve with chicken or your favorite main dish.
Makes 4 servings.

Cheese & Bacon Potato Bake

 1 (13¾-fluid ounce) can
    COLLEGE INN® Chicken or
    Beef Broth
 5 medium potatoes, pared and
    thinly sliced (about 5 cups)
 1 large onion, thinly sliced
 6 slices bacon
 3 tablespoons all-purpose flour
 1 cup shredded sharp Cheddar
    cheese (4 ounces)

In medium saucepan, over medium-high heat, heat broth to a boil; reduce heat. Add potatoes and onion; cover and simmer 5 minutes. Drain, reserving 1½ cups broth. In skillet, over medium-high heat, cook bacon until crisp. Remove and crumble bacon; pour off all but 3 tablespoons drippings. Blend flour into reserved drippings. Gradually add reserved broth; cook over medium heat, stirring constantly, until thickened. Stir in cheese until melted. In greased 2-quart baking dish, layer ⅓ each potato-onion mixture, sauce and bacon. Repeat layers twice. Bake at 400°F for 35 minutes or until done.
Makes 6 servings.

Sunny Fries

 1 14-oz. pkg. frozen cottage
    fries french fried potatoes
¼ lb. VELVEETA Pasteurized
    Process Cheese Spread,
    cubed
 2 tablespoons milk
½ teaspoon dry mustard

Prepare potatoes as directed on package. Combine process cheese spread, milk and mustard in saucepan; stir over low heat until process cheese spread is melted. Serve over hot cooked potatoes.
4 servings.

Preparation time: 5 minutes
Cooking time: 15 minutes

Microwave: Prepare potatoes as directed on package. Microwave process cheese spread, milk and mustard in 1-quart microwave-safe bowl on High 2½ to 3½ minutes or until process cheese spread is melted, stirring every minute. Serve over hot cooked potatoes.

Galbani® Fontina Potato Surprise

2½ pounds potatoes
 3 tablespoons butter or
    margarine, melted
¼ cup freshly grated imported
    Parmesan cheese
 1 egg
 1 egg white
⅛ teaspoon salt
⅛ teaspoon ground nutmeg
 4 tablespoons fine dry bread
    crumbs, divided
 8 ounces GALBANI® Fontina, cut
    into chunks
¼ cup freshly grated sharp
    Provolone cheese
¼ pound prosciutto, cut into
    small pieces
 2 tablespoons butter or
    margarine, cut into small
    pieces

Cook potatoes in boiling water in large saucepan over medium-low heat until tender. Drain. Cool slightly; pare. Press potatoes through food mill or mash until smooth. Combine potatoes, melted butter, Parmesan cheese, egg, egg white, salt and nutmeg in large bowl until smooth; set aside.

Sprinkle ½ of the bread crumbs in well-buttered 9-inch round baking dish. Tilt dish to coat. Spread about ½ of the potato mixture on bottom and sides of dish. Combine Fontina, Provolone and prosciutto in small bowl. Sprinkle over potato mixture in dish. Cover with remaining potato mixture; sprinkle with remaining bread crumbs. Dot with pieces of butter. Bake in preheated 350°F oven 40 minutes or until thin crust forms. Let stand 5 minutes. Invert baking dish onto serving plate, tapping gently to remove. Serve immediately.
Makes 4 to 6 servings.

*Favorite recipe from **Bel Paese Sales Co., Inc.***

Risotto with Vegetables

- 2 tablespoons butter or margarine
- 2 tablespoons vegetable oil
- 1 medium onion, chopped
- 1 clove garlic, minced
- 1 cup sliced mushrooms
- 1 cup uncooked Arborio or long grain rice*
- Pinch saffron (optional)
- 2 cups hot chicken broth, divided
- 1/4 teaspoon TABASCO® pepper sauce
- 1 to 1 1/2 cups hot water, divided
- 1 package (9 ounces) frozen artichoke hearts, cooked and drained
- 1/2 cup fresh or canned roasted red peppers, coarsely chopped**

In medium skillet heat butter and oil; cook onion, garlic and mushrooms 5 minutes or until onions are translucent. Add rice; cook 1 to 2 minutes or until partly translucent. Stir in saffron, if desired.

Add 1/2 cup hot broth and Tabasco® sauce; stir constantly until rice absorbs broth. Add remaining broth and hot water, 1/2 cup at a time; stir constantly from bottom and sides of pan and wait until rice just begins to dry out before adding more liquid. Cook and stir until rice is tender but firm to the bite, and is the consistency of creamy rice pudding. (The total amount of liquid used will vary. Watch rice carefully to ensure proper consistency.) Total cooking time is about 30 minutes. Stir in artichokes and roasted peppers. Serve with additional Tabasco® sauce, if desired.
Makes 6 servings.

*Arborio rice gives the best results. Do not use converted rice.

**To roast peppers, hold over source of heat with a fork until skin blisters. Cool slightly; peel and chop.

Skillet Potatoes

- 3 tablespoons butter or margarine
- 1 cup sliced celery
- 1/2 cup chopped onion
- 2 cloves garlic, minced
- 1 can (10 3/4 ounces) CAMPBELL'S® Condensed Chicken Broth
- 1/4 cup water
- 4 cups cubed potatoes
- 1 cup carrots cut into julienne strips
- 1/8 teaspoon pepper
- Chopped fresh parsley

1. In 10-inch skillet over medium heat, in hot butter, cook celery, onion and garlic until vegetables are tender, stirring occasionally.
2. Add broth, water, potatoes, carrots and pepper to skillet. Heat to boiling; reduce heat to low. Cover; simmer 15 minutes or until potatoes are tender.
3. Uncover; over medium heat, simmer 5 minutes or until broth is slightly thickened, stirring often. Sprinkle with parsley before serving.
Makes about 5 cups or 6 servings.

Spicy Rice

- 2 tablespoons CRISCO® Oil
- 1 cup uncooked long grain rice
- 1 small onion, halved lengthwise and thinly sliced
- 2 cups water
- 2 tablespoons raisins
- 1 teaspoon salt
- 3 whole cloves
- 1 bay leaf
- 1/8 teaspoon ground cardamom
- 1/8 teaspoon pepper

Heat Crisco® Oil in large saucepan. Add rice and onion. Cook over moderate heat, stirring constantly, until golden brown. Add remaining ingredients. Heat to boiling. Cover. Reduce heat. Simmer 20 to 25 minutes, or until rice is tender. Remove and discard cloves and bay leaf.
6 servings.

Tex-Mex Rice and Beans

- 1/2 cup chopped onion
- 1 garlic clove, minced
- 1 tablespoon oil
- 1 can (15 oz.) red kidney beans, drained
- 1 can (10 1/2 oz.) condensed beef bouillon
- 1 medium green pepper, diced
- 1/2 cup barbecue sauce
- 1 1/2 cups MINUTE® Rice

Cook and stir onion and garlic in hot oil in large skillet until onion is tender but not browned. Stir in beans, bouillon, green pepper and barbecue sauce. Bring to a full boil. Stir in rice. Cover; remove from heat. Let stand 5 minutes. Fluff with fork.
Makes 4 servings.

Microwave Directions: Omit oil. Mix all ingredients in microwavable dish. Cover and cook at HIGH 5 minutes. Stir; cover and cook at HIGH 3 minutes longer. Stir; cover and let stand 5 minutes.
Makes 4 servings.

Fried Potato Wedges

- 4 medium white potatoes, baked
- CRISCO® Oil for frying

Cut each potato into 6 wedges. Heat 2 to 3 inches Crisco® Oil in deep-fryer or large saucepan to 375°F. Fry half the wedges at a time 2 to 3 minutes, or until golden brown. Drain on paper towels. Serve immediately.
4 to 6 servings.

Pecan-Stuffed Squash

1 (13¾-fluid ounce) can
  COLLEGE INN® Beef or
  Chicken Broth
2 small acorn squash, halved
  and seeded
⅓ cup BLUE BONNET® Margarine
2 cups dry herb-seasoned
  stuffing mix
1 (2-ounce) package
  PLANTERS® Pecan Pieces
⅓ cup seedless raisins

Reserve ⅔ cup broth; pour remaining broth into shallow baking dish. Place squash cut-side down in broth. Bake at 400°F for 25 to 35 minutes. In medium saucepan, over medium-high heat, heat reserved broth and margarine until margarine melts; stir in stuffing mix, pecans and raisins. Turn squash over, cut-side up; spoon stuffing into squash cavities. Bake 20 minutes more or until squash is done, basting with broth after 10 minutes.
Makes 4 servings.

Microwave: Reserve ⅔ cup broth. In 2-quart microwave-proof oblong dish, place squash cut-side down in remaining broth. Microwave, uncovered, on HIGH (100% power) for 6 to 7 minutes. In 1-quart microwave-proof bowl, place reserved broth and margarine. Microwave, uncovered, on HIGH for 1 to 2 minutes until margarine melts. Stir in stuffing mix, pecans and raisins. Turn squash over, cut-side up; spoon stuffing into squash cavities. Microwave, uncovered, on HIGH for 5 to 6 minutes until stuffing is heated through and squash is done. Let stand 5 minutes before serving.

Golden Squash Bake

8 cups sliced yellow crookneck
  squash, cooked and drained
6 slices bacon, cooked and
  crumbled
2 eggs
1 cup BORDEN® or MEADOW
  GOLD® Cottage Cheese
2 tablespoons flour
2 teaspoons WYLER'S® or
  STEERO® Chicken-Flavor
  Instant Bouillon
1 cup (4 ounces) shredded
  sharp Cheddar cheese

Preheat oven to 350°. In large bowl, combine eggs, cottage cheese, flour and bouillon. Add squash; mix well. Turn into greased 12×7-inch baking dish. Top with Cheddar cheese and bacon. Bake 20 to 25 minutes. Let stand 5 minutes before serving. Refrigerate leftovers.
Makes 6 to 8 servings.

Southern-Style Squash and Okra

2 small onions, sliced and
  separated into rings
3 medium crookneck squash,
  cut into ¼-inch slices
1 package (10 ounces) frozen
  whole okra, thawed and cut
  into bite-size pieces
2 tablespoons butter or
  margarine
1 clove garlic, minced
1 teaspoon salt
⅛ teaspoon pepper
½ teaspoon dried thyme,
  crushed
1 tablespoon lemon juice
¼ cup grated Cheddar cheese
  (1 ounce)

Place onion slices, squash and okra on 24×18-inch piece of heavy-duty foil. Dot with butter. Sprinkle with garlic, salt, pepper, thyme and lemon juice. Fold and seal foil edges tightly. Grill packet, on covered grill, over medium-hot **KINGSFORD® Charcoal Briquets** 25 to 30 minutes or until tender, turning packet over once. To serve, unwrap foil packet and sprinkle with Cheddar cheese.
Makes 4 to 6 servings.

Creamy Baked Mashed Potatoes

1 envelope LIPTON® Vegetable
  Recipe Soup Mix
4 cups hot mashed potatoes*
1 cup shredded Cheddar or
  Swiss cheese (about
  4 ounces)
½ cup chopped green onions
  (optional)
1 egg, slightly beaten
⅛ teaspoon pepper

Preheat oven to 375°.

In lightly greased 1½-quart casserole, thoroughly combine all ingredients except ¼ cup cheese. Bake 40 minutes. Top with remaining cheese and bake an additional 5 minutes or until cheese is melted.
Makes about 8 servings.

*Do not use salt when preparing hot mashed potatoes.

Microwave Directions: In lightly greased 1½-quart casserole, thoroughly combine all ingredients except ¼ cup cheese. Heat covered at HIGH (Full Power), turning casserole occasionally, 7 minutes or until heated through. Top with remaining cheese, then let stand covered 5 minutes.

Saucy Garden Patch Vegetables

1 can (11 ounces) condensed Cheddar cheese soup
1/2 cup sour cream
1/4 cup milk
1/2 teaspoon DURKEE Seasoned Salt
1 bag (16 ounces) frozen vegetable combination (broccoli, corn, red pepper), thawed and drained
1 bag (16 ounces) frozen vegetable combination (brussels sprouts, carrots, cauliflower), thawed and drained
1 cup (4 ounces) shredded Cheddar cheese
1 can (2.8 ounces) DURKEE French Fried Onions

Preheat oven to 375°. In large bowl, combine soup, sour cream, milk, seasoned salt, vegetables, *1/2 cup* cheese and *1/2 can* French Fried Onions. Spoon into 8×12-inch baking dish. Bake, covered, at 375° for 40 minutes or until vegetables are done. Top with remaining cheese and onions; bake, uncovered, 3 minutes or until onions are golden brown.
Makes 8 to 10 servings.

Microwave Directions: Prepare vegetable mixture as above; spoon into 8×12-inch microwave-safe dish. Cook, covered, on HIGH 10 to 12 minutes or until vegetables are done. Stir vegetables halfway through cooking time. Top with remaining cheese and onions; cook, uncovered, 1 minute or until cheese melts. Let stand for 5 minutes.

Chinese Spinach

3 tablespoons CRISCO® Oil
1 tablespoon soy sauce
1 teaspoon lime juice
1/2 teaspoon sugar
1/8 teaspoon pepper
1 clove garlic, minced
1/2 cup diagonally sliced green onion, 1-inch slices
12 ounces fresh spinach, trimmed, washed and torn into bite-size pieces
1/4 cup sliced water chestnuts
1 jar (2 ounces) sliced pimiento, drained

Heat Crisco® Oil, soy sauce, lime juice, sugar and pepper in large skillet. Add garlic. Stir-fry over medium-high heat about 1 minute, or until garlic is light brown. Add onion. Stir-fry 1 minute. Add spinach, water chestnuts and pimiento. Stir-fry 2 to 3 minutes longer, or until spinach is tender.
4 to 6 servings.

Spinach Almond Casserole

1 recipe Sesame Vegetable Topping (see Index)
2 packages (10 ounces each) frozen chopped spinach, thawed
2 tablespoons CRISCO® Oil
1/4 cup chopped onion
2 tablespoons chopped celery
2 tablespoons all-purpose flour
1 teaspoon salt
1/2 teaspoon dried dill weed
1/8 teaspoon pepper
1 cup half-and-half
1 egg, slightly beaten
3 tablespoons chopped almonds

Prepare Sesame Vegetable Topping as directed. Set aside. Preheat oven to 325°F.

Press excess moisture from spinach. Set aside.

Heat Crisco® Oil in medium saucepan. Add onion and celery. Sauté over moderate heat until tender. Remove from heat. Stir in flour, salt, dill weed and pepper. Return to heat. Blend in half-and-half. Cook, stirring constantly, until bubbly. Remove from heat. Blend in egg. Stir in spinach and almonds. Transfer to lightly oiled 1-quart casserole. Sprinkle with Sesame Vegetable Topping. Bake at 325°F, 35 to 40 minutes, or until hot and topping is light brown.
6 to 8 servings.

Crisp Onion-Roasted Potatoes

1 envelope LIPTON® Onion or Onion-Mushroom Recipe Soup Mix
1/2 cup olive or vegetable oil
1/4 cup butter or margarine, melted
1 teaspoon thyme leaves (optional)
1 teaspoon marjoram leaves (optional)
1/4 teaspoon pepper
2 pounds all-purpose potatoes, cut into quarters

Preheat oven to 450°.

In shallow baking or roasting pan, thoroughly blend all ingredients except potatoes. Add potatoes and turn to coat thoroughly. Bake, stirring potatoes occasionally, 60 minutes or until potatoes are tender and golden brown. Garnish, if desired, with chopped parsley.
Makes about 8 servings.

Vegetable Sunburst

- 3 medium carrots, thinly sliced (about 3 cups)
- 3 small zucchini, thinly sliced (about 3 cups)
- 1 cup (4 ounces) shredded Cheddar cheese
- 1 can (2.8 ounces) DURKEE French Fried Onions
- 1 can (10¾ ounces) condensed cream of celery soup
- ¼ cup milk
- ½ teaspoon DURKEE Seasoned Salt
- ¼ teaspoon DURKEE Garlic Powder
- ¼ teaspoon DURKEE Leaf Oregano

Preheat oven to 350°. In medium saucepan, cook carrots in boiling water to cover just until tender-crisp. Place hot carrots under cold running water until cool enough to handle; drain. In 1½-quart casserole, arrange *half* the carrots around edge of dish; place *half* the zucchini in center. Sprinkle ½ *cup* cheese and ½ *can* French Fried Onions over vegetables. In small bowl, combine soup, milk and seasonings. Pour *half* the soup mixture over onions. Arrange remaining zucchini around edge of casserole and remaining carrots in center. Pour remaining soup mixture over vegetables. Bake, covered, at 350° for 30 minutes or until vegetables are tender. Top with remaining cheese and onions; bake, uncovered, 5 minutes or until onions are golden brown.
Makes 4 to 6 servings.

Microwave Directions: Place carrots and ½ cup water in medium microwave-safe bowl; cook on HIGH 5 to 7 minutes or until carrots are tender-crisp. Stir carrots halfway through cooking time. Drain. Prepare soup mixture as above. In 1½-quart microwave-safe casserole, layer vegetables, cheese, onions and soup mixture as above. Cook, covered, 8 to 10 minutes or until vegetables are tender. Rotate dish halfway through cooking time. Top with remaining cheese and onions; cook, uncovered, 1 minute or until cheese melts. Let stand 5 minutes.

Skewered Vegetables

- 2 medium zucchini, cut into 1½-inch slices
- 8 small boiling onions
- 8 fresh medium mushrooms
- 2 tablespoons butter or margarine, melted
- 4 cherry tomatoes
  Salt and pepper

In medium saucepan, cook zucchini and onions, covered, in boiling water to cover for 1 minute. Remove with slotted spoon and drain. Alternately thread zucchini, onions and mushrooms on 4 skewers. Brush with melted butter.

Grill vegetables, on covered grill, over medium-hot **KINGSFORD® Charcoal Briquets** 6 minutes or until tender, carefully turning skewers once. Add cherry tomatoes to end of skewers during last minute of grilling. Season to taste with salt and pepper. Serve immediately.
Makes 4 servings.

Polynesian Vegetables

- 1 can (20 ounces) DOLE® Pineapple Chunks
- ½ cup chopped onion
- 2 cloves garlic, pressed
- 3 tablespoons soy sauce
- 1 tablespoon sesame oil
- 1 tablespoon cornstarch
- ½ teaspoon salt
- 2 DOLE™ Carrots, thinly sliced on diagonal (2 cups)
- 1 bunch DOLE™ Broccoli, cut into flowerets (2 cups)
- 1 DOLE™ Red or Green Bell Pepper, seeded and cut into chunks
- 2 to 3 tablespoons sesame seeds, toasted

To Microwave: Drain pineapple juice into 2½-quart microwave-safe casserole dish. Stir in onion, garlic, soy sauce, oil, cornstarch and salt. Microwave on HIGH about 4 minutes, stirring after 2 minutes. Add carrots; stir to coat. Cover. Microwave on HIGH 5 to 6 minutes. Stir in broccoli and bell pepper; microwave on HIGH 3 to 5 minutes longer or until vegetables are tender-crisp. Remove cover. Stir in pineapple; continue microwaving on HIGH 2 to 3 minutes. Let stand 5 minutes before serving. Sprinkle with sesame seeds.
Makes 6 servings.

Stuffed Tomatoes

- 6 to 8 medium tomatoes
- 2 tablespoons CRISCO® Oil
- ⅓ cup chopped celery
- 2 tablespoons chopped onion
- 2 cups cooked brown rice
- ¼ cup grated Parmesan cheese
- 1 tablespoon snipped fresh parsley
- 1 teaspoon dried basil leaves
- ⅛ teaspoon pepper
- ⅛ teaspoon garlic powder

Cut thin slice from top of each tomato. Set tops aside. Scoop out center of tomatoes; chop pulp and set aside. Place shells upside down on paper towels to drain.

Preheat oven to 350°F. Heat Crisco® Oil in medium saucepan. Add celery and onion. Sauté over moderate heat until celery is tender. Remove from heat. Add reserved tomato pulp, rice, Parmesan cheese, parsley, basil, pepper and garlic powder. Mix well. Fill tomato shells with rice mixture. Replace tomato tops, if desired.

Lightly oil 9-inch pie plate or round baking dish. Place tomatoes in dish. Cover with aluminum foil. Bake at 350°F, 30 to 45 minutes, or until tomatoes are tender.
6 to 8 servings.

Note: Use 1 lightly oiled custard cup for each tomato instead of pie plate or baking dish, if desired.

Grilled Tomatoes

**2 large tomatoes
2 tablespoons olive or vegetable oil
1½ teaspoons chopped fresh basil or ½ teaspoon dried basil, crushed
Salt and pepper**

In covered grill, arrange medium-hot **KINGSFORD® Charcoal Briquets** on one side of grill. Slice each tomato in half crosswise; remove excess juice and seeds. Drizzle tomato halves with oil. Place in foil pan. Place foil pan on edge of grill not directly over coals. Cook tomatoes, on covered grill, 10 to 14 minutes or until heated through. Sprinkle cut surfaces with basil, salt and pepper. Garnish with fresh basil, if desired.
Makes 4 servings.

Swiss Vegetable Medley

**1 bag (16 ounces) frozen vegetable combination (broccoli, carrots, cauliflower), thawed and drained
1 can (10¾ ounces) condensed cream of mushroom soup
1 cup (4 ounces) shredded Swiss cheese
⅓ cup sour cream
¼ teaspoon DURKEE Ground Black Pepper
1 jar (4 ounces) diced pimiento, drained (optional)
1 can (2.8 ounces) DURKEE French Fried Onions**

Preheat oven to 350°. In large bowl, combine vegetables, soup, *½ cup* cheese, the sour cream, pepper, pimiento and *½ can* French Fried Onions. Pour into shallow 1-quart casserole. Bake, covered, at 350° for 30 minutes or until vegetables are done. Sprinkle remaining cheese and onions in diagonal rows across top; bake, uncovered, 5 minutes or until onions are golden brown.
Makes 6 servings.

Microwave Directions: Prepare vegetable mixture as above; pour into shallow 1-quart microwave-safe casserole. Cook, covered, on HIGH 8 to 10 minutes or until vegetables are done. Stir vegetables halfway through cooking time. Top with remaining cheese and onions as above; cook, uncovered, 1 minute or until cheese melts. Let stand 5 minutes.

Fresh Vegetable Ring

**2 cups broccoli flowerets
2 cups cauliflowerets
1 small zucchini, cut into ¼-inch slices
1 small yellow squash, cut into ¼-inch slices
1 can (10¾ ounces) CAMPBELL'S® Condensed Chicken Broth
6 medium CAMPBELL'S FRESH® Mushrooms, halved
Sweet red pepper strips for garnish
2 teaspoons cornstarch
1 teaspoon chopped fresh basil leaves or ½ teaspoon dried basil leaves, crushed
1 teaspoon wine vinegar**

To Microwave:
1. Arrange broccoli in a circle around rim of a 12-inch round microwave-safe platter. Arrange cauliflower next to broccoli. Arrange alternate slices of zucchini and yellow squash next to cauliflower, leaving space in center of platter. Pour ¼ cup of the broth over vegetables. Cover with vented plastic wrap; microwave on HIGH 5 minutes, rotating dish once during cooking.
2. Place mushrooms in center of platter. Garnish with red pepper strips. Cover; microwave on HIGH 2 minutes or until vegetables are tender-crisp. Let stand, covered, while preparing sauce.
3. To make sauce: In small microwave-safe bowl, combine remaining broth, cornstarch, basil and vinegar; stir until smooth. Cover with vented plastic wrap; microwave on HIGH 2 minutes or until mixture boils, stirring twice during cooking. Spoon over vegetables in platter.
Makes 6 servings.

Tangy Blue Cheese Vegetables

**1 package (3 ounces) cream cheese, softened
¼ cup (2 ounces) crumbled blue cheese
¾ cup milk
1 jar (4½ ounces) whole mushrooms, drained
1 bag (16 ounces) frozen vegetable combination (peas, carrots, cauliflower), thawed and drained
1 can (2.8 ounces) DURKEE French Fried Onions**

Preheat oven to 375°. In medium saucepan, combine cream cheese, blue cheese and milk. Cook and stir over medium heat until smooth. Stir in mushrooms, vegetables and ½ *can* French Fried Onions; pour into 1-quart casserole. Bake, covered, at 375° for 30 minutes or until vegetables are done. Top with remaining onions; bake, uncovered, 3 minutes or until onions are golden brown.
Makes 4 to 6 servings.

Microwave Directions: In 1-quart microwave-safe casserole, combine cream cheese, blue cheese and milk. Cook, covered, on HIGH 5 to 6 minutes or until cheeses melt, stirring mixture halfway through cooking time. Add mushrooms, vegetables and ½ *can* onions; cook, covered, 5 to 7 minutes or until vegetables are done. Stir halfway through cooking time. Top with remaining onions; cook, uncovered, 1 minute. Let stand for 5 minutes.

Grill-Baked Sweet Potatoes

4 medium sweet potatoes
  Vegetable oil
4 tablespoons butter or
  margarine
4 tablespoons brown sugar

Tear off four 6×9-inch pieces of heavy-duty foil. Brush sweet potatoes with oil. Pierce several times with fork. Wrap potatoes in foil. Grill potatoes, on uncovered grill, over medium-hot **KINGSFORD®** Charcoal Briquets about 1 hour or until tender, turning once. Remove foil. Open potatoes with tines of fork and push ends to fluff. Top each with 1 tablespoon butter and 1 tablespoon brown sugar.
Makes 4 servings.

Pronto Zucchini

4 cups mushroom slices
4 cups zucchini slices
¼ cup PARKAY Margarine
½ cup spaghetti sauce
¼ lb. VELVEETA Pasteurized
  Process Cheese Spread,
  cubed
2 teaspoons dried oregano
  leaves, crushed

In large skillet, saute vegetables in margarine until crisp-tender. Drain. Reduce heat to low. Add sauce, process cheese spread and oregano; stir until process cheese spread is melted.
4 to 6 servings.

Preparation time: 10 minutes
Cooking time: 15 minutes

Variation: Substitute 2 tablespoons chopped fresh oregano leaves for dried oregano leaves.

Sesame Vegetable Topping

2 tablespoons CRISCO® Oil
2 tablespoons finely chopped
  onion
2 teaspoons sesame seeds
½ cup buttery round cracker
  crumbs

Heat Crisco® Oil in small skillet. Add onion. Sauté over moderate heat until tender-crisp. Add sesame seeds. Cook, stirring constantly, 1 minute. Remove from heat. Stir in cracker crumbs. Use as a topping for vegetable dishes.
About ½ cup.

Sweet 'n Sour Stir Fry

2 tablespoons oil
1 cup thinly sliced carrots
1 cup snow peas (about
  4 ounces)
1 small green pepper, cut into
  chunks
1 cup sliced water chestnuts
1 medium tomato, cut into
  wedges
½ cup sliced cucumber, halved
¾ cup WISH-BONE® Sweet 'n
  Spicy French Dressing
2 tablespoons brown sugar
2 teaspoons soy sauce

In medium skillet, heat oil and cook carrots, snow peas and green pepper over medium heat, stirring frequently, 5 minutes or until crisp-tender. Add water chestnuts, tomato, cucumber and sweet 'n spicy French dressing blended with brown sugar and soy sauce. Simmer covered 5 minutes or until vegetables are tender. Top, if desired, with sesame seeds.
Makes about 6 servings.
Note: Also terrific with Wish-Bone® Lite Sweet 'n Spicy French, Russian or Lite Russian Dressing.

Almondine Butter Sauce

½ cup sliced almonds
⅓ cup butter or margarine
¼ cup REALEMON® Lemon Juice
  from Concentrate

In small skillet, over medium low heat, cook almonds in margarine until golden; remove from heat. Stir in ReaLemon® brand. Serve warm over cooked vegetables or fish.
Makes ⅔ cup.

Easy "Hollandaise" Sauce

½ lb. VELVEETA Pasteurized
  Process Cheese Spread,
  cubed
¼ cup milk
¼ teaspoon paprika
1 egg, beaten
2 teaspoons lemon juice

Combine process cheese spread, milk and paprika in saucepan; stir over low heat until process cheese spread is melted. Stir small amount of hot mixture into egg; return to hot mixture. Cook, stirring constantly, over low heat until thickened. Stir in juice. Serve over hot cooked vegetables or fish.
1¼ cups.

Preparation time: 5 minutes
Cooking time: 15 minutes

Microwave: Microwave process cheese spread, milk and paprika in 1-quart microwave-safe bowl. Microwave on High 2½ to 3½ minutes or until process cheese spread is melted, stirring every minute. Stir small amount of hot mixture into egg; return to hot mixture. Microwave on Medium (50%) 1 to 1½ minutes or until thickened, stirring every 30 seconds. Stir in juice. Serve over hot cooked vegetables or fish.

Stir-Fried Vegetables with Bulgur

2 tablespoons vegetable oil
2 cups broccoli flowerets
1 cup thinly sliced carrots
1 cup bulgur wheat
1 small clove garlic, minced
1 tablespoon sesame seed
1 teaspoon dried oregano
  leaves, crushed
1¾ cups V8® Vegetable Juice
1 cup thinly sliced zucchini
1 cup sliced CAMPBELL'S
  FRESH® Mushrooms
  (4 ounces)
¼ cup sliced green onions
½ cup shredded Swiss cheese
  (2 ounces)

1. In 10-inch skillet or wok over medium-high heat, in hot oil, cook broccoli, carrots, bulgur, garlic, sesame seed and oregano, stirring quickly and frequently (stir-frying), about 2 minutes.
2. Add V8 juice, zucchini, mushrooms and green onions. Heat to boiling; reduce heat to low. Cover; simmer 15 minutes or until all liquid is absorbed, stirring occasionally.
3. Stir in cheese.
Makes 5 cups or 10 side-dish servings.

Per serving: 141 calories, 4 g protein, 5 g fat, 20 g carbohydrate, 173 mg sodium, 6 mg cholesterol.

Italian Vegetable Sauté

2 tablespoons CRISCO® Oil
1 clove garlic, minced
¼ teaspoon dried oregano leaves
¼ teaspoon dried marjoram
  leaves
2 cups julienne-cut zucchini
1 small onion, thinly sliced and
  separated into rings
1 can (16 ounces) whole
  tomatoes, drained, cut up
2 tablespoons sliced, pitted
  black olives (optional)
½ teaspoon salt
⅛ teaspoon pepper
2 tablespoons grated Parmesan
  cheese

Heat Crisco® Oil in large skillet. Add garlic, oregano and marjoram. Sauté over moderate heat until garlic is light brown. Add zucchini and onion. Stir to coat. Sauté 5 to 7 minutes, or until tender. Stir in tomatoes, olives (optional), salt and pepper. Cook until heated through. Stir in Parmesan cheese.
4 to 6 servings.

Spicy Vegetable Stir-Fry

¾ to 1 pound fresh broccoli
¼ cup CRISCO® Oil
1 medium zucchini, cut into
  julienne strips
1 small onion, halved lengthwise
  and thinly sliced
⅛ teaspoon dried crushed red
  pepper
1 cup sliced fresh mushrooms
2 tablespoons shelled sunflower
  seeds
2 teaspoons soy sauce

Trim and discard tough ends from broccoli stalks. Cut stalks into thin slices. Separate heads into flowerets.
  Heat Crisco® Oil in large skillet. Add broccoli, zucchini, onion and red pepper. Stir-fry over medium-high heat about 5 minutes, or until broccoli is tender-crisp. Add mushrooms. Stir-fry 1 minute longer, or until mushrooms are tender. Stir in sunflower seeds and soy sauce.
4 to 6 servings.

Citrus Candied Sweet Potatoes

2 (16- or 18-ounce) cans sweet
  potatoes, drained
1¼ cups firmly packed light brown
  sugar
2 tablespoons cornstarch
¾ cup orange juice
¼ cup REALEMON® Lemon Juice
  from Concentrate
2 tablespoons margarine or
  butter, melted

Preheat oven to 350°. In 2-quart shallow baking dish, arrange sweet potatoes. In medium bowl, combine sugar and cornstarch; add orange juice, ReaLemon® brand and margarine. Pour over sweet potatoes. Bake 50 to 55 minutes, basting occasionally with sauce.
Makes 6 to 8 servings.
  Microwave: Arrange sweet potatoes as above. Increase cornstarch to 3 tablespoons. In 1-quart glass measure, combine sugar and cornstarch. Add orange juice, ReaLemon® brand and margarine. Cook on 100% power (high) 5 to 8 minutes until slightly thickened, stirring every 2 minutes. Pour over sweet potatoes; cook on 100% power (high) 8 minutes, basting after 4 minutes. Let stand 2 minutes before serving.

PIZZA & SANDWICHES

A treasury of ideas for two American classics. Homemade pizza, fresh from the oven, will become a delicious tradition with these easy-to-prepare recipes. Sandwiches with star quality—glamorous enough for company— turn lunches and midnight snacks into delectable feasts. Perk up a casual supper with tacos, fajitas or extra-special burgers.

Classic Pizza

½ tablespoon active dry yeast
1 teaspoon sugar
½ cup very warm water (105°F to 115°F)
1¾ cups all-purpose flour
¾ teaspoon salt
2 tablespoons olive oil
1 medium onion, chopped
1 medium clove garlic, minced
1 can (14½ ounces) whole peeled tomatoes, undrained, chopped
2 tablespoons tomato paste
1 teaspoon dried oregano, crumbled
½ teaspoon dried basil, crumbled
⅛ teaspoon black pepper
1¾ cups shredded mozzarella cheese
½ cup grated Parmesan cheese
½ small red bell pepper, chopped
½ small green bell pepper, chopped
⅓ cup pitted ripe olives, cut into halves
4 fresh medium mushrooms, sliced
1 can (2 ounces) flat anchovy fillets, drained

1. Sprinkle yeast and ½ teaspoon of the sugar over warm water in small bowl; stir until yeast is dissolved. Let stand until mixture is bubbly.
2. Place 1½ cups of the flour and ¼ teaspoon of the salt in medium bowl; stir in yeast mixture and 1 tablespoon of the oil, stirring until a smooth, soft dough forms. Knead on floured surface, using as much remaining flour as needed to form stiff elastic dough. Let dough rise, covered, in greased bowl in warm place until doubled in bulk, 30 to 45 minutes.
3. Meanwhile, heat remaining 1 tablespoon oil in medium saucepan over medium heat. Add onion; cook until soft, about 5 minutes. Add garlic; cook 30 seconds. Add tomatoes, tomato paste, oregano, basil, remaining ½ teaspoon sugar, remaining ½ teaspoon salt and the black pepper. Heat to boiling; reduce heat to medium-low. Simmer, uncovered, stirring occasionally, until sauce is thick, 10 to 15 minutes. Transfer sauce to bowl; let cool.
4. Heat oven to 450°F. Punch dough down. Knead briefly on lightly floured surface to distribute air bubbles; let dough rest 5 minutes. Flatten dough into circle on lightly floured surface. Roll out dough, into 10-inch circle. Place circle in greased 12-inch pizza pan; pat dough out to edges of pan. Let stand, covered, 15 minutes.
5. Mix mozzarella and Parmesan cheeses in small bowl. Spread sauce evenly over pizza dough. Sprinkle with two-thirds of the cheeses. Arrange bell peppers, olives, mushrooms and anchovies on top of pizza. Sprinkle remaining cheeses on top of pizza. Bake until crust is golden brown, about 20 minutes. Cut into wedges to serve.
Makes 4 to 6 servings.

Bagel Pizza

2 tablespoons prepared pizza
sauce
1 bagel, cut in half
2 teaspoons grated Parmesan
cheese
2 teaspoons sliced green onion
2 slices LITE-LINE® Mozzarella
Flavor Process Cheese
Product*
2 teaspoons finely chopped
green pepper
2 pitted ripe olives, sliced

Spread 1 tablespoon pizza sauce on
each bagel half. Top with equal portions of remaining ingredients. Place
on baking sheet; bake at 400° for 4 to
5 minutes *or* broil until Lite-line slice
begins to melt.
Makes 1 serving; 293 calories.
*"½ the calories"—8% milkfat
product. Caloric values by product
analyses and recipe calculation.

Pizza Bread Pronto

½ pound sliced SWIFT
PREMIUM® or MARGHERITA®
Deli Peperoni
Butter or margarine, softened
4 mini French rolls, 8 inches
long, sliced lengthwise
Grated Parmesan cheese
1 can (8 ounces) pizza sauce
Sliced mozzarella cheese
Dried oregano leaves

Spread butter over cut sides of rolls
and sprinkle with Parmesan cheese.
Broil, 4 inches from heat, until lightly
browned. Spread several tablespoons
pizza sauce over each. Layer peperoni
over sauce. Top with mozzarella
cheese and sprinkle with oregano.
Broil until cheese melts. Serve hot.
Makes 8 servings.

Turkey Pizza Nicoise

2 cups julienned strips cooked
BUTTERBALL® turkey
(³/₄ pound)
3 tablespoons olive oil
3 tablespoons red wine vinegar
2 cloves garlic, minced
1 to 2 teaspoons dried tarragon
leaves, crushed
1 can (8 ounces) pizza sauce
1 prepared pizza crust, 10-inch
diameter
1½ cups (6 ounces) finely
shredded Swiss cheese,
divided
1 can (2¼ ounces) sliced black
olives, drained
1 medium tomato, cut into
½-inch wedges
1 tablespoon capers
2 tablespoons grated Parmesan
cheese

Preheat oven to 400°F. Combine oil,
vinegar, garlic and tarragon in medium bowl. Add turkey; toss gently to
coat. Cover and marinate in refrigerator 1 hour. Spread pizza sauce over
crust. Sprinkle 1 cup Swiss cheese on
sauce. Arrange olives, tomatoes and
capers over pizza. Top with marinated
turkey. Sprinkle with Parmesan
cheese and remaining ½ cup Swiss
cheese. Bake in oven 10 to 15 minutes
or until cheese melts and is golden.
Yield: 4 servings.

English Muffin Pizzas

2 English muffins, split and
toasted
¼ cup PREGO® Spaghetti Sauce
¼ cup shredded mozzarella
cheese (1 ounce)
Pepperoni or frankfurter slices
for garnish
VLASIC® or EARLY
CALIFORNIA® Sliced Olives,
green pepper or mushrooms
for garnish

To Microwave:
1. Spread each muffin half with 1 tablespoon spaghetti sauce; sprinkle
with 1 tablespoon cheese. Top with
garnish, if desired.
2. Arrange pizzas in circular pattern
on microwave-safe plate lined with paper towels. Microwave, uncovered, on
HIGH 1½ minutes or until cheese
melts, rotating plate once during
cooking.
Makes 4 pizzas.

Mini Tortilla Pizzas

2 tablespoons oil
1 medium green pepper,
coarsely chopped
1 envelope LIPTON® Onion or
Onion-Mushroom Recipe
Soup Mix
1 can (8 ounces) tomato sauce
1 cup water
1 teaspoon chili powder
½ teaspoon ground cumin
(optional)
2 cups cut-up cooked chicken
4 corn or flour tortillas
2 cups shredded Monterey Jack
or Cheddar cheese
(8 ounces)

Preheat oven to 375°.
In large saucepan, heat oil and cook
green pepper over medium heat until
tender. Stir in onion recipe soup mix,
tomato sauce, water, chili powder and
cumin. Bring to a boil, then simmer,
stirring occasionally, 10 minutes. Stir
in chicken.
Meanwhile, on baking sheet, arrange tortillas. If desired, lightly
brush tortillas with additional oil for
extra crispness. Spoon chicken mixture evenly on tortillas, then top with
cheese. Bake 15 minutes or until
cheese is melted and sauce is bubbling. Serve, if desired, with sour
cream, chopped tomato and additional shredded cheese. Garnish, if desired, with jalapeño peppers.
Makes 4 servings.

Neapolitan Pizza

1 pouch CAMPBELL'S® Onion
　　Soup and Recipe Mix
2 cups all-purpose flour
1 tablespoon sugar
1 package active dry yeast
3/4 cup very warm water (120° to
　　130°F.)
2 tablespoons olive or vegetable
　　oil
2 CAMPBELL'S FRESH®
　　Tomatoes, thinly sliced
1 jar (6 ounces) marinated
　　artichoke hearts, drained
　　and cut up
2 cups shredded mozzarella
　　cheese (8 ounces)

1. In medium bowl, combine soup mix, 1 cup of the flour, sugar and yeast; mix well. With mixer at low speed, gradually pour warm water and oil into dry ingredients; beat until just mixed. With mixer at medium speed, beat 4 minutes, scraping bowl often.
2. With spoon, stir in about 3/4 cup flour or enough to make a soft dough. Turn dough onto lightly floured surface; knead until smooth and elastic, about 5 minutes, adding more flour as necessary.
3. Grease 14-inch pizza pan or baking sheet. On floured surface, roll dough to 14-inch round. Transfer to pizza pan. Turn edge under to form rim.
4. Let rise in warm place, 20 minutes.
5. Preheat oven to 400°F. Bake crust 5 minutes; remove from oven. Arrange tomato slices and artichoke hearts over crust; sprinkle with cheese. Bake 15 minutes more or until lightly browned.
Makes 4 servings.
Note: Add your favorite pizza toppings, such as anchovies, mushrooms, green pepper strips, roasted red peppers, pepperoni or cooked Italian sausage.

Pineapple Pizza

2 cans (8 ounces each) DOLE®
　　Crushed Pineapple
1/2 cup bottled pizza sauce
1 clove garlic, pressed
1 teaspoon dried oregano,
　　crumbled
1/2 loaf frozen bread dough,
　　thawed
1/2 pound Italian sausage,
　　crumbled, cooked
1 small DOLE™ Green Bell
　　Pepper, seeded and sliced
1/4 cup chopped green onion
2 cups shredded mozzarella
　　cheese
2 tablespoons grated Parmesan
　　cheese

Preheat oven to 500°F. Drain pineapple well, pressing out excess juice with back of spoon. In small bowl, combine pizza sauce, garlic and oregano. Roll and stretch thawed dough to fit greased 12-inch pizza pan. Spread dough with pizza sauce mixture. Top with sausage, green pepper, onion, pineapple and cheeses. Bake in preheated oven 12 to 15 minutes or until pizza is bubbly and crust is browned.
Makes 4 servings.

Party Pizza

1/2 pound ECKRICH® Beef
　　Smoked Sausage, cut into
　　1/4-inch slices
1 loaf (16 ounces) frozen bread
　　dough, thawed
　　Cornmeal
2 tablespoons butter or
　　margarine
1 1/2 cups green bell pepper strips
1 1/2 cups sliced onions
8 ounces fresh mushrooms,
　　sliced
3 cups (12 ounces) shredded
　　mozzarella cheese, divided
1 jar (8 ounces) pizza sauce
1 teaspoon dried oregano leaves
1/2 teaspoon dried basil leaves
1/2 teaspoon fennel seeds
1/2 cup grated Parmesan cheese

Let bread dough warm and start to rise. Preheat oven to 425°F. Sprinkle cornmeal in 12-inch circle on buttered pizza pan or baking sheet. Place bread dough on cornmeal; stretch and pull to fit 12-inch circle. Bake 7 minutes. Remove from oven. Melt butter in medium skillet over medium-high heat; add green peppers, onions and mushrooms. Saute until vegetables just begin to lose their crispness. Stir in sausage. Cover bread with 1/2 of the mozzarella cheese. Combine pizza sauce, oregano, basil and fennel seeds in small bowl; spread over mozzarella cheese. Top with sausage mixture. Return to oven and bake 20 to 25 minutes more or until done. Top with remaining 1 1/2 cups mozzarella cheese; sprinkle with Parmesan cheese. Return to oven and bake until mozzarella melts, about 5 minutes more. To serve, cut into wedges or squares.
Makes 1 pizza, 12-inch diameter.

Layered Picnic Club Sandwich

1 loaf unsliced round bread
　　(about 9-inch diameter)
3/4 cup WISH-BONE® Creamy
　　Italian Dressing
　　Lettuce leaves
1/3 pound sliced Swiss cheese
3/4 pound sliced cooked roast
　　beef
1/2 pound sliced cooked turkey
1 large tomato, sliced

Cut bread in half horizontally; hollow out center of each half, leaving 1/4-inch shell.

Spread 1/3 cup creamy Italian dressing into each shell; line bottom shell with lettuce. Into bottom shell, layer cheese, roast beef, remaining dressing, turkey, then tomato. Top with lettuce; replace top shell. To serve, cut into wedges.
Makes about 6 servings.
Note: Also terrific with Wish-Bone® Lite Creamy Italian, Thousand Island, Lite Thousand Island or Chunky Blue Cheese Dressing.

Thick 'n Cheesy Vegetable Pizza

2 loaves (1 pound each) frozen bread dough, thawed
1 envelope LIPTON® Vegetable Recipe Soup Mix
¼ cup olive or vegetable oil
2 tablespoons chopped fresh basil leaves*
1 large clove garlic, finely chopped
¼ teaspoon pepper
2 cups shredded mozzarella cheese (about 6 ounces)
1 cup fresh or canned sliced mushrooms
1 medium tomato, coarsely chopped

Preheat oven to 425°.

Into lightly oiled 12-inch pizza pan, press dough to form crust; set aside.

In small bowl, blend vegetable recipe soup mix, oil, basil, garlic and pepper; spread evenly on dough. Top with remaining ingredients. Bake 20 minutes or until cheese is melted and crust is golden brown. To serve, cut into wedges.

Makes about 6 servings.

Substitution: Use 2 teaspoons dried basil leaves.

Egg Salad Magnifique

1 8-ounce package PHILADELPHIA BRAND Cream Cheese, softened
½ cup KRAFT Real Mayonnaise
1 tablespoon KRAFT Cream Style Prepared Horseradish
6 hard-cooked eggs, chopped
1 6-ounce package frozen crabmeat, thawed, drained
½ cup chopped celery
½ cup chopped red or green pepper
6 croissants, split
Lettuce

Combine cream cheese, mayonnaise and horseradish, mixing until well blended. Add eggs, crabmeat, celery and peppers; mix lightly. Chill. Fill croissants with lettuce and egg mixture.

6 sandwiches.

Vegetarian Sandwiches

Cucumber Sauce (recipe follows)
¾ cup V8® Vegetable Juice
¼ cup brown rice, uncooked
2 eggs, beaten
½ cup shredded mozzarella cheese (2 ounces)
1 cup canned chick peas, drained and mashed
¼ cup fresh whole wheat bread crumbs
2 tablespoons chopped walnuts
1 tablespoon finely chopped onion
1 small clove garlic, minced
Generous dash ground red pepper (cayenne)
3 whole wheat pita breads (sandwich pockets), cut in half crosswise
CAMPBELL'S FRESH® Butterhead Lettuce Leaves

1. Prepare Cucumber Sauce.
2. In small saucepan over high heat, heat V8 juice to boiling. Stir in rice; reduce heat to low. Cover; simmer 45 minutes or until rice is tender and liquid is absorbed, stirring occasionally.
3. In medium bowl, stir together cooked rice, eggs, cheese, chick peas, crumbs, walnuts, onion, garlic and pepper until well mixed. Chill slightly, until firm enough to shape. Shape mixture into 6 patties.
4. Spray 10-inch nonstick skillet with vegetable cooking spray. Over medium heat, cook patties, 3 at a time, 8 minutes or until browned on both sides.
5. In each pita bread half, arrange lettuce and one bean patty; top with Cucumber Sauce.

Makes 6 sandwiches.

CUCUMBER SAUCE: In small bowl, stir together ½ cup plain low-fat yogurt, ½ cup chopped, seeded and peeled cucumber and ⅛ teaspoon dried dill weed, crushed. Cover; refrigerate until serving time.

Makes 1 cup.

Per serving: 268 calories, 12 g protein, 7 g fat, 39 g carbohydrate, 492 mg sodium, 100 mg cholesterol.

Frisco Bay Sandwiches

1 6½-oz. can tuna, drained, flaked
¼ lb. VELVEETA Pasteurized Process Cheese Spread, cubed
1 cup chopped apple
½ cup celery slices
MIRACLE WHIP Salad Dressing
6 croissants, split
Lettuce

Combine tuna, process cheese spread, apples, celery and enough salad dressing to moisten; mix lightly. Fill croissants with lettuce and tuna mixture.

6 sandwiches.

Preparation time: 10 minutes

Grilled Smoked Turkey 'n Muenster Sandwiches

1/4 cup WISH-BONE® Thousand Island or Lite Thousand Island Dressing
6 slices pumpernickel bread (about 3/4 inch thick)
1/4 pound sliced Muenster cheese
1/2 pound sliced smoked or unsmoked cooked turkey breast
3 tablespoons butter or margarine, softened

Evenly spread Thousand Island dressing on each bread slice. Equally top 3 bread slices with 1/2 of the cheese, turkey, then remaining cheese; top with remaining bread slices, dressing side down. Evenly spread butter on outside of bread slices.

In large skillet, cook sandwiches, covered, over medium heat, turning once and pressing down sandwiches occasionally, 8 minutes or until cheese is melted.
Makes 3 hearty sandwiches.

Beef Fajitas

1/2 cup REALIME® Lime Juice from Concentrate
1/4 cup vegetable oil
2 cloves garlic, finely chopped
1 (1- to 1 1/2-pound) flank steak
10 (6-inch) flour tortillas, warmed according to package directions
Garnishes: shredded lettuce, chopped tomatoes, chopped green onion, shredded Cheddar cheese, sliced ripe olives, guacamole, sour cream, picante sauce

In small bowl, combine ReaLime® brand, oil and garlic; pour over meat. Refrigerate 6 hours or overnight, turning occasionally. Remove meat from marinade; grill or broil as desired, basting frequently with marinade. Slice meat diagonally into thin strips; place on tortillas. Top with one or more of the garnishes; fold tortillas. Serve immediately. Refrigerate leftovers.
Makes 10 fajitas.

Bacon & Chicken Sandwiches

1 (5-ounce) can cooked white meat chicken, drained
1 small stalk celery, thinly sliced
1 green onion, sliced
1/2 cup plain nonfat yogurt
Pepper to taste
3 hamburger buns, toasted
3 canned pineapple rings, well drained
3 slices ARMOUR® Lower Salt Bacon, cooked crisp and crumbled

Combine chicken, celery, onion, yogurt and pepper in small bowl. If desired, place lettuce leaf on bottom of each bun; place pineapple ring on lettuce. Top each with one third of the chicken mixture and bacon.
Makes 3 servings.

Nutrition Information Per Serving: 268 calories, 18.6 g protein, 5.7 g fat, 33.2 g carbohydrates, 40 mg cholesterol, 567 mg sodium.

Beef and Bean Chimichangas

1 pound ground beef
2 tablespoons CRISCO® Oil
1 medium onion, chopped
2 cloves garlic, minced
1 can (16 ounces) whole tomatoes, drained, cut up
1/3 cup salsa
1 1/2 teaspoons chili powder
3/4 teaspoon ground coriander
1/2 teaspoon ground thyme
1/2 teaspoon salt
1/8 teaspoon cayenne
1/8 teaspoon ground cumin
1 cup refried beans
CRISCO® Oil for frying
6 eight-inch flour tortillas
3/4 cup shredded Monterey Jack cheese (optional)

Place ground beef in medium skillet. Brown over medium-high heat. Drain. Remove beef from skillet; set aside. Place 2 tablespoons Crisco® Oil in same skillet. Add onion and garlic. Sauté over moderate heat until onion is tender. Stir in ground beef, tomatoes, salsa, chili powder, coriander, thyme, salt, cayenne and cumin. Cook over medium-low heat, stirring occasionally, 10 to 15 minutes, or until mixture is thickened. Remove from heat. Stir in refried beans.

Heat 2 inches Crisco® Oil in deep-fryer or large saucepan to 375°F. Meanwhile, place 1/2 cup beef mixture in center of each tortilla. Fold opposite sides of tortilla to center over beef mixture. Fold ends toward center; secure with wooden pick.

Fry 1 to 2 chimichangas at a time, 1 1/2 to 2 minutes, or until golden brown. Drain on paper towels. Sprinkle top of each chimichanga with 2 tablespoons Monterey Jack cheese (optional). Serve immediately with *salsa,* if desired.
6 servings.

Turkey Cranberry Croissant

Thin-sliced cooked BUTTERBALL® turkey (1 pound)
1 package (8 ounces) cream cheese, softened
¼ cup orange marmalade
½ cup chopped pecans
6 croissants or rolls, split
¾ cup whole berry cranberry sauce
Lettuce leaves

Combine cream cheese, marmalade and pecans in small bowl. Spread top and bottom halves of croissants with cream cheese mixture. Layer turkey on bottom halves. Spoon 2 tablespoons cranberry sauce over turkey. Add lettuce and croissant top.
Yield: 6 sandwiches.

Lipton Onion Burgers

1 envelope LIPTON® Onion, Onion-Mushroom, Beefy Onion or Beefy Mushroom Recipe Soup Mix
2 pounds ground beef
½ cup water

In large bowl, combine all ingredients; shape into 8 patties. Grill or broil until done. Serve, if desired, on hamburger rolls.
Makes 8 servings.
Microwave Directions: Prepare patties as above. In oblong baking dish, arrange 4 patties and heat uncovered at HIGH (Full Power) 6 minutes, turning patties once. Repeat with remaining patties. Let stand covered 5 minutes. Serve as above.

Arizona's 7-Layer Taco Sandwich

1 pound thinly sliced BUTTERBALL® Deli Turkey Breast
½ cup coarsely chopped ripe olives
½ teaspoon chili powder
½ teaspoon ground cumin
¼ teaspoon salt
½ cup mayonnaise
½ cup sour cream
½ cup sliced green onions
4 large oval slices French bread, about ½ inch thick
1 large tomato, sliced
1 ripe avocado, peeled, sliced
¾ cup (3 ounces) shredded Cheddar cheese
¾ cup (3 ounces) shredded Monterey Jack cheese
Lettuce leaves
Salsa

Preheat oven to 350°F. Combine olives, chili powder, cumin and salt in medium bowl; reserve two tablespoons. Stir mayonnaise, sour cream and onions into remaining olive mixture. Using ½ of the mayonnaise mixture, spread on 1 side of each bread slice. Top with tomato and turkey. Spread remaining mayonnaise mixture on top of turkey. Top with avocado slices. Sprinkle with cheeses. Transfer sandwiches to baking sheet. Bake until hot, about 15 minutes. Top with reserved olive mixture. Serve on lettuce leaves with salsa.
Makes 4 open-faced sandwiches.

Garden-Fresh Pitas

1½ cups cut-up cooked chicken (about 9 ounces)
⅓ cup WISH-BONE® Creamy Italian or Lite Creamy Italian Dressing
¼ cup finely chopped celery
4 small pita breads, split
Lettuce leaves
1 medium tomato, sliced
½ cup thinly sliced cucumber

In medium bowl, combine chicken, creamy Italian dressing and celery; cover and chill. To serve, line breads with lettuce, tomato and cucumber; spoon in chicken mixture.
Makes 4 servings.

Fiesta Burgers

1 lb. ground beef
⅔ cup crushed corn chips
½ cup chili sauce
¼ lb. VELVEETA Pasteurized Process Cheese Spread, sliced
4 hard rolls, split
Lettuce
4 red onion slices
Guacamole
Chopped tomato

Combine meat, chips and ¼ cup chili sauce; mix lightly. Shape into four patties; place on rack of broiler pan. Broil on both sides to desired doneness. Top with process cheese spread; broil until process cheese spread begins to melt. Spread rolls with remaining chili sauce. For each sandwich, cover bottom half of roll with lettuce, onion and patty. Top with remaining ingredients, additional chips and top half of roll.
4 sandwiches

Preparation time: 10 minutes
Broiling time: 15 minutes

Seafood Salad Sandwiches

1 envelope LIPTON® Vegetable
    Recipe Soup Mix
3/4 cup sour cream
1/4 cup mayonnaise
1 teaspoon lemon juice
1/2 cup chopped celery
1 tablespoon fresh or frozen
    chopped chives (optional)
    Hot pepper sauce to taste
1/8 teaspoon pepper
2 packages (6 ounces each)
    frozen crabmeat, thawed
    and well drained*
4 hard rolls, halved
    Lettuce leaves

In large bowl, blend vegetable recipe
soup mix, sour cream, mayonnaise,
lemon juice, celery, chives, hot pepper
sauce and pepper. Stir in crabmeat;
chill. To serve, line rolls with lettuce,
then fill with crab mixture.
Makes 4 hearty sandwiches.
    Variations: Use 1 package (12
ounces) frozen cleaned shrimp, cooked
and coarsely chopped; *OR* 2 packages
(8 ounces each) sea legs, thawed,
drained and chopped; *OR* 1 can (13
ounces) tuna, drained and flaked; *OR*
2 cans (4½ ounces each) medium or
large shrimp, drained and chopped;
OR 2 cans (6½ ounces each) crabmeat, drained and flaked.

Middle East Pita Pockets

1/2 cup canned chick peas,
    drained
1/4 cup water
2 tablespoons sesame seeds
1 tablespoon lemon juice
1 clove garlic
1/2 teaspoon TABASCO® pepper
    sauce
1/2 teaspoon salt
1/2 cup chopped cucumber
1/2 cup julienne strips yellow
    squash
1/2 cup julienne strips zucchini
1/4 cup sliced radishes
1/4 cup sliced green onions
2 pita breads, 6 inches in
    diameter

In container of blender or food processor combine chick peas, water, sesame
seeds, lemon juice, garlic, Tabasco®
sauce and salt. Cover; blend until
smooth. In medium bowl mix cucumber, yellow squash, zucchini, radishes
and green onions. Cut pita breads in
half to form pockets. Spoon vegetable
mixture into each pocket. Spoon chick
pea sauce over vegetables.
Makes 2 servings.

Turkey-Topped Biscuits

1 tablespoon butter or
    margarine
1/2 pound ground turkey
1 tablespoon grated Parmesan
    cheese
1/2 teaspoon rubbed sage
1/2 teaspoon fennel seed
1/4 teaspoon garlic powder
1/8 teaspoon salt
1/8 teaspoon pepper
1/2 cup chopped onion
1 medium apple, chopped
3/4 cup V8® Vegetable Juice
1/4 cup raisins
1/4 teaspoon ground cinnamon
4 hot biscuits, split

1. In 10-inch skillet over medium
heat, in hot butter, cook turkey, Parmesan, sage, fennel, garlic powder,
salt and pepper until turkey is
browned, stirring to separate turkey.
2. Add onion and apple; cook until
tender, stirring often. Stir in V8 juice,
raisins and cinnamon. Cook, uncovered, 15 minutes or until slightly
thickened.
3. To serve: Spoon turkey mixture
onto bottom halves of biscuits; cover
with biscuit tops.
Makes 4 servings.

Per serving: 280 calories, 14 g protein, 12 g fat, 31 g carbohydrate, 607
mg sodium, 47 mg cholesterol.

Chili Dogs

1 can (11¼ ounces)
    CAMPBELL'S® Condensed
    Chili Beef Soup
2 tablespoons water
2 tablespoons ketchup
6 frankfurters
6 PEPPERIDGE FARM®
    Frankfurter Rolls, split
3 slices American cheese, cut
    into triangles

To Microwave:
1. In small microwave-safe bowl, combine soup, water and ketchup. Cover
with vented plastic wrap; microwave
on HIGH 3 minutes or until very hot,
stirring once during cooking.
2. Arrange frankfurters on 10-inch
microwave-safe plate lined with paper
towels. Microwave, uncovered, on
HIGH 2 minutes or until hot.
3. Place cooked frankfurters in rolls.
Spoon a heaping tablespoon of soup
mixture over each. Arrange cheese
triangles over soup mixture.
4. Arrange rolls on same plate lined
with clean paper towels. Microwave,
uncovered, on HIGH 1 minute or until
cheese melts.
Makes 6 servings.

Golden Gate Grill

3/4 pound thinly sliced BUTTERBALL® Deli Turkey Breast
1 egg, beaten
1/4 cup milk or half and half
8 large oval slices sourdough French bread
Grated Parmesan or Romano cheese
1 tomato, sliced thin
1 small avocado, peeled, sliced
2 tablespoons chopped fresh cilantro
4 slices red onion, separated into rings
4 slices Monterey Jack cheese
2 tablespoons butter or margarine, softened
1 clove garlic, minced
1/8 to 1/4 teaspoon crushed red pepper

Combine egg and milk in shallow dish. Dip 1 side of each bread slice in egg mixture, then in Parmesan cheese. Arrange turkey on undipped side of 4 slices of the bread. Place tomato, avocado, cilantro and red onion on turkey. Top with Monterey Jack cheese and remaining bread, dipped side up. Combine butter, garlic and red pepper. Preheat large skillet over medium heat. Melt 1 tablespoon of the butter mixture in skillet. Brown both sides of 2 sandwiches until crisp. Repeat with remaining butter and sandwiches. Serve immediately.
Makes 4 sandwiches.

Santa Monica Sandwich

Sliced cooked BUTTERBALL® turkey (3/4 pound)
4 to 8 slices cooked bacon, cut into halves crosswise
4 slices buttered toast
Avocado Sauce (recipe follows)
Orange sections

Place 2 to 4 halves of bacon between sliced turkey on each piece of toast. Top with Avocado Sauce and orange sections.
Yield: 4 open-faced sandwiches.

Avocado Sauce

1 ripe avocado
2 tablespoons mayonnaise
2 teaspoons lemon juice
1/4 teaspoon onion powder

Cut avocado in half; remove pit. Pare. Mash avocado and blend with remaining ingredients in small bowl.
Yield: 2/3 cup.

Chili Burritos

1 pound ground beef
1/4 cup chopped green pepper
1 can (11 ounces) CAMPBELL'S® Condensed Zesty Tomato Soup/Sauce
1 tablespoon chili powder
1 tablespoon Worcestershire sauce
8 (8-inch) flour tortillas
Guacamole for garnish
Chopped CAMPBELL'S FRESH® Tomatoes for garnish
Shredded Cheddar cheese for garnish

To Microwave:
1. Crumble beef into 2-quart microwave-safe casserole; stir in green pepper. Cover with lid; microwave on HIGH 5 minutes or until beef is no longer pink, stirring once during cooking to break up meat. Spoon off fat.
2. Stir in soup, chili powder and Worcestershire. Cover; microwave on HIGH 5 minutes or until hot and bubbling.
3. Wrap stack of tortillas in damp paper towels. Microwave on HIGH 1 minute or until warm. Spoon heaping 1/4 cup meat mixture onto each tortilla. Fold in sides and roll up to make burritos. Garnish with guacamole, tomatoes and cheese.
Makes 8 burritos or 4 servings.
Note: You can also serve the filling mixture on hamburger rolls.

Nutty Burgers

1 1/2 pounds ground beef
1 medium onion, finely chopped
1 clove garlic, minced
1 cup dry bread crumbs
1/3 cup grated Parmesan cheese
2/3 cup pine nuts
1/3 cup chopped parsley
2 eggs
1 1/2 teaspoons salt
1 teaspoon pepper

In large bowl, combine all ingredients. Shape into 6 thick patties. Grill patties, on covered grill, over medium-hot **KINGSFORD® Charcoal Briquets** 5 minutes on each side or until done. Serve on French bread and garnish with chopped green onion, if desired.
Makes 6 servings.

Quick 'n Easy Tacos

1 pound ground beef
1 can (14½ ounces) whole peeled tomatoes, undrained and coarsely chopped
1 medium green pepper, finely chopped
1 envelope LIPTON® Onion, Onion-Mushroom or Beefy Mushroom Recipe Soup Mix
1 tablespoon chili powder
3 drops hot pepper sauce
8 taco shells
Taco Toppings*

In medium skillet, brown ground beef over medium-high heat; drain. Stir in tomatoes, green pepper, onion recipe soup mix, chili powder and hot pepper sauce. Bring to a boil, then simmer 15 minutes or until slightly thickened. Serve in taco shells with assorted Taco Toppings.
Makes about 4 servings.

Taco Toppings: Use shredded Cheddar or Monterey Jack cheese, shredded lettuce, chopped tomatoes, sliced pitted ripe olives, sour cream or taco sauce.

Microwave Directions: In 2-quart casserole, heat ground beef with green pepper, uncovered, at HIGH (Full Power) 4 minutes, stirring once; drain. Stir in tomatoes, onion recipe soup mix, chili powder and hot pepper sauce. Heat uncovered, stirring occasionally, 7 minutes or until heated through. Let stand uncovered 5 minutes. Serve as above.

Sloppy Joes

2 pounds ground beef
1 envelope LIPTON® Onion, Onion-Mushroom, Beefy Mushroom or Beefy Onion Recipe Soup Mix
1 can (15 ounces) tomato sauce
½ cup sweet pickle relish

In large skillet, brown ground beef over medium-high heat; drain. Stir in remaining ingredients. Simmer, stirring occasionally, 10 minutes. Serve, if desired, over toasted hamburger rolls.
Makes about 8 servings.

Microwave Directions: In 2-quart casserole, heat ground beef, uncovered, at HIGH (Full Power) 7 minutes; drain. Stir in remaining ingredients. Heat covered, stirring occasionally, 4 minutes or until heated through. Let stand covered 5 minutes. Serve as above.

Stuffed Cheese Burgers

1½ cups shredded Monterey Jack cheese (about 8 ounces)
1 can (2¼ ounces) chopped black olives
⅛ teaspoon hot pepper sauce
1¾ pounds ground beef
¼ cup finely chopped onion
1 teaspoon salt
½ teaspoon pepper
6 hamburger buns
Butter or margarine, melted

In large bowl, combine cheese, olives and hot pepper sauce. Divide mixture evenly and shape into 6 balls. Mix ground beef with onion, salt and pepper; shape into 12 thin patties. Place 1 cheese ball in center of each of 6 patties and top each with a second patty. Seal edges to enclose cheese balls. Lightly oil grid. Grill patties, on covered grill, over medium-hot **KINGSFORD® Charcoal Briquets** 5 to 6 minutes on each side or until done.

Split buns, brush with butter and place, cut-side down, on grill to heat through. Serve Cheese Burgers on buns.
Makes 6 servings.

Avocado & Bacon Pitas

2 (6-inch) pita breads, cut in half
4 leaves leaf lettuce, washed and drained
12 slices ARMOUR® Lower Salt Bacon, cut in half and cooked crisp
1 avocado, peeled, pitted and sliced
1 (15¼-ounce) can pineapple spears, well drained
4 radishes, thinly sliced
8 tablespoons bottled low sodium, reduced calorie zesty Italian salad dressing

Open sliced edges of pita bread halves. Line with leaf lettuce. Divide bacon, avocado, pineapple and radishes evenly among bread pockets. Before serving, spoon 2 tablespoons of the dressing over top of each sandwich.
Makes 4 sandwiches.

Nutrition Information Per Sandwich: 319 calories, 10.1 g protein, 17.2 g fat, 35.2 g carbohydrates, 18 mg cholesterol, 558 mg sodium.

Tuna Melt

1 (6½-ounce) can tuna, drained
⅓ cup chopped tomato
¼ cup chopped green pepper
¼ cup mayonnaise or salad dressing
8 slices bread
8 slices BORDEN® Process American Cheese Food
Margarine or butter, softened

In medium bowl, combine tuna, tomato, pepper and mayonnaise; spread equal amounts on 4 slices bread. Top each with 2 cheese food slices then remaining bread slices. Spread margarine on outside of each sandwich. Grill. Serve immediately. Refrigerate leftovers.
Makes 4 sandwiches.

Barbecue Ham Sandwiches

1 cup catsup
3 tablespoons REALEMON®
  Lemon Juice from
  Concentrate
¼ cup chopped onion
¼ cup firmly packed brown sugar
2 tablespoons Worcestershire
  sauce
1 teaspoon prepared mustard
1 pound thinly sliced cooked
  ham
  Buns or hard rolls

In medium saucepan, combine all ingredients except ham and buns. Simmer uncovered 5 minutes. Add ham; heat through. Serve on buns. Refrigerate leftovers.
Makes 6 to 8 sandwiches.
Microwave: In 2-quart round baking dish, combine ingredients as above. Cover with wax paper; microwave on full power (high) 3 minutes. Stir in ham; cover with wax paper and microwave on full power (high) 3 to 4 minutes or until hot. Serve as above.

The California Classic

¼ cup MIRACLE WHIP Salad
  Dressing
1 teaspoon KRAFT Pure
  Prepared Mustard
4 rye bread slices
  Alfalfa sprouts
4 cooked turkey slices
¼ lb. VELVEETA Pasteurized
  Process Cheese Spread,
  sliced
  Thin tomato slices
  Peeled avocado slices

Combine salad dressing and mustard; mix well. Spread bread slices with salad dressing mixture. For each sandwich, top one bread slice with sprouts, turkey, process cheese spread, tomatoes, avocados and second bread slice.
2 sandwiches.

Preparation time: 10 minutes
Variation: Substitute salami slices or boiled ham slices for turkey.

Texas-Style Steak on Hot Bread

½ cup olive or vegetable oil
¼ cup lime juice
¼ cup red wine vinegar
1 medium onion, finely chopped
1 clove garlic, minced
1 teaspoon chili powder
½ teaspoon salt
¼ teaspoon ground cumin
1 beef skirt or flank steak (about
  1½ pounds)
1 round loaf French or
  sourdough bread
1 cup salsa
1 cup guacamole

In shallow glass dish, combine oil, lime juice, vinegar, onion, garlic, chili powder, salt and cumin. With meat mallet, pound steak to ¼-inch thickness. Place steak in marinade; turn to coat. Cover and refrigerate several hours or overnight, turning several times. Drain steak; discard marinade. Grill steak, on covered grill, over medium-hot **KINGSFORD® Charcoal Briquets** 4 to 8 minutes on each side, or until done. Cut bread into 1-inch slices and toast on grill. Heat salsa. Carve steak into ¾-inch diagonal strips. Arrange steak on toasted bread. Top with hot salsa and guacamole.
Makes 4 to 6 servings.

Loaf Sandwiches with Bacon & Ham

¼ cup unsalted margarine or
  butter, melted
1 to 2 teaspoons garlic powder
1 large loaf French bread
3 ounces ARMOUR® Lower Salt
  Ham, thinly sliced
2 ounces ARMOUR® Lower Salt
  Monterey Jack Cheese,
  thinly sliced
6 cherry tomato slices
6 slices ARMOUR® Lower Salt
  Bacon, cut in half and
  cooked crisp
12 (¼-inch) zucchini slices

Combine margarine and garlic powder in small bowl; set aside. Make 6 diagonal cuts at equal distances along loaf of bread, cutting ¾ of the way through loaf. Spread margarine mixture on cut sides of bread. Evenly distribute ham and cheese among cuts. Place 1 tomato slice, 2 bacon pieces and 2 zucchini slices in each cut. If desired, wrap entire loaf with foil and bake in 375°F. oven about 15 to 20 minutes, or until cheese is melted. Cut into 6 servings.
Makes 6 servings.

Nutritional Information Per Serving: 380 calories, 14.1 protein, 16.3 g fat, 44 g carbohydrates, 23 mg cholesterol, 701 mg sodium.

EGGS, CHEESE & BRUNCH DISHES

Transform lazy weekend brunches and informal Sunday-night suppers into special events with these innovative ideas for casual dining. Create light and airy souffles, quiches rich with eggs and meat, and waffles and pancakes that rise above the crowd. You'll turn ham and eggs into a gourmet treat.

Vegetable Egg Bake

6 SWIFT PREMIUM® BROWN 'N SERVE™ Microwave Sausage Links, thawed
1½ cups frozen vegetable mix containing broccoli, carrots, water chestnuts and red bell peppers
2 tablespoons chopped onion
6 eggs
3 tablespoons milk
¼ teaspoon salt
Dash ground black pepper
½ cup (2 ounces) shredded Monterey Jack cheese

Microwave Directions: Coarsely chop frozen vegetables. Place vegetables and onion in 10×6×1½-inch microwave-safe baking dish. Cover with vented plastic wrap and *microwave* on High (100%) 4 minutes or until vegetables are crisp-tender, stirring once. Drain well. Beat together eggs, milk, salt and pepper in medium bowl. Pour egg mixture over vegetables: cover with waxed paper. Place baking dish on inverted microwave-safe dinner plate in microwave oven. *Microwave* on 70% (Medium-High) 5 minutes or until eggs are partially set, pushing cooked edges to center once during cooking. Push cooked edges to center again and arrange sausage on top of vegetable-egg mixture. Cover loosely and *microwave* on 70% 1½ to 2 minutes. Sprinkle cheese over sausage and eggs; *microwave* on 70% 1½ to 2 minutes more or until center is almost set.
Makes 6 servings.

Bacon & Broccoli Frittata

6 eggs, beaten
¼ cup skim milk
⅛ teaspoon white pepper
2 tablespoons unsalted margarine or butter
1 cup fresh or frozen broccoli flowerets, thawed if frozen
¼ cup *each* chopped red and green pepper
8 slices ARMOUR® Lower Salt Bacon, cooked crisp
1 cup (4 ounces) shredded ARMOUR® Lower Salt Cheddar Cheese

Preheat oven to 350°F. Combine eggs, milk and white pepper in medium bowl; set aside. Melt margarine in large ovenproof skillet or metal casserole over medium heat. Add broccoli and red and green peppers; sauté for 5 minutes. Pour egg mixture over vegetables. Arrange bacon on top; sprinkle with cheese. Bake about 15 to 20 minutes, or until cheese is melted and eggs are set. Cut and serve immediately. Garnish with halved cherry tomatoes and parsley, if desired.
Makes 4 servings.

Nutrition Information Per Serving: 360 calories, 22 g protein, 29 g fat, 6.1 g carbohydrates, 453 mg cholesterol, 478 mg sodium.

Tempting Cheese Crepes

²/₃ cup flour
½ teaspoon salt
3 eggs, beaten
1 cup milk
**2 8-ounce packages *Light*
   PHILADELPHIA BRAND
   Neufchâtel Cheese, softened**
¼ cup sugar
**1 teaspoon vanilla
   Strawberry-Banana Topping**

Combine flour, salt and eggs; beat until smooth. Gradually add milk, mixing until well blended. For each crepe, pour ¼ cup batter into hot, lightly greased 8-inch skillet or crepe pan, tilting skillet to cover bottom. Cook over medium-high heat until lightly browned on both sides, turning once.

Combine neufchâtel cheese, sugar and vanilla, mixing until well blended. Spread approximately ¼ cup neufchâtel cheese mixture onto each crepe. Fold in thirds. Place in 13×9-inch baking dish. Bake at 350°, 15 to 20 minutes or until thoroughly heated. Serve with Strawberry-Banana Topping.
8 servings.

Preparation Tip: Lightly grease and preheat the skillet or crepe pan until a drop of water sizzles when sprinkled on. If the skillet isn't really hot, crepes may be too thick and stick to the pan.

Strawberry-Banana Topping

**1 10-ounce package frozen
   strawberries, thawed**
1 tablespoon cornstarch
1 banana, sliced

Drain strawberries, reserving liquid. Add enough water to reserved liquid to measure 1¼ cups; gradually add to cornstarch in saucepan, stirring until well blended. Bring to boil over medium heat, stirring constantly. Boil 1 minute. Stir in fruit.
2 cups.

Baked Sausage Squares

**1 roll (16 ounces) ECKRICH®
   Country Sausage**
**2 cups Cheddar cheese
   croutons**
5 eggs, beaten
¾ cup milk
½ teaspoon salt
½ teaspoon dry mustard

Preheat oven to 350°F. Slice sausage into 12 patties and cook according to package directions. Place croutons in buttered 8-inch square baking pan. Arrange sausage patties on croutons. Combine remaining ingredients in medium bowl; pour over sausage and croutons. Bake 25 minutes or until eggs are set. To serve, cut into rectangles.
Makes 6 servings.

"Philly" Brunch Quiche

Pastry for 1-crust 10-inch pie
**1 8-ounce package
   PHILADELPHIA BRAND
   Cream Cheese, cubed**
1 cup milk
4 eggs, beaten
¼ cup chopped onion
1 tablespoon PARKAY Margarine
1 cup finely chopped ham
¼ cup chopped pimento
¼ teaspoon dill weed
Dash of pepper

On lightly floured surface, roll pastry to 12-inch circle. Place in 10-inch pie plate. Turn under edge; flute. Prick bottom and sides of pastry with fork. Bake at 400°, 12 to 15 minutes or until pastry is lightly browned.

Combine cream cheese and milk in saucepan; stir over low heat until smooth. Gradually add cream cheese mixture to eggs, mixing until well blended. Saute onions in margarine. Add onions and remaining ingredients to cream cheese mixture; mix well. Pour into pastry shell. Bake at 350°, 35 to 40 minutes or until set. Garnish with ham slices and fresh dill, if desired.
8 servings.

Variations: Substitute ¼ cup finely chopped green pepper for dill weed.

Substitute 10-ounce package frozen chopped spinach, cooked, drained, 1 cup (4 ounces) shredded KRAFT 100% Natural Swiss Cheese and 6 crisply cooked bacon slices, crumbled, for ham, pimento and dill weed.

Substitute 4-ounce package pepperoni slices, chopped, ¼ cup (1 ounce) KRAFT Grated Parmesan Cheese and ½ teaspoon dried oregano leaves, crushed, for ham, pimento and dill weed. Place pepperoni on bottom of baked pastry shell; continue as directed.

Banana Nut Pancakes

2 ripe, medium DOLE® Bananas
¾ cup milk
1 egg, lightly beaten
1 tablespoon vegetable oil
1 cup pancake and waffle mix
½ cup chopped walnuts
**⅛ teaspoon ground cinnamon
   Banana slices and additional
   chopped nuts**

Mash bananas in medium bowl (1 cup). Stir in milk, egg and oil. In medium bowl, combine pancake mix, nuts and cinnamon. Stir banana mixture into dry ingredients until just moistened. For each pancake, pour ¼ cup batter onto lightly greased hot skillet. Brown on underside until bubbles appear on surface. Turn and brown other side. Serve with banana slices and additional nuts.
Makes 4 to 5 servings.

Turkey and Caper Quiche

¾ cup diced cooked
　　BUTTERBALL® turkey
Pastry for single 9-inch pie
　　crust*
½ cup (2 ounces) shredded
　　Swiss cheese
⅓ cup diced tomato
¼ cup minced onion
1 teaspoon capers
3 eggs, beaten
1 tablespoon Dijon mustard
1 teaspoon seasoned salt
1 cup half and half

Preheat oven to 350°F. Line 9-inch quiche dish or pie pan with pastry. Trim edges and flute. Layer turkey, cheese, tomato, onion and capers in crust. Blend eggs, mustard, salt and half and half in small bowl. Pour mixture into pie crust. Bake in oven 40 to 50 minutes or until knife inserted 1 inch from center comes out clean.
Yield: 4 servings.

　*Substitute frozen 9-inch deep dish pie crust, thawed, for pastry. Omit quiche dish; bake directly in foil pan.

Breakfast Pizza

6 ECKRICH® SMOK-Y-LINKS®
　　Sausages, cut into ¼-inch
　　slices
Pastry for single crust 9-inch
　　pie
2 cups (8 ounces) shredded
　　Swiss cheese
4 eggs
1½ cups sour cream
2 tablespoons chopped parsley

Preheat oven to 425°F. Roll out pastry and fit into 12-inch pizza pan. Bake, on lowest oven rack, 5 minutes. Cool. Sprinkle sausage and cheese over crust. Lightly beat eggs in medium bowl. Stir in sour cream and parsley until smooth. Pour over sausage and cheese. Bake 20 to 25 minutes more. Cool 5 minutes before cutting.
Makes 4 to 5 servings.

Swiss Chicken Quiche

1 (9-inch) unbaked pastry shell,
　　pricked
2 cups cubed cooked chicken or
　　turkey
1 cup (4 ounces) shredded
　　Swiss cheese
2 tablespoons flour
1 tablespoon WYLER'S® or
　　STEERO® Chicken-Flavor
　　Instant Bouillon
1 cup BORDEN® or MEADOW
　　GOLD® Milk
3 eggs, well beaten
¼ cup chopped onion
2 tablespoons chopped green
　　pepper
2 tablespoons chopped pimiento

Preheat oven to 425°. Bake pastry shell 8 minutes; remove from oven. Reduce oven temperature to 350°. In medium bowl, toss cheese with flour and bouillon; add remaining ingredients. Mix well. Pour into prepared shell. Bake 40 to 45 minutes or until set. Let stand 10 minutes before serving. Garnish as desired. Refrigerate leftovers.
Makes 6 servings.

Savory Onion Cheese Tart

1 envelope LIPTON® Golden
　　Onion Recipe Soup Mix
1 cup milk
1 egg, slightly beaten
½ teaspoon rosemary leaves
1 package (8 ounces) mozzarella
　　cheese, shredded
1 package (15 ounces)
　　refrigerated pie crusts for
　　2 (9-inch) crusts

In small bowl, thoroughly blend golden onion recipe soup mix, milk, egg and rosemary. Stir in cheese. Freeze 1 hour or refrigerate at least 2 hours until mixture is slightly thickened and not runny.

Preheat oven to 375°. On two aluminum-foil-lined baking sheets, unfold pie crusts. Fold crust edges over 1 inch to form rim. Brush, if desired, with 1 egg yolk beaten with 2 tablespoons water. Fill center of each prepared crust with ½ soup mixture; spread evenly to rim. Bake 25 minutes or until crusts are golden brown. To serve, cut into wedges.
Makes 2 tarts.
　Freezing/Reheating Directions: Tarts can be baked, then frozen. Simply wrap in heavy-duty aluminum foil; freeze. To reheat, unwrap and bake at 350° until heated through.

Quiche Florentine

1 15-oz. pkg. PILLSBURY All
　　Ready Pie Crust
2 cups (8 ozs.) VELVEETA
　　Shredded Pasteurized
　　Process Cheese Food
⅓ cup (1½ ozs.) KRAFT 100%
　　Grated Parmesan Cheese
1 10-oz. pkg. frozen chopped
　　spinach, thawed, well-
　　drained
4 crisply cooked bacon slices,
　　crumbled
¾ cup milk
3 eggs, beaten
¼ teaspoon pepper

Prepare pie crust according to package directions for filled one-crust pie using 9-inch pie plate. (Refrigerate remaining crust for later use.) In large bowl, combine remaining ingredients; mix well. Pour into unbaked pie crust. Bake at 350°, 35 to 40 minutes or until knife inserted in center comes out clean. Let stand 10 minutes before serving.
6 to 8 servings.

Preparation time: 15 minutes
Baking time: 40 minutes plus standing time

B.L.T.E. Breakfast Pockets

4 slices bacon, cooked and
    crumbled
6 eggs
⅓ cup BORDEN® or MEADOW
    GOLD® Milk
1 teaspoon WYLER'S® or
    STEERO® Chicken-Flavor
    Instant Bouillon
1 tablespoon margarine or
    butter
½ cup chopped tomato
3 (5-inch) pita bread rounds, cut
    in half
6 lettuce leaves
6 slices BORDEN® Process
    American Cheese Food

In medium bowl, beat eggs, milk and
bouillon. In medium skillet, melt
margarine; add egg mixture. Cook
and stir until eggs are set; remove
from heat. Stir in bacon and tomato.
Fill each pita bread half with lettuce,
cheese food slice and ½ cup egg mixture. Serve immediately. Refrigerate
leftovers.
Makes 6 sandwiches.

Southwestern Egg Puff

1 lb. VELVEETA Mexican
    Pasteurized Process Cheese
    Spread with Jalapeño
    Pepper, cubed
2 cups cottage cheese
6 eggs, beaten
½ cup picante sauce
¼ cup PARKAY Margarine,
    melted
¼ cup flour
½ teaspoon baking powder
½ teaspoon seasoned salt
1 12-oz. can whole kernel corn
    with sweet peppers, drained

In large bowl, combine ingredients;
mix well. Pour into greased 12×8-
inch baking dish. Bake at 350°, 35 to
40 minutes or until golden brown. Top
with additional picante sauce, sour
cream and avocado slices, if desired.
4 to 6 servings.

Preparation time: 10 minutes
Baking time: 40 minutes

Variation: Substitute VELVEETA
Pasteurized Process Cheese Spread
for Process Cheese Spread with Jalapeño Pepper.

Souper Easy Quiche

4 eggs
1 can (11 ounces) CAMPBELL'S®
    Condensed Cheddar Cheese
    Soup/Sauce
½ cup light cream
1 cup shredded sharp Cheddar
    cheese
½ cup diced cooked ham
½ cup drained, cooked, chopped
    broccoli
1 9-inch unbaked piecrust
    (recipe follows)
Ground nutmeg

1. In medium bowl, beat eggs until
foamy. Gradually add soup and
cream, mixing well.
2. Sprinkle cheese, ham and broccoli
evenly over piecrust. Pour soup mixture over all. Sprinkle with nutmeg.
3. Bake at 350°F. 50 minutes or until
center is set. Let stand 10 minutes before serving.
Makes 6 servings.
PIECRUST: In medium bowl, stir together 1 cup all-purpose flour and ½
teaspoon salt. With pastry blender,
cut in ⅓ cup shortening until mixture
resembles coarse crumbs. Add 2 to 3
tablespoons cold water, a tablespoon
at a time, mixing lightly with fork until pastry holds together. Form into a
ball. On lightly floured surface, roll
dough to a 13-inch round. Transfer to
9-inch pie plate. Trim edge, leaving ½
inch pastry beyond edge of pie plate.
Fold overhang under pastry; pinch a
high edge. Flute edge.

English Breakfast

8 SWIFT PREMIUM® BROWN 'N
    SERVE™ Microwave Sausage
    Links
18 ounces frozen shredded hash
    brown potatoes
5 eggs
¼ cup milk
2 tablespoons chopped onion
1 tablespoon chopped fresh
    parsley
1 teaspoon dry mustard
½ teaspoon salt
¼ teaspoon ground black pepper
1 cup (4 ounces) shredded
    sharp Cheddar cheese,
    divided
4 tomato slices, cut into halves

Microwave Directions: Place frozen
potatoes in 11×7×2-inch microwave-
safe baking dish or shallow 2-quart
oval microwave-safe dish. Cover with
vented plastic wrap. *Microwave* on
High (100%) 3 minutes; break up and
rearrange partially thawed potatoes.
Cover and *microwave* 4 to 5 minutes
more or until hot, stirring every 2
minutes. Combine eggs, milk, onion,
parsley, mustard, salt and pepper in
small bowl. Pour over potatoes. Sprinkle with ½ cup of the cheese. Cover
with waxed paper. *Microwave* on High
4 minutes, stirring every 2 minutes to
bring cooked egg mixture to center of
dish. Remove from microwave oven;
let stand, covered, while heating sausage according to package directions.
Arrange hot sausage down center of
egg mixture. Sprinkle with remaining
½ cup cheese. Place 4 tomato halves
along each lengthwise edge of dish.
Cover with waxed paper and *microwave* on High 2 minutes or until
cheese melts.
Makes 4 servings.

Oatmeal Griddlecakes

8 SIZZLEAN® Breakfast Strips
1½ cups uncooked rolled oats
2 cups milk
1 cup all-purpose flour
2 tablespoons packed dark brown sugar
2 teaspoons baking powder
1 teaspoon salt
3 eggs, lightly beaten
¼ cup butter or margarine, melted, cooled
Pancake syrup

Cook Sizzlean® strips according to package directions. Dice and set aside. Mix oats and milk in large bowl and set aside until all milk has been absorbed. Combine flour, brown sugar, baking powder and salt in small bowl. Add eggs and diced Sizzlean® pieces to oat mixture; mix well. Stir in flour mixture. Add butter and stir only long enough to blend batter. Do not overmix.

Lightly grease griddle or heavy skillet and heat over medium heat until water drop flicked onto it "dances" and instantly evaporates. Pour or ladle batter into pan to form 3½-inch-diameter pancakes. Cook 2 to 3 minutes until small bubbles form on pancake surface and begin to break.

Flip over and brown other side. Stack cooked pancakes on heated platter and keep warm. Repeat cooking procedure using remaining batter. Serve pancakes hot with pancake syrup and additional cooked Sizzlean® strips, if desired.
Makes 5 servings.

Chocolate Waffles

1 cup unsifted all-purpose flour
¾ cup sugar
½ cup HERSHEY'S Cocoa
½ teaspoon baking powder
½ teaspoon baking soda
¼ teaspoon salt
1 cup buttermilk
2 eggs
¼ cup butter or margarine, melted

Combine flour, sugar, cocoa, baking powder, baking soda and salt in medium bowl. Add buttermilk and eggs; beat with wooden spoon just until blended. Gradually add melted butter, beating until smooth. Bake in waffle iron according to manufacturer's directions. Serve warm with pancake syrup or, for dessert, with ice cream, fruit-flavored syrups and sweetened whipped cream.
10 to 12 four-inch waffles.

Mandarin Orange French Toast

1 can (11 ounces) DOLE® Mandarin Orange Segments
1 tablespoon grated orange peel
½ cup orange juice
1 tablespoon brown sugar
2 teaspoons cornstarch
1 teaspoon vanilla extract
Dash ground nutmeg
2 eggs, lightly beaten
½ cup half-and-half
4 slices (½ inch thick each) stale French bread or thick-sliced white bread
2 tablespoons butter or margarine
¼ cup DOLE™ Sliced Natural Almonds, toasted, optional

Drain syrup from oranges into saucepan. Stir in orange peel and juice, brown sugar, cornstarch, vanilla and nutmeg. Cook over low heat, stirring, until sauce thickens slightly and turns clear. Remove from heat; add orange segments.

In pie plate, combine eggs and half-and-half. Dip bread in egg mixture, saturating both sides. Melt butter in large skillet until hot. Cook soaked bread in skillet until golden brown on each side. Place 2 slices French toast on each plate; top with Mandarin orange sauce. Sprinkle with almonds, if desired.
Makes 2 servings.

Gingery Banana Waffles

3 cups flour
4 teaspoons baking powder
2 teaspoons ground cinnamon
1½ teaspoons ground ginger
1 teaspoon salt
4 eggs
⅔ cup brown sugar, packed
2 extra-ripe, medium DOLE™ Bananas
1¼ cups milk
½ cup molasses
½ cup butter or margarine, melted
4 firm, medium DOLE™ Bananas, sliced
Maple syrup

Preheat waffle iron. In large bowl, combine flour, baking powder, cinnamon, ginger and salt. In medium bowl, beat eggs with brown sugar until light and fluffy. Puree extra-ripe bananas in blender (1 cup). Beat pureed bananas, milk, molasses and butter into egg mixture; add to dry ingredients. Stir until just moistened.

For each waffle, cook ¾ cup batter in waffle iron until golden brown. Serve with sliced bananas and syrup.
Makes 8 servings.

Peach Melba Pancakes

1 package (6 ounces) GREAT STARTS® Frozen Pancakes with Sausages
1 tablespoon raspberry preserves
1 teaspoon water
3 fresh or canned peach slices

To Microwave:
1. Prepare pancakes with sausages according to package directions.
2. In microwave-safe custard cup, stir preserves and water. Microwave, uncovered, on HIGH 30 seconds or until hot. Arrange peach slices over hot pancakes; top with raspberry mixture.
Makes 1 serving.

Cheese Strata

6 slices bread, crusts removed
3 cups (12 ounces) shredded Monterey Jack, Cheddar and/or Swiss cheese, divided
6 eggs
2 cups milk
1 tablespoon LAWRY'S® Minced Onion with Green Onion Flakes
1 teaspoon LAWRY'S® Seasoned Salt

Arrange bread slices in bottom of lightly buttered 13×9-inch baking dish. Sprinkle with 1½ cups of the cheese. Beat eggs, milk and seasonings in medium bowl until well blended. Pour over cheese. Sprinkle with remaining 1½ cups cheese. Bake at 350°F 35 minutes or until light golden brown. Let stand 5 minutes before serving.
Makes 6 servings.

Mexican Variation: Pour 1 bottle (8½ ounces) LAWRY'S® Chunky Taco Sauce over strata 5 minutes before baking time is completed; continue baking.

Herb Variation: Add 2 tablespoons LAWRY'S® Pinch of Herbs to egg mixture; continue as directed.

Mushroom Variation: Cook and stir ½ pound sliced mushrooms in 2 tablespoons butter or margarine in medium skillet over medium-high heat until mushrooms are soft. Remove from heat; stir in 1 package (0.75 ounces) LAWRY'S® Mushroom Gravy Mix. Add to egg mixture; continue as directed.

Cornmeal Bacon Shortcakes

1¼ cups all-purpose flour
¾ cup cornmeal
2 tablespoons sugar
1½ tablespoons low sodium baking powder
¾ cup unsalted margarine or butter, cold
12 slices ARMOUR® Lower Salt Bacon, cooked crisp and finely crumbled
⅓ cup skim milk
1 egg

Preheat oven to 400°F. Combine flour, cornmeal, sugar and baking powder. Cut in margarine until mixture is crumbly. Stir in bacon. Add milk and egg; stir until just moistened. Do not overmix. Spray 6 shortcake or muffin tin cups with nonstick cooking spray. Spoon ⅓ cup of the batter into each cup. Bake about 10 to 12 minutes, or until golden brown. Garnish with fresh basil, if desired.
Makes 6 shortcakes or muffins.

Nutrition Information Per Cake: 452 calories, 9.7 g protein, 30.6 g fat, 39.5 g carbohydrates, 57.7 mg cholesterol, 271 mg sodium.

Greek-Style Puffy Pancake

Puffy Pancake (recipe follows)
2 cups sliced CAMPBELL'S FRESH® Mushrooms (8 ounces)
1 large onion, sliced
1 cup shredded carrots
¾ cup V8® Vegetable Juice
1 teaspoon cornstarch
½ teaspoon dried basil leaves, crushed
¾ cup crumbled feta cheese, divided (4 ounces)
2 tablespoons VLASIC® or EARLY CALIFORNIA® Sliced Pitted Ripe Olives
2 tablespoons chopped fresh parsley

1. Prepare Puffy Pancake.
2. Meanwhile, spray 10-inch nonstick skillet with vegetable cooking spray. Over medium-high heat, cook mushrooms, onion and carrots 5 minutes or until vegetables are tender, stirring often.
3. In small bowl, stir together V8 juice, cornstarch and basil. Stir V8 mixture into skillet; cook 4 minutes or until slightly thickened, stirring often.
4. Sprinkle ½ of the feta onto pancake. Spoon vegetable mixture over feta. Sprinkle with remaining feta, olives and parsley. Cut into wedges.
Makes 4 servings.
PUFFY PANCAKE: Turn oven to 450°F. Place 10-inch ovenproof skillet on middle rack in oven 5 minutes. Meanwhile, in medium bowl with mixer at medium speed, beat ½ cup all-purpose flour, ½ cup skim milk, 2 eggs and ⅛ teaspoon salt until well blended. Add 1 tablespoon vegetable oil to skillet, tilting to coat bottom and sides. Pour batter into pan. Bake 10 minutes. Reduce heat to 350°F.; bake 10 minutes more or until puffed and browned.

Per serving: 272 calories, 12 g protein, 16 g fat, 26 g carbohydrate, 637 mg sodium, 163 mg cholesterol.

Hash-and-Egg Brunch

1 can (12 ounces) corned beef, cut into chunks
3 cups frozen hash brown potatoes, thawed
1 can (10¾ ounces) condensed cream of celery soup
1 can (2.8 ounces) DURKEE French Fried Onions
¼ teaspoon DURKEE Ground Black Pepper
6 eggs
½ cup (2 ounces) shredded Cheddar cheese

Preheat oven to 400°. In large bowl, combine corned beef, potatoes, soup, *½ can* French Fried Onions and the pepper. Spoon evenly into 8×12-inch baking dish. Bake, covered, at 400° for 20 minutes or until heated through. Using back of spoon, make 6 wells in hash mixture. Break 1 egg into each well. Bake, uncovered, 15 to 20 minutes or until eggs are cooked to desired doneness. Sprinkle cheese down center of dish and top with remaining onions. Bake, uncovered, 1 to 3 minutes or until onions are golden brown.
Makes 6 servings.

Microwave Directions: Prepare corned beef mixture as above; spoon into 8×12-inch microwave-safe dish. Do not add eggs. Cook, uncovered, on HIGH 10 minutes. Rotate dish halfway through cooking time. Place eggs in hash as above. Using a toothpick, pierce each egg yolk and white twice. Cook, covered, 5 to 6 minutes or until eggs are cooked to desired doneness. Rotate dish halfway through cooking time. Top with cheese and remaining onions; cook, uncovered, 1 minute or until cheese melts. Let stand for 5 minutes.

Colorful Ham Omelet

3 tablespoons unsalted margarine or butter, divided
¼ cup finely chopped onion
¼ cup *each* finely chopped red and green pepper
½ cup (2 ounces) ARMOUR® Lower Salt Ham cut into ¼-inch cubes
6 eggs
¼ cup (1 ounce) shredded ARMOUR® Lower Salt Cheddar Cheese

Melt 1 tablespoon of the margarine in small skillet or omelet pan over medium heat. Add onion and red and green peppers; sauté about 3 to 5 minutes, or until tender. Add ham cubes; heat thoroughly. Remove and set aside.

Melt 1 tablespoon of the margarine in same pan over medium heat; add 3 well-beaten eggs. Cook eggs, pulling edges toward center, until almost set. Spoon half of the ham mixture over eggs. Cover and continue cooking until set. *Do not overcook.* Fold half of the omelet over other half. Sprinkle half of the cheese over top. Gently slide onto serving plate. Repeat with remaining ingredients. Serve immediately. Garnish with cilantro, if desired.
Makes 2 servings.

Microwave Directions: Place 1 tablespoon of the margarine, onion, red and green peppers, and ham in small microwave-safe dish. Cook on High power for 3 minutes; set aside. Separate eggs; beat egg whites in medium bowl until soft peaks form. Beat egg yolks with 2 tablespoons water in small bowl. Gently fold yolk mixture into whites. Melt remaining 2 tablespoons margarine in microwave-safe 9-inch pie plate; swirl to coat bottom. Carefully pour half of the egg mixture into pie plate. Cook on Medium power (50%) about 7 to 9 minutes or until almost set. Spoon half of the ham mixture and cheese over eggs. Cook on

Medium-High power (70%) for 2 more minutes, or until eggs are set. Fold and remove omelet from pie plate as above. Repeat with remaining ingredients. Garnish as above.

Nutrition Information Per Serving: 497 calories, 27 g protein, 42 g fat, 6.4 g carbohydrates, 851 mg cholesterol, 500 mg sodium.

Sausage-Asparagus Souffle Sandwiches

6 ounces ECKRICH® Smoked Sausage, cut into 18 slices
Water
¼ teaspoon salt
18 asparagus spears
3 English muffins, split, toasted
3 eggs, separated
½ teaspoon Worcestershire sauce
½ teaspoon Dijon mustard
Dash ground black pepper
¾ cup (3 ounces) shredded Cheddar cheese

Bring ½ inch water and the salt to a boil in large skillet over high heat. Place asparagus in boiling water. Reduce heat to low; cover and simmer 5 minutes or until asparagus is crisp-tender. Meanwhile, arrange muffin halves in 13×9×2-inch baking pan. Arrange 3 asparagus spears on each muffin half.

Preheat oven to 350°F. Beat egg whites in medium bowl until stiff, but not dry. Beat egg yolks with Worcestershire sauce, mustard and pepper in small bowl; fold into whites. Fold in cheese. Top each sandwich with souffle mixture and 3 slices of the sausage. Bake 15 minutes.
Makes 3 servings.

Pineapple Brunch Casserole

1 can (8 ounces) DOLE®
Crushed Pineapple
1 cup biscuit mix
1 cup milk
4 eggs, lightly beaten
6 tablespoons butter or
margarine, melted
1 teaspoon Dijon mustard
½ teaspoon onion powder
Pinch ground nutmeg
4 ounces cooked ham, diced
1 cup shredded Monterey Jack
or sharp Cheddar cheese
2 green onions, finely chopped

Preheat oven to 350°F. Drain pineapple. Reserve 2 tablespoons pineapple for garnish, if desired. Combine biscuit mix, milk, eggs, butter, mustard, onion powder and nutmeg in blender or in large mixer bowl until smooth. Stir in ham, cheese, onions and pineapple. Pour into greased 9-inch pie plate. Bake in preheated oven 35 to 40 minutes or until set. Garnish with reserved pineapple, if desired.
Makes 6 servings.

Huevos Rancheros

2 tablespoons vegetable oil
1 small onion, chopped
1 green pepper, chopped
1 tomato, peeled and chopped
1 can (8 ounces) tomato sauce
½ cup water
1 clove garlic, minced
1 teaspoon dried oregano leaves
½ teaspoon salt
½ to 1 teaspoon TABASCO®
pepper sauce
6 eggs
Tortillas or toasted English
muffins

In large skillet heat oil; add onion and green pepper. Cook 5 minutes or until tender. Add tomato, tomato sauce, water, garlic, oregano, salt and Tabasco® sauce. Cover; simmer 20 minutes. Break eggs, 1 at a time, into cup and slip into sauce. Cover; simmer over low heat 5 minutes or until eggs are set. Serve over tortillas or English muffins.
Makes 6 servings.

Eggs Arnold

¼ cup butter or margarine
2 medium onions, peeled, thinly
sliced
8 eggs
½ cup milk
1 teaspoon TABASCO® pepper
sauce
¼ teaspoon salt
2 tablespoons chopped parsley
4 English muffins
1 tablespoon spicy brown
mustard
3 ounces thinly sliced salami

In medium skillet melt butter; cook onions over low heat about 15 to 20 minutes or until lightly golden. Meanwhile, in large bowl beat together eggs, milk, Tabasco® sauce and salt. When onions are cooked, stir in egg mixture. When edges begin to set, draw cooked portions toward center so uncooked portion flows to bottom. Stir constantly; cook over low heat about 4 to 6 minutes or until eggs are cooked throughout, but still moist. Gently stir in parsley. Split and toast English muffins; spread with mustard. Top with salami slices and egg mixture. Serve with additional Tabasco® sauce, if desired.
Makes 4 servings.

Fresh Asparagus Soufflé

1 pound fresh asparagus, cut
into 1-inch pieces
¼ cup butter or margarine
¼ cup flour
½ teaspoon dried thyme leaves
½ teaspoon TABASCO® pepper
sauce
¼ teaspoon salt
1¼ cups milk
4 eggs, separated
¾ cup grated Parmesan cheese
¼ teaspoon cream of tartar

Preheat oven to 375°F. Prepare collar for 1½-quart greased straight-sided soufflé dish as follows: Fold 26-inch-long sheet of waxed paper in half lengthwise; grease 1 side and wrap around soufflé dish, greased-side-in, so 3 inches extend above top edge of dish. Tie in place with string.

In medium saucepan cook asparagus in 1 inch boiling water 5 minutes or until crisp-tender. Drain; set aside. In same saucepan melt butter; blend in flour, thyme, Tabasco® sauce and salt. Gradually add milk. Stir constantly; bring to a boil over medium heat and boil 1 minute. In medium bowl beat egg yolks. Gradually add ¼ of hot sauce; stir constantly. Gradually stir egg yolk mixture into remaining sauce in pan. Add cheese and asparagus; mix well. Cool slightly.

In large bowl of electric mixer at high speed beat egg whites with cream of tartar until whites are stiff, but not dry. Gently fold in sauce mixture. Spoon into prepared soufflé dish. Bake 40 to 45 minutes or until golden brown. Remove collar. Serve immediately.
Makes 4 servings.

Savory Sunday Eggs

1/4 **pound bulk pork sausage**
1/2 **cup chopped onion**
8 **eggs, beaten**
1/2 **cup milk**
  Dash of pepper
1 **8-ounce package**
  PHILADELPHIA BRAND
  Cream Cheese, cubed
  Chopped chives

Brown sausage in large skillet; drain. Add onions; cook until tender. Add combined eggs, milk and pepper. Cook slowly, stirring occasionally, until eggs begin to set. Add cream cheese; continue cooking, stirring occasionally, until cream cheese is melted and eggs are set. Sprinkle with chives.
6 servings.

Sausage 'n Egg Brunch Special

1/2 **pound ECKRICH® Smoked**
  Sausage
12 **ounces frozen shredded hash**
  brown potatoes, thawed
1/2 **cup sour cream**
1/4 **cup milk**
1/2 **cup (2 ounces) shredded**
  sharp Cheddar cheese
1 **tablespoon chopped chives**
4 **eggs**

Preheat oven to 350°F. Combine potatoes, sour cream, milk, cheese and chives in medium bowl. Spoon into buttered shallow 2-quart rectangular casserole. Bake 40 minutes. Cut sausage into halves lengthwise, then cut crosswise into bite-sized pieces. Arrange down center of casserole. Bake 10 minutes more. Shape a well in each corner of the potato mixture. Break an egg into each well. Bake 10 to 12 minutes more or until eggs reach desired doneness. Serve immediately.
Makes 4 servings.

Sausage Omelet

1 **package (8 ounces) SWIFT**
  PREMIUM® BROWN 'N
  SERVE™ Sausage Links
1/4 **cup chopped onion**
1/4 **cup chopped green bell**
  pepper
5 **eggs**
1/4 **cup milk**
1 **tomato, chopped**
1 1/2 **tablespoons butter or**
  margarine

Heat sausage in heavy 8-inch oven-proof skillet according to package directions. Remove sausage and keep warm. Saute onion and green pepper in same skillet over medium-high heat until vegetables are tender. Combine eggs and milk in medium bowl. Add onion, green pepper and tomato. Melt butter in same skillet over low heat. Add egg mixture and cook until eggs are almost set. Arrange sausage on top of eggs. To finish cooking top of omelet, broil, 4 inches from heat, until center is firm and top is lightly browned. Cut into wedges and serve immediately.
Makes 5 servings.

Cream Cheese Kugel

1 **8-ounce package**
  PHILADELPHIA BRAND
  Cream Cheese, softened
1/4 **cup PARKAY Margarine,**
  melted
4 **eggs, beaten**
1/2 **cup milk**
1/4 **cup sugar**
1/2 **teaspoon salt**
4 **cups (8 ounces) fine noodles,**
  cooked, drained
1/2 **cup raisins**
1/4 **teaspoon cinnamon**

Combine cream cheese and margarine, mixing until well blended. Blend in eggs, milk, sugar and salt. Add noodles and raisins; mix well. Pour mixture into 12×8-inch baking dish. Sprinkle with cinnamon. Bake at 375°, 30 minutes or until set.
6 to 8 servings.

Variation: Substitute 8 1/4-ounce can crushed pineapple, drained, for raisins.

Microwave: Prepare recipe as directed except for baking. Microwave on High 8 minutes, turning dish after 4 minutes. Microwave on Medium (50%) 9 to 12 minutes or until center is set.

Frittata Romano

6 **eggs**
1/2 **teaspoon TABASCO® pepper**
  sauce
1/4 **teaspoon salt**
1 **cup canned or thawed frozen**
  artichoke hearts, drained,
  sliced
1 **jar (3 ounces) pimiento,**
  drained
1/3 **cup grated Parmesan cheese**
2 **tablespoons olive or vegetable**
  oil
2 **medium cloves garlic, minced**

Preheat broiler. In large bowl beat eggs with Tabasco® sauce and salt. Gently fold in artichoke slices, pimiento and cheese. In 8- or 9-inch skillet with ovenproof handle,* heat oil; cook garlic until golden. Pour in egg mixture; cook over low heat. When edges begin to set, draw cooked portions toward center so uncooked portion flows to bottom. Cook until eggs are almost set. Place skillet under broiler 2 to 3 minutes or until eggs are set. To serve, loosen edges with spatula. Place large plate over skillet; invert frittata onto plate. Place serving plate on frittata and invert again so that top is up.
Makes 4 servings.

*If handle is not ovenproof, wrap with a double thickness of heavy-duty aluminum foil.

Phyllo Spinach Pie

1 container (15 ounces) ricotta cheese
1 package (10 ounces) frozen chopped spinach, cooked and squeezed dry
2 eggs, slightly beaten
2 tablespoons grated Parmesan cheese
1 envelope LIPTON® Vegetable Recipe Soup Mix
1/4 teaspoon ground nutmeg
2 cups fresh or canned sliced mushrooms
15 phyllo strudel sheets
1/2 cup butter or margarine, melted

Preheat oven to 375°.

In large bowl, thoroughly combine ricotta, spinach, eggs, Parmesan cheese, vegetable recipe soup mix and nutmeg; stir in mushrooms and set aside.

Unfold phyllo strudel sheets; cover with wax paper, then damp cloth. Brush 1 sheet at a time with melted butter. Place 6 buttered sheets across 9-inch pie plate, extending sheets over sides; press gently into pie plate. Place an additional 6 buttered sheets in opposite direction across 9-inch pie plate, extending sheets over sides, to form a cross; press gently into pie plate. Turn spinach mixture into prepared pie plate; gently fold sheets over spinach mixture to cover. Form remaining 3 buttered sheets into a ball and place on center of pie; brush with butter. Bake 35 minutes or until golden. Let stand 10 minutes before serving.
Makes about 8 servings.

Freezing Directions: Pie can be frozen up to 1 month. Simply prepare as above, but do not brush with butter or bake. Wrap in heavy-duty aluminum foil; freeze. To serve, unwrap, then brush with butter as above and bake at 375°, 40 minutes or until golden. Let stand as above.

Scotch Eggs

1/2 pound ground cooked ham
2 eggs
1/2 teaspoon dried thyme leaves
1/4 teaspoon TABASCO® pepper sauce
1 teaspoon prepared mustard
8 hard-cooked eggs, peeled
1 1/2 cups dry bread crumbs
Vegetable oil

In medium bowl mix ham, raw eggs, thyme, Tabasco® sauce and mustard. Pat ham mixture around hard-cooked eggs to make even coating; roll in bread crumbs. In large heavy saucepot heat about 2 inches oil over medium-high heat to 375°F. Fry coated eggs, a few at a time, 2 to 3 minutes or until golden brown. Drain on paper towels. Serve warm.
Makes 8 servings.

Broccoli-Mushroom Omelet

6 eggs, separated
1/4 cup evaporated skim milk
1/4 cup grated Parmesan cheese
1/8 teaspoon pepper
1 cup shredded Swiss cheese (4 ounces), divided
1 cup broccoli flowerets
1 cup sliced CAMPBELL'S FRESH® Mushrooms (4 ounces)
1/2 cup diced sweet red pepper
1/2 teaspoon dried Italian seasoning, crushed
1 1/2 cups V8® Vegetable Juice
1 tablespoon cornstarch

1. Preheat oven to 350°F. In large bowl with mixer at high speed, beat egg whites until stiff but not dry. In small bowl with mixer at high speed, beat egg yolks, milk, Parmesan cheese and pepper until foamy. Carefully fold egg yolk mixture and 1/2 cup of the Swiss cheese into beaten egg whites.

2. Spray oven-safe 10-inch nonstick skillet with vegetable cooking spray. Over medium heat, heat skillet; add egg mixture. Cook over low heat 5 minutes or until golden on underside. Place skillet in oven; bake 10 minutes or until top is puffed and golden brown.

3. Meanwhile, to prepare sauce: Spray another 10-inch nonstick skillet with vegetable cooking spray. Cook broccoli, mushrooms, red pepper and Italian seasoning until vegetables are tender-crisp, stirring often.

4. In small bowl, stir together V8 juice and cornstarch. Gradually stir V8 mixture into vegetable mixture. Over medium heat, heat until mixture boils and thickens, stirring often.

5. To serve: Running spatula under omelet, slide omelet onto serving plate. Sprinkle with remaining 1/2 cup Swiss cheese. Spoon sauce over omelet; cut into wedges.
Makes 6 servings.

Per serving: 203 calories, 15 g protein, 15 g fat, 9 g carbohydrate, 407 mg sodium, 295 mg cholesterol.

Campbelled Eggs

1 can (about 11 ounces) CAMPBELL'S® Condensed Nacho Cheese Soup/Dip, Cream of Chicken Soup or Cream of Mushroom Soup
8 eggs
Chopped fresh parsley for garnish

To Microwave:
1. In 3-quart microwave-safe casserole, stir soup until smooth. Add eggs; beat until smooth.
2. Cover with lid; microwave on HIGH 6 1/2 minutes or until eggs are nearly set, stirring 3 times during cooking. Let stand, covered, 2 minutes. Garnish with parsley.
Makes 4 servings.

BREADS, ROLLS & COFFEE CAKES

Fill your kitchen with the aroma of fresh-baked breads and rolls, and take pride in the delectable results. Your family will rave over homemade doughnuts and coffee cakes for breakfast, fruit-filled muffins for afternoon snacks, and crusty loaves or rolls for any time. And many are surprisingly easy to make!

Chocolate Spice Surprise Muffins

⅓ cup firmly packed light brown sugar
¼ cup margarine or butter, softened
1 egg
1 cup BORDEN® or MEADOW GOLD® Milk
2 cups biscuit baking mix
⅓ cup unsweetened cocoa
1 (9-ounce) package NONE SUCH® Condensed Mincemeat, crumbled
18 solid milk chocolate candy drops
½ cup confectioners' sugar
1 tablespoon water

Preheat oven to 375°. In large mixer bowl, beat brown sugar and margarine until fluffy. Add egg and milk; mix well. Stir in biscuit mix, cocoa and mincemeat until moistened. Fill greased or paper baking cup–lined muffin cups ¾ full. Top each with candy drop; press into batter. Bake 15 to 20 minutes. Cool 5 minutes; remove from pan. Meanwhile, in small bowl, mix confectioners' sugar and water; drizzle over warm muffins.
Makes about 1½ dozen.

Louisiana Corn Muffins

1 cup flour
1 cup yellow cornmeal
2 tablespoons sugar
2½ teaspoons baking powder
½ teaspoon salt
1 cup milk
½ cup vegetable oil
2 eggs, lightly beaten
½ teaspoon TABASCO® pepper sauce
1 can (8¾ ounces) whole kernel corn, drained, or 1 cup fresh or thawed frozen corn kernels

Preheat oven to 400°F. Grease twelve 3×1¼-inch muffin cups. In large bowl combine flour, cornmeal, sugar, baking powder and salt. In medium bowl combine milk, oil, eggs and Tabasco® sauce. Make a well in center of dry ingredients; add milk mixture and stir just to combine. Stir in corn. Spoon batter into prepared muffin cups. Bake 15 to 20 minutes or until a cake tester inserted in center comes out clean. Cool 5 minutes on wire rack. Remove from pans. Serve warm.
Makes 12 muffins.

Microwave Directions: Prepare muffin batter as directed above. Spoon approximately ⅓ cup batter into each of 6 paper baking cup–lined 6-ounce custard cups or microwave-safe muffin pan cups. Cook uncovered on High 4 to 5½ minutes or until cake tester inserted in center comes out clean; turn and rearrange cups or turn muffin pan ½ turn once during cooking. Cool 5 minutes on wire rack. Remove from pans. Repeat procedure with remaining batter. Serve warm.

Chocolate Chip Bran Muffins

1½ cups bran flakes cereal
½ cup boiling water
1 cup buttermilk or sour milk*
¼ cup vegetable oil
1 egg, slightly beaten
1¼ cups unsifted all-purpose flour
½ cup sugar
1 teaspoon baking soda
¼ teaspoon salt
½ cup HERSHEY'S MINI CHIPS Semi-Sweet Chocolate
¼ cup finely chopped dried apricots
¾ cup bran flakes cereal

Microwave: Combine 1½ cups bran flakes cereal and boiling water in medium bowl; blend well. Cool. Add buttermilk, oil and egg; blend well. Combine flour, sugar, baking soda and salt in medium bowl; stir in cereal mixture, MINI CHIPS Chocolate and apricots just until dry ingredients are moistened.

Place 6 paper muffin cups (2½ inches in diameter) in microwave cupcake or muffin maker or in 6-ounce micro-proof custard cups. Fill each cup half full with batter. Sprinkle 2 teaspoons bran flakes cereal on top of each muffin. Microwave at HIGH (100%) for 2½ to 3½ minutes, turning ¼ turn at end of each minute, or until cake tester comes out clean. (Tops may still appear moist.) Let stand several minutes. (Moist spots will disappear upon standing.) Repeat cooking procedure with remaining batter. Serve warm.
About 1½ dozen muffins.
*To sour milk: Use 1 tablespoon vinegar plus milk to equal 1 cup.

Pineapple Carrot Raisin Muffins

2 cups all-purpose flour
1 cup sugar
2 teaspoons baking powder
½ teaspoon ground cinnamon
¼ teaspoon ground ginger
½ cup shredded carrots
½ cup raisins
½ cup chopped walnuts
1 can (8 ounces) DOLE® Crushed Pineapple
2 eggs
1 teaspoon vanilla
½ cup butter or margarine, melted

In large bowl, combine flour, sugar, baking powder and spices. Stir in carrots, raisins and nuts. In small bowl, combine undrained pineapple, eggs and vanilla. Add liquid mixture to flour mixture; stir just until moistened. Batter will be lumpy; do not overmix. Stir in butter. Spoon batter evenly into 12 greased 2¾-inch muffin cups. Bake in preheated 375° oven 20 to 25 minutes or until golden brown. Remove to wire rack to cool.
Makes 1 dozen muffins.

Golden Oatmeal Muffins

1 package DUNCAN HINES® Butter Recipe Golden Cake Mix
1 cup quick-cooking oats
¼ teaspoon salt
¾ cup milk
2 large eggs, slightly beaten
2 tablespoons butter or margarine, melted
Honey or jam

1. Preheat oven to 400°F. Grease 24 muffin cups.
2. Combine dry cake mix, oats and salt in bowl. Beat together milk, eggs and butter. Add to dry ingredients, stirring just until moistened. Spoon into muffin cups, filling two-thirds full.
3. Bake at 400°F for 13 minutes or until golden brown. Serve with honey or your favorite jam.
24 muffins.

Honey-Lemon Muffins

¾ cup ROMAN MEAL® Original Wheat, Rye, Bran, Flax Cereal
1½ cups all-purpose flour
1 tablespoon baking powder
½ teaspoon salt
1 egg, slightly beaten
1 cup plain yogurt
½ cup vegetable oil
½ cup honey
2 teaspoons grated lemon peel
1 to 2 tablespoons lemon juice

In large bowl, combine cereal, flour, baking powder and salt. In small bowl, mix egg, yogurt, oil, honey, lemon peel and juice. Add liquid mixture to flour mixture; stir just until moistened. Batter will be lumpy; do not overmix. Spoon batter evenly into 12 greased 2½-inch muffin cups. Bake in preheated 375° oven 20 to 25 minutes or until golden brown. Remove to wire rack to cool.
Makes 1 dozen muffins.

Cranberry Muffins and Creamy Orange Spread

**2 cups flour
6 tablespoons sugar
2 teaspoons baking powder
½ teaspoon salt
¾ cup milk
½ cup PARKAY Margarine, melted
1 egg, beaten
¾ cup coarsely chopped cranberries
Creamy Orange Spread:
1 8-ounce package PHILADELPHIA BRAND Cream Cheese, softened
1 tablespoon sugar
1 tablespoon orange juice
1 teaspoon grated orange peel**

Combine flour, 4 tablespoons sugar, baking powder and salt; mix well. Add combined milk, margarine and egg, mixing just until moistened. Fold in combined remaining sugar and cranberries. Spoon into greased medium-size muffin pan, filling each cup ⅔ full. Bake at 400°, 20 to 25 minutes or until golden brown.

Combine cream cheese, sugar, orange juice and peel, mixing until well blended. Chill. Serve with muffins. *1 dozen.*

Variation: Substitute *Light* PHILADELPHIA BRAND Neufchâtel Cheese for Cream Cheese.

Raisin Scones

**2 cups all-purpose flour
2 tablespoons sugar
2 teaspoons baking powder
½ teaspoon baking soda
½ teaspoon salt
½ teaspoon ground nutmeg
½ cup butter or margarine, cut into chunks
1 cup SUN-MAID® Raisins
¾ cup buttermilk
1 egg white, lightly beaten, for glaze
Sugar, for glaze**

In large bowl, combine flour, 2 tablespoons sugar, the baking powder, soda, salt and nutmeg. Cut in butter until mixture resembles coarse meal. Mix in raisins, then mix in buttermilk with fork. Gather dough into ball and knead on lightly floured board about 2 minutes. Roll or pat dough out ¾ inch thick. With sharp knife, cut into 3-inch triangles. Space apart on greased baking sheets. Brush tops with egg white; sprinkle with sugar. Bake in preheated 425°F oven for about 15 minutes or until nicely browned. Serve warm with butter or jam.
Makes about 1 dozen scones.

Lemon Tea Muffins

**2 cups unsifted flour
2 teaspoons baking powder
½ teaspoon salt
1 cup margarine or butter, softened
1 cup granulated sugar
4 eggs, separated
½ cup REALEMON® Lemon Juice from Concentrate
¼ cup finely chopped nuts
2 tablespoons light brown sugar
¼ teaspoon ground nutmeg**

Preheat oven to 375°. Stir together flour, baking powder and salt; set aside. In large mixer bowl, beat margarine and granulated sugar until fluffy. Add egg yolks; beat until light. Gradually stir in ReaLemon® brand alternately with dry ingredients (*do not overmix*). In small mixer bowl, beat egg whites until stiff but not dry; fold one-third egg whites into lemon mixture. Fold remaining egg whites into lemon mixture. Fill paper-lined or greased muffin cups ¾ full. Combine remaining ingredients; sprinkle evenly over muffins. Bake 15 to 20 minutes. Cool 5 minutes; remove from pan. Serve warm.
Makes about 1½ dozen.

Moist Orange Mince Muffins

**2 cups unsifted flour
½ cup sugar
1 tablespoon baking powder
1 teaspoon salt
½ teaspoon baking soda
1 egg, slightly beaten
1 (8-ounce) container BORDEN® LITE-LINE® or VIVA® Orange Yogurt
⅓ cup BORDEN® or MEADOW GOLD® Milk
⅓ cup vegetable oil
1 (9-ounce) package NONE SUCH® Condensed Mincemeat, finely crumbled
⅓ cup BAMA® Orange Marmalade, melted, optional**

Preheat oven to 400°. In medium bowl, combine dry ingredients; set aside. In medium bowl, combine egg, yogurt, milk, oil and mincemeat; mix well. Stir into flour mixture only until moistened. Fill greased or paper baking cup-lined muffin cups ¾ full. Bake 20 to 25 minutes or until golden brown. Immediately turn out of pan. Brush warm muffins with marmalade if desired.
Makes about 1½ dozen.

Walnut Streusel Muffins

3 cups all-purpose flour
1½ cups packed brown sugar
¾ cup butter or margarine
1 cup chopped DIAMOND®
   Walnuts
2 teaspoons baking powder
1 teaspoon *each* ground nutmeg
   and ginger
½ teaspoon *each* baking soda
   and salt
1 cup buttermilk or soured milk
2 eggs, beaten

In medium bowl, combine 2 cups of the flour and the sugar; cut in butter to form fine crumbs. In small bowl, combine ¾ cup of the crumbs and ¼ cup of the walnuts; set aside. Into remaining crumb mixture, stir in remaining 1 cup flour, the baking powder, spices, soda, salt and remaining ¾ cup walnuts. In another small bowl, combine buttermilk and eggs; stir into dry ingredients just to moisten. Spoon into 18 greased or paper-lined 2¾-inch muffin cups, filling about ⅔ full. Top each with a generous spoonful of reserved crumb-nut mixture. Bake in preheated 350°F oven 20 to 25 minutes or until springy to the touch. Cool in pans 10 minutes. Loosen and remove from pans. Serve warm.
Makes 1½ dozen muffins.

Blueberry Muffins

1 package DUNCAN HINES®
   Deluxe White Cake Mix
2 tablespoons all-purpose flour
1 teaspoon baking powder
⅔ cup milk
3 large eggs
⅓ cup CRISCO® Oil or PURITAN®
   Oil
1 cup rinsed fresh or well-
   drained, thawed, frozen
   blueberries

1. Preheat oven to 375°F. Line 24 muffin cups with paper liners.
2. Combine dry cake mix, flour and baking powder in large bowl. Beat milk, eggs and oil together with fork; add to mixture in bowl and stir just until dry ingredients are moistened. Fold in blueberries.
3. Spoon batter into muffin cups, filling one-third full.
4. Bake at 375°F for 15 to 20 minutes or until golden brown.
24 muffins.

Treasure Bran Muffins

1¼ cups whole bran cereal
1 cup milk
¼ cup oil
1 egg, beaten
1¼ cups flour
½ cup sugar
1 tablespoon baking powder
½ teaspoon salt
½ cup raisins

* * *

1 8-ounce package
   PHILADELPHIA BRAND
   Cream Cheese, softened
¼ cup sugar
1 egg, beaten

Combine cereal and milk; let stand 2 minutes. Add combined oil and egg; mix well. Add combined dry ingredients, mixing just until moistened. Stir in raisins. Spoon into greased and floured medium-size muffin pan, filling each cup ⅔ full.

Combine cream cheese, sugar and egg, mixing until well blended. Drop rounded measuring tablespoonfuls of cream cheese mixture onto batter. Bake at 375°, 25 minutes.
1 dozen.

Molasses Muffins

1⅔ cups unsifted all-purpose flour
3 tablespoons sugar
2 teaspoons baking powder
1 teaspoon ground ginger
½ teaspoon salt
½ cup dark molasses
2 eggs, slightly beaten
¼ cup CRISCO® Oil
¼ cup milk

Preheat oven to 400°F. Place paper liners in 12 muffin cups. Set aside.

Mix flour, sugar, baking powder, ginger and salt in medium mixing bowl. Make a well in center of mixture. Set aside. Blend remaining ingredients in small mixing bowl. Pour into well in dry ingredients. Stir just until ingredients are moistened. Pour into lined muffin cups, filling each about two-thirds full. Bake at 400°F, about 15 minutes, or until centers spring back when touched lightly.
1 dozen muffins.
Variation: Orange Raisin Muffins. Follow recipe above, omitting ginger. Add ½ cup raisins and 2 teaspoons grated orange peel to dry ingredients.

Southern Hush Puppies

CRISCO® Oil for frying
¾ cup yellow cornmeal
⅓ cup unsifted all-purpose flour
1½ teaspoons baking powder
½ teaspoon salt
½ cup buttermilk
1 egg
¼ cup finely chopped onion

Heat 2 to 3 inches Crisco® Oil in deep-fryer or large saucepan to 375°F. Mix cornmeal, flour, baking powder and salt in medium mixing bowl. Add remaining ingredients. Mix well. Drop batter by tablespoonfuls into hot Crisco® Oil. Fry a few at a time, 3 to 4 minutes, or until golden brown. Drain on paper towels. Repeat with remaining batter. Serve immediately or keep warm in 175°F oven.
About 1 dozen hush puppies.

Italian Pepperoni Puffs

2¼ to 2¾ cups unsifted all-purpose flour, divided
1 package (¼ ounce) active dry yeast
1 tablespoon sugar
1 teaspoon garlic salt
½ teaspoon Italian seasoning
¼ teaspoon onion powder
¾ cup very warm water (120° to 130°F)
2 tablespoons CRISCO® Oil
1 egg
½ cup grated Parmesan cheese
¼ cup finely chopped pepperoni
CRISCO® Oil for frying

Mix 1½ cups flour, yeast, sugar, garlic salt, Italian seasoning and onion powder in large mixing bowl. Add warm water, Crisco® Oil and egg. Beat with electric mixer at low speed until ingredients are moistened, scraping bowl constantly. Beat at medium speed 3 minutes, scraping bowl occasionally. Stir in Parmesan cheese and enough remaining flour to make a slightly stiff dough.

Knead dough on lightly floured surface 5 to 8 minutes, or until smooth and elastic, adding additional flour as necessary. Place in lightly oiled medium mixing bowl. Turn dough over to coat both sides with Crisco® Oil. Cover; let rise in warm place 40 to 50 minutes, or until doubled.

Punch down dough. Place on lightly floured surface. Divide dough in half. Roll each half to ⅛-inch thickness. Cut into 2-inch rounds. Place ½ teaspoon chopped pepperoni in center of half of the rounds. Brush edges with water. Top with remaining rounds. Press edges together with fork to seal. Cover; let rise in warm place about 30 minutes, or until doubled.

Heat 2 to 3 inches Crisco® Oil in deep-fryer or large saucepan to 365°F. Fry 3 or 4 puffs at a time, 3 to 4 minutes, or until golden brown, turning over several times. Drain on paper towels. Sprinkle with *grated Parmesan cheese*, if desired. Serve warm.
1½ to 2 dozen puffs.

Raised Doughnuts

3½ to 4½ cups unsifted all-purpose flour, divided
¾ cup sugar, divided
2 packages (¼ ounce each) active dry yeast
1 teaspoon salt
1 cup milk
¼ cup vegetable shortening
2 eggs, slightly beaten
CRISCO® Oil for frying

Mix 2 cups flour, ¼ cup sugar, yeast and salt in large mixing bowl. Set aside. Combine milk and shortening in small saucepan. Cook over moderate heat until very warm (120° to 130°F). Add to flour mixture. Add eggs. Beat with electric mixer at low speed 1 minute, scraping bowl constantly. Beat at medium speed 3 minutes, scraping bowl occasionally. Stir in enough remaining flour to make a soft dough.

Knead dough on lightly floured surface 5 to 8 minutes, or until smooth and elastic, adding additional flour as necessary (dough will be slightly sticky). Place in lightly oiled medium mixing bowl. Turn dough over to coat both sides with Crisco® Oil. Cover; let rise in warm place 40 to 50 minutes, or until doubled.

Oil baking sheet. Set aside. Punch down dough. Place on lightly floured surface. Divide dough in half. Roll each half to ½-inch thickness. Cut into 2½-inch rounds with doughnut cutter. Place doughnuts and holes on prepared baking sheet. Cover; let rise in warm place about 30 minutes, or until doubled.

Heat 2 to 3 inches Crisco® Oil in deep-fryer or large saucepan to 375°F. Fry 2 or 3 doughnuts at a time, 1 to 1½ minutes, or until golden brown, turning over once. To fry holes, place several at a time in hot Crisco® Oil. Fry 45 to 60 seconds, or until golden brown, turning over occasionally. Drain on paper towels. Place remaining ½ cup sugar in large plastic food storage bag. Add a few doughnuts and holes at a time; shake to coat.
1½ dozen doughnuts and 1½ dozen holes.

Variation: Glazed Raised Doughnuts. Follow recipe above, except reduce sugar to ¼ cup and do not shake doughnuts in sugar. Before frying doughnuts, combine 1 cup confectioners sugar, 2 tablespoons milk, 1 tablespoon honey and 1 teaspoon grated lemon or orange peel in small mixing bowl. Beat at medium speed with electric mixer until smooth. After frying, dip one side of warm doughnuts in glaze. Cool doughnuts, glazed side up, on wire rack over waxed paper.

Jamaican Sweet Buns

    2 cups all-purpose flour
    1/4 cup sugar
    4 teaspoons baking powder
    2 teaspoons grated lemon peel
    1/4 teaspoon salt
    1/2 cup butter or margarine
    1/2 cup milk
    2 egg yolks, lightly beaten
    3/4 cup SUN-MAID® Raisins
    3/4 cup shredded coconut
    1 egg white, beaten, for glaze
      Sugar, for glaze

In medium bowl, combine flour, the 1/4 cup sugar, the baking powder, peel and salt. Cut in butter until mixture resembles coarse meal. Combine milk and yolks; mix into flour mixture to form soft dough. Mix in raisins and coconut just to blend. Evenly divide dough into six 4-inch greased tart pans; flatten tops. Brush generously with egg white; sprinkle heavily with sugar (about 2 teaspoons on each). Space apart on baking sheet. Bake in preheated 450°F oven about 15 minutes or until springy to the touch and well browned. Cool in pans. Serve with whipped sweet butter.
Makes 6 buns.

French Breakfast Puffs

    1 1/2 cups unsifted all-purpose flour
    1/2 cup confectioners sugar
    1 teaspoon baking powder
    1 teaspoon salt
    3/4 teaspoon ground nutmeg
    1/2 cup milk
    1/2 cup water
    1/4 cup CRISCO® Oil
    1 1/2 teaspoons grated lemon peel
    3 eggs
      CRISCO® Oil for frying
      Confectioners sugar

Mix flour, 1/2 cup confectioners sugar, baking powder, salt and nutmeg in small mixing bowl. Set aside. Combine milk, water, Crisco® Oil and lemon peel in medium saucepan. Heat to rolling boil over medium-high heat. Add flour mixture all at once. Beat with wooden spoon until mixture pulls away from sides of pan into a ball. Remove from heat; cool slightly. Add eggs, one at a time, beating after each addition.

Heat 2 to 3 inches Crisco® Oil in deep-fryer or large saucepan to 350°F.

Drop dough by tablespoonfuls into hot Crisco® Oil. Fry 3 or 4 puffs at a time, 4 to 6 minutes, or until golden brown, turning over several times. Drain on paper towels. Sprinkle top of each puff with confectioners sugar.
About 32 puffs.

Lemon Pecan Sticky Rolls

    1/2 cup granulated sugar
    1/2 cup firmly packed light brown sugar
    1/4 cup margarine or butter
    1/4 cup REALEMON® Lemon Juice from Concentrate
    1/2 teaspoon ground cinnamon
    1/2 cup chopped pecans
    2 (8-ounce) packages refrigerated crescent rolls

Preheat oven to 375°. In small saucepan, combine sugars, margarine, ReaLemon® brand and cinnamon. Bring to a boil; boil 1 minute. Reserving 1/4 cup, pour remaining sugar mixture into 9-inch round layer cake pan. Sprinkle with nuts. Separate rolls into 8 rectangles; spread with reserved sugar mixture. Roll up jellyroll-fashion, beginning with short side; seal edges. Cut in half. Place rolls, cut-side down, in prepared pan. Bake 30 to 35 minutes or until dark golden brown. Loosen sides. Immediately turn onto serving plate; do not remove pan. Let stand 5 minutes; remove pan. Serve warm.
Makes 16 rolls.

Paul Bunyan Sticky Buns

    1 package (16 ounces) hot roll mix
    1/2 cup butter or margarine, melted
    2 tablespoons water
    1 cup packed brown sugar
    1 cup chopped DIAMOND® Walnuts
    3/4 cup granulated sugar
    1 tablespoon ground cinnamon

Prepare dough as package directs for rolls. Knead gently on lightly floured board 1 minute. Place dough in lightly greased bowl; turn once to grease surface. Cover; let rise in warm place (85°F) until doubled, about 1 hour. To prepare syrup, in small saucepan, combine 1/4 cup of the butter, the water and brown sugar. Stir over medium heat until sugar dissolves. Bring to boil; reduce heat to low and simmer gently 1 minute. Pour at once into 11×7-inch baking pan, tilting to spread syrup evenly. Sprinkle 1/2 cup of the walnuts over syrup layer; set aside. After dough has risen, turn out onto lightly floured board. Let rest 5 minutes, then stretch and roll into 30×5-inch rectangle. Brush with remaining 1/4 cup butter. In small bowl, combine granulated sugar and cinnamon; sprinkle over butter. Arrange remaining 1/2 cup walnuts on top. Starting from 5-inch side, roll up loosely, jelly-roll fashion, pinching edges to seal. Cut roll into 6 equal pieces. Place cut sides up in prepared pan, spreading pinwheels open a little. Cover; let rise in warm place 35 to 45 minutes or until almost doubled. Cover lower shelf of oven with foil. Bake buns on center shelf of preheated 375°F oven 25 to 35 minutes or until golden. Immediately invert onto tray. Cool 5 minutes. Serve warm.
Makes 6 large buns.

Easy Apple Kuchen

2 envelopes active dry yeast
¼ cup warm water (about 110°F)
2 large eggs
1 package DUNCAN HINES®
    Deluxe Yellow Cake Mix
1¼ cups all-purpose flour
1½ cups sugar
1 tablespoon ground cinnamon
⅓ cup butter or margarine
6 medium apples or 2 cans
    (20 ounces each) pie-sliced
    apples, drained

1. Dissolve yeast in warm water in large mixer bowl. Blend in eggs and half of dry cake mix. Beat for 1 minute at medium speed. Add remaining cake mix and beat for 3 minutes at medium speed. (Batter should be quite stiff but not doughlike.) Let rest 5 minutes.
2. Sprinkle flour on board. Scrape batter out onto prepared board. Knead batter until flour is worked in, about 100 strokes. Place in greased bowl, cover, and let rise in warm, draft-free place for 30 minutes.
3. For topping, mix sugar and cinnamon in bowl; cut in butter with pastry blender or 2 knives.
4. Preheat oven to 350°F. Grease 13×9×2-inch pan and 8×8×2-inch pan. Pare, core and slice apples.
5. Punch down dough with greased fingertips. Spread dough to ¼- to ⅓-inch thickness on bottom of pans. Arrange apple slices in rows on top. Sprinkle with topping. Let rise in warm place for 30 minutes.
6. Bake at 350°F for 25 to 30 minutes or until toothpick inserted in center comes out clean. Serve warm.
24 servings.

Crullers

1 8-ounce package
    PHILADELPHIA BRAND
    Cream Cheese, softened
⅓ cup PARKAY Margarine
1 cup flour
    Dash of salt
    Sugar

Combine cream cheese and margarine, mixing until well blended. Add flour and salt; mix well. Shape dough into ball; chill 1 hour. On lightly floured surface, roll dough to 12×6-inch rectangle. Cut dough into twenty-four ½-inch strips. Fry in deep hot oil, 375°, 1 to 2 minutes or until golden brown, turning once using tongs. Drain on paper towels. Roll in sugar.
2 dozen.

Fruity Swirl Coffeecake

1 8-ounce package
    PHILADELPHIA BRAND
    Cream Cheese, softened
1 cup sugar
½ cup PARKAY Margarine
2 eggs
½ teaspoon vanilla
1¾ cups flour
1 teaspoon baking powder
½ teaspoon baking soda
¼ teaspoon salt
¼ cup milk
½ cup KRAFT Red Raspberry
    Preserves

Combine cream cheese, sugar and margarine, mixing until well blended. Add eggs, one at a time, mixing well after each addition. Blend in vanilla. Add combined dry ingredients alternately with milk, mixing well after each addition. Pour into greased and floured 13×9-inch baking pan; dot with preserves. Cut through batter with knife several times for marble effect. Bake at 350°, 35 minutes.
12 servings.

Blueberries 'n Cheese Coffeecake

½ cup PARKAY Margarine
1¼ cups granulated sugar
2 eggs
2¼ cups flour
1 tablespoon baking powder
1 teaspoon salt
¾ cup milk
¼ cup water
2 cups blueberries
1 8-ounce package
    PHILADELPHIA BRAND
    Cream Cheese, cubed
1 teaspoon grated lemon peel

*   *   *

¼ cup granulated sugar
¼ cup flour
1 teaspoon grated lemon peel
2 tablespoons PARKAY
    Margarine
    Powdered sugar

Beat margarine and granulated sugar until light and fluffy. Add eggs, one at a time, mixing well after each addition. Add combined 2 cups flour, baking powder and salt alternately with combined milk and water, mixing well after each addition. Toss blueberries with remaining flour; fold into batter with cream cheese and peel. Pour into greased and floured 13×9-inch baking pan.

Combine granulated sugar, flour and peel; cut in margarine until mixture resembles coarse crumbs. Sprinkle over batter. Bake at 375°, 1 hour. Cool. Sprinkle with powdered sugar before serving.
12 servings.

Variation: Substitute 2 cups frozen blueberries, thawed, well-drained, for fresh blueberries.

Apricot Crumble Cake

1 8-ounce package
    PHILADELPHIA BRAND
    Cream Cheese, softened
1/2 cup PARKAY Margarine
1 1/4 cups granulated sugar
1/4 cup milk
2 eggs
1 teaspoon vanilla
1 3/4 cups flour
1 teaspoon baking powder
1/2 teaspoon baking soda
1/4 teaspoon salt
1 10-ounce jar KRAFT Apricot or
    Peach Preserves
2 cups flaked coconut
2/3 cup packed brown sugar
1 teaspoon cinnamon
1/3 cup PARKAY Margarine,
    melted

Combine cream cheese, margarine and granulated sugar, mixing at medium speed on electric mixer until well blended. Gradually add milk, mixing well after each addition. Blend in eggs and vanilla. Add combined dry ingredients to cream cheese mixture; mix well. Pour half of batter into greased and floured 13×9-inch baking pan. Dot with preserves; cover with remaining batter. Bake at 350°, 35 to 40 minutes or until wooden pick inserted in center comes out clean.

Combine coconut, brown sugar, cinnamon and margarine; mix well. Spread onto cake; broil 3 to 5 minutes, or until golden brown.
16 servings.

Cream Cheese Swirl Coffee Cake

2 (3-ounce) packages cream
    cheese, softened
2 tablespoons confectioners'
    sugar
2 tablespoons REALEMON®
    Lemon Juice from
    Concentrate
2 cups unsifted flour
1 teaspoon baking powder
1 teaspoon baking soda
1/4 teaspoon salt
1 cup granulated sugar
1/2 cup margarine or butter,
    softened
3 eggs
1 teaspoon vanilla extract
1 (8-ounce) container BORDEN®
    or MEADOW GOLD® Sour
    Cream
Cinnamon-Nut Topping*

Preheat oven to 350°. In small bowl, beat cheese, confectioners' sugar and ReaLemon® brand until smooth; set aside. Stir together flour, baking powder, baking soda and salt; set aside. In large mixer bowl, beat granulated sugar and margarine until fluffy. Add eggs and vanilla; mix well. Add dry ingredients alternately with sour cream; mix well. Pour half of batter into greased and floured 10-inch tube pan. Spoon cheese mixture on top of batter to within 1/2 inch of pan edge. Spoon remaining batter over filling, spreading to pan edge. Sprinkle with Cinnamon-Nut Topping. Bake 40 to 45 minutes or until wooden pick inserted near center comes out clean. Cool 10 minutes; remove from pan. Serve warm.
Makes one 10-inch cake.

Cinnamon-Nut Topping: Combine 1/4 cup finely chopped nuts, 2 tablespoons granulated sugar and 1/2 teaspoon ground cinnamon.

Orange Wake-Up Cake

1 package DUNCAN HINES®
    Butter Recipe Golden Cake
    Mix
2/3 cup water
3 large eggs
1/2 cup (1 stick) butter or
    margarine, softened
2 tablespoons grated orange
    peel
1/2 cup chopped pecans
1/3 cup packed brown sugar
1/4 cup fine graham cracker
    crumbs
2 tablespoons butter or
    margarine, melted
1 1/2 teaspoons ground cinnamon
1 cup confectioners' sugar
2 tablespoons hot water
1/4 teaspoon vanilla extract

1. Preheat oven to 375°F. Grease and flour two 9×1 1/2-inch round layer pans.
2. Combine dry cake mix, water, eggs and 1/2 cup butter in large mixer bowl. Mix cake as directed on package. Fold in 1 tablespoon of the orange peel. Divide batter evenly in pans.
3. For topping, combine pecans, brown sugar, graham cracker crumbs, 2 tablespoons butter, remaining orange peel and cinnamon; mix well. Sprinkle evenly over batter in pans.
4. Bake at 375°F for 25 to 30 minutes or until toothpick inserted in center comes out clean.
5. For glaze,* mix confectioners' sugar, hot water and vanilla until smooth. Drizzle over warm cakes. Serve warm or cool in pans.
12 to 16 servings.
*Or heat 2/3 cup DUNCAN HINES® Vanilla Frosting in a small saucepan over medium heat, stirring constantly, until thin.

Soda Bread

3 cups unsifted all-purpose flour
3 tablespoons sugar
2 teaspoons baking powder
1 teaspoon baking soda
1 teaspoon salt
1½ cups buttermilk
1 egg, slightly beaten
3 tablespoons CRISCO® Oil
½ cup raisins

Preheat oven to 350°F. Oil 8-inch round baking dish. Set aside.

Mix flour, sugar, baking powder, baking soda and salt in medium mixing bowl. Add buttermilk, egg and Crisco® Oil. Stir with fork until ingredients are moistened. Stir in raisins. Pour into prepared dish.

Bake at 350°F, 35 to 40 minutes, or until wooden pick inserted in center comes out clean. Cool 10 minutes. Remove from dish. Cool completely on wire rack.

One 8-inch round loaf.

Gingerbread

¼ cup butter or margarine, softened
¼ cup packed brown sugar
¼ cup honey
¼ cup molasses
2 eggs, lightly beaten
¾ cup orange juice
2 cups all-purpose flour
1 teaspoon baking powder
¾ teaspoon salt
½ teaspoon baking soda
1½ teaspoons ground ginger
1 teaspoon ground cinnamon
1 teaspoon ground nutmeg
Grated peel of 1 orange
¾ cup SUN-MAID® Zante Currants

In large bowl, beat butter and brown sugar until smooth and thick. Add honey and molasses and beat again until smooth. Blend in eggs and then orange juice.

In medium bowl, combine flour, baking powder, salt, baking soda, ginger, cinnamon and nutmeg. Stir in orange peel and currants. Add flour mixture to butter mixture, stirring until blended. Pour the batter into greased 8×8×2-inch pan. Bake in preheated 350°F oven 40 minutes or until pick inserted in the center comes out clean. Cool in pan on wire rack 15 minutes before cutting and serving.
Makes 8 servings.

Golden Fruit Loaves

1 package DUNCAN HINES®
   Butter Recipe Golden Cake
   Mix
1½ cups chopped candied mixed
   fruit (6 ounces)
½ cup all-purpose flour
½ teaspoon baking powder
½ teaspoon baking soda
1 cup milk
2 large eggs
2 tablespoons butter or
   margarine, softened

1. Preheat oven to 350°F. Grease and flour two 8½×4½×2½-inch loaf pans.
2. Sprinkle 2 tablespoons dry cake mix over candied fruit; stir to coat.
3. Combine remaining cake mix, flour, baking powder and baking soda in large mixer bowl. Add milk, eggs and butter. Blend at low speed, then beat 2 minutes at medium speed. Fold in fruit. Divide batter evenly in pans.
4. Bake at 350°F for 45 to 50 minutes or until toothpick inserted in center comes out clean. Cool in pans on racks 20 minutes. Remove from pans; cool completely on racks.
2 medium loaves.

Golden Apple Boston Brown Bread

¼ cup butter or margarine, softened
⅓ cup honey
⅓ cup light molasses
1 cup whole wheat flour
1 cup rye flour
1 cup yellow cornmeal
2 teaspoons baking soda
½ teaspoon salt
2 cups buttermilk
2 cups coarsely chopped
   Washington Golden
   Delicious apples

In large bowl, cream butter, honey and molasses. In medium bowl, combine flours, cornmeal, baking soda and salt. Add flour mixture to butter mixture alternately with buttermilk, mixing well after each addition. Stir in apples. Pour batter into 2 greased 8½×4½×2½-inch loaf pans. Bake in preheated 350° oven 1 hour or until toothpick inserted into center comes out clean. Let cool in pans on wire racks 10 minutes. Loosen edges; remove from pans. Cool slightly on wire racks; serve warm.
Makes 2 loaves.

Variation: To steam brown bread, divide batter evenly between 2 greased 1-pound coffee cans, filling cans about three-fourths full. Cover tops of cans with aluminum foil; tie foil to cans with string. Place rack in large kettle; add boiling water to depth of 1 inch. Place cans on rack; cover kettle. Steam over low heat 3 hours or until toothpick inserted near center comes out clean. If necessary, add more boiling water to kettle during steaming. Cool as above.

*Favorite recipe from **Washington Apple Commission***

Old-Fashioned Apple Loaf

2 cups unsifted all-purpose flour
2 teaspoons baking powder
1 teaspoon apple pie spice*
1/2 teaspoon salt
1/4 teaspoon baking soda
2/3 cup chunky applesauce
1/2 cup granulated sugar
2 eggs
1/4 cup CRISCO® Oil
2 tablespoons milk
2 tablespoons chopped walnuts
2 teaspoons butter or margarine
1 teaspoon packed brown sugar

Preheat oven to 350°F. Oil and flour 8×4-inch loaf pan. Set aside.

Mix flour, baking powder, apple pie spice, salt and baking soda in medium mixing bowl. Set aside. Combine applesauce, granulated sugar, eggs, Crisco® Oil and milk in large mixing bowl. Mix well. Add flour mixture. Beat at medium speed with electric mixer just until combined, scraping bowl occasionally. Pour into prepared loaf pan.

Combine walnuts, butter and brown sugar in small mixing bowl. Mix with fork until crumbly. Sprinkle down center of loaf. Bake at 350°F, 35 to 45 minutes, or until golden brown and wooden pick inserted in center comes out clean. Immediately remove from pan. Cool on wire rack.
1 loaf.

*Substitute 3/4 teaspoon ground cinnamon, dash ground nutmeg and dash ground cloves for apple pie spice, if desired.

Golden Raisin Spice Bread

2 cups unsifted flour
2 teaspoons baking powder
1 teaspoon ground cinnamon
1/2 teaspoon ground nutmeg
1/2 teaspoon salt
1 cup sugar
1/2 cup margarine or butter, softened
3 eggs
1/2 cup milk
1/2 cup REALEMON® Lemon Juice from Concentrate
1 cup golden seedless raisins

Preheat oven to 350°. Stir together flour, baking powder, cinnamon, nutmeg and salt; set aside. In large mixer bowl, beat sugar and margarine until fluffy. Add eggs, 1 at a time; beat well. Add milk alternately with dry ingredients; stir well. Stir in ReaLemon® brand and raisins. Turn into greased and floured 9×5-inch loaf pan. Bake 55 to 60 minutes or until wooden pick inserted near center comes out clean. Cool 10 minutes; remove from pan. Cool completely. Store tightly wrapped.
Makes one 9×5-inch loaf.

Lemon Bread

2 cups unsifted flour
1 teaspoon baking powder
1/2 teaspoon baking soda
1/4 teaspoon salt
1 1/2 cups sugar
1/2 cup margarine or butter, softened
3 eggs
1/2 cup REALEMON® Lemon Juice from Concentrate
1/2 cup BORDEN® or MEADOW GOLD® Milk
3/4 cup chopped pecans, optional Clear Lemon Glaze*

Preheat oven to 350°. Stir together flour, baking powder, baking soda and salt; set aside. In large mixer bowl, beat sugar and margarine until fluffy. Add eggs, 1 at a time; beat well. Gradually beat in ReaLemon® brand. Add milk alternately with dry ingredients; stir well. Add pecans if desired. Turn into greased and floured 9×5-inch loaf pan. Bake 50 to 55 minutes or until wooden pick inserted near center comes out clean. Remove from oven; drizzle with Clear Lemon Glaze. Cool 15 minutes; remove from pan. Cool completely. Store tightly wrapped.
Makes one 9×5-inch loaf.
***CLEAR LEMON GLAZE:** In small saucepan, combine 2 tablespoons sugar and 2 teaspoons ReaLemon® brand; heat until sugar dissolves.

Chocolate Chip Banana Bread

2 cups unsifted all-purpose flour
1 cup sugar
1 teaspoon baking powder
1 teaspoon salt
1/2 teaspoon baking soda
1 cup mashed ripe bananas (about 3 small)
1/2 cup shortening
2 eggs
1 cup HERSHEY'S MINI CHIPS Semi-Sweet Chocolate
1/2 cup chopped walnuts

Grease bottom only of 9×5×3-inch loaf pan; set aside. Combine all ingredients except MINI CHIPS Chocolate and walnuts in large mixer bowl; blend well on medium speed. Stir in MINI CHIPS Chocolate and walnuts.

Pour into prepared pan. Bake at 350° for 60 to 70 minutes or until cake tester comes out clean. Cool 10 minutes; remove from pan. Cool completely on wire rack.
1 loaf.

Pumpkin Nut Bread

3½ cups unsifted flour
2 teaspoons baking soda
1½ teaspoons ground cinnamon
½ teaspoon baking powder
2 cups sugar
⅔ cup shortening
4 eggs
1 (16-ounce) can pumpkin (about 2 cups)
½ cup water
1 (9-ounce) package NONE SUCH® Condensed Mincemeat, crumbled
1 cup chopped nuts

Preheat oven to 350°. Stir together flour, baking soda, cinnamon and baking powder; set aside. In large mixer bowl, beat sugar and shortening until fluffy. Add eggs, pumpkin and water; mix well. Stir in flour mixture, mincemeat and nuts. Turn into 2 greased 9×5-inch loaf pans. Bake 55 to 60 minutes or until wooden pick inserted near center comes out clean. Cool 10 minutes; remove from pan. Cool completely.
Makes two 9×5-inch loaves.

Favorite Banana Bread

1 8-ounce package PHILADELPHIA BRAND Cream Cheese, softened
1 cup sugar
¼ cup PARKAY Margarine
1 cup mashed ripe banana
2 eggs
2¼ cups flour
1½ teaspoons baking powder
½ teaspoon baking soda
1 cup chopped nuts

Combine cream cheese, sugar and margarine, mixing until well blended. Blend in banana and eggs. Add combined remaining ingredients, mixing just until moistened. Pour into greased and floured 9×5-inch loaf pan. Bake at 350°, 1 hour and 10 minutes or until wooden pick inserted near center comes out clean. Cool 5 minutes; remove from pan. Serve with additional cream cheese, if desired.
1 loaf.

Beer Cheese Bread

1½ cups unsifted all-purpose flour
½ cup whole wheat flour
2 tablespoons sugar
1½ teaspoons baking powder
1 teaspoon instant minced onion
¾ teaspoon baking soda
½ teaspoon salt
2 cups shredded Cheddar cheese (about 8 ounces)
1 cup beer
2 eggs
⅓ cup CRISCO® Oil

Preheat oven to 350°F. Oil and flour 9×5-inch loaf pan. Set aside.

Mix all-purpose flour, whole wheat flour, sugar, baking powder, onion, baking soda and salt in medium mixing bowl. Add remaining ingredients. Beat with electric mixer at medium speed about 1 minute, scraping bowl occasionally. Pour into prepared pan.

Bake at 350°F, 50 to 60 minutes, or until wooden pick inserted in center comes out clean. Immediately remove from pan. Cool on wire rack.
1 loaf.

V8 Cheese Bread

5½ to 6 cups all-purpose flour, divided
2 packages active dry yeast
1½ teaspoons salt
1 cup V8® Vegetable Juice
¾ cup water
3 tablespoons butter or margarine
1½ cups shredded Cheddar cheese (6 ounces)
1 egg

1. In large bowl, combine 2 cups of the flour, yeast and salt; set aside. In small saucepan over medium heat, heat V8 juice, water and butter until warm (115° to 120°F.)
2. Stir V8 mixture into flour mixture. With mixer at low speed, beat 30 seconds. Add cheese and egg. With mixer at high speed, beat 3 minutes. Stir in 2½ cups of the remaining flour.
3. Turn dough onto lightly floured surface; knead until smooth and elastic, about 6 minutes, adding remaining flour while kneading. Shape dough into ball; place in large greased bowl, turning dough to grease top. Cover; let rise in warm place until doubled in bulk, about 1 hour.
4. Spray two 8- by 4-inch loaf pans with vegetable cooking spray. Punch dough down; divide in half. Shape into 2 loaves. Place in pans. Cover; let rise in warm place until doubled, about 45 minutes.
5. Preheat oven to 375°F. Bake 35 minutes or until golden and loaves sound hollow when lightly tapped with fingers. Remove from pans; cool on wire racks.
Makes 2 loaves, 12 slices each.

Per slice: 79 calories, 2 g protein, 3 g fat, 12 g carbohydrate, 118 mg sodium, 12 mg cholesterol.

Wholesome Wheat Bread

5½ to 6 cups whole wheat flour
2 packages active dry yeast
1 teaspoon salt
1 teaspoon ground cinnamon
1 cup KARO® Dark Corn Syrup
1 cup water
½ cup HELLMANN'S® or BEST FOODS® Real Mayonnaise
2 eggs

In large mixer bowl, combine 2 cups of the flour, the yeast, salt and cinnamon. In medium saucepan, combine corn syrup, water and real mayonnaise; heat mixture over medium heat, stirring occasionally, until very warm (120° to 130°). Pour hot mixture into flour mixture; beat at medium speed 2 minutes. Reduce speed to low; beat in 2 more cups of the flour and the eggs until well mixed. Beat at medium speed 2 minutes. By hand, stir in enough of the remaining flour to make dough easy to handle. Turn out onto lightly floured surface. Knead 10 minutes or until dough is smooth and elastic, adding as much remaining flour as needed to prevent sticking. Shape dough into a ball. Place in large, greased bowl; turn dough once to grease surface. Cover with towel; let rise in warm place (85°) until doubled, about 1 hour.

Punch dough down; divide in half. Cover; let rest 10 minutes. Shape each half into 8×4-inch oval. Place on large, greased and floured baking sheet. Cut 3 slashes, ¼ inch deep, in top of each loaf. Cover; let rise in warm place until doubled, about 1½ hours. Bake in preheated 350° oven 30 to 40 minutes or until loaves are browned and sound hollow when tapped. Immediately remove from baking sheet to wire racks to cool.
Makes 2 loaves.

Mexican Corn Bread

1 cup yellow cornmeal
⅔ cup unsifted all-purpose flour
2 teaspoons baking powder
½ teaspoon salt
¾ cup dairy sour cream
2 eggs
¼ cup CRISCO® Oil
2 cups shredded Cheddar cheese (about 8 ounces), divided
1 can (8¾ ounces) whole kernel corn, drained
1 can (4 ounces) chopped green chilies, drained

Preheat oven to 350°F. Oil 8-inch square baking pan. Set aside.

Mix cornmeal, flour, baking powder and salt in small mixing bowl. Set aside. Blend sour cream, eggs and Crisco® Oil in medium mixing bowl. Add cornmeal mixture, 1½ cups Cheddar cheese, corn and chilies. Mix well. Pour into prepared pan. Sprinkle with remaining ½ cup Cheddar cheese. Bake at 350°F, 30 to 35 minutes, or until wooden pick inserted in center comes out clean. Cut into squares and serve warm.
One 8-inch square pan.

Cinnamon-Raisin Swirl Loaf

2 cups SUN-MAID® Raisins
Water
6¾ to 7¼ cups all-purpose flour
2 packages active dry yeast
2 cups milk
¾ cup granulated sugar
¼ cup butter or margarine
2 teaspoons salt
3 eggs
2 teaspoons ground cinnamon
Powdered Sugar Icing (recipe follows)

In small bowl, combine raisins with enough hot tap water to cover. Plump 5 minutes; drain well. Set aside. In large bowl, combine 3 cups of the flour and the yeast. In medium saucepan, heat milk, ¼ cup of the granulated sugar, the butter and salt over low heat just until warm (115° to 120°F) and until butter is almost melted, stirring constantly. Add to flour mixture; add eggs. Beat at low speed of electric mixer for ½ minute, scraping sides of bowl constantly. Beat 3 minutes at high speed, scraping bowl occasionally. Stir in plumped raisins. Stir in as much remaining flour as can be mixed in with a spoon. Turn out onto lightly floured board. Knead in enough remaining flour to make a moderately stiff dough that is smooth and elastic (6 to 8 minutes total). Shape into a ball. Place dough in lightly greased bowl; turn once to grease surface. Cover; let rise in warm place (85°F) until doubled, about 1¼ hours.

Punch dough down; divide in half. Cover; let rest 10 minutes. Roll each half into 15×7-inch rectangle. Brush entire surface lightly with water. Combine remaining ½ cup granulated sugar and the cinnamon; sprinkle ½ of the sugar mixture over each rectangle. Roll up, jelly-roll fashion, starting from a 7-inch side; pinch edges and ends to seal. Place, sealed edges down, in 2 greased 9×5×3-inch loaf pans. Cover; let rise in warm place until nearly doubled, 35 to 45 minutes. Bake in preheated 375°F oven 35 to 40 minutes or until bread sounds hollow when tapped, covering bread with foil the last 15 minutes to prevent overbrowning. Remove bread from pans; cool completely on wire racks. Drizzle with Powdered Sugar Icing.
Makes 2 loaves.

POWDERED SUGAR ICING: In medium bowl, combine 1 cup sifted powdered sugar, ¼ teaspoon vanilla and enough milk (about 1½ tablespoons) to make of drizzling consistency.

Cheese Casserole Bread

- **2 cups warm milk (105° to 115°)**
- **2 packages active dry yeast**
- **3 tablespoons sugar**
- **1 tablespoon butter**
- **½ teaspoon salt**
- **4½ cups all-purpose flour**
- **6 ounces Cheddar cheese, cut into ½-inch cubes**

In large bowl, combine milk and yeast; stir to dissolve yeast. Add sugar, butter and salt; stir until butter is melted. Stir in 3 cups of the flour; beat until smooth. Stir in remaining flour and cheese; mix well. Pour batter into well-buttered 1½-quart round casserole. Cover with waxed paper; let rise in warm place (85°) until doubled, about 1 hour. Remove waxed paper. Bake in preheated 350° oven 50 to 55 minutes or until toothpick inserted into center comes out clean. Let cool in dish on wire rack 10 minutes. Loosen edge; remove from dish. Cool slightly on wire rack; serve warm with butter.
Makes 1 loaf.

*Favorite recipe from **American Dairy Association***

Double-Braided Saffron Bread

- **4½ to 5½ cups unsifted all-purpose flour, divided**
- **2 tablespoons sugar**
- **1 package (¼ ounce) active dry yeast**
- **1½ teaspoons salt**
- **⅓ cup CRISCO® Oil**
- **1 cup very warm water (120° to 130°F)**
- **⅛ teaspoon powdered saffron**
- **4 eggs**
- **1 teaspoon cold water**

Mix 1¼ cups flour, sugar, yeast and salt in large mixing bowl. Stir in Crisco® Oil. Combine warm water and saffron in small bowl. Stir until saffron is dissolved. Add to flour mixture. Beat with electric mixer at medium speed 3 minutes, scraping bowl occasionally. Separate 1 egg; set yolk aside. Add egg white to flour mixture. Add remaining 3 eggs and ½ cup flour. Beat at medium speed 1 minute, scraping bowl occasionally. Stir in enough remaining flour to make soft dough.

Knead dough on lightly floured surface 8 to 10 minutes, or until smooth and elastic, adding additional flour as necessary. Place in lightly oiled large mixing bowl. Turn dough over to coat both sides with Crisco® Oil. Cover; let rise in warm place 1 to 1½ hours, or until doubled.

Oil baking sheet. Set aside. Punch down dough. Place on lightly floured surface. Set aside two thirds of dough. Divide remaining dough into 6 equal portions. Roll each portion with floured fingers into a 10-inch-long piece. Braid 3 pieces together. Braid remaining 3 pieces. Set aside.

Divide remaining dough into 6 equal portions. Roll each portion with floured fingers into a 12-inch-long piece. Braid 3 pieces together. Braid remaining 3 pieces. For each loaf, center 1 small braid on top of 1 large braid. Press ends together to seal. Place both loaves on prepared baking sheet.

Blend reserved egg yolk and cold water in small bowl. Brush on both loaves. Cover; let rise in warm place about 1 hour, or until doubled. Preheat oven to 400°F. Bake loaves at 400°F, 20 to 25 minutes, or until loaves are golden brown and sound hollow when tapped lightly. Cool on wire rack.
2 loaves.

Savory Bubble Cheese Bread

- **6 to 7 cups flour, divided**
- **2 tablespoons sugar**
- **4 teaspoons instant minced onion**
- **2 teaspoons salt**
- **2 packages active dry yeast**
- **½ teaspoon caraway seeds**
- **1¾ cups milk**
- **½ cup water**
- **3 tablespoons butter or margarine**
- **1 teaspoon TABASCO® pepper sauce**
- **2 cups (8 ounces) shredded sharp Cheddar cheese, divided**
- **1 egg, lightly beaten**

In large bowl of electric mixer combine 2½ cups flour, sugar, onion, salt, yeast and caraway seeds. In small saucepan combine milk, water and butter. Heat milk mixture until very warm (120°F. to 130°F.); stir in Tabasco® sauce.

With mixer at medium speed gradually add milk mixture to dry ingredients; beat 2 minutes. Add 1 cup flour. Beat at high speed 2 minutes. With wooden spoon stir in 1½ cups cheese and enough flour to make a stiff dough. Turn dough out onto lightly floured surface. Knead 8 to 10 minutes or until dough is smooth and elastic, adding as much remaining flour as needed to prevent sticking. Place in large greased bowl and invert dough to bring greased side up. Cover with towel; let rise in warm place (90°F. to 100°F.) 1 hour or until doubled in bulk.

Punch dough down. Divide dough into 16 equal pieces; shape each piece into a ball. Place ½ the balls in well-greased 10-inch tube pan. Sprinkle with remaining ½ cup cheese. Arrange remaining balls on top. Cover with towel; let rise in warm place 45 minutes or until doubled in bulk. Preheat oven to 375°F. Brush bread with egg. Bake 40 to 50 minutes or until golden brown. Remove from pan. Cool completely on wire rack.
Makes one 10-inch round loaf.

Mexicali Corn Bread

Milk
1 (13¾-fluid ounce) can
 COLLEGE INN® Chicken
 Broth
1 (15-ounce) package corn bread
 mix
½ teaspoon chili powder
4 eggs, lightly beaten
1 cup grated Monterey Jack
 cheese with jalapeño
 peppers (4 ounces)
1 (8¾-ounce) can whole kernel
 sweet corn, drained
1 (2-ounce) jar diced pimientos,
 drained

Add enough milk to chicken broth to make 2½ cups liquid; set aside. In large bowl, stir together corn bread mix and chili powder; stir in eggs and reserved broth mixture until just blended. Stir in cheese, corn and pimientos. Pour into greased 13×9×2-inch baking dish. Bake at 400°F for 25 to 30 minutes or until toothpick inserted in center comes out clean. Cut into squares to serve.
Makes 8 to 10 servings.

Poppy Seed Bread

1 cup sugar
½ cup butter or margarine,
 softened
2 eggs
1 teaspoon grated lemon peel
2 extra-ripe, medium DOLE™
 Bananas
2 cups flour
2 teaspoons baking powder
½ teaspoon salt
¼ teaspoon ground cinnamon
¼ cup poppy seeds

Preheat oven to 350°F. In large bowl, beat sugar and butter until light and fluffy. Beat in eggs and lemon peel. Puree bananas in blender (1 cup). In small bowl, combine flour, baking powder, salt and cinnamon. Add dry ingredients to egg mixture alternately with pureed bananas, ending with dry ingredients. Stir in poppy seeds. Spoon into greased 9×5-inch loaf pan.

Bake in preheated oven 60 to 70 minutes or until wooden pick inserted in center comes out clean. Cool slightly in loaf pan before turning out onto wire rack to cool completely.
Makes 1 loaf.

Cottage Herb Rolls

1 package active dry yeast
¼ cup warm water
2½ cups unsifted flour
¼ cup sugar
1 teaspoon oregano leaves
1 teaspoon salt
½ cup cold margarine or butter
1 cup BORDEN® or MEADOW
 GOLD® Cottage Cheese
1 egg, beaten
Melted margarine or butter

Dissolve yeast in warm water. In large bowl, combine flour, sugar, oregano and salt; mix well. Cut in cold margarine until mixture resembles coarse cornmeal. Blend in cheese, egg and yeast. Turn onto well-floured surface; knead. Shape into ball; place in well-greased bowl. Brush top with melted margarine. Cover; let rise until doubled. Punch down; shape as desired. Brush with melted margarine; cover. Let rise again until nearly doubled. Bake in preheated 375° oven 12 to 15 minutes. Serve warm.
Makes 1½ to 2 dozen.

Braided Sesame Ring

7 to 8 cups all-purpose flour
2 packages active dry yeast
¼ cup sugar
1 teaspoon salt
1½ cups very warm water (120° to
 130°)
½ cup HELLMANN'S® or BEST
 FOODS® Real Mayonnaise
4 eggs
2 tablespoons sesame seeds

In large bowl, combine 2 cups of the flour, the yeast, sugar and salt. Gradually beat in water until smooth. Add 2 more cups flour, the real mayonnaise and 3 of the eggs; beat well. Stir in enough of the remaining flour to make dough easy to handle. Turn out onto lightly floured surface. Knead 10 minutes or until dough is smooth and elastic, adding as much remaining flour as needed to prevent sticking. Shape dough into ball. Place in large, greased bowl; turn dough once to grease surface. Cover with towel; let rise in warm place (85°) until doubled, about 1 hour.

Punch dough down; divide into 3 equal pieces. Cover; let rest 10 minutes. Roll each piece into 24-inch rope. Place side-by-side on large greased baking sheet; loosely braid ropes. Shape braid into circle, pinching ends together to seal. Cover; let rise in warm place until doubled, about 1½ hours. In small bowl, beat remaining egg; brush over surface of dough. Sprinkle with sesame seeds. Bake in preheated 375° oven 40 minutes or until loaf is browned and sounds hollow when tapped. Remove to wire rack to cool.
Makes 1 loaf.

COOKIES & CANDIES

A batch of ideas for sweet snacking. You'll find crisp lunch-box treats, delicate cookies for the tea table, brownies to cure the "midnight munchies," and lovely frosted cookies for holiday baking. Try these foolproof candies, too—in no time, you can whip up indulgent confections that look professional and taste scrumptious.

Peanut Butter Cutouts

1½ cups all-purpose flour
¾ teaspoon baking soda
⅛ teaspoon salt
½ cup MAZOLA® Margarine, softened
½ cup SKIPPY® Creamy Peanut Butter
½ cup granulated sugar
½ cup packed brown sugar
1 egg
Colored sugars (optional)

In small bowl, combine flour, baking soda and salt. In large bowl, beat margarine and peanut butter until well blended. Beat in granulated and brown sugars until blended. Beat in egg. Gradually beat in flour mixture until well mixed. Divide dough into thirds. Wrap each portion; refrigerate until firm, about 3 hours. Roll out dough, one third at a time, ¼ inch thick on lightly floured surface. Cut out with cookie cutters. Place 2 inches apart on ungreased cookie sheets. If desired, sprinkle cookies with colored sugars. Bake in preheated 350° oven 8 to 10 minutes or until lightly browned. Remove to wire racks to cool.
Makes about 4 dozen cookies.

Santa Lollipop Cookies: Prepare cookie dough as above. Place lollipop sticks 3 inches apart on ungreased cookie sheets. Roll out dough ⅛ inch thick. Cut out with 4-inch Santa cookie cutter; place over 1 end of each lollipop stick. Bake as above. Decorate as desired.
Makes 3 dozen cookies.

Macaroon Kiss Cookies

⅓ cup butter or margarine, softened
1 package (3 ounces) cream cheese, softened
¾ cup sugar
1 egg yolk
2 teaspoons almond extract
2 teaspoons orange juice
1¼ cups unsifted all-purpose flour
2 teaspoons baking powder
¼ teaspoon salt
5 cups (14-ounce package) flaked coconut
54 HERSHEY'S KISSES Chocolates (9-ounce package), unwrapped

Cream butter, cream cheese and sugar in large mixer bowl until light and fluffy. Add egg yolk, almond extract and orange juice; beat well. Combine flour, baking powder and salt; gradually add to creamed mixture. Stir in 3 cups of the coconut. Cover tightly; chill 1 hour or until firm enough to handle.

Shape dough into 1-inch balls; roll in remaining coconut. Place on ungreased cookie sheet. Bake at 350° for 10 to 12 minutes or until lightly browned. Remove from oven; immediately press unwrapped KISS on top of each cookie. Cool 1 minute. Carefully remove from cookie sheet; cool completely on wire rack.
About 4½ dozen cookies.

Thumbprint Cookies

- 1 package (4-serving size) JELL-O® Instant Pudding and Pie Filling, any flavor
- 1 package (10 ounces) pie crust mix
- 2 tablespoons butter or margarine, melted
- 4 to 5 tablespoons cold water
- 1 package (4 ounces) BAKER'S® GERMAN'S® Sweet Chocolate, broken into squares
  Whole or chopped toasted nuts

Combine pudding mix and pie crust mix in medium bowl; add butter and 4 tablespoons of the water. Mix with fork until soft dough forms. (If dough is too dry, add 1 tablespoon water.) Shape dough into 1-inch balls. Place 1 inch apart on ungreased baking sheets; press thumb deeply into center of each.

Cut each square of chocolate in half. Press 1 half into center of each cookie. Bake in preheated 350° oven for about 15 minutes or until lightly browned. Immediately press nuts lightly into chocolate centers. Remove from baking sheets and cool on wire racks.
Makes 3 dozen.

Coconut Thumbprints: Prepare Thumbprint Cookies as directed, omitting chocolate and nuts. Mix 1⅓ cups (about) BAKER'S® ANGEL FLAKE® Coconut with ½ cup sweetened condensed milk; spoon into centers of cookies before baking.

Jam Thumbprints: Prepare Thumbprint Cookies as directed, omitting chocolate and nuts. Spoon ½ teaspoon jam into center of each cookie after baking.

Cream Cheese and Jelly Thumbprints: Prepare Thumbprint Cookies as directed, omitting chocolate and nuts. Using 1 package (3 ounces) cream cheese, softened, spoon ½ teaspoon cream cheese into center of each cookie before baking and top each with ½ teaspoon jelly after baking.

Lemon Sugar Cookies

- 3 cups unsifted flour
- 2 teaspoons baking powder
- ½ teaspoon salt
- 2 cups sugar
- 1 cup shortening
- 2 eggs
- ¼ cup REALEMON® Lemon Juice from Concentrate
  Additional sugar

Preheat oven to 350°. Stir together flour, baking powder and salt; set aside. In large mixer bowl, beat sugar and shortening until fluffy; beat in eggs. Stir in dry ingredients, then ReaLemon® brand; mix well. Chill 2 hours. Shape into 1¼-inch balls; roll in additional sugar. Place 2 inches apart on greased baking sheets; flatten. Bake 8 to 10 minutes or until lightly browned.
Makes about 8 dozen.

Fruited Shortbread Cookies

- 2½ cups unsifted flour
- 1 teaspoon baking soda
- 1 teaspoon cream of tartar
- 1 cup margarine or butter, softened
- 1½ cups confectioners' sugar
- 1 egg
- 1 (9-ounce) package NONE SUCH® Condensed Mincemeat, crumbled
- 1 teaspoon vanilla extract
  Lemon Frosting, optional
  Candied cherries or nuts, optional

Preheat oven to 375°. Stir together flour, baking soda and cream of tartar; set aside. In large mixer bowl, beat margarine and sugar until fluffy. Add egg; mix well. Stir in mincemeat and vanilla. Add flour mixture; mix well (dough will be stiff). Roll into 1¼-inch balls. Place on ungreased baking sheets; flatten slightly. Bake 10 to 12 minutes or until lightly browned. Cool. Frost with Lemon Frosting and garnish with candied cherries or nuts if desired.
Makes about 3 dozen.
LEMON FROSTING: In small mixer bowl, beat 2 cups confectioners' sugar, 2 tablespoons softened margarine or butter, 2 tablespoons water and ½ teaspoon grated lemon rind until well blended.
Makes about ⅔ cup.

Wheat Germ Cookies

- 1 package DUNCAN HINES® Deluxe Yellow Cake Mix
- 1 large egg
- 3 tablespoons brown sugar
- ¼ cup CRISCO® Oil or PURITAN® Oil
- 2 tablespoons butter or margarine, melted
- ½ cup wheat germ
- 2 tablespoons water
- ½ cup chopped nuts

1. Preheat oven to 375°F.
2. Combine dry cake mix, egg, brown sugar, oil, butter, wheat germ and water in bowl. Mix with spoon. (Dough will be stiff.) Stir in nuts.
3. Drop by teaspoonfuls, 2 inches apart, on ungreased cookie sheets.
4. Bake at 375°F for 10 minutes for chewy cookies, 12 minutes for crispy cookies. Cool 1 minute on cookie sheet, then remove to rack to finish cooling.
About 3 dozen cookies.

Chocolate Cookie Sandwiches

½ cup shortening
1 cup sugar
1 egg
1 teaspoon vanilla
1½ cups unsifted all-purpose flour
⅓ cup HERSHEY'S Cocoa
½ teaspoon baking soda
½ teaspoon salt
¼ cup milk
   Creme Filling

Cream shortening, sugar, egg and vanilla in large mixer bowl until light and fluffy. Combine flour, cocoa, baking soda and salt; add alternately with milk to creamed mixture until ingredients are combined.

Drop by teaspoonfuls onto ungreased cookie sheet. Bake at 375° for 11 to 12 minutes or just until soft-set (*do not overbake*). Cool 1 minute. Remove from cookie sheet; cool completely on wire rack. Prepare Creme Filling. Spread bottom of one cookie with about 1 tablespoon filling; cover with another cookie. Repeat with remaining cookies and filling.
About 15 filled cookies.

Creme Filling

2 tablespoons butter or margarine, softened
2 tablespoons shortening
½ cup marshmallow creme
¾ teaspoon vanilla
⅔ cup confectioners' sugar

Cream butter and shortening in small mixer bowl; gradually beat in marshmallow creme. Blend in vanilla and confectioners' sugar; beat to spreading consistency.

Chocolate Chip Whole Wheat Cookies

¾ cup shortening
1½ cups packed light brown sugar
1 egg
¼ cup water
1 teaspoon vanilla
1 cup unsifted whole wheat flour
½ teaspoon baking soda
½ teaspoon salt
2 cups quick-cooking oats
1 cup chopped dried apricots or raisins
1 cup HERSHEY'S MINI CHIPS Semi-Sweet Chocolate

Cream shortening and brown sugar in large mixer bowl until light and fluffy. Add egg, water and vanilla; beat well. Combine whole wheat flour, baking soda and salt; stir into creamed mixture. Stir in oats, dried apricots and MINI CHIPS Chocolates.

Drop by teaspoonfuls onto lightly greased cookie sheet; flatten slightly. Bake at 350° for 10 to 12 minutes or until golden brown. Remove from cookie sheet; cool completely on wire rack.
About 5 dozen cookies.

Reese's Chewy Chocolate Cookies

1¼ cups butter or margarine, softened
2 cups sugar
2 eggs
2 teaspoons vanilla
2 cups unsifted all-purpose flour
¾ cup HERSHEY'S Cocoa
1 teaspoon baking soda
½ teaspoon salt
2 cups (12-ounce package) REESE'S Peanut Butter Chips

Cream butter and sugar in large mixer bowl until light and fluffy. Add eggs and vanilla; beat well. Combine flour, cocoa, baking soda and salt; gradually blend into creamed mixture. Stir in peanut butter chips.

Drop by teaspoonfuls onto ungreased cookie sheet. Bake at 350° for 8 to 9 minutes. *Do not overbake.* (Cookies will be soft; they will puff during baking and flatten upon cooling.) Cool until set, about 1 minute. Remove from cookie sheet; cool completely on wire rack.
About 4½ dozen cookies.

Hershey's™ Great American Chocolate Chip Cookies

1 cup butter, softened
¾ cup sugar
¾ cup packed light brown sugar
1 teaspoon vanilla
2 eggs
2¼ cups unsifted all-purpose flour
1 teaspoon baking soda
½ teaspoon salt
2 cups (12-ounce package) HERSHEY'S Semi-Sweet Chocolate Chips
1 cup chopped nuts (optional)

Cream butter, sugar, brown sugar and vanilla in large mixer bowl until light and fluffy. Add eggs; beat well. Combine flour, baking soda and salt; gradually add to creamed mixture. Beat well. Stir in chocolate chips and nuts.

Drop by teaspoonfuls onto ungreased cookie sheet. Bake at 375° for 8 to 10 minutes or until lightly browned. Cool slightly. Remove from cookie sheet; cool completely on wire rack.
About 6 dozen cookies.

Milk Chocolate Chip Cookies: Substitute 2 cups (11.5-ounce package) HERSHEY'S Milk Chocolate Chips for the semi-sweet chocolate chips.

Black-Eyed Susans

Filling:
  1 cup chopped SUN-MAID®
    Muscat Raisins
  ½ cup orange juice
  ½ teaspoon grated orange peel
  ¼ cup sugar
    Dash salt
Dough:
  ½ cup butter or margarine,
    softened
  ½ cup peanut butter
  1 cup sugar
  1 egg
  1 teaspoon vanilla
  1¼ cups all-purpose flour
  ½ teaspoon baking powder
  ¼ teaspoon salt

To prepare Filling: In small saucepan, combine all filling ingredients. Cook over medium heat, stirring frequently, until sugar dissolves and mixture thickens slightly. Cool while preparing dough.

To prepare Dough: In medium bowl, cream butter, peanut butter, sugar, egg and vanilla. In small bowl, sift flour with baking powder and salt; stir into creamed mixture. Cover and chill dough several hours. Roll out dough on lightly floured board to ⅛-inch thickness. Cut into 3-inch rounds with cookie cutter. Place 2 teaspoons of filling in centers of *half* the dough rounds. Cut small circles from centers of remaining dough rounds.* Place on top of raisin-filled rounds. Press edges together lightly to seal. Place on greased baking sheets. Bake in preheated 350°F oven 10 to 12 minutes or until golden brown. Cool on baking sheets a few minutes. Remove to wire rack to cool completely.
Makes about 1½ dozen cookies.

*A doughnut cutter works well. Simply cut ½ of dough with holes and ½ without.

Easy Peanut Butter Cookies

  1 (14-ounce) can EAGLE® Brand
    Sweetened Condensed Milk
    (NOT evaporated milk)
  ¾ cup peanut butter
  2 cups biscuit baking mix
  1 teaspoon vanilla extract
    Granulated sugar

Preheat oven to 375°. In large mixer bowl, beat sweetened condensed milk and peanut butter until smooth. Add biscuit mix and vanilla; mix well. Shape into 1-inch balls. Roll in sugar. Place 2 inches apart on ungreased baking sheets. Flatten with fork. Bake 6 to 8 minutes or until *lightly* browned (do not overbake). Cool. Store tightly covered at room temperature.
Makes about 5 dozen.

Peanut Blossoms: Shape as above; *do not flatten.* Bake as above. Press solid milk chocolate candy in center of each ball immediately after baking.

Peanut Butter & Jelly Gems: Press thumb in center of each ball of dough; fill with jelly, jam or preserves. Bake as above.

Any-Way-You-Like'm Cookies: Stir 1 cup semi-sweet chocolate chips *or* chopped peanuts *or* raisins *or* flaked coconut into dough. Proceed as above.

Chocolate Spice Cookies

  2 cups unsifted flour
  ½ cup unsweetened cocoa
  1 teaspoon baking soda
  ½ teaspoon salt
  1¼ cups sugar
  ¾ cup shortening
  ¼ cup margarine or butter,
    softened
  2 eggs
  2 teaspoons vanilla extract
  1 (9-ounce) package NONE
    SUCH® Condensed
    Mincemeat, crumbled
  1 cup chopped nuts, optional

Preheat oven to 350°. Stir together flour, cocoa, baking soda and salt; set aside. In large mixer bowl, beat sugar, shortening and margarine until fluffy. Beat in eggs and vanilla. Add flour mixture; mix well. Stir in mincemeat and nuts if desired. Roll into 1¼-inch balls; place 2 inches apart on ungreased baking sheets. Flatten slightly. Bake 8 to 10 minutes or until almost no imprint remains when lightly touched.
Makes about 4 dozen.

Lemon Tea Cookies

  3¼ cups unsifted all-purpose flour
  1½ teaspoons baking powder
  ¼ teaspoon salt
  ¾ cup butter or margarine,
    softened
  ¾ cup granulated sugar
  ¾ cup confectioners sugar
  ½ cup CRISCO® Oil
  2 eggs
  2 teaspoons grated lemon peel
  2 teaspoons lemon extract
    Granulated sugar

Mix flour, baking powder and salt in small mixing bowl. Set aside. Cream butter, granulated sugar and confectioners sugar in large mixing bowl. Blend in Crisco® Oil, eggs, lemon peel and lemon extract. Stir in flour mixture. Cover and refrigerate about 2 hours.

Preheat oven to 350°F. Shape dough into 1-inch balls. Place 2 to 3 inches apart on ungreased baking sheet. Flatten to ⅛-inch thickness with bottom of drinking glass dipped in granulated sugar. Bake at 350°F, 10 to 12 minutes, or until edges are light golden brown. Remove cookies from pan immediately. Cool on wire rack.
6 to 7 dozen cookies.

Variation: Lemon Crisps. Follow recipe above, except shape dough into ¾-inch balls and flatten to 1⁄16-inch thickness with sugar-dipped glass. Bake 7 to 9 minutes, or until edges are light golden brown.

Quick Pudding Cookies

**1 package (4-serving size)
    JELL-O® Instant Pudding
    and Pie Filling, any flavor
1 cup all-purpose biscuit mix
1/4 cup vegetable oil
1 egg, slightly beaten
3 tablespoons water**

Combine pudding mix and biscuit mix in medium bowl. Stir in oil, egg and water, blending well. Drop from teaspoon 2 inches apart onto ungreased baking sheets. Bake in preheated 375° oven for about 12 minutes, or until lightly browned. Remove from baking sheets and cool on wire racks. Store in tightly covered container.
Makes about 2 dozen.
Note: Cookie dough may be pressed through cookie press, or rolled into 1-inch balls and flattened on baking sheets with fork or glass dipped in flour; reduce water to 2 tablespoons.
Quick Pudding Chip Cookies: Prepare Quick Pudding Cookies as directed, stirring in 1/2 cup BAKER'S® Semi-Sweet Chocolate Flavored Chips just before baking.

Super Chocolate Chunk Cookies

**1/2 cup butter or margarine,
    softened
1/2 cup granulated sugar
1/4 cup firmly packed brown sugar
1 teaspoon vanilla
1 egg
1 cup flour
1/2 teaspoon baking soda
1/2 teaspoon salt
1 package (8 squares) BAKER'S®
    Semi-Sweet Chocolate, cut
    into chunks*
3/4 cup chopped walnuts**

Beat butter, sugars, vanilla and egg until light and fluffy. Mix flour with soda and salt; blend into butter mixture. Stir in chocolate chunks and nuts. Chill 1 hour. Drop 2 inches apart, from heaping tablespoon, onto ungreased baking sheets. Bake at 350° about 15 minutes, or until lightly browned.
Makes 1 1/2 to 2 dozen.
Double-Dip Chocolate Chunk Cookies: Prepare Super Chocolate Chunk Cookies, melting 1 square of the semi-sweet chocolate; cool slightly and add with the butter-sugar mixture; omit the nuts. Melt and cool 4 oz. sweet cooking chocolate; partially dip the cooled baked cookies into the chocolate. Let stand or chill until chocolate is firm.
Super Coconut Chocolate Chunk Cookies: Prepare Super Chocolate Chunk Cookies, adding 1 1/3 cups (about) BAKER'S® ANGEL FLAKE® Coconut with the chocolate and nuts.
Super Peanut Butter Chocolate Chunk Cookies: Prepare Super Chocolate Chunk Cookies, adding 1/2 cup peanut butter with the butter-sugar mixture, increasing the brown sugar to 1/2 cup and using peanuts instead of walnuts.
*Or use 2 packages (4 ounces each) BAKER'S® GERMAN'S® Sweet Chocolate, cut into chunks.
Note: Recipe may be doubled, tripled or quadrupled. Dough may be chilled 4 hours or overnight; let stand at room temperature about 15 minutes before baking.

Lemon Blossom Cookies

**2 cups margarine or butter,
    softened
1 1/2 cups confectioners' sugar
1/4 cup REALEMON® Lemon Juice
    from Concentrate
4 cups unsifted flour
    Finely chopped nuts, optional
    Assorted fruit preserves and
    jams or pecan halves**

Preheat oven to 350°. In large mixer bowl, beat margarine and sugar until fluffy. Add ReaLemon® brand; beat well. Gradually add flour; mix well. Chill 2 hours. Shape into 1-inch balls; roll in nuts if desired. Place 1 inch apart on greased baking sheets. Press thumb in center of each ball; fill with preserves or pecan. Bake 14 to 16 minutes or until lightly browned.
Makes about 6 dozen.

Coconut Macaroons

**1 1/3 cups (about) BAKER'S®
    ANGEL FLAKE® Coconut
1/3 cup sugar
3 tablespoons flour
1/8 teaspoon salt
2 egg whites
1/2 teaspoon almond extract**

Combine coconut, sugar, flour and salt in mixing bowl. Stir in egg whites and almond extract; mix well. Drop from teaspoon onto lightly greased baking sheets. Garnish with candied cherry halves, if desired. Bake at 325° for 20 to 25 minutes, or until edges of cookies are golden brown. Remove from baking sheets immediately.
Makes about 18.
Raisin Macaroons: Prepare Coconut Macaroons as directed, adding 1/3 cup raisins before baking.
Chip Macaroons: Prepare Coconut Macaroons as directed, adding 1/3 cup BAKER'S® Semi-Sweet Chocolate Flavored Chips before baking.
Nut Macaroons: Prepare Coconut Macaroons as directed, adding 1/3 cup chopped pecans or almonds before baking.
Fruited Macaroons: Prepare Coconut Macaroons as directed, adding 1/3 cup chopped mixed candied fruit before baking. Garnish with candied cherry halves, maraschino cherries or whole almonds, if desired.

Chocolate Kahlúa® Bears

1/4 cup KAHLÚA®
2 squares (1 ounce each)
    unsweetened chocolate
2/3 cup shortening
1 2/3 cups sugar
2 eggs
2 teaspoons vanilla
2 cups sifted all-purpose flour
2 teaspoons baking powder
3/4 teaspoon salt
1/2 teaspoon ground cinnamon
    Chocolate Icing (recipe
    follows)

To Kahlúa® in measuring cup, add enough water to make 1/3 cup liquid. In small saucepan over low heat, melt chocolate; cool. In large bowl, beat shortening, sugar, eggs and vanilla until light and fluffy. Stir in chocolate. In small bowl, combine flour, baking powder, salt and cinnamon. Add dry ingredients to egg mixture alternately with 1/3 cup liquid. Cover; refrigerate until firm. Roll out dough, one fourth at a time, about 1/4 inch thick on well-floured surface. Cut out with bear-shaped or other cookie cutters. Place 2 inches apart on ungreased cookie sheets. Bake in preheated 350° oven 8 to 10 minutes. Remove to wire racks to cool. Spread Chocolate Icing in thin, even layer on cookies. Let stand until set; decorate as desired.
Makes about 2 1/2 dozen cookies.
CHOCOLATE ICING: In medium saucepan, combine 6 squares (1 ounce each) semisweet chocolate, 1/3 cup butter or margarine, 1/4 cup Kahlúa® and 1 tablespoon light corn syrup. Cook over low heat until chocolate melts, stirring to blend. Add 3/4 cup sifted powdered sugar; beat until smooth. If necessary, beat in additional Kahlúa® to make spreading consistency.

Melting Moments

1 cup flour
2 tablespoons cornstarch
1/2 cup unsifted confectioners
    sugar
1 cup butter or margarine,
    softened
1 1/3 cups (about) BAKER'S®
    ANGEL FLAKE® Coconut

Mix flour with cornstarch and sugar in a bowl. Blend in butter to form a soft dough. Cover and chill, if necessary, until dough is firm enough to handle. Shape into small balls, about 3/4 inch in diameter. Roll in coconut and place on ungreased baking sheets, about 1 1/2 inches apart. Flatten with lightly floured fork, if desired. Bake at 300° for 20 to 25 minutes, or until lightly browned.
Makes about 3 dozen.
Almond Melting Moments: Prepare Melting Moments as directed, adding 2 teaspoons almond extract with the butter.

Chocolate Fruit Truffles

2 1/2 cups vanilla wafer crumbs
    (about 65 wafers)
1 (14-ounce) can EAGLE® Brand
    Sweetened Condensed Milk
    (NOT evaporated milk)
1 (9-ounce) package NONE
    SUCH® Condensed
    Mincemeat, crumbled
1 cup chopped cashews *or*
    almonds
1/2 cup chopped candied cherries
2 tablespoons unsweetened
    cocoa
1/2 teaspoon almond extract
    Confectioners' sugar
    Additional candied cherries,
    optional

In large bowl, combine all ingredients except confectioners' sugar and additional candied cherries until well blended. Chill 4 hours or overnight. Dip hands in confectioners' sugar; shape mixture into 1-inch balls. (Rechill if mixture becomes too soft.) Roll in confectioners' sugar. Place on wax paper-lined baking sheets; chill 2 hours or until firm. Store tightly covered in refrigerator. Garnish with additional candied cherries if desired.
Makes about 6 dozen.

Tip: Flavor of these candies improves after 24 hours. They can be made ahead and stored in refrigerator for several weeks.

Coconut Washboards

2 cups flour
3/4 teaspoon CALUMET® Baking
    Powder
1/4 teaspoon cinnamon
1/4 teaspoon nutmeg
1/8 teaspoon salt
3/4 cup butter
1 cup firmly packed brown sugar
1 egg
1 teaspoon vanilla
1/2 teaspoon almond extract
1 1/3 cups (about) BAKER'S®
    ANGEL FLAKE® Coconut

Mix flour with baking powder, spices and salt. Cream butter. Gradually add sugar, beating until light and fluffy. Add egg, vanilla and almond extract; beat well. Add flour mixture, blending well. Stir in coconut. Divide dough into 2 parts. Chill, if necessary, until dough is easily handled. Spread or pat each half into a 10×9-inch rectangle. Cut each rectangle into 4 strips lengthwise. Cut each strip into 10 pieces. Place about 2 inches apart on ungreased baking sheets. Using a floured fork, gently press ridges into cookies. Bake at 375° for 8 to 10 minutes, or until golden brown.
Makes about 6 1/2 dozen.

Lollipop Cookies

1 package (3-dozen-size) sugar
   or peanut butter cookie mix
12 to 14 wooden sticks
   Sugar, for flattening cookies
   SUN-MAID® Raisins
   Dried mixed fruit, snipped

Prepare cookie dough and sheet according to package directions. Roll dough with your hands into 1½-inch balls. Place about 2 inches apart on cookie sheets. Insert wooden stick halfway into each ball of dough. Dip bottom of glass into sugar and flatten cookies. Decorate cookies as desired with raisins and mixed fruit. Bake in preheated oven according to temperature and time on cookie mix package. Remove to wire rack to cool.
Makes about 1 dozen cookies.

Pinwheels and Checkerboards

2 cups flour
1 teaspoon CALUMET® Baking
   Powder
½ teaspoon salt
⅔ cup butter or margarine
1 cup sugar
1 egg
1 teaspoon vanilla
2 squares BAKER'S®
   Unsweetened Chocolate,
   melted

Mix flour, baking powder and salt. Cream butter. Gradually add sugar and continue beating until light and fluffy. Add egg and vanilla; beat well. Gradually add flour mixture, mixing well after each addition. Divide dough in half; blend chocolate into one half. Use prepared doughs to make Pinwheels or Checkerboards.

Pinwheels: Roll chocolate and vanilla doughs separately between sheets of waxed paper into 12×8-inch rectangles. Remove top sheets of paper and invert vanilla dough onto chocolate dough. Remove remaining papers. Roll up as for jelly roll; then wrap in waxed paper. Chill until firm, at least 3 hours (or freeze 1 hour). Cut into ¼-inch slices and place on baking sheets. Bake at 375° about 10 minutes, or until cookies just begin to brown around edges. Cool on racks.
Makes about 4½ dozen.

Checkerboards: Set out small amount of milk. Roll chocolate and vanilla doughs separately on lightly floured board into 9×4½-inch rectangles. Brush chocolate dough lightly with milk and top with vanilla dough. Using a long sharp knife, cut lengthwise into 3 strips, 1½ inches wide. Stack strips, alternating colors and brushing each layer with milk. Cut lengthwise again into 3 strips, ½ inch wide. Invert middle section so that colors are alternated; brush sides with milk. Press strips together lightly to form a rectangle. Wrap in waxed paper. Chill overnight. Cut into ⅛-inch slices, using a very sharp knife. Place on baking sheets. Bake at 375° for about 8 minutes, or just until white portions begin to brown. Cool on racks.
Makes about 5 dozen.

Kris Kringle Cookies

1⅓ cups butter or margarine,
   softened
1⅓ cups granulated sugar
2 eggs
2⅔ cups all-purpose flour
¼ teaspoon salt
1½ cups SUN-MAID® Raisins,
   chopped
½ cup chopped candied ginger*
1 egg white, beaten, for glaze
   Colored sugars, dragées,
   candied fruits and
   DIAMOND® Walnuts, for
   garnish

In large bowl, cream butter, granulated sugar and eggs. Stir in flour and salt, mixing until blended. Stir in raisins and ginger. Cover and chill dough. Roll out dough on lightly floured board to ⅛-inch thickness; cut into desired shapes with sharp-edged cookie cutters. Space apart on greased baking sheets. Brush with beaten white; sprinkle with additional granulated sugar, or decorate with colored sugars, dragées, candied fruits and walnuts, if desired. Bake in preheated 350°F oven 12 to 15 minutes or until golden. Cool 2 to 3 minutes in pan; remove to wire rack to cool completely.
Makes 1½ to 2 dozen large cookies.

*An additional ½ cup of raisins may be substituted for candied ginger; add 1 tablespoon ground ginger.

Gingerbread People

1 package DUNCAN HINES®
   Deluxe Spice Cake Mix
2 teaspoons ground ginger
2 large eggs
⅓ cup CRISCO® Oil or PURITAN®
   Oil
⅓ cup dark molasses
½ cup all-purpose flour
   Dark raisins

1. Combine all ingredients, except raisins, in large bowl; mix well (mixture will be soft). Refrigerate 2 hours.
2. Preheat oven to 375°F. Roll dough to ¼-inch thickness on lightly floured surface. Cut with 6-inch cookie cutter. Place on ungreased cookie sheets. Press raisins in dough for eyes and buttons.
3. Bake at 375°F for 8 to 10 minutes or until edges just start to brown. Cool several minutes on cookie sheet, then remove to racks to finish cooling.
About 14 six-inch cookies.

Holiday Chocolate Cookies

1/2 cup butter or margarine, softened
3/4 cup sugar
1 egg
1 teaspoon vanilla
1 1/2 cups unsifted all-purpose flour
1/3 cup HERSHEY'S Cocoa
1/2 teaspoon baking powder
1/2 teaspoon baking soda
1/4 teaspoon salt
Decorator's Frosting

Cream butter, sugar, egg and vanilla in large mixer bowl until light and fluffy. Combine remaining ingredients except Decorator's Frosting; add to creamed mixture, blending well.

Roll a small portion of dough at a time on lightly floured surface to 1/4-inch thickness. (If too soft, chill dough until firm enough to roll.) Cut with 2 1/2-inch cutter; place on ungreased cookie sheet. Bake at 325° for 5 to 7 minutes or until only a slight indentation remains when touched lightly. Cool 1 minute. Remove from cookie sheet; cool completely on wire rack. Prepare Decorator's Frosting and decorate with holiday designs or messages.
About 3 dozen cookies.

Decorator's Frosting

1 1/2 cups confectioners' sugar
2 tablespoons shortening
2 tablespoons milk
1/2 teaspoon vanilla
Red, green or yellow food color

Combine all ingredients except food color in small mixer bowl; beat until smooth and of spreading consistency. Tint with drops of food color, blending well.

Confetti Cones

1/2 cup butter or margarine, melted
1/2 cup granulated sugar
2/3 cup all-purpose flour
1 teaspoon vanilla
2 egg whites
1/2 cup DIAMOND® Walnuts, finely chopped
Colored sugar (about 2 tablespoons)

In medium bowl, combine butter, sugar, flour, vanilla and unbeaten egg whites; beat just until smooth. Stir in walnuts. Drop batter by teaspoonfuls about 4 inches apart onto lightly greased baking sheet and spread slightly.* Sprinkle with colored sugar. Bake in preheated 350°F oven 8 to 10 minutes or until edges are lightly browned. Remove each with broad spatula, quickly shaping into cone. Set in bottle neck or tiny jar a few minutes to set shape. Store in tightly covered container to keep crisp.
About 2 1/2 dozen (3-inch) cookies.

*Bake no more than 6 at a time until you get used to making cones. To speed baking, start second sheet when first one is half baked. Cookies may also be left flat or placed on side of small bottle to make rounded "tiles."

Candy Bar Cookies

1 package DUNCAN HINES® Deluxe Yellow Cake Mix
1/2 cup CRISCO® Oil or PURITAN® Oil
1 large egg
1 package (14 ounces) vanilla caramels
1/3 cup evaporated milk
1/3 cup butter or margarine
1 2/3 cups confectioners' sugar
1 cup chopped pecans
1 package (6 ounces) semisweet chocolate pieces (1 cup)

1. Preheat oven to 350°F.
2. For crust, combine dry cake mix, oil and egg in bowl with pastry blender. Spread evenly over bottom of ungreased 13×9×2-inch pan.
3. Bake at 350°F for 15 to 20 minutes or until light golden brown. Prepare filling while crust is baking.
4. Combine caramels and evaporated milk in top of double boiler; heat until caramels melt, stirring occasionally. Add butter; stir until melted. Remove from heat. Stir in confectioners' sugar and pecans. Spread hot caramel mixture over warm, baked crust.
5. Melt semisweet chocolate pieces over hot water in top of double boiler. Spread in very thin layer over caramel filling. Refrigerate; cut into bars when cool.
About 4 dozen small bars.

Walnut Jam Crescents

2/3 cup butter or margarine
1 1/3 cups all-purpose flour
1/2 cup dairy sour cream
2/3 cup raspberry jam or orange marmalade
2/3 cup DIAMOND® Walnuts, finely chopped

In medium bowl, cut butter into flour until mixture resembles fine crumbs. Add sour cream and mix until stiff dough is formed. Divide evenly into 2 portions. Shape each into a ball, flatten slightly, wrap in waxed paper and chill well. Working with one portion of dough at a time, roll dough into 11-inch round on lightly floured pastry cloth or board. Spread with 1/3 cup of the jam and sprinkle with 1/3 cup of the walnuts. Cut into quarters, then cut each quarter into 3 wedges. Roll up, one at a time, starting from outer edge, and place, in crescent shape, on lightly greased cookie sheets. Repeat with second portion of dough. Bake in preheated 375°F oven 25 to 30 minutes or until lightly browned. Remove to wire racks to cool.
Makes 2 dozen crescents.

Jelly Jewels

1 package DUNCAN HINES®
   Deluxe Yellow Cake Mix
3/4 cup CRISCO® shortening
2 large egg yolks
1 tablespoon milk
2 large egg whites
2 tablespoons water
1¼ cups ground nuts
   Red or green jelly

1. Preheat oven to 375°F. Grease cookie sheets.
2. Combine dry cake mix, shortening, egg yolks and milk; mix well. Shape into 1-inch balls.
3. Combine egg whites and water. Beat with fork until blended. Dip balls in egg white mixture, then roll in nuts. Place 2 inches apart on cookie sheets.
4. Bake at 375°F for 12 to 15 minutes or until golden brown. Immediately press thumb or thimble into center of each cookie making a depression. Cool several minutes on cookie sheets, then remove to racks to finish cooling. Before serving, fill depressions with jelly.
About 4 dozen 2-inch cookies.

Slice 'n' Bake Lemon Cookies

2¼ cups unsifted flour
¼ teaspoon baking soda
½ cup margarine or butter, softened
½ cup shortening
½ cup granulated sugar
½ cup firmly packed light brown sugar
1 egg
3 tablespoons REALEMON® Lemon Juice from Concentrate
   Egg white, beaten
   Sliced almonds

Stir together flour and baking soda; set aside. In large mixer bowl, beat margarine, shortening and sugars until fluffy. Add egg; mix well. Gradually add dry ingredients and ReaLemon® brand; mix well. Chill 2 hours; form into two 10-inch rolls. Wrap well; freeze until firm. Preheat oven to 350°. Cut rolls into ¼-inch slices; place 1 inch apart on greased baking sheets. Brush with egg white; top with almonds. Bake 10 to 12 minutes or until lightly browned.
Makes about 5 dozen.

Granola Cookies

1 cup sugar
½ cup CRISCO® Oil
⅓ cup honey
2 eggs
¼ cup water
2 cups unsifted all-purpose flour
1¾ cups quick-cooking rolled oats
1 teaspoon baking soda
1 teaspoon salt
1 teaspoon ground cinnamon
½ cup chopped dried apricots
½ cup raisins
½ cup chopped nuts
½ cup miniature semisweet chocolate chips
½ cup flaked coconut

Preheat oven to 350°F. Grease baking sheet. Set aside.
   Mix sugar, Crisco® Oil, honey, eggs and water in large mixing bowl. Add flour, oats, baking soda, salt and cinnamon. Mix well. Stir in remaining ingredients.
   Drop by teaspoonfuls about 2 inches apart onto prepared baking sheet. Bake at 350°F, about 8 minutes, or until almost no indentation remains when touched lightly. Cool on wire rack.
4½ to 5 dozen cookies.
   Variation: Granola Bars. Follow recipe above, except spread dough in greased and floured 15×10-inch jelly roll pan. Bake at 350°F, about 15 minutes, or until top is light brown. Cool completely on wire rack. Cut into 48 bars.

Swiss Cinnamon Cookies

3 egg whites
3¼ cups powdered sugar (approximately)
3 cups DIAMOND® Walnuts, finely ground
1 tablespoon ground cinnamon
   Chopped DIAMOND® Walnuts, colored sugars, candied cherries, dragées, for garnish

In medium bowl, beat egg whites until foamy. Gradually beat in 2 cups of the sugar. Beat until mixture holds soft peaks, 3 to 4 minutes; remove ¾ cup of the batter, cover and set aside. Mix the 3 cups walnuts, the cinnamon and ¾ cup more of the sugar into larger egg white-sugar portion. Working with a third of the dough at a time, roll out to ⅛-inch thickness on pastry cloth or board heavily dusted with powdered sugar. Cut into desired shapes with cookie cutters. Place on greased or parchment-lined baking sheets. With tip of knife, spread reserved egg white mixture ⅛ inch thick onto top of each cookie, spreading almost to edges. Decorate immediately, as desired, with chopped walnuts, colored sugars, candied cherries and dragées. Bake in preheated 300°F oven 12 to 14 minutes or until cookies are just set and very lightly browned. Remove to wire racks to cool completely. Store in airtight container. Cookies can be securely wrapped and frozen up to 2 months.
Makes about 3 dozen (3-inch) cookies.

Lacy Chocolate Crisps

- ½ cup light corn syrup
- ⅓ cup butter or margarine
- 1 package (4 oz.) BAKER'S® GERMAN'S® Sweet Chocolate
- ½ cup firmly packed light brown sugar
- 1 cup flour
- ⅔ cup BAKER'S® ANGEL FLAKE® Coconut

Bring corn syrup to a boil. Add butter and chocolate. Cook and stir over low heat until smooth. Remove from heat; stir in sugar, flour and coconut. Drop from tablespoon onto lightly greased baking sheets, leaving 3 inches between. Bake at 300° for 15 minutes, or until wafers bubble vigorously and develop lacy holes. Cool on sheets 2 minutes; lift with spatula and finish cooling on racks. (If wafers harden on sheets, return briefly to oven.) If desired, roll warm wafers around wooden spoon handle; cool. Fill with tinted sweetened whipped cream.
Makes 2½ dozen.

Florentines

- ½ cup flour
- ¼ teaspoon baking soda
  Dash of salt
- ¼ cup butter or margarine
- ⅓ cup firmly packed brown sugar
- 2 tablespoons light corn syrup
- 1 egg, well beaten
- ½ cup BAKER'S® ANGEL FLAKE® Coconut
- ½ teaspoon vanilla
- 2 squares BAKER'S® Semi-Sweet Chocolate
- 1 tablespoon butter or margarine

Mix flour, soda and salt. Cream ¼ cup butter. Gradually add sugar and beat until light and fluffy. Add corn syrup and egg; blend well. Stir in flour mixture, coconut and vanilla. Drop by half teaspoonfuls onto greased baking sheets, leaving 2 inches between. Bake at 350° about 10 minutes. Cool on baking sheets 1 minute, remove quickly and finish cooling on racks. (If wafers harden on sheets, return briefly to oven.) Melt chocolate and 1 tablespoon butter in saucepan over very low heat, stirring constantly until smooth. Drizzle over wafers.
Makes 4 dozen.

Lemony Spritz Sticks

- 1 cup butter or margarine, softened
- 1 cup confectioners' sugar
- ¼ cup REALEMON® Lemon Juice from Concentrate
- 2½ cups unsifted flour
- ¼ teaspoon salt
  Chocolate Glaze
  Finely chopped nuts

Preheat oven to 375°. In large mixer bowl, beat butter and sugar until fluffy. Add ReaLemon® brand; beat well. Stir in flour and salt; mix well. Place dough in cookie press with star-shaped plate. Press dough into 3-inch strips onto greased baking sheets. Bake 5 to 6 minutes or until lightly browned on ends. Cool 1 to 2 minutes; remove from baking sheets. Cool completely. Dip ends of cookies in Chocolate Glaze then nuts.
Makes about 8½ dozen.

Tip: When using electric cookie gun, use decorator tip. Press dough into ½×3-inch strips onto greased baking sheets. Bake 8 to 10 minutes or until lightly browned on ends.

CHOCOLATE GLAZE: In small saucepan, melt 3 ounces sweet cooking chocolate and 2 tablespoons margarine or butter.
Makes about ⅓ cup.

Almond Shortbread Cookies

- 2½ cups unsifted flour
- 1 teaspoon baking soda
- 1 teaspoon cream of tartar
- 1 cup margarine or butter, softened
- 1½ cups confectioners' sugar
- 1 egg
- 1 (9-ounce) package NONE SUCH® Condensed Mincemeat, crumbled
- ½ cup sliced almonds
- ½ teaspoon almond extract
  Almond Frosting
  Additional sliced almonds

Preheat oven to 375°. Stir together flour, baking soda and cream of tartar; set aside. In large mixer bowl, beat margarine and sugar until fluffy. Add egg; mix well. Stir in mincemeat, ½ cup almonds and extract. Add flour mixture; mix well (dough will be stiff). Roll into 1¼-inch balls. Place on ungreased baking sheets; flatten slightly. Bake 10 to 12 minutes or until lightly browned. Cool. Frost with Almond Frosting and garnish with additional almonds if desired.
Makes about 3 dozen.

ALMOND FROSTING: In small mixer bowl, combine 2¼ cups confectioners' sugar, 3 tablespoons margarine or butter, softened, 3 tablespoons water and ½ teaspoon almond extract; beat well.
Makes about 1 cup.

Pecan Tassies

1 8-ounce package
   PHILADELPHIA BRAND
   Cream Cheese, softened
1 cup PARKAY Margarine
2 cups flour
2 eggs, beaten
1½ cups packed brown sugar
2 teaspoons vanilla
1½ cups chopped pecans

Combine cream cheese and margarine, mixing until well blended. Add flour; mix well. Chill. Divide dough into quarters; divide each quarter into 12 balls. Press each ball onto bottom and sides of miniature muffin pans. Combine eggs, brown sugar and vanilla; stir in pecans. Spoon into pastry shells, filling each cup. Bake at 325°, 30 minutes or until pastry is golden brown. Cool 5 minutes; remove from pans. Sprinkle with powdered sugar, if desired.
4 dozen.

Raisin Oatmeal Crispies

1 cup butter or margarine,
   softened
1 cup sugar
3 cups rolled oats, uncooked
¾ cup all-purpose flour
1 teaspoon baking soda
½ teaspoon ground cloves
½ teaspoon ground cinnamon
1 cup SUN-MAID® Raisins
¼ cup milk

In large bowl, blend together butter and sugar; add oats. Sift flour with baking soda, cloves and cinnamon. Add to oats mixture, blending well. Stir in raisins and milk; mix thoroughly. Roll dough into 1-inch balls. Place 3 inches apart on greased baking sheets. Bake in preheated 350°F oven 12 to 15 minutes or until golden brown.
Makes about 4 dozen cookies.

"Philly" Apricot Cookies

1½ cups PARKAY Margarine
1½ cups granulated sugar
1 8-ounce package
   PHILADELPHIA BRAND
   Cream Cheese, softened
2 eggs
2 tablespoons lemon juice
1½ teaspoons grated lemon peel
4½ cups flour
1½ teaspoons baking powder
   KRAFT Apricot Preserves
   Powdered sugar

Combine margarine, granulated sugar and cream cheese, mixing until well blended. Blend in eggs, juice and peel. Add combined flour and baking powder; mix well. Chill several hours. Shape level measuring tablespoonfuls of dough into balls. Place on ungreased cookie sheet; flatten slightly. Indent centers; fill with preserves. Bake at 350°, 15 minutes. Cool; sprinkle with powdered sugar.
Approximately 7 dozen.

Walnutty Ribbons

2 cups all-purpose flour
½ teaspoon baking powder
½ cup butter or margarine,
   softened
¾ cup sugar
1 egg
2 teaspoons rum flavoring
1 teaspoon vanilla
1 teaspoon grated lemon peel
1 tablespoon milk
1 cup finely chopped DIAMOND®
   Walnuts
⅓ cup orange marmalade (or
   other jam)

In medium bowl, sift flour with baking powder; set aside. In large bowl, cream butter, sugar, egg, rum, vanilla and peel. Blend in flour mixture and milk to make a stiff dough. Divide into 4 equal portions and shape each into a roll about 12 inches long. Transfer to lightly greased cookie sheets, placing rolls about 3 inches apart. Make a wide depression down center of each roll with handle of knife. In small bowl, mix walnuts with marmalade. Spoon ¼ of the mixture down center of each roll. Bake in preheated 350°F oven 15 to 20 minutes or until edges are lightly browned. Slide rolls off onto wire racks to cool. Cut into 1¼-inch slices to serve.
Makes about 3 dozen cookies.

Reese's Cookies

1 cup shortening, *or* ¾ cup
   butter or margarine,
   softened
1 cup sugar
½ cup packed light brown sugar
1 teaspoon vanilla
2 eggs
2 cups unsifted all-purpose flour
1 teaspoon baking soda
1 cup REESE'S Peanut Butter
   Chips
1 cup HERSHEY'S Semi-Sweet
   Chocolate Chips

Cream shortening or butter, sugar, brown sugar and vanilla in large mixer bowl until light and fluffy. Add eggs; beat well. Combine flour and baking soda; add to creamed mixture. Stir in peanut butter chips and chocolate chips.

Drop by teaspoonfuls onto ungreased cookie sheet. Bake at 350° for 10 to 12 minutes or until lightly browned. Cool slightly. Remove from cookie sheet; cool completely on wire rack.
About 5 dozen cookies.

Macaroon Almond Crumb Bars

1 (18¼- or 18½-ounce) package chocolate cake mix
¼ cup vegetable oil
2 eggs
1 (14-ounce) can EAGLE® Brand Sweetened Condensed Milk (NOT evaporated milk)
½ to 1 teaspoon almond extract
1½ cups coconut macaroon crumbs (about 8 macaroons)
1 cup chopped slivered almonds

Preheat oven to 350° (325° for glass dish). In large mixer bowl, combine cake mix, oil and *1 egg*. Beat on medium speed until crumbly. Press firmly on bottom of greased 13×9-inch baking pan. In medium mixing bowl, combine sweetened condensed milk, remaining egg and extract; mix well. Add *1 cup* macaroon crumbs and almonds. Spread evenly over prepared crust. Sprinkle with remaining *½ cup* crumbs. Bake 30 to 35 minutes or until lightly browned. Cool thoroughly. Cut into bars. Store loosely covered at room temperature.
Makes 36 bars.

Chocolate Crackles

10 tablespoons butter or margarine
6 tablespoons HERSHEY'S Cocoa
1 cup sugar
2 teaspoons baking powder
½ teaspoon salt
2 eggs
1 teaspoon vanilla
2 cups unsifted all-purpose flour
½ cup chopped nuts
Confectioners' sugar

Microwave: Microwave butter in medium micro-proof bowl at HIGH (100%) for 45 to 60 seconds or until melted. Add cocoa; blend well. Beat in sugar, baking powder, salt, eggs and vanilla. Stir in flour and nuts. Refrigerate at least 8 hours or until firm.

Shape dough into 1-inch balls; roll in confectioners' sugar. Cover microproof plate with wax paper. Place 8 balls 2 inches apart in circular shape on wax paper. Microwave at MEDIUM (50%) for 1½ to 2 minutes or until surface is dry but cookies are soft when touched. Cool on wax paper on countertop. Repeat cooking procedure with remaining dough. Before serving, sprinkle with additional confectioners' sugar.
About 4 dozen cookies.

Toffee Bars

½ cup margarine or butter
1 cup oats
½ cup firmly packed brown sugar
½ cup unsifted flour
½ cup finely chopped walnuts
¼ teaspoon baking soda
1 (14-ounce) can EAGLE® Brand Sweetened Condensed Milk (NOT evaporated milk)
2 teaspoons vanilla extract
1 (6-ounce) package semi-sweet chocolate chips

Preheat oven to 350°. In medium saucepan, melt *6 tablespoons* margarine; stir in oats, sugar, flour, nuts and baking soda. Press firmly on bottom of greased 13×9-inch baking pan; bake 10 to 15 minutes or until lightly browned. Meanwhile, in medium saucepan, combine remaining *2 tablespoons* margarine and sweetened condensed milk. Over medium heat, cook and stir until mixture thickens slightly, about 15 minutes. Remove from heat; stir in vanilla. Pour over crust. Return to oven; bake 10 to 15 minutes longer or until golden brown. Remove from oven; immediately sprinkle chips on top. Let stand 1 minute; spread while still warm. Cool to room temperature; chill thoroughly. Cut into bars. Store tightly covered at room temperature.
Makes 36 bars.

Rich Lemon Bars

1½ cups plus 3 tablespoons unsifted flour
½ cup confectioners' sugar
¾ cup cold margarine or butter
4 eggs, slightly beaten
1½ cups granulated sugar
1 teaspoon baking powder
½ cup REALEMON® Lemon Juice from Concentrate
Additional confectioners' sugar

Preheat oven to 350°. In medium bowl, combine *1½ cups* flour and confectioners' sugar; cut in margarine until crumbly. Press onto bottom of lightly greased 13×9-inch baking pan; bake 15 minutes. Meanwhile, in large bowl, combine eggs, granulated sugar, baking powder, ReaLemon® brand and remaining *3 tablespoons* flour; mix well. Pour over baked crust; bake 20 to 25 minutes or until golden brown. Cool. Cut into bars. Sprinkle with additional confectioners' sugar. Store covered in refrigerator; serve at room temperature.
Makes 30 bars.

Lemon Pecan Bars: Omit 3 tablespoons flour in lemon mixture. Sprinkle ¾ cup finely chopped pecans over top of lemon mixture. Bake as above.

Coconut Lemon Bars: Omit 3 tablespoons flour in lemon mixture. Sprinkle ¾ cup flaked coconut over top of lemon mixture. Bake as above.

Frosted Toffee Bars

2 cups QUAKER® Oats (Quick or Old Fashioned), uncooked
½ cup packed brown sugar
½ cup margarine, melted
½ cup semisweet chocolate chips
¼ cup chopped peanuts

In medium bowl, combine oats, sugar and margarine; mix well. Spread in greased 9-inch square pan. Bake in preheated 350° oven 13 minutes or until light golden brown; cool. In small, heavy saucepan over low heat, melt chips. Spread over oat mixture; sprinkle with nuts. Refrigerate until chocolate is set. Cut into 2×1½-inch bars. Store in tightly covered container in refrigerator.
Makes about 2 dozen bars.

Triple Layer Cookie Bars

½ cup margarine or butter
1½ cups graham cracker crumbs
1 (7-ounce) package flaked coconut (2⅔ cups)
1 (14-ounce) can EAGLE® Brand Sweetened Condensed Milk (NOT evaporated milk)
1 (12-ounce) package semi-sweet chocolate chips
½ cup creamy peanut butter

Preheat oven to 350° (325° for glass dish). In 13×9-inch baking pan, melt margarine in oven. Sprinkle crumbs evenly over margarine. Top evenly with coconut then sweetened condensed milk. Bake 25 minutes or until lightly browned. In small saucepan, over low heat, melt chips with peanut butter. Spread evenly over hot coconut layer. Cool 30 minutes. Chill thoroughly. Cut into bars. Store loosely covered at room temperature.
Makes 36 bars.

Chocolate 'n' Oat Bars

1 cup unsifted flour
1 cup quick-cooking oats
¾ cup firmly packed light brown sugar
½ cup margarine or butter, softened
1 (14-ounce) can EAGLE® Brand Sweetened Condensed Milk (NOT evaporated milk)
1 cup chopped nuts
1 (6-ounce) package semi-sweet chocolate chips

Preheat oven to 350° (325° for glass dish). In large bowl, combine flour, oats, sugar and margarine; mix well. Reserving ½ cup oat mixture, press remainder on bottom of 13×9-inch baking pan. Bake 10 minutes. Pour sweetened condensed milk evenly over crust. Sprinkle with nuts and chocolate chips. Top with remaining oat mixture; press down firmly. Bake 25 to 30 minutes or until lightly browned. Cool. Cut into bars. Store covered at room temperature.
Makes 36 bars.

Coconut Dream Bars

1 cup flour
¼ cup firmly packed brown sugar
⅓ cup softened butter or margarine
2 eggs
¾ cup firmly packed brown sugar
¼ cup flour
½ teaspoon CALUMET® Baking Powder
1⅓ cups (about) BAKER'S® ANGEL FLAKE® Coconut
1 teaspoon vanilla
1 cup chopped walnuts

Combine 1 cup flour and ¼ cup brown sugar. Add butter and mix until blended. Press into ungreased 9-inch square pan; bake at 350° for 15 minutes. Meanwhile, beat eggs until thick and light in color. Gradually beat in ¾ cup brown sugar and continue beating until mixture is light and fluffy. Mix ¼ cup flour with the baking powder; fold into egg mixture. Mix in coconut, vanilla and nuts. Spread over baked crust in pan. Bake 20 to 25 minutes longer or until lightly browned. Cool; cut in bars, triangles or squares.
Makes about 2 dozen.

Lemon Bars

1 package DUNCAN HINES® Deluxe Lemon Supreme Cake Mix
3 large eggs
⅓ cup CRISCO® Shortening
½ cup sugar
½ teaspoon baking powder
¼ teaspoon salt
2 teaspoons grated lemon peel
¼ cup lemon juice
Confectioners' sugar

1. Preheat oven to 350°F.
2. Combine dry cake mix, 1 egg and shortening in bowl; mix until crumbly. Measure 1 cup and set aside. Pat remaining mixture lightly in ungreased 13×9×2-inch pan.
3. Bake at 350°F for 15 minutes or until light brown.
4. Beat remaining 2 eggs, sugar, baking powder, salt, lemon peel and lemon juice until light and foamy. Pour over hot crust; sprinkle with reserved 1 cup crumb mixture.
5. Bake at 350° for 15 minutes or until light brown. Sprinkle with confectioners' sugar. Cool on rack; cut into bars.
2½ dozen bars.

Festive Cookie Bars

Bottom Layer:
- 1¼ cups all-purpose flour
- 1 teaspoon granulated sugar
- 1 teaspoon baking powder
  Dash salt
- ⅔ cup butter or margarine
- 2 tablespoons cold coffee or water
- 1 egg yolk
- 1 package (12 ounces) real semisweet chocolate pieces

Top Layer:
- ½ cup butter or margarine, softened
- 1 cup granulated sugar
- 1 tablespoon vanilla
- 2 eggs plus 1 egg white
- 1 cup SUN-MAID® Raisins
- 1 cup DIAMOND® Walnuts
  Powdered sugar, for garnish

To prepare bottom layer: In large bowl, combine flour, granulated sugar, baking powder and salt. Cut in butter until mixture resembles coarse crumbs. In small bowl, mix coffee and egg yolk to blend; stir into flour mixture to moisten evenly. Form dough into a roll. With floured fingertips, press evenly onto bottom of greased 15×10-inch jelly-roll pan. (Layer will be thin.) Bake in preheated 350°F oven 10 minutes. Sprinkle chocolate pieces evenly over crust; return to oven 2 minutes to melt chocolate. Remove from oven; spread evenly with spatula. Allow to stand several minutes to set.

To prepare top layer: In large bowl, cream butter, granulated sugar and vanilla. Beat in eggs and egg white, one at a time, mixing well after each addition. (Mixture will appear slightly curdled.) Stir in raisins and walnuts. Spread evenly over chocolate layer. Return to oven; bake 20 to 25 minutes or until top is browned. Dust with powdered sugar. Cool in pan; cut into bars.
Makes 3½ to 4 dozen bars.
Note: Cookies freeze well.

Pecan Pie Bars

- 2 cups unsifted flour
- ½ cup confectioners' sugar
- 1 cup cold margarine or butter
- 1 (14-ounce) can EAGLE® Brand Sweetened Condensed Milk (NOT evaporated milk)
- 1 egg
- 1 teaspoon vanilla extract
- 1 (6-ounce) package almond brickle chips
- 1 cup chopped pecans

Preheat oven to 350° (325° for glass dish). In medium bowl, combine flour and sugar; cut in margarine until crumbly. Press firmly on bottom of 13×9-inch baking pan. Bake 15 minutes. Meanwhile, in medium bowl, beat sweetened condensed milk, egg and vanilla. Stir in chips and pecans. Spread evenly over crust. Bake 25 minutes or until golden brown. Cool. Cut into bars. Store covered in refrigerator.
Makes 36 bars.

Crunch Bars

- 5 cups bite-size crispy rice or wheat square cereal
- ½ cup margarine or butter
- 1 cup butterscotch *or* peanut butter flavored chips
- 1 (3½-ounce) can flaked coconut (1⅓ cups)
- 1 (14-ounce) can EAGLE® Brand Sweetened Condensed Milk (NOT evaporated milk)
- 1 cup chopped pecans

Preheat oven to 350° (325° for glass dish). Coarsely crush *3 cups* cereal. In 13×9-inch baking pan, melt margarine in oven. Sprinkle crushed cereal over margarine; top evenly with chips, coconut, sweetened condensed milk, nuts and *2 cups* uncrushed cereal. Press down firmly. Bake 25 to 30 minutes or until lightly browned. Cool thoroughly. Cut into bars. Store loosely covered at room temperature.
Makes 36 bars.

Layered Lemon Crumb Bars

- 1 (14-ounce) can EAGLE® Brand Sweetened Condensed Milk (NOT evaporated milk)
- ½ cup REALEMON® Lemon Juice from Concentrate
- 1 teaspoon grated lemon rind
- ⅔ cup margarine or butter, softened
- 1 cup firmly packed light brown sugar
- 1½ cups unsifted flour
- 1 cup oats
- 1 teaspoon baking powder
- ½ teaspoon salt
- ½ teaspoon ground cinnamon
- ½ teaspoon ground nutmeg

Preheat oven to 350° (325° for glass dish). In small bowl, combine sweetened condensed milk, ReaLemon® brand and lemon rind; set aside. In large mixer bowl, beat margarine and sugar until fluffy; add dry ingredients. Mix until crumbly. Spread half the oat mixture into lightly greased 13×9-inch baking pan. Press down firmly; spread lemon mixture evenly over crust. Sprinkle remaining oat mixture evenly over lemon layer. Bake 20 to 25 minutes or until lightly browned. Chill. Cut into bars. Store covered in refrigerator.
Makes 36 bars.

Jungle Bars

- 2 ripe, medium DOLE™ Bananas
- 8 ounces dried figs
- 8 ounces dried apricots
- 8 ounces DOLE™ Pitted Dates
- 8 ounces DOLE™ Raisins
- 2 cups granola
- 8 ounces DOLE™ Chopped Natural Almonds, toasted
- 1 cup flaked coconut

Coarsely chop bananas, figs, apricots, dates, raisins and granola in food processor or run through food grinder. Stir in almonds. Press mixture into greased 13×9-inch baking dish. Sprinkle with coconut. Cover; refrigerate 24 hours to allow flavors to blend. Cut into squares.
Makes 24 bars.

Magic Cookie Bars

- ½ cup margarine or butter
- 1½ cups graham cracker *or* other crumbs*
- 1 (14-ounce) EAGLE® Brand Sweetened Condensed Milk (NOT evaporated milk)
- 1 cup semi-sweet chocolate chips *or* other toppings**
- 1 (3½-ounce) can flaked coconut (1⅓ cups)
- 1 cup chopped nuts***

Preheat oven to 350° (325° for glass dish). In 13×9-inch baking pan, melt margarine in oven. Sprinkle crumbs over margarine; pour sweetened condensed milk evenly over crumbs. Sprinkle with chips then coconut and nuts; press down firmly. Bake 25 to 30 minutes or until lightly browned. Cool. Chill thoroughly if desired. Cut into bars. Store loosely covered at room temperature.
Makes 36 bars.

*Crumbs: Vanilla wafer, chocolate wafer, ginger snap cookie, quick-cooking oats, wheat germ.

**Toppings: Peanut butter flavored chips, butterscotch flavored chips, plain multi-colored candy-coated chocolate pieces, raisins, chopped dried apricots, almond brickle chips, banana chips, chopped candied cherries, small gumdrop candies, miniature marshmallows.

***Nuts: Walnuts, pecans, almonds, peanuts, cashews, macadamia nuts.

Flavor Variations:

Mint: Combine ½ teaspoon peppermint extract and 4 drops green food coloring if desired with sweetened condensed milk. Proceed as above.

Mocha: Add 1 tablespoon instant coffee and 1 tablespoon chocolate flavored syrup with sweetened condensed milk. Proceed as above.

Peanut Butter: Combine ⅓ cup peanut butter with sweetened condensed milk. Proceed as above.

Maple: Combine ½ to 1 teaspoon maple flavoring with sweetened condensed milk. Proceed as above.

Seven Layer Magic Cookie Bars: Add 1 (6-ounce) package butterscotch flavored chips after chocolate chips.

Lebkuchen Jewels

- ¾ cup packed brown sugar
- 1 egg
- 1 cup honey
- 1 tablespoon grated lemon peel
- 1 teaspoon lemon juice
- 2¾ cups all-purpose flour
- 1 teaspoon *each* ground nutmeg, cinnamon and cloves
- ½ teaspoon *each* baking soda and salt
- 1 cup SUN-MAID® Golden Raisins
- ½ cup *each* mixed candied fruits and citron
- 1 cup chopped DIAMOND® Walnuts
- Lemon Glaze (recipe follows)
- Candied cherries and citron, for garnish

In large bowl, beat sugar and egg until smooth and fluffy. Add honey, lemon peel and juice; beat well. In medium bowl, sift flour with nutmeg, cinnamon, cloves, baking soda and salt; gradually mix into egg-sugar mixture on low speed. Stir in fruits and nuts. Spread batter into greased 15×10-inch jelly-roll pan. Bake in preheated 375°F oven 20 minutes or until lightly browned. Cool slightly in pan; brush with Lemon Glaze. Cool; cut into diamonds. Decorate with candied cherries and slivers of citron, if desired. Store in covered container up to 1 month.
Makes about 4 dozen.

LEMON GLAZE: In small bowl, combine 1 cup sifted powdered sugar with enough lemon juice (1½ to 2 tablespoons) to make a thin glaze.

Chocolate Streusel Bars

- 1¾ cups unsifted flour
- 1½ cups confectioners' sugar
- ½ cup unsweetened cocoa
- 1 cup cold margarine or butter
- 1 (8-ounce) package cream cheese, softened
- 1 (14-ounce) can EAGLE® Brand Sweetened Condensed Milk (NOT evaporated milk)
- 1 egg
- 2 teaspoons vanilla extract
- ½ cup chopped walnuts, optional

Preheat oven to 350°. In large bowl, combine flour, sugar and cocoa; mix well. Cut in margarine until crumbly (mixture will be dry). Reserving 2 cups crumb mixture, press remainder firmly on bottom of 13×9-inch baking pan. Bake 15 minutes. Meanwhile, in large mixer bowl, beat cheese until fluffy. Gradually beat in sweetened condensed milk until smooth. Add egg and vanilla; mix well. Pour evenly over baked crust. Combine reserved crumb mixture with nuts if desired; sprinkle evenly over cheese mixture. Bake 25 minutes or until bubbly. Cool. Chill. Cut into bars. Store covered in refrigerator.
Makes 24 to 36 bars.

Apple Raisin Snack Bars

1 1/2 cups old fashioned or quick oats, uncooked
3/4 cup flour
1/2 cup packed brown sugar
1/4 cup granulated sugar
3/4 cup PARKAY Margarine
* * *
2 8-ounce packages PHILADELPHIA BRAND Cream Cheese, softened
2 eggs
1 cup chopped apple
1/3 cup raisins
1 tablespoon granulated sugar
1/2 teaspoon cinnamon

Combine oats, flour and sugars; cut in margarine until mixture resembles coarse crumbs. Reserve 1 cup oat mixture; press remaining mixture onto bottom of greased 13×9-inch baking pan. Bake at 350°, 15 minutes.

Combine cream cheese and eggs, mixing until well blended. Pour over crust. Top with combined remaining ingredients; sprinkle with reserved oat mixture. Bake at 350°, 25 minutes. Cool; cut into bars.
Approximately 1 1/2 dozen.
Variation: Substitute *Light* PHILADELPHIA BRAND Neufchâtel Cheese for Cream Cheese.

Raspberry Oatmeal Bars

1 package DUNCAN HINES® Deluxe Yellow Cake Mix
2 1/2 cups quick-cooking oats
3/4 cup (1 1/2 sticks) butter or margarine, melted
1 cup (12-ounce jar) raspberry preserves or jam*
1 tablespoon water

1. Preheat oven to 375°F. Grease 13×9×2-inch pan.
2. Combine dry cake mix and oats in large bowl; add melted butter and stir until crumbly. Measure half of crumb mixture (about 3 cups) into pan. Press firmly to cover bottom. Combine preserves and water; stir until blended. Spread over crumb mixture in pan. Sprinkle remaining crumb mixture over preserves; pat firmly to make top even.
3. Bake at 375°F for 18 to 23 minutes or until top is very light brown. Cool in pan on rack; cut into bars. Store in airtight container.
4 dozen bars.
*Apricot, blackberry or strawberry preserves can be substituted.

Fruit & Nut Snack Bars

1/2 cup margarine or butter, softened
1 1/4 cups granulated sugar
3 eggs
1 1/3 cups (one-half jar) NONE SUCH® Ready-to-Use Mincemeat (Regular *or* Brandy & Rum)
1/2 cup chopped pecans
2 (1-ounce) squares unsweetened chocolate, melted
1/4 teaspoon salt
1 1/2 cups unsifted flour
Confectioners' sugar
Pecan halves, optional

Preheat oven to 350°. In large mixer bowl, beat margarine and granulated sugar until fluffy. Add eggs; beat well. Stir in mincemeat, chopped pecans, chocolate and salt; mix well. Stir in flour. Spread evenly into lightly greased 13×9-inch baking pan. Bake 30 minutes or until wooden pick inserted near center comes out clean. Cool. Sprinkle with confectioners' sugar. Cut into bars. Garnish with pecan halves if desired.
Makes 24 to 36 bars.

Chocolate Mint Cheesecake Bars

1 1/4 cups unsifted flour
1 cup confectioners' sugar
1/2 cup unsweetened cocoa
1/4 teaspoon baking soda
1 cup cold margarine or butter
1 (8-ounce) package cream cheese, softened
1 (14-ounce) can EAGLE® Brand Sweetened Condensed Milk (NOT evaporated milk)
2 eggs
1 1/2 teaspoons peppermint extract
2 to 3 drops green food coloring, optional
Chocolate Glaze

Preheat oven to 350°. In large bowl, combine flour, sugar, cocoa and baking soda; mix well. Cut in margarine until crumbly (mixture will be dry). Press firmly on bottom of 13×9-inch baking pan. Bake 15 minutes. Meanwhile, in large mixer bowl, beat cheese until fluffy. Gradually beat in sweetened condensed milk until smooth. Add eggs, extract and food coloring if desired; mix well. Pour evenly over baked crust. Bake 20 minutes or until lightly browned around edges. Cool. Drizzle with Chocolate Glaze. Chill. Cut into bars. Store covered in refrigerator.
Makes 24 to 36 bars.
CHOCOLATE GLAZE: Combine 1 cup confectioners' sugar, 2 tablespoons unsweetened cocoa, 1 tablespoon melted margarine or butter, 2 tablespoons water and 1/2 teaspoon vanilla extract; mix well.
Makes about 1/2 cup.

Apple Crumb Squares

2 cups QUAKER® Oats (Quick or Old Fashioned), uncooked
1½ cups all-purpose flour
¾ cup margarine, melted
1 cup firmly packed brown sugar
1 teaspoon cinnamon
½ teaspoon salt (optional)
½ teaspoon baking soda
¼ teaspoon ground nutmeg
1 cup applesauce
½ cup chopped nuts

Heat oven to 375°F. Grease 13×9-inch baking pan. Combine all ingredients *except* applesauce and nuts; mix until crumbly. Reserve 1 cup mixture. Press remaining mixture onto bottom of prepared pan. Bake 15 minutes; cool. Spread applesauce over partially baked crust; sprinkle with nuts. Top with reserved 1 cup oat mixture. Bake 13 to 15 minutes or until golden brown. Cool in pan on wire rack; cut into 2-inch squares.
Makes about 2 dozen squares.

Chocolate Pecan Bars

1¼ cups unsifted flour
1 cup confectioners' sugar
½ cup unsweetened cocoa
1 cup cold margarine or butter
1 (14-ounce) can EAGLE® Brand Sweetened Condensed Milk (NOT evaporated milk)
1 egg
2 teaspoons vanilla extract
1½ cups chopped pecans

Preheat oven to 350° (325° for glass dish). In large bowl, combine flour, sugar and cocoa; cut in margarine until crumbly. Press firmly on bottom of 13×9-inch baking pan. Bake 15 minutes. Meanwhile, in medium bowl, beat sweetened condensed milk, egg and vanilla. Stir in pecans. Spread evenly over baked crust. Bake 25 minutes or until lightly browned. Cool. Cut into bars. Store covered in refrigerator.
Makes 36 bars.

Marble Squares

½ cup PARKAY Margarine
¾ cup water
1½ 1-ounce squares unsweetened chocolate
2 cups flour
2 cups sugar
1 teaspoon baking soda
½ teaspoon salt
2 eggs, beaten
½ cup sour cream

* * *

1 8-ounce package PHILADELPHIA BRAND Cream Cheese, softened
⅓ cup sugar
1 egg
1 6-ounce package semi-sweet chocolate pieces

Combine margarine, water and chocolate in saucepan; bring to a boil. Remove from heat. Stir in combined flour, sugar, baking soda and salt. Add eggs and sour cream; mix well. Pour into greased and floured 15×10×1-inch jelly roll pan.

Combine cream cheese and sugar, mixing until well blended. Blend in egg. Spoon over chocolate batter. Cut through batter with knife several times for marble effect. Sprinkle with chocolate pieces. Bake at 375°, 25 to 30 minutes or until wooden pick inserted in center comes out clean.
Approximately 2 dozen.

Pineapple Dream Bars

½ cup butter or margarine, softened
1 cup dark brown sugar, packed
1⅓ cups flour
1 can (8¼ ounces) DOLE® Crushed Pineapple
2 eggs
1 teaspoon baking powder
1 teaspoon ground cinnamon
¼ teaspoon ground nutmeg
¼ teaspoon salt
1 teaspoon rum extract
1½ cups flaked coconut
1 cup chopped walnuts
½ cup chopped maraschino cherries

Preheat oven to 350°F. In medium mixer bowl, beat butter and ⅓ cup brown sugar. Blend in 1 cup flour until mixture is crumbly. Pat into bottom of 13×9-inch baking pan. Bake in preheated oven 10 to 15 minutes or until golden. Keep oven hot, but remove pan to cool.

Drain pineapple well, pressing out excess liquid with back of spoon. In large bowl, beat eggs with remaining ⅔ cup brown sugar until thick. In small bowl, combine remaining ⅓ cup flour, baking powder, cinnamon, nutmeg and salt. Stir dry ingredients and extract into egg mixture. Fold in pineapple, coconut, nuts and cherries. Spread over baked crust. Bake 30 minutes longer or until set. Cool slightly on wire rack before cutting into bars.
Makes 18 bars.

Peanutty Chocolate Snack Squares

5 graham crackers, broken into squares
1/2 cup sugar
1 cup light corn syrup
1 cup HERSHEY'S Semi-Sweet Chocolate Chips
1 cup peanut butter
1 cup dry roasted peanuts

Microwave: Line bottom of 8-inch square pan with graham cracker squares, cutting to fit as necessary. Combine sugar and corn syrup in 2-quart micro-proof bowl. Microwave at HIGH (100%), stirring every 2 minutes, until mixture boils; boil 3 minutes. Stir in chocolate chips, peanut butter and peanuts. Pour over crackers; spread carefully. Cover; refrigerate until firm. Cut into 2-inch squares.
16 squares.

Minty Chocolate Squares

1 6-ounce package semi-sweet chocolate pieces
1 cup PARKAY Margarine
1 3/4 cups graham cracker crumbs
1 cup flaked coconut
1/2 cup chopped nuts
2 8-ounce packages PHILADELPHIA BRAND Cream Cheese, softened
1 cup sifted powdered sugar
1/2 teaspoon mint extract
Few drops green food coloring (optional)

Melt 1/3 cup chocolate pieces with 3/4 cup margarine over low heat, stirring until smooth. Add combined crumbs, coconut and nuts; mix well. Press onto bottom of ungreased 13×9-inch baking pan; chill. Combine cream cheese, sugar, extract and food coloring, mixing until well blended. Spread over crust; chill. Melt remaining chocolate pieces with remaining margarine over low heat, stirring until smooth. Spread over cream cheese layer; chill. Cut into squares. Serve chilled.
Approximately 3 dozen.

Pumpkin Cheesecake Bars

1 (16-ounce) package pound cake mix
3 eggs
2 tablespoons margarine or butter, melted
4 teaspoons pumpkin pie spice
1 (8-ounce) package cream cheese, softened
1 (14-ounce) can EAGLE® Brand Sweetened Condensed Milk (NOT evaporated milk)
1 (16-ounce) can pumpkin (about 2 cups)
1/2 teaspoon salt
1 cup chopped nuts

Preheat oven to 350°. In large mixer bowl, on low speed, combine cake mix, *1 egg*, margarine and *2 teaspoons* pumpkin pie spice until crumbly. Press onto bottom of 15×10-inch jellyroll pan. In large mixer bowl, beat cheese until fluffy. Gradually beat in sweetened condensed milk then remaining *2 eggs*, pumpkin, remaining *2 teaspoons* pumpkin pie spice and salt; mix well. Pour over crust; sprinkle with nuts. Bake 30 to 35 minutes or until set. Cool. Chill; cut into bars. Store covered in refrigerator.
Makes 48 bars.

Almond & Fruit Meringue Bars

3 cups sifted all-purpose flour
3/4 cup granulated sugar
1/2 teaspoon salt
1 cup butter or margarine, cold
2 eggs, separated
1/4 cup water
1/8 teaspoon cream of tartar
3/4 cup sifted powdered sugar
1 teaspoon vanilla
1/4 teaspoon ground cinnamon
3 tablespoons finely chopped candied fruits
3/4 cup chopped almonds

In large bowl, combine flour, granulated sugar and salt. Cut in butter until mixture resembles coarse meal. In small bowl, beat egg yolks lightly with water; sprinkle over flour mixture, tossing to moisten evenly. Shape dough into ball. If dough is too soft to handle, cover and refrigerate until firm. In small mixer bowl, beat egg whites with cream of tartar at high speed until soft peaks form. Gradually beat in powdered sugar until whites are glossy and stand in stiff peaks. Gently fold vanilla, cinnamon and candied fruits into meringue; set aside. Divide dough in half. Roll out each half into 12×8-inch rectangle on lightly floured surface. Spread half the meringue mixture over each rectangle; sprinkle with almonds. Cut each rectangle into sixteen 4×1 1/2-inch bars. Place on ungreased cookie sheets. Bake in preheated 350° oven 15 to 18 minutes or until lightly browned. Remove to wire racks to cool.
Makes 32 bars.

*Favorite recipe from **Almond Board of California***

Peanut Butter Paisley Brownies

1/2 cup butter or margarine, softened
1/4 cup peanut butter
1 cup sugar
1 cup packed light brown sugar
3 eggs
1 teaspoon vanilla
2 cups unsifted all-purpose flour
2 teaspoons baking powder
1/4 teaspoon salt
1/2 cup (5.5-ounce can) HERSHEY'S Syrup

Blend butter and peanut butter in large mixer bowl. Add sugar and brown sugar; beat well. Add eggs, one at a time, beating well after each addition. Blend in vanilla. Combine flour, baking powder and salt; add to peanut butter mixture.

Spread half the batter in greased 13×9-inch pan. Spoon syrup over top. Carefully spread with remaining batter. Swirl with spatula or knife for marbled effect. Bake at 350° for 35 to 40 minutes or until lightly browned. Cool; cut into squares.
About 3 dozen brownies.

Lemon Iced Ambrosia Bars

1 1/2 cups unsifted flour
1/3 cup confectioners' sugar
3/4 cup cold margarine or butter
2 cups firmly packed light brown sugar
4 eggs, beaten
1 cup flaked coconut
1 cup finely chopped pecans
3 tablespoons flour
1/2 teaspoon baking powder
Lemon Icing*

Preheat oven to 350°. In medium bowl, combine flour and confectioners' sugar; cut in margarine until crumbly. Press onto bottom of lightly greased 13×9-inch baking pan; bake 15 minutes. Meanwhile, in large bowl, combine remaining ingredients except icing; mix well. Spread evenly over baked crust; bake 20 to 25 minutes. Cool. Spread with Lemon Icing; chill. Cut into bars. Store covered in refrigerator.
Makes 36 bars.
*LEMON ICING: Combine 2 cups confectioners' sugar, 3 tablespoons REALEMON® Lemon Juice from Concentrate and 2 tablespoons softened margarine; mix until smooth.
Makes about 2/3 cup.

Double-Deck Brownies

2/3 cup flour
1/2 teaspoon CALUMET® Baking Powder
1/4 teaspoon salt
2 eggs
1 cup sugar
1/2 cup butter or margarine, melted and cooled
1/3 cup BAKER'S® ANGEL FLAKE® Coconut
1/4 teaspoon almond extract
2 squares BAKER'S® Unsweetened Chocolate, melted
1 square BAKER'S® Semi-Sweet Chocolate, melted

Mix flour, baking powder and salt. Beat eggs thoroughly. Gradually add sugar and continue beating until light and fluffy. Blend in butter; then stir in flour mixture. Measure 1/2 cup into small bowl. Stir in coconut and almond extract; set aside. Add unsweetened chocolate to remaining batter; spread in greased 8-inch square pan. Drop coconut batter by teaspoonfuls over chocolate batter. Then spread carefully to form a thin layer. Bake at 350° for 30 to 35 minutes or until lightly browned. Cool in pan. Drizzle with semi-sweet chocolate. Cut into squares or bars.
Makes about 20.

Lemony Raisin-Coconut Squares

Crust:
1/4 cup butter or margarine, softened
1/2 cup packed light brown sugar
1 cup all-purpose flour
1/4 cup toasted shredded coconut*
Topping:
2 eggs
1 cup packed light brown sugar
1 tablespoon grated lemon peel
1/4 cup lemon juice
1/4 teaspoon salt
1 1/2 cups SUN-MAID® Raisins
3/4 cup toasted shredded coconut*
Powdered sugar, for garnish

To prepare crust: In small bowl, cream butter and the 1/2 cup brown sugar. Blend in flour and the 1/4 cup coconut. Mixture will be dry. Grease 9-inch square cake pan. Line bottom and 2 opposite sides with foil, allowing foil to extend slightly beyond edges; generously grease foil. Press crust mixture evenly into bottom of pan. Bake in preheated 350°F oven about 12 minutes or until edges brown lightly. Remove from oven.

To prepare topping: In medium bowl, beat eggs until foamy with electric mixer. Add the 1 cup brown sugar, the lemon peel and juice, and salt. Beat 2 minutes. Stir in raisins and coconut. Spread topping evenly over crust. Bake 20 to 25 minutes or until top begins to brown. Cool in pan. Loosen edges with sharp knife. Grasp foil edges and lift out of pan. With sharp knife, cut into 16 squares. Dust with powdered sugar, if desired.
Makes 16 squares.
*To toast 1 cup coconut, spread in shallow baking pan. Bake in 350°F oven about 10 minutes or until lightly browned, stirring occasionally. Cool.

Cheesecake Bars

2 cups unsifted flour
1½ cups firmly packed brown sugar
1 cup cold margarine or butter
1½ cups quick-cooking oats
2 (8-ounce) packages cream cheese, softened
½ cup granulated sugar
3 eggs
¼ cup BORDEN® or MEADOW GOLD® Milk
1 teaspoon vanilla extract
¼ cup REALEMON® Lemon Juice from Concentrate

Preheat oven to 350°. In bowl, combine flour and brown sugar; cut in margarine until crumbly. Stir in oats. Reserving *1½ cups* mixture, press remainder into 15×10-inch jellyroll pan; bake 10 minutes. Meanwhile, in large mixer bowl, beat cheese and granulated sugar until fluffy. Add eggs; beat well. Add milk and vanilla, then ReaLemon® brand; beat well. Pour over crust; sprinkle with reserved mixture. Bake 25 minutes or until lightly browned. Cool. Refrigerate.
Makes 40 bars.

Rocky Road Frosted Brownies

1 (9-inch) square pan of baked brownies, cooled
1 square (1 ounce) unsweetened chocolate
2 tablespoons butter or margarine, softened
1½ cups sifted powdered sugar
4 teaspoons milk
½ cup miniature marshmallows
½ cup coarsely chopped DIAMOND® Walnuts

In top of double boiler, melt chocolate over hot, not boiling, water. In medium bowl, combine chocolate, butter, powdered sugar and milk; beat smooth. Spread over top of cooled brownies. Sprinkle with marshmallows and walnuts. With small spatula, swirl frosting around marshmallows and walnuts. Let frosting set before cutting.
Makes 16 squares.

Best Brownies

½ cup butter or margarine, melted
1 cup sugar
1 teaspoon vanilla
2 eggs
½ cup unsifted all-purpose flour
⅓ cup HERSHEY'S Cocoa
¼ teaspoon baking powder
¼ teaspoon salt
½ cup chopped nuts (optional)
Creamy Brownie Frosting

Blend butter, sugar and vanilla in large bowl. Add eggs; using a wooden spoon, beat well. Combine flour, cocoa, baking powder and salt; gradually blend into egg mixture. Stir in nuts.

Spread in greased 9-inch square pan. Bake at 350° for 20 to 25 minutes or until brownie begins to pull away from edges of pan. Cool; frost with Creamy Brownie Frosting. Cut into squares.
About 16 brownies.

Creamy Brownie Frosting

3 tablespoons butter or margarine, softened
3 tablespoons HERSHEY'S Cocoa
1 tablespoon light corn syrup or honey
½ teaspoon vanilla
1 cup confectioners' sugar
1 to 2 tablespoons milk

Cream butter, cocoa, corn syrup and vanilla in small mixer bowl. Add confectioners' sugar and milk; beat to spreading consistency.
About 1 cup frosting.

Scrumptious Chocolate Layer Bars

2 cups (12-ounce package) HERSHEY'S Semi-Sweet Chocolate Chips
1 package (8 ounces) cream cheese
½ cup plus 2 tablespoons (5-ounce can) evaporated milk
1 cup chopped walnuts
¼ cup sesame seeds (optional)
½ teaspoon almond extract
3 cups unsifted all-purpose flour
1½ cups sugar
1 teaspoon baking powder
½ teaspoon salt
1 cup butter or margarine
2 eggs
½ teaspoon almond extract

Combine chocolate chips, cream cheese and evaporated milk in medium saucepan. Cook over low heat, stirring constantly, until chips are melted and mixture is smooth. Remove from heat; stir in walnuts, sesame seeds and ½ teaspoon almond extract. Blend well; set aside.

Combine remaining ingredients in large mixer bowl; blend well on low speed until mixture resembles coarse crumbs. Press half the mixture in greased 13×9-inch pan; spread with chocolate mixture. Sprinkle rest of crumbs over filling. (If mixture softens and forms a stiff dough, pinch off small pieces to use as topping.) Bake at 375° for 35 to 40 minutes or until golden brown. Cool; cut into bars.
About 3 dozen bars.

Dorchester Fudge

- 1 package (8 squares) BAKER'S® Semi-Sweet Chocolate, finely chopped
- ½ cup marshmallow topping
- ½ cup chopped nuts* (optional)
- ¼ cup butter or margarine, at room temperature
- ½ teaspoon vanilla
- 1½ cups sugar
- ⅔ cup evaporated milk

Place chocolate in a bowl with marshmallow topping, nuts, butter and vanilla; set aside. Combine sugar and milk in 2-quart saucepan. Cook and stir over medium heat until mixture comes to a *full rolling boil*. Keep at full rolling boil 5 minutes, stirring constantly. Carefully pour boiling sugar syrup over chocolate mixture and stir until chocolate is melted. Pour into buttered 8-inch square pan. Chill until firm, about 1 hour. Cut into squares.
Makes 1½ pounds or about 3 dozen pieces.

*Or use 1 cup BAKER'S® ANGEL FLAKE® Coconut.

Mocha Almond Fudge: Prepare Dorchester Fudge as directed, using chopped toasted blanched almonds for the nuts and adding 2 teaspoons MAXWELL HOUSE® or YUBAN® Instant Coffee to milk mixture.

Peanut Butter Fudge: Prepare Dorchester Fudge as directed, substituting ½ cup peanut butter for the nuts and butter.

Fudge Shapes: Prepare Dorchester Fudge as directed, omitting the nuts; cool slightly and pour fudge mixture onto waxed paper on baking sheet. Top with waxed paper and roll with rolling pin until ½ inch thick. Remove top paper; run tines of fork across surface, scoring fudge. Chill until firm; then cut into shapes with small cookie cutters. Garnish with toasted almonds, if desired.

Raspberry Fudge Balls

- 1 8-ounce package PHILADELPHIA BRAND Cream Cheese, softened
- 1 6-ounce package semi-sweet chocolate pieces, melted
- ¾ cup vanilla wafer crumbs
- ¼ cup KRAFT Raspberry Preserves, strained
- Finely chopped almonds
- Cocoa
- Powdered sugar

Combine cream cheese and chocolate, mixing until well blended. Stir in crumbs and preserves. Chill several hours or overnight. Shape into 1-inch balls; roll in almonds, cocoa or sugar.
Approximately 3 dozen.

Chocolate Truffles

- ½ cup unsalted butter, softened
- 2½ cups confectioners' sugar
- ½ cup HERSHEY'S Cocoa
- ¼ cup heavy or whipping cream
- 1½ teaspoons vanilla
- Centers: Pecan or walnut halves, whole almonds, candied cherries, after-dinner mints
- Coatings: Confectioners' sugar, flaked coconut, chopped nuts

Cream butter in large mixer bowl. Combine 2½ cups confectioners' sugar and the cocoa; add alternately with cream and vanilla to butter. Blend well. Chill until firm. Shape small amount of mixture around desired center; roll into 1-inch balls. Drop into desired coating and turn until well covered. Chill until firm.
About 3 dozen truffles.

Variation: Chocolate Rum Truffles: Decrease vanilla to 1 teaspoon and add ½ teaspoon rum extract.

Creamy White Fudge

- 1½ pounds white confectioners' coating*
- 1 (14-ounce) can EAGLE® Brand Sweetened Condensed Milk (NOT evaporated milk)
- ⅛ teaspoon salt
- ¾ to 1 cup chopped nuts
- 1½ teaspoons vanilla extract

In heavy saucepan, over low heat, melt coating with sweetened condensed milk and salt. Remove from heat; stir in nuts and vanilla. Spread evenly into wax paper-lined 8- or 9-inch square pan. Chill 2 hours or until firm. Turn fudge onto cutting board; peel off paper and cut into squares. Store tightly covered at room temperature.
Makes about 2¼ pounds.

Microwave: In 2-quart glass measure, combine coating, sweetened condensed milk and salt. Microwave on full power (high) 3 to 5 minutes or until coating melts, stirring after 3 minutes. Stir in nuts and vanilla. Proceed as above.

Praline Fudge: Omit vanilla. Add 1 teaspoon maple flavoring and 1 cup chopped pecans. Proceed as above.

Confetti Fudge: Omit nuts. Add 1 cup chopped mixed candied fruit. Proceed as above.

Rum Raisin Fudge: Omit vanilla. Add 1½ teaspoons white vinegar, 1 teaspoon rum flavoring and ¾ cup raisins. Proceed as above.

Cherry Fudge: Omit nuts. Add 1 cup chopped candied cherries.

*White confectioners' coating can be purchased in candy specialty stores.

Chocolate-Almond Fudge

4 cups sugar
1³/₄ cups (7-ounce jar) marshmallow creme
1¹/₂ cups (12-ounce can) evaporated milk
1 tablespoon butter or margarine
2 cups (12-ounce package) HERSHEY'S MINI CHIPS Semi-Sweet Chocolate
1 HERSHEY'S Milk Chocolate Bar with Almonds (8 ounces), chopped
1 teaspoon vanilla
³/₄ cup chopped slivered almonds

Butter 9-inch square pan; set aside. Combine sugar, marshmallow creme, evaporated milk and butter in heavy 4-quart saucepan. Cook over medium heat, stirring constantly, until mixture comes to a full rolling boil; boil and stir 7 minutes. Remove from heat; *immediately* add MINI CHIPS Chocolate and chocolate bar pieces, stirring until completely melted. Blend in vanilla; stir in almonds. Pour into prepared pan; cool completely. Cut into 1-inch squares.
About 5 dozen candies.

Double-Decker Fudge

1 cup REESE'S Peanut Butter Chips
1 cup HERSHEY'S Semi-Sweet Chocolate Chips
2¹/₄ cups sugar
1³/₄ cups (7-ounce jar) marshmallow creme
³/₄ cup evaporated milk
¹/₄ cup butter
1 teaspoon vanilla

Measure peanut butter chips into one bowl and chocolate chips into another; set aside. Butter 8-inch square pan; set aside. Combine sugar, marshmallow creme, evaporated milk and butter in heavy 3-quart saucepan. Cook over medium heat, stirring constantly, until mixture boils; continue cooking and stirring for 5 minutes.

Remove from heat; stir in vanilla. Immediately stir half the hot mixture into peanut butter chips until completely melted. Quickly pour into prepared pan. Stir remaining hot mixture into chocolate chips until completely melted. Quickly spread over top of peanut butter layer; cool until set. Cut into 1-inch squares. Store in airtight container in cool, dry place.
About 4 dozen candies.

Chocolate "Philly" Fudge

4 cups sifted powdered sugar
1 8-ounce package PHILADELPHIA BRAND Cream Cheese, softened
4 1-ounce squares unsweetened chocolate, melted
1 teaspoon vanilla
Dash of salt
¹/₂ cup chopped nuts

Gradually add sugar to cream cheese, mixing well after each addition. Add remaining ingredients; mix well. Spread into greased 8-inch square pan. Chill several hours; cut into squares.
1³/₄ pounds.
Variations: Omit vanilla and nuts; add few drops peppermint extract and ¹/₄ cup crushed peppermint candy. Sprinkle with additional ¹/₄ cup crushed peppermint candy before chilling.

Omit nuts; add 1 cup shredded coconut. Garnish with additional coconut.

Omit nuts; add ¹/₂ cup chopped maraschino cherries, drained. Garnish with whole cherries.

Rich Cocoa Fudge

3 cups sugar
²/₃ cup HERSHEY'S Cocoa
¹/₈ teaspoon salt
1¹/₂ cups milk
¹/₄ cup butter or margarine
1 teaspoon vanilla

Butter 8- or 9-inch square pan; set aside. Combine sugar, cocoa and salt in heavy 4-quart saucepan; stir in milk. Cook over medium heat, stirring constantly, until mixture comes to full rolling boil. Boil, without stirring, to soft-ball stage, 234°F on a candy thermometer (or until syrup, when dropped into very cold water, forms a soft ball that flattens when removed from water). Bulb of candy thermometer should not rest on bottom of saucepan.

Remove from heat. Add butter and vanilla; *do not stir.* Cool at room temperature to 110°F (lukewarm). Beat until fudge thickens and loses some of its gloss. Quickly spread in prepared pan; cool. Cut into 1- to 1¹/₂-inch squares.
About 3 dozen candies.
Variations: Nutty Rich Cocoa Fudge: Beat cooked fudge as directed. *Immediately* stir in 1 cup broken almonds, pecans or walnuts and quickly spread in prepared pan.

Marshmallow-Nut Cocoa Fudge: Increase cocoa to ³/₄ cup. Cook fudge as directed. Add 1 cup marshmallow creme with butter and vanilla; *do not stir.* Cool to 110°F (lukewarm). Beat 10 minutes; stir in 1 cup broken nuts and pour into prepared pan. (Fudge does not set until poured into pan).

Easy Rocky Road

2 cups (12-ounce package)
  HERSHEY'S Semi-Sweet
  Chocolate Chips
¼ cup butter or margarine
2 tablespoons shortening
3 cups miniature marshmallows
¾ cup coarsely chopped nuts

Microwave: Butter 8-inch square pan; set aside. Place chocolate chips, butter and shortening in large micro-proof bowl. Microwave at MEDIUM (50%) for 5 to 7 minutes or until chips are softened and mixture is melted and smooth when stirred. Add marshmallows and nuts; blend well. Spread evenly in prepared pan. Cover; chill until firm. Cut into 2-inch squares. *16 squares.*

Foolproof Dark Chocolate Fudge

3 (6-ounce) packages semi-
  sweet chocolate chips
1 (14-ounce) can EAGLE® Brand
  Sweetened Condensed Milk
  (NOT evaporated milk)
  Dash salt
½ to 1 cup chopped nuts
1½ teaspoons vanilla extract

In heavy saucepan, over low heat, melt chips with sweetened condensed milk and salt. Remove from heat; stir in nuts and vanilla. Spread evenly into wax paper-lined 8- or 9-inch square pan. Chill 2 hours or until firm. Turn fudge onto cutting board; peel off paper and cut into squares. Store loosely covered at room temperature.
Makes about 2 pounds.

Microwave: In 1-quart glass measure, combine chips with sweetened condensed milk. Microwave on full power (high) 3 minutes. Stir until chips melt and mixture is smooth. Stir in remaining ingredients. Proceed as above.

Creamy Dark Chocolate Fudge: Melt 2 cups CAMPFIRE® Miniature Marshmallows with chips and sweetened condensed milk. Proceed as above.

Milk Chocolate Fudge: Omit 1 (6-ounce) package semi-sweet chocolate chips. Add 1 cup milk chocolate chips. Proceed as above.

Creamy Milk Chocolate Fudge: Omit 1 (6-ounce) package semi-sweet chocolate chips. Add 1 cup milk chocolate chips and 2 cups CAMPFIRE® Miniature Marshmallows. Proceed as above.

Mexican Chocolate Fudge: Reduce vanilla to 1 teaspoon. Add 1 tablespoon instant coffee and 1 teaspoon ground cinnamon to sweetened condensed milk. Proceed as above.

Butterscotch Fudge: Omit chocolate chips and vanilla. In heavy saucepan, melt 2 (12-ounce) packages butterscotch flavored chips with sweetened condensed milk. Remove from heat; stir in 2 tablespoons white vinegar, ⅛ teaspoon salt, ½ teaspoon maple flavoring and 1 cup chopped nuts. Proceed as above.

Coconut Granola Snack

1⅓ cups (about) BAKER'S®
  ANGEL FLAKE® Coconut
½ cup quick cooking rolled oats
2 tablespoons firmly packed
  brown sugar
¼ cup chopped pitted dried
  prunes
¼ cup chopped dried apricots
2 tablespoons sesame seed
2 tablespoons oil
2 tablespoons honey
¼ cup seedless raisins

Mix coconut with cereal, brown sugar, prunes, apricots and sesame seed in large bowl. Combine oil and honey in saucepan and bring to a boil over medium heat. Pour over cereal mixture and mix to coat well. Spread evenly in 13×9-inch pan. Bake at 325° for 20 minutes, stirring several times to toast evenly. Sprinkle with raisins and spread out on a tray to cool. Break into small pieces and store in airtight container.
Makes 3½ cups.

Fudgy Chocolate Truffles

½ cup margarine or butter
¾ cup unsweetened cocoa
1 (14-ounce) can EAGLE® Brand
  Sweetened Condensed Milk
  (NOT evaporated milk)
1 teaspoon vanilla extract *or*
  rum flavoring
  Additional unsweetened cocoa

In heavy saucepan, over low heat, melt margarine. Add *¾ cup* cocoa then sweetened condensed milk; mix until smooth and well blended. Over medium heat, cook and stir until thickened and smooth, about 5 minutes. Remove from heat; stir in vanilla. Chill 3 hours or until firm. Shape into 1¼-inch balls. Roll in additional cocoa. Chill until firm. Store covered in refrigerator.
Makes about 4 dozen.

Microwave: In 1-quart glass measure, melt margarine on 100% power (high) 1 minute. Add ¾ cup cocoa then sweetened condensed milk; mix until smooth and well blended. Cook on 100% power (high) 2 to 3 minutes or until thickened, stirring after each minute until smooth. Proceed as above.

Bonbon Cups

1 package (8 squares) BAKER'S®
  Semi-Sweet Chocolate
1 cup sifted confectioners sugar
1 tablespoon milk
1 tablespoon light corn syrup
½ cup chopped mixed candied
  fruits
1 teaspoon rum extract
  (optional)
2 tablespoons butter or
  margarine

Melt 4 squares of the chocolate in saucepan over very low heat, stirring constantly until smooth. Remove from heat. Add sugar, milk and corn syrup. Stir in fruits and extract. Spoon into 3 dozen paper or aluminum foil bonbon cups; chill.

Melt remaining 4 squares chocolate with the butter in saucepan over very low heat, stirring constantly until smooth. Cool slightly; spoon onto fruit filling in cups, mounding the chocolate. Chill until firm. Store in refrigerator.
Makes 3 dozen.

Chocolate Creams

1 package (8 squares) BAKER'S®
  Semi-Sweet Chocolate
½ cup butter or margarine
1¾ cups sifted confectioners
  sugar
2 tablespoons light cream or
  half and half
1 teaspoon vanilla
1 cup finely chopped nuts or
  grated BAKER'S® Semi-
  Sweet Chocolate

Melt chocolate with butter in saucepan over very low heat, stirring constantly until smooth. Blend in sugar, cream and vanilla. Chill about 30 minutes. Shape into ½-inch balls and roll in nuts. Store in refrigerator.
Makes about 4½ dozen.

Chocolatey Peanut Treats

1 8-ounce container Soft
  PHILADELPHIA BRAND
  Cream Cheese
½ cup peanut butter
1 6-ounce package semi-sweet
  chocolate pieces, melted
2¼ cups graham cracker crumbs
⅔ cup finely chopped peanuts

Combine cream cheese and peanut butter, mixing until well blended. Blend in chocolate. Stir in graham cracker crumbs; mix well. Shape into 1-inch balls. Roll in peanuts; chill.
4 dozen.
Variation: Omit peanuts. Prepare, shape and chill dough as directed. Roll in powdered sugar just before serving.

Coconut Date Slices

1 cup chopped or cut dates
¾ cup sugar
2 eggs, well beaten
1 cup chopped walnuts
1 teaspoon vanilla
2 cups POST Toasties Corn
  Flakes or POST 40% Bran
  Flakes
⅔ cup (about) BAKER'S® ANGEL
  FLAKE® Coconut

Combine dates, sugar and eggs in 10-inch skillet. Cook over medium heat, stirring constantly, until mixture pulls away from sides of pan, about 5 minutes. Remove from heat. Stir in nuts and vanilla, then carefully stir in cereal and cool slightly. Moisten hands in cold water and shape mixture into two 6-inch logs, about 1½ inches in diameter. Roll in coconut, wrap in waxed paper and chill at least 1 hour. Cut into thin (about ⅜-inch) slices.
Makes 3 dozen.

Coconut Rum Balls

4 cups vanilla wafer crumbs
1¼ cups (about) BAKER'S®
  ANGEL FLAKE® Coconut
1 cup finely chopped nuts
1 can (14 ounces) sweetened
  condensed milk
½ cup rum*
  Confectioners sugar

Combine crumbs, coconut and nuts in bowl. Stir in condensed milk and rum, mixing well. Shape into 1-inch balls and roll in confectioners sugar to coat. Cover and store in refrigerator. Roll again in sugar just before serving.
Makes 6 dozen.
*Or use ½ cup water and 1 teaspoon rum extract.
Note: For best flavor store 24 hours; candies may be stored for several weeks. Recipe may be halved using ⅔ cup sweetened condensed milk.

Chocolate-Coconut Clusters

1 package (8 squares) BAKER'S®
  Semi-Sweet Chocolate
1⅓ cups (about) BAKER'S®
  ANGEL FLAKE® Coconut*

Melt chocolate in saucepan over very low heat, stirring constantly. Add coconut and mix lightly until completely coated. Drop from teaspoon onto waxed paper. Chill until chocolate is firm.
Makes about 2 dozen.
Microwave: Place unwrapped chocolate in nonmetal pie plate. Heat in microwave oven at medium power for 2 minutes. Stir and heat 30 seconds longer. Proceed as directed.

Buckeyes

**2 (3-ounce) packages cream
  cheese, softened
1 (14-ounce) can EAGLE® Brand
  Sweetened Condensed Milk
  (NOT evaporated milk)
2 (12-ounce) packages peanut
  butter flavored chips
1 cup finely chopped peanuts
½ pound chocolate
  confectioners' coating***

In large mixer bowl, beat cheese until fluffy. Gradually beat in sweetened condensed milk until smooth. In heavy saucepan, over low heat, melt peanut butter chips; stir into cheese mixture. Add nuts. Chill 2 to 3 hours; shape into 1-inch balls. In small heavy saucepan, over low heat, melt confectioners' coating. With wooden pick, dip each peanut ball into melted coating, not covering completely. Place on wax paper-lined baking sheets until firm. Store covered at room temperature or in refrigerator.
Makes about 7 dozen.

*Chocolate confectioners' coating can be purchased in candy specialty stores.

Chocolate Pecan Critters

**1 (11½-ounce) package milk
  chocolate chips
1 (6-ounce) package semi-sweet
  chocolate chips
¼ cup margarine or butter
1 (14-ounce) can EAGLE® Brand
  Sweetened Condensed Milk
  (NOT evaporated milk)
⅛ teaspoon salt
2 cups coarsely chopped pecans
2 teaspoons vanilla extract
  Pecan halves**

In heavy saucepan, over medium heat, melt chips and margarine with sweetened condensed milk and salt. Remove from heat; stir in chopped nuts and vanilla. Drop by teaspoonfuls onto wax paper-lined baking sheets. Top with pecan halves. Chill. Store tightly covered.
Makes about 5 dozen.

Microwave: In 2-quart glass measure, microwave chips, margarine, sweetened condensed milk and salt on full power (high) 3 minutes, stirring after 1½ minutes. Stir to melt chips; stir in chopped nuts and vanilla. Proceed as above.

Chocolate-Dipped Morsels

**4 squares BAKER'S® Semi-
  Sweet Chocolate
  Assorted morsel centers***

Melt chocolate in saucepan over very low heat, stirring constantly until smooth. Insert wooden picks or skewers into fruit and marshmallow centers. Dip quickly, one at a time, into chocolate. (To dip pretzels or nuts, stir into chocolate; then remove with fork.) Let stand or chill on rack or waxed paper until chocolate is firm. For best eating quality, chill dipped fresh or canned fruits and serve the same day.
Makes 1 to 1½ dozen.

***Suggested Morsel Centers.**
Fruits: Firm strawberries, ½-inch banana slices, fresh pineapple wedges or drained canned pineapple chunks, peeled orange slices, orange wedges, well-drained stemmed maraschino cherries, dried figs, dried dates or dried apricots.

Unsalted Pretzels and Large Marshmallows.

Nuts: Walnuts or pecan halves or whole almonds or Brazil nuts.

Strawberry Bon Bons

**1 (14-ounce) can EAGLE® Brand
  Sweetened Condensed Milk
  (NOT evaporated milk)
2 (7-ounce) packages flaked
  coconut (5⅓ cups)
1 (8-serving size) package
  strawberry flavor gelatin
1 cup ground blanched almonds
1 teaspoon almond extract
  Red food coloring
2¼ cups sifted confectioners'
  sugar
3 tablespoons BORDEN®
  Whipping Cream
  Green food coloring**

In large bowl, combine sweetened condensed milk, coconut, ⅓ cup gelatin, almonds, extract and enough red food coloring to tint mixture a strawberry shade. Chill 1 hour or until firm enough to handle. Using about ½ tablespoon for each, form into strawberry shapes. Sprinkle remaining gelatin onto wax paper; roll each strawberry in gelatin to coat. Place on wax paper-lined baking sheets; chill. In small bowl, combine sugar, cream and green food coloring. Using pastry bag with open star tip, pipe small amount on top each strawberry. Store covered at room temperature or in refrigerator.
Makes about 60 candies.

Tip: Green tube decorator icing can be used to make strawberry "stems." Omit confectioners' sugar, cream and green food coloring.

Peanut Butter Logs

1 (12-ounce) package peanut butter flavored chips
1 (14-ounce) can EAGLE® Brand Sweetened Condensed Milk (NOT evaporated milk)
1 cup CAMPFIRE® Miniature Marshmallows
1 cup chopped peanuts

In heavy saucepan, over low heat, melt chips with sweetened condensed milk. Add marshmallows; stir until melted. Remove from heat; cool 20 minutes. Divide in half; place each portion on a 20-inch piece of wax paper. Shape each into 12-inch log. Roll in nuts. Wrap tightly; chill 2 hours or until firm. Remove paper; cut into 1/4-inch slices.
Makes two 12-inch logs.

Microwave: In 2-quart glass measure, microwave chips, sweetened condensed milk and marshmallows on full power (high) 4 minutes or until melted, stirring after 2 minutes. Let stand at room temperature 1 hour. Proceed as above.

Peanut Butter Fudge: Stir peanuts into mixture. Spread into wax paper-lined 8- or 9-inch square pan. Chill 2 hours or until firm. Turn fudge onto cutting board; peel off paper and cut into squares.

Milk Chocolate Bourbon Balls

1 (12-ounce) package vanilla wafer cookies, finely crushed (about 3 cups crumbs)
5 tablespoons bourbon or brandy
1 (11 1/2-ounce) package milk chocolate chips
1 (14-ounce) can EAGLE® Brand Sweetened Condensed Milk (NOT evaporated milk)
Finely chopped nuts

In medium mixing bowl, combine crumbs and bourbon. In heavy saucepan, over low heat, melt chips. Remove from heat; add sweetened condensed milk. Gradually add crumb mixture; mix well. Let stand at room temperature 30 minutes or chill. Shape into 1-inch balls; roll in nuts. Store tightly covered.
Makes about 5 1/2 dozen.

Tip: Flavor of these candies improves after 24 hours. They can be made ahead and stored in freezer. Thaw before serving.

Layered Mint Chocolate Candy

1 (12-ounce) package semi-sweet chocolate chips
1 (14-ounce) can EAGLE® Brand Sweetened Condensed Milk (NOT evaporated milk)
2 teaspoons vanilla extract
6 ounces white confectioners' coating*
1 tablespoon peppermint extract
Few drops green or red food coloring, optional

In heavy saucepan, over low heat, melt chips with 1 cup sweetened condensed milk. Stir in vanilla. Spread half the mixture into wax paper-lined 8- or 9-inch square pan; chill 10 minutes or until firm. Hold remaining chocolate mixture at room temperature. In heavy saucepan, over low heat, melt coating with remaining sweetened condensed milk. Stir in peppermint extract and food coloring if desired. Spread on chilled chocolate layer; chill 10 minutes longer or until firm. Spread reserved chocolate mixture on n nt layer. Chill 2 hours or until firm. Turn onto cutting board; peel off paper and cut into squares. Store loosely covered at room temperature.
Makes about 1 3/4 pounds.

*White confectioners' coating can be purchased in candy specialty stores.

Fruit Bon Bons

1 (14-ounce) can EAGLE® Brand Sweetened Condensed Milk (NOT evaporated milk)
2 (7-ounce) packages flaked coconut (5 1/3 cups)
1 (6-ounce) package fruit flavor gelatin, any flavor
1 cup ground blanched almonds
1 teaspoon almond extract
Food coloring, optional

In large mixing bowl, combine sweetened condensed milk, coconut, 1/3 cup gelatin, almonds, extract and enough food coloring to tint mixture desired shade. Chill 1 hour or until firm enough to handle. Using about 1/2 tablespoon mixture for each, shape into 1-inch balls. Sprinkle remaining gelatin onto wax paper; roll each ball in gelatin to coat. Place on wax paper-lined baking sheets; chill. Store covered at room temperature or in refrigerator.
Makes about 5 dozen.

Fresh 'n Fruity Pops

1 envelope KNOX® Unflavored Gelatine
½ cup cold water
1 cup fruit juice, heated to boiling
Suggested Fresh Fruits*
¼ cup sugar or 6 packets aspartame sweetener
1 tablespoon lemon juice

In medium bowl, sprinkle unflavored gelatine over cold water; let stand 1 minute. Add hot juice and stir until gelatine is completely dissolved, about 5 minutes. Stir in remaining ingredients. Pour into 6 (5-ounce) Popsicle molds or paper cups; freeze until partially frozen, about 30 minutes. Insert wooden ice cream sticks; freeze until firm, about 4 hours. To serve, let stand at room temperature 5 minutes; remove from mold.
Makes 6 pops.

*Suggested Fresh Fruits: Use any of the following, pureed, to equal 1 cup—bananas, blueberries, pitted cherries, cantaloupe, nectarines, plums, peaches or strawberries.

Crunchy Clusters

1 (12-ounce) package semi-sweet chocolate chips *or* 3 (6-ounce) packages butterscotch flavored chips
1 (14-ounce) can EAGLE® Brand Sweetened Condensed Milk (NOT evaporated milk)
1 (3-ounce) can chow mein noodles *or* 2 cups pretzel sticks, broken into ½-inch pieces
1 cup dry roasted peanuts *or* whole roasted almonds

In heavy saucepan, over low heat, melt chips with sweetened condensed milk. Remove from heat. In large mixing bowl, combine noodles and nuts; stir in chocolate mixture. Drop by tablespoonfuls onto wax paper-lined baking sheets; chill 2 hours or until firm. Store loosely covered in cool dry place.
Makes about 3 dozen.

Microwave: In 2-quart glass measure, combine chips and sweetened condensed milk. Microwave on full power (high) 3 minutes, stirring after 1½ minutes. Stir until smooth. Proceed as above.

Creamy Cocoa Taffy

1¼ cups sugar
¾ cup light corn syrup
⅓ cup HERSHEY'S Cocoa
⅛ teaspoon salt
2 teaspoons white vinegar
¼ cup evaporated milk
1 tablespoon butter

Butter 9-inch square pan; set aside. Combine sugar, corn syrup, cocoa, salt and vinegar in heavy 2-quart saucepan. Cook over medium heat, stirring constantly, until mixture boils; add evaporated milk and butter. Continue to cook, stirring occasionally, to firm-ball stage, 248°F on a candy thermometer (or until syrup, when dropped into very cold water, forms a firm ball that does not flatten when removed from water). Bulb of candy thermometer should not rest on bottom of saucepan.

Pour mixture into prepared pan. Let stand until taffy is cool enough to handle. Butter hands; stretch taffy, folding and pulling until light in color and hard to pull. Place taffy on table; pull into ½-inch-wide strips (twist two strips together, if desired). Cut into 1-inch pieces with buttered scissors. Wrap individually in plastic wrap.
About 1¼ pounds candy.

Chocolate Brittle Drops

4 squares BAKER'S® Semi-Sweet Chocolate
1½ cups (½ pound) coarsely crushed peanut brittle

Melt chocolate in saucepan over very low heat, stirring constantly. Remove from heat and stir in peanut brittle. Drop from teaspoon onto waxed paper. Let stand until chocolate is firm.
Makes about 2 dozen.

Caramel Peanut Balls

3 cups *finely* chopped dry roasted peanuts
1 (14-ounce) can EAGLE® Brand Sweetened Condensed Milk (NOT evaporated milk)
1 teaspoon vanilla extract
½ pound chocolate confectioners' coating*

In heavy saucepan, combine nuts, sweetened condensed milk and vanilla. Over medium heat, cook and stir 8 to 10 minutes or until mixture forms ball around spoon and pulls away from side of pan. Cool 10 minutes. Chill if desired. Shape into 1-inch balls. In small heavy saucepan, over low heat, melt confectioners' coating. With wooden pick, dip each ball into melted coating, covering half of ball. Place on wax paper-lined baking sheets until firm. Store covered at room temperature or in refrigerator.
Makes about 4½ dozen.

**Chocolate confectioners' coating can be purchased in candy specialty stores.

Apricot Almond Chewies

4 cups finely chopped dried apricots (about 1 pound)
4 cups flaked coconut or coconut macaroon crumbs (about 21 macaroons)
2 cups slivered almonds, toasted and finely chopped
1 (14-ounce) can EAGLE® Brand Sweetened Condensed Milk (NOT evaporated milk)
Whole almonds, optional

In large mixing bowl, combine all ingredients except whole almonds. Chill 2 hours. Shape into 1-inch balls. Top each with whole almond if desired. Store tightly covered in refrigerator. *Makes about 6 1/2 dozen.*

Easiest-Ever Cocoa Fudge

3 2/3 cups (1-pound package) confectioners' sugar, sifted
1/2 cup HERSHEY'S Cocoa
1/2 cup butter or margarine, cut into pieces
1/4 cup milk
1/2 cup chopped nuts (optional)
1 tablespoon vanilla

Microwave: Butter 8-inch square pan; set aside. Combine confectioners' sugar, cocoa, butter and milk in medium micro-proof bowl. Microwave at HIGH (100%) for 2 to 3 minutes or until butter is melted. Stir until mixture is smooth. Stir in nuts and vanilla; blend well. Spread evenly in prepared pan; cool. Cut into 1-inch squares. Store, covered, in refrigerator. *About 5 dozen candies.*

Chipper Peanut Candy

1 (6-ounce) package butterscotch flavored chips
1 (14-ounce) can EAGLE® Brand Sweetened Condensed Milk (NOT evaporated milk)
1 cup peanut butter
2 cups crushed WISE® Potato Chips
1 cup coarsely chopped peanuts

In heavy saucepan, melt butterscotch chips with sweetened condensed milk and peanut butter. Over medium heat, cook and stir until well blended. Remove from heat. Add potato chips and nuts; mix well. Press into aluminum foil-lined 8- or 9-inch square pan. Chill. Turn candy onto cutting board; peel off foil and cut into squares. Store loosely covered at room temperature. *Makes about 2 pounds.*
Microwave: In 2-quart glass measure, combine sweetened condensed milk, butterscotch chips and peanut butter. Microwave on full power (high) 4 minutes, stirring after 2 minutes. Proceed as above.

Almond Toffee

1 cup butter or margarine
1 cup sugar
3 tablespoons water
1 tablespoon light corn syrup
1/3 cup chopped toasted blanched almonds
1 package (8 squares) BAKER'S® Semi-Sweet Chocolate
2/3 cup chopped toasted blanched almonds

Melt butter in heavy 2-quart saucepan over very low heat. Add sugar and stir until mixture starts to boil. Combine water and corn syrup; blend into sugar mixture. Cook and stir over medium heat until mixture comes to a boil. Reduce heat; cover and cook 3 minutes. Uncover and cook gently, stirring frequently to prevent burning, until a small amount of mixture forms a hard and brittle thread in cold water (or to a temperature of 300°). Remove from heat. Stir in 1/3 cup almonds. Spread evenly in well-buttered 15×10-inch jelly roll pan. Let stand until almost cool to the touch.
Melt 4 squares of the chocolate in saucepan over very low heat, stirring constantly until smooth. Spread over toffee; then sprinkle with 1/3 cup of the remaining almonds. Let stand until chocolate is firm. Turn toffee out onto waxed paper. (Toffee may break.) Melt remaining 4 squares chocolate and spread over toffee. Sprinkle with remaining 1/3 cup almonds. Let stand until chocolate is firm. Break into pieces.
Makes about 1 1/2 pounds.

Gelatin Jiggles

4 packages (4-serving size) or 2 packages (8-serving size) JELL-O® Brand Gelatin, any flavor
2 1/2 cups boiling water or fruit juice

Completely dissolve gelatin in boiling water. Pour into 9-inch square pan. Chill until firm, about 4 hours. Cut with small cookie cutters that have been dipped in warm water, or cut into 1-inch squares. Carefully transfer cutouts to serving plates, using broad spatula that has been dipped in warm water. Flake remaining gelatin with fork; reserve for another use. *Makes about 1 1/2 dozen cutouts.*
Note: To cut letters or shapes, place paper or cardboard pattern on firm gelatin; cut with sharp knife that has been dipped in warm water.

DESSERTS

For the perfect finale to a great meal, turn to these delectable desserts. You'll find smooth Bavarian creams and mousses, fruity parfaits, elegant chocolate souffles, rich puddings, and a mouth-watering selection of cheesecakes. Provide a light touch with a refreshing fruit mold or tangy sorbet.

Cocoa Bavarian Cream

  2 envelopes unflavored gelatine
1½ cups cold milk
1¼ cups sugar
  ¾ cup HERSHEY'S Cocoa
  1 tablespoon light corn syrup
  3 tablespoons butter or
      margarine
1¾ cups milk
1½ teaspoons vanilla
10 to 12 ladyfingers, split
  1 cup heavy or whipping cream

Sprinkle gelatine onto 1½ cups milk in medium saucepan; let stand 3 to 4 minutes to soften. Combine sugar and cocoa; add to gelatine mixture in saucepan. Add corn syrup. Cook over medium heat, stirring constantly, until mixture boils. Remove from heat; stir in butter until melted. Blend in 1¾ cups milk and the vanilla; pour into large mixer bowl. Cool; chill until almost set.

Meanwhile, line bottom and side of 1½-quart mold with ladyfingers, rounded sides against mold. Whip cream until stiff. Beat chilled chocolate mixture until smooth. Add whipped cream to chocolate on low speed just until blended. Pour into ladyfinger-lined mold; chill until set. Unmold before serving.
12 servings.

Chocolate Mousse à l'Orange

  2 cups (12-ounce package)
      HERSHEY'S Semi-Sweet
      Chocolate Chips
  1 block (1 ounce) HERSHEY'S
      Unsweetened Baking
      Chocolate
  6 tablespoons water
  6 egg yolks, at room
      temperature
  2 to 3 tablespoons orange-
      flavored liqueur
1½ cups heavy or whipping cream
  6 egg whites, at room
      temperature
  ½ cup sugar
      Sweetened whipped cream
      Orange slices, cut into wedges
      (optional)

Melt chocolate chips and baking chocolate with water in top of double boiler over hot, not boiling, water; stir until smooth. Remove from heat. With wire whisk, beat egg yolks, one at a time, into chocolate mixture; cool to lukewarm. Stir in orange-flavored liqueur. Whip cream until stiff; fold into chocolate mixture.

Beat egg whites in large mixer bowl until foamy. Gradually add sugar; beat until stiff peaks form. Fold in chocolate-cream mixture. Spoon into dessert dishes. Cover; chill several hours or until firm. Garnish with sweetened whipped cream and orange wedges.
16 servings.

Acapulco Flan

20 KRAFT Caramels
2 tablespoons water
1 8-ounce package
   PHILADELPHIA BRAND
   Cream Cheese, softened
1/2 cup sugar
6 eggs, beaten
1 teaspoon vanilla
2 cups milk

Melt caramels with water over low heat, stirring until smooth. Pour into greased 9-inch layer pan. Combine cream cheese and sugar, mixing until well blended. Blend in eggs and vanilla. Gradually add milk, mixing until well blended. Set layer pan in baking pan on oven rack; slowly pour milk mixture over caramel sauce. Pour boiling water into baking pan to 1/2-inch depth. Bake at 350°, 45 minutes or until knife inserted 2 inches from edge of pan comes out clean. Remove from water immediately; cool 5 minutes. Invert onto serving dish with rim. Serve warm or chilled.
6 to 8 servings.

Strawberries 'n Cream Fool

1 envelope KNOX® Unflavored
   Gelatine
1/4 cup cold water
1 package (10 ounces) frozen
   strawberries in light syrup,
   thawed
1/4 cup frozen orange juice
   concentrate, partially
   thawed and undiluted
1/4 cup sugar
1 teaspoon finely chopped
   crystallized ginger (optional)
1 container (8 ounces) frozen
   whipped topping, thawed*

In medium saucepan, sprinkle unflavored gelatine over cold water; let stand 1 minute. Stir over low heat until gelatine is completely dissolved, about 3 minutes.

In blender or food processor, process strawberries, orange juice concentrate, sugar and ginger. While processing, through feed cap, gradually add gelatine mixture and process until blended. In large bowl, blend 1 cup strawberry mixture with whipped topping. Turn into serving bowl. Gently fold in remaining strawberry mixture, just until marbled; chill until set, about 2 hours. Serve, if desired, with angel food or pound cake.
Makes 8 servings; 165 calories per serving.
   ***Substitution:** Use 1 cup (1/2 pint) whipping or heavy cream, whipped. 163 calories per serving.*

Mt. Gretna Chocolate Fondue

4 squares (4 ounces)
   HERSHEY'S Unsweetened
   Baking Chocolate
1 cup light cream
1 cup sugar
1/4 cup creamy peanut butter
1 1/2 teaspoons vanilla
   Fondue Dippers

Combine chocolate and cream in medium saucepan. Cook over low heat, stirring constantly, until chocolate is melted and mixture is smooth. Add sugar and peanut butter; continue cooking until slightly thickened. Remove from heat; stir in vanilla. Pour into fondue pot or chafing dish; serve warm with Fondue Dippers.
About 2 cups fondue.
   Fondue Dippers: In advance, prepare a selection of the following: marshmallows; angel food, sponge or pound cake pieces; strawberries; grapes; pineapple chunks; mandarin orange segments; cherries; fresh fruit slices. (Drain fruit well. Brush fresh fruit with lemon juice to prevent fruit from turning brown.)

Butterscotch Apple Squares

1/4 cup margarine or butter
1 1/2 cups graham cracker crumbs
2 small all-purpose apples,
   pared and chopped (about
   1 1/4 cups)
1 (6-ounce) package
   butterscotch flavored chips
1 (14-ounce) can EAGLE® Brand
   Sweetened Condensed Milk
   (NOT evaporated milk)
1 (3 1/2-ounce) can flaked
   coconut (1 1/3 cups)
1 cup chopped nuts

Preheat oven to 350° (325° for glass dish). In 3-quart shallow baking pan (13×9-inch), melt margarine in oven. Sprinkle crumbs evenly over margarine; top with apples. In heavy saucepan, over medium heat, melt chips with sweetened condensed milk. Pour butterscotch mixture evenly over apples. Top with coconut and nuts; press down firmly. Bake 25 to 30 minutes or until lightly browned. Cool. Chill thoroughly. Garnish as desired. Refrigerate leftovers.
Makes 12 servings.
   Microwave: In 2 1/2-quart shallow baking dish (12×7-inch), microwave margarine on full power (high) 1 minute or until melted. Sprinkle crumbs evenly over margarine; top with apples. In 1-quart glass measure, microwave chips with sweetened condensed milk on 2/3 power (medium-high) 2 to 3 minutes. Mix well. Pour butterscotch mixture evenly over apples. Top with coconut and nuts. Press down firmly. Microwave on full power (high) 8 to 9 minutes. Proceed as above.

Banana Mocha Layered Dessert

1 cup whipping cream
2 tablespoons sugar
1 teaspoon instant coffee powder
½ teaspoon vanilla extract
3 firm, medium DOLE™ Bananas
1 package (8½ ounces) chocolate wafer cookies

In large mixer bowl, beat cream, sugar, coffee powder and vanilla until stiff peaks form. Slice bananas. Crumble half the wafers into bottom of 8-inch square pan. Top with half the banana slices. Spread with half the mocha cream. Repeat layers. Refrigerate until ready to serve. Garnish with additional banana slices, if desired.
Makes 8 servings.

Delightful Dessert Pancake

1 8-ounce package *Light* PHILADELPHIA BRAND Neufchâtel Cheese, softened
3 tablespoons honey
1 teaspoon grated lemon peel
1 teaspoon lemon juice
* * *
½ cup milk
½ cup flour
¼ teaspoon salt
2 eggs, beaten
1 tablespoon PARKAY Margarine
2 cups assorted fruit
¼ cup toasted flake coconut

Combine neufchâtel cheese, honey, peel and juice, mixing until well blended. Chill.

Gradually add milk to combined flour and salt; beat until smooth. Beat in eggs. Heat heavy 10-inch ovenproof skillet in 450° oven until very hot. Add margarine to coat skillet; pour in batter immediately. Bake on lowest oven rack at 450°, 10 minutes. Reduce oven temperature to 350°; continue baking 10 minutes or until golden brown. Fill with fruit; sprinkle with coconut. Serve immediately with neufchâtel cheese mixture.
6 to 8 servings.

Mexicana Bread Pudding

1 cup SUN-MAID® Raisins
1 cup orange juice
¾ cup packed brown sugar
½ teaspoon *each* ground cinnamon and grated orange peel
¼ teaspoon ground nutmeg
5 cups lightly packed 1-inch French bread cubes (about 6 ounces)
2½ cups shredded Monterey Jack cheese
½ cup chopped DIAMOND® Walnuts
Cream, lightly sweetened whipped cream or ice cream (optional)

In small saucepan, combine raisins, juice, sugar, cinnamon, peel and nutmeg. Bring to boil over medium heat, stirring occasionally. In large bowl, toss bread with raisin mixture. Add 2 cups of the cheese and the walnuts; toss. Turn into buttered 1½-quart baking dish; sprinkle remaining ½ cup cheese on top. Bake in preheated 375°F oven 15 to 20 minutes or until cheese is melted. Serve warm, topped with cream, if desired.
Makes 6 servings.

Tropical Crisp

1 DOLE™ Fresh Pineapple
4 DOLE™ Bananas
1 cup brown sugar, packed
1 cup flour
¾ cup rolled oats
½ cup flaked coconut
½ teaspoon ground nutmeg
½ cup butter or margarine, softened

Preheat oven to 350°F. Twist crown from pineapple. Cut pineapple lengthwise into quarters. Remove fruit from shells with curved knife. Trim off core and cut fruit into chunks. Cut bananas into chunks. In 9-inch baking dish, toss bananas and pineapple with ¼ cup brown sugar. In medium bowl, combine remaining ¾ cup brown sugar, flour, oats, coconut and nutmeg. Cut in butter until crumbly. Sprinkle over fruit mixture. Bake in preheated oven 45 to 50 minutes or until topping is crisp and juices have begun to bubble around edges.
Makes 8 servings.

Baked Honey Apples

2 to 3 apples, cored and sliced into ¾-inch rings
½ cup butter or margarine
⅓ cup honey

Arrange 2 or 3 apple rings on each of four 12×12-inch pieces of heavy-duty foil. Dot with butter; drizzle with honey. Fold foil loosely around apples; seal edges. Grill packets, on covered grill, over medium-hot **KINGSFORD® Charcoal Briquets** 12 to 15 minutes or until apples are crisp-tender, turning packets once.
Makes 4 servings.

Thanksgiving Cranberry Cobbler

- 1 package DUNCAN HINES®
  Deluxe Yellow Cake Mix
- 1/2 teaspoon ground cinnamon
- 1/4 teaspoon ground nutmeg
- 1 cup (2 sticks) butter or
  margarine, softened
- 1/2 cup chopped nuts
- 1 can (21 ounces) peach pie
  filling
- 1 can (16 ounces) whole
  cranberry sauce
  Vanilla ice cream or sweetened
  whipped cream

1. Preheat oven to 350°F.
2. Combine dry cake mix, cinnamon and nutmeg in bowl. Cut in butter with pastry blender or two knives until crumbly. Stir in nuts; set aside.
3. Combine peach pie filling and cranberry sauce in ungreased 13×9×2-inch pan; mix well. Sprinkle crumb mixture over fruit.
4. Bake at 350°F for 45 to 50 minutes or until golden brown. Serve warm with ice cream or whipped cream.
16 servings.

Swedish Apple Cake

- 1 cup packed brown sugar
- 2 tablespoons all-purpose flour
- 1/4 teaspoon ground nutmeg
- 1/8 teaspoon salt
- 1 cup water
- 2 tablespoons butter or
  margarine
- 1 can (20 ounces) apple pie
  filling
- 1 package DUNCAN HINES®
  Deluxe Lemon Supreme
  Cake Mix
- 3 large eggs
- 1/3 cup CRISCO® Oil or PURITAN®
  Oil
- 1 1/4 cups water

1. For sauce, combine brown sugar, flour, nutmeg and salt in small baking dish. Gradually stir in 1 cup water. Add butter; set aside.
2. Spread apple pie filling in 13×9×2-inch pan.
3. Combine dry cake mix, eggs, oil and 1 1/4 cups water in large mixer bowl. Mix as directed on package. Spread batter evenly over apples.
4. Preheat oven to 350°F. Bake cake and sauce for 43 to 48 minutes or until toothpick inserted in center of cake comes out clean.
5. To serve, spoon warm cake and apples in serving bowls and top with sauce.
16 to 20 servings.

Fruit Crumble

- 4 cups thinly sliced peeled
  apples
- 1/4 cup packed brown sugar
- 1 teaspoon lemon juice
- 1/4 teaspoon ground cinnamon
- 2 tablespoons butter or
  margarine
- 1 cup coarsely crushed
  PEPPERIDGE FARM® Irish
  Oatmeal, Hazelnut or Lemon
  Nut Crunch Cookies
- 1/2 cup chopped walnuts
  (optional)

To Microwave:
1. In large bowl, toss together apples, brown sugar, lemon juice and cinnamon. Spoon mixture into 9-inch microwave-safe pie plate; set aside.
2. Place butter in medium microwave-safe bowl. Cover; microwave on HIGH 30 seconds or until melted. Stir in cookies and walnuts. Sprinkle over apple mixture.
3. Microwave, uncovered, on HIGH 7 minutes or until apples are tender, rotating dish twice during cooking. Let stand, uncovered, 5 minutes.
Makes 6 servings.
Note: Substitute a 21-ounce can of apple or cherry pie filling for fresh apples. Omit brown sugar. Microwave as directed above.

Gelatin Ice Cream Dessert

- 1 package (4-serving size)
  JELL-O® Brand Gelatin, any
  flavor
- 1 cup boiling water
- 2 cups (1 pint) ice cream, any
  flavor

Completely dissolve gelatin in boiling water. Add ice cream by spoonfuls, stirring until ice cream is melted. Pour into individual dessert glasses or serving bowl. Chill until set, about 30 minutes. Garnish with fresh fruit, if desired.
Makes 3 cups or 6 servings.

Peanut Butter Snacking Cups

- 3/4 cup graham cracker crumbs
- 3 tablespoons butter or
  margarine, melted
- 3 1/2 cups (8 ounces) COOL WHIP®
  Non-Dairy Whipped Topping,
  thawed
- 1 cup milk
- 1/2 cup chunky peanut butter
- 1 package (4-serving size)
  JELL-O® Vanilla Flavor
  Instant Pudding and Pie
  Filling
- 1/4 cup strawberry preserves

Line 12-cup muffin pan with paper baking cups. Combine crumbs and butter; mix well. Press about 1 tablespoon of the crumb mixture into each cup. Top each with about 1 tablespoon of the whipped topping. Gradually blend milk into peanut butter in bowl. Add pudding mix. With electric mixer at low speed, beat until blended, 1 to 2 minutes. Fold in remaining whipped topping. Spoon into crumb-lined cups. Top each cup with 1 teaspoon of the preserves. Freeze about 4 hours; peel off papers.
Makes 12 servings.

Cherry-Topped Icebox Cake

20 whole graham crackers
2 cups cold milk
1 package (6-serving size)
    JELL-O® Vanilla or Chocolate
    Flavor Instant Pudding and
    Pie Filling
1¾ cups thawed COOL WHIP®
    Non-Dairy Whipped Topping
2 cans (21 ounces each) cherry
    pie filling

Line 13×9-inch pan with some of the graham crackers, breaking crackers, if necessary. Pour cold milk into bowl. Add pudding mix. With electric mixer at low speed, beat until well blended, 1 to 2 minutes. Let stand 5 minutes; then blend in whipped topping. Spread half of the pudding mixture over crackers. Add another layer of crackers. Top with remaining pudding mixture and remaining crackers. Spread cherry pie filling over crackers. Chill about 3 hours.
Makes 12 servings.

Chocolate-Frosted Icebox Cake: Prepare Cherry-Topped Icebox Cake as directed, substituting ¾ cup ready-to-spread chocolate fudge frosting for the cherry pie filling. Carefully spread frosting over top layer of graham crackers.

Very Berry Sorbet

1 envelope KNOX® Unflavored
    Gelatine
½ cup sugar
1½ cups water
2 cups pureed strawberries or
    raspberries (about
    1½ pints)*
½ cup creme de cassis (black
    currant) liqueur or cranberry
    juice cocktail
2 tablespoons lemon juice

In medium saucepan, mix unflavored gelatine with sugar; blend in water. Let stand 1 minute. Stir over low heat until gelatine is completely dissolved, about 5 minutes. Let cool to room temperature; stir in remaining ingredients. Pour into 9-inch square baking pan; freeze 3 hours or until firm.

With electric mixer or food processor, beat mixture until smooth. Return to pan; freeze 2 hours or until firm. To serve, let stand at room temperature 15 minutes or until slightly softened. Spoon into dessert dishes or stemmed glassware. Garnish, if desired, with fresh fruit.
Makes 8 servings; 119 calories per serving with creme de cassis; 78 calories per serving with cranberry juice cocktail.

*****Substitution:** Use 1 package (10 ounces) frozen strawberries or raspberries, partially thawed and pureed.

Pots de Crème au Chocolat

2 squares (2 ounces)
    HERSHEY'S Unsweetened
    Baking Chocolate, broken
    into pieces
1 cup light cream
⅔ cup sugar
2 egg yolks, slightly beaten
2 tablespoons butter or
    margarine, softened
1 teaspoon vanilla
    Sweetened whipped cream
    Candied violets (optional)

Combine baking chocolate pieces and cream in medium saucepan. Cook over medium heat, stirring constantly with wire whisk, until chocolate flecks disappear and mixture is hot. Add sugar and continue cooking and stirring until mixture begins to boil. Remove from heat; gradually add to beaten egg yolks, stirring constantly. Stir in butter and vanilla. Pour into six crème pots or demitasse cups; press plastic wrap directly onto surface. Chill several hours or until set. Garnish with sweetened whipped cream and candied violets.
6 servings.

Strawberry Ice

1 quart strawberries, cleaned
    and hulled
1 cup sugar
½ cup water
3 tablespoons REALEMON®
    Lemon Juice from
    Concentrate
    Few drops red food coloring,
    optional

In blender container, combine sugar, water and ReaLemon® brand; mix well. Gradually add strawberries; blend until smooth, adding food coloring if desired. Pour into 8-inch square pan; freeze about 1½ hours. In small mixer bowl, beat until slushy. Return to freezer. Place in refrigerator 1 hour before serving to soften. Return leftovers to freezer.
Makes 6 servings.

Tortoni Squares

1 envelope unflavored gelatin
½ cup cold water
2 8-ounce containers Soft
    PHILADELPHIA BRAND
    Cream Cheese
2 tablespoons sugar
1 17-ounce can apricot halves,
    drained, chopped
2 tablespoons chopped
    almonds, toasted
¼ teaspoon rum flavoring
2 cups thawed frozen whipped
    topping
2 cups macaroon cookies,
    crumbled

Soften gelatin in water; stir over low heat until dissolved. Cool. Combine cream cheese and sugar, mixing until well blended. Gradually add gelatin mixture, mixing until blended. Stir in apricots, almonds and flavoring. Fold in whipped topping. Place macaroons on bottom of 9-inch square baking pan; top with cream cheese mixture. Chill until set; cut into squares.
9 servings.

Creamy Lemon Sherbet

1 cup sugar
2 cups (1 pint) BORDEN® or MEADOW GOLD® Whipping Cream, unwhipped
½ cup REALEMON® Lemon Juice from Concentrate
Few drops yellow food coloring

In medium bowl, combine sugar and cream, stirring until sugar is dissolved. Stir in ReaLemon® brand and food coloring. Pour into 8-inch square pan or directly into sherbet dishes. Freeze 3 hours or until firm. Remove from freezer 5 minutes before serving. Return leftovers to freezer.
Makes about 3 cups.

Creamy Lime Sherbet: Substitute REALIME® Lime Juice from Concentrate for ReaLemon® brand and green food coloring for yellow.

Peach Cream Cake

1 (7-inch) prepared loaf angel food cake, frozen
1 (14-ounce) can EAGLE® Brand Sweetened Condensed Milk (NOT evaporated milk)
1 cup cold water
1 (3½-ounce) package instant vanilla pudding and pie filling mix
1 teaspoon almond extract
2 cups (1 pint) whipping cream, whipped
4 cups sliced, pared fresh peaches *or* 1 (20-ounce) package frozen sliced peaches, thawed

Cut cake into ¼-inch slices; arrange half the slices on bottom of 13×9-inch baking dish. In large mixer bowl, combine sweetened condensed milk and water; mix well. Add pudding mix; beat until well blended. Chill 5 minutes. Stir in extract; fold in whipped cream. Pour half the cream mixture over cake slices; arrange half the peach slices on top. Repeat layering, ending with peach slices. Chill 4 hours or until set. Cut into squares to serve. Refrigerate leftovers.
Makes 10 to 12 servings.

Frozen Chocolate Graham Cups

1½ cups cold milk
1 package (4-serving size) JELL-O® Chocolate Flavor Instant Pudding and Pie Filling
1 cup thawed COOL WHIP® Non-Dairy Whipped Topping
7 whole graham crackers, broken in pieces
½ cup miniature marshmallows
¼ cup chopped salted peanuts

Pour cold milk into bowl. Add pudding mix. With electric mixer at low speed, beat until well blended, 1 to 2 minutes. Let stand 5 minutes. Fold in whipped topping, crackers, marshmallows and peanuts. Spoon into muffin pan lined with paper baking cups. Freeze until firm, about 3 hours. Garnish with additional whipped topping, if desired.
Makes about 8 servings.

Frozen Vanilla Graham Cups: Prepare Frozen Chocolate Graham Cups as directed, substituting vanilla flavor instant pudding and pie filling for the chocolate flavor pudding and ¼ cup chopped nuts or slivered almonds and ¼ cup diced maraschino cherries for the marshmallows and peanuts.
Makes 6 servings.

Sparkling Lemon-Lime Sorbet

1 envelope KNOX® Unflavored Gelatine
½ cup sugar
1 cup water
1 cup Champagne, sauterne or ginger ale
½ cup fresh lemon juice (about 3 lemons)
⅓ cup fresh lime juice (about 3 limes)

In medium saucepan, mix unflavored gelatine with sugar; blend in water. Let stand 1 minute. Stir over low heat until gelatine is completely dissolved, about 5 minutes. Let cool to room temperature; stir in remaining ingredients. Pour into 9-inch square baking pan; freeze 3 hours or until firm.

With electric mixer or food processor, beat mixture until smooth. Return to pan; freeze 2 hours or until firm. To serve, let stand at room temperature 15 minutes or until slightly softened. Spoon into dessert dishes or stemmed glassware. Garnish, if desired, with fresh mint.
Makes 6 servings; 110 calories per serving with Champagne or sauterne; 90 calories per serving with ginger ale.

Variation: For a Sparkling Citrus Mint Sorbet, increase water to 2 cups; omit Champagne. After gelatine is dissolved, add ¼ cup loosely packed mint leaves and simmer over low heat 5 minutes; strain. Let cool to room temperature, then proceed as above.
78 calories per serving.

Frozen Passion

2 (14-ounce) cans EAGLE® Brand Sweetened Condensed Milk (NOT evaporated milk)
1 (2-liter) bottle *or* 5 (12-ounce) cans carbonated beverage, any flavor

In ice cream freezer container, combine ingredients; mix well. Freeze according to manufacturer's instructions. Store leftovers in freezer.
Makes 2 to 3 quarts.

Passion Shakes: In blender container, combine *one-half* can sweetened condensed milk, *1 (12-ounce) can* carbonated beverage and *3 cups* ice. Blend until smooth. Repeat for additional shakes. Store leftovers in freezer.
Makes 1 or 2 quarts.

Melon Sorbet Cooler

1 envelope KNOX® Unflavored Gelatine
1/2 cup sugar
1 cup water
2 1/2 cups pureed cantaloupe (about 1 large)*
1/3 cup rum (optional)
2 tablespoons lemon juice

In medium saucepan, mix unflavored gelatine with sugar; blend in water. Let stand 1 minute. Stir over low heat until gelatine is completely dissolved, about 5 minutes. Let cool to room temperature; stir in remaining ingredients. Pour into 9-inch square baking pan; freeze 3 hours or until firm.

With electric mixer or food processor, beat mixture until smooth. Return to pan; freeze 2 hours or until firm. To serve, let stand at room temperature 15 minutes or until slightly softened. Garnish, if desired, with fresh mint.
Makes about 8 servings.

***Variation:** Use 2 1/2 cups pureed honeydew melon (about 1/2 medium).

Pudding Ice Cream

2 cups cold light cream or half and half
1 package (4-serving size) JELL-O® Vanilla or Chocolate Flavor Instant Pudding and Pie Filling
3 1/2 cups (8 ounces) COOL WHIP® Non-Dairy Whipped Topping, thawed

Pour cold cream into bowl. Add pudding mix. With electric mixer at low speed, beat until well blended, 1 to 2 minutes. Let stand 5 minutes. Fold in whipped topping. Pour into 2-quart covered plastic container. Freeze until firm, about 6 hours.
Makes 6 cups or 12 servings.

Toffee Crunch Pudding Ice Cream: Prepare Pudding Ice Cream as directed, using vanilla flavor pudding mix and folding in 2/3 cup crushed chocolate-covered toffee bars with the whipped topping.

Rum Raisin Pudding Ice Cream: Prepare Pudding Ice Cream as directed, using vanilla flavor pudding mix. Soak 1/2 cup chopped raisins in 2 tablespoons light rum; fold in with the whipped topping.

Rocky Road Pudding Ice Cream: Prepare Pudding Ice Cream as directed, using chocolate flavor pudding mix and folding in 1 cup miniature marshmallows and 1/2 cup chopped walnuts with the whipped topping.

Cinnamon Walnut Pudding Ice Cream: Prepare Pudding Ice Cream as directed, using vanilla flavor pudding mix and adding 2 tablespoons light brown sugar and 1/2 teaspoon cinnamon to the pudding mix. Add 1/2 cup finely chopped walnuts with the whipped topping.

Fruit Pudding Ice Cream: Prepare Pudding Ice Cream as directed, folding in 1 cup pureed fruit (strawberries, peaches or raspberries) with the whipped topping.

Chocolate Chip Pudding Ice Cream: Prepare Pudding Ice Cream as directed, using chocolate flavor pudding mix and folding in 3/4 cup BAKER'S® Real Semi-Sweet Chocolate Chips with the whipped topping.

Banana Bonanza Ice Cream

2 cups milk
2 cups whipping cream
2 eggs, beaten
1 1/4 cups sugar
2 extra-ripe, medium DOLE™ Bananas
1/2 teaspoon vanilla extract
1/4 teaspoon salt
1/8 teaspoon ground nutmeg

In large saucepan, combine milk, cream, eggs and sugar. Cook and stir over low heat until mixture thickens slightly and coats metal spoon. Cool to room temperature. Puree bananas in blender (1 cup). In large bowl, combine cooled custard, pureed bananas, vanilla, salt and nutmeg. Pour into ice cream freezer can. Freeze according to manufacturer's directions.
Makes 2 quarts.

Almond Creme

2 packages (4 ounces each) BAKER'S® GERMAN'S® Sweet Chocolate
1/4 cup water
2/3 cup sweetened condensed milk
2 cups heavy cream
1/2 teaspoon vanilla
1/2 cup toasted slivered blanched almonds

Melt chocolate in water in saucepan over very low heat, stirring constantly until smooth. Cool. Combine chocolate, condensed milk, cream and vanilla in large bowl of electric mixer. Chill; then whip until soft peaks form. Fold in almonds. Spoon into 9-inch square pan or 1 1/2-quart freezer container. Freeze until firm, about 5 hours. Garnish with additional toasted almonds, if desired.
Makes 8 to 10 servings.

Frozen Chocolate Banana Loaf

1½ cups chocolate wafer cookie crumbs (about 30 wafers)
¼ cup sugar
3 tablespoons margarine or butter, melted
1 (14-ounce) can EAGLE® Brand Sweetened Condensed Milk (NOT evaporated milk)
⅔ cup chocolate flavored syrup
2 small ripe bananas, mashed (¾ cup)
2 cups (1 pint) BORDEN® or MEADOW GOLD® Whipping Cream, whipped (*do not use non-dairy whipped topping*)

Line 9×5-inch loaf pan with aluminum foil, extending foil above sides of pan; butter foil. Combine crumbs, sugar and margarine; press firmly on bottom and halfway up sides of prepared pan. In large bowl, combine sweetened condensed milk, syrup and bananas; mix well. Fold in whipped cream. Pour into prepared pan; cover. Freeze 6 hours or until firm. To serve, remove from pan; peel off foil. Garnish as desired; slice. Return leftovers to freezer.
Makes 8 to 10 servings.

Raspberry Freeze

¼ cup honey
1 8-ounce package PHILADELPHIA BRAND Cream Cheese, softened
1 10-ounce package frozen raspberries, partially thawed, undrained
1 cup banana slices
2 cups KRAFT Miniature Marshmallows
1 cup whipping cream, whipped

Gradually add honey to cream cheese, mixing until well blended. Stir in fruit; fold in marshmallows and whipped cream. Pour into lightly oiled 9-inch square pan; freeze. Place in refrigerator 30 minutes before serving. Cut into squares.
9 servings.

Variations: Prepare mixture as directed. Spoon raspberry mixture into ten 5-ounce paper drinking cups; insert wooden sticks in center. Freeze.

Prepare mixture as directed. Pour raspberry mixture into lightly oiled 9-inch springform pan with ring insert; freeze. Place in refrigerator 1 hour before serving. Loosen dessert from rim of pan; remove rim of pan.

Frozen Pudding Sandwiches

1½ cups cold milk
½ cup peanut butter (optional)*
1 package (4-serving size) JELL-O® Instant Pudding and Pie Filling, any flavor
24 graham cracker squares*

Gradually add milk to peanut butter in bowl, blending until smooth. Add pudding mix. With electric mixer at low speed, beat until well blended, 1 to 2 minutes. Let stand 5 minutes. Spread filling about ½ inch thick on 12 of the graham cracker squares. Top with remaining squares, pressing lightly and smoothing around edges with spatula. Freeze until firm, about 3 hours. Sandwiches can be stored, wrapped, in freezer 3 to 4 days.
Makes 12 sandwiches.

*When omitting peanut butter, reduce squares to 18; makes 9 sandwiches.

Frozen Chocolate Bombe

1 purchased pound cake
¼ cup almond liqueur*
1¾ cups heavy cream**
3 tablespoons sugar**
¾ teaspoon vanilla**
2 squares BAKER'S® Semi-Sweet Chocolate, melted and cooled
¼ cup chopped pecans
2 tablespoons finely chopped drained maraschino cherries
3 squares BAKER'S® Semi-Sweet Chocolate
2 tablespoons butter or margarine

Thinly slice pound cake; diagonally cut each piece in half. Line 1½-quart bowl with plastic wrap or strips of waxed paper; then line with cake pieces, trimming as necessary to line bowl completely. Sprinkle cake with liqueur. Set aside remaining cake pieces.

Whip the cream with sugar and vanilla until soft peaks form. Fold melted chocolate into half of the whipped cream. Spoon into cake-lined bowl. Fold pecans and cherries into remaining whipped cream; spoon into bowl over chocolate mixture. Cover completely with remaining cake pieces. Freeze until firm, about 4 hours.

Melt 3 squares chocolate with the butter in saucepan over very low heat, stirring constantly until smooth. Cool slightly. Invert frozen bombe onto serving plate. Remove plastic wrap. Spread chocolate quickly and evenly over cake. Freeze about 10 minutes, or until chocolate is firm. If frozen longer, remove from freezer 20 minutes before serving (for ease in cutting).
Makes 8 to 10 servings.

*Or use ¼ cup fruit nectar and ⅛ teaspoon almond extract

**Or use 3½ cups thawed COOL WHIP® Whipped Topping.

Aloha Cheesecake

1 cup vanilla wafer crumbs
¼ cup PARKAY Margarine, melted

* * *

2 8-ounce packages
    PHILADELPHIA BRAND
    Cream Cheese, softened
⅓ cup sugar
2 tablespoons milk
2 eggs
½ cup chopped macadamia nuts, toasted
1 8¼-ounce can crushed pineapple, drained
1 kiwi, peeled, sliced

Combine crumbs and margarine; press onto bottom of 9-inch springform pan. Bake at 350°, 10 minutes.

Combine cream cheese, sugar and milk, mixing at medium speed on electric mixer until well blended. Add eggs, one at a time, mixing well after each addition. Stir in nuts; pour over crust. Bake at 350°, 45 minutes. Loosen cake from rim of pan; cool before removing rim of pan. Chill. Before serving, top with fruit.
10 to 12 servings.

Miniature Cheesecakes

⅓ cup graham cracker crumbs
1 tablespoon sugar
1 tablespoon PARKAY Margarine, melted

* * *

1 8-ounce package
    PHILADELPHIA BRAND
    Cream Cheese, softened
¼ cup sugar
1½ teaspoons lemon juice
½ teaspoon grated lemon peel
¼ teaspoon vanilla
1 egg
    KRAFT Strawberry or Apricot Preserves

Combine crumbs, sugar and margarine. Press rounded measuring tablespoonful of crumb mixture onto bottom of each of six paper-lined muffin cups. Bake at 325°, 5 minutes.

Combine cream cheese, sugar, juice, peel and vanilla, mixing at medium speed on electric mixer until well blended. Blend in egg; pour over crust, filling each cup ¾ full. Bake at 325°, 25 minutes. Cool before removing from pan. Chill. Top with preserves just before serving.
6 servings.

Variation: Substitute fresh fruit for KRAFT Preserves.

Make Ahead: Wrap chilled cheesecakes individually in plastic wrap; freeze. Let stand at room temperature 40 minutes before serving.

Chocolate Caramel Pecan Cheesecake

2 cups vanilla wafer crumbs
6 tablespoons PARKAY Margarine, melted

* * *

1 14-ounce bag KRAFT Caramels
1 5-ounce can evaporated milk
1 cup chopped pecans, toasted
2 8-ounce packages
    PHILADELPHIA BRAND
    Cream Cheese, softened
½ cup sugar
1 teaspoon vanilla
2 eggs
½ cup semi-sweet chocolate pieces, melted

Combine crumbs and margarine; press onto bottom and sides of 9-inch springform pan. Bake at 350°, 10 minutes.

In 1½-quart heavy saucepan, melt caramels with milk over low heat, stirring frequently, until smooth. Pour over crust. Top with pecans. Combine cream cheese, sugar and vanilla, mixing at medium speed on electric mixer until well blended. Add eggs, one at a time, mixing well after each addition. Blend in chocolate; pour over pecans. Bake at 350°, 40 minutes. Loosen cake from rim of pan; cool before removing rim of pan. Chill. Garnish with whipped cream, additional chopped nuts and maraschino cherries, if desired.
10 to 12 servings.

Northwest Cheesecake Supreme

1 cup graham cracker crumbs
3 tablespoons sugar
3 tablespoons PARKAY Margarine, melted

* * *

4 8-ounce packages
    PHILADELPHIA BRAND
    Cream Cheese, softened
1 cup sugar
3 tablespoons flour
4 eggs
1 cup sour cream
1 tablespoon vanilla
1 21-ounce can cherry pie filling

Combine crumbs, sugar and margarine; press onto bottom of 9-inch springform pan. Bake at 325°, 10 minutes.

Combine cream cheese, sugar and flour, mixing at medium speed on electric mixer until well blended. Add eggs, one at a time, mixing well after each addition. Blend in sour cream and vanilla; pour over crust. Bake at 450°, 10 minutes. Reduce oven temperature to 250°; continue baking 1 hour. Loosen cake from rim of pan; cool before removing rim of pan. Chill. Top with cherry pie filling just before serving.
10 to 12 servings.

Variation: Substitute 1½ cups finely chopped nuts and 2 tablespoons sugar for graham cracker crumbs and sugar in crust.

Peaches in Port

6 to 8 large fresh peaches,
peeled and cut into sixths
2 teaspoons lemon juice
1/4 cup tawny port wine
2 tablespoons butter or
margarine

Arrange peaches on 24×18-inch piece of heavy-duty foil. Sprinkle with lemon juice and port; dot with butter. Fold foil loosely around fruit and seal edges tightly. Grill packet, on covered grill, over medium-hot **KINGS-FORD® Charcoal Briquets** about 15 minutes or until fruit is hot, turning packet once.
Makes 4 to 6 servings.

Frozen Mocha Cheesecake

1 1/4 cups chocolate wafer cookie
crumbs (about 24 wafers)
1/4 cup margarine or butter,
melted
1/4 cup sugar
1 (8-ounce) package cream
cheese, softened
1 (14-ounce) can EAGLE® Brand
Sweetened Condensed Milk
(NOT evaporated milk)
2/3 cup chocolate flavored syrup
1 to 2 tablespoons instant
coffee
1 teaspoon hot water
1 cup (1/2 pint) BORDEN® or
MEADOW GOLD® Whipping
Cream, whipped
Additional chocolate crumbs,
optional

Combine crumbs, margarine and sugar; press firmly on bottom and up side of 8- or 9-inch springform pan or 13×9-inch baking pan. In large mixer bowl, beat cheese until fluffy. Gradually beat in sweetened condensed milk and chocolate syrup until smooth. In small bowl, dissolve coffee in water; add to cheese mixture. Mix well. Fold in whipped cream. Pour into prepared pan; cover. Freeze 6 hours or overnight. Garnish with additional chocolate crumbs if desired. Return leftovers to freezer.
Makes one 8- or 9-inch cheesecake.

Butterscotch Cheesecake

1/3 cup margarine or butter,
melted
1 1/2 cups graham cracker crumbs
1/3 cup firmly packed brown sugar
1 (14-ounce) can EAGLE® Brand
Sweetened Condensed Milk
(NOT evaporated milk)
3/4 cup cold water
1 (3 5/8-ounce) package
butterscotch pudding and
pie filling mix
3 (8-ounce) packages cream
cheese, softened
3 eggs
1 teaspoon vanilla extract
Whipped cream
Crushed hard butterscotch
candy

Preheat oven to 375°. Combine margarine, crumbs and sugar; press firmly on bottom of 9-inch springform pan. In medium saucepan, combine sweetened condensed milk and water; mix well. Stir in pudding mix. Over medium heat, cook and stir until thickened and bubbly. In large mixer bowl, beat cheese until fluffy. Beat in eggs and vanilla then pudding mixture. Pour into prepared pan. Bake 50 minutes or until golden brown around edge (center will be soft). Cool to room temperature. Chill thoroughly. Garnish with whipped cream and crushed candy. Refrigerate leftovers.
Makes one 9-inch cheesecake.

Piña Colada Cheesecake

1 1/2 cups vanilla wafer or graham
cracker crumbs
1/2 cup flaked coconut, optional
3 tablespoons butter or
margarine, melted
1 can (8 ounces) DOLE®
Crushed Pineapple
3 packages (8 ounces each)
cream cheese, softened
3 eggs
1 cup sugar
1 cup dairy sour cream
3 tablespoons dark rum
2 teaspoons coconut extract
Pineapple Topping (recipe
follows)

Preheat oven to 350°. In medium bowl, combine cookie crumbs, coconut and butter. Press onto bottom and sides of 9-inch springform pan. Bake 10 minutes. Cool.

Drain pineapple. In large bowl, beat cream cheese, eggs and sugar. Stir pineapple, sour cream, rum and coconut extract into cream cheese mixture. Pour into prepared crust. Bake in preheated oven 50 to 55 minutes or until set. Cool to room temperature; refrigerate until chilled. Spread Pineapple Topping over cheesecake just before serving.
Makes 16 servings.
PINEAPPLE TOPPING: In saucepan, combine 20 ounces (1 can) undrained Dole® Crushed Pineapple, 1/2 cup sugar, 1 tablespoon dark rum and 1 tablespoon cornstarch. Cook, stirring constantly, until thickened and clear. Cool.

"Philly" Fruit Clouds

1 8-ounce package
  PHILADELPHIA BRAND
  Cream Cheese, softened
½ cup sugar
1 tablespoon lemon juice
2 teaspoons grated lemon peel
1 cup whipping cream, whipped
  Assorted fruit

Combine cream cheese, sugar, juice and peel, mixing until well blended. Fold in whipped cream. With back of spoon, shape on wax paper-lined cookie sheet to form ten shells; freeze. Fill each shell with fruit. Garnish with fresh mint, if desired.
10 servings.

Variations: Prepare cream cheese mixture as directed. Spread into 8-inch square pan; freeze. Cut into squares; top with fruit.

Substitute *Light* PHILADELPHIA BRAND Neufchâtel Cheese for Cream Cheese.

Cheddar Cheese Pears

3 fresh pears, peeled, cored and
  cut into halves *or* 1 can
  (29 ounces) pear halves,
  drained
2 teaspoons grated lemon peel
2 tablespoons fresh lemon juice
½ cup shredded Cheddar cheese
  (about 2 ounces)

Arrange pears on large square of heavy-duty foil. Sprinkle lemon peel and juice over pears. Fill pear halves with cheese. Fold up foil around pears; seal edges tightly. Grill packet over medium-hot **KINGSFORD® Charcoal Briquets** 15 minutes or until pears are hot and cheese is soft.
Makes 6 servings.

Hot Fruit Compote

1 (20-ounce) can pineapple
  chunks, drained
1 (17-ounce) can pitted dark
  sweet cherries, drained
1 (16-ounce) can sliced peaches,
  drained
1 (16-ounce) can pear halves,
  drained
1 (11-ounce) can mandarin
  orange segments, drained
¼ cup margarine or butter
½ cup firmly packed light brown
  sugar
½ cup orange juice
¼ cup REALEMON® Lemon Juice
  from Concentrate
½ teaspoon ground cinnamon
  Sour cream and brown sugar

Preheat oven to 350°. In 13×9-inch baking dish, combine fruits. In small saucepan, melt margarine; add sugar, orange juice, ReaLemon® brand and cinnamon. Pour mixture over fruits. Bake 20 minutes or until hot. Serve warm with sour cream and brown sugar.
Makes 8 to 10 servings.

Fresh Pineapple Melba

2 packages (10 ounces each)
  frozen raspberries, thawed
  Sugar
2 tablespoons cornstarch
3 tablespoons raspberry-
  flavored brandy
1 DOLE™ Fresh Pineapple
3 cups (1½ pints) vanilla ice
  cream
  Fresh raspberries for garnish,
  optional

In 2-quart saucepan, combine raspberries and their juice, sugar to taste and cornstarch. Stir until cornstarch is dissolved. Cook over medium heat, stirring constantly, until sauce turns clear and is slightly thickened. Remove from heat. Stir in brandy. Place plastic wrap directly on surface of sauce to cover. Refrigerate.

Twist crown from pineapple. Cut pineapple lengthwise into quarters. Remove fruit from shells with curved knife. Trim off core and cut fruit into chunks. Refrigerate, covered, until serving time.

To serve, spoon pineapple into 6 dessert dishes. Top each with scoop of ice cream. Drizzle with raspberry sauce; garnish with fresh raspberries, if desired.
Makes 6 servings.

Almond-Crumb Peaches

8 PEPPERIDGE FARM® Almond
  Supreme Cookies, finely
  crushed
2 tablespoons almond-flavored
  liqueur
4 ripe peaches, halved and
  pitted
  Whipped cream for garnish

To Microwave:
1. In small bowl, stir together cookies and liqueur.
2. Arrange peaches, cut-side up, in circular pattern on 10-inch microwave-safe plate. Spoon some of the cookie mixture into center of each peach. Microwave, uncovered, on HIGH 4 minutes or until peaches are tender, rotating dish once during cooking. Garnish with whipped cream.
Makes 4 servings.

Note: You can substitute 8 canned peach halves, drained, for fresh peaches. Reduce cooking time to 2 minutes or until peaches are heated through.

Fruit Kabobs with Whiskey Baste

2 tablespoons honey
2 tablespoons whiskey
1 tablespoon lemon juice
1 can (8 ounces) pineapple chunks, drained
1 large banana, diagonally sliced into 1-inch pieces
1 orange, peeled and sectioned
8 maraschino cherries

In large bowl, combine honey, whiskey and lemon juice; add pineapple chunks, banana pieces, orange sections and cherries. Gently toss to coat fruit well. Cover and refrigerate up to 2 hours or until ready to grill.

Remove fruit with slotted spoon, reserving whiskey baste. Alternately thread fruit on skewers. Grill fruit kabobs, on covered grill, over medium-low **KINGSFORD® Charcoal Briquets** 5 to 10 minutes or until fruit is warmed through, basting frequently with whiskey baste.
Makes 4 servings.

Spiced Lemon Pears

1½ cups water
1 cup firmly packed light brown sugar
¼ cup REALEMON® Lemon Juice from Concentrate
2 cinnamon sticks
6 whole cloves
4 fresh pears, halved, pared and core removed

In large saucepan, combine all ingredients except pears. Bring to a boil; cook and stir until sugar dissolves. Add pears; cover and simmer 10 minutes or until pears are tender. Serve warm or chilled as a dessert, meat accompaniment or salad.
Makes 4 servings.

Microwave: In 2-quart round baking dish, combine all ingredients except pears. Cover with plastic wrap; microwave on full power (high) 6 minutes or until mixture boils. Stir; add pears. Cover; microwave 6 minutes or until tender. Proceed as above.

Snow Topped Apples

2 medium baking apples
2 teaspoons raisins
2 teaspoons chopped nuts
Dash of cinnamon
2 teaspoons PARKAY Margarine
2 tablespoons *Light* PHILADELPHIA BRAND Neufchâtel Cheese

Core apples; remove peel around top of apples. Place each in 10-ounce custard cup. Fill center of apples with combined raisins, nuts and cinnamon; dot with margarine. Bake at 375°, 25 to 30 minutes or until soft. Top warm apples with neufchâtel cheese. Sprinkle with additional chopped nuts, if desired.
2 servings.

Variation: Substitute Soft PHILADELPHIA BRAND Cream Cheese for Neufchâtel Cheese.

Microwave: Prepare apples as directed. Cover custard cups with plastic wrap vented at one edge. Microwave on High 2½ to 3 minutes or until apples are soft. Serve as directed.

Bananas Foster

4 firm, small DOLE™ Bananas
½ cup brown sugar, packed
¼ cup butter or margarine
Dash cinnamon
⅓ cup light rum
Coffee or vanilla ice cream

Cut bananas into halves lengthwise, then crosswise. In 10-inch skillet, heat brown sugar and butter until sugar is melted. Cook and stir 2 minutes or until slightly thickened. Add bananas; cook slowly 1 to 2 minutes or until bananas are heated and glazed. Sprinkle lightly with cinnamon. Add rum. Carefully ignite rum with long match. Spoon liquid over bananas until flames die out, about 1 minute. Serve warm over ice cream.
Makes 4 servings.

Cherry Crunch

1 can (21 ounces) cherry pie filling
1 teaspoon lemon juice
1 package DUNCAN HINES® Deluxe White Cake Mix
½ cup chopped nuts, if desired
½ cup (1 stick) butter or margarine, melted
Sweetened whipped cream or ice cream

1. Preheat oven to 350°F.
2. Spread pie filling in bottom of ungreased 8×8×2-inch pan. Sprinkle with lemon juice. Combine dry cake mix, nuts and melted butter (mixture will be crumbly). Sprinkle over pie filling.
3. Bake at 350°F for 40 to 50 minutes or until golden brown. Serve warm with sweetened whipped cream or ice cream.
12 servings.

Fruited Tilt

1 package (4-serving size)
   JELL-O® Brand Gelatin, any
   flavor
3/4 cup boiling water
1/2 cup cold water
   Ice cubes
1 cup sliced or diced fresh fruit*
1 cup thawed COOL WHIP® Non-
   Dairy Whipped Topping

Dissolve gelatin in boiling water. Combine cold water and ice cubes to make 1¼ cups. Add to gelatin, stirring until slightly thickened. Remove any unmelted ice. Fold in fruit. Spoon half of the fruited gelatin into individual parfait glasses. Tilt glasses in refrigerator by catching bases between bars of rack and leaning tops against wall; chill until set. Spoon whipped topping into glasses; top with remaining fruited gelatin. Stand glasses upright. Chill about 30 minutes.
Makes 6 to 8 servings.

*Do not use fresh pineapple, kiwifruit, mango, papaya or figs.

Molded Strawberries Romanoff

1 pint strawberries, hulled
2 tablespoons sugar
2 packages (4-serving size) or
   1 package (8-serving size)
   JELL-O® Brand Strawberry
   Flavor Gelatin
2 cups boiling water
2 tablespoons brandy*
1 tablespoon orange liqueur*
1¾ cups thawed COOL WHIP®
   Non-Dairy Whipped Topping

Slice strawberries, reserving a few whole berries for garnish, if desired. Sprinkle sliced berries with sugar; let stand 15 minutes. Drain, reserving liquid. Add enough cold water to liquid to make 1 cup. Dissolve gelatin in boiling water. Measure 3/4 cup of the gelatin and add brandy, orange liqueur and 1/2 cup of the measured liquid. Chill until slightly thickened. Fold in whipped topping. Pour into 6-cup mold. Chill until set but not firm.

Add remaining measured liquid to remaining gelatin. Chill until thickened; fold in sliced berries. Spoon over creamy layer in mold. Chill until firm, about 4 hours. Unmold. Garnish with reserved berries.
Makes 6 cups or 12 servings.

Substitution: Use 1/2 teaspoon brandy extract and 3 tablespoons orange juice for the brandy and orange liqueur.

Apple Custard Dessert

1 package DUNCAN HINES®
   Butter Recipe Golden Cake
   Mix
1 cup shredded or flaked
   coconut
1/2 cup (1 stick) butter or
   margarine
6 medium apples, pared, cored
   and cut in eighths (about
   6 cups)
1 cup water
1/4 cup lemon juice

1. Preheat oven to 350°F. Grease 13×9×2-inch baking pan.
2. Combine dry cake mix and coconut in large bowl. Cut in butter with pastry blender or two knives until crumbly.
3. Arrange apple slices in greased pan. Sprinkle crumb mixture over apples. Combine water and lemon juice; pour over all.
4. Bake at 350°F for 45 to 50 minutes or until top is lightly browned and set. Cool before serving.
12 to 16 servings.

Pears au Chocolat

4 fresh pears
1/2 cup sugar
1 cup water
1 teaspoon vanilla
6 tablespoons finely chopped
   nuts
2 tablespoons confectioners'
   sugar
1 teaspoon milk
   Chocolate Sauce

Core pears from bottom, leaving stems intact. Peel pears. Slice piece off bottom to make a flat base. Combine sugar and water in medium saucepan; add pears. Cover; simmer over low heat 10 to 20 minutes (depending on ripeness) or just until pears are soft. Remove from heat; add vanilla. Cool pears in syrup; chill. Combine nuts, confectioners' sugar and milk in small bowl. To serve, drain pears; spoon nut mixture into cavities. Place pears on dessert plates. Prepare Chocolate Sauce; pour or spoon sauce onto each pear. Serve with remaining sauce.
4 servings.

Chocolate Sauce

6 tablespoons water
6 tablespoons sugar
1/4 cup butter or margarine
1¹/3 cups HERSHEY'S MINI CHIPS
   Semi-Sweet Chocolate

Combine water, sugar and butter in small saucepan; bring to full boil. Remove from heat; stir in MINI CHIPS Chocolate. Stir until chocolate has completely melted; beat or whisk until smooth. Cool.

Fruit Juice Gelatine Cooler

- 1 envelope KNOX® Unflavored Gelatine
- 2 to 4 tablespoons sugar
- 2 cups fruit juice, heated to boiling*

In medium bowl, mix unflavored gelatine with sugar; add hot juice and stir until gelatine is completely dissolved, about 5 minutes. Pour into 2-cup bowl, mold or dessert dishes; chill until firm, about 3 hours. To serve, unmold onto serving platter.
Makes about 4 servings.

*Do not use fresh or frozen pineapple juice.

Lime Chiffon Squares

- 1/4 cup margarine or butter, melted
- 1 cup graham cracker crumbs
- 1 (3-ounce) package lime flavor gelatin
- 1 cup boiling water
- 1 (14-ounce) can EAGLE® Brand Sweetened Condensed Milk (NOT evaporated milk)
- 1 (8-ounce) can crushed pineapple, undrained
- 2 tablespoons REALIME® Lime Juice from Concentrate
- 4 cups CAMPFIRE® Miniature Marshmallows
- 1 cup (1/2 pint) BORDEN® or MEADOW GOLD® Whipping Cream, whipped

Combine margarine and crumbs; press firmly on bottom of 9-inch square *or* 12×7-inch baking dish. In large mixing bowl, dissolve gelatin in water; stir in sweetened condensed milk, pineapple and ReaLime® brand. Fold in marshmallows and whipped cream. Pour into prepared dish. Chill 2 hours or until set. Garnish as desired. Refrigerate leftovers.
Makes 10 to 12 servings.

Flaming Pineapple

- 1 fresh pineapple
- 1/2 cup packed light brown sugar
- 1/2 teaspoon ground cinnamon
- 1/8 teaspoon freshly ground nutmeg
- 1/4 cup butter or margarine
- 1/2 cup light rum
  Ice cream, whipped cream or chilled soft custard (optional)

Cut pineapple in half lengthwise, leaving on green top. Cut each half lengthwise into four sections. Carefully cut pineapple away from peel. Remove core, then cut pineapple into 1-inch chunks; rearrange pineapple chunks on peel. Place in large baking pan or foil pan. Sprinkle with brown sugar, cinnamon and nutmeg; dot with butter. Place pan on edge of grill. Heat pineapple, on covered grill, over medium-hot **KINGSFORD® Charcoal Briquets** 10 minutes; remove pan from grill.

In small saucepan, heat rum on range-top over low heat just until hot. Carefully ignite with match; pour flaming rum over pineapple, stirring sauce and spooning over pineapple. Serve with ice cream.
Makes 8 servings.

Fruit Whip

- 3/4 cup boiling water
- 1 package (4-serving size) JELL-O® Brand Gelatin, any flavor
- 1/2 cup cold water or fruit juice Ice cubes
- 1 cup fresh or canned fruit (optional)*

Pour boiling water into blender. Add gelatin. Cover and blend at low speed until gelatin is completely dissolved, about 30 seconds. Combine cold water and ice cubes to make 1 1/4 cups. Add to gelatin and stir until ice is partially melted; then blend at high speed for 30 seconds. Pour into dessert glasses or serving bowl. Spoon in fruit. Chill until firm, 20 to 30 minutes. Dessert layers as it chills. Garnish with additional fruit and mint, if desired.
Makes 4 1/2 cups or 6 servings.

*See note, page 310 (Fruited Tilt).

Applesauce Yogurt Dessert

- 1 package (4-serving size) JELL-O® Brand Sugar Free Gelatin, any red flavor
- 1 cup boiling water
- 3/4 cup chilled unsweetened applesauce
- 1/4 teaspoon cinnamon
- 1/2 cup vanilla yogurt

Dissolve gelatin in boiling water. Measure 3/4 cup of the gelatin; add applesauce and cinnamon. Pour into individual dessert glasses or serving bowl. Chill until set but not firm.

Chill remaining gelatin until slightly thickened. Blend in yogurt. Spoon over gelatin in glasses. Chill until set, about 2 hours. Garnish with additional yogurt and mint leaves, if desired.
Makes 2 cups or 4 servings.

Microwave Hershey Bar Mousse

1 HERSHEY'S Milk Chocolate
    Bar (8 ounces), broken into
    pieces
1/4 cup water
2 eggs, beaten
1 cup heavy or whipping cream

Microwave: Combine chocolate bar pieces and water in medium microproof bowl. Microwave at HIGH (100%) for 1½ to 2 minutes or until chocolate is softened and mixture is melted and smooth when stirred. Stir in eggs. Microwave at MEDIUM (50%) for 1½ to 2½ minutes or until mixture is hot; *do not boil*. Cool slightly. Whip cream until stiff; fold into cooled chocolate mixture. Pour into 8-inch square pan. Cover; freeze until firm. Cut into squares.
4 servings.

Ice Cream and Orange Dessert

3/4 cup boiling water
1 package (4-serving size)
    JELL-O® Brand Orange,
    Peach or Lemon Flavor
    Gelatin
1 cup (1/2 pint) vanilla ice cream
1/2 cup crushed ice
1 medium orange, peeled and
    cut into bite-size pieces

Pour boiling water into blender. Add gelatin. Cover and blend at low speed until gelatin is completely dissolved, about 30 seconds. Add ice cream and crushed ice. Blend at high speed until ice is melted, about 30 seconds. Pour into bowl. Stir in orange. Chill until firm, about 1 hour. When ready to serve, spoon into flat-bottom ice cream cups or dessert dishes.
Makes about 3 cups or 6 servings.

Self-Layering Dessert

3/4 cup boiling water
1 package (4-serving size)
    JELL-O® Brand Gelatin, any
    flavor
1/2 cup cold water
    Ice cubes
1/2 cup thawed COOL WHIP® Non-
    Dairy Whipped Topping

Pour boiling water into blender. Add gelatin. Cover and blend at low speed until gelatin is completely dissolved, about 30 seconds. Combine cold water and ice cubes to make 1¼ cups. Add to gelatin and stir until ice is partially melted. Then add whipped topping; blend at high speed for 30 seconds. Pour into dessert glasses. Chill about 30 minutes. Dessert layers as it chills. Garnish as desired.
Makes 3 cups or 6 servings.

Piña Colada Ring

2 envelopes unflavored gelatin
2 1/4 cups (18 ounces) pineapple
    juice, unsweetened
1 package (8 ounces) Neufchatel
    cheese
1/3 cup sugar
1 teaspoon grated orange rind
1 teaspoon grated lemon rind
1 1/2 teaspoons rum extract
1/2 cup dry CARNATION® Nonfat
    Dry Milk
1/2 cup ice water
2 tablespoons lemon juice
1/2 cup toasted flake coconut
    Fresh fruit

Soften gelatin in pineapple juice; heat to dissolve. Pour into blender container. Add Neufchatel cheese, sugar, rinds, and rum extract. Cover; blend until smooth. Pour into large bowl. Chill until mixture mounds from a spoon. Place nonfat dry milk, ice water, and lemon juice in small mixer bowl. Beat on high speed until stiff peaks form, 4 to 6 minutes. Fold into gelatin mixture. Spoon into 6-cup ring mold. Chill until firm. Unmold onto serving platter. Sprinkle with toasted coconut. Garnish outer edge and center of mold with fresh fruit.
Makes 6 cups.

Fruited Fruit Juice Gelatin

2 packages (4-serving size) or
    1 package (8-serving size)
    JELL-O® Brand Orange
    Flavor Sugar Free Gelatin*
1 1/2 cups boiling water
1 cup cold apple juice*
    Ice cubes
1 1/2 cups diced apples*

Completely dissolve gelatin in boiling water. Combine cold fruit juice and ice cubes to make 2½ cups. Add to gelatin, stirring until slightly thickened. Remove any unmelted ice. Stir in apples. Pour into bowl or individual dessert glasses. Chill until set, about 4 hours. Garnish with celery leaves and additional fruit, if desired.
Makes 5 cups or 10 servings.
*Additional Flavor Combinations: Use strawberry flavor gelatin with canned pineapple juice, 1½ cups diced apples and ¼ cup chopped nuts.

Use raspberry flavor gelatin with cranberry juice cocktail, 1½ cups diced oranges, 2 tablespoons chopped nuts and ¼ cup chopped celery.

Use strawberry-banana flavor gelatin with orange juice and 1½ cups sliced bananas.

Use strawberry flavor gelatin with grape juice and 1½ cups seedless green grapes.

Chocolate-Berry Parfaits

Chocolate Cream Pudding (see Index)
1 package (10 ounces) frozen sliced strawberries, thawed, or 1 cup sweetened sliced fresh strawberries
1 cup heavy or whipping cream*
¼ cup confectioners' sugar*
Fresh strawberries (optional)

Prepare Chocolate Cream Pudding; cool completely. Drain strawberries; puree in blender or sieve to equal ½ to ¾ cup. Beat cream and confectioners' sugar until stiff; fold in strawberry puree. Alternately layer chocolate pudding and strawberry cream in parfait glasses. Chill until set. Garnish with strawberries.
8 to 10 servings.

*You may substitute 2 cups frozen non-dairy whipped topping, thawed, for the cream and confectioners' sugar.

Fresh Fruit Parfaits

1 envelope KNOX® Unflavored Gelatine
1¾ cups cold water
9 packets aspartame sweetener or 3 tablespoons sugar
⅓ cup fresh lemon juice (about 2 lemons)
1 medium peach or nectarine, sliced
1 medium banana, sliced
1½ cups seedless green grapes, halved
1½ cups sliced strawberries

In medium saucepan, sprinkle unflavored gelatine over ½ cup cold water; let stand 1 minute. Stir over low heat until gelatine is completely dissolved, about 3 minutes. Stir in sweetener until dissolved, then add lemon juice and remaining 1¼ cups water.

In large bowl, combine fruit. Into 6 (8 ounce) parfait or dessert glasses, evenly divide fruit. Evenly pour gelatine mixture over fruit to cover; chill until firm, about 3 hours.
Makes 6 servings; 80 calories per serving with aspartame sweetener; 98 calories per serving with sugar.

Cookies and Cream Parfaits

1 envelope KNOX® Unflavored Gelatine
¼ cup cold water
2 cups (1 pint) vanilla or chocolate ice cream, softened
1 cup (½ pint) whipping or heavy cream
22 chocolate sandwich cookies
1 teaspoon vanilla extract

In small saucepan, sprinkle unflavored gelatine over cold water; let stand 1 minute. Stir over low heat until gelatine is completely dissolved, about 3 minutes. Remove from heat and let stand until lukewarm, about 1 minute.

In blender or food processor, process ice cream, whipping cream, 10 cookies and vanilla until blended. While processing, through feed cap, gradually add lukewarm gelatine mixture and process until blended. Let stand until mixture is slightly thickened, about 5 minutes.

Meanwhile, coarsely crush remaining 12 cookies. In parfait glasses or dessert dishes, alternately layer gelatine mixture with crushed cookies; chill until set, about 2 hours. Garnish, if desired, with whipped cream and additional cookies.
Makes about 6 servings.

Elegant Chocolate Mousse

3 squares BAKER'S® Unsweetened Chocolate
¾ cup water
¾ cup sugar
⅛ teaspoon salt
3 egg yolks, slightly beaten
1½ teaspoons vanilla
1¾ cups heavy cream*
3 tablespoons sugar*
¾ teaspoon vanilla*

Melt chocolate in water in saucepan over very low heat, stirring constantly until smooth. Stir in ¾ cup sugar and the salt. Bring to a boil over medium heat, stirring constantly. Reduce heat and simmer 5 minutes, stirring constantly.

Blend a small amount of the hot mixture into egg yolks; stir into remaining hot mixture. Cook and stir 1 minute longer. Cool to room temperature; then add 1½ teaspoons vanilla. Whip the cream with 3 tablespoons sugar and ¾ teaspoon vanilla until soft peaks form. Gradually blend in chocolate mixture. Spoon into 9-inch square pan or 1½-quart freezer container. Freeze until firm, at least 6 hours.
Makes 8 servings.

*Or use 3½ cups thawed COOL WHIP® Non-Dairy Whipped Topping.

Quick Chocolate Mousse

1 (14-ounce) can EAGLE® Brand Sweetened Condensed Milk (NOT evaporated milk)
1 (4-serving size) package *instant* chocolate flavor pudding and pie filling mix
1 cup cold water
1 cup (½ pint) BORDEN® or MEADOW GOLD® Whipping Cream, whipped

In large mixer bowl, beat sweetened condensed milk, pudding mix and water; chill 5 minutes. Fold in whipped cream. Spoon into serving dishes; chill. Garnish as desired.
Makes 8 to 10 servings.

Fruit Glazed Baked Custards

3 eggs
1 (14-ounce) can EAGLE® Brand Sweetened Condensed Milk (NOT evaporated milk)
1 cup water
1 teaspoon vanilla extract
½ cup red currant jelly
2 tablespoons orange-flavored liqueur *or* orange juice
1 tablespoon cornstarch
Few drops red food coloring, optional
Fresh strawberries or other fruit

Preheat oven to 350°. In medium mixing bowl, beat eggs; stir in sweetened condensed milk, water and vanilla. Pour equal portions of mixture into six 6-ounce custard cups. Set cups in shallow pan; fill pan with 1 inch hot water. Bake 45 to 50 minutes or until knife inserted in center comes out clean. Cool. In small saucepan, combine jelly, liqueur and cornstarch. Cook and stir until jelly melts and mixture comes to a boil. Stir in food coloring if desired. Cool to room temperature. Invert custards onto serving plates. Top with sauce and strawberries. Refrigerate leftovers.
Makes 6 servings.

Creamy Banana Pudding

1 (14-ounce) can EAGLE® Brand Sweetened Condensed Milk (NOT evaporated milk)
1½ cups cold water
1 (3½-ounce) package instant vanilla pudding and pie filling mix
2 cups (1 pint) BORDEN® or MEADOW GOLD® Whipping Cream, whipped
36 vanilla wafers
3 medium bananas, sliced and dipped in lemon juice

In large mixing bowl, combine sweetened condensed milk and water. Add pudding mix; beat until well blended. Chill 5 minutes. Fold in whipped cream. Spoon *1 cup* pudding mixture into 2½-quart round glass serving bowl. Top with one-third each of the vanilla wafers, bananas and pudding. Repeat layering twice, ending with pudding mixture. Chill thoroughly. Garnish as desired. Refrigerate leftovers.
Makes 8 to 10 servings.
Tip: Mixture can be layered in individual serving dishes.

Strawberry-Chocolate Bavarian Cream

1 package (10 ounces) frozen sliced strawberries, thawed
2 envelopes unflavored gelatine
½ cup sugar
1 cup HERSHEY'S Semi-Sweet Chocolate Chips
2¼ cups milk
1 teaspoon vanilla
2 cups heavy or whipping cream
1 teaspoon vanilla
2 or 3 drops red food color

Drain strawberries; reserve syrup. Add water to syrup to equal ¾ cup. Stir gelatine into liquid; set aside. Puree or mash berries to equal ½ cup; reserve.

Combine sugar, chocolate chips and ½ cup of the milk in medium saucepan. Cook over low heat, stirring constantly, until mixture is smooth and very hot. Add gelatine mixture, stirring until gelatine is dissolved. Remove from heat; add remaining 1¾ cups milk and 1 teaspoon vanilla. Pour into bowl; chill, stirring occasionally, until mixture mounds when dropped from a spoon.

Whip 1 cup of the cream until stiff; fold into chocolate mixture. Pour into oiled 5- or 6-cup mold; chill until firm. Whip remaining 1 cup cream and 1 teaspoon vanilla in small mixer bowl until stiff. Fold in reserved puree and food color. Unmold Bavarian; garnish with strawberry mixture.
8 to 10 servings.

Old-Fashioned Rice Pudding

4 cups cold milk
1 cup MINUTE® Rice
1 package (4-serving size) JELL-O® Vanilla or Coconut Cream Flavor Pudding and Pie Filling
¼ cup raisins (optional)
1 egg, well beaten
¼ teaspoon ground cinnamon
⅛ teaspoon ground nutmeg

Combine milk, rice, pudding mix, raisins and egg in medium saucepan. Bring to a full boil over medium heat, stirring constantly. Remove from heat. Cool 5 minutes, stirring twice. Pour into individual dessert dishes or serving bowl. Sprinkle with cinnamon and nutmeg; serve warm. (For chilled pudding, place plastic wrap directly on hot pudding. Cool slightly; then chill about 1 hour. Stir before serving; sprinkle with cinnamon and nutmeg.)
Makes 10 servings.
Old-Fashioned Fruited Rice Pudding: Add 1 can (17½ oz.) drained fruit cocktail to pudding after cooling 5 minutes. Garnish as desired.

Peanut Butter Shells with Chocolate-Almond Cream

2 cups (12-ounce package) REESE'S Peanut Butter Chips
2 tablespoons shortening*
Chocolate-Almond Cream Filling

Melt peanut butter chips and shortening in top of double boiler over hot, not boiling, water; stir until smooth. Remove from heat; cool slightly. Place 15 paper baking cups (2¾ inches in diameter) in muffin pans. Using a narrow, soft-bristled pastry brush, thickly and evenly coat the inside pleated surface and bottom of each cup with peanut butter mixture. (Reserve any remaining peanut butter mixture for touch-up.) Chill 10 minutes; coat any thin spots. (If peanut butter mixture thickens, stir over hot water until mixture becomes fluid again.) Cover; chill at least 1 hour or until firm.

Remove only a few peanut butter shells from refrigerator at a time; carefully peel paper from each cup. (Unfilled cups will keep for weeks in an airtight container in the refrigerator.) Fill each cup with Chocolate-Almond Cream Filling; chill several hours or overnight.
15 desserts.
*Do not substitute butter, margarine or oil.

Chocolate-Almond Cream Filling

1 HERSHEY'S Milk Chocolate Bar with Almonds (8 ounces)
1½ cups miniature or 15 large marshmallows
⅓ cup milk
1 cup heavy or whipping cream

Cut chocolate bar in pieces, chopping almonds into small pieces. Place in top of double boiler and melt with marshmallows and milk over hot, not boiling, water. Stir until chocolate and marshmallows are melted and mixture is smooth. Remove from heat; cool. Whip cream until stiff and fold into chocolate mixture. Cover; chill until ready to use.
Tip: You may prepare the shells weeks in advance of use, but for best results make the filling no earlier than a day ahead of serving time.

Creamy Low-Calorie Rice Pudding

1 package (4-serving size) JELL-O® Sugar Free Vanilla Pudding and Pie Filling
3 cups skim or low-fat milk
½ cup MINUTE® Rice
¼ cup raisins
⅛ teaspoon ground cinnamon

Combine all ingredients in medium saucepan. Bring to a boil over medium heat, stirring constantly. Pour into 1-quart casserole or individual dessert dishes. Place plastic wrap directly on surface of hot pudding. Chill 30 minutes; remove plastic wrap. Sprinkle with additional cinnamon, if desired.
Makes 8 servings.

Quick Bavarian

¾ cup boiling water
1 package (4-serving size) JELL-O® Brand Gelatin, any flavor
½ cup cold water
Ice cubes
1 cup thawed COOL WHIP® Non-Dairy Whipped Topping

Pour boiling water into blender. Add gelatin. Cover and blend at low speed until gelatin is completely dissolved, about 30 seconds. Combine cold water and ice cubes to make 1¼ cups. Add to gelatin and stir until ice is partially melted. Then add whipped topping; blend at high speed for 30 seconds. Pour into serving bowl. Chill 30 minutes.
Makes 4 cups or 8 servings.

Pudding Tart-in-a-Dish

1 package (4-serving size) JELL-O® Pudding and Pie Filling, any flavor except Lemon
2 cups milk
½ cup graham cracker crumbs or cookie crumbs
2 to 3 teaspoons butter or margarine, melted

Combine pudding mix and milk in medium saucepan; blend well. Cook and stir over medium heat until mixture comes to a full boil. Cool 5 minutes, stirring twice.

Combine crumbs and butter; mix well. Press mixture on bottom and sides of individual dessert glasses. Spoon pudding into crumb-lined glasses. Chill. Garnish with prepared whipped topping and additional crumbs, if desired.
Makes about 2½ cups or 4 servings.

Pudding in a Cloud

1 package (4-serving size) JELL-O® Pudding and Pie Filling, any flavor except Lemon
2 cups milk
2 cups thawed COOL WHIP® Non-Dairy Whipped Topping

Combine pudding mix and milk in medium saucepan; blend well. Cook and stir over medium heat until mixture comes to a full boil. Pour into bowl; cover surface of pudding with plastic wrap. Chill.

Spoon ⅓ cup of the whipped topping into each of 6 dessert glasses. Using the back of a spoon, make a depression in the center and spread topping up the sides of each glass. Spoon pudding mixture into glasses. Chill.
Makes about 3½ cups or 6 servings.

Fruit and Juice Pudding

1 can (17 ounces) fruit cocktail
1 package (4-serving size) JELL-O® Vanilla Flavor Pudding and Pie Filling
1⅔ cups milk

Microwave:* Drain fruit cocktail, reserving ⅓ cup syrup; set aside. Combine pudding mix and milk in 1½-quart microwave-safe bowl; blend well. Add reserved syrup. Cook at HIGH 3 minutes. Stir well and cook 2 minutes longer; then stir again and cook 1 minute or until mixture comes to a boil. Cover surface of pudding with plastic wrap. Chill. Fold in fruit. Spoon into individual dessert dishes.
Makes 3 cups or 6 servings.

*Ovens vary. Cooking time is approximate.

Layered Cookie Pudding

4 cookies, coarsely crumbled
1 cup thawed COOL WHIP® Non-Dairy Whipped Topping
2 cups cold milk
1 package (4-serving size) JELL-O® Instant Pudding and Pie Filling, any flavor

Gently fold cookies into whipped topping. Pour cold milk into bowl. Add pudding mix. With electric mixer at low speed, beat until well blended, 1 to 2 minutes. Pour half of the pudding into individual dessert glasses, filling each glass half full. Spoon 3 to 4 tablespoons of the whipped topping mixture over pudding in glasses. Spoon remaining pudding over whipped topping mixture. Garnish with additional whipped topping and halved cookies or whole strawberries, if desired.
Makes about 3 cups or 5 to 6 servings.

"Philly" Banana Pudding

12 vanilla wafers
1 8-ounce container Soft PHILADELPHIA BRAND Cream Cheese
2 tablespoons milk
2 tablespoons sugar
1 teaspoon vanilla
2 cups thawed frozen whipped topping
2 medium bananas, sliced

Line bottom and sides of 1-quart serving bowl with wafers. Combine cream cheese, milk, sugar and vanilla, mixing until well blended. Fold in remaining ingredients. Spoon into bowl; chill.
6 servings.

Quick Coffee Fluff

1 tablespoon MAXWELL HOUSE® or YUBAN® Instant Coffee
2¼ cups cold milk
1 envelope DREAM WHIP® Whipped Topping Mix
1 package (6-serving size) JELL-O® Vanilla Flavor Instant Pudding and Pie Filling
½ teaspoon cinnamon (optional)
½ cup chopped nuts (optional)

Dissolve coffee in milk in bowl. Add whipped topping mix, pudding mix and cinnamon. With electric mixer at low speed, beat until well blended, about 1 minute. Gradually increase beating speed and beat until mixture forms soft peaks, 3 to 6 minutes. Fold in nuts. Spoon into individual dessert glasses. Chill. Garnish with additional whipped topping and pecan halves.
Makes 8 or 9 servings.

Coconut Pecan Sauce

1 (14-ounce) can EAGLE® Brand Sweetened Condensed Milk (NOT evaporated milk)
2 egg yolks, beaten
¼ cup margarine or butter
½ cup flaked coconut
½ cup chopped pecans
1 teaspoon vanilla extract

In heavy saucepan, combine sweetened condensed milk, egg yolks and margarine. Over medium heat, cook and stir until thickened and bubbly, about 8 minutes. Stir in remaining ingredients. Serve warm over ice cream or cake.
Makes about 2 cups.
  Microwave: In 1-quart glass measure, combine sweetened condensed milk, egg yolks and margarine. Cook on 70% power (medium-high) 4 to 5 minutes, stirring after 3 minutes. Proceed as above.
  To Reheat: In small heavy saucepan, combine desired amount of sauce with small amount of water. Over low heat, stir constantly until heated through.

Baked Almond Pudding

¼ cup firmly packed brown sugar
¾ cup slivered almonds, toasted
1 (14-ounce) can EAGLE® Brand Sweetened Condensed Milk (NOT evaporated milk)
5 eggs
1 cup (½ pint) BORDEN® or MEADOW GOLD® Whipping Cream
½ teaspoon almond extract
Additional toasted almonds, optional

Preheat oven to 325°. In 8-inch round layer cake pan, sprinkle sugar; set aside. In blender or food processor container, grind nuts; add sweetened condensed milk, eggs, *½ cup* cream and extract. Blend thoroughly. Pour into prepared pan; set in larger pan. Fill larger pan with 1 inch hot water. Bake 40 to 45 minutes or until knife inserted near center comes out clean. Cool. Chill thoroughly; invert onto serving plate. Beat remaining cream for garnish; top with additional almonds if desired. Refrigerate leftovers.
Makes 8 to 10 servings.

Hot Fudge Sauce

1 (6-ounce) package semi-sweet chocolate chips or
  4 (1-ounce) squares semi-sweet chocolate
2 tablespoons margarine or butter
1 (14-ounce) can EAGLE® Brand Sweetened Condensed Milk (NOT evaporated milk)
2 tablespoons water
1 teaspoon vanilla extract

In heavy saucepan, over medium heat, melt chips and margarine with sweetened condensed milk, water and vanilla. Cook and stir constantly until thickened, about 5 minutes. Serve warm over ice cream. Refrigerate leftovers.
Makes about 2 cups.
  Mocha: Add 1 teaspoon instant coffee. Proceed as above.
  Microwave: In 1-quart glass measure, combine ingredients. Cook on 100% power (high) 3 to 3½ minutes, stirring after each minute.
  To Reheat: In small heavy saucepan, combine desired amount of sauce with small amount of water. Over low heat, stir constantly until heated through.

Pudding Tortoni

1¼ cups cold milk
1 package (4-serving size) JELL-O® Pistachio or Vanilla Flavor Instant Pudding and Pie Filling
1¾ cups thawed COOL WHIP® Non-Dairy Whipped Topping
¾ cup BAKER'S® ANGEL FLAKE® Coconut, toasted*
¼ cup chopped drained maraschino cherries
½ teaspoon almond extract

Pour cold milk into bowl. Add pudding mix. With electric mixer at low speed, beat until well blended, 1 to 2 minutes. Blend in whipped topping. Fold in coconut, cherries and almond extract. Spoon into muffin pan lined with paper baking cups. Freeze until firm, about 3 hours.
Makes 3½ cups or 6 servings.
  ***To toast coconut:** Spread coconut in a thin layer in shallow pan. Toast in preheated 350° oven for 7 to 12 minutes or until lightly browned, stirring frequently.

Easy Lemon Pudding

1 (14-ounce) can EAGLE® Brand Sweetened Condensed Milk (NOT evaporated milk)
2½ cups cold water
2 (3¾-ounce) packages instant lemon pudding and pie filling mix

In large mixing bowl, combine sweetened condensed milk and water. Add pudding mix; beat until well blended. Chill thoroughly. Serve in individual dessert dishes or fill 12 medium-size cream puffs. Refrigerate leftovers.
Makes 6 to 8 servings.

Chocolate Cream Pudding

cup sugar
¼ **cup HERSHEY'S Cocoa**
⅓ **cup cornstarch**
¼ **teaspoon salt**
3 **cups milk**
3 **egg yolks, slightly beaten**
2 **tablespoons butter or margarine**
1½ **teaspoons vanilla**

Combine sugar, cocoa, cornstarch and salt in heavy saucepan; add milk and egg yolks. Cook over medium heat, stirring constantly, until mixture boils; boil and stir 1 minute. Remove from heat; blend in butter and vanilla. Pour into bowl or individual dessert dishes; press plastic wrap directly onto surface of pudding. Cool; chill until set.
6 to 8 servings.

Ginger Mandarin Sauce over Vanilla Ice Cream

1 **can (20 ounces) lychee fruit**
1 **can (11 ounces) DOLE® Mandarin Orange Segments**
1 **tablespoon cornstarch**
½ **cup orange juice**
¼ **cup sugar**
2 **tablespoons butter or margarine**
2 **tablespoons finely chopped crystallized ginger**
1 **teaspoon grated orange peel Vanilla ice cream**

Drain lychees and orange segments; reserve syrup. In saucepan, dissolve cornstarch in orange juice; add reserved syrup and sugar. Cook, stirring, until sauce boils and thickens. Stir in butter, ginger, orange peel and fruit. Heat through. Serve sauce warm or at room temperature over ice cream. Store leftover sauce in covered container in refrigerator up to 1 week.
Makes 4 cups sauce.

Coconut Fudge Sauce

1 **(6-ounce) package semi-sweet chocolate chips** *or*
4 **(1-ounce) squares semi-sweet chocolate**
1 **(14-ounce) can EAGLE® Brand Sweetened Condensed Milk (NOT evaporated milk)**
1 **(15-ounce) can COCO LOPEZ® Cream of Coconut**

In heavy saucepan, over medium heat, melt chips with sweetened condensed milk. Cook, stirring constantly, until sauce is slightly thickened, about 5 minutes. Gradually stir in cream of coconut; heat through. Serve warm over ice cream or with fresh fruit. Refrigerate leftovers.
Makes about 3½ cups.
   Microwave: In 1-quart glass measure, combine chips and sweetened condensed milk. Microwave on full power (high) 3 to 3½ minutes, stirring after each minute. Gradually stir in cream of coconut; microwave on full power (high) 2 minutes, stirring after each minute.

Pineapple Orange Dessert Sauce

1 **can (20 ounces) DOLE® Pineapple Chunks, undrained**
½ **cup orange juice**
1 **tablespoon cornstarch**
1 **tablespoon sugar**
1 **teaspoon ground ginger**
1 **teaspoon grated orange peel Vanilla ice cream DOLE™ Blanched Slivered Almonds, toasted**

In saucepan, combine pineapple chunks, orange juice, cornstarch, sugar, ginger and orange peel. Cook and stir until sauce boils and thickens. Cool to room temperature. Spoon sauce over ice cream. Sprinkle with almonds.
Makes 2 cups sauce.

Chocolate Custard Sauce

1 **egg, slightly beaten**
¼ **cup sugar**
¼ **teaspoon salt**
1½ **cups milk**
1 **square BAKER'S® Unsweetened Chocolate, melted**
½ **teaspoon vanilla**

Combine egg, sugar, salt and milk in saucepan. Cook and stir over medium heat until mixture begins to thicken slightly and coats a metal spoon, about 5 minutes. Remove from heat. Stir in chocolate and vanilla. Beat with hand or electric mixer until blended. Cover surface with plastic wrap. Chill. Serve over fruit, desserts or cake. Store any leftover sauce in refrigerator.
Makes 1½ cups.

Toasted Almond Souffle

1 8-ounce package
  PHILADELPHIA BRAND
  Cream Cheese, softened
1/3 cup sugar
1/2 teaspoon almond extract
1/4 teaspoon salt
4 eggs, separated
1/2 cup half and half
2 tablespoons sliced almonds

Combine cream cheese, sugar, extract and salt, mixing until well blended. Lightly beat egg yolks; blend into cream cheese mixture. Gradually add half and half. Beat egg whites until stiff peaks form. Fold into cream cheese mixture; pour into 1½-quart souffle dish. With tip of spoon, make slight indentation or "track" around top of souffle 1 inch from edge to form top hat. Top with almonds. Bake at 325°, 50 minutes or until light golden brown.
6 to 8 servings.

Microwave Classic Chocolate Sauce

2 squares (2 ounces)
  HERSHEY'S Unsweetened
  Baking Chocolate
2 tablespoons butter or
  margarine
1 cup sugar
1/4 teaspoon salt
3/4 cup evaporated milk
1/2 teaspoon vanilla

Microwave: Place baking chocolate and butter in small micro-proof bowl. Microwave at HIGH (100%) for 1 minute or until chocolate is softened and mixture is melted and smooth when stirred. Add sugar, salt and evaporated milk; blend well. Microwave an additional 2 to 3 minutes, stirring with wire whisk after each minute, or until mixture is smooth and hot. Stir in vanilla. Serve warm.
About 1½ cups sauce.

Bananas Coco Lopez

4 firm medium bananas, peeled
  and sliced
  REALEMON® Lemon Juice
  from Concentrate
1 cup COCO LOPEZ® Cream of
  Coconut
1/4 teaspoon ground cinnamon
1/2 teaspoon vanilla extract

Dip sliced bananas in ReaLemon® brand. In large skillet or chafing dish, combine cream of coconut and cinnamon; bring to a boil. Add bananas and vanilla. Over medium heat, cook and stir 2 to 3 minutes. Serve warm over ice cream or cake.
Makes 4 to 6 servings.

Microwave: Dip sliced bananas in ReaLemon® brand. In 2-quart glass measure, combine cream of coconut and cinnamon. Microwave on full power (high) 2 minutes or until mixture boils. Add bananas and vanilla. Microwave on full power (high) 1½ to 2 minutes or until bananas are heated through *(do not overheat).*

Black Russian Mini Soufflés

3 squares (1 ounce each) semi-
  sweet chocolate
1 envelope KNOX® Unflavored
  Gelatine
1/2 cup sugar
2 eggs, separated
1 cup milk
3 tablespoons coffee liqueur
2 tablespoons vodka
1 cup (½ pint) whipping or
  heavy cream, whipped

With vegetable peeler, make chocolate curls and shavings from 1 square chocolate; reserve for garnish.

In medium saucepan, mix unflavored gelatine with 1/4 cup sugar; blend in egg yolks beaten with milk. Let stand 1 minute. Stir over low heat until gelatine is completely dissolved, about 5 minutes. Add remaining 2 squares chocolate and continue cooking, stirring constantly, until chocolate is melted. With wire whisk or rotary beater, beat mixture until chocolate is blended. Stir in liqueur and vodka. Pour into large bowl and chill, stirring occasionally, until mixture mounds slightly when dropped from spoon, about 40 minutes.

In large bowl, beat egg whites until soft peaks form; gradually add remaining 1/4 cup sugar and beat until stiff. Fold into gelatine mixture.

Fold 1 cup whipped cream into gelatine mixture. Spoon into 6 (5-ounce) wine or Champagne glasses, each with 1½-inch collar; chill until set, about 2 hours. Remove collars, then gently pat reserved chocolate shavings onto sides. Top with remaining whipped cream and reserved chocolate curls.
Makes 6 servings.

To Make Soufflé Collars: Cut 6 (3×6-inch) strips of wax paper or aluminum foil. Fold each in half lengthwise so that each strip measures 1½×6 inches. Wrap 1 strip around each of 6 wine or Champagne glasses forming a 1-inch collar; secure with tape.

Hot Chocolate Soufflé

1 tablespoon plus 1 cup sugar, divided
3/4 cup HERSHEY'S Cocoa
1/2 cup unsifted all-purpose flour
1/4 teaspoon salt
2 cups milk
6 egg yolks, well beaten
2 tablespoons butter
1 teaspoon vanilla
8 egg whites, at room temperature
1/4 teaspoon cream of tartar
Sweetened whipped cream (optional)

Lightly butter 2½-quart soufflé dish; sprinkle with 1 tablespoon sugar, tilting to coat. Measure length of heavy-duty aluminum foil to fit around soufflé dish; fold in thirds lengthwise. Lightly oil one side of collar; tape securely to outside of dish (oiled side in), allowing collar to extend at least 2 to 3 inches above rim. Set aside.

Combine cocoa, 3/4 cup sugar, the flour and salt in medium saucepan; gradually blend in milk. Cook over medium heat, stirring constantly with wire whisk, until mixture boils; remove from heat. Gradually stir small amount of chocolate mixture into beaten egg yolks; blend well. Return egg mixture to chocolate mixture in pan. Add butter and vanilla, stirring until combined. Set aside; cool to lukewarm.

Beat egg whites with cream of tartar in large mixer bowl until soft peaks form. Add remaining 1/4 cup sugar, 2 tablespoons at a time, beating until stiff peaks form. Gently fold one-third of the chocolate mixture into beaten egg whites. Fold in remaining chocolate mixture, half at a time, just until combined.

Gently pour mixture, without stirring, into prepared dish; smooth top with spatula. Place dish in larger pan; place in oven on bottom rack. Pour hot water into pan to depth of 1 inch (be sure bottom of foil collar does not touch water bath). Bake at 350° for 1 hour and 10 minutes or until cake tester inserted halfway between edge and center comes out clean. Carefully remove foil. Serve immediately with sweetened whipped cream. *8 to 10 servings.*

Fruited Chocolate Trifle

2/3 cup sugar
2 tablespoons cornstarch
1/8 teaspoon salt
2 eggs, slightly beaten
3 cups milk, scalded
3 squares BAKER'S® Unsweetened Chocolate
3 tablespoons almond liqueur*
12 ladyfingers, split
1 pint fresh strawberries, hulled and halved
1 can (16 ounces) apricot halves, drained

Combine sugar, cornstarch and salt in bowl. Add eggs and mix well. Gradually pour in hot milk, stirring constantly. Return to saucepan. Cook and stir over very low heat until mixture is smooth and thickened. Remove from heat. Add chocolate and liqueur; stir until chocolate is melted. Cool slightly.

Arrange half of the ladyfingers, fruits and chocolate custard in layers in a serving dish; repeat layers with remaining ingredients. Chill at least 2 hours. Before serving, garnish with sweetened whipped cream and additional strawberries, if desired.
Makes 8 to 10 servings.

*Or use 1/2 teaspoon almond extract.

Individual Fudge Soufflés

1/2 cup butter or margarine, softened
1¼ cups sugar
1 teaspoon vanilla
4 eggs
2/3 cup milk
1/2 teaspoon instant coffee granules
2/3 cup unsifted all-purpose flour
2/3 cup HERSHEY'S Cocoa
1½ teaspoons baking powder
1 cup heavy or whipping cream
2 tablespoons confectioners' sugar

Grease and sugar eight 5- or 6-ounce custard cups or ramekins; set aside. Cream butter, sugar and vanilla in large mixer bowl until light and fluffy. Add eggs, one at a time, beating well after each addition. Scald milk; remove from heat and add coffee granules, stirring until dissolved. Combine flour, cocoa and baking powder; add alternately with milk-coffee mixture to creamed mixture. Beat 1 minute on medium speed.

Divide batter evenly among prepared custard cups. Place in two 8-inch square pans; place pans in oven. Pour hot water into pans to depth of 1/8 inch. Bake at 325° for 40 to 45 minutes for custard cups (50 to 55 minutes for ramekins), adding more water if necessary, until cake tester inserted halfway between edge and center comes out clean. Remove pans from oven and allow custard cups to stand in water 5 minutes. Remove custard cups from water; cool slightly. Serve in custard cups or invert onto dessert dishes. Beat cream with confectioners' sugar until stiff; spoon onto warm soufflés.
8 servings.

Hawaiian Trifle

2 packages (3⅛ ounces each) vanilla flavor pudding and pie filling mix (not instant)
2 cups milk
1½ cups DOLE® Chilled Pineapple Juice
2 cups whipping cream
1 package (16 ounces) frozen pound cake, thawed
½ cup cream sherry
1 cup raspberry jam, melted
1 can (20 ounces) DOLE® Crushed Pineapple
Maraschino cherries, optional

Prepare pudding mix according to package directions, using milk and pineapple juice as liquid. Place saucepan in bowl of ice water to cool pudding; stir often. In medium bowl, beat 1 cup cream until soft peaks form; fold into cooled pudding. Cut pound cake in half lengthwise. Drizzle sherry over cake; cut cake into chunks.

Spoon 1 cup pudding into 2½- to 3-quart glass serving bowl. Top with half the cake and half the jam. Reserve ½ cup undrained pineapple for garnish. Spoon half the remaining pineapple on top of jam in serving bowl. Spoon half the remaining pudding on top. Repeat layering with remaining ingredients, ending with pudding. Refrigerate, covered, overnight.

In medium bowl, beat remaining 1 cup cream until soft peaks form; spread over top of trifle. Drain reserved ½ cup pineapple. Garnish trifle with pineapple and maraschino cherries, if desired.
Makes 8 servings.

Peach Melba Trifle

1 (14-ounce) can EAGLE® Brand Sweetened Condensed Milk (NOT evaporated milk)
1½ cups cold water
1 (4-serving size) package *instant* vanilla flavor pudding and pie filling mix
2 cups (1 pint) BORDEN® or MEADOW GOLD® Whipping Cream, whipped
¼ cup plus 1 tablespoon dry sherry *or* orange juice
6 cups angel food cake cubes (about 10 ounces)
1½ pounds fresh peaches, pared and sliced *or* 1 (29-ounce) can sliced peaches, drained
½ cup red raspberry preserves
Toasted almonds and additional preserves, optional

In large bowl, combine sweetened condensed milk and water. Add pudding mix; beat well. Chill 5 minutes. Fold in whipped cream and *1 tablespoon* sherry. Place *3 cups* cake cubes in 3- to 4-quart glass serving bowl. Sprinkle with *2 tablespoons* sherry. Top with half the peach slices, *½ cup* preserves and half the pudding mixture. Repeat layering with remaining cake, sherry, peach slices and pudding. Garnish with almonds and preserves if desired. Chill thoroughly. Refrigerate leftovers.
Makes 10 to 12 servings.

Chilly Strawberry Souffles

1 10-ounce package frozen strawberries, thawed
2 envelopes unflavored gelatin
2¼ cups cold water
1 8-ounce package *Light* PHILADELPHIA BRAND Neufchâtel Cheese, softened
¼ cup sugar
1 tablespoon lemon juice
Few drops red food coloring (optional)
2 cups thawed frozen whipped topping

Drain strawberries, reserving liquid. Chop strawberries. Soften gelatin in ½ cup water; stir over low heat until dissolved. Add remaining water. Combine neufchâtel cheese and sugar, mixing until well blended. Gradually add gelatin mixture to neufchâtel cheese mixture, mixing until well blended. Stir in reserved liquid, juice and food coloring. Chill, stirring occasionally, until thickened but not set. Beat with electric mixer or wire whisk until smooth. Fold in strawberries and whipped topping. Wrap 3-inch collar of foil around individual dessert dishes; secure with tape. Pour mixture into dishes; chill until firm. Remove collar before serving.
8 to 10 servings.

Variations: Substitute PHILADELPHIA BRAND Cream Cheese for Neufchâtel Cheese. Increase sugar to ⅔ cup. Substitute 1 cup whipping cream, whipped, for whipped topping.

Substitute 1-quart souffle dish for individual dessert dishes.

PIES & PASTRIES

Though Americans did not invent the pie, it must be America's most popular dessert. All your favorites are here—aromatic fruit pies, smooth custard pies topped with meringue, chocolate pies, and rich nut pies. When time is short, concoct a superb pie from pantry-shelf ingredients.

Easy Chocolate Mousse Pie

Graham Cracker Crust
1 package (8 ounces) cream cheese, softened
1/2 cup HERSHEY'S Cocoa
1 cup confectioners' sugar
1 1/2 teaspoons vanilla
2 cups heavy or whipping cream

Prepare Graham Cracker Crust; set aside. Beat cream cheese and cocoa in large mixer bowl until fluffy and well blended. Gradually add confectioners' sugar; blend well. Stir in vanilla. Whip cream until stiff; fold into cheese mixture. Pour into cooled crust; chill until firm. Garnish as desired.
8 servings.

Graham Cracker Crust

1 1/2 cups graham cracker crumbs
1/3 cup butter or margarine, melted
3 tablespoons sugar

Combine graham cracker crumbs, melted butter and sugar in small bowl. Press mixture firmly onto bottom and up side of 9-inch pie pan. Bake at 350° for 10 minutes; cool.

ReaLemon Meringue Pie

1 (9-inch) baked pastry shell
1 2/3 cups sugar
6 tablespoons cornstarch
1/2 cup REALEMON® Lemon Juice from Concentrate
4 eggs, separated*
1 1/2 cups boiling water
2 tablespoons margarine or butter
1/4 teaspoon cream of tartar
Mint leaves, optional

Preheat oven to 350°. In heavy saucepan, combine *1 1/3 cups* sugar and cornstarch; add ReaLemon® brand. In small bowl, beat egg yolks; add to lemon mixture. Gradually add water, stirring constantly. Over medium heat, cook and stir until mixture boils and thickens, about 8 to 10 minutes. Remove from heat. Add margarine; stir until melted. Pour into prepared pastry shell. In small mixer bowl, beat egg whites with cream of tartar until soft peaks form; gradually add remaining *1/3 cup* sugar, beating until stiff but not dry. Spread on top of pie, sealing carefully to edge of shell. Bake 12 to 15 minutes or until golden brown. Cool. Chill before serving. Garnish with mint if desired. Refrigerate leftovers.
Makes one 9-inch pie.
  *Use only Grade A clean, uncracked eggs.

Eggnog Pie

1 cup cold dairy or canned eggnog
1 package (6-serving size) JELL-O® Vanilla Flavor Instant Pudding and Pie Filling
1 tablespoon rum or ¼ teaspoon rum extract
¼ teaspoon nutmeg
3½ cups (8 ounces) COOL WHIP® Non-Dairy Whipped Topping, thawed
1 prepared 8- or 9-inch graham cracker crumb crust, cooled

Pour cold eggnog into bowl. Add pie filling mix, rum and nutmeg. With electric mixer at low speed, beat until blended, about 1 minute. Let stand 5 minutes. Fold in 2 cups of the whipped topping. Spoon into pie crust. Chill until firm, about 2 hours. Garnish with remaining whipped topping. Sprinkle with additional nutmeg, if desired.
Makes one 8- or 9-inch pie.

German Sweet Chocolate Pie

1 unbaked 9-inch pie shell
⅓ cup butter or margarine
⅓ cup packed brown sugar
⅓ cup chopped pecans
⅓ cup BAKER'S® ANGEL FLAKE® Coconut
1 package (6-serving size) JELL-O® Vanilla Flavor Pudding and Pie Filling
1 package (4 ounces) BAKER'S® GERMAN'S® Sweet Chocolate, broken in pieces
2½ cups milk
1 cup thawed COOL WHIP® Non-Dairy Whipped Topping

Prick pie shell thoroughly with fork. Bake in preheated 425° oven for 5 to 8 minutes or until shell begins to brown. Remove from oven.

Meanwhile, combine butter, brown sugar, nuts and coconut in medium saucepan. Heat over medium heat until butter and sugar are melted, stirring occasionally. Spread in bottom of hot pie shell. Return to 425° oven for 5 minutes or until bubbly; cool.

Combine pie filling mix, chocolate and milk in medium saucepan. Cook and stir over medium heat until mixture comes to a full boil. Remove from heat and beat to blend, if necessary. Cool 5 minutes, stirring twice. Pour over coconut mixture in pie shell. Cover surface with plastic wrap. Chill about 4 hours. Before serving, remove plastic wrap. Garnish with whipped topping and sprinkle with additional coconut, if desired.
Makes one 9-inch pie.

Strawberry Bavarian Pie

1 package (4-serving size) JELL-O® Brand Strawberry Flavor Gelatin
¼ cup sugar
1 cup boiling water
¼ cup cold water
1 pint strawberries, hulled and halved
1¾ cups thawed COOL WHIP® Non-Dairy Whipped Topping
1 baked 9-inch pie shell, cooled

Dissolve gelatin and sugar in boiling water. Add cold water. Chill until thickened. Arrange strawberries in bottom of pie shell. With electric mixer at medium speed, beat thickened gelatin until fluffy, thick and about doubled in volume. Blend in 1 cup of the whipped topping. Chill until mixture mounds. Spoon over berries in pie shell. Chill about 4 hours. Garnish with remaining whipped topping and additional berries, if desired.
Makes one 9-inch pie.

Strawberry Yogurt Pie

1 pint fresh strawberries*
1 envelope KNOX® Unflavored Gelatine
½ cup sugar
2 eggs, separated
½ cup milk
½ pint (8 ounces) strawberry yogurt
1 teaspoon lemon juice
4 drops red food coloring (optional)
1 (9-inch) prepared chocolate crumb crust or graham cracker crust

In blender or food processor, puree enough strawberries to equal ¾ cup; reserve remaining whole strawberries for garnish.

In medium saucepan, mix unflavored gelatine with ¼ cup sugar; blend in egg yolks beaten with milk. Let stand 1 minute. Stir over low heat until gelatine is completely dissolved, about 5 minutes. With wire whisk or rotary beater, blend in pureed strawberries, yogurt, lemon juice and food coloring. Pour into large bowl and chill, stirring occasionally, until mixture mounds slightly when dropped from spoon, about 40 minutes.

In medium bowl, beat egg whites until soft peaks form; gradually add remaining ¼ cup sugar and beat until stiff. Fold into gelatine mixture. Turn into prepared crust; chill until firm, about 3 hours. Garnish with reserved strawberries.
Makes 8 servings; 206 calories per serving with chocolate crumb crust; 227 calories per serving with graham cracker crust.

***Substitution:** Use 1 package (12 ounces) frozen unsweetened strawberries, thawed.

Almond Ginger Ice Cream Pie

Almond Crust (recipe follows)
1 can (20 ounces) DOLE®
    Crushed Pineapple
1 quart vanilla ice cream,
    softened
½ cup DOLE™ Blanched Slivered
    Almonds, toasted
¼ cup crystallized ginger,
    chopped
3 tablespoons almond-flavored
    liqueur
1 tablespoon grated orange peel

Prepare Almond Crust. Drain pineapple; reserve all but ½ cup juice. In large bowl, combine pineapple, reserved juice and remaining ingredients. Spoon into prepared crust; freeze overnight or until firm. Let soften slightly before slicing. Garnish as desired.
Makes 8 to 10 servings.
ALMOND CRUST: In bowl, combine 1½ cups vanilla wafer crumbs, ⅔ cup toasted ground Dole™ Almonds and ¼ cup melted butter or margarine. Press onto bottom and sides of 9-inch pie plate. Freeze until ready to use.

Dutch Apple Raisin Pie

1½ cups SUN-MAID® Raisins
1 cup water
½ cup sugar
1 tablespoon all-purpose flour
½ teaspoon ground cinnamon
¼ teaspoon salt
1 tablespoon lemon juice
4 cups pared and sliced apples
    (4 to 6 apples)
Pastry for double-crust 9-inch
    pie
1 egg, beaten, for glaze
Sugar, for glaze

In large saucepan over low heat, simmer raisins in water until liquid is almost absorbed, 5 to 7 minutes. Meanwhile, in small bowl, mix sugar, flour, cinnamon and salt. Stir into raisin mixture along with lemon juice and apples. Turn into pastry-lined 9-inch pie plate. Cover with top crust, seal and flute edges. Cut slits for steam to escape. Brush with beaten egg and sprinkle with sugar. Bake in preheated 425°F oven 10 minutes; reduce heat to 350°F and bake 45 to 55 minutes longer or until crust is golden brown. Cool on wire rack. Serve warm or at room temperature.
Makes one 9-inch pie.
Note: If desired, sprinkle filling with grated Cheddar cheese just before covering with top crust.

Create-a-Crust Apple Pie

2 medium all-purpose apples,
    pared and sliced (about
    2 cups)
1 tablespoon REALEMON®
    Lemon Juice from
    Concentrate
½ cup plus 2 tablespoons biscuit
    baking mix
1 (14-ounce) can EAGLE® Brand
    Sweetened Condensed Milk
    (NOT evaporated milk)
1½ cups water
3 eggs
¼ cup margarine or butter,
    softened
1½ teaspoons vanilla extract
½ teaspoon ground cinnamon
½ teaspoon ground nutmeg

Preheat oven to 350°. In medium bowl, toss apples with ReaLemon® brand, then *2 tablespoons* biscuit mix. Arrange on bottom of buttered 10-inch pie plate. In blender container, combine remaining ingredients. Blend on low speed 3 minutes. Let stand 5 minutes. Pour evenly over apples. Bake 35 to 40 minutes or until golden brown around edge. Cool slightly; serve warm or chilled with vanilla ice cream. Refrigerate leftovers.
Makes one 10-inch pie.

Brandied Fruit Pie

1 KEEBLER® Ready-Crust®
    Graham Cracker Pie Crust
2 packages (8 ounces each)
    mixed, pitted dried fruit
¾ cup plus 1 tablespoon water
¼ cup plus 1 tablespoon brandy
    or cognac
5 thin slices lemon
¾ cup packed brown sugar
1 teaspoon ground cinnamon
¼ teaspoon ground nutmeg
¼ teaspoon ground cloves
¼ teaspoon salt
½ cup graham cracker crumbs
¼ cup butter or margarine,
    melted
Hard sauce or whipped cream
    (optional)
Lemon slices for garnish

In medium saucepan, combine dried fruit, ¾ cup of the water, ¼ cup of the brandy and the 5 lemon slices. Simmer over low heat 10 minutes or until liquid is absorbed. Remove and discard lemon slices. Stir in sugar, spices, salt, remaining 1 tablespoon water and remaining 1 tablespoon brandy; pour into pie crust. Sprinkle graham cracker crumbs evenly over top of pie. Drizzle melted butter over crumbs. Bake in preheated 350° oven 30 minutes. Cool on wire rack. Serve warm or at room temperature. If desired, serve with hard sauce or whipped cream; garnish with lemon slices.
Makes 8 servings.

Cherry Cheese Pie

- 1 (9-inch) graham cracker crumb crust
- 1 (8-ounce) package cream cheese, softened
- 1 (14-ounce) can EAGLE® Brand Sweetened Condensed Milk (NOT evaporated milk)
- 1/3 cup REALEMON® Lemon Juice from Concentrate
- 1 teaspoon vanilla extract
  Canned cherry pie filling, chilled

In large bowl, beat cheese until fluffy. Gradually add sweetened condensed milk; beat until smooth. Stir in ReaLemon® brand and vanilla. Pour into prepared crust. Chill 3 hours or until set. Top with desired amount of pie filling before serving. Refrigerate leftovers.
Makes one 9-inch pie.
  Topping Variations:
  Ambrosia: In small saucepan, combine 1/2 cup BAMA® Peach or Apricot preserves, 1/4 cup flaked coconut, 2 tablespoons orange-flavored liqueur and 2 teaspoons cornstarch; cook and stir until thickened. Remove from heat. Chill thoroughly. Arrange fresh orange sections (1 or 2 oranges) on top of pie; drizzle with sauce.
Makes about 1/2 cup.
  Glazed Strawberry: In saucepan, combine 3 tablespoons BAMA® Apple Jelly and 1 tablespoon ReaLemon® brand. Cook and stir until jelly melts. Combine 1/2 teaspoon cornstarch and 1 tablespoon water; add to jelly mixture. Cook and stir until thickened and clear. Cool 10 minutes. Arrange sliced strawberries over top of pie; spoon glaze over strawberries.
  Cranberry Nut: In small bowl, combine 1 cup chilled cranberry-orange relish, 1/2 cup chopped walnuts and 1 teaspoon grated orange rind. Spread over pie. Garnish with orange twists if desired.
Makes about 1 cup.

Apple Chess Pie

- 1 (9-inch) unbaked pastry shell
- 4 eggs
- 1 (14-ounce) can EAGLE® Brand Sweetened Condensed Milk (NOT evaporated milk)
- 1 cup applesauce
- 1/2 cup margarine or butter, melted
- 1/4 cup REALEMON® Lemon Juice from Concentrate
- 2 tablespoons cornmeal

Preheat oven to 425°. Bake pastry shell 8 minutes; remove from oven. Reduce oven temperature to 350°. In large mixer bowl, beat eggs. Add remaining ingredients except pastry shell; mix well. Pour into prepared pastry shell. Bake 40 to 45 minutes or until knife inserted near center comes out clean. Cool. Serve warm or chilled. Refrigerate leftovers.
Makes one 9-inch pie.

Caribbean Fudge Pie

- 1/4 cup butter or margarine, softened
- 3/4 cup packed brown sugar
- 3 eggs
- 1 package (12 ounces) real semisweet chocolate pieces
- 2 teaspoons instant coffee powder
- 1 teaspoon rum flavoring
- 1/4 cup all-purpose flour
- 1 cup coarsely broken DIAMOND® Walnuts
- 1 (9-inch) unbaked pie shell
- 1/2 cup DIAMOND® Walnut halves

In large bowl, cream butter and brown sugar. Add eggs, one at a time, beating well after each addition. In top of double boiler, melt chocolate over hot, not boiling, water and add to creamed mixture with coffee and rum flavoring. Stir in flour and the 1 cup walnuts. Pour into unbaked pie shell and decorate top with the 1/2 cup walnut halves. Bake, below oven center, in preheated 375°F oven 25 minutes or until knife inserted near center comes out clean. Cool on wire rack. Store in refrigerator, covered. Serve topped with whipped cream or ice cream, if desired.
Makes 8 servings.

Kansas City Pie

- 1 1/4 cups finely chopped pecans
- 3/4 cup flour
- 1/4 cup PARKAY Margarine, melted
- 2 8-ounce packages PHILADELPHIA BRAND Cream Cheese, softened
- 1 1/2 cups powdered sugar
- 1 8-ounce container (3 cups) frozen whipped topping, thawed
- 2 4-ounce packages chocolate instant pudding and pie filling mix
- 2 2/3 cups milk

Combine pecans, flour and margarine; press onto bottom of 9-inch springform pan. Bake at 375°, 20 minutes. Cool.

Combine cream cheese and sugar, mixing until well blended. Fold in 1 1/2 cups whipped topping; spread over crust. Prepare mix as directed on package for pudding, except use 2 2/3 cups milk. Spoon over cream cheese layer. Chill several hours or overnight. Loosen pie from rim of pan; remove rim of pan. Spread remaining whipped topping over pudding layer just before serving.
10 to 12 servings.

Classic Banana Cream Pie

2 eggs
1/2 cup plus 2 tablespoons sugar
1/4 cup flour
2 cups milk, scalded
1/2 cup unsalted butter or
    margarine
1 tablespoon vanilla extract
5 firm, medium DOLE™ Bananas
1 baked 9-inch pastry shell
1 cup whipping cream

In heavy saucepan, beat eggs, 1/2 cup sugar and flour until pale lemon color. Gradually beat hot milk into egg mixture. Cook, stirring constantly, over medium heat until sauce thickens, about 5 minutes. Remove from heat. Stir in butter and vanilla until blended. Place plastic wrap directly on surface of filling to cover. Cool.

To assemble pie, slice bananas; reserve a few slices for garnish, if desired. Fold remaining bananas into filling; spoon into baked pastry shell. Beat cream with remaining 2 tablespoons sugar until soft peaks form. Spread on top of pie.
Makes 8 servings.

Banana Layered Pie

2 1/4 cups cold milk
1 package (6-serving size)
    JELL-O® Vanilla Flavor
    Instant Pudding and Pie
    Filling
1 baked 9-inch pie shell or
    prepared graham cracker
    crumb crust, cooled
2 medium bananas
1/2 cup thawed COOL WHIP® Non-
    Dairy Whipped Topping
    Lemon juice

Pour cold milk into bowl. Add pie filling mix. With electric mixer at low speed, beat until blended, about 1 minute. Pour 1/2 cup of the pie filling into pie shell.

Slice 1 banana; arrange slices on filling in shell. Top with 3/4 cup of the pie filling.

Blend whipped topping into remaining pie filling. Spread over filling in pie shell. Chill about 3 hours. Slice remaining banana; brush with lemon juice. Arrange banana slices on pie. Garnish with additional whipped topping, if desired.
Makes one 9-inch pie.

Sweet Potato Pecan Pie

1 (9-inch) unbaked pastry shell
1 pound (2 medium) yams or
    sweet potatoes, cooked and
    peeled
1/4 cup margarine or butter
1 (14-ounce) can EAGLE® Brand
    Sweetened Condensed Milk
    (NOT evaporated milk)
1 teaspoon grated orange rind
1 teaspoon vanilla extract
1 teaspoon ground cinnamon
1/2 teaspoon ground nutmeg
1/4 teaspoon salt
2 eggs
    Pecan Topping

Preheat oven to 350°. In large mixer bowl, beat hot yams with margarine until smooth. Add remaining ingredients except pastry shell and Pecan Topping; mix well. Pour into pastry shell. Bake 30 minutes. Remove from oven; spoon Pecan Topping evenly over top. Return to oven; bake 20 to 25 minutes or until golden brown. Cool. Serve warm or chilled. Refrigerate leftovers.
Makes one 9-inch pie.
PECAN TOPPING: In small mixer bowl, combine 1 egg, 3 tablespoons dark corn syrup, 3 tablespoons firmly packed light brown sugar, 1 tablespoon margarine, melted, and 1/2 teaspoon maple flavoring; mix well. Stir in 1 cup chopped pecans.

Fluffy Grasshopper Pie

2 cups finely crushed creme-
    filled chocolate sandwich
    cookies (about 20 cookies)
1/4 cup margarine or butter,
    melted
1 (8-ounce) package cream
    cheese, softened
1 (14-ounce) can EAGLE® Brand
    Sweetened Condensed Milk
    (NOT evaporated milk)
3 tablespoons REALEMON®
    Lemon Juice from
    Concentrate
1/4 cup green creme de menthe
1/4 cup white creme de cacao
1 (4-ounce) container frozen
    non-dairy whipped topping,
    thawed or 1 cup (1/2 pint)
    BORDEN® or MEADOW
    GOLD® Whipping Cream,
    stiffly whipped

Combine crumbs and margarine; press firmly on bottom and up side of buttered 9-inch pie plate. Chill. Meanwhile, in large mixer bowl, beat cheese until fluffy; gradually beat in sweetened condensed milk until smooth. Stir in ReaLemon® brand and liqueurs. Fold in whipped topping. Chill 20 minutes; pile into crust. Chill or freeze 4 hours or until set. Garnish as desired. Refrigerate or freeze leftovers.
Makes one 9-inch pie.

Impossible Pie

1 (14-ounce) can EAGLE® Brand
    Sweetened Condensed Milk
    (NOT evaporated milk)
1½ cups water
½ cup biscuit baking mix
3 eggs
¼ cup margarine or butter,
    softened
1½ teaspoons vanilla extract
1 cup flaked coconut

Preheat oven to 350°. In blender container, combine all ingredients except coconut. Blend on low speed 3 minutes. Pour mixture into buttered 10-inch pie plate; let stand 5 minutes. Sprinkle coconut over top. Carefully place in oven; bake 35 to 40 minutes or until knife inserted near edge comes out clean. Cool slightly; serve warm or cool. Refrigerate leftovers.
Makes one 10-inch pie.

Tip: Pie can be baked in buttered 9-inch pie plate but it will be extremely full.

Impossible Lemon Pie: Add 3 tablespoons REALEMON® Lemon Juice from Concentrate and 1 tablespoon grated lemon rind to ingredients in blender.

Banana Mocha Ice Cream Pie

1 pint chocolate ice cream,
    softened
1 pint coffee ice cream,
    softened
¼ cup coffee-flavored liqueur
1 firm, medium DOLE™ Banana,
    peeled, diced
    Chocolate Cookie Crust
    (recipe follows)

Combine softened ice creams with liqueur. Fold in diced banana. Pour into prepared Chocolate Cookie Crust. Freeze until firm. Garnish with sliced bananas and mocha-flavored candies. *Makes one 8- or 9-inch pie.*
CHOCOLATE COOKIE CRUST: Combine 2 cups chocolate wafer crumbs and ½ cup melted butter. Blend well. Pour into buttered 8- or 9-inch pie pan. Press evenly over bottom and sides of pan. Chill.

Chocolate Turtle Pie

¼ cup caramel- or butterscotch-
    flavored dessert topping
1 baked 8- or 9-inch pie shell,
    cooled
¾ cup pecan halves
1 package (4-serving size)
    JELL-O® Chocolate Flavor
    Pudding and Pie Filling
1¾ cups milk
1¾ cups thawed COOL WHIP®
    Non-Dairy Whipped Topping

Place caramel topping in small saucepan. Heat over medium heat until topping comes to a boil, stirring constantly. Pour into pie shell. Arrange pecans on topping and chill.

Combine pie filling mix and milk in medium saucepan; blend well. Cook and stir over medium heat until mixture comes to a full boil. Cool 5 minutes, stirring twice. Pour over nuts in pie shell. Cover surface with plastic wrap. Chill about 3 hours. Remove plastic wrap. Pipe whipped topping around edge of pie. Drizzle with additional topping and garnish with additional pecans, if desired.
Makes one 8- or 9-inch pie.

Cookies in a Crust

1 KEEBLER® Ready-Crust®
    Butter Flavored Pie Crust
2 eggs
⅓ cup all-purpose flour
⅓ cup granulated sugar
⅓ cup packed brown sugar
½ cup butter or margarine,
    melted, cooled
1 package (6 ounces) semisweet
    chocolate chips
⅔ cup chopped walnuts
    Whipped cream (optional)

In large bowl, beat eggs until foamy. Add flour and sugars; blend thoroughly. Mix in melted butter. Stir in chips and walnuts; pour into pie crust. Bake in preheated 325° oven 1 hour or until golden brown. Cool on wire rack. If desired, garnish with whipped cream.
Makes 8 servings.

Peach Surprise Pie

2 8-ounce packages *Light*
    PHILADELPHIA BRAND
    Neufchâtel Cheese, softened
¼ cup sugar
½ teaspoon vanilla
    Pastry for 1-crust 9-inch pie,
    baked
1 16-ounce can peach slices,
    drained
¼ cup KRAFT Red Raspberry
    Preserves
1 teaspoon lemon juice

Combine neufchâtel cheese, sugar and vanilla, mixing until well blended. Spread onto bottom of crust; chill several hours or overnight. Top with peaches just before serving. Combine preserves and juice, mixing until well blended. Spoon over peaches. Garnish with fresh mint, if desired.
6 to 8 servings.

Black Bottom Pie

9-inch pastry shell or crumb crust
½ cup sugar
⅓ cup HERSHEY'S Cocoa
¼ cup butter or margarine, softened
1 envelope unflavored gelatine
¼ cup cold water
2 cups milk
4 egg yolks
½ cup sugar
¼ cup cornstarch
1 teaspoon vanilla
2 tablespoons rum
4 egg whites
½ cup sugar
Grated chocolate

Bake pastry shell; set aside. Combine ½ cup sugar, the cocoa and butter in medium bowl; set aside. Sprinkle gelatine onto cold water in small bowl; let stand 1 minute to soften. Place bowl in pan of simmering water to dissolve gelatine. Combine milk, egg yolks, ½ cup sugar and the cornstarch in medium saucepan. Cook over medium heat, stirring constantly, until mixture boils; boil and stir 1 minute. Remove from heat; measure 1½ cups of the custard and blend into cocoa-sugar mixture. Add vanilla and pour into cooled shell; chill until set.

Combine dissolved gelatine with remaining custard; add rum and set aside. Beat egg whites in small mixer bowl until foamy; gradually add ½ cup sugar and beat until stiff peaks form. Fold egg whites into gelatine-custard mixture. Chill 15 minutes or until partially set. Spoon over chocolate custard in crust. Chill until set. Garnish with grated chocolate.
8 servings.

Frozen Peanut Butter Pie

3½ cups (8 ounces) COOL WHIP® Non-Dairy Whipped Topping, thawed
1 prepared 9-inch graham cracker crumb crust, cooled
⅓ cup strawberry jam
1 cup cold milk
½ cup chunky peanut butter
1 package (4-serving size) JELL-O® Vanilla Flavor Instant Pudding and Pie Filling

Spread 1 cup of the whipped topping in bottom of pie crust; freeze for about 10 minutes. Carefully spoon jam over whipped topping.

Gradually add milk to peanut butter in bowl, blending until smooth. Add pie filling mix. With electric mixer at low speed, beat until well blended, 1 to 2 minutes. Fold in remaining whipped topping. Spoon over jam in pie crust. Freeze until firm, about 4 hours. Garnish with additional whipped topping and chopped nuts, if desired.
Makes one 9-inch pie.

Margarita Pie

½ cup margarine or butter
1¼ cups finely crushed pretzels
¼ cup sugar
1 (14-ounce) can EAGLE® Brand Sweetened Condensed Milk (NOT evaporated milk)
⅓ cup REALIME® Lime Juice from Concentrate
2 to 4 tablespoons tequila
2 tablespoons triple sec or other orange-flavored liqueur
1 cup (½ pint) BORDEN® or MEADOW GOLD® Whipping Cream, whipped
Additional whipped cream, orange twists and mint leaves or pretzels for garnish, optional

In small saucepan, melt margarine; stir in pretzel crumbs and sugar. Mix well. Press crumbs on bottom and up side of buttered 9-inch pie plate; chill. In large bowl, combine sweetened condensed milk, ReaLime® brand, tequila and triple sec; mix well. Fold in whipped cream. Pour into prepared crust. Freeze or chill until firm, 4 hours in freezer or 2 hours in refrigerator. Garnish as desired. Refrigerate or freeze leftovers.
Makes one 9-inch pie.

Cranberry Crumb Pie

1 (9-inch) unbaked pastry shell
1 (8-ounce) package cream cheese, softened
1 (14-ounce) can EAGLE® Brand Sweetened Condensed Milk (NOT evaporated milk)
¼ cup REALEMON® Lemon Juice from Concentrate
3 tablespoons light brown sugar
2 tablespoons cornstarch
1 (16-ounce) can whole berry cranberry sauce
¼ cup cold margarine or butter
⅓ cup unsifted flour
¾ cup chopped walnuts

Preheat oven to 425°. Bake pastry shell 8 minutes; remove from oven. Reduce oven temperature to 375°. In large mixer bowl, beat cheese until fluffy. Gradually beat in sweetened condensed milk until smooth. Stir in ReaLemon® brand. Pour into prepared pastry shell. In small bowl, combine *1 tablespoon* sugar and cornstarch; mix well. Stir in cranberry sauce. Spoon evenly over cheese mixture. In medium mixing bowl, cut margarine into flour and remaining *2 tablespoons* sugar until crumbly. Stir in nuts. Sprinkle evenly over cranberry mixture. Bake 45 to 50 minutes or until bubbly and golden. Cool. Serve at room temperature or chill thoroughly. Refrigerate leftovers.
Makes one 9-inch pie.

Traditional Pumpkin Pie

1 (9-inch) unbaked pastry shell
1 (16-ounce) can pumpkin (about 2 cups)
1 (14-ounce) can EAGLE® Brand Sweetened Condensed Milk (NOT evaporated milk)
2 eggs
1 teaspoon ground cinnamon
½ teaspoon ground ginger
½ teaspoon ground nutmeg
½ teaspoon salt

Preheat oven to 425°. In large mixer bowl, combine all ingredients except pastry shell; mix well. Pour into prepared pastry shell. Bake 15 minutes. Reduce oven temperature to 350°; continue baking 35 to 40 minutes or until knife inserted 1 inch from edge comes out clean. Cool. Garnish as desired. Refrigerate leftovers.
Makes one 9-inch pie.
Topping Variations:
Sour Cream Topping: In medium mixing bowl, combine 1½ cups BORDEN® or MEADOW GOLD® Sour Cream, 2 tablespoons sugar and 1 teaspoon vanilla extract. After 30 minutes of baking, spread evenly over top of pie; bake 10 minutes longer. Garnish as desired.
Streusel Topping: In medium mixing bowl, combine ½ cup firmly packed light brown sugar and ½ cup unsifted flour; cut in ¼ cup cold margarine or butter until crumbly. Stir in ¼ cup chopped nuts. After 30 minutes of baking, sprinkle on top of pie; bake 10 minutes longer.

Orange 'n Vanilla Mousse Pie

1 envelope KNOX® Unflavored Gelatine
¼ cup cold water
1 cup (½ pint) whipping or heavy cream, heated to boiling
1 package (8 ounces) cream cheese, softened
1 can (6 ounces) frozen orange juice concentrate, partially thawed and undiluted
¾ cup confectioners sugar
1½ teaspoons vanilla extract
1 (9-inch) graham cracker crust

In blender, sprinkle unflavored gelatine over cold water; let stand 1 minute. Add hot cream and process at low speed until gelatine is completely dissolved, about 2 minutes. Add cream cheese, orange juice concentrate, sugar and vanilla; process until blended. Chill blender container until mixture is slightly thickened, about 15 minutes. Pour into prepared crust; chill until firm, about 3 hours. Garnish, if desired, with whipped cream and orange slices.
Makes about 8 servings.

No-Bake Pumpkin Pie

1 egg
1 (14-ounce) can EAGLE® Brand Sweetened Condensed Milk (NOT evaporated milk)
1 teaspoon ground cinnamon
½ teaspoon *each* ground ginger, nutmeg and salt
1 envelope KNOX® Unflavored Gelatine
2 tablespoons water
1 (16-ounce) can pumpkin (about 2 cups)
1 KEEBLER® Ready-Crust® Graham Cracker Pie Crust

In medium bowl, beat egg; beat in sweetened condensed milk and spices. In medium saucepan, sprinkle gelatine over water; let stand 1 minute. Over *low* heat, stir until gelatine dissolves. Add sweetened condensed milk mixture; over *low* heat, cook and stir constantly until mixture thickens slightly, 5 to 10 minutes. Remove from heat. Add pumpkin. Pour into crust. Chill 4 hours or until set. Garnish as desired. Refrigerate leftovers.
Makes one pie.

Paradise Pumpkin Pie

Pastry for 1-crust 9-inch pie
1 8-ounce package PHILADELPHIA BRAND Cream Cheese, softened
¼ cup sugar
½ teaspoon vanilla
1 egg

* * *

1¼ cups canned pumpkin
1 cup evaporated milk
½ cup sugar
2 eggs, beaten
1 teaspoon cinnamon
¼ teaspoon ground ginger
¼ teaspoon ground nutmeg
Dash of salt
Maple syrup
Pecan halves

On lightly floured surface, roll pastry to 12-inch circle. Place in 9-inch pie plate. Turn under edge; flute. Combine cream cheese, sugar and vanilla, mixing at medium speed on electric mixer until well blended. Blend in egg. Spread onto bottom of pastry shell.
Combine all remaining ingredients except syrup and pecans; mix well. Carefully pour over cream cheese mixture. Bake at 350°, 65 minutes. Cool. Brush with syrup; top with pecan halves.
8 servings.

Fluffy Orange Pie

2 cups vanilla wafer crumbs (about 50 wafers)
⅓ cup margarine or butter, melted
1 (8-ounce) package cream cheese, softened
1 (14-ounce) can EAGLE® Brand Sweetened Condensed Milk (NOT evaporated milk)
1 (6-ounce) can frozen orange juice concentrate, thawed
1 cup (½ pint) BORDEN® or MEADOW GOLD® Whipping Cream, whipped

Combine crumbs and margarine; press firmly on bottom and up side of 9-inch pie plate. Chill. Meanwhile, in large mixer bowl, beat cheese until fluffy; gradually beat in sweetened condensed milk then juice concentrate until smooth. Fold in whipped cream. Pile into crust. Chill 2 hours or until set. Garnish as desired. Refrigerate leftovers.
Makes one 9-inch pie.

Frozen Peach Cream Pies

1 (8-ounce) package cream cheese, softened
1 (14-ounce) can EAGLE® Brand Sweetened Condensed Milk (NOT evaporated milk)
2 cups chopped pared fresh, canned or frozen peaches, pureed (about 1½ cups)
1 tablespoon REALEMON® Lemon Juice from Concentrate
¼ teaspoon almond extract
Few drops yellow and red food coloring, optional
1 (8-ounce) container frozen non-dairy whipped topping, thawed
2 (6-ounce) packaged graham cracker crumb crusts
Additional peach slices

In large mixer bowl, beat cheese until fluffy. Gradually beat in sweetened condensed milk, then pureed peaches, ReaLemon® brand, extract and food coloring if desired. Fold in whipped topping. Pour equal portions into crusts. Freeze 4 hours or until firm. Remove from freezer 5 minutes before serving. Garnish with additional peaches. Return ungarnished leftovers to freezer.
Makes 2 pies.

Chess Pie

½ cup butter or margarine, softened
½ cup packed brown sugar
½ cup granulated sugar
4 eggs
½ teaspoon salt
1 teaspoon grated lemon peel
1 teaspoon lemon juice
1 teaspoon vanilla
1 cup finely chopped DIAMOND® Walnuts
1 cup finely chopped SUN-MAID® Raisins
1 (9-inch) unbaked pie shell
Walnut Cream Topping:
1 cup whipping cream
2 tablespoons powdered sugar
½ cup finely chopped or ground DIAMOND® Walnuts

In medium bowl, cream butter and brown and granulated sugars until fluffy. Beat in eggs, one at a time, until well blended. Stir in salt, lemon peel and juice, vanilla, walnuts and raisins. (Mixture will appear slightly curdled.) Pour into unbaked pie shell. Bake, below oven center, in preheated 350°F oven 40 to 45 minutes or until just barely set in center. Top will be a deep brown. Cool on wire rack. Serve with Walnut Cream Topping.
Makes 8 servings.

To prepare Walnut Cream Topping: In medium bowl, beat cream until soft peaks form. Fold in powdered sugar and walnuts.

Simply Superb Pecan Pie

3 eggs, beaten
1 cup sugar
½ cup dark corn syrup
1 teaspoon vanilla
6 tablespoons butter or margarine, melted, cooled
1 cup pecan pieces or halves
1 (9-inch) unbaked pie shell

In large bowl, beat eggs, sugar, corn syrup, vanilla and butter. Stir in pecans. Pour into unbaked pie shell. Bake in preheated 350° oven 45 to 60 minutes or until knife inserted halfway between outside and center comes out clean. Cool on wire rack.
Makes one 9-inch pie.

Favorite recipe from National Pecan Marketing Council, Inc.

Coconut Chocolate Pie

4 squares BAKER'S® Semi-Sweet Chocolate*
¼ cup butter or margarine
1 can (13 ounces) evaporated milk
1⅓ cups (about) BAKER'S® ANGEL FLAKE® Coconut
3 eggs, slightly beaten
½ cup sugar
1 unbaked 9-inch Pie Shell (see page 331)

Melt chocolate with butter in saucepan over very low heat, stirring constantly until smooth. Remove from heat. Blend in milk, coconut, eggs and sugar; pour into pie shell. Bake at 400° for 30 minutes. Cool. Top with sweetened whipped cream or ice cream, if desired.
Makes one 9-inch pie.
*Or use 1 package (4 ounces) BAKER'S® GERMAN'S® Sweet Chocolate

Berry-Bottomed Walnut Pie

Cranberry Filling (recipe
    follows)
2 eggs
³/₄ cup dark corn syrup
¹/₃ cup packed brown sugar
3 tablespoons butter or
    margarine, melted
1 teaspoon grated orange peel
2 cups DIAMOND® Walnuts
1 (9-inch) unbaked pie shell
    Sweetened whipped cream, for
    garnish

Prepare Cranberry Filling; cool. In medium bowl, beat eggs, corn syrup, sugar, butter and orange peel. Mix in walnuts. Spread Cranberry Filling evenly in pie shell. Top with walnut mixture. Bake in preheated 350°F oven about 45 minutes or until filling is set and crust is browned. Cool on wire rack. Serve at room temperature. Top with sweetened whipped cream, if desired.
Makes one 9-inch pie.
CRANBERRY FILLING: In medium saucepan, combine 1½ cups fresh cranberries, 6 tablespoons orange juice and 3 tablespoons granulated sugar. Bring to boil over high heat. Reduce heat to medium; cook 3 minutes. In small dish, mix 2 teaspoons cornstarch with 1 tablespoon water. Stir into cranberry mixture. Cook and stir until mixture is the consistency of thick jam.

Fresh Pineapple Pie

Nut Crust (recipe follows)
1 large DOLE™ Fresh Pineapple
¹/₂ cup sugar
2 tablespoons cornstarch
1 teaspoon grated lemon peel
¹/₈ teaspoon ground nutmeg
1¹/₂ cups water
3 drops yellow food coloring,
    optional

Prepare Nut Crust. Twist crown from pineapple. Cut pineapple lengthwise into quarters. Remove fruit from shells with curved knife. Trim off core and cut fruit into bite-size chunks. In large saucepan, combine sugar, cornstarch, lemon peel and nutmeg. Stir in water and food coloring. Cook, stirring constantly, until sauce is clear and thickened. Remove from heat. Add pineapple. Cool. Spoon pineapple mixture into prepared crust. Refrigerate, covered, overnight.
Makes 6 to 8 servings.
NUT CRUST: Preheat oven to 400°F. In large bowl, combine 1³/₄ cups vanilla wafer crumbs, ²/₃ cup ground toasted walnuts, 5 tablespoons melted butter or margarine and 1 tablespoon sugar. Press onto bottom and sides of 9-inch pie plate. Bake in preheated oven 8 minutes. Cool.

Classic Meringue Pie

²/₃ cup sugar
¹/₃ cup flour
¹/₂ teaspoon salt
2³/₄ cups milk
2 squares BAKER'S®
    Unsweetened Chocolate
3 eggs, separated
2 teaspoons butter or margarine
2 teaspoons vanilla
1 baked 9-inch Pie Shell, cooled
    (recipe follows)
6 tablespoons sugar

Mix ²/₃ cup sugar, the flour and salt in saucepan. Gradually stir in milk; add chocolate. Cook and stir over medium heat until mixture is smooth and thickened; then cook and stir 5 minutes longer. Remove from heat. Beat egg yolks slightly. Stir a small amount of the hot mixture into egg yolks, mixing well. Return to remaining hot mixture in saucepan. Cook 2 minutes longer. Blend in butter and vanilla. Cover surface with plastic wrap and cool 30 minutes without stirring. Pour into pie shell.

Beat egg whites until foamy throughout. Gradually add 6 tablespoons sugar and continue beating until meringue forms stiff peaks. Pile lightly on filling; then spread to edge of pie shell to seal well. Bake at 425° for 8 minutes, or until meringue is lightly browned. Cool to room temperature before serving.
Makes one 9-inch pie.

Pie Shell

1¹/₄ cups flour
¹/₂ teaspoon salt
¹/₂ cup shortening
3 tablespoons (about) cold water

Mix flour and salt in bowl. Lightly cut in shortening with a pastry blender until mixture resembles coarse meal. Sprinkle in water, a small amount at a time, mixing lightly with pastry blender or fork until all particles are moistened and cling together when pastry is pressed into a ball. Cover with a damp cloth and let stand a few minutes. Roll pastry thin (less than ¹/₈ inch) on lightly floured board. Line a 7-, 8- or 9-inch pie pan with pastry. Trim 1 inch larger than pan; fold under to form standing rim; flute edge.

For a baked pie shell, prick pastry thoroughly with fork. Bake at 425° for 12 to 15 minutes or until lightly browned. Cool.

Microwave Hershey Bar Pie

Chocolate Crumb Crust or
Graham Cracker Crust (see
Index)
1 HERSHEY'S Milk Chocolate
Bar (8 ounces), broken into
pieces
1/3 cup milk
1 1/2 cups miniature marshmallows
1 cup heavy or whipping cream
Sweetened whipped cream
Chilled cherry pie filling

Bake crumb crust; set aside. Combine chocolate bar pieces, milk and miniature marshmallows in medium microproof bowl. Microwave at HIGH (100%) for 1 1/2 to 2 1/2 minutes or until chocolate is softened and mixture is melted and smooth when stirred. Cool completely.

Whip cream until stiff; fold into chocolate mixture. Spoon into crust. Cover; chill several hours or until firm. Garnish with sweetened whipped cream; serve with chilled cherry pie filling.
8 servings.

Chocolate Crumb Crust

1/2 cup butter or margarine
1 1/2 cups graham cracker crumbs
6 tablespoons HERSHEY'S
Cocoa
1/3 cup confectioners' sugar

Grease micro-proof 9-inch pie plate. In small micro-proof bowl, microwave butter at HIGH (100%) for 1 minute or until melted. Stir in graham cracker crumbs, cocoa and confectioners' sugar until well blended. Press on bottom and up side of prepared pie plate. Microwave an additional 1 to 1 1/2 minutes until bubbly. (Do not overcook.) Cool crust completely before filling.

Harvest Cherry Pie

Pastry for 2-crust pie
1 1/3 cups (one-half jar) NONE
SUCH® Ready-to-Use
Mincemeat (Regular *or*
Brandy & Rum)
3/4 cup chopped nuts
1 (21-ounce) can cherry pie
filling
1 egg yolk plus 2 tablespoons
water, optional

Place rack in lower half of oven; preheat oven to 425°. In small bowl, stir together mincemeat and nuts; turn into pastry-lined 9-inch pie plate. Spoon cherry pie filling over mincemeat. Cover with top crust; cut slits near center. Seal and flute. For a more golden crust, mix egg yolk and water; brush over entire surface of pie. Bake 25 to 30 minutes or until golden brown. Serve warm or cool. Garnish as desired.
Makes one 9-inch pie.

Praline Ice Cream Pudding Pie

2 tablespoons light brown sugar
2 tablespoons butter or
margarine
1/3 cup chopped nuts
1 lightly baked 9-inch pie shell*
1 1/2 cups cold milk
1 cup (1/2 pint) vanilla ice cream,
softened
1 package (6-serving size)
JELL-O® Butter Pecan Flavor
Instant Pudding and Pie
Filling

Combine brown sugar, butter and nuts in small saucepan. Heat over medium heat until butter is melted. Pour into pie shell. Bake in preheated 450° oven for 5 minutes or until bubbly. Cool on wire rack.

Combine milk and ice cream in medium bowl until thoroughly blended. Add pie filling mix. With electric mixer at low speed, beat until blended, about 1 minute. Pour immediately over nut mixture in pie shell. Chill until set, about 3 hours. Garnish with whipped topping and pecan halves or chopped nuts, if desired.
Makes one 9-inch pie.
*Decrease recommended baking time by 5 minutes.

Peachy Mince Pie with Cheddar Crust

1 (9-ounce) package pie crust
mix
1 cup (4 ounces) shredded
sharp Cheddar cheese
1 jar NONE SUCH® Ready-to-Use
Mincemeat (Regular *or*
Brandy & Rum)
1 (16-ounce) can sliced peaches,
drained
1 egg yolk plus 2 tablespoons
water, optional

Place rack in lower half of oven; preheat oven to 425°. Prepare pie crust mix as package directs for 2-crust pie, adding cheese. Turn mincemeat into pastry-lined 9-inch pie plate. Top with peach slices. Cover with top crust; cut slits near center. Seal and flute. For a more golden crust, mix egg yolk and water; brush over entire surface of pie. Bake 20 minutes or until golden. Serve warm or cool. Garnish as desired.
Makes one 9-inch pie.

Single Pie Crust

1⅓ cups unsifted all-purpose flour
½ teaspoon salt
6 tablespoons CRISCO® Oil
3 tablespoons milk

Preheat oven to 375°F. Combine flour and salt in medium mixing bowl. Blend Crisco® Oil and milk. Add to flour mixture. Stir with fork until mixture forms a ball. Shape into ball; flatten slightly. Place between sheets of waxed paper. Roll to a circle 2 inches larger than inverted 9-inch pie plate. Remove top sheet of waxed paper. Carefully slide your hand under bottom sheet of waxed paper. Turn over into pie plate so waxed paper is on top, easing pastry to fit pie plate. Remove waxed paper. Trim and flute edges. Prick thoroughly with fork. Bake at 375°F, 12 to 15 minutes, or until light golden brown. Cool.
One 9-inch pie crust.

Fresh Strawberry Pie

1 (9-inch) baked pastry shell
1¼ cups sugar
1 tablespoon cornstarch
1½ cups water
3 tablespoons REALEMON® Lemon Juice from Concentrate
1 (4-serving size) package strawberry flavor gelatin
1 quart fresh strawberries, cleaned and hulled

In medium saucepan, combine sugar and cornstarch; add the water and ReaLemon® brand. Over high heat, bring to a boil. Reduce heat; cook and stir until slightly thickened and clear, 4 to 5 minutes. Add gelatin; stir until dissolved. Cool to room temperature. Stir in strawberries; turn into prepared pastry shell. Chill 4 to 6 hours or until set. Refrigerate leftovers.
Makes one 9-inch pie.

Classic Raisin Pie

2 cups SUN-MAID® Raisins
1 cup *each* orange juice and water
½ cup sugar
2 tablespoons cornstarch
1 teaspoon ground allspice
½ cup chopped DIAMOND® Walnuts
1 tablespoon lemon juice
Pastry for double-crust 9-inch pie
1 egg, beaten, for glaze
Sugar, for glaze

In medium saucepan, combine raisins, orange juice and water; bring to boil over high heat. Reduce heat to low; simmer 5 minutes. In small bowl, combine sugar, cornstarch and allspice; mix well. Stir into raisin mixture. Cook and stir in walnuts and lemon juice. Cool 10 minutes; pour into pastry-lined 9-inch pie plate. Cover with top crust; seal and flute edges. Cut leaves from leftover pastry to decorate top of pie, if desired. Cut slits for steam to escape. Brush with beaten egg; sprinkle generously with sugar. Bake in preheated 425°F oven 10 minutes; reduce heat to 375°F and bake 25 to 30 minutes longer or until filling is bubbly and crust is golden. Cover with foil, if needed, to prevent overbrowning. Cool on wire rack about ½ hour before cutting. Serve warm or at room temperature with ice cream or whipped cream, if desired.
Makes one 9-inch pie.

Pastry for Two-Crust Pie

2⅔ cups unsifted all-purpose flour
1 teaspoon salt
¾ cup CRISCO® Oil
6 tablespoons milk

Combine flour and salt in medium mixing bowl. Blend Crisco® Oil and milk. Add to flour mixture. Stir with fork until mixture forms a ball. Divide dough in half; set one half aside. Shape remaining half into a ball; flatten slightly. Place between sheets of waxed paper. Roll to a circle at least 2 inches larger than inverted 9-inch pie plate. Remove top sheet of waxed paper. Carefully slide your hand under bottom sheet of waxed paper. Turn over into pie plate so waxed paper is on top, easing pastry to fit pie plate. Remove waxed paper. Add filling. Roll out remaining dough. Place over filling. Trim and flute edges. Cut slits in top so steam can escape. Bake according to pie recipe.
One 9-inch double pie crust.

Lemon Pastry

1 cup unsifted flour
½ teaspoon salt
⅓ cup shortening
1 egg, beaten
1 tablespoon REALEMON® Lemon Juice from Concentrate

Preheat oven to 400°. In medium bowl, combine flour and salt; cut in shortening until crumbly. In small bowl, beat egg and ReaLemon® brand. Sprinkle over flour mixture; stir until dough forms a ball. On floured surface, roll out to about ⅛-inch thickness. Line 9-inch pie plate; flute edges. Prick with fork. Bake 12 to 15 minutes or until golden.
Makes one 9-inch pastry shell.

Coconut Custard Pie

1 (9-inch) unbaked pastry shell
1 cup flaked coconut
3 eggs
1 (14-ounce) can EAGLE® Brand Sweetened Condensed Milk (NOT evaporated milk)
1¼ cups hot water
1 teaspoon vanilla extract
¼ teaspoon salt
⅛ teaspoon ground nutmeg

Preheat oven to 425°. Toast ½ cup coconut; set aside. Bake pastry shell 8 minutes; cool slightly. Meanwhile, in medium mixing bowl, beat eggs. Add sweetened condensed milk, water, vanilla, salt and nutmeg; mix well. Stir in remaining ½ cup coconut. Pour into prepared pastry shell. Sprinkle with toasted coconut. Bake 10 minutes. Reduce oven temperature to 350°; continue baking 25 to 30 minutes or until knife inserted near center comes out clean. Cool. Chill if desired. Refrigerate leftovers.
Makes one 9-inch pie.
Custard Pie: Omit coconut. Proceed as above.

Strawberry Tart Glace

Pastry for 1-crust 9-inch pie
2 8-ounce packages *Light* PHILADELPHIA BRAND Neufchâtel Cheese, softened
½ cup sugar
1 tablespoon milk
¼ teaspoon vanilla
1 quart strawberries, hulled
1 tablespoon cornstarch
¼ cup water
Few drops red food coloring (optional)

On lightly floured surface, roll pastry to 12-inch circle. Place in 10-inch quiche dish. Prick bottom and sides of pastry with fork. Bake at 450°, 9 to 11 minutes or until golden brown.
Combine neufchâtel cheese, ¼ cup sugar, milk and vanilla, mixing at medium speed on electric mixer until well blended. Spread onto bottom of crust. Puree 1 cup strawberries. Top neufchâtel cheese mixture with remaining strawberries. Combine remaining sugar and cornstarch in saucepan; gradually add pureed strawberries and water. Cook, stirring constantly, over medium heat until mixture is clear and thickened. Stir in food coloring. Pour over strawberries; chill.
8 servings.
Variations: Substitute PHILADELPHIA BRAND Cream Cheese for Neufchâtel Cheese.
Substitute 9-inch pie plate for 10-inch quiche dish.
Substitute almond extract for vanilla.

Banana Cream Cheese Pie

1 (9-inch) graham cracker crumb crust or baked pastry shell
1 (8-ounce) package cream cheese, softened
1 (14-ounce) can EAGLE® Brand Sweetened Condensed Milk (NOT evaporated milk)
⅓ cup REALEMON® Lemon Juice from Concentrate
1 teaspoon vanilla extract
3 to 4 medium bananas, sliced and dipped in additional ReaLemon® brand and drained

In large mixer bowl, beat cheese until fluffy. Gradually beat in sweetened condensed milk until smooth. Stir in ReaLemon® brand and vanilla. Line crust with *2 sliced bananas.* Pour filling over bananas; cover. Chill 3 hours or until set. Just before serving, arrange remaining banana slices on top of pie. Refrigerate leftovers.
Makes one 9-inch pie.

Cinnamon Fruit Tart with Sour Cream Filling

1 envelope KNOX® Unflavored Gelatine
¼ cup cold water
1 cup (8 ounces) creamed cottage cheese
¾ cup canned pineapple juice
½ cup sour cream
½ cup milk
¼ cup sugar
1 teaspoon lemon juice
Cinnamon Graham Cracker Crust (recipe follows)
Suggested Fresh Fruit*
2 tablespoons orange or apricot marmalade, melted

In small saucepan, sprinkle unflavored gelatine over cold water; let stand 1 minute. Stir over low heat until gelatine is completely dissolved, about 3 minutes.
In blender or food processor, process cottage cheese, pineapple juice, sour cream, milk, sugar and lemon juice until blended. While processing, through feed cap, gradually add gelatine mixture and process until blended. Pour into Cinnamon Graham Cracker Crust; chill until firm, about 3 hours. To serve, top with Suggested Fresh Fruit, then brush with marmalade.
Makes 12 servings, 223 calories per serving.
***Suggested Fresh Fruit:** Use any combination of the following to equal 2 cups—sliced strawberries, kiwi or oranges; blueberries or raspberries.*
CINNAMON GRAHAM CRACKER CRUST: In small bowl, combine 2 cups graham cracker crumbs, 1 tablespoon sugar, ½ teaspoon ground cinnamon and ¼ cup melted butter. Press into 10-inch tart pan. Bake at 375°, 8 minutes; cool.

Mini Fruit Cheese Tarts

24 (2- or 3-inch) prepared tart-size crusts
1 (8-ounce) package cream cheese, softened
1 (14-ounce) can EAGLE® Brand Sweetened Condensed Milk (NOT evaporated milk)
⅓ cup REALEMON® Lemon Juice from Concentrate
1 teaspoon vanilla extract
   Assorted fruit (strawberries, blueberries, bananas, raspberries, orange segments, cherries, kiwifruit, grapes, pineapple, etc.)
¼ cup BAMA® Apple Jelly, melted

In large mixer bowl, beat cheese until fluffy. Gradually beat in sweetened condensed milk until smooth. Stir in ReaLemon® brand and vanilla. Spoon equal portions into crusts. Top with fruit; brush with jelly. Chill 2 hours or until set. Refrigerate leftovers.
Makes 24 tarts.

Plum Pudding Pie

⅓ cup plus 2 tablespoons KAHLÚA®
½ cup golden raisins
½ cup chopped pitted dates
⅓ cup chopped candied cherries
½ cup chopped walnuts
⅓ cup dark corn syrup
½ teaspoon pumpkin pie spice
¼ cup butter or margarine, softened
¼ cup packed brown sugar
2 tablespoons all-purpose flour
¼ teaspoon salt
2 eggs, slightly beaten
1 (9-inch) unbaked pie shell
1 cup whipping cream
   Maraschino cherries (optional)

In medium bowl, combine ⅓ cup of the Kahlúa®, the raisins, dates and cherries; mix well. Cover; let stand 1 to 4 hours. Stir in walnuts, corn syrup and spice. In large bowl, cream butter, sugar, flour and salt. Stir in eggs. Add fruit mixture; blend well. Pour into unbaked pie shell. Bake in preheated 350° oven 35 minutes or until filling is firm and crust is golden. Cool completely on wire rack. When ready to serve, in small bowl, beat whipping cream with remaining 2 tablespoons Kahlúa® just until soft peaks form. Spoon cream into pastry bag fitted with large star tip and pipe decoratively on top. If desired, garnish with maraschino cherries.
Makes 8 servings.

Strawberry and Cream Napoleons

1 package (17¼ ounces) frozen puff pastry sheets, thawed according to package directions
1 envelope KNOX® Unflavored Gelatine
¼ cup cold water
2 cups (1 pint) whipping or heavy cream
¼ cup raspberry liqueur
½ cup confectioners sugar
½ cup strawberry preserves, heated
4 cups sliced strawberries (about 2 pints)
   Strawberry Glaze (recipe follows)

Preheat oven to 425°.
   On lightly floured surface, unfold pastry sheets, then cut each lengthwise into 3 rectangles. Cut each rectangle in half crosswise.* Place on ungreased baking sheets and bake 20 minutes or until puffed and golden. On wire rack, cool completely.
   Chill large mixing bowl at least 15 minutes. Meanwhile, in small saucepan, sprinkle unflavored gelatine over cold water; let stand 1 minute. Stir over low heat until gelatine is completely dissolved, about 3 minutes. In chilled bowl, while beating cream on low speed, gradually add gelatine mixture and liqueur, then beat on medium speed until thickened, about 5 minutes. Add sugar, then beat on high speed until soft peaks form, about 2 minutes.
   To serve, with long, serrated knife, cut each pastry rectangle in half horizontally. Reserve the 8 best rectangles for tops. Evenly brush 8 rectangles with ½ preserves, then top with ½ strawberries and ½ cream mixture. Repeat layers, ending with reserved pastry tops. Decoratively drizzle tops with Strawberry Glaze.
Makes 8 large napoleons.
   Hint: For smaller napoleons, cut each pastry rectangle in thirds crosswise and proceed as above.
STRAWBERRY GLAZE: In small bowl, thoroughly blend ½ cup sifted confectioners sugar, 2 teaspoons water and 1 teaspoon strawberry preserves, heated.

Raisin Sour Cream Pie

¾ cup sugar
2 tablespoons cornstarch
¼ teaspoon salt
2 eggs, beaten
2 cups dairy sour cream
1 cup SUN-MAID® Raisins
2 tablespoons lemon juice
1 (9-inch) pie shell, baked, or crumb crust

In top of double boiler, blend together sugar, cornstarch and salt. In small bowl, combine beaten eggs, 1½ cups of the sour cream, the raisins and lemon juice. Stir into sugar mixture. Set over hot, not boiling, water and cook until thick, stirring frequently. Pour into baked pie shell. When cool, top with remaining ½ cup sour cream. Chill several hours.
Makes one 9-inch pie.

Napoleons

**2 sheets (17¼-ounce package)
    frozen puff pastry
Chocolate Cream Filling
Vanilla Frosting
Chocolate Glaze**

Thaw folded pastry sheets as directed; gently unfold. Roll each on floured surface to 15×12-inch rectangle. Place on ungreased cookie sheets; prick each sheet thoroughly with fork. Bake at 350° for 18 to 22 minutes or until puffed and lightly browned. Cool completely on cookie sheets. Prepare Chocolate Cream Filling.

Cut one rectangle lengthwise into three equal pieces. Place one piece on serving plate; spread with one-fourth of the Chocolate Cream Filling. Top with second piece of pastry; spread with one-fourth of the filling. Place remaining piece on top; set aside. Repeat procedure with remaining pastry and filling.

Prepare Vanilla Frosting; spread half the frosting on each Napoleon. Prepare Chocolate Glaze; drizzle half of the glaze in decorative design over frosting on each rectangle. Cover; chill at least 1 hour or until filling is firm. Cut each rectangle into six pieces.
12 servings.

Chocolate Cream Filling

**½ cup sugar
3 tablespoons cornstarch
1½ cups milk
3 egg yolks, slightly beaten
¾ cup HERSHEY'S MINI CHIPS
    Semi-Sweet Chocolate
½ teaspoon vanilla**

Combine sugar, cornstarch and milk in medium saucepan. Cook over medium heat, stirring constantly, until mixture just begins to boil. Remove from heat. Gradually stir small amount of mixture into egg yolks; blend well. Return egg mixture to mixture in pan. Cook over medium heat, stirring constantly, 1 minute. Remove from heat; add MINI CHIPS Chocolate and vanilla, stirring until chips are melted and mixture is smooth. Press plastic wrap directly onto surface. Cool; chill thoroughly.

Vanilla Frosting

**1½ cups confectioners' sugar
1 tablespoon light corn syrup
¼ teaspoon vanilla
1 to 2 tablespoons hot water**

Combine confectioners' sugar, corn syrup, vanilla and hot water in small mixer bowl; beat to spreading consistency.

Chocolate Glaze

**¼ cup butter or margarine
⅓ cup HERSHEY'S Cocoa**

Melt butter in small saucepan. Remove from heat; stir in cocoa until smooth. Cool slightly.

Chocolate-Almond Tarts

**Chocolate Tart Shells
¾ cup sugar
¼ cup HERSHEY'S Cocoa
2 tablespoons cornstarch
2 tablespoons flour
¼ teaspoon salt
2 cups milk
2 egg yolks, slightly beaten
2 tablespoons butter or
    margarine
¼ teaspoon almond extract
Sliced almonds**

Prepare Chocolate Tart Shells; set aside. Combine sugar, cocoa, cornstarch, flour and salt in medium saucepan; blend in milk and egg yolks. Cook over medium heat, stirring constantly, until mixture boils; boil and stir 1 minute. Remove from heat; blend in butter and almond extract.

Pour into cooled shells; press plastic wrap directly onto surface. Chill. Garnish tops with sliced almonds.
6 tarts.

Chocolate Tart Shells

**1½ cups vanilla wafer crumbs
    (about 45 wafers)
⅓ cup confectioners' sugar
¼ cup HERSHEY'S Cocoa
6 tablespoons butter or
    margarine, melted**

Combine crumbs, confectioners' sugar, cocoa and melted butter in medium bowl; stir until completely blended. Divide mixture among six 4-ounce tart pans; press mixture firmly onto bottoms and up sides of pans. Bake at 350° for 5 minutes. Cool.

German Apple Torte

**⅓ cup PARKAY Margarine
⅓ cup sugar
1 egg
1¼ cups flour**

* * *

**2 8-ounce packages *Light*
    PHILADELPHIA BRAND
    Neufchâtel Cheese, softened
½ cup sugar
2 tablespoons flour
½ teaspoon vanilla
2 eggs
1¼ cups peeled chopped apple
¼ cup sliced almonds
⅓ cup KRAFT Grape or Red
    Currant Jelly, heated**

Beat margarine and sugar until light and fluffy. Blend in egg. Add flour; mix well. Spread dough onto bottom and 1¼ inches up sides of 9-inch springform pan. Bake at 425°, 5 to 7 minutes or until crust is lightly browned.

Combine neufchâtel cheese, sugar, flour and vanilla, mixing at medium speed on electric mixer until well blended. Add eggs, one at a time, mixing well after each addition. Pour into crust. Top with apples and almonds. Bake at 425°, 10 minutes. Reduce oven temperature to 350°; continue baking 30 minutes. Drizzle with jelly. Loosen cake from rim of pan; cool before removing rim of pan. Chill several hours or overnight.
10 to 12 servings.

Chocolate-Filled Cream Puffs

1 cup water
1/2 cup butter or margarine
1/4 teaspoon salt
1 cup unsifted all-purpose flour
4 eggs
Chocolate Cream Filling
Confectioners' sugar

Heat water, butter and salt to rolling boil in medium saucepan. Add flour all at once; stir vigorously over low heat about 1 minute or until mixture leaves side of pan and forms a ball. Remove from heat; add eggs, one at a time, beating well after each addition until smooth and velvety.

Drop by scant 1/4 cupfuls onto ungreased cookie sheet. Bake at 400° for 35 to 40 minutes or until puffed and golden brown. While puff is warm, horizontally slice off small portion of top; reserve tops. Remove any soft filaments of dough; cool puffs. Prepare Chocolate Cream Filling; fill puffs. Replace tops; dust with confectioners' sugar. Chill.
About 12 cream puffs.

Chocolate Cream Filling

1 1/4 cups sugar
1/3 cup HERSHEY'S Cocoa
1/3 cup cornstarch
1/4 teaspoon salt
3 cups milk
3 egg yolks, slightly beaten
2 tablespoons butter or margarine
1 1/2 teaspoons vanilla

Combine sugar, cocoa, cornstarch and salt in medium saucepan; stir in milk. Cook over medium heat, stirring constantly, until mixture boils; boil and stir 1 minute. Remove from heat. Gradually stir small amount of chocolate mixture into egg yolks; blend well. Return egg mixture to chocolate mixture in pan; stir and heat just until boiling. Remove from heat; blend in butter and vanilla. Pour into bowl; press plastic wrap directly onto surface. Cool.

Variation—Miniature Cream Puffs: Drop dough by level teaspoonfuls onto ungreased cookie sheet. Bake at 400° for about 15 minutes. Fill as directed above.
About 8 dozen miniature cream puffs.

"Philly" Cream Puff Ring

1 cup water
1/2 cup PARKAY Margarine
1 cup flour
1/4 teaspoon salt
4 eggs
2 8-ounce packages
    PHILADELPHIA BRAND
    Cream Cheese, softened
1 1/2 cups powdered sugar
1 teaspoon vanilla
1 cup whipping cream, whipped
2 bananas, sliced
1 1-ounce square unsweetened
    chocolate, melted
1 tablespoon milk

Bring water and margarine to boil. Add flour and salt; stir vigorously over low heat until mixture forms ball. Remove from heat. Add eggs, one at a time, beating well after each addition. Drop ten 1/2 cupfuls of dough on lightly greased cookie sheet to form 9-inch ring. Bake at 400°, 50 to 55 minutes or until golden brown. Remove from cookie sheet immediately; cool.

Combine cream cheese, 1 cup sugar and vanilla, mixing until well blended. Reserve 1/2 cup cream cheese mixture; fold whipped cream and bananas into remaining mixture. Chill. Carefully cut top from ring; fill with whipped cream mixture. Replace top. Add remaining sugar, chocolate and milk to reserved cream cheese mixture; mix well. Spread over ring.
10 servings.

Glazed Apple Cream Tart

1/2 cup plus 2 tablespoons
    margarine or butter,
    softened
1/4 cup firmly packed light brown
    sugar
1 cup unsifted flour
1/4 cup quick-cooking oats
1/4 cup finely chopped walnuts
1 (14-ounce) can EAGLE® Brand
    Sweetened Condensed Milk
    (NOT evaporated milk)
1 (16-ounce) container BORDEN®
    or MEADOW GOLD® Sour
    Cream
1/2 cup frozen apple juice
    concentrate, thawed
2 eggs, beaten
1 teaspoon vanilla extract
2 medium all-purpose apples,
    pared and thinly sliced
    (about 2 cups)
1/2 cup BAMA® Apricot Preserves
5 teaspoons water
1 teaspoon cornstarch

Preheat oven to 350°. In small mixer bowl, beat 1/2 cup margarine and sugar until fluffy. Stir in flour, oats and nuts; press firmly on bottom and halfway up side of lightly greased 9-inch springform pan. Bake 15 to 20 minutes or until golden. Meanwhile, in medium bowl, combine sweetened condensed milk and sour cream; add juice concentrate, eggs and vanilla. Mix well. Pour into prepared crust. Bake 30 to 35 minutes or until center is set. Cool. In medium saucepan, melt remaining 2 tablespoons margarine. Add apples; cook and stir until tender. Arrange on top of tart. In small saucepan, combine preserves, water and cornstarch; cook and stir until slightly thickened. Spoon over apples. Chill. Refrigerate leftovers.
Makes one 9-inch tart.

CAKES

Every celebration is a good reason to show off your baking skills with a tender cake, high and moist. A specially filled angel cake will draw raves at a party. Delight the children with whimsical shapes and decorations. And for the birthday honoree, present the traditional chocolate layer cake.

Almond Lemon Pound Cake

2 cups cake flour
1/2 teaspoon cream of tartar
1/2 teaspoon salt
1 cup butter or margarine, softened
1 cup granulated sugar
4 eggs
5 tablespoons lemon juice
1¼ cups BLUE DIAMOND® Chopped Natural Almonds, toasted
1/2 cup powdered sugar
1/2 teaspoon vanilla

In small bowl, combine flour, cream of tartar and salt. In large bowl, cream butter and granulated sugar. Add eggs, 1 at a time, beating well after each addition. Beat in 2 tablespoons of the lemon juice. Gradually add flour mixture; mix thoroughly. Fold in 1 cup of the almonds. Pour batter into greased 9×5×3-inch loaf pan. Sprinkle top with remaining ¼ cup almonds. Bake in preheated 325° oven 1 hour or until toothpick inserted into center comes out clean. Meanwhile, in small saucepan, combine powdered sugar, remaining 3 tablespoons lemon juice and the vanilla. Stir over medium heat until sugar is dissolved. Remove cake from oven. Drizzle hot glaze over top. Let cool in pan on wire rack 15 minutes. Loosen edges; remove from pan. Cool completely on wire rack.
Makes 1 loaf.

Pumpkin-Bran Cake

2 cups NABISCO® 100% Bran
1/2 cup milk
3 eggs
1 can (16 ounces) solid pack pumpkin
3/4 cup BLUE BONNET® Margarine, melted
2½ cups all-purpose flour
2 cups granulated sugar
1½ teaspoons pumpkin pie spice
1 teaspoon baking soda
1/2 teaspoon DAVIS® Baking Powder
1¼ cups PLANTERS® Walnuts, chopped
2 teaspoons grated orange peel
1/2 cup powdered sugar
1 to 1½ teaspoons milk

In large bowl, combine bran, ½ cup milk and the eggs; let stand 5 minutes. Blend in pumpkin and margarine. Stir in flour, granulated sugar, spice, baking soda, baking powder, ¾ cup of the walnuts and the orange peel. Pour into greased 13×9×2-inch pan; sprinkle with remaining ½ cup walnuts. Bake in preheated 325° oven 1 hour or until toothpick inserted into center comes out clean. Let cool in pan on wire rack 10 minutes. Loosen edges; remove from pan. Invert cake again so nut side is up. Cool completely on wire rack. In small bowl, mix powdered sugar and 1 teaspoon milk. Add additional milk, if necessary, to make desired consistency. Drizzle glaze over cake.
Makes about 12 servings.

Chocolatetown Special Cake

½ cup HERSHEY'S Cocoa
½ cup boiling water
⅔ cup shortening
1¾ cups sugar
1 teaspoon vanilla
2 eggs
2¼ cups unsifted all-purpose flour
1½ teaspoons baking soda
½ teaspoon salt
1⅓ cups buttermilk or sour milk*

Stir together cocoa and boiling water in small bowl until smooth; set aside. Cream shortening, sugar and vanilla in large mixer bowl until light and fluffy. Add eggs; beat well. Combine flour, baking soda and salt; add alternately with buttermilk to creamed mixture. Blend in cocoa mixture.

Pour into three greased and floured 8-inch or two 9-inch layer pans. Bake at 350° for 25 to 30 minutes for 8-inch pans or 35 to 40 minutes for 9-inch pans, or until cake tester comes out clean. Cool 10 minutes; remove from pans. Cool completely; frost as desired.

8 to 10 servings.

*To sour milk: Use 4 teaspoons vinegar plus milk to equal 1⅓ cups.

Pound Cake

1 package (2-layer size) yellow cake mix or pudding-included cake mix
1 package (4-serving size) JELL-O® Vanilla, Butterscotch, Butter Pecan or Lemon Flavor Pudding and Pie Filling
1 cup (½ pint) sour cream or plain yogurt
⅓ cup vegetable oil
4 eggs
⅛ to ¼ teaspoon mace (optional)

Combine all ingredients in large bowl. With electric mixer at low speed, blend just to moisten, scraping sides of bowl often. Then beat at medium speed for 4 minutes. Pour batter into 2 greased and floured 9×5-inch loaf pans. Bake in preheated 350° oven for 40 to 45 minutes or until cake tester inserted in center of cake comes out clean and cakes begin to pull away from sides of pans. Cool in pans on wire rack 15 minutes. Remove from pans and finish cooling on wire racks. Sprinkle with confectioners sugar, if desired.

Makes two 9×5-inch loaves.

Tomato Soup Spice Cake

1 tablespoon sugar
1 box (about 18 ounces) spice cake mix
1 can (10¾ ounces) CAMPBELL'S® Condensed Tomato Soup
2 eggs
2 tablespoons water
1 cup sour cream
¼ cup packed brown sugar
1 teaspoon vanilla extract

To Microwave:
1. Generously grease 14-cup microwave-safe Bundt® pan. Sprinkle pan with sugar.
2. In large bowl, combine cake mix, soup, eggs and water. With mixer, beat 2 minutes or until well mixed, constantly scraping side and bottom of bowl.
3. Pour into prepared pan. Microwave, uncovered, at 50% power 9 minutes, rotating pan once during cooking.
4. Increase power to HIGH. Microwave, uncovered, 5 minutes or until toothpick inserted into cake comes out clean. Let stand directly on countertop 15 minutes. Invert onto serving plate; cool completely.
5. In small bowl, stir together sour cream, brown sugar and vanilla until sugar dissolves. Spoon evenly over cooled cake.

Makes 12 servings.

Cherry Nut Cake

1 8-ounce package PHILADELPHIA BRAND Cream Cheese, softened
1 cup PARKAY Margarine
1½ cups granulated sugar
1½ teaspoons vanilla
4 eggs
2¼ cups sifted cake flour
1½ teaspoons baking powder
¾ cup chopped maraschino cherries, well-drained
½ cup chopped pecans

* * *

½ cup finely chopped pecans
1½ cups sifted powdered sugar
2 tablespoons milk

Combine cream cheese, margarine, granulated sugar and vanilla, mixing at medium speed on electric mixer until well blended. Add eggs, one at a time, mixing well after each addition. Sift together 2 cups flour and baking powder. Gradually add to cream cheese mixture; mix well. Toss remaining flour with cherries and pecans; fold into batter.

Grease 10-inch tube or fluted tube pan; sprinkle with finely chopped pecans. Pour batter into pan. Bake at 325°, 1 hour and 10 minutes. Cool 5 minutes; remove from pan. Cool. Glaze with combined powdered sugar and milk. Garnish with additional pecan halves and maraschino cherry halves, if desired.

10 to 12 servings.

Variations: Substitute ¾ cup chopped dried apricots for maraschino cherries and 2 tablespoons orange juice and 1 teaspoon grated orange peel for milk.

Substitute 2 cups all-purpose flour for sifted cake flour.

Omit finely chopped nuts. Pour batter into three greased and floured 1-pound coffee cans. Bake at 325°, 1 hour.

Make ahead: Bake cake; wrap securely in plastic wrap. Freeze. Thaw, wrapped, at room temperature for 12 hours.

French Apple Cake

3 cooking apples, pared, cored
   and sliced (about 3 cups)
2/3 cup sugar
1 tablespoon all-purpose flour
1/2 teaspoon ground cinnamon
2 tablespoons butter or
   margarine, melted
2 tablespoons lemon juice
1 package DUNCAN HINES®
   Deluxe White Cake Mix
3 large eggs
1/3 cup CRISCO® Oil or PURITAN®
   Oil
1 1/4 cups water

1. Preheat oven to 350°F. Grease
13×9×2-inch pan.
2. Arrange apples in pan. Mix sugar,
flour and cinnamon; sprinkle over apples. Combine melted butter and
lemon juice; drizzle over apples.
3. Place dry cake mix, eggs, oil and
water in large mixer bowl. Mix cake
as directed on package. Turn batter
into pan over apples and spread
evenly.
4. Bake at 350°F for 40 to 50 minutes
or until toothpick inserted in center
comes out clean. Cool 1 to 2 minutes
in pan. Invert on large platter or tray;
remove pan after 1 to 2 minutes.
Serve warm.
12 to 16 servings.

Cinnamon
Ripple Cake

1 package DUNCAN HINES®
   Deluxe Angel Food Cake Mix
1 1/3 cups water
3 1/2 teaspoons ground cinnamon
3/4 cup whipping cream
1/2 cup cold milk
1/3 cup confectioners' sugar
1 teaspoon vanilla extract

1. Preheat oven to 375°F.
2. Prepare cake with water as directed on package. Spoon one-fourth
of batter into ungreased 10-inch tube
pan and spread evenly. With small
fine sieve, sprinkle one teaspoon cinnamon over batter. Repeat layering
two more times, ending with batter.
3. Bake at 375°F for 30 to 40 minutes
or until top crust is golden brown,
firm and looks very dry. Do not underbake.
4. To cool cake, hang pan upside down
on bottle or funnel. When completely
cooled, remove from pan.
5. To serve, beat whipping cream and
milk in chilled bowl with chilled
beaters until thick. Blend in confectioners' sugar, vanilla extract and remaining 1/2 teaspoon cinnamon. Cut
cake into slices and top with cinnamon cream.
12 to 16 servings.

Carrot Cake

2 1/4 cups unsifted all-purpose flour
1 1/2 cups sugar
2 teaspoons baking soda
1 1/2 teaspoons ground cinnamon
1/2 teaspoon ground nutmeg
1/2 teaspoon salt
1 cup CRISCO® Oil
3 eggs
1/2 cup milk
2 cups shredded carrot
1 1/2 cups flaked coconut
3/4 cup chopped nuts
1/2 cup currants or raisins
Frosting:
1 package (3 ounces) cream
   cheese, softened
2 tablespoons butter or
   margarine, softened
2 tablespoons milk
1/4 teaspoon vanilla
   Dash salt
2 to 2 1/4 cups confectioners
   sugar

Preheat oven to 325°F. Oil and flour
13×9-inch baking pan. Set aside.
   Mix flour, sugar, baking soda, cinnamon, nutmeg and salt in large mixing
bowl. Add Crisco® Oil, eggs, milk and
carrot. Beat with electric mixer at low
speed until ingredients are moistened, scraping bowl constantly. Beat
at medium speed 2 minutes, scraping
bowl occasionally. Stir in coconut,
nuts and currants. Pour into prepared
pan. Bake at 325°F, 55 to 60 minutes,
or until wooden pick inserted in center comes out clean. Cool completely
on wire rack.
   For frosting, blend cream cheese
and butter in small mixing bowl. Add
milk, vanilla and salt. Mix well. Stir
in enough confectioners sugar until
thick enough to spread. Spread on
cooled cake.
One 13×9-inch cake.

Angel Food à
la Flambé

1 package DUNCAN HINES®
   Deluxe Angel Food Cake Mix
1 1/3 cups water
6 canned apricot halves
1 cup strawberry preserves
1/4 cup plus 2 tablespoons rum

1. Preheat oven to 375°F.
2. Prepare cake with water as directed on package. Pour batter into
ungreased 10-inch tube pan. Cut
through batter with knife or spatula
to remove large air bubbles.
3. Bake at 375° for 30 to 40 minutes
or until top crust is golden brown,
firm and dry. Do not underbake. To
cool, hang pan upside down on funnel
or bottle at least 1 1/2 hours; remove
from pan.
4. Arrange apricot halves on top of
cooled cake.
5. Combine strawberry preserves and
2 tablespoons rum in small saucepan.
Heat until warm. Glaze cake and
apricots with warm mixture. Heat 1/4
cup rum in small saucepan, then ignite with match and spoon over cake.
12 servings.

Marble Chiffon Cake

⅓ cup HERSHEY'S Cocoa
2 tablespoons sugar
¼ cup water
2 tablespoons vegetable oil
2 cups unsifted all-purpose flour
1½ cups sugar
3 teaspoons baking powder
1 teaspoon salt
½ cup vegetable oil
7 egg yolks, at room
    temperature
¾ cup cold water
2 teaspoons vanilla
7 egg whites, at room
    temperature
½ teaspoon cream of tartar
Cocoa Glaze

Combine cocoa, 2 tablespoons sugar, ¼ cup water and 2 tablespoons oil in small bowl until smooth; set aside. Combine flour, 1½ cups sugar, the baking powder and salt in large mixer bowl; add ½ cup oil, the egg yolks, ¾ cup cold water and the vanilla. Beat on low speed until combined. Beat 5 minutes on high speed. With clean beaters, beat egg whites and cream of tartar in another large mixer bowl until stiff peaks form.

Pour batter in thin stream over entire surface of egg whites; fold in lightly; using rubber spatula. Remove one-third of the batter to another bowl; gently fold in chocolate mixture. Pour half the vanilla batter into ungreased 10-inch tube pan; spread half the chocolate batter over vanilla. Repeat layers; gently swirl with spatula or knife for marbled effect. Bake at 325° for 65 to 70 minutes or until cake springs back when touched lightly. Invert cake over heat-proof funnel or bottle until completely cool. Loosen cake from pan; invert onto serving plate. Spread top with Cocoa Glaze.
12 to 16 servings.

Cocoa Glaze

2 tablespoons butter or
    margarine
¼ cup HERSHEY'S Cocoa
3 tablespoons water
½ teaspoon vanilla
1¼ cups confectioners' sugar

Melt butter in small saucepan over low heat. Stir in cocoa and water. Cook, stirring constantly, until mixture thickens; *do not boil.* Remove from heat. Stir in vanilla. Gradually add confectioners' sugar; beat with wire whisk until smooth.

Chocolate Almond Cake l'Orange

6 tablespoons butter or
    margarine
1 cup sugar
⅛ teaspoon salt
3 eggs
4 squares BAKER'S®
    Unsweetened Chocolate,
    melted and cooled
¾ cup ground almonds
¼ cup dry bread crumbs
3 tablespoons orange liqueur
1 teaspoon vanilla

Cream butter. Gradually beat in sugar and salt and continue beating until light and fluffy. Add eggs, one at a time, beating thoroughly after each. Stir in chocolate, almonds, bread crumbs, 2 tablespoons of the liqueur and the vanilla.

Pour into greased and floured 8-inch layer pan. Bake at 375° about 25 minutes, or until cake tester inserted in center comes out clean. Cool in pan 5 minutes. Invert onto rack and drizzle with remaining 1 tablespoon liqueur. Cool. Garnish with sweetened whipped cream and thinly slivered orange rind, if desired.
Makes one 8-inch cake.

Chocolate Yogurt Cake

2 cups unsifted all-purpose flour
1½ cups sugar
½ cup unsweetened cocoa
2 teaspoons baking soda
1 teaspoon salt
1 cup plain yogurt
3 eggs
⅔ cup CRISCO® Oil
1½ teaspoons vanilla
Frosting:
1 package (6 ounces) semisweet
    chocolate chips
¼ cup butter or margarine
⅔ cup plain yogurt
½ teaspoon vanilla
⅛ teaspoon salt
2½ to 3 cups confectioners sugar

Preheat oven to 350°F. Grease and flour two 9-inch round layer pans. Set aside.

Mix flour, sugar, cocoa, baking soda and salt in large mixing bowl. Add yogurt, eggs, Crisco® Oil and vanilla. Beat with electric mixer at low speed until ingredients are moistened, scraping bowl constantly. Beat at medium speed 2 minutes, scraping bowl occasionally. Pour into prepared pans. Bake at 350°F, 30 to 35 minutes, or until wooden pick inserted in center comes out clean. Cool 10 minutes. Remove from pans. Cool completely on wire rack.

For frosting, combine chocolate chips and butter in small saucepan. Cook over low heat, stirring constantly, until melted. Transfer mixture to medium mixing bowl. Cool slightly. Blend in yogurt, vanilla and salt. Stir in enough confectioners sugar until frosting is thick enough to spread. Fill and frost cooled cake.
One 2-layer cake.

Petits Fours

1 package DUNCAN HINES®
  Deluxe White or Yellow Cake
  Mix
3 large eggs
1/3 cup CRISCO® Oil or PURITAN®
  Oil
1 1/4 cups water
3 cups granulated sugar
1/4 teaspoon cream of tartar
1 1/2 cups hot water
1 teaspoon vanilla extract
2 1/4 cups confectioners' sugar
  Food coloring, if desired
  Frosted roses or candy
  decorations, if desired

1. Line 15 1/2×10 1/2×1-inch jelly roll pan with waxed paper. Preheat oven to 350°F.
2. Combine dry cake mix, eggs, oil and 1 1/4 cups water in large mixer bowl. Mix cake as directed on package. Turn batter into pan and spread evenly.
3. Bake at 350°F for 25 to 30 minutes or until toothpick inserted in center comes out clean. Immediately turn cake out onto towel and peel off paper. Cool.
4. Cut cooled cake into seventy 1 1/2-inch shapes. Place on racks with waxed paper under racks.
5. For frosting, combine granulated sugar, cream of tartar, and 1 1/2 cups hot water in heavy saucepan. Cook over medium heat until syrup reaches 226°F on candy thermometer. Cool until lukewarm (110°F). Stir in vanilla extract. Gradually beat in confectioners' sugar until frosting is of good pouring consistency. Tint frosting with food coloring, if desired.
6. Pour frosting over cakes on racks. After frosting one rack, remove frosting from waxed paper and return to bowl of frosting. If frosting becomes too thick, heat over hot water or add a few drops of hot water. Repeat until all cakes are frosted. Decorate with frosted roses or candy decorations.
70 cakes.

Kahlúa® Sweetheart Cake

3/4 cup unsweetened cocoa
1 teaspoon instant coffee
  crystals
1 cup boiling water
1/2 cup plus 2 tablespoons
  KAHLÚA®
1/2 cup butter or margarine,
  softened
1/4 cup shortening
1 3/4 cups sugar
3 eggs
1 teaspoon vanilla
2 cups sifted all-purpose flour
1 1/2 teaspoons baking soda
3/4 teaspoon salt
1/4 teaspoon baking powder
  KAHLÚA® Fudge Frosting
  (recipe follows)

In small heatproof bowl, blend cocoa, coffee and water. Stir in 1/2 cup Kahlúa®; cool. In large bowl, beat butter, shortening, sugar, eggs and vanilla until light and fluffy. In small bowl, combine flour, baking soda, salt and baking powder. Add flour mixture to butter mixture alternately with cocoa mixture, beating well after each addition. Line bottoms of two 9-inch round pans with parchment paper; lightly grease sides of pans. Divide batter evenly between prepared pans. Bake in preheated 350° oven 25 to 30 minutes or just until toothpick inserted into center comes out clean. Do not overbake. Let cool in pans on wire racks 5 minutes. Loosen edges; remove from pans. Peel off parchment paper; cool completely on wire racks. Prepare Kahlúa® Fudge Frosting. Brush bottom of each layer with 1 tablespoon of remaining Kahlúa®. Fill and frost layers with frosting. Decorate as desired. Let stand until frosting is set.
Makes 10 to 12 servings.

KAHLÚA® FUDGE FROSTING: In medium saucepan, combine 1 package (6 ounces) semisweet chocolate chips, 1/4 cup *each* Kahlúa® and half-and-half and 1 cup butter or margarine. Stir over medium heat until chocolate melts. Remove from heat; blend in 2 1/2 cups powdered sugar. Beat until frosting is cool and holds its shape. (Pan may be placed over ice water to hasten cooling.)

Easy German Chocolate Cake

1 package DUNCAN HINES®
  Deluxe Swiss Chocolate
  Cake Mix
3 large eggs
1/2 cup CRISCO® Oil or PURITAN®
  Oil
1 1/4 cups water
1 cup chopped nuts
1/3 cup butter or regular
  margarine, melted
1 cup packed light brown sugar
1 can (3 1/2 ounces) flaked
  coconut
1/4 cup milk

1. Preheat oven to 350°F. Grease and flour 13×9×2-inch pan.
2. Combine dry cake mix, eggs, oil and water in large mixer bowl. Mix cake as directed on package. Stir in 1/2 cup nuts. Turn batter into pan and spread evenly.
3. Bake at 350°F for 35 to 40 minutes or until toothpick inserted in center comes out clean. Cool in pan on rack.
4. For topping, combine butter, brown sugar, coconut, milk and remaining 1/2 cup nuts. Spread evenly over cooled cake. Place under broiler and broil 2 to 3 minutes or until bubbly.
12 to 16 servings.

Cool and Minty Party Cake

1 (14-ounce) can EAGLE® Brand Sweetened Condensed Milk (NOT evaporated milk)
2 teaspoons peppermint extract
8 drops green food coloring
2 cups (1 pint) BORDEN® or MEADOW GOLD® Whipping Cream, whipped (do not use non-dairy whipped topping)
1 (18¼- or 18½-ounce) package white cake mix
Green creme de menthe
1 (8-ounce) container frozen non-dairy whipped topping, thawed

In large mixing bowl, combine sweetened condensed milk, extract and food coloring. Fold in whipped cream. Pour into aluminum foil-lined 9-inch round layer cake pan; cover. Freeze at least 6 hours or overnight. Meanwhile, prepare and bake cake mix as package directs for two 9-inch round layers. Remove from pans; cool thoroughly. With table fork, poke holes in layers 1 inch apart halfway through each layer. Spoon small amounts of creme de menthe in holes. Place 1 cake layer on serving plate; top with ice cream layer then second cake layer. Trim ice cream layer to fit cake layers. Frost quickly with topping. Return to freezer until ready to serve. Garnish as desired.
Makes one 9-inch cake.
Tip: Cake can be made 1 week ahead and stored in freezer.

Lickety-Split Cocoa Cake

1½ cups unsifted all-purpose flour
1 cup sugar
¼ cup HERSHEY'S Cocoa
1 teaspoon baking soda
½ teaspoon salt
1 cup water
¼ cup plus 2 tablespoons vegetable oil
1 tablespoon vinegar
1 teaspoon vanilla

Combine flour, sugar, cocoa, baking soda and salt in large bowl. Add water, oil, vinegar and vanilla; stir with spoon or wire whisk just until batter is smooth and ingredients are well blended.
Pour into greased and floured 9-inch layer pan or 8-inch square pan. Bake at 350° for 35 to 40 minutes or until cake tester comes out clean. Cool in pan; frost as desired.
6 to 8 servings.

Martha Washington Devil's Food Cake

4 squares BAKER'S® Unsweetened Chocolate
2 cups sugar
1½ cups buttermilk or sour milk
2 cups flour
1½ teaspoons CALUMET® Baking Powder
1 teaspoon baking soda
1 teaspoon salt
¾ cup butter or margarine
3 eggs
1 teaspoon vanilla
Classic Fudge Frosting (see Index)

Melt chocolate in saucepan over very low heat, stirring constantly until smooth. Add ½ cup of the sugar and ½ cup of the buttermilk; stir until well blended. Cool thoroughly. Mix flour, baking powder, soda and salt. Cream butter. Gradually beat in remaining 1½ cups sugar and continue beating until light and fluffy. Add eggs, one at a time, beating thoroughly after each. Blend in about one-fourth of the flour mixture. Blend in chocolate mixture and vanilla. Alternately add remaining flour mixture and remaining 1 cup buttermilk, beating after each addition until smooth.
Pour into 2 greased and floured 9-inch layer pans. Bake at 350° about 40 minutes, or until cake tester inserted in centers comes out clean. Cool in pans 10 minutes. Remove from pans and finish cooling on racks. Spread frosting between layers and over top and sides.
Makes one 9-inch layer cake.

Cocoa-Spice Snackin' Cake

¼ cup butter or margarine, melted
¼ cup HERSHEY'S Cocoa
¾ cup applesauce
1¼ cups unsifted all-purpose flour
1 cup sugar
¾ teaspoon baking soda
½ teaspoon cinnamon
¼ teaspoon nutmeg
¼ teaspoon salt
1 egg, beaten
½ cup chopped nuts

Combine melted butter and cocoa; blend in applesauce. Combine flour, sugar, baking soda, cinnamon, nutmeg and salt in large bowl. Blend in cocoa mixture and egg until dry ingredients are moistened. Stir in nuts.
Spread in greased 9-inch square pan. Bake at 350° for 30 to 35 minutes or until cake tester comes out clean. Cool in pan.
8 to 10 servings.

Mocha Almond Roll

3/4 cup cake flour
1 teaspoon baking powder
1/4 teaspoon salt
3 eggs
1 cup granulated sugar
1/3 cup water
1 1/2 teaspoons vanilla
1/2 teaspoon almond extract
  Powdered sugar
1 cup BLUE DIAMOND®
  Blanched Almond Paste
2 3/4 cups whipping cream
6 squares (1 ounce each)
  semisweet chocolate,
  chopped
3 tablespoons coffee-flavored
  liqueur
  Chocolate curls (optional)

In small bowl, combine flour, baking powder and salt. In large bowl, beat eggs until foamy. Gradually beat in granulated sugar. Beat in water, 1/2 teaspoon of the vanilla and the almond extract. Gradually beat in flour mixture until smooth. Lightly grease 15 1/2×10 1/2×1-inch jelly-roll pan; line with waxed paper and grease again. Pour batter into prepared pan. Bake in preheated 375° oven 12 to 15 minutes or until toothpick inserted into center comes out clean. Immediately invert cake onto towel sprinkled with powdered sugar; remove waxed paper. While still warm, roll up cake and towel beginning at short end; cool completely. Roll almond paste between 2 pieces of waxed paper into 15×10-inch rectangle. In small saucepan over low heat, stir 3/4 cup of the cream and the chocolate until smooth. Remove from heat; stir occasionally until thickened. In medium bowl, beat remaining 2 cups cream, 3/4 cup powdered sugar, the liqueur and remaining 1 teaspoon vanilla until soft peaks form. Beat in 1/3 cup chocolate mixture until stiff peaks form. Unroll cake; spread with remaining chocolate mixture. Place almond paste on top. Spread 1 1/4 cups whipped cream mixture over almond paste, leaving 1-inch border at 1 short end; roll up cake from opposite end. Frost cake with remaining whipped cream mixture; refrigerate. If desired, garnish with chocolate curls.
Makes 8 to 10 servings.

Drum Layer Cake

1 package DUNCAN HINES®
  Deluxe Cake Mix (any flavor)
3 large eggs
  CRISCO® Oil or PURITAN® Oil
  Water
5 cups confectioners' sugar
3/4 cup CRISCO® Shortening
1/3 cup non-dairy creamer
2 teaspoons vanilla extract
1/2 cup water
1/2 teaspoon salt
  Licorice twists and strings
2 lollipops

1. Preheat oven to 350°F. Grease and flour two 8×1 1/2-inch round layer pans.
2. Combine dry cake mix, eggs and the amount of oil and water listed on package in large mixer bowl. Mix, bake and cool cake as directed on package.
3. For decorator frosting, beat confectioners' sugar, shortening, non-dairy creamer, vanilla extract, 1/2 cup water and salt in large mixer bowl. Beat 3 minutes at medium speed, then 5 minutes at high speed. Add more confectioners' sugar to thicken or water to thin frosting as needed.
4. Spread frosting between cooled layers and on sides and top of cake. Cut lengths of licorice twists and make pattern around sides of cake. For top and bottom borders, braid three licorice strings together and place on cake. Place lollipops on top for drumsticks.
12 to 16 servings.

German Chocolate Cake

1 package (4 ounces) BAKER'S®
  GERMAN'S® Sweet
  Chocolate
1/2 cup boiling water
2 cups flour
1 teaspoon baking soda
1/2 teaspoon salt
1 cup butter or margarine
2 cups sugar
4 egg yolks
1 teaspoon vanilla
1 cup buttermilk
4 egg whites
  Coconut-Pecan Filling and
  Frosting

Melt chocolate in boiling water. Cool. Mix flour, soda and salt. Cream butter and sugar until light and fluffy. Add egg yolks, one at a time, beating thoroughly after each. Blend in vanilla and chocolate. Alternately add flour mixture and buttermilk, beating after each addition until smooth. Beat egg whites until stiff peaks form. Fold into batter.

Pour into three 9-inch layer pans, lined on bottoms with waxed paper. Bake at 350° for 30 to 35 minutes, or until a cake tester inserted in centers comes out clean. Immediately run spatula around pans between cakes and sides. Cool in pans 15 minutes. Remove from pans; remove paper and finish cooling on racks. Spread filling and frosting between layers and over top of cake.
Makes one 9-inch layer cake.
COCONUT-PECAN FILLING AND FROSTING: Combine 1 cup evaporated milk or heavy cream, 1 cup sugar, 3 slightly beaten egg yolks, 1/2 cup butter or margarine and 1 teaspoon vanilla in saucepan. Cook and stir over medium heat until mixture thickens, about 12 minutes. Remove from heat and stir in 1 1/3 cups (about) BAKER'S® ANGEL FLAKE® Coconut and 1 cup chopped pecans. Cool until of spreading consistency, beating occasionally.
Makes 2 1/2 cups.

Choco-Coconut Cake Roll

4 egg whites, at room
  temperature
1/2 cup sugar
4 egg yolks, at room
  temperature
1/3 cup sugar
1 teaspoon vanilla
1/2 cup unsifted all-purpose flour
1/3 cup HERSHEY'S Cocoa
1/2 teaspoon baking powder
1/4 teaspoon baking soda
1/8 teaspoon salt
1/3 cup water
  Cherry-Coconut Filling
  Confectioners' sugar

Line 15 1/2×10 1/2×1-inch jelly roll pan with aluminum foil; generously grease foil. Set aside. Beat egg whites in large mixer bowl until foamy; gradually add 1/2 cup sugar and beat until stiff peaks form. Set aside.

Beat egg yolks in small mixer bowl 3 minutes on high speed. Gradually add 1/3 cup sugar and the vanilla; continue beating 2 additional minutes. Combine flour, cocoa, baking powder, baking soda and salt; add alternately with water to egg yolk mixture, beating on low speed just until batter is smooth. Gradually fold chocolate mixture into beaten egg whites until mixture is well blended.

Spread batter evenly in prepared pan. Bake at 375° for 12 to 15 minutes or until cake springs back when touched lightly. Invert onto towel sprinkled with confectioners' sugar; carefully peel off foil. Immediately roll cake and towel together starting from narrow end; place on wire rack to cool completely.

Prepare Cherry-Coconut Filling. Carefully unroll cake; remove towel. Spread cake with filling; reroll and chill. Sprinkle with confectioners' sugar just before serving.
8 to 10 servings.

Cherry-Coconut Filling

1 cup heavy or whipping cream
3 tablespoons confectioners'
  sugar
  Few drops red food color
  (optional)
1/3 cup chopped maraschino
  cherries, well drained
1/2 cup flaked coconut

Beat cream until slightly thickened. Add confectioners' sugar and food color; beat until stiff. Fold in cherries and coconut.

Chocolate Sheet Cake

1 1/4 cups margarine or butter
1/2 cup unsweetened cocoa
1 cup water
2 cups unsifted flour
1 1/2 cups firmly packed brown
  sugar
1 teaspoon baking soda
1 teaspoon ground cinnamon
1/2 teaspoon salt
1 (14-ounce) can EAGLE® Brand
  Sweetened Condensed Milk
  (NOT evaporated milk)
2 eggs
1 teaspoon vanilla extract
1 cup confectioners' sugar
1 cup nuts

Preheat oven to 350°. In small saucepan, melt *1 cup* margarine; stir in *1/4 cup* cocoa, then water. Bring to a boil; remove from heat. In large mixer bowl, combine flour, brown sugar, baking soda, cinnamon and salt. Add cocoa mixture; beat well. Stir in *1/3 cup* sweetened condensed milk, eggs and vanilla. Pour into greased 15×10-inch jellyroll pan. Bake 15 minutes or until cake springs back when lightly touched. In small saucepan, melt remaining *1/4 cup* margarine; add remaining *1/4 cup* cocoa and remaining sweetened condensed milk. Stir in confectioners' sugar and nuts. Spread on *warm* cake.
Makes one 15×10-inch cake.

Strawberry Tunnel Cream Cake

1 (10-inch) prepared round angel
  food cake
2 (3-ounce) packages cream
  cheese, softened
1 (14-ounce) can EAGLE® Brand
  Sweetened Condensed Milk
  (NOT evaporated milk)
1/3 cup REALEMON® Lemon Juice
  from Concentrate
1 teaspoon almond extract
2 to 4 drops red food coloring,
  optional
1 cup chopped fresh
  strawberries
1 (12-ounce) container frozen
  non-dairy whipped topping,
  thawed (5 1/4 cups)
  Additional fresh strawberries,
  optional

Invert cake onto serving plate. Cut 1-inch slice crosswise from top of cake; set aside. With sharp knife, cut around cake 1 inch from center hole and 1 inch from outer edge, leaving cake walls 1 inch thick. Remove cake from center, leaving 1-inch-thick base on bottom of cake. Reserve cake pieces. In large mixer bowl, beat cheese until fluffy. Gradually beat in sweetened condensed milk until smooth. Stir in ReaLemon® brand, extract and food coloring if desired. Stir in reserved torn cake pieces and chopped strawberries. Fold in *1 cup* whipped topping. Fill cavity of cake with strawberry mixture; replace top slice of cake. Chill 3 hours or until set. Frost with remaining whipped topping; garnish with strawberries if desired. Store in refrigerator.
Makes one 10-inch cake.

Cranberry Pudding Cake with Sauce

1 package (2-layer size) yellow cake mix*
1 package (4-serving size) JELL-O® Lemon Flavor Instant Pudding and Pie Filling
4 eggs
1 cup (½ pint) sour cream*
¼ cup vegetable oil
½ cup chopped nuts
1 can (16 ounces) whole berry cranberry sauce or jellied cranberry sauce cut in small cubes
1 package (4-serving size) JELL-O® Lemon Flavor Pudding and Pie Filling
½ cup sugar
¼ teaspoon salt
1 tablespoon butter or margarine

Combine cake mix, instant pudding mix, eggs, sour cream, oil and nuts in large bowl. With electric mixer at low speed, blend just to moisten, scraping sides of bowl often. Then beat at medium speed for 4 minutes. Fold in half of the cranberry sauce. Pour batter into 2 greased and floured 9×5-inch loaf pans. Bake in preheated 350° oven for 50 to 55 minutes or until cake tester inserted in center of cake comes out clean and cake begins to pull away from sides of pan. Do not underbake. Cool in pans on wire rack 15 minutes. Remove from pans and finish cooling on wire rack.

Add water to remaining cranberry sauce to make 2½ cups. Combine pudding mix, sugar, salt and measured liquid in medium saucepan. Cook and stir over medium heat until mixture comes to a full boil and is thickened. Remove from heat. Stir in butter. Serve warm over cake.
Makes two 9×5-inch loaves.

   Substitution: Use pudding-included cake mix, decreasing sour cream to ¾ cup.

Golden Crunch Cake

2 cups fine vanilla wafer crumbs
1 cup finely chopped pecans
½ cup sugar
¼ cup (½ stick) butter or margarine
1 package DUNCAN HINES® Butter Recipe Golden Cake Mix
3 large eggs
½ cup (1 stick) butter or margarine, softened
⅔ cup water

1. Preheat oven to 375°F. Grease two 9×5×3-inch pans.
2. Combine wafer crumbs, pecans and sugar in bowl. Add ¼ cup butter and cut in with pastry blender until crumbs are fine. Divide evenly in pans; press on bottom and sides.
3. Combine dry cake mix, eggs, ½ cup butter and water in large mixer bowl. Mix cake as directed on package. Divide batter evenly in pans.
4. Bake at 375°F for 50 to 60 minutes or until toothpick inserted in center comes out clean. Cool in pans on racks 5 minutes. Carefully loosen cake from pans and turn upside down on racks; cool completely.
20 servings.

Mocha Fudge Pudding Cake

¾ cup sugar
1 cup unsifted all-purpose flour
2 teaspoons baking powder
¼ teaspoon salt
½ cup butter or margarine
1 square (1 ounce) HERSHEY'S Unsweetened Baking Chocolate
½ cup milk
1 teaspoon vanilla
½ cup sugar
½ cup packed light brown sugar
¼ cup HERSHEY'S Cocoa
1 cup hot strong coffee
Ice cream

Combine ¾ cup sugar, the flour, baking powder and salt in medium bowl. Melt butter with baking chocolate in small saucepan over low heat; add to dry ingredients with milk and vanilla. Beat until smooth. Pour into 8- or 9-inch square pan.

Combine ½ cup sugar, the brown sugar and cocoa in small bowl; sprinkle evenly over batter. Pour coffee over top; *do not stir.* Bake at 350° for 40 minutes or until center is almost set. Serve warm with ice cream.
8 to 10 servings.

Banana Mocha Cake

2 extra-ripe, medium DOLE™ Bananas
1 teaspoon instant coffee powder
1¼ cups flour
⅔ cup sugar
¼ cup cornstarch
3 tablespoons cocoa
1 teaspoon baking soda
½ teaspoon salt
⅓ cup vegetable oil
1 egg, lightly beaten
1 tablespoon vinegar
1 teaspoon vanilla extract
Silky Mocha Frosting (recipe follows)

Preheat oven to 350°F. Puree bananas in blender (1 cup). Stir coffee powder into pureed bananas. In 9-inch square baking pan, combine flour, sugar, cornstarch, cocoa, baking soda and salt. Blend well. Make a well in center of dry ingredients. Add banana mixture, oil, egg, vinegar and vanilla. Stir in dry mixture with fork until well blended. Bake in preheated oven 30 minutes. Cool completely on wire rack. Spread cake with Silky Mocha Frosting.
Makes 12 servings.
SILKY MOCHA FROSTING: In large mixer bowl, combine 3 tablespoons butter or margarine, 1½ cups sifted powdered sugar, 2 tablespoons cocoa and 1 teaspoon instant coffee powder. Add 2 tablespoons milk and ½ teaspoon vanilla extract. Beat until smooth.

Pineapple Upside-Down Cake

1 can (20 ounces) DOLE®
    Pineapple Slices
2/3 cup butter or margarine
2/3 cup brown sugar, packed
10 maraschino cherries
3/4 cup granulated sugar
2 eggs, separated
1 teaspoon grated lemon peel
1 teaspoon lemon juice
1 teaspoon vanilla extract
1½ cups flour
1¾ teaspoons baking powder
¼ teaspoon salt
½ cup dairy sour cream

Preheat oven to 350°F. Drain pineapple; reserve 2 tablespoons liquid. In 9- or 10-inch cast iron skillet, melt ⅓ cup butter. Remove from heat. Add brown sugar and stir until blended. Arrange pineapple slices in skillet. Place 1 cherry in center of each slice.

In large bowl, beat remaining ⅓ cup butter with ½ cup granulated sugar until fluffy. Beat in egg yolks, lemon peel and juice, and vanilla. In medium bowl, combine flour, baking powder and salt. Blend dry ingredients into creamed mixture alternately with sour cream and reserved pineapple liquid. In large bowl, beat egg whites until soft peaks form. Gradually beat in remaining ¼ cup granulated sugar until stiff peaks form. Fold into batter. Spread evenly over pineapple in skillet.

Bake in preheated oven about 35 minutes or until cake springs back when touched. Let stand in skillet on wire rack 10 minutes. Invert onto serving plate. Serve warm or cold.
Makes 8 to 10 servings.

Strawberries & Cream Angel Cake

1 (10-inch) prepared angel food cake
2 (3-ounce) packages cream cheese, softened
1 (14-ounce) can EAGLE® Brand Sweetened Condensed Milk (NOT evaporated milk)
⅓ cup REALEMON® Lemon Juice from Concentrate
1 teaspoon almond extract
2 to 3 drops red food coloring, optional
1 cup (½ pint) BORDEN® or MEADOW GOLD® Whipping Cream, whipped
1 cup chopped fresh strawberries
    Additional fresh strawberries, optional

Cut 1-inch slice crosswise from top of cake; set aside. With sharp knife, cut around cake 1 inch from center hole and 1 inch from outer edge, leaving cake wall 1 inch thick. Remove cake from center, leaving 1-inch-thick base on bottom of cake. Tear cake removed from center into bite-size pieces; reserve. In large mixer bowl, beat cheese until fluffy. Gradually beat in sweetened condensed milk until smooth. Stir in ReaLemon® brand, almond extract and food coloring if desired. Fold in whipped cream. Reserve two-thirds of cream mixture; refrigerate. Fold strawberries and reserved torn cake pieces into remaining cream mixture; fill cake cavity. Replace top slice of cake; frost with reserved cream mixture. Chill 3 hours or until set. Garnish with additional strawberries if desired. Store in refrigerator.
Makes one 10-inch cake.

Fudgey Pecan Cake

¾ cup butter or margarine, melted
1½ cups sugar
1½ teaspoons vanilla
3 egg yolks
½ cup plus 1 tablespoon HERSHEY'S Cocoa
½ cup unsifted all-purpose flour
3 tablespoons vegetable oil
3 tablespoons water
¾ cup finely chopped pecans
3 egg whites, at room temperature
⅛ teaspoon cream of tartar
⅛ teaspoon salt
    Royal Glaze (see Index)
    Pecan halves (optional)

Line bottom of 9-inch springform pan with aluminum foil; butter foil and side of pan. Set aside. Combine ¾ cup melted butter, the sugar and vanilla in large mixer bowl; beat well. Add egg yolks, one at a time, beating well after each addition. Blend in cocoa, flour, oil and water; beat well. Stir in chopped pecans. Beat egg whites, cream of tartar and salt in small mixer bowl until stiff peaks form. Carefully fold into chocolate mixture. Pour into prepared pan. Bake at 350° for 45 minutes or until top begins to crack slightly. (Cake will not test done in center.) Cool 1 hour. Cover; chill until firm. Remove side of pan.

Prepare Royal Glaze. Pour over cake, allowing glaze to run down side. With narrow metal spatula, spread glaze evenly on top and side. Allow to harden. Garnish with pecan halves.
10 to 12 servings.

Rum-Nut Pudding Cake

1 cup chopped pecans or
    walnuts
1 package (2-layer size) yellow
    cake mix*
1 package (4-serving size)
    JELL-O® Vanilla or Butter
    Pecan Flavor Instant
    Pudding and Pie Filling
4 eggs
3/4 cup water*
1/4 cup vegetable oil
2/3 cup dark rum
1 cup sugar
1/2 cup butter or margarine

Sprinkle nuts evenly in bottom of greased and floured 10-inch tube or fluted tube pan. Combine cake mix, pudding mix, eggs, 1/2 cup of the water, the oil and 1/3 cup of the rum in large bowl. With electric mixer at low speed, blend just to moisten, scraping sides of bowl often. Then beat at medium speed for 4 minutes. Pour batter into pan. Bake in preheated 325° oven for about 1 hour or until cake tester inserted in center comes out clean and cake begins to pull away from sides of pan. Do not underbake. Cool in pan on wire rack 15 minutes.

Meanwhile, combine sugar, butter and remaining 1/4 cup water in small saucepan. Cook and stir over medium-high heat until mixture comes to a boil; boil 5 minutes, stirring constantly. Stir in remaining rum and bring just to a boil.

Invert cake onto serving plate and prick with cake tester or wooden pick. Carefully spoon warm syrup over warm cake. Garnish with whipped topping and pecans, if desired.
Makes one 10-inch cake.

*Substitution: Use pudding-included cake mix, reducing water in batter to 1/4 cup.

Surprise Carrot Cake

1 8-ounce package
    PHILADELPHIA BRAND
    Cream Cheese, softened
1/4 cup sugar
1 egg, beaten

* * *

2 cups flour
1 3/4 cups sugar
2 teaspoons baking soda
2 teaspoons cinnamon
1 teaspoon salt
1 cup oil
3 eggs, beaten
3 cups shredded carrot
1/2 cup chopped nuts

Combine cream cheese, sugar and egg, mixing until well blended. Set aside.

Combine dry ingredients. Add combined oil and eggs, mixing just until moistened. Fold in carrots and nuts. Reserve 2 cups batter; pour remaining batter into greased and floured 9-inch bundt pan. Pour cream cheese mixture over batter; carefully spoon reserved batter over cream cheese mixture, spreading to cover. Bake at 350°, 55 minutes or until wooden pick inserted in center comes out clean. Cool 10 minutes; remove from pan. Cool thoroughly. Sprinkle with powdered sugar, if desired.
12 servings.

Variation: Substitute *Light* PHILADELPHIA BRAND Neufchâtel Cheese for Cream Cheese.

Kentucky Jam Cake

1 1/2 cups flour
1 teaspoon baking soda
1/2 teaspoon salt
1 teaspoon allspice
1/4 teaspoon cinnamon
3/4 cup buttermilk
2 tablespoons whiskey, bourbon
    or fruit juice
1/3 cup shortening
1/2 cup granulated sugar
1/2 cup firmly packed brown sugar
3 eggs, separated
1/2 cup seedless raspberry or
    blackberry jam
2 squares BAKER'S®
    Unsweetened Chocolate,
    melted and cooled
1 cup raisins
1/2 cup chopped nuts*

Mix flour, soda, salt and spices. Combine buttermilk and whiskey. Cream shortening. Gradually beat in sugars and continue beating until light and fluffy. Add egg yolks and beat thoroughly. Alternately add flour and buttermilk mixtures, beating after each addition until smooth. Blend in jam and chocolate. Fold in raisins and nuts. Beat egg whites until stiff peaks form; fold into batter.

Pour into well-greased 9-inch tube pan. Bake at 350° for 50 to 55 minutes, or until cake tester inserted in center of cake comes out clean. Cool in pan 15 minutes. Remove sides of pan and finish cooling upright on rack. Loosen from tube and bottom; invert onto rack. Wrap in aluminum foil or plastic wrap. Store in refrigerator at least 2 days to mellow flavors. Serve at room temperature. Sprinkle with confectioners sugar and garnish with raspberries, if desired.
Makes one 9-inch cake.

*Or use 8 squares Baker's® Semi-Sweet Chocolate, cut into large (3/8-inch) chunks.

Pudding Poke Cake

1 package (2-layer size) yellow cake mix or pudding-included cake mix*
Ingredients for cake mix
2 packages (4-serving size) JELL-O® Chocolate Flavor Instant Pudding and Pie Filling*
1 cup confectioners sugar
4 cups cold milk

Prepare and bake cake as directed on package for 13×9-inch cake. Remove from oven. Poke holes at once down through cake to pan with round handle of wooden spoon. (Or poke holes with plastic drinking straw, using turning motion to make large holes.) Holes should be at 1-inch intervals.

Only after the holes are made, combine pudding mix with sugar in large bowl. Gradually stir in milk. Beat with electric mixer at low speed for not more than 1 minute. Do not overbeat. Quickly, before pudding thickens, pour about half of the thin pudding evenly over warm cake and into holes. (This will make stripes in cake.) Allow remaining pudding to thicken slightly; then spoon over the top, swirling it to "frost" the cake. Chill at least 1 hour. Store cake in refrigerator.
Makes one 13×9-inch cake.

Peanut Butter Poke Cake: Prepare Pudding Poke Cake as directed, using chocolate flavor instant pudding and pie filling. Add ½ cup peanut butter to pudding mix and confectioners sugar with ½ cup of the milk; blend well before adding remaining milk and beating.

*Additional Flavor Combinations: Use yellow cake mix with butterscotch or pistachio flavor pudding mix.

Use chocolate cake mix with chocolate, vanilla, coconut cream, banana cream or pistachio flavor pudding mix.

Use lemon cake mix with lemon flavor pudding mix.

Use white cake mix with butterscotch, chocolate, pistachio or vanilla pudding mix.

Easy Pina Colada Cake

1 (18¼- to 18½-ounce) package yellow cake mix*
1 (4-serving size) package *instant* vanilla flavor pudding and pie filling mix
1 (15-ounce) can COCO LOPEZ® Cream of Coconut
½ cup plus 2 tablespoons rum
⅓ cup vegetable oil
4 eggs
1 (8-ounce) can crushed pineapple, *well drained*
Whipped cream, pineapple chunks, maraschino cherries, toasted coconut for garnish

Preheat oven to 350°. In large mixer bowl, combine cake mix, pudding mix, *½ cup* cream of coconut, *½ cup* rum, oil and eggs. Beat on medium speed 2 minutes. Stir in pineapple. Pour into well-greased and floured 10-inch bundt or tube pan. Bake 50 to 55 minutes. Cool 10 minutes. Remove from pan. With a table knife or skewer, poke holes about 1 inch apart in cake almost to bottom. Combine remaining cream of coconut and remaining *2 tablespoons* rum; slowly spoon over cake. Chill thoroughly. Garnish as desired. Store in refrigerator.
Makes one 10-inch cake.

*If cake mix with "pudding in" is used, omit pudding mix.

Old-Fashioned Lemon Pudding Cake

3 eggs, separated
1 cup sugar
¼ cup unsifted flour
¼ teaspoon salt
1 cup BORDEN® or MEADOW GOLD® Milk
¼ cup REALEMON® Lemon Juice from Concentrate

Preheat oven to 325°. In small mixer bowl, beat egg whites until stiff but not dry; set aside. In medium bowl, combine sugar, flour and salt. In small bowl, beat egg yolks; stir in milk and ReaLemon® brand. Add to flour mixture; mix well. Fold in egg whites; pour into 1-quart baking dish. Place in larger pan; fill with 1 inch hot water. Bake 50 to 55 minutes or until top is well browned. Cool about 30 minutes before serving. Spoon pudding over cake in serving dishes. Refrigerate leftovers.
Makes 6 to 8 servings.

Individual Servings: Pour mixture into 8 (6-ounce) custard cups; place in shallow pan. Fill with 1 inch hot water. Bake 35 to 40 minutes.

Chocolate Swirl Cake

1 cup butter or margarine, softened
2 cups sugar
2 teaspoons vanilla
3 eggs
2¾ cups unsifted all-purpose flour
1 teaspoon baking soda
½ teaspoon salt
1 cup buttermilk or sour milk*
1 cup HERSHEY'S Syrup
¼ teaspoon baking soda
1 cup flaked coconut (optional)

Cream butter, sugar and vanilla in large mixer bowl until light and fluffy. Add eggs; beat well. Combine flour, 1 teaspoon baking soda and the salt; add alternately with buttermilk to creamed mixture. Combine syrup and ¼ teaspoon baking soda. Measure 2 cups batter into small bowl; blend in syrup mixture.

Add coconut to remaining batter; pour into greased and floured 12-cup Bundt pan or 10-inch tube pan. Pour chocolate batter over vanilla batter in pan; *do not mix.* Bake at 350° about 70 minutes or until cake tester comes out clean. Cool 15 minutes; remove from pan. Cool completely; glaze or frost as desired.
12 to 16 servings.

*To sour milk: Use 1 tablespoon vinegar plus milk to equal 1 cup.

Strawberries Romanoff on Angel Slices

**1 package DUNCAN HINES®
  Deluxe Angel Food Cake Mix**
1⅓ cups water
**1½ pints fresh strawberries,
  hulled and halved
  lengthwise**
⅓ cup orange juice
**3 tablespoons orange-flavored
  liqueur**
2 tablespoons sugar
1 cup whipping cream
½ teaspoon vanilla extract

1. Preheat oven to 375°F.
2. Prepare cake with water as directed on package. Pour batter into ungreased 10-inch tube pan. Cut through batter with knife or spatula to remove large air bubbles.
3. Bake at 375°F for 30 to 40 minutes or until top crust is golden brown, firm and dry. Do not underbake. To cool, hang pan upside down on funnel or bottle at least 1½ hours.
4. Place strawberries in bowl. Combine orange juice, 2 tablespoons of the liqueur and sugar; pour over strawberries. Cover with plastic wrap. Refrigerate, occasionally spooning liquid over strawberries.
5. Beat whipping cream until soft peaks form. Beat in remaining 1 tablespoon liqueur and vanilla extract. Beat until thick. Refrigerate until ready to use.
6. To serve, cut cake into slices. Spoon some strawberrries and liquid over cake slices; top with whipped cream.
12 to 16 servings.

New Orleans Crumb Cake

**1 package DUNCAN HINES®
  Deluxe Devil's Food Cake
  Mix**
3 large eggs
**½ cup CRISCO® Oil or PURITAN®
  Oil**
1⅓ cups water
1 cup graham cracker crumbs
**3 tablespoons CRISCO®
  Shortening, melted**
**1 package (6 ounces) semisweet
  chocolate pieces (1 cup)**
½ cup chopped nuts
  **Sweetened whipped cream, if
  desired**

1. Preheat oven to 350°F. Grease and flour 13×9×2-inch pan.
2. Combine dry cake mix, eggs, oil and water in large mixer bowl. Mix cake as directed on package. Turn batter into pan and spread evenly.
3. Combine graham cracker crumbs and melted shortening; mix well. Stir in chocolate pieces and nuts. Sprinkle evenly over batter.
4. Bake at 350°F for 40 to 50 minutes or until toothpick inserted in center comes out clean. Cool in pan on rack. Serve with whipped cream.
16 servings.

Birthday Cakelets

**2 packages DUNCAN HINES®
  Deluxe Devil's Food Cake
  Mix**
6 large eggs
**1 cup CRISCO® Oil or PURITAN®
  Oil**
2⅔ cups water
2 cups light corn syrup
4 large egg whites
⅛ teaspoon salt
  Red food coloring
½ teaspoon peppermint extract

1. Preheat oven to 350°F. Grease and flour two 13×9×2-inch pans.
2. Combine dry cake mix, whole eggs, oil and water in large mixer bowl. Mix, bake and cool cakes as directed on package. Freeze cooled cakes at least 2 hours.
3. For frosting, heat syrup to boiling. Beat egg whites in large mixer bowl at medium speed until frothy. Add salt and continue beating until soft peaks form. Turn mixer to high speed and gradually add hot corn syrup, beating until soft peaks form. Fold in food coloring to tint delicate pink. Fold in peppermint extract.
4. Draw heart on 3-inch square of cardboard; cut out. Set heart pattern on lower left corner of one cake. Cut around pattern through cake. Cut out 11 more hearts before removing cake pieces. Repeat with remaining cake.
5. Frost sides and tops of each cake heart. Insert pink birthday candle in center of each heart.
24 servings.

Cream Cheese Frosting

**4 squares BAKER'S® Semi-
  Sweet Chocolate**
**1 package (3 ounces) cream
  cheese, at room temperature**
1 tablespoon light cream or milk
¼ teaspoon salt
1 cup sifted confectioners sugar
½ teaspoon vanilla

Melt chocolate in saucepan over very low heat, stirring constantly until smooth. Remove from heat. Blend in cream cheese, cream and salt. Gradually beat in sugar and continue beating until smooth. Add vanilla.
Makes 1 cup, or enough to cover tops of two 8-inch layers, the top of one 9-inch square cake or the tops of 1 dozen cupcakes.

Lemon Icing

2 tablespoons margarine or
    butter
3 to 4 teaspoons REALEMON®
    Lemon Juice from
    Concentrate
1 cup confectioners' sugar

In small saucepan, melt margarine with ReaLemon® brand; remove from heat. Stir in sugar; mix well. Drizzle warm icing over 10-inch bundt or tube cake, coffee cake or sweet rolls.
Makes about 1/2 cup.

Continental Flair Frosting

1 cup sugar
1 cup heavy cream or
    evaporated milk
4 squares BAKER'S®
    Unsweetened Chocolate
1/2 cup butter or margarine, at
    room temperature
1 teaspoon rum extract or
    vanilla

Combine sugar and cream in saucepan. Bring to a boil over medium heat, stirring constantly. Reduce heat and simmer gently for 6 minutes. Remove from heat. Add chocolate and stir until chocolate is melted. Blend in butter and rum extract. Chill until mixture begins to thicken; then beat until thick, creamy and of spreading consistency.
Makes about 2 1/2 cups, or enough to cover tops and sides of two 8- or 9-inch cake layers, the top and sides of one 9-inch square or 13×9-inch cake, or the tops of 24 cupcakes.
Note: Recipe may be halved.

Classic Fudge Frosting

4 squares BAKER'S®
    Unsweetened Chocolate
2 tablespoons butter or
    margarine
1 pound (4 cups) confectioners
    sugar
Dash of salt
1/2 cup milk
1 teaspoon vanilla

Melt chocolate with butter over very low heat, stirring constantly until smooth. Remove from heat. Combine sugar, salt, milk and vanilla. Add chocolate, blending well. If necessary, let stand until of spreading consistency, stirring occasionally. Spread quickly, adding a small amount of additional milk if frosting thickens.
Makes about 2 1/2 cups, or enough to cover tops and sides of two 8- or 9-inch layers, the top and sides of one 9-inch square or 13×9-inch cake, or the tops of 24 cupcakes.

Chocolate Cream Cheese Frosting

3 packages (3 ounces each)
    cream cheese, softened
1/3 cup butter or margarine,
    softened
5 cups confectioners' sugar
1 cup HERSHEY'S Cocoa
5 to 7 tablespoons light cream

Blend cream cheese and butter in large mixer bowl. Combine confectioners' sugar and cocoa; add alternately with cream to cream cheese mixture. Beat to spreading consistency.
About 3 cups frosting.

Royal Glaze

8 squares (8 ounces)
    HERSHEY'S Semi-Sweet
    Baking Chocolate, broken
    into pieces*
1/2 cup heavy or whipping cream

Combine chocolate pieces and cream in small saucepan. Cook over very low heat, stirring constantly, until chocolate is melted and mixture is smooth; *do not boil.* Remove from heat; cool, stirring occasionally, until mixture begins to thicken, about 10 to 15 minutes.
About 1 cup.
  *You may substitute 1 1/3 cups HERSHEY'S Semi-Sweet Chocolate Chips for the baking chocolate.

Quick Fluffy Frosting

1 1/2 cups cold milk
1 envelope DREAM WHIP®
    Whipped Topping Mix
1 package (4-serving size)
    JELL-O® Instant Pudding
    and Pie Filling, any flavor

Pour milk into deep narrow bowl; add whipped topping mix and pudding mix. With electric mixer at low speed, beat until well blended. Gradually increase beating speed to high and whip until mixture forms soft peaks, 4 to 6 minutes. Makes enough to frost 2-layer 9-inch cake. Store frosted cake in refrigerator.
Makes about 3 cups.

Chocolate Butter Frosting

6 tablespoons butter or margarine
Dash of salt
1 pound (4 cups) confectioners sugar
2 squares BAKER'S® Unsweetened Chocolate, melted and cooled
4 tablespoons (about) milk
1½ teaspoons vanilla

Cream butter with salt. Gradually beat in part of the sugar. Blend in chocolate. Alternately add remaining sugar with milk until of spreading consistency, beating after each addition until smooth. Blend in vanilla.
Makes 3 cups, or enough to cover tops and sides of two 8- or 9-inch layers or the top and sides of one 13×9-inch cake.

Quick Chocolate Frosting

4 squares (4 ounces) HERSHEY'S Unsweetened Baking Chocolate
¼ cup butter or margarine
3 cups confectioners' sugar
1 teaspoon vanilla
⅛ teaspoon salt
⅓ cup milk

Melt baking chocolate and butter in small saucepan over very low heat, stirring constantly, until chocolate is melted and mixture is smooth. Pour into small mixer bowl; add confectioners' sugar, vanilla and salt. Blend in milk; beat to spreading consistency.
(If frosting is too thick, add additional milk, 1 teaspoonful at a time, until frosting is desired consistency.)
About 2 cups frosting.

Chocolate Satin Glaze

2 tablespoons sugar
2 tablespoons water
½ cup HERSHEY'S MINI CHIPS Semi-Sweet Chocolate

Combine sugar and water in small saucepan; cook over medium heat, stirring constantly, until mixture boils and sugar is dissolved. Remove from heat; immediately add MINI CHIPS Chocolate, stirring until melted. Continue stirring until glaze is desired consistency.
About ½ cup glaze.

Chocolate Glaze

3 squares BAKER'S® Semi-Sweet Chocolate*
3 tablespoons water
1 tablespoon butter or margarine
1 cup sifted confectioners sugar
Dash of salt
½ teaspoon vanilla

Place chocolate, water and butter in saucepan. Stir constantly over very low heat until mixture is smooth. Remove from heat. Combine sugar and salt in bowl. Gradually blend in chocolate mixture and vanilla. For thinner glaze, add a small amount of hot water. For thicker glaze, cool until of desired consistency.
Makes about ¾ cup, or enough for a 9- or 10-inch tube cake, 8- or 9-inch layer cake, 13×9-inch cake or a 10-inch cake roll.
*Or, use 1 package (4 ounces) BAKER'S® GERMAN'S® Sweet Chocolate.

Chocolate-Coconut Frosting

⅓ cup sugar
1 tablespoon cornstarch
¾ cup evaporated milk
1 HERSHEY'S Milk Chocolate Bar (4 ounces), broken into pieces
1 tablespoon butter or margarine
1 cup flaked coconut
½ cup chopped nuts

Combine sugar and cornstarch in small saucepan; blend in evaporated milk. Cook over medium heat, stirring constantly, until mixture boils; remove from heat. Add chocolate bar pieces and butter; stir until chocolate is melted and mixture is smooth. Stir in coconut and nuts. Immediately spread on cake.
About 2 cups frosting.

Bittersweet Glaze

2 squares BAKER'S® Unsweetened Chocolate
2 tablespoons butter or margarine
Dash of salt
1¾ cups confectioners sugar
3 tablespoons (about) hot water

1. Melt chocolate with butter in saucepan over very low heat, stirring constantly until smooth. Remove from heat and add salt. Alternately add sugar with water until of spreading consistency.
Makes 1 cup, or enough for a 9- or 10-inch tube cake, 9-inch square cake, 10-inch cake roll or about 3½ dozen cookies.

Fudge 'n' Banana Cupcakes

> 1 package DUNCAN HINES®
>   Deluxe Devil's Food Cake
>   Mix
> 3 large eggs
> ½ cup CRISCO® Oil or PURITAN®
>   Oil
> 1⅓ cups water
> ½ cup (1 stick) butter or
>   margarine
> 2 ounces (2 squares)
>   unsweetened chocolate
> 1 pound confectioners' sugar
> ½ cup half-and-half
> 1 teaspoon vanilla extract
> 4 medium bananas
> 2 tablespoons lemon juice

1. Preheat oven to 350°F. Line 24 muffin cups with paper baking cups.
2. Combine dry cake mix, eggs, oil and water in large mixer bowl. Mix, bake and cool cupcakes as directed on package.
3. For frosting*, melt butter and chocolate in heavy saucepan over low heat. Remove from heat. Add confectioners' sugar alternately with half-and-half, mixing until smooth after each addition. Beat in vanilla extract. Add more confectioners' sugar to thicken or milk to thin as needed.
4. Using small paring knife, remove cone-shaped piece from top center of each cupcake. Dot top of each cone with frosting. Frost top of each cupcake spreading frosting down into cone-shaped hole. Slice bananas and dip in lemon juice. Stand three banana slices in each hole. Set cone-shaped pieces, pointed-side-up, on banana slices.
24 cupcakes.

*Or use 1 can Duncan Hines® Dark Dutch Fudge or Chocolate Frosting.

Creme-Filled Cupcakes

> ¾ cup shortening
> 1¼ cups sugar
> 2 eggs
> 1 teaspoon vanilla
> 1¾ cups unsifted all-purpose flour
> ½ cup HERSHEY'S Cocoa
> 1 teaspoon baking soda
> ½ teaspoon salt
> 1 cup milk
>   Vanilla Creme

Cream shortening and sugar in large mixer bowl. Add eggs and vanilla; blend well. Combine flour, cocoa, baking soda and salt; add alternately with milk to creamed mixture. Fill paper-lined muffin cups (2½ inches in diameter) two-thirds full with batter. Bake at 375° for 20 to 25 minutes or until cake tester comes out clean. Cool completely.

Prepare Vanilla Creme; spoon into pastry bag with open star tip. Insert tip into center of top of cupcake; gently squeeze until cupcake begins to peak. Cover top with swirl of filling. (Or cut a 1½-inch cone from top of cupcake. Fill; replace cone. Swirl filling over top.)
About 2 dozen cupcakes.

Vanilla Creme

> ¼ cup unsifted all-purpose flour
> ½ cup milk
> ¼ cup butter or margarine,
>   softened
> ¼ cup shortening
> 2 teaspoons vanilla
> ¼ teaspoon salt
> 4 cups confectioners' sugar

Combine flour and milk in small saucepan; cook over low heat, stirring constantly with wire whisk, until mixture thickens and just begins to boil. Remove from heat; chill. Cream butter and shortening in large mixer bowl; blend in vanilla, salt and the chilled flour mixture. Gradually add confectioners' sugar; beat to spreading consistency.

Chocolate Zucchini Cupcakes

> 1½ cups unsifted all-purpose flour
> ¾ cup sugar
> ¼ cup unsweetened cocoa
> 1½ teaspoons baking soda
> ½ teaspoon salt
> 1 cup shredded, peeled zucchini
> ⅓ cup CRISCO® Oil
> ⅓ cup buttermilk
> 1 egg
> 1 teaspoon vanilla

Frosting:
> 1½ cups confectioners sugar
> 2 tablespoons butter or
>   margarine, softened
> 2 to 3 tablespoons milk, divided
> ¼ teaspoon vanilla

Preheat oven to 350°F. Place paper liners in 12 muffin cups. Set aside.

Mix flour, sugar, cocoa, baking soda and salt in medium mixing bowl. Add remaining cake ingredients. Beat with electric mixer at low speed until ingredients are moistened, scraping bowl constantly. Beat at high speed 1 minute, scraping bowl occasionally. Pour into lined muffin cups, filling each about ⅔ full. Bake at 350°F, 20 to 25 minutes, or until wooden pick inserted in center comes out clean. Remove from pan. Cool completely on wire rack.

For frosting, combine confectioners sugar, butter, 1 tablespoon milk and vanilla in small mixing bowl at low speed until smooth, scraping bowl frequently. Beat in additional milk until thick enough to spread. Spread on cooled cupcakes.
1 dozen cupcakes.

Black Bottom Cupcakes

2 packages (3 ounces each) cream cheese, softened
1⅓ cups sugar
1 egg
1 package (6 ounces) chocolate chips
1½ cups flour
¼ cup unsweetened cocoa
1 teaspoon baking soda
½ teaspoon salt
2 extra-ripe, medium DOLE™ Bananas
⅓ cup vegetable oil
1 teaspoon vanilla extract
1 firm, large DOLE™ Banana

Preheat oven to 350°F. Line 18 muffin cups with paper liners. In small bowl, beat cream cheese and ⅓ cup sugar until light and fluffy. Add egg; beat until well blended. Stir in chocolate chips. Set aside.

In large bowl, combine remaining 1 cup sugar, flour, cocoa, baking soda and salt; mix well. Puree extra-ripe bananas in blender (1 cup). Combine pureed bananas with oil and vanilla. Stir banana mixture into dry ingredients until smooth.

Divide batter evenly among prepared muffin cups. Thinly slice firm banana; place 2 slices in center of batter in each muffin cup. Divide cream cheese mixture evenly over bananas in muffin cups. Bake in preheated oven 30 minutes or until wooden pick inserted in center comes out clean. Cool in pan on wire rack.
Makes 18 cupcakes.

Chocolatetown Cupcakes

½ cup butter or margarine, softened
1 cup sugar
1 teaspoon vanilla
4 eggs
1¼ cups unsifted all-purpose flour
¾ teaspoon baking soda
1½ cups (16-ounce can) HERSHEY'S Syrup

Cream butter, sugar and vanilla in large mixer bowl until light and fluffy. Add eggs; beat well. Combine flour and baking soda; add alternately with syrup to creamed mixture. Fill paper-lined muffin cups (2½ inches in diameter) half full with batter. Bake at 375° for 15 to 20 minutes or until cake tester comes out clean. Cool; frost as desired.
About 2½ dozen cupcakes.

Chocolate Butterscotch Chip Cupcakes

½ cup cake flour
1 package (6 ounces) butterscotch-flavored pieces (1 cup), divided
1 package (6 ounces) semisweet chocolate pieces (1 cup), divided
1 package DUNCAN HINES® Deluxe White Cake Mix
3 egg whites or 3 whole eggs
⅓ cup CRISCO® Oil or PURITAN® Oil
1¼ cups water

1. Preheat oven to 350°F. Line 24 muffin cups with paper baking cups.
2. Combine cake flour, ½ cup butterscotch pieces and ½ cup chocolate pieces in small bowl.
3. Combine dry cake mix, egg whites or whole eggs, oil and water in large mixer bowl. Mix cake as directed on package. Stir in chocolate-butterscotch mixture. Spoon batter into muffin cups, filling about two-thirds full.
4. Bake at 350°F for 18 to 23 minutes or until toothpick inserted in centers comes out clean. Cool in pans on racks 10 minutes. Remove from pans; cool completely on racks.
5. For chocolate-butterscotch frosting, melt remaining ½ cup butterscotch and ½ cup chocolate pieces in small saucepan over low heat; stir until smooth. Spread over cooled cupcakes.
24 cupcakes.

Sherried Fruit-Spice Cake

½ cup cream sherry
½ cup SUN-MAID® Raisins
½ cup finely chopped dried figs
½ cup chopped pitted prunes
½ cup finely chopped dried apricots
1½ cups milk
5 cups all-purpose flour
⅔ cup granulated sugar
1 package active dry yeast
½ teaspoon salt
¾ cup butter or margarine, softened
½ cup packed brown sugar
2 eggs
1 teaspoon ground cinnamon
½ teaspoon ground nutmeg
⅛ teaspoon ground cloves
1 cup chopped DIAMOND® Walnuts
Sherry Icing (recipe follows)
DIAMOND® Walnut halves, for garnish
Dried figs, prunes or apricots, for garnish

In small saucepan over low heat, warm sherry; add the 1/2 cup each raisins, figs, prunes and apricots. Remove from heat. Let stand, covered, several hours or overnight. In small saucepan over low heat, scald milk; cool to lukewarm (110° to 115°F). In large bowl, combine 1 1/2 cups of the flour, 1/3 cup of the granulated sugar, the yeast and salt. Add milk, stirring until combined. Cover; let rise in warm place (85°F) until doubled, 45 to 60 minutes.

Stir yeast mixture down. In large bowl, beat butter, brown sugar and remaining 1/3 cup granulated sugar until fluffy. Add eggs, one at a time, beating 1 minute after each addition. Stir in fruit-sherry and yeast mixtures. In medium bowl, combine remaining 3 1/2 cups flour, the cinnamon, nutmeg and cloves. Stir into dough along with the 1 cup walnuts. Place dough into greased and lightly floured 10-inch fluted tube- pan. Cover; let rise in warm place until nearly doubled, about 1 1/2 hours. Bake in preheated 350°F oven about 1 hour or until cake pulls away from edge of pan. Cover with foil the last 15 minutes, if necessary, to prevent overbrowning. Loosen edges and invert onto wire rack; cool completely. Glaze cake with Sherry Icing. Top with walnut halves. Garnish with figs, prunes and apricots, if desired.
Makes one 10-inch cake.
SHERRY ICING: In medium bowl, combine 1 cup sifted powdered sugar, 1/2 teaspoon vanilla and enough cream sherry (1 to 2 tablespoons) to make of drizzling consistency.

Ever-So-Easy Fruitcake

2 1/2 cups unsifted flour
1 teaspoon baking soda
2 eggs, slightly beaten
1 jar NONE SUCH® Ready-to-Use Mincemeat (Regular *or* Brandy & Rum)
1 (14-ounce) can EAGLE® Brand Sweetened Condensed Milk (NOT evaporated milk)
2 cups (1 pound) mixed candied fruit
1 cup coarsely chopped nuts

Preheat oven to 300°. Grease and flour 10-inch bundt pan. Combine flour and baking soda; set aside. In large bowl, combine remaining ingredients; blend in dry ingredients. Pour batter into prepared pan. Bake 1 hour and 45 to 50 minutes or until wooden pick comes out clean. Cool 15 minutes. Turn out of pan. Garnish as desired.
Makes one 10-inch cake.

Tip: To substitute condensed mincemeat for ready-to-use mincemeat, crumble 2 (9-ounce) packages None Such® Condensed Mincemeat into small saucepan; add 1 1/2 cups water. Boil briskly 1 minute. Cool. Proceed as above.

Chocolate Fruitcake: Prepare fruitcake batter as above, adding 3 (1-ounce) squares unsweetened chocolate, melted. For glaze, melt 3 (1-ounce) squares semi-sweet chocolate with 2 tablespoons margarine or butter. Spoon over fruitcake.

Fruitcake-in-a-Can: Grease three 1-pound coffee cans; fill each can with about 2 2/3 cups batter. Bake 1 hour and 20 to 25 minutes. *Or,* grease eight 10 3/4-ounce soup cans; fill each with 1 cup batter. Bake 50 to 55 minutes.

Fruitcake Bars: Grease 15×10-inch jellyroll pan; spread batter evenly in pan. Bake 40 to 45 minutes. Cool. Glaze if desired. Makes about 4 dozen bars.

Fruitcake Loaves: Grease two 9×5-inch loaf pans. Pour half the batter into each pan. Bake 1 hour and 20 to 25 minutes.

Fruitcake Cookies: Drop by rounded tablespoonfuls, 2 inches apart, onto greased baking sheets. Bake 15 to 18 minutes. Makes about 5 1/2 dozen cookies.

Fruitcake Mini Loaves: Grease twelve 4 1/2×2 1/2-inch loaf pans. Fill each pan 2/3 full. Bake 35 to 40 minutes.

Spicy Walnut Fruitcake

1 cup DIAMOND® Walnuts, coarsely chopped
1 cup SUN-MAID® Raisins
1 cup pitted dates, coarsely chopped
2/3 cup SUN-MAID® Zante Currants
1/2 cup sliced dried apricots
1/2 cup halved candied cherries
1/4 cup chopped candied orange peel
1/4 cup chopped candied lemon peel
1/3 cup butter or margarine, softened
1/2 cup sugar
1/2 teaspoon salt
1 teaspoon ground cinnamon
1/2 teaspoon *each* ground allspice, nutmeg and mace
1/4 teaspoon ground ginger
2 eggs, beaten
1/8 teaspoon baking soda
1/4 cup molasses
1 cup all-purpose flour
Powdered Sugar Glaze (recipe follows)
DIAMOND® Walnut halves and candied fruit, for garnish

In large bowl, combine chopped walnuts, fruits and peels; mix well. In another large bowl, cream butter, sugar, salt and spices until fluffy. Beat in eggs. Add soda, molasses and flour; mix to moderately stiff batter. Stir in walnut-fruit mixture. Pack batter into well-greased and floured 6-cup mold or pan. Bake in preheated 275°F oven about 2 1/2 hours or until center springs back when lightly touched. Cool completely, then loosen edges and remove from pan. Wrap in foil and store at least 48 hours in a cool, dry place. Before serving, glaze with Powdered Sugar Glaze and decorate with walnut halves and candied fruits.
Makes one cake.
POWDERED SUGAR GLAZE: In small bowl, combine 1 cup sifted powdered sugar, 1/2 teaspoon vanilla and enough milk (1 to 2 tablespoons) to make of drizzling consistency.

Festive Cranberry Torte

1 8-ounce package
   PHILADELPHIA BRAND
   Cream Cheese, softened
¼ cup sugar
½ cup whipping cream, whipped
1 10¾-ounce frozen pound
   cake, thawed
1 14-ounce jar cranberry orange
   sauce

Combine cream cheese and sugar, mixing until well blended. Fold in whipped cream. Split cake horizontally into four layers. Spread bottom layer with ½ cup cranberry orange sauce; top with second layer. Spread second layer with ⅔ cup cream cheese mixture; top with third layer. Spread third layer with ½ cup cranberry orange sauce. Cover with top cake layer. Frost top and sides of torte with remaining cream cheese mixture. Chill several hours or overnight. Top with remaining cranberry orange sauce just before serving. Garnish with whole cranberries and fresh mint, if desired.
10 to 12 servings.
   Variation: Substitute *Light* PHILADELPHIA BRAND Neufchâtel Cheese for Cream Cheese.

Black Forest Torte

1 (18¼- or 18½-ounce) package
   chocolate cake mix
1 (21-ounce) can cherry pie
   filling, drained and chilled,
   reserving ½ cup sauce
1 (6-ounce) package semi-sweet
   chocolate chips
1 (14-ounce) can EAGLE® Brand
   Sweetened Condensed Milk
   (NOT evaporated milk)
½ teaspoon almond extract

Preheat oven to 350°. Prepare and bake cake mix as package directs for two 9-inch round layers. Remove from pans; cool thoroughly. In heavy saucepan, over medium heat, melt chips with sweetened condensed milk. Cook and stir until mixture thickens, about 10 minutes. Cool 20 minutes. Meanwhile, combine cherries, reserved sauce and extract. Place 1 cake layer on serving plate, top side up. With sharp knife, remove crust from top of cake layer to within ½ inch of edge; top with half the chocolate mixture then the cherries. Top with second cake layer and remaining chocolate mixture. Garnish as desired.
Makes one 9-inch cake.

A Very Special Walnut Torte

Crust:
   ½ cup butter or margarine,
      softened
   ¼ cup sifted powdered sugar
   1 cup all-purpose flour
   2 squares (1 ounce each)
      semisweet chocolate, melted
Filling:
   3 cups granulated sugar
   ⅓ cup light corn syrup
   1 cup butter or margarine
   1 cup whipping cream
   6 cups DIAMOND® Walnuts
   2 squares (1 ounce each)
      semisweet chocolate, melted

To prepare crust: In medium bowl, cream butter and powdered sugar. At low speed, gradually add flour just until blended. With floured hands, pat dough into bottom of 9-inch springform pan. Prick with fork. Bake in preheated 350°F oven 10 minutes. Lower heat to 300°F; bake 20 to 25 minutes longer or until golden. Cool. Spread melted chocolate in thin layer over crust; set aside.
   To prepare filling: In Dutch oven over low heat, warm granulated sugar, stirring as it begins to melt. Stir occasionally until it becomes liquid and turns caramel color, 20 to 30 minutes. Stir in corn syrup, butter and cream. Cook over medium heat

until 240°F registers on candy thermometer (soft-ball stage). Stir in walnuts; immediately pour over prepared crust, pressing flat. Cool completely in refrigerator. Remove sides of springform pan. Drizzle chocolate over torte. Bring to room temperature. Cut in thin wedges with a sharp knife. This is a confection-like torte, and is best eaten out of hand.
Makes 16 servings.

Viennese Cherry Cheese Torte

1 package DUNCAN HINES®
   Butter Recipe Golden Cake
   Mix
3 large eggs
½ cup (1 stick) butter or
   margarine, softened
⅔ cup water
1 package (8 ounces) plus
   1 package (3 ounces) cream
   cheese, softened
⅔ cup sugar
¼ teaspoon ground nutmeg
2 tablespoons milk
1 can (21 ounces) cherry pie
   filling

1. Preheat oven to 375°F. Grease and flour two 8×1½- or 9×1½-inch round layer pans.
2. Combine dry cake mix, eggs, butter and water in large mixer bowl. Mix, bake and cool as directed on package. Refrigerate layers to make splitting easier. Split each cake into 2 thin layers.
3. For filling, beat cream cheese, sugar, nutmeg and milk until smooth.
4. Place one layer on cake plate. Spread with ½ cup cream cheese filling; top with ½ cup cherry filling. Repeat layers, ending with cake layer. Spread remaining cream cheese filling over top layer and top with remaining cherry filling. Refrigerate until ready to serve.
12 to 16 servings.

Chocolate Almond "Philly" Torte

1 8-ounce package PHILADELPHIA BRAND Cream Cheese, softened
¼ cup PARKAY Margarine
1 cup sugar
2 eggs
½ teaspoon vanilla
1½ cups flour
1 teaspoon baking soda
½ teaspoon baking powder
½ cup milk
2 1-ounce squares unsweetened chocolate, melted
Almond and Chocolate "Philly" Cream Frostings

Combine cream cheese, margarine and sugar, mixing until well blended. Blend in eggs and vanilla. Add combined dry ingredients alternately with milk, mixing well after each addition. Blend in chocolate. Spread batter into wax paper-lined 15×10×1-inch jelly roll pan. Bake at 350°, 12 to 15 minutes or until wooden pick inserted in center comes out clean. Cool thoroughly. Cut crosswise into four equal sections; remove from pan. Spread three sections with almond frosting; chill until frosting is firm. Stack. Top with remaining layer; frost top and sides with chocolate frosting. *12 servings.*

Almond and Chocolate "Philly" Cream Frostings

1 8-ounce package PHILADELPHIA BRAND Cream Cheese, softened
6½ cups sifted powdered sugar
½ cup whipping cream
½ cup chopped almonds, toasted
2 1-ounce squares unsweetened chocolate, melted

Beat cream cheese at medium speed on electric mixer. Gradually add 5 cups sugar, mixing well after each addition. Add whipping cream, beating at high speed until creamy. Divide mixture in half. Add remaining sugar and almonds to one half, mixing until well blended. Stir chocolate into remaining half. Chill chocolate frosting until thickened for spreading consistency.

Open House Ribbon Torte

1 package DUNCAN HINES® Deluxe Fudge Marble Cake Mix
3 large eggs
⅓ cup CRISCO® Oil or PURITAN® Oil
1¼ cups water
1 cup whipping cream
1 cup milk
1 package (4-serving-size) chocolate instant pudding and pie filling mix

1. Preheat oven to 350°F. Grease and flour two 8×1½- or 9×1½-inch round layer pans.
2. Combine dry cake mix, eggs, oil and water in large mixer bowl. Mix as directed on package but do not add contents of small packet. Turn half of batter (about 2½ cups) into one pan. Blend contents of small packet into remaining batter and turn into remaining pan.
3. Bake and cool layers as directed on package. Chill cooled layers to make splitting easier. Split each layer into two thin layers.
4. Whip cream until stiff. Blend in milk and pudding mix. Let set for 1 minute.
5. Place one chocolate layer on plate. Spread one-fourth pudding mixture over layer. Top with remaining layers, alternating light and dark layers and spreading pudding mixture between layers. Frost top layer with pudding mixture. Refrigerate until ready to serve.
12 to 16 servings.

Viennese Chocolate Torte

1 cup flour
½ teaspoon salt
½ cup ground walnuts
¾ cup unsalted butter
1¼ cups confectioners sugar
8 egg yolks
1 package (8 squares) BAKER'S® Semi-Sweet Chocolate, melted and cooled
1 teaspoon vanilla
8 egg whites
1 cup (10-ounce jar) apricot jam
Continental Flair Frosting, half recipe (see Index)
Sweetened whipped cream or thawed COOL WHIP® Whipped Topping

Mix flour, salt and walnuts. Cream butter. Gradually beat in sugar and continue beating until light and fluffy. Add egg yolks, a few at a time, beating thoroughly after each addition. Gradually stir in chocolate. Add flour mixture and vanilla, stirring just to blend. Beat egg whites until soft peaks form. Blend about ¼ cup of the beaten egg whites into the chocolate mixture; gently fold in remaining egg whites.

Pour into 2 greased and floured 9-inch layer pans. Bake at 350° for 40 to 45 minutes, or until cake tester inserted in centers comes out clean. Cool in pans 10 minutes. Remove from pans and finish cooling on racks.

Split layers horizontally, making 4 layers. Stir jam in saucepan over low heat until melted. Spread about ⅓ cup over tops of three layers. Stack on a rack placed on a tray; top with fourth layer. Prepare frosting as directed, cooling only slightly. Pour quickly over cake, covering top and sides. Place cake on serving plate. If desired, spoon frosting drippings into plastic-lined decorating bag fitted with writing tip; pipe a name or greeting on cake. Store in refrigerator at least one day to mellow flavors. Serve at room temperature with sweetened whipped cream.
Makes one 9-inch torte.

ACKNOWLEDGMENTS

The publishers would like to thank the companies and organizations listed below for the use of their recipes in this book.

American Dairy Association
Armour Swift-Eckrich
Bel Paese Sales Company, Inc.
Best Foods, a Division of CPC International Inc.
Blue Diamond Growers
Borden Kitchens, Borden, Inc.
Campbell Soup Company
Carnation, Nestlé Food Company
The Creamette Company
Diamond Walnut Growers, Inc.
The Dole Food Company
Durkee-French Foods, A Division of Reckitt & Colman Inc.
Filippo Berio Olive Oil
Hershey Chocolate U.S.A.
The HVR Company
Kahlúa Liqueur
Keebler Company
Kellogg Company
Kikkoman International Inc.
The Kingsford Products Company

Kraft General Foods, Inc.
Lawry's® Foods, Inc.
Thomas J. Lipton, Inc.
McIlhenny Company
Mrs. Paul's Kitchens, Inc.
Nabisco Brands, Inc.
National Live Stock and Meat Board
National Pecan Marketing Council
National Pork Producers Council
Norseland Foods, Inc.
Pepperidge Farm Incorporated
Pet Incorporated
The Procter & Gamble Company, Inc.
The Quaker Oats Company
Roman Meal Company
StarKist Seafood Co.
Sun-Maid Growers of California
USA Rice Council
Vlasic Foods, Inc.
Washington Apple Commission

PHOTO CREDITS

The publishers would like to thank the companies and organizations listed below for the use of their photographs in this book.

Armour Swift-Eckrich
Borden Kitchens, Borden, Inc.
Campbell Soup Company
Diamond Walnut Growers, Inc.
The Dole Food Company
Kikkoman International Inc.
Kraft General Foods, Inc.
Thomas J. Lipton, Inc.
The Procter & Gamble Company, Inc.

INDEX